The Portfolio Journey

The Portfolio Journey

A Creative Guide to Keeping Student-Managed
Portfolios in the Classroom

Tom Crockett

1998
Teacher Ideas Press
A Division of
Libraries Unlimited, Inc.
Englewood, Colorado

This book is dedicated to Meredith,
the constant companion of my journey.

TEACHER IDEAS PRESS
A Division of
Libraries Unlimited, Inc.
P.O. Box 6633
Englewood, CO 80155-6633
1-800-237-6124
www.lu.com/tip

Production Editor: Kevin W. Perizzolo
Copy Editor: Jason Cook
Proofreader: Melissa Root
Indexer: Linda Running Bentley
Typesetter: Kay Minnis

Library of Congress Cataloging-in-Publication Data

Crockett, Tom, 1957–
    The portfolio journey : a creative guide to keeping student-
managed portfolios in the classroom / Tom Crockett.
        xvi, 243 p. 22x28 cm.
    Includes bibliographical references and index.
    ISBN 1-56308-454-6
    1. Portfolios in education. I. Title.
LB1029.P67C76   1998
371.39--dc21   97-52984
                                                    CIP

Following the sun we left the old world.

—Inscription on one of Columbus' caravels.

Contents

Part 3
Preparing for the Journey

Part 4
On the Road

Part 5
Coming Home

Preface

Several years ago, while I was still teaching in the classroom, an observer to one of my classes commented that if there was an art to teaching, I must surely have the gift for it. Praise often makes me uncomfortable, and my first instinct was to dismiss my success with students as being a matter of chance or luck (but I knew this was not an honest response to a genuine compliment). I thanked the person who had made the observation and went on with my teaching.

The comment stayed with me, though. I couldn't seem to get it out of my head. What bothered me most was that it didn't seem to describe my experience as a teacher very accurately. It didn't feel like I had any kind of gift for teaching. Giftedness always implies that something comes naturally to someone, and I certainly fumbled and stumbled my way through my first several years of teaching. I became depressed, angry, frustrated, and disillusioned on a regular basis. The other thing about giftedness that bothered me was the idea that some people would be effective teachers but most would not, and there was really nothing to be done about it. I believe that I *learned* how to be an effective teacher, that I worked at it, that I was flexible enough to adjust my style and methods over time. Teaching seemed like more of a discipline to me. The more I learned and the more I practiced effective techniques, the better I became at teaching.

Rather than having a gift for teaching, I now tend to see teaching as a path I began to follow. I was on a journey, and like all characters in heroic myths who begin journeys, I began mine ill-prepared for what I would face. I think most teachers begin their teaching journeys this way. Even the best schools of education can only do so much to prepare people for teaching. Despite the best in training, we all must face the obstacles and challenges of our journeys in our own way.

Some people turn back early in their journey. They come to realize that this is not the right path for them. Others get stuck at a certain point, often repeating the same strategies that fail to take them forward. These teachers often spend much of their time looking backward, remembering some point in their journey where these strategies succeeded. You may have encountered some of these teachers on your journey. There are, however, teachers who continue to move forward, forging new alliances, gathering magical tools, seeking and heeding the advice of mentors, modeling the successful behaviors and techniques of others, and discarding failed strategies and attitudes along the way.

This was the journey I made. That I became an effective teacher had less to do with any gift and more to do with a natural propensity for flexibility and improvisation. I just kept trying new things. I held onto what worked and left the rest behind. This book is a part of what worked.

My own personal journey in education has taken me from being a teacher to being a teacher of teachers. There have been milestones in this journey that I can see from where I am today and for which I am thankful. I realize now that I was well prepared for this journey long before I ever began. I had parents who supported me with love and attention, and for whom no accomplishment of mine was a surprise. I had grandparents on one side of my family who encouraged me to learn by reading, and I had grandparents on the other side who gave me the opportunity to learn by experiencing the natural world. Miss Lee, in the fifth grade, helped me become hooked on a lifelong habit of reading. Don Cox taught me that a high school teacher could be both a teacher and a friend. In college, I was lucky enough to have four mentors of radically different temperaments. I have tried to blend the patience and grace of Wally Dreyer and the discipline and eloquence of Ken Daley with the intellectual precision of Robert McCullough and the compassion, humor, and humanity of David Johnson. These early teachers will always be a part of the teacher and person I am.

When I began teaching, I was lucky enough to have worked with Vic Frailing, from whom I learned about quiet tenacity, strength, and perseverance, and Claudia Sweeney, who showed me the power of unconditional love. When I became a member of the Polaroid Education Program's national training staff, I was thrown in constant contact with some of the most dynamic educators I could ever hope to meet. Phillip Seymour, Paul Zappala, Peggy Hooberman, Tim Gangwer, Dalton Cason, Pat Thomas, Gloria Henry, Ginny Graves, and Mark Zimmerman helped me refine my ideas of what effective teaching and effective portfolios are all about.

In the past seven years, I have presented hundreds of workshops for thousands of teachers, and I have learned much from the educators with whom I have worked. Fellow teachers like Debbie Cooke, Laurie Marshall, Karen Musser, Dina Hall, Gail Hunt, Gary Taylor, Kathleen Hull, Jane Duhl, Marge Pollard, and Christine Ejlali have been an inspiration. There is no way I can adequately thank the many teachers in my workshops who offered their advice and feedback on the ideas that would become the Portfolio Journey. They shared their ideas with passion and enthusiasm, as great teachers always do.

I have been extremely fortunate to have met and learned from so many teachers on my journey. When you meet people who help you on your journey, you may be lucky enough to be able to help them in their journey at the same time. I think that, most often, the best hope you have of making restitution for the assistance you have received is simply to offer what help you can to the fellow travelers you meet along the way. This act plots you on a great map that stretches backward in time to mark the first teacher and forward in time for as long as there will be people to teach. I hope that by writing this book I add a little mark on that map.

Introduction
The Portfolio Journey

It is not on any map: true places never are.
—Herman Melville (*Moby-Dick*, 1851)

Imagine that you are about to take a great journey. You can go anywhere you choose. You can go forward in time or backward. You can journey beneath the ocean to the center of the earth, or drift to the farthest point in the farthest galaxy from your home. You can explore places that have never been explored, or simply see things you've never seen before. Where you are going, no one will know who you are. Because no one will know where you have been or from where you come, it would be helpful to take along some things to show the people whom you meet. This is a way of introducing yourself to others. You will want to take things that show where you have been and of what you are capable. As you travel, you will grow and change. You will be able to do new things, and you will do old things better. It would be helpful if you collected samples of your new skills while you travel. When you return home, you will have wonderful evidence of the person you have become. Remember, you can go anywhere, but you should be prepared to end up anywhere. How will you prepare for your journey?

It is not much of a stretch to realize that this journey is the journey of *growing up*. It is education, experience, challenge, and change. A portfolio is the suitcase you will carry. It is what you will pack to take with you on your journey. It is what you will fill as you travel, and it is the record you will have with you when you return.

The Portfolio Journey: A Creative Guide to Keeping Student-Managed Portfolios in the Classroom is a teacher's guide, manual, and activity book for creating, maintaining, and working with student-managed portfolios. Its premise is that the metaphor of travel can be used to inspire and organize students to keep their own portfolios. It introduces the idea of portfolios and walks a teacher through the processes of planning, preparing, organizing, maintaining, evaluating, and maximizing the value inherent in student portfolios.

If you are not familiar with the idea of student portfolios or are unconvinced of the need for them, Chapter 1 of this book would be a good place to start. If you think portfolios might be a good idea but have questions about the logistics of keeping them, *The Portfolio Journey* will provide some answers.

Student portfolios are now mandated in a number of states and are being adopted by many local school systems. The idea of student portfolios as assessment tools has passed the test phase. They are now a part of teachers' and students' lives. This book is not a scholarly exploration or defense of portfolios. It grew out of my own classroom experience; the writing of two books on portfolios (*It's About Who I Am: A Student's Guide to Portfolios* and *Telling Our Stories: An Instant Image Portfolio Guide*); and my interaction with thousands of educators over the past several years in my role as a curriculum developer, a writer, and a teacher trainer. As I spoke to educators about portfolios, it became clear to me that although sensitive, intelligent teachers could understand the value of student portfolios, they had serious questions about managing the process of keeping them. *The Portfolio Journey* is written for these teachers: educators interested in practical and innovative classroom ideas. It is not a how-it-should-be-done book but rather a fun and inspirational how-it-*might*-be-done book.

The *Portfolio Journey* ideas are geared toward teachers of first- through eighth-grade students. I have tried to create worksheets and materials that are adaptable, but you may need to customize some materials to make them more age-appropriate for the students you teach.

This brings me to another important point of *The Portfolio Journey*: This is a "bring your own brain" expedition. So many books for teachers are written to the lowest common denominator. This book isn't. It begins with the premise that you are an intelligent, committed, caring, and creative teacher. I know you are intelligent because you are reading this book. You are looking for new ideas and new information, a sure sign of intelligence. I also know that you are committed and caring. If you weren't committed to being the best teacher you can be, you wouldn't be searching to improve your skills by learning about student portfolios. If you didn't truly care about the students you teach, you could find a lot of other things to take up your spare time. The one quality that you might take issue with is creativity. Well, don't! A lot of people have convinced themselves that they aren't very creative. Allow me to redefine creativity in a much more user-friendly fashion. Creativity is the collision of practice and playfulness. If you practice something enough, you will develop facility for that thing. If you keep a playful attitude, you will find new combinations, new connections, new innovations—all the things associated with creativity.

The teacher presently using portfolios will find new ideas and a new way of thinking about portfolios. The teacher new to portfolios should be able to launch them successfully and imaginatively with the help of the material in this book. *The Portfolio Journey* does require your creativity, though. Does this book have illustrations, worksheets, reproducible pages? Sure, but they are meant to inspire, motivate, and suggest possibilities to you. Use them as they are or modify them. Scan them into your computer and change things. Cut and paste with scissors and glue before you photocopy the worksheets, or start from scratch and create your own materials. The instructions as well are meant as a starting point. I have tried to be thorough and give you plenty of advice, but these processes will only really become yours once you begin working with them and altering them to meet your own special needs. If something doesn't work for you, change it. Save what works and create your own variations. Can you add activities and elements to a Portfolio Journey portfolio? Of course! The whole process will probably not fully come alive until you do begin to add your own creative innovations. There are other good books available on portfolios (some of them are listed in the appendix). You might want to add some of the ideas from these books to your students' portfolios. You may already have ideas or processes you want to incorporate. Remember, this is *your* journey.

The Portfolio Journey is not a blueprint. It is truly a guidebook, and, as in all guidebooks, you will decide your own itinerary. Take what is useful to you, but don't be afraid to explore on your own. Bon voyage!

The Teacher as Pathfinder

In Part 1 of the Portfolio Journey you will:

- Gather some opinions about whether the journey is worth making.
- Look at some illustrations to help you remember the teaching styles that will best serve a Portfolio Journey teacher.
- Study a map of the places to which your students will be traveling.

Portfolio
A Tool for Tomorrow's Traveler

> The traveler must be somebody and come from somewhere so his definite character and moral traditions may supply an origin and a point of comparison for his observations.
>
> —George Santayana

One of the first questions you hear when traveling is, "Where are you from?" The next question is usually some variation of, "What do you do?" or "What brings you here?" These questions help people understand others in a more personal context. They are also part of the initial probing for common ground that occurs between strangers. Establishing context and finding common ground are natural ways to begin a discussion of student portfolios. Our Portfolio Journey will, as Santayana suggests, begin from a specific somewhere.

It is the rare teacher today who does not have at least some passing knowledge of student portfolios. Novice teachers, fresh from schools of education, have most likely been encouraged to keep their own portfolios. Art teachers and writing teachers have already been keeping student portfolios for a number of years. Some teachers have participated in districtwide cycles of adopting and experimenting with student portfolios. Even teachers who have never experimented with keeping student portfolios in their classrooms have some idea of what they are.

What typically makes the subject of student portfolios confusing is that the term *student portfolio* has many definitions. To an art teacher, a portfolio is a collection of a student's best work. To a writing teacher, a portfolio documents a student's writing process. To some teachers, a portfolio is a clearly defined and carefully structured element of an alternative assessment program. For still other teachers, a portfolio is a student-centered scrapbook created for reflection and self-assessment.

None of these definitions is incorrect. Portfolios can contain both finished work and work in progress. Portfolios can be used to grade, rank, and evaluate students. They can also be used to help students better understand their academic experiences. Portfolios can serve many purposes. To begin our Portfolio Journey, though, we must establish context and find common ground. This chapter answers three questions that will form the basis of our Portfolio Journey: What is a student portfolio? Why keep portfolios? and, How do portfolios become tools for lifelong learning? ✪

What Is a Student Portfolio?

A portfolio is evidence, usually bound in some form of container, that suggests or demonstrates a person's skills and abilities.

You won't find this definition in a dictionary. It is a definition based on how educators have come to use the word *portfolio*. This definition has precedent in how the portfolios of artists, graphic designers, and illustrators are described and certainly includes these kinds of portfolios. However, the portfolio we think of when we imagine an artist's portfolio is only one manifestation of a lifelong process: It is the form a portfolio takes at a specific point in time, in response to a specific set of circumstances.

Our simple definition of a portfolio shifts emphasis to where it belongs—the contents. A portfolio is a collection of evidence. The contents, or evidence, may be referred to as samples, examples, documents, records, or products. Because they have been assembled together, they provide evidence of a person's skills and abilities. The portfolio is the story told by the careful selection, organization, and presentation of that evidence.

This definition is open. It allows portfolios to take various forms, to serve various purposes, and to fulfill various criteria. Eventually, you may want to elaborate and add qualifiers to this definition. Reading this book, you will take a journey of sorts. How you apply what you find in this book will take you to a unique destination. All that matters as we begin this journey is that we agree to share this definition. ✪

Why Keep Portfolios?

1. The Habit of Saving   2. A Strong Sense of Self
3. Another Way of Knowing   4. Finding a Path

When the idea of student portfolios was first introduced and discussed in a big way in education, it was an idea linked to the alternative assessment movement. Portfolios were proposed as being an alternative to grading. Portfolios were described as being a more authentic form of assessment. To this day, when most teachers think of portfolios, they think of them as being assessment tools. Though this is not an unsound justification for the use of portfolios, it overlooks several, perhaps more important, reasons for encouraging students to keep portfolios.

1. The Habit of Saving

Perhaps the single most important reason for keeping student portfolios is to prepare students for the world in which they will work—a world in which the economic structure is rapidly changing.

If you think about the careers we traditionally associate with portfolios, the jobs of artist, architect, designer, actor, or model might come to mind. Portfolios probably evolved as tools in such professions because they require a visual product. Saying that you have ability as an artist, architect, designer, actor, or model and showing that you have ability are very different ways of presenting evidence. More importantly, though, these careers require constant publicity. Again and again, artists, architects, designers, actors, and models have to sell their abilities to new clients. They need an organized way of presenting themselves and their skills.

Most careers don't require this, or at least they didn't until recently. In the late-industrial-age, manufacturing-based model of employment, one left high school well prepared for a job on the assembly line, or one left college well prepared for a job in management. Whichever course, one could depend on a well-paying job, with benefits and regular promotion until retirement. In this model, a portfolio would have been redundant. Though the employee may have worked on a number of different projects over their years spent with a company, the memory of what they accomplished, their capabilities, resided within the community of the company. The employee was promoted (the corporate version of getting a new job) based on their abilities, but no one had to be reminded of what those abilities were. The company knew who the employees were and what they could do.

This model is changing. Through automation and computerization, companies are caring for their employees only up to the point where they can be replaced by a machine that costs less. Through downsizing and restructuring, companies are laying off employees in management and sales, often out-sourcing—hiring freelancers/temporary employees or temporary services—work traditionally done within the company. Some estimates suggest that by the turn of the century, fifty percent of all jobs will be temporary or part-time work.

Today's students will not climb the corporate ladder; they will climb a ladder they create by moving from company to company to advance. Many of them will create their own job opportunities in new markets we can only imagine. They will have freelance jobs and form temporary alliances with other freelance agents around specific projects. In the economic world in which today's students are coming of age, portfolios will no longer be an option.

This is not to suggest that students should begin developing career portfolios in the second grade. Still, we can help prepare them by beginning the process of keeping portfolios while they are young. Creating a useful portfolio involves skills that can be developed in school. If students learn to save and document their achievements, they will be a step ahead of those who don't. If they learn to transform their portfolio contents into an effective presentation of their abilities, they will be learning to add value to information by organizing and prioritizing it. If they learn to use their portfolios as interviewing tools, they will be better prepared to find and get the jobs they want.

This one reason, even if we had no other reasons, should be enough to make portfolios an essential element of our classrooms. The goal of all teachers is to help prepare their students for the world they will face. Our students will not face the world we knew. Student portfolios are a powerful way of teaching students the habit of saving.

2. A Strong Sense of Self

Imagine for a moment what it would be like to change jobs and supervisors every year. You would spend the first part of the year just getting to know what your new supervisor expected of you. Just as you began to feel comfortable with your new job, you would be preparing yourself to begin again, at a new job, with a new supervisor. Add to this the frustration of knowing that each of your future employers would know you through the eyes of your previous employers, at least initially. What if nothing of what you had done in your previous job could be used to establish your position in your new job, to build a relationship with your new supervisor? What if you were neither encouraged nor allowed to bring samples of your previous work with you to your new job? If this scenario sounds like a frustrating and unpleasant way to work, keep in mind that it is not much different from what our students face for roughly twelve or more years of their lives.

We pass our students along from one teacher to the next with nothing more than a folder of grades, test scores, and teacher comments. In the absence of any other indicators, our students often gauge their self-esteem and self-concept from how well liked they are by any one teacher. Some students pursue our attention by the academic work they do; some use their social skills. Other students use negative behaviors to get attention. The common denominator is that they are struggling to define who they are.

What children want to know, perhaps more than anything else, is who they are. They look for indicators of who they are in relation to others. They model and try different behaviors and different patterns. The more tools we provide to help them define themselves in a positive way, the more we free them from being dependent on the opinion of any one individual. A portfolio is just such a tool.

We are aware that our students don't often develop a sense of continuity about their education. They live in the moment and don't seem to see their own progress. Part of this is undoubtedly in the nature of being young, but how much of it could be changed if we were to provide better tools and processes? A portfolio, again, is just such a tool. A portfolio allows students to move from assignment to assignment, project to project, grade to grade, and school to school with samples of their achievements.

Many teachers avoid looking at a student's permanent record of grades and test scores because they want to approach each child as free from preconceived ideas as possible. A portfolio, however, is a different kind of a record. Rather than being biography, what other people thought were students' capabilities, portfolios are autobiography, what those students proved were their capabilities. What if you had the chance to sit down with each of your new students for ten minutes at the beginning of each school year and review their portfolios with them? What might you learn by seeing the actual work they had done and hearing their comments about that work?

Returning to our original analogy, if you had to change jobs and supervisors every year, wouldn't you want just such an opportunity? Wouldn't you want to be able to sit down with your new supervisor and present samples of work you had done and evidence of projects to which you had contributed? Wouldn't your growing portfolio help you to see the progress you were making in developing skills? What if you found yourself working for someone who didn't value your abilities? Wouldn't your portfolio, the evidence of your abilities, help you to maintain your sense of self-worth through such a difficult experience? If the answer to any of these questions is yes, you have another reason for encouraging the development of student portfolios in your classroom.

3. Another Way of Knowing

You may have noticed that the two previous reasons for keeping student portfolios are student-centered. Giving students an advantage in a changing economic landscape and providing them with tools for developing a positive self-concept may benefit teachers as well, but these justifications for keeping portfolios primarily benefit students. When considering portfolios as assessment tools, the same frame of reference should be used. To the extent that a portfolio is used to grade, rank, and formally evaluate a student, it serves the interests of the school, the system, or the state. Though it is certainly possible to use portfolios in this way, this process usually drains the life from an otherwise vital process. If you want your portfolios to have any of the powerful potential for change that has been discussed, they must first and foremost not interfere with the needs of the student, the teacher, or the parent.

Portfolios are effective tools for student self-assessment. When students play an active role in selecting the materials that go into their portfolios, they come to own and value the evidence of their academic achievements. When the contents of a portfolio are dictated by the needs of standardization for formal assessment, students quickly lose interest in them. Portfolios become yet another process over which students have little control or influence.

Portfolios can be extremely useful to teachers who want to help students develop a sense of their academic achievements. They are an effective focus for dialogue and discussion. When portfolios are used to evaluate a teacher's performance, however, teachers quickly learn to create portfolios that fit this model—the portfolio equivalent of teaching to the test.

Parents often find portfolios a much friendlier entrée into their child's academic and social world. Rather than discussing the abstraction of grades and grade point averages, most parents would rather look at a child's work and talk about how they can help their child do better. Student/teacher/parent conferences built around portfolios can be learning experiences for everyone involved. Again, though, when portfolios are prescribed for formal assessment and are used to rank and evaluate students, the role and room for parental involvement often are squeezed from the process.

The best assessment use for student portfolios—the use for which the material in this book is based—is informal student assessment with three primary clients: students, teachers, and parents. Informal assessment means that portfolios are not used for ranking and formally evaluating students. This is not to suggest that grades must be totally divorced from portfolios. It is possible to assign grades for the management and maintenance of student portfolios, or portfolios can contain work that was at one point graded. Portfolios should not, however, be graded wholly, as a single entity, nor should student grades be derived from portfolios. (Teachers whose school systems or schools have mandated portfolios as formal assessment tools might consider keeping two separate but related portfolios for each student.)

Students will find that portfolios help them understand their strengths and abilities. Portfolios show them that they are making progress academically. Portfolios also can allow students to document effort and achievement in areas that often go unnoticed. Teachers will find that portfolios help them guide and mentor their students. Portfolios can help teachers find a student's strengths and the mode of communication with which that student is most comfortable. Parents will find that portfolio contents are easier to discuss with their children than grades and scores, making conferences and review sessions more beneficial.

When used as an informal assessment tool in the hands of students, teachers, and parents, portfolios can provide a new window onto student achievement in school. Portfolios give students another way of knowing who they are.

4. Finding a Path

By itself, a portfolio is a powerful tool. It can help prepare students for an economic future that will put a premium on career flexibility and personal marketing. It is both a process and a product for helping students develop and define a positive self-image. It can be a powerful tool for self-assessment and communication. With a little guidance, portfolios can also be used to help students plan and set effective goals and objectives.

In life, we don't always know where we are going. Sometimes we are not even certain of where we have been. When we travel, we consult maps regularly to decide where we are going and how best to get there. We look at where we have been to help us decide where we will go next. A portfolio can be a kind of map. If we have kept it well, it will tell us where we have been. It can also help us think about where we might go next. By finding the patterns and the resources within our portfolios, we can set reasonable objectives and monitor our progress toward our destination.

A teacher might establish a goal at the beginning of a school year, such as: Each student will be able to demonstrate an understanding of local or state history by the end of the year. This goal could be represented by a point plotted on a map as a destination. Goals might be linked to requirements established by the curriculum. They might be goals that a teacher deems important. Goals might also be arrived at by a process that reflects both teacher and student input.

The first question after establishing such a goal might be: What are some ways of reaching this goal? Traditional teaching options might include drill and test, lecture, cooperative group work for projects, research and report, and field trips and experiential learning, among others. These options, or combinations of these options, might also be plotted as points on a map. Now we have a goal and some sense of how we are going to get there.

Portfolios enter the process by asking the next question: What resources do individual students have that could help them reach the goal? Remember that the goal is to *demonstrate* knowledge or understanding. Some students excel at memorizing facts and taking tests; others express themselves better through more open-ended writing. Some students need projects to be able to express themselves fully; other students might need to perform or present information. This is the sort of information that a portfolio can reveal. It can help give a teacher more flexibility in the assignments that will be used to demonstrate knowledge or understanding.

The third and fourth questions in the process involve portfolios to their fullest potential: How will we know we are progressing toward our goal? and, How will we know when we have arrived? A portfolio can serve as the repository for evidence of progress toward and attainment of goals. By reviewing the portfolio regularly, both the teacher and the student can evaluate progress, change direction, and set new goals and objectives.

Practicing this process models effective goal-setting behavior for students. Setting reasonable goals with clear objectives is one of the traits present in just about everyone's list of attributes of successful people. ✪

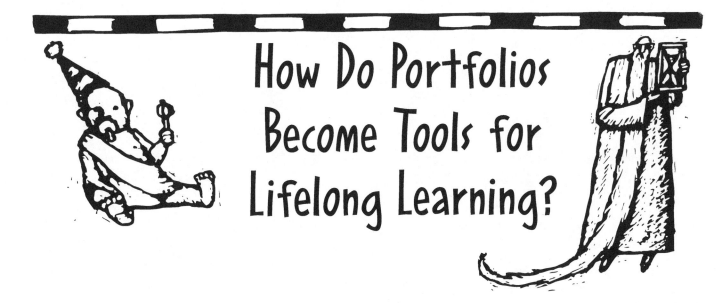

How Do Portfolios Become Tools for Lifelong Learning?

Though this book presents a creative metaphor and approach to keeping student portfolios for grades one through eight, it is based on a larger vision. This vision is one in which portfolios are life tools, begun at the earliest age and continued well into the adult years of life. Though it is not essential, for the purposes of this book, that you embrace this entire vision, it does lend perspective to the work you do with students between the first and the eighth grades.

To be relevant and appropriate throughout an entire lifetime, it is essential that portfolios change and adapt over time. For young children, portfolios are simple collections. They should be fun and mostly visual. In the elementary and middle grades, portfolios undergo a transition from guided collections to more organized and focused presentations. In high school, portfolios begin to reflect the need for a more sophisticated and compact presentation tool. The portfolio of a student at the high school level is still general but should be transitioned into a more career- and path-specific document during the college or advanced education phase. After college, the portfolio becomes a job-search and career-maintenance tool. Finally, it becomes the basis for legacy work done later in life.

Portfolios truly are the ultimate tool for tomorrow's traveler. They help students keep track of where they have been. They help students develop the habit of recording and documenting their travels. They give students a firm sense of their identity and potential. They aid students in developing a sense of continuity about their journey, keeping them on course when they need reassurance and suggesting new paths when they need a change. They also help teachers and parents to be better guides and resources. Finally, they help shape the skills our students will need to become successful travelers. If our students can select goals and pursue objectives that match their abilities, there is nowhere they cannot go. ✪

Traveling Hats
New Roles for the Portfolio Journey Teacher

Management of Savages

A frank, joking, but determined manner, joined with an air of showing more confidence in the good faith of the natives than you really feel, is best. It is observed, that a sea-captain generally succeeds in making an excellent impression on savages: they thoroughly appreciate common sense, truth, and uprightness; and are not half such fools as strangers usually account them. If a savage does mischief, look upon him as you would on a kicking mule or a wild animal, whose nature it is to be unruly, and keep your temper quite unruffled.

—Sir Francis Galton (*The Art of Travel*, 1867)

Remember how you felt when you first started teaching: the excitement, the exhilaration, the sheer terror. Maybe there are still days when you could easily imagine yourself as a Victorian explorer confronting "the savage natives." It's not that you aren't well prepared. It isn't that you aren't well intentioned and optimistic. It's not that you don't have anything but the highest hopes for your students, but sometimes, well sometimes, they can seem like little savages. In that case, Sir Francis Galton's advice is probably as good as any you will find.

As good as this advice may be, however, it's not enough for a Portfolio Journey teacher. One thing that teachers who embrace portfolios find is that this position places new demands on their sense of their role in the classroom. No longer is it good enough to be the dispenser of knowledge. Portfolio teachers must be flexible and versatile. They must assume different roles at different times. They must be able to dispense knowledge when appropriate. They must also be planners. They must be able to introduce new processes and understand the difference between teaching and mentoring. They must be grand facilitators; they must motivate. They must be curators and cheerleaders, critics and promoters. They must model the behaviors and attitudes they are championing, and they must love what they do and respect those for whom they do it.

Is this a description of yourself? If you're reading this book, it probably describes yourself more closely than you think. You probably assume most if not all of these roles every day. The Portfolio Journey is based on your ability as a teacher to assume four distinct roles in the classroom. Each of these roles corresponds to a phase of the Portfolio Journey. Respectively, these phases are planning and preparing, assembling and maintaining, refining and developing, and displaying and utilizing. These are key steps in the development of creative student portfolios.

Keeping student portfolios in today's busy classrooms is not easy. It requires perseverance and commitment on the part of students. There is no magic to guarantee that this process will be easy, but the following ideas can make a great difference in the success of your Portfolio Journey:

The Secrets of Successful Portfolio Programs

1. The portfolio process must be fun. It must capture the imagination of both teachers and students.

2. Portfolios must be student-managed. They must be created and maintained by students with guidance from teachers and parents.

3. Portfolios must become teaching tools. They must be integrated into every subject within the curriculum.

4. Portfolios need to be shared. Portfolios that are shared regularly are respected, valued, and cared for.

To more easily associate your role as teacher with each phase of portfolio development, the remaining parts of this book are organized by "archetypal" roles of the Portfolio Journey teacher. When planning and preparing, you will be assuming the role of *Travel Agent*. When helping students assemble and maintain their portfolios, you will be playing the role of *Travel Consultant*. To refine and develop their portfolios, your students will need you to be a kind of *Tour Guide*. When you assist in the display and effective use of portfolios, you will be acting as a *Curator*.

As the Travel Agent for the Portfolio Journey, you will be expected to plan and prepare yourself and your classroom for the journey. Travel Agents must be good at visualizing destinations. They should also be comfortable researching and planning for the portfolio process. The steps you take as a Travel Agent, such as reading this book and learning about the portfolio process, are steps taken, for the most part, before you introduce the Portfolio Journey to your students.

As a Travel Consultant, you will be introducing processes and procedures. You will also be helping your students with the packing and organization of their portfolios. During this phase, you may be operating in the more traditional role of teacher as knowledge dispenser. Though students may eventually come to organize their portfolios in ways they have been involved in determining, it helps in the beginning to have everyone working from the same model.

As a Tour Guide, you will be facilitating the process of travel and collection. You will be offering advice and serving as a resource to your student travelers. By the processes you initiate, you will be guiding students through editing and refinement of their portfolios. You must be willing to act as a guide, a facilitator, and a mentor to help students develop their abilities of self-reflection and self-assessment.

Finally, as a Curator, you will be motivating students to continue to collect and save. You will be modeling a positive and enthusiastic attitude. The Curator helps students find larger audiences for the portfolios they have assembled. The Curator also brings parents and students together to review and reflect on school work using the portfolio.

The illustrations that follow (pp. 14–21) expand on these roles. The remaining parts of this book are organized around the roles of Travel Agent, Travel Consultant, Tour Guide, and Curator. You may find it useful to keep a notebook of ideas you want to implement in your Portfolio Journey (the illustrations that follow might be used as subject dividers in such a notebook).

(Text continues on p. 22.)

The Travel Agent

The role of Travel Agent suggests planning and preparation. Keeping student portfolios truly is a journey, and, like any journey, it demands our attention even before we depart. A successful portfolio experience requires planning. You must understand and prepare for the logistics of keeping portfolios. It also helps to reflect on why you are choosing to keep student portfolios. A good Travel Agent tries to learn as much as possible about the destinations of their clients.

A good Travel Agent has

Vision

As a Portfolio Journey teacher, you must be able to see where your students are going. You needn't know the details, but you should know the territory. A portfolio program will succeed or fail in your classroom in direct correlation to how clearly you can imagine it. Some people need support to realize a dream. If you need help, try forming a portfolio brainstorming team with other teachers. Seek input from different sources. Learn about portfolios. Think about what this journey might mean to you and your students.

What Travel Agents Do

☑ They learn all they can about the portfolio process, yet are comfortable with the idea that their own Portfolio Journeys will be unique adventures.

☑ They set initial goals and objectives (we call them destinations) for student portfolios while, at the same time, understanding that those goals will be modified along the way.

☑ They decide what kinds of evidence (or souvenirs) will be most useful to their students.

They imagine where their students might go.

The Travel Consultant

Though the Travel Agent helps you plan where you will go and how you will get there, it is the Travel Consultant who helps you with the practical matters that will make your journey a success. In the role of Travel Consultant, you will introduce the portfolio process to your students, showing them what to pack and how to organize and annotate.

A good Travel Consultant is

Organized

Teachers who use portfolios in the classroom find that being organized is the single biggest influence on whether the portfolio process works. Being organized means that you know and are able to communicate to your students a system for saving, annotating, handling, and storing portfolios. Being organized does not mean being inflexible. You will need to re-evaluate your organization procedures on a fairly regular basis.

What Travel Consultants Do

☑ They prepare some of the materials they will use to teach their students about portfolios and the Portfolio Journey, and they set the mood for travel and exploration in their classrooms.

☑ They help students construct their basic portfolio containers (we call them trunks), and they teach students how to edit their own portfolios individually and in special portfolio review teams.

☑ They teach their students the basics of saving evidence, and they establish the process and procedure of annotating portfolio contents and documenting portfolio reviews.

☑ They encourage students to think about their own abilities and strengths, interests and experiences through the creation of student passports.

They help their students organize and pack.

The Tour Guide

The Tour Guide takes over once the journey has begun. Some of the Tour Guide's responsibilities include keeping travelers on schedule, pointing out important sights, handling problems and making special arrangements on the road, and keeping travelers motivated. Student portfolios require the same kind of attention. Once the portfolio process has been introduced, you will need to guide students through editing, reflection, refinement, and assessment.

A good Tour Guide is a Facilitator

A teacher will tell you how to make a fire. A mentor will teach you how to make fire, but only when you really want to know how. A master will show you how to make a fire. A facilitator will help you figure out how to make fire. Each of these approaches has its place in education, but facilitated learning has the highest long-term effect on learners. Keeping portfolios, like traveling, is not always easy. It requires perseverance and patience. A good Tour Guide handles difficulties and setbacks with patience and good humor.

What Tour Guides Do

☑ They help students refine their working portfolios into display portfolios (or suitcases) through a process of self-reflection and cooperative assessment.

☑ They teach their students how to create special portfolios (or *daypacks*) customized for specific needs and they facilitate the creation of project portfolios (or kits) focused to document extended projects and detail process work.

☑ They help students understand the progress they are making by establishing a special rubric system for portfolio work.

They help make their students' journeys rewarding.

The Curator

The Curator helps students share their portfolios with peers, faculty, family, and the community. The Curator also acts as a facilitator between students and those who might view student portfolios. Curators often have to educate their audience by placing artifacts in context. A good Curator can also help a student make better use of the materials they have gathered. Finally, a Curator can use the process of sharing to motivate students to value their own work.

A good Curator has a lot of Enthusiasm

A Portfolio Journey teacher must infect students with enthusiasm and excitement. Students learn most of what they learn by modeling your behavior. As a Curator for your students' portfolio work, you must be part cheerleader and part coach. This does not mean that you must be artificial in your praise. On the contrary, though a Curator should always be supportive, the praise must be sincere or it becomes self-defeating.

What Curators Do

☑ They create opportunities for students to share their portfolios with peers, friends, family, faculty, and the community through activities that range from the informal to the formal.

☑ They facilitate involvement with their children's education through student/teacher/parent portfolio review sessions after school and during conferences.

☑ They teach students how to use their portfolios for interviews and presentations.

☑ They model successful portfolio behaviors and attitudes by maintaining their own portfolios in the classroom.

They help their students take pride in their journeys.

The secrets of successful portfolios are not so secret. They seem to be common-sense solutions to genuine concerns about the practical aspects of establishing a portfolio program in schools. Teachers genuinely want to know if portfolios will be boring for them and for their students. They are concerned about increased administrative and custodial work that will take them away from teaching. They want to know when and how they can fit portfolio maintenance into their schedules. Teachers want to know how they can use portfolios without encumbering the curriculum. They also want to know if the process of maintaining portfolios will be a battle of wills with students who tend to lose interest quickly in new things.

The Portfolio Journey addresses these concerns through techniques and strategies grounded in the reality of the classroom but buoyant with the vision of the enchanted classroom we all hope to provide for our children and our students.

Charting a Course
The Landscape of the Portfolio Journey

He had bought a large map
representing the sea,
Without the least vestige of land:
And the crew were much pleased
when they found it to be
A map they could all understand.

—Lewis Carroll (*The Hunting of the Snark:
An Agony in Eight Fits*, 1876)

In the early days of sea travel, what is sometimes called the Age of Discovery, ships had both captains and pilots. The captain commanded and controlled the ship and the crew, but a seaworthy captain always deferred to the pilot on matters of navigation. The pilot was responsible for getting a ship, its cargo and crew, to a destination and back again. For most sailors, navigation beyond sight of land was a mystery. The craft of navigation was shrouded in secrecy as a way of protecting the status and importance of the pilot. Sea charts were rare and often unreliable. What was reliable was a pilot's rudder. The rudder was a book of notations, course calculations, sketches, and commentary assembled by an individual pilot. Rudders were valuable because they reflected the knowledge and wisdom a pilot gained from personal experience. The rudder of a pilot showed how a ship could sail from one place to another across a vast ocean. It contained the information that formed the basis for making navigational decisions.

Before beginning your Portfolio Journey, it may be useful to glimpse into the rudder of one who has made that journey. The Portfolio Journey is based on certain assumptions about effective teaching and education. It is not essential that you agree with or put into practice all these principles, but you should at least know what they are.

As mentioned in Chapter 2, portfolios tend to both reflect and initiate changes in the way we educate children. Portfolios require teachers to be flexible about the roles they assume in the classroom. They tend to push teachers into a more student-centered model of education. They even encourage us to introduce more democratic or consensus-based decision making. This can be frightening, but it needn't be. These things will tend to grow out of the process of keeping portfolios. Just let it happen. Embrace the changes with which you are comfortable.

Five principles of education form the landscape upon which the Portfolio Journey is made. Can you make the Portfolio Journey without accepting the principles? Probably; but the experience will be much richer and more successful if you can accept and begin to put into practice these ideas about what makes education successful. Are these the only principles you need to be an effective teacher? Of course not; but if you embrace at least these five principles in your classroom, you will be the kind of teacher that students need.

The five principles are not new, and they are not a secret. The only thing unusual about their presentation here is that they are presented as a related package. You will find that these ideas support and complement each other. Their coordinated use exponentially increases the benefit of any of the ideas used individually. These principles will help you chart a course for your portfolio journey.

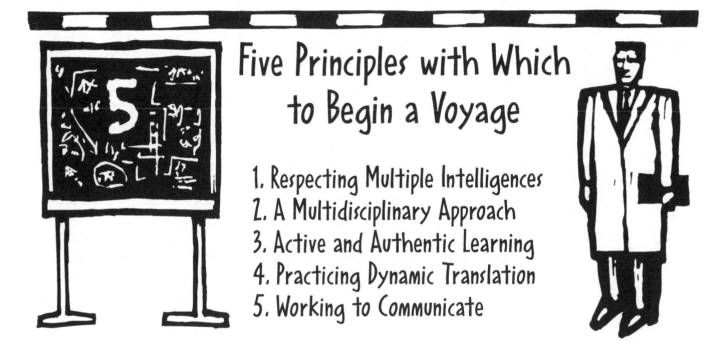

Five Principles with Which to Begin a Voyage

1. Respecting Multiple Intelligences
2. A Multidisciplinary Approach
3. Active and Authentic Learning
4. Practicing Dynamic Translation
5. Working to Communicate

1. Respecting Multiple Intelligences

Multiple intelligence theory is hardly new. Howard Gardner's groundbreaking book *Frames of Mind* (New York: Basic Books, 1983) recognized seven intelligences. Teachers soon found that the intelligences Gardner identified—verbal-linguistic, bodily-kinesthetic, logical-mathematical, visual-spatial, musical-rhythmic, interpersonal, and intrapersonal— were quite useful in understanding more students' learning patterns. More recently, Gardner has added an additional intelligence—what he calls naturalistic intelligence—bringing the current total of identified intelligences to eight. Gardner suggested that the way we teach and what we choose to evaluate only address one or two of the eight possible types of intelligence.

The reason that portfolios fit together so well with multiple intelligence theory is that effective portfolios reflect many more intelligences or modes of expression and problem solving than traditional report cards or standardized tests. As an organizing principle for a portfolio, multiple intelligence theory has some interesting benefits. It helps teachers attend to all the intelligence domains in a classroom. It encourages the use of alternative media such as video or audio recordings, computer diskettes, and photographs.

For the purposes of the Portfolio Journey, you might want to think about the different intelligences as being your students' countries of origin. Like the country and culture you have been raised in, your particular intelligence will color and influence the way you see the world and the way you express yourself to the world. Respecting multiple intelligences should be as natural as respecting the culture and traditions of a visitor from another country.

Do you need to believe that there are actually eight identifiable intelligences? No; but if you assume that this is true and act accordingly, better teaching and more inclusive behavior—the validation and acceptance of a wider range of intelligences—on the Portfolio Journey will follow.

2. A Multidisciplinary Approach

This is an easy one. A multidisciplinary approach just makes sense. It reflects real-life and real-world tasks. For example, in real life, one doesn't spend forty minutes using math skills and only math skills. In real life, math skills must be integrated with myriad other skills. We don't think of them as being separate and isolated. We might have to teach fundamental skills using brief, isolated activities, but we should quickly provide interesting, multidisciplinary tasks in which those skills, among others, are required.

The Portfolio Journey itself is a multidisciplinary experience. Along the way, your students will find themselves using writing and reading skills. They will be using math and art skills. They will be learning geography and history, cooperative social skills, and independent thought. They will be practicing reflection and analysis, problem solving, and communication skills. None of these skills will be developed in a vacuum. They will grow out of a set of related, multidisciplinary activities.

Embracing a multidisciplinary approach is about designing meaningful experiences for your students. What our students seem to have the hardest time with is continuity. They tend to see every activity as an isolated element. Effective teachers are bridge builders. They are masters at defining relationships.

3. Active and Authentic Learning

These two principles are so closely related that they can be discussed together. Active learning simply means that students learn best by doing. Are there different learning styles? Certainly; but what matters is that you activate those learning styles. The most effective way of doing this is to create experiences in which students can use the knowledge they are learning. Meaningful experiences in which students must create and develop products allow them to use knowledge as well as reflect their level of knowledge.

Authentic learning is simply striving to make tasks relevant to students. Projects and products that are student-centered go a long way toward making this goal a reality, but sometimes it can be difficult to find relevant projects. When this happens, it is time to call on the power of imagination. If you can't think of a natural reason why a fifth-grade student would need to know about a specific formula in geometry, can you invent an imaginative world or scenario where that knowledge would be useful?

Documentation of these active and authentic learning projects and products will be the core of your students' portfolios. Some projects will be saved in their original form; others will be photographed, sketched, photocopied, or described in writing. Some events and performances will be recorded on audiocassette; others might be videotaped; still others might be recorded on computer diskette.

For the Portfolio Journey, active and authentic learning means that, rather than sitting in hotel rooms watching television broadcasts about the world, your students will be out in the streets of the countries they are exploring. They will be working with farmers and craftspeople, exploring museums and temples, cooking meals, playing games. They will be learning by doing, engaged by their own natural curiosity.

4. Practicing Dynamic Translation

The idea behind dynamic translation is that real understanding, deep learning, occurs when one takes an idea and translates it into a different medium. Furthermore, the more media an idea is filtered through, the greater one's understanding of that idea. This might mean that ideas one learns by reading should be expressed by transforming them into a piece of music, a play, a painting, or a machine. Concepts one encounters through film might be expressed in written pieces or as oral presentations. If conducting a hands-on experiment in a science lab results in learning something new, one might try using that knowledge to improve performance in an athletic event or to invent a new solution to a common problem.

Portfolios support this kind of learning because they maintain the connection between projects and help students develop a sense of continuity. Dynamic translation focuses on key concepts. It sometimes sacrifices breadth of learning for depth of learning, but it more closely resembles real-world tasks. Breakthrough inventions and discoveries are more likely to be made by specialists who explore beyond the boundaries of their disciplines. Dynamic translation trains students in this kind of thinking.

For the Portfolio Journey, dynamic translation might be seen as analogous to the process of learning about another country. As you explore a new culture, you often find that key concepts are expressed again and again in music, dance, drama, literature, social order, myth, custom, and so on. Once you have identified the concept, you come to understand each of its expressions more fully.

5. Working to Communicate

As cited in the first chapter of this book, one of the primary reasons for keeping a portfolio is to help prepare students for the world of work. In a society driven by information, communication is a critical skill. Students who are practiced and skilled at communicating are much more likely to be successful. A portfolio is an excellent place to show off communication skills. Visual communication—written words and images—fits well in a portfolio. Other forms of communication—presentation and performance—can be documented through photographs and included in portfolios. The skills of communication need to be encouraged, fostered, and taught.

One thing that can help us better teach communication skills is the knowledge that projects and products must be shared. Without sharing, the process has not been concluded. Portfolios can be communication tools. They can help students present themselves to others; but to do this, the portfolios must be shared.

In *The Portfolio Journey*, the idea of working to communicate is similar to the idea of traveling with a purpose. When you travel to learn, to gather information and experience for the pursuit of a creative endeavor, travel becomes more meaningful. ✪

Looking over the Pilot's Shoulder

So, are you interested in what this landscape looks like? Do you want to see how the roles of the portfolio teacher discussed in Chapter 2 (Travel Agent, Travel Consultant, Tour Guide, and Curator) can be integrated with the five principles? The maps that follow present this information in a visual format. As you look at the maps, imagine yourself and your classroom. What would your maps look like? In Part 2, you will begin creating the maps and making the plans necessary for launching your students on a Portfolio Journey.

(Text continues on p. 35.)

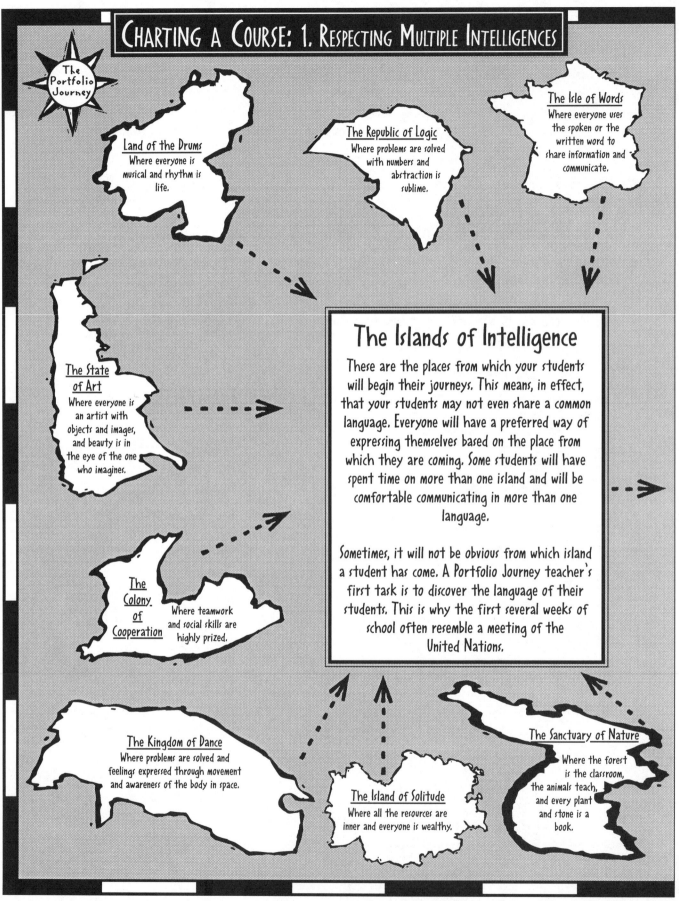

CHARTING A COURSE: 1. RESPECTING MULTIPLE INTELLIGENCES

The Portfolio Journey

Land of the Drums
Where everyone is musical and rhythm is life.

The Republic of Logic
Where problems are solved with numbers and abstraction is sublime.

The Isle of Words
Where everyone uses the spoken or the written word to share information and communicate.

The State of Art
Where everyone is an artist with objects and images, and beauty is in the eye of the one who imagines.

The Colony of Cooperation
Where teamwork and social skills are highly prized.

The Islands of Intelligence

These are the places from which your students will begin their journeys. This means, in effect, that your students may not even share a common language. Everyone will have a preferred way of expressing themselves based on the place from which they are coming. Some students will have spent time on more than one island and will be comfortable communicating in more than one language.

Sometimes, it will not be obvious from which island a student has come. A Portfolio Journey teacher's first task is to discover the language of their students. This is why the first several weeks of school often resemble a meeting of the United Nations.

The Kingdom of Dance
Where problems are solved and feelings expressed through movement and awareness of the body in space.

The Island of Solitude
Where all the resources are inner and everyone is wealthy.

The Sanctuary of Nature
Where the forest is the classroom, the animals teach, and every plant and stone is a book.

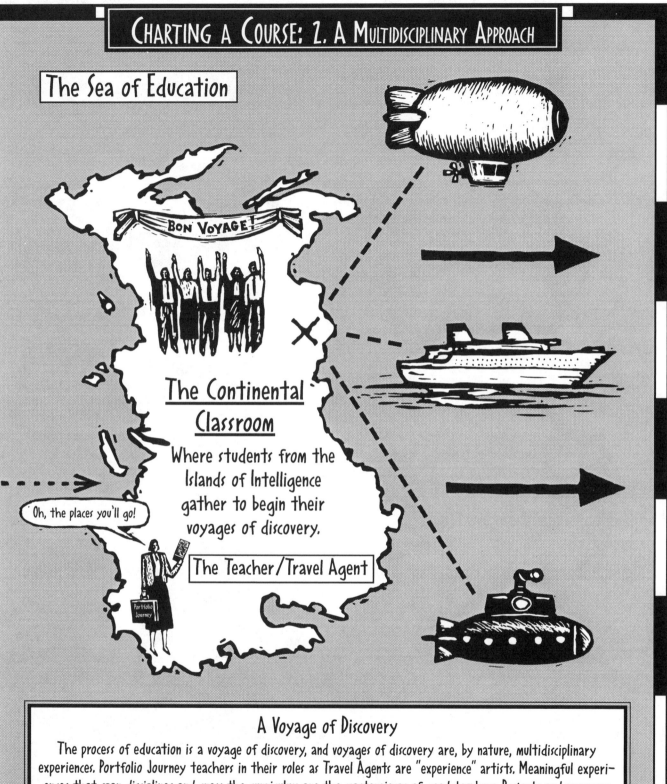

A Voyage of Discovery

The process of education is a voyage of discovery, and voyages of discovery are, by nature, multidisciplinary experiences. Portfolio Journey teachers in their roles as Travel Agents are "experience" artists. Meaningful experiences that span disciplines and cross the curriculum are the masterpieces of good teachers. Projects and processes that link literature to math, history to science, or art to geography allow more students the chance for success and show respect for a variety of intelligences.

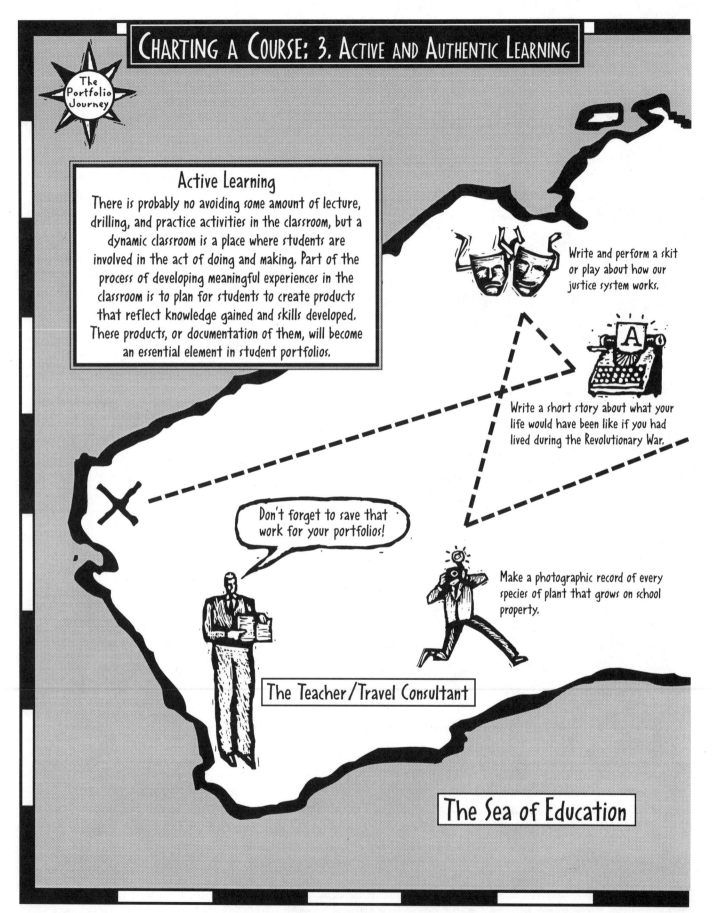

CHARTING A COURSE: 3. ACTIVE AND AUTHENTIC LEARNING

The Portfolio Journey

Active Learning

There is probably no avoiding some amount of lecture, drilling, and practice activities in the classroom, but a dynamic classroom is a place where students are involved in the act of doing and making. Part of the process of developing meaningful experiences in the classroom is to plan for students to create products that reflect knowledge gained and skills developed. These products, or documentation of them, will become an essential element in student portfolios.

Write and perform a skit or play about how our justice system works.

Write a short story about what your life would have been like if you had lived during the Revolutionary War.

Don't forget to save that work for your portfolios!

Make a photographic record of every species of plant that grows on school property.

The Teacher/Travel Consultant

The Sea of Education

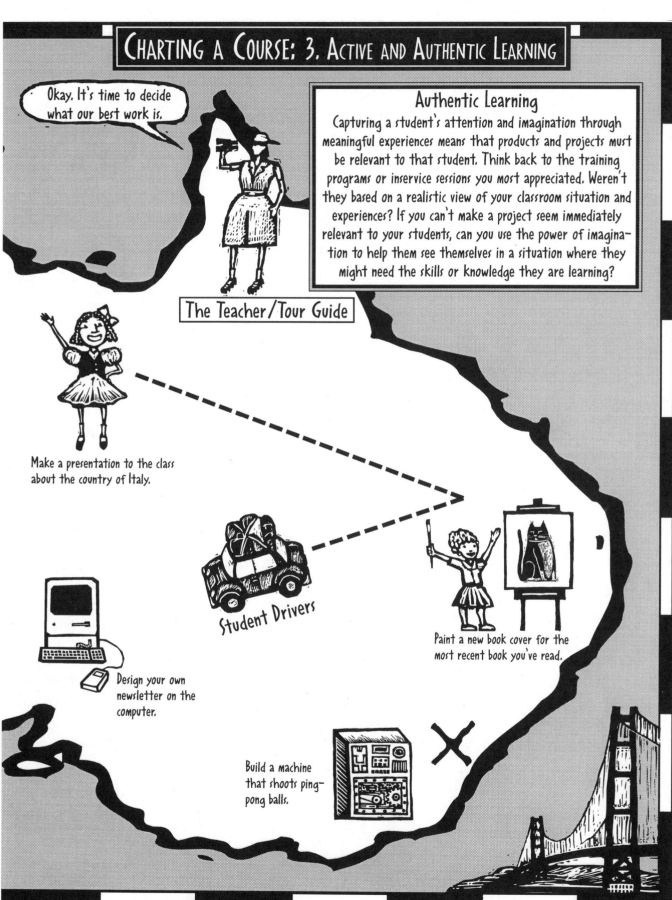

CHARTING A COURSE: 3. ACTIVE AND AUTHENTIC LEARNING

Okay. It's time to decide what our best work is.

Authentic Learning

Capturing a student's attention and imagination through meaningful experiences means that products and projects must be relevant to that student. Think back to the training programs or inservice sessions you most appreciated. Weren't they based on a realistic view of your classroom situation and experiences? If you can't make a project seem immediately relevant to your students, can you use the power of imagination to help them see themselves in a situation where they might need the skills or knowledge they are learning?

The Teacher/Tour Guide

Make a presentation to the class about the country of Italy.

Student Drivers

Paint a new book cover for the most recent book you've read.

Design your own newsletter on the computer.

Build a machine that shoots ping-pong balls.

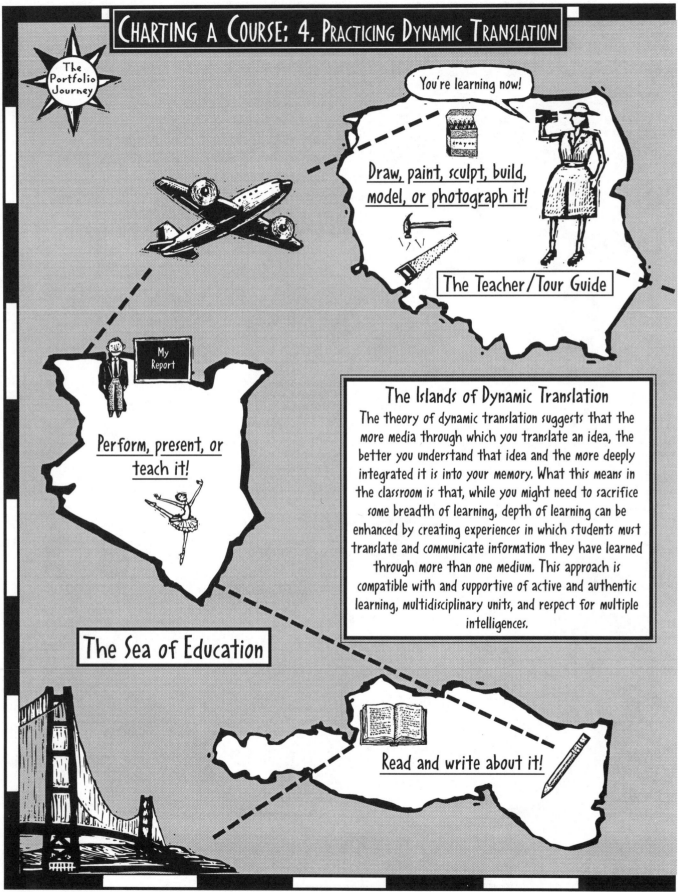

CHARTING A COURSE: WORKING TO COMMUNICATE

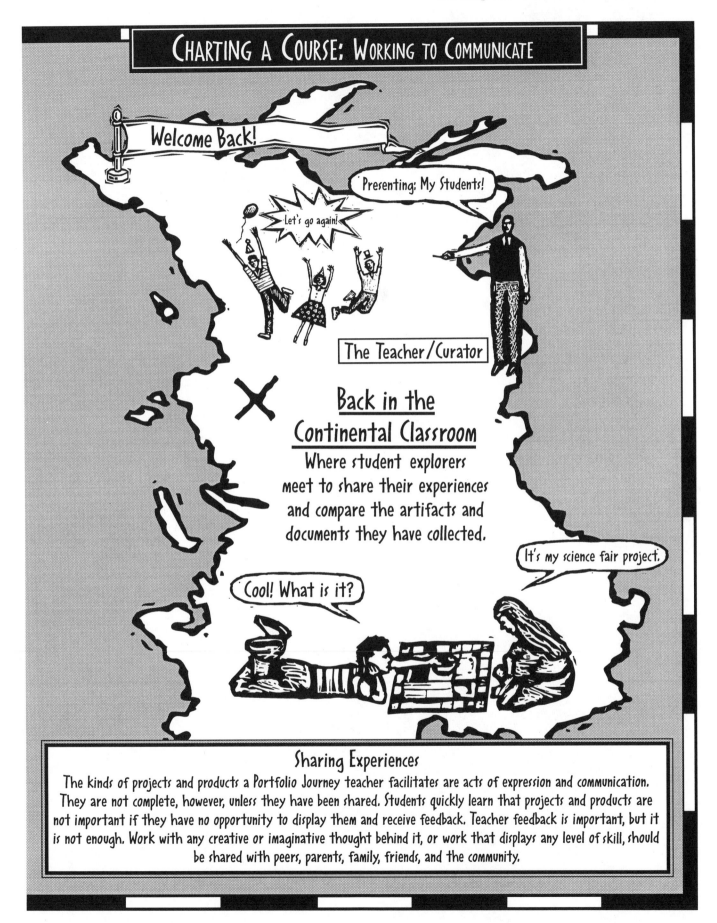

Sharing Experiences

The kinds of projects and products a Portfolio Journey teacher facilitates are acts of expression and communication. They are not complete, however, unless they have been shared. Students quickly learn that projects and products are not important if they have no opportunity to display them and receive feedback. Teacher feedback is important, but it is not enough. Work with any creative or imaginative thought behind it, or work that displays any level of skill, should be shared with peers, parents, family, friends, and the community.

Planning the Journey

The Portfolio Journey

The Teacher as Travel Agent

In Part 2 of the Portfolio Journey you will:

ⓔ Plan the journey your students will take during the school year, including the important sites to see, the challenges to embrace, and the destinations to be reached.

ⓔ Identify the souvenirs you will want your students to collect on their journeys.

ⓔ Select the four kinds of luggage (portfolios) you will be carrying on your journey.

ⓔ Prepare the mood and atmosphere of your classroom for travels, both real and imagined.

Destinations
Establishing Criteria for Portfolios

"Would you tell me, please, which way I ought to go from here?"
"That depends a good deal on where you want to get to," said the Cat.
"I don't much care where—" said Alice.
"Then it doesn't matter which way you go," said the Cat.
"—so long as I get *somewhere*," Alice added as an explanation.
"Oh, you're sure to do that," said the Cat, "if you only walk long enough."

—Lewis Carroll (*Alice in Wonderland*)

It is possible to imagine the portfolio Alice might keep if she follows her whims and the advice of the Cheshire Cat. It would be filled with odds and ends, samples of whatever seemed, at the time, like something to keep. When, after walking *long enough*, Alice eventually arrives somewhere, her portfolio might reflect where she had been and what she had done. Then again, it might not.

Now you are ready to begin planning your Portfolio Journey. For Part 2 of this book, remember that you will be acting as a Travel Agent. Your role will be to plan for the journey your students will take. You have already begun learning about the portfolio process. Now it is time to develop more specific elements of the Portfolio Journey.

Establishing criteria for portfolios, knowing where we are going, is an essential step in the process of planning for successful portfolios. Establishing portfolio criteria gives a purpose to the act of collecting. We may not be able to predict where our students will end up or what routes they will take, but we should agree on some destinations. Whether these destinations are a part of a visionary future or the practical pieces of an economic puzzle, we still need them. Establishing criteria for portfolios is like climbing to the top of the nearest mountain and thinking about where we might go from there.

When discussing criteria for portfolios, it is important to remember that we are not yet discussing the specifics of what will be included in each portfolio. Establishing criteria is the first step in imagining what purpose a student portfolio might serve, what its contents might be. This is the point where we ask ourselves as teachers: What do we want our students to be able to do when they leave the education system? What skills and abilities will best serve them in adult life? All students are not created equal. The criteria we establish will not make them equal. Some students will master some skills, while other students will perfect a different set of abilities. Establishing appropriate criteria will help ensure that, although we recognize each individual student as a unique person, we expect each of our students to succeed.

In a perfect world, those with an interest and a stake in the education of children would cooperate and collaborate to establish the criteria for an effective portfolio. Society, as the most generalized of the stakeholders, would help decide what skills would best serve its economic prosperity and social stability. Parents would suggest criteria that, once fulfilled, would best ensure economic and emotional success, security, and happiness for their children. School administrators, tasked with managing and monitoring the process of education, would want the criteria to be achievable and demonstrable. Teachers would outline the process of achieving these criteria as a series of steps appropriate for their students. As primary guides, teachers would want criteria that they deem important, criteria that challenge and motivate their students. At some point during the process, students would begin providing input as to the skills and abilities they want and need.

A student portfolio program should, in many respects, reflect the mission of education. Certainly, some of the standards that a school system has adopted will find their way into portfolio criteria. The criteria for a student portfolio program, though, will differ in focus and in vision. To be successful as a tool in the short term, a portfolio must be focused. For long-term success, however, a portfolio must have a vision.

This chapter is about finding a vision, or (in the context of our travel metaphor) finding a destination. It guides you through the processes of forming a portfolio planning team, finding a vision, and translating your vision into developmentally appropriate indicators. It also shows you how to build on your initial vision and how to see that vision in visual form as an actual map. ✪

Vision
A Strategy for Finding a Destination

Vision: The place we hope the education process will take our students. It is the destination we want our students to reach.

Focus: The signs that will indicate that our students are reaching that destination.

Traveling Companions: Forming a Portfolio Planning Team

When planning a student portfolio program, it can be very helpful to work with colleagues. Working toward a vision and a focus is best accomplished by brainstorming. Bringing together a small group of people to imagine what purpose a portfolio might serve and what it might contain has some distinct advantages. Because the end product is to be a portfolio capable of reflecting the achievements of a diverse group of students, diversity among the planners can be beneficial. Even working with just one other person when planning a portfolio will provide a different perspective and different emphasis. Large groups can brainstorm, but translating group-creative sessions into plans is work for smaller teams of five to seven teachers.

In addition to the size of the group doing the planning, the level or scope of the planning being done is also a consideration. For an individual teacher or a small group within a school, the best kind of team is simply a teacher portfolio cooperative. A group like this can assign itself some background reading in student portfolios. They can meet informally to complete structured activities such as those provided in this chapter, or simply to share ideas. This is the best approach for teachers who are experimenting with student portfolios in their classrooms outside of any school or system-wide mandate for portfolios.

If teachers at a certain grade level agree to adopt student portfolios, it can help to form several small teams to work toward vision and focus. It is useful to meet as a large group on a regular basis to maintain the grade-wide perspective, but more progress will be made (and will be made sooner) if the real developmental work is done in smaller teams. This strategy can also be used for teachers who are united by the special needs of their students.

Though portfolios can have a profound effect on students during the course of a single school year, the real potential of portfolios is most fully realized with the continuity provided by a school-wide program. When a school adopts student portfolios, it sends a strong message to students and to parents about the importance of portfolios. When portfolio planning involves an entire school, it is still best to keep the teams organized by grade level or special needs. At the school level, the vision will be shared, but the focus or theme might vary from grade to grade, just as the treatment or metaphor might vary from class to class. Schoolwide adoption also offers the possibility of involving parents in the planning process from the beginning.

Beyond school-wide adoption of student portfolios is system-wide adoption. This type of planning is beyond the focus of this book, but it is essentially the same process on a much larger scale and longer timeline. Though system-wide adoption can be a long and difficult process, it will, if done correctly, clarify the mission of a school system and provide added continuity for parents and students.

Starting There and Working to Here: Finding a Vision

After you have formed a portfolio planning team or support group (or if you are working alone), the next step is to begin brainstorming around a deceptively simple question: *What should the portfolio of a graduating high school senior demonstrate or evidence?*

Asking this question is what is meant by "starting there." Even if you normally teach, for example, second-grade students, imagine that each of your students is graduating from high school and moving into the adult world. What skills or abilities should they possess? Answering this question will provide you with a vision for the portfolio program. Your answer should be in the form of a list, of particular skills or abilities, prepared from the point of view of a caring mentor. It should be student-centered, and it should look to the future. It might be prioritized according to what each student will need to survive physically, emotionally, and economically. Don't worry at this point about whether you believe you can or cannot teach these skills or abilities. A Portfolio Journey "Visioning Worksheet" to use for your brainstorming follows. If you are working with a team, photocopy and distribute the worksheet to each team member. Following this worksheet is a sample completed worksheet (p. 42) showing some of the skills and abilities that teachers have suggested when visioning such a portfolio. Remember, this is a student-centered list. It is a "wish list" of sorts. Don't censor your ideas at this stage: Be optimistic! Be idealistic!

Establishing Portfolio Criteria
Visioning Worksheet
When my students graduate from high school, they will have:

_____
_____
_____
_____
_____
_____
_____
_____
_____
_____
_____
_____
_____
_____
_____
_____
_____
_____
_____
_____
_____
_____
_____
_____
_____
_____
_____
_____
_____
_____

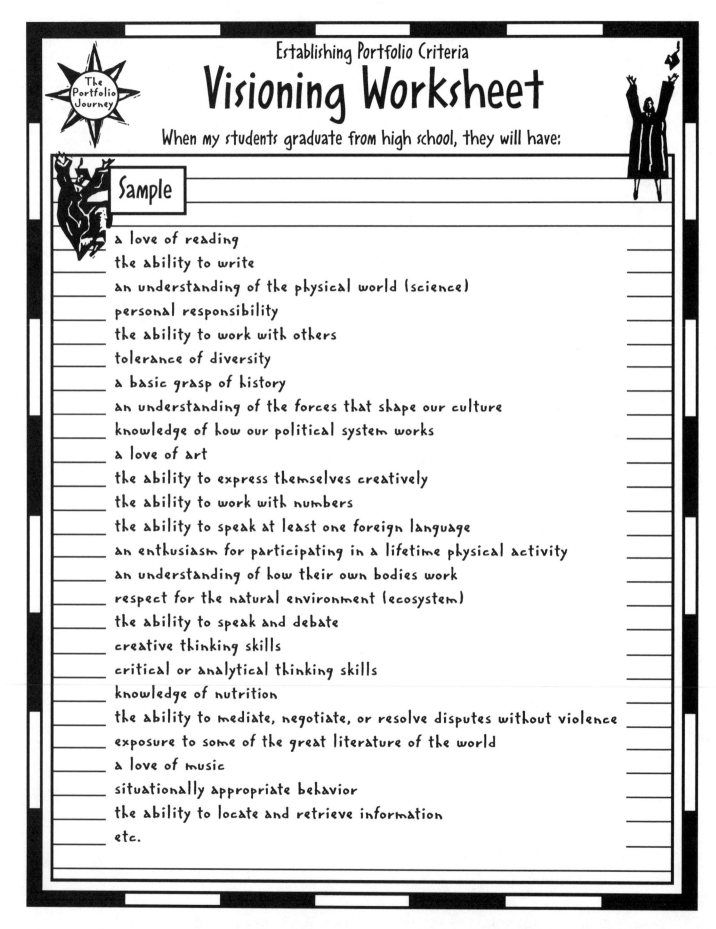

Establishing Portfolio Criteria

Visioning Worksheet

When my students graduate from high school, they will have:

Sample

a love of reading

the ability to write

an understanding of the physical world (science)

personal responsibility

the ability to work with others

tolerance of diversity

a basic grasp of history

an understanding of the forces that shape our culture

knowledge of how our political system works

a love of art

the ability to express themselves creatively

the ability to work with numbers

the ability to speak at least one foreign language

an enthusiasm for participating in a lifetime physical activity

an understanding of how their own bodies work

respect for the natural environment (ecosystem)

the ability to speak and debate

creative thinking skills

critical or analytical thinking skills

knowledge of nutrition

the ability to mediate, negotiate, or resolve disputes without violence

exposure to some of the great literature of the world

a love of music

situationally appropriate behavior

the ability to locate and retrieve information

etc.

On the sample worksheet, notice that none of the suggestions is yet specific. They don't suggest how a student will gain these skills or abilities, or at what grade. They don't quantify or qualify. They don't even provide any markers for what would indicate that a student had achieved them. These are broad goals, not objectives. It is even debatable whether some of these goals could be met. This is okay: This list should be broad and visionary.

The next step is to focus on each of the items in your list. If some of the items overlap and can be condensed, consolidate them now. You should now have a list that inspires you. Locate each goal at the end of a timeline that begins in elementary school and ends in the twelfth grade. Ask yourself what kind of indicators or evidence would demonstrate progress toward each goal. This may take some time, but it is time well spent. When, on your timeline, should these indicators appear? When placing the indicators on your timeline, don't worry about whether your placement of indicators is developmentally correct (you will be most accurate about the grades you teach). A Portfolio Journey "Timeline Worksheet" to use for organizing your thoughts follows (p. 44). Photocopy the worksheet first because each worksheet should track only one goal from your "Visioning Worksheet."

Knowing Your Role: Translating Your Vision

At this point, you should have lists that begin to show some of the evidence you hope to see in student portfolios at the grade you teach. Basically, you began with a list for the entire journey and then worked your way backwards to the part of the journey for which you will be responsible. You will not be with students for their entire journey, but you will be planning part of their trip. What can *you* do to help each student reach these goals?

From your timeline, assemble a list of the indicators that fall around the grade you teach. Include indicators from the grade before and the grade beyond yours to reflect a range of student development. A Portfolio Journey "Trip Planning Worksheet 1" to use for creating this list of the specific indicators you have selected or identified for your students follows (p. 45).

Necessary Diversions: Building on Your Vision

At this point, it might be necessary to add to your list. You probably have some succinct and admirable goals with what you think are practical and achievable indicators. You are probably developing a sense for what kinds of work students might be saving in their portfolios, but other people may have already set the expectations for what your students should be doing in class. You may already have certain portfolio standards to which you must adhere. You certainly already have content and skill standards that you are required to teach. Now is the time to build these mandated standards into the portfolio description.

Begin by listing mandated standards on the Portfolio Journey "Trip Planning Worksheet 2" (p. 46). Incorporate mandated standards into the objectives you have arrived at through your visioning and timeline worksheets. Combine similar objectives where possible. Integrating content areas can also be effective: You might ask students to write about their artwork or create artwork related to a science concept. For instance, if one of your objectives is for students to understand the relationship of primary, secondary, and tertiary colors, you might expect to see a painting that demonstrates the ability to mix colors. You might also expect students to provide a written explanation of the process they used to create the

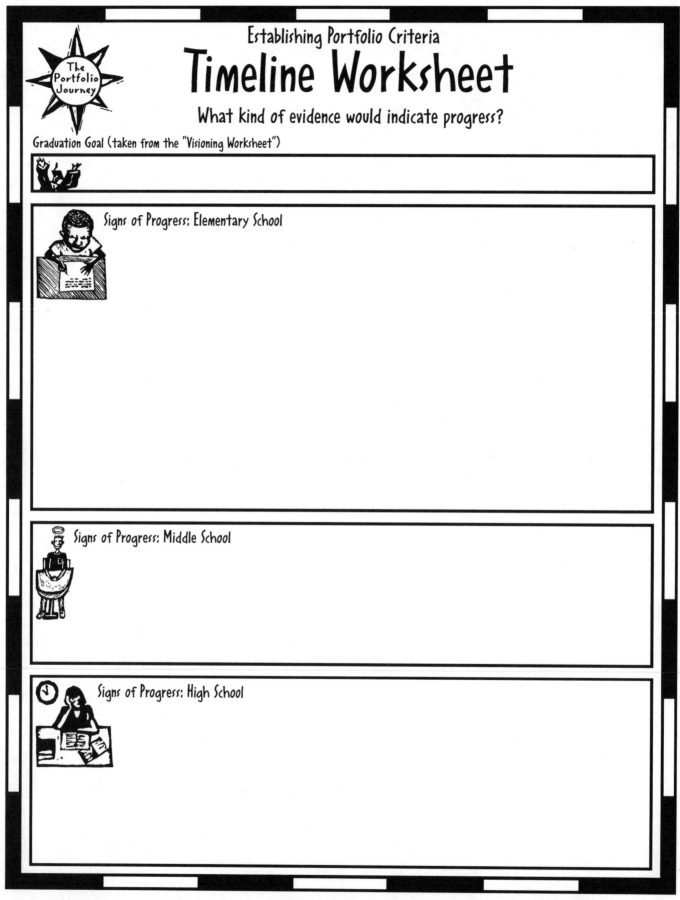

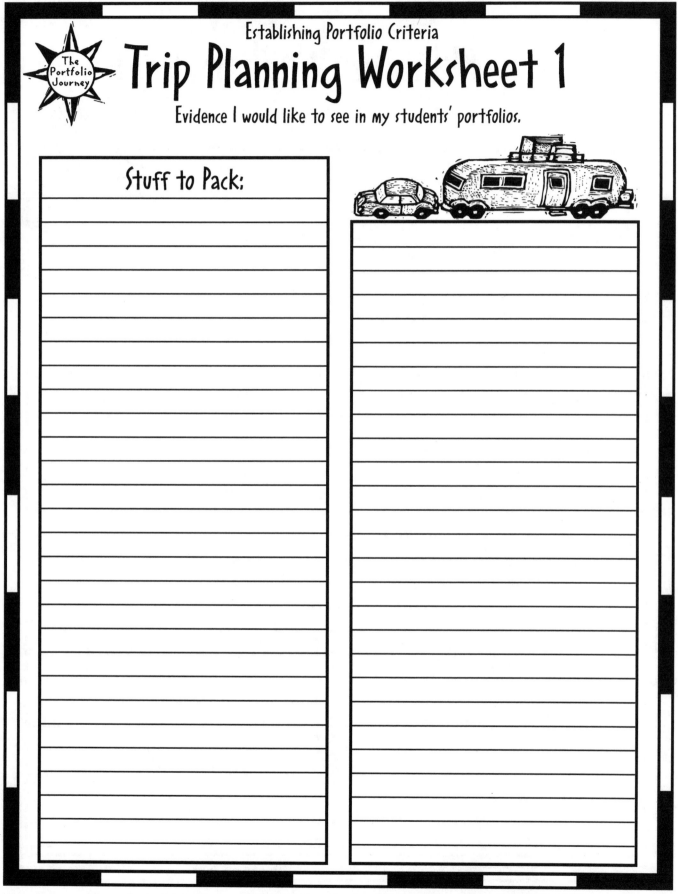

Establishing Portfolio Criteria

Trip Planning Worksheet 1

Evidence I would like to see in my students' portfolios.

Stuff to Pack:

Establishing Portfolio Criteria

Trip Planning Worksheet 2

Standards that I know my students will need to meet.

Still More Stuff to Pack:

painting. The writing sample might include standards mandated by the school or system. As a teacher, if you have been teaching for a number of years, you probably already have a good sense of what kinds of work you want your students to do and to save. You might, at this point, review your lesson plans from years past to add ideas to "Trip Planning Worksheet 2."

Mapping the Territory: Another Way of Seeing Your Vision

You are now much closer to realizing the purpose and contents for your students' portfolios. You have a vision, which you have integrated with preexisting requirements. In the next chapter, "Appropriate Souvenirs: What to Put into Portfolios," we will work on focus. Before moving on, though, I invite you try an activity—"Mapping the Territory." This engaging activity is ideal for the beginning of the school year, but is can also be done whenever you want to step back and see the big picture. It will help fix a sense of the journey and the destination in your mind. It is important not to rush or force an activity like this. It should be done playfully and with humor. "Mapping the Territory" can be very fun when done as or shared with a team.

Recall the idea of dynamic translation mentioned in Chapter 3. "Mapping the Territory" is an example of a dynamic translation activity. So far in this chapter, we have worked mostly with ideas and words. Now we are going to translate our ideas and words into images. This is an exercise for the imagination.

To begin, find the largest sheet of paper (24 by 30 inches or larger) that you can comfortably draw upon when laid in front of you. Using a pencil, lightly draw the outline or boundaries of a continent, so that the continent fills the entire sheet of paper. Draw some lakes, some rivers, some swamps, and some wetlands. Add some hills and mountain ranges, deserts and grasslands, forests and tundra. Draw these regions lightly, using pencil, so that you can move them later, if necessary. If you don't like to draw, cut out small pictures from magazines to represent the terrain of your continent.

Now imagine the Portfolio Journey as a real journey across a continent. Allow yourself to slip into the metaphor of traveling across a vast, unknown continent with your students. Look back at the lists you have compiled for your educational vision. Find a starting point on one side of your continent (if you are doing this activity at midyear, you might locate your class somewhere in the middle of the continent). Map the process that will take your students from where they are now to having full portfolios that richly reflect their abilities and experiences. Begin this process now, continuing as you learn more about the Portfolio Journey in the chapters ahead. Draw landforms, landmarks, cities, towns, or special places to represent the goals of your vision. Which goals do you anticipate will be difficult to achieve? You might draw imposing terrain for such goals to signify the difficulty of attaining them.

If you anticipate traveling in such a way as to cover a certain portion of the continent in a certain portion of the school year, you might add milestones—the little indicators that will let you know that you are achieving your goals. How will you travel? Will you plot a course in a straight line to cross the continent in the shortest possible distance, or will you meander and explore? How comfortable will you be with detours? Will you allow your students to help decide some of the course as they progress?

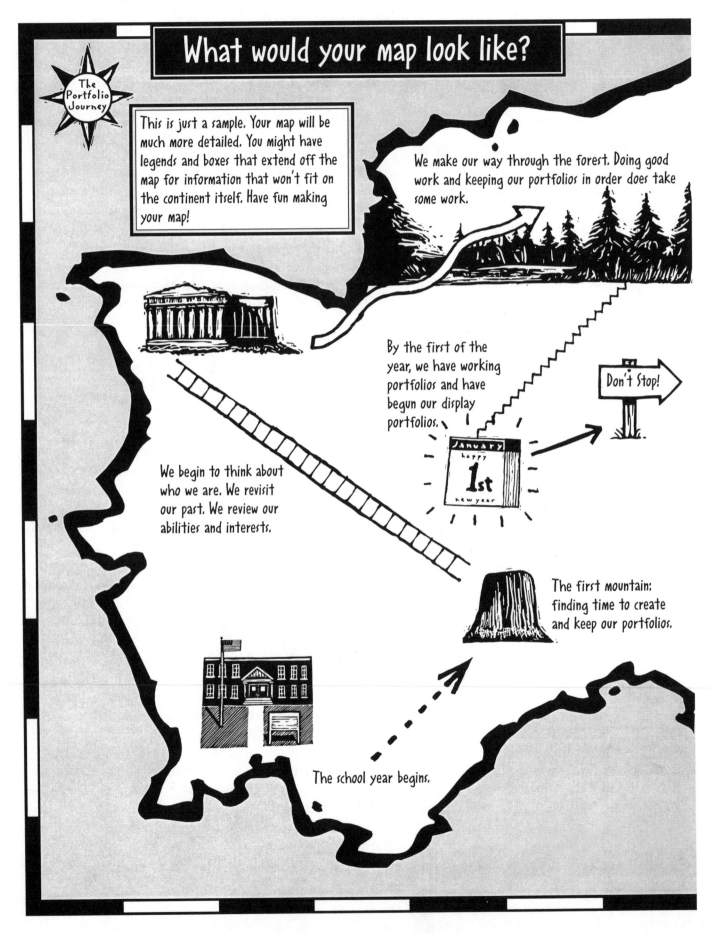

What would your map look like?

The Portfolio Journey

This is just a sample. Your map will be much more detailed. You might have legends and boxes that extend off the map for information that won't fit on the continent itself. Have fun making your map!

We make our way through the forest. Doing good work and keeping our portfolios in order does take some work.

By the first of the year, we have working portfolios and have begun our display portfolios.

Don't Stop!

January happy 1st new year

We begin to think about who we are. We revisit our past. We review our abilities and interests.

The first mountain: finding time to create and keep our portfolios.

The school year begins.

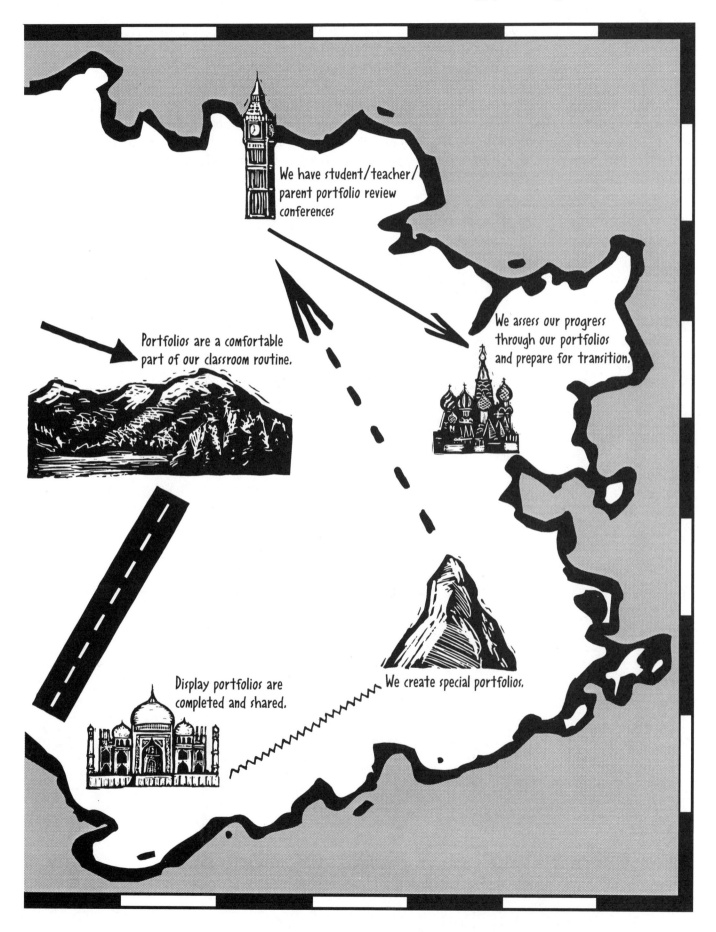

Draw as much detail as you can. Once you have a fairly detailed picture of your journey, use ink and colored markers to add sparkle to your map. Refer to your map often throughout your Portfolio Journey, comparing your planned progress to your actual progress. Use it like a visual journal to map the route actually taken and compare it to the planned route. Or, better still, post the map on a wall in your classroom so that everyone (students, parents, teachers, and administrators) can visualize the territory ahead. Remember, flexibility is a virtue. Deviating from the planned route is not a weakness. It is usually caused by the discovery of unforeseen obstacles or a better route. Explorers who are flexible are usually the ones who are most successful. ✪

Appropriate Souvenirs
What to Put into Portfolios

Two most necessary items of any African outfit, however small, are a portable table and a stout portable chair, and it would be better if the traveller took two or three chairs with him (as they are very light and portable) so as to be able to offer a seat to any native of importance who may visit his tent—an attention generally much appreciated.

—H. H. Johnston (*Hints on Outfit*, 1889)

In his book *Hints on Outfit*, H. H. Johnston was sharing with fellow travelers of his time what he had learned from years of travel. Specifically, he was suggesting what travelers might want to take with them on their journeys. In this chapter, we shall be doing something similar. There is no one right way to keep student portfolios. That said, though, it does not follow that one should just save bits and pieces of everything.

In Chapter 4, you began the process of defining what kind of portfolio your students might keep. You began by clarifying a vision. It is now time to work on focus. Where a vision is broad, focus is narrow. Having a focus is what keeps a portfolio from being just a simple collection of a student's work. Focus is the set of criteria that will organize the collection. A focus comes from selecting or establishing a portfolio purpose and a unifying theme. The purpose and theme should, when outlined in concrete and practical steps, help you realize the vision you intend for your students. Your theme will provide the structure for your students' portfolios.

You may be wondering whether *travel* isn't the theme of your students' portfolios. After all, it is the metaphor we have been using and will continue to use throughout this book. Travel is a powerful metaphor, and it is the idea you will be using to organize the process of keeping student portfolios. Remember that your student-centered goals should include making the portfolio process fun (and rich, and imaginative, and exciting) and making portfolios student-managed. Though *travel* is an engaging metaphor for drawing students into the process of keeping portfolios, your theme—your focus—must reflect your vision and must be academically sound and defensible.

Before selecting a theme, it is important to understand that there are three basic purposes for portfolios. There may well be others, but if you understand these three, you will have a sound foundation for selecting a theme. You may have many reasons for using student portfolios, but your purpose will help you define the materials that will be saved in a portfolio. The three purposes for portfolios that we will be discussing are *presentational*, *documentary*, and *exploratory*. Effective portfolios are flexible tools, and there is often an overlap among these purposes. As you will learn in Chapter 6, these three purposes are reflected, to different degrees, in each of the four types of portfolios discussed in *The Portfolio Journey*. In other words, *The Portfolio Journey* gives you the option of achieving each of these purposes through different portfolio types, but, at any one time, the emphasis for a particular portfolio usually lies in one area: presentation, documentation, or exploration.

Presentational Portfolio
A Tool for Communication

A presentational portfolio is used to display a person's abilities to others. It might be used as a requirement for graduation, for a job application, or for college admission. It tends to show only the very best work of which a student is capable. Any portfolio can be used for presentation, but a presentational portfolio is designed to be exhibited for others. When we think of an artist's or a designer's portfolio, we are thinking of a presentational portfolio.

Documentary Portfolio
A Collection of Student Work

A documentary portfolio is a collection of work. It may not be the best work of which a student is capable, but it is usually significant work. The documentary portfolio is not shaped as deliberately as a presentational portfolio. Any portfolio can be used for documentation, but when one is trying to amass a broad range of evidence, perhaps demonstrating many skills, one collects that work in a documentary portfolio. The documentary portfolio is closest to what most people expect of a traditional student portfolio.

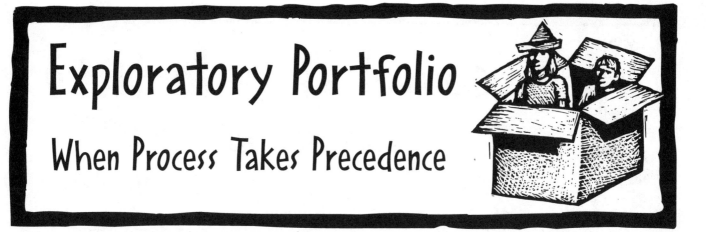

Exploratory Portfolio
When Process Takes Precedence

An exploratory portfolio turns the process of keeping a portfolio into a more active learning experience. Exploratory portfolios are used as teaching tools in the classroom. They actually help to shape the learning experience. Students are expected to review their work and revise or branch out into other assignments, based on what they discover. Any portfolio can be used for exploration, but in the exploratory portfolio, work is valued for the processes revealed and the discoveries made.

A theme for student portfolios should, as stated above, reflect the vision you have for your students' education. If, for instance, for the question *What should the portfolio of a graduating high school senior demonstrate or evidence?* (from Chapter 4), if you decided that communication skills were of primary importance, your theme might focus attention on that area. In other words, the portfolio contents would reflect a student's ability to communicate. If you decided that information handling skills were one of your top requirements for a successful high school graduate, your theme or emphasis should reflect this. If you or your planning team answered "flexibility and a wide range of skills," you might choose *diversity through multiple intelligences* as your theme. In this case, you would want to highlight the widest possible range of experiences and expertise.

Selecting a theme does not preclude gathering evidence in support of other elements of your vision. It merely provides a strong focus. It is, in a sense, the compass for your Portfolio Journey. It will keep you on course and make the process of building portfolios meaningful.

It is possible to imagine many strong themes for student portfolios. You might keep Creative and Critical Thinking Skills Portfolios, Creative Expression Portfolios, Life Skills Portfolios, Problem Solving Portfolios, Conflict Resolution Portfolios, or Personal History Portfolios. Notice, though, that each of these themes has several things in common. First, they are visionary—they take a long-range and caring view of the needs of students as people. Second, they are broad enough to allow for a wide range of experiences and a variety of forms of evidence. Third, they are focused enough to allow you to easily communicate your reasons for using portfolios to students, parents, and administrators.

Portfolio themes and portfolio purposes should be complementary. They are concepts that go hand-in-hand. To demonstrate what is meant by purposes and themes of portfolios being complementary, a discussion follows with examples of three themes for portfolios—the Communications Portfolio, the Information Skills Portfolio, and the Multiple Intelligences Portfolio. ✪

Theme: # Communications Portfolio
Purpose: ## Presentational

In our world, information comes to us and passes from us in three main channels: the written word, the spoken word, and the realized image. When information passes from us, it is called communication. There can be little doubt that successful people are successful communicators. Our information-age economy places a premium on the skills of communication. A presentational portfolio, one that highlights a student's abilities, is a natural vehicle for demonstrating communication skills. Most teachers would be pleased if their students could successfully communicate their ideas through writing, speech, and imagery. To that end, it is possible to focus a student portfolio around evidence of communication skills within the three primary channels of communication.

A Communications Portfolio for a student might contain samples of work from each of the three main channels of communication—writing, speaking, and image making—as well as from a fourth category, for crossover skills. It might include the following:

- Elements of Writing

    1. Samples that demonstrate a grasp of spelling and punctuation
    2. Samples that show control of organization and sequence
    3. Samples of prewriting, such as clustering
    4. Samples of handwriting and keyboarding skills
    5. Samples demonstrating research skills

- Written Work

    1. Samples of outlines
    2. Samples of descriptive writing
    3. Samples of imaginative writing
    4. Samples of analytical writing
    5. Samples of narrative writing, storytelling, and journalism
    6. Samples of expressive writing, such as poetry
    7. Samples of motivational writing, such as letters to the editor
    8. Samples of technical writing, such as reports

- Elements of Speaking

    1. Presentation outlines
    2. Samples of notes used for a presentation
    3. Photographs of graphics used for a presentation
    4. Samples of scripts

- Oral Presentations

    1. Video- or audiocassettes of oral reports (presenting data)
    2. Video- or audiocassettes of dramatic readings (telling stories)
    3. Video- or audiocassettes of debates (arguing or defending)
    4. Video- or audiocassettes of persuasive speeches (effecting change)
    5. Video- or audiocassettes of improvisation (spontaneity/flexibility)
    6. Video- or audiocassettes of discussions (developmental thought)
    7. Video- or audiocassettes of songs or poetry (expression)

- Elements of Image Making

    1. Sketches, diagrams, and visual planning
    2. Samples of media exploration
    3. Samples of the ability to organize images for display
    4. Samples of the ability to establish visual criteria
    5. Samples of the ability to substitute images for words
    6. Samples of the ability to alter or manipulate existing imagery

- Realized Images

    1. Samples of student-generated imagery (photographs, drawings, paintings, sculptures, collages, models, videotaped dance pieces, constructions, computer graphics, films, videos, animations, etc.) that

        a. express an abstraction through symbol or metaphor
        b. communicate information
        c. explore the range of a medium
        d. tell a story
        e. imagine new connections
        f. advocate change
        g. document a moment in time

- Crossover Skills

    1. Samples of the ability to combine words and images effectively, which might include

        a. photo-essays
        b. graphic illustrations with text
        c. posters
        d. newsletters, newspapers, yearbooks
        e. art and literary publications
        f. bulletin boards
        g. science fair projects
        h. interactive multimedia displays

    2. Samples of the ability to integrate imagery with live presentations, such as

        a. slides
        b. overhead transparencies
        c. display graphics (charts, graphs, etc.)

The Communications Portfolio would draw samples from all the content areas. Many of the pieces chosen for the portfolio would overlap categories. A single report, for instance, might provide evidence of all the elements of writing, as well as for the ability to generate imagery that conveys information. It might also serve as evidence of the ability to combine words and images for effective communication. A Communications Portfolio might be developed as a documentary or exploratory portfolio, but if it is to be presentational, it should be built around a small, focused selection of the very best examples of a student's work. An effective presentational portfolio should be able to communicate a person's strengths at a glance. When used in formal situations, such as student/teacher/parent reviews, the presentation time for a Communications Portfolio, including time for discussion, should be about twenty minutes. ✪

Theme: # Information Skills Portfolio
Purpose: Documentary

As important as communication is to success in an information-based economy, two additional skill sets are of equal importance. In addition to communication, the ability to effectively handle information involves access and transformation. Access skills are what might also be called research skills. This is the set of skills that allows one to tap into data and find relevant information. The ability to transform data is the process by which one adds value to information. Adding value to information is done by organizing, arranging, combining, connecting, abstracting, condensing, linking, contextualizing, or otherwise transforming that information.

An Information Skills Portfolio is built around evidence of work in the areas of accessing, transforming, and communicating. As a documentary portfolio, this collection need not have only finished pieces or even necessarily a student's best work. To document the skills of access, transformation, and communication, an Information Skills Portfolio might include the following:

- Access Skills

    1. Samples of the ability to extract information by reading
    2. Samples of the ability to extract information by listening
    3. Samples of the ability to extract information by observing
    4. Samples of the ability to use reference materials
    5. Samples of the ability to record information or experience accurately with written words, spoken words, and realized images

6. Samples demonstrating the use of recording tools (cameras, tape recorders, video cameras, etc.)
7. Samples of interviews
8. Samples of the ability to understand traditional information sources (libraries, journal abstracts, encyclopedias, etc.)
9. Samples of the ability to access digital information (computers, online databases, CD-ROMs, etc.)
10. Samples of the ability to use innovative information sources (museum collections, genealogies, archives, etc.)

- Transformation Skills

    1. Samples of the ability to organize data into useful patterns (graphs, charts, etc.)
    2. Samples of the ability to arrange information (database construction, multimedia design, etc.)
    3. Samples of the ability to link related or unrelated information to reveal new connections (hypertext, hypermedia, invention, etc.)
    4. Samples of mental flexibility (brainstorming, etc.)
    5. Samples of the ability to incubate ideas (preparing to have new ideas by research and immersion in a subject area)
    6. Samples of the ability to translate ideas from one field or area of study into another
    7. Samples of the ability to imagine written, spoken, or graphic information arranged in new patterns

- Communication Skills

    1. Samples of the ability to communicate information effectively with written words, spoken words, and realized images
    2. Samples of the ability to express abstract concepts and feelings with written words, spoken words, and realized images
    3. Samples of the ability to motivate and effect change with written words, spoken words, and realized images
    4. Samples of the use of imaginative forms of communication
    5. Samples that evidence social skills (effective teamwork, leadership ability, etc.)

This list of samples that might be included in an Information Skills Portfolio is by no means complete. It is a starting point. A documentary portfolio is intended as a broad collection of evidence of a student's ability. It is, by nature, larger and more comprehensive than a presentational portfolio. Though a presentational portfolio may contain examples of work in progress, its focus is finished work. To focus on exploring process, an exploratory portfolio is the best choice. ✪

Theme: Multiple Intelligences Portfolio
Purpose: Exploratory

The Multiple Intelligences Portfolio is an idea based on the theories of Harvard professor Dr. Howard Gardner (see Chapter 3, page 24). As an organizing principle for an exploratory portfolio, the idea of multiple intelligences is useful because it encourages more inclusive portfolios that reflect a wider range of students' school experiences. Two of the things that differentiate an exploratory portfolio from presentational and documentary portfolios are inclusion of process materials—evidence of the steps a student uses to achieve a finished product—and the use of portfolio criteria to encourage students to explore new ways of relating to the work they do in school. An exploratory portfolio built around Gardner's eight intelligences would encourage students to investigate each of the intelligences within themselves.

In addition to the samples suggested as appropriate for the Communications and Information Skills Portfolios (presentational and documentary), an exploratory portfolio might include rough drafts; outlines; sketches; notes; storyboards; photographs of models; and video- and audiocassettes of rehearsals, improvisations, practice sessions, and so on. Though this kind of exploratory portfolio might contain all kinds of material, it is critical to include evidence of each of the seven intelligences:

- Verbal-Linguistic Intelligence
  Samples of a student's ability to express thought, feeling, or abstract content through language

- Bodily-Kinesthetic Intelligence
  Samples of a student's ability to express thought physically through dance, movement, athletic performance, or motor skills

- Logical-Mathematical Intelligence
  Samples of a student's ability to solve problems or express abstract concepts through numbers or formulas, or to apply rules of logic to thought problems

- Visual-Spatial Intelligence
  Samples of a student's ability to generate or work with imagery, to manipulate objects in space, to assemble and construct things, or to express thought or feeling through realized imagery

- Musical-Rhythmic Intelligence
  Samples of a student's ability to express thought through musical performance

- Interpersonal Intelligence
  Samples of a student's ability to interact constructively with others—to organize, to lead, to facilitate, to mediate, or to work on cooperative projects

- Intrapersonal Intelligence
  Samples of a student's ability for self-reflection, self-assessment, or evaluating and tapping into inner resources

- Naturalistic Intelligence
  Samples of a student's ability to recognize and differentiate between species and subspecies of plants and animals, to understand the complex relationships and dynamics of an ecosystem, or to classify organic and inorganic phenomena

Teachers who use exploratory portfolios tend to design activities and assignments to meet the criteria they have established for portfolios. There is nothing wrong with this, so long as the criteria are ambitious and grounded with a positive vision. Multiple intelligences, as a theory, can incite a powerful vision of what education should be. ✪

So Which Path Is Best?

This chapter has provided examples of the three types of student portfolios. The *presentational* portfolio is used to show samples of the very best work of which a student is capable. It tends to be compact and heavily edited. If a portfolio is to be used to showcase a student's abilities, the presentational portfolio is the type to use. The *documentary* portfolio represents the most traditional idea of what a portfolio should be. It contains some process samples, some finished work, and is a repository for student work. This is a balanced portfolio, the type most teachers attempt to keep. Whereas a documentary portfolio reflects the work done in class, an *exploratory* portfolio actually drives the work done in class. It is not just a passive collection of student work but a tool for expanding horizons.

That said, it is important to remember that one needn't choose just one type of portfolio. As you will learn in the next chapter, a working portfolio, what is called a *trunk*, begins as something most like a documentary portfolio. As it is edited, it becomes more like what has been described as a presentational portfolio. This is called a display portfolio, or *suitcase*. An even more focused variation of the presentational portfolio is called a special portfolio, or *daypack*. The project portfolio, or *kit*, is a way of bringing an exploratory component to the evidence collected. It is possible also to keep portfolios within portfolios. A presentational portfolio or an exploratory portfolio might reside as a small binder within a larger, documentary portfolio. What is most important is that you understand the basic types of portfolios—presentational, documentary, and exploratory—and collect evidence in support of them. As you become more comfortable with keeping portfolios, your focus may also evolve.

The second most important element to selecting a portfolio path is to establish a theme that will allow you to decide what to include and what to exclude. The Communications Portfolio, the Information Skills Portfolio, and the Multiple Intelligences Portfolio are broad and visionary organizing themes. They are not, however, the only themes. Effective portfolios can, as mentioned earlier, be organized around a great variety of themes. Writing skills, whole language development, multicultural education, learning styles theory, or any number of academically valid ideas would make interesting and exciting themes. The important thing is to select a theme that resonates with your vision of education. It should motivate you, excite you, and encourage you to facilitate the very best student portfolios. Even if you are only experimenting (perhaps you will change your theme next year), select a type and a theme and work with them.

Before going further, it might be useful to sit down and try out a theme. A Portfolio Journey "Theme Outline Worksheet" to use for sketching a thematic contents outline similar to that listed for each of the three sample portfolio themes follows (p. 61). Even if you choose to use one of these sample themes, it is helpful to practice sketching the outline yourself, so that you can customize it and add new ideas. You might want to photocopy the worksheet, saving the original as a master for future outlining.

Now you should have an outline of what your students' portfolios might contain. This will be your guide, your compass, to keep your students' portfolios on course. By the way, if you have been photocopying the worksheets from the book and doing your work on the photocopies, it might be time to think about collating them in a binder. You might use plastic drop-in pages or a three-hole punch to prepare the worksheets for insertion. Keeping your notes and plans together in one place will facilitate your Portfolio Journey. Not only will this help you to become better organized, it will help you to present your portfolio ideas more professionally to parents, teachers, and administrators. ✪

Appropriate Souvenirs

Theme Outline Worksheet

Imagining Portfolios with Purpose

Theme:

Type:

Outline the theme and type of portfolio you would like to have your students build. Refer to the "Visioning" and "Trip Planning Worksheets" from chapter 4.

Appropriate Souvenirs
Five Kinds of Portfolio Evidence

To be even more specific about the kinds of evidence you might save in a student portfolio, you can think of appropriate souvenirs, portfolio contents, as falling into five categories: found samples, processed samples, revisions, reflections, and portfolio projects.

Found Samples

Found samples are pretty much what the name implies. These are pieces done to fulfill class assignments. They may be graded by the teacher or ungraded, but they are the most basic kind of portfolio document. Any work a student does may potentially be selected for the portfolio. The issue of grading often comes up when discussing portfolios. Many proponents of portfolios believe that portfolio work should not be graded. I think this position is somewhat extreme. I realize that grading, as an activity in itself, affects students in different ways. For some, it provides motivation; for others, it can be inhibiting. The issue of grading is easy to resolve if you understand the range or categories of evidence that you will be including in a portfolio. There is nothing wrong with including in portfolios student work that has been graded by the teacher and returned to the student. This is just an example of a found sample, and students should, at some point, have the option of shifting that piece into their display portfolios (if they are proud of and pleased with the grade), keeping it in their working portfolio (if they are not bothered by the grade but think that the piece is not typical of their best work), or editing it out of their portfolio altogether during the editing process (if they are not satisfied with their grade). Found samples may be written work, photographs of projects, video- or audiocassettes of performances, or artwork.

Processed Samples

Processed samples extend the value of found samples. Processing is the act of self-assessment and self-analysis that can be applied to any project. Once a paper, project, or any other kind of student work has been graded and returned to a student, it can be added, as is, to the portfolio—this would be a found sample. If, however, students were asked to evaluate their work, assessing the fairness of the grade and the quality of their work and highlighting areas where improvement could be made on the next project, this would be a processed sample. Processing can become an integral part of the Portfolio Journey through the use of the annotation methods listed in Chapter 8. Processed samples are significantly more useful in portfolios than simple found samples. They help students build a sense of continuity from project to project, they teach students the skills of self-analysis, and they empower students to become active partners in the evaluation process, as opposed to passive receptors. The processing itself should not be graded, but it may be appropriate to encourage it through the use of bonus or penalty points.

Revisions

Revisions are samples of student work that have been graded and then revised or rewritten. In many cases, it will not make sense to have students take the time necessary for rewriting or revising their work. For the kind of work that will be transitioned from students' working portfolios to their display portfolios, however, revision is important. Revisions incorporate changes recommended by teachers and by the students themselves during the processing phase. Major written projects and some kinds of artwork or performances should be revised if they are to be saved for display or special portfolios. Revisions are not something students (or non-students, for that matter) naturally want to do. It is much easier to just move on and leave that work behind. The revision process should be encouraged by offering students the chance to actually present their portfolios, or work from their portfolios, to an audience. This will be discussed in more detail in Chapter 13.

Reflections

Reflection is related to the processed sample, but whereas processing is applied to individual samples of student work, reflection is applied to the portfolio as a whole. Reflection is a chance for students to draw some conclusions about who they are, based on the evidence in their portfolios. Reflection presents a natural opportunity for building self-esteem. A strong sense of self-worth, backed up by evidence in a portfolio, is an empowering combination for anyone. Because portfolios are open-ended documents, no two portfolios will ever be the same. Students are not in competition for a limited number of outstanding marks on a grading curve. Students who come to know that their strength lies in interpersonal communication skills can have a dynamic and impressive portfolio without necessarily being an "A" student.

Portfolio Projects

This category covers work designed and instigated by teachers or students for the sole purpose of inclusion in student portfolios. This kind of work occurs most frequently with exploratory portfolios. When a discovery made from a review of portfolio contents illuminates a particular strength, an area of interest, or a challenge to overcome, it is sometimes appropriate to assign a project in response to that discovery. These kinds of projects may or may not be graded, but they should be processed and evaluated so that students will come to value this work as much as they do their other projects. An example of a portfolio project: A student discovers that his or her display portfolio, though filled with fine samples of creative writing, is lacking essays or analytical kinds of writing. The student, concluding that the portfolio should better reflect an analytical or problem solving capacity, chooses to do some analytical or critical writing just for their display portfolio.

As you are thinking about appropriate souvenirs for your students' portfolios, remember that you can best reflect the range and diversity of your students' educational experiences by expanding your ideas about media and about what can be documented and saved. Don't overlook the potential of photography, videocassettes, audiocassettes, digitally scanned material stored on computer diskettes, and other emerging media.

Some of the things you may already be doing in your classroom might find a place in your students' portfolios: For instance, you might include the following:

- interviews
- two- and three-dimensional artwork
- photographs of projects, artwork, or performances
- peer evaluations
- self-assessments
- computer programs
- multimedia projects
- musical pieces (recorded or scored)
- logs and journals
- observation checklists
- performance video- or audiocassettes
- cooperative work (use a single photograph photocopied for each team member to represent the project)
- simulations
- games
- programs from performances
- award certificates and honors
- and the list could go on and on and on . . . ❂

In the next chapter, you will become acquainted with the four types of portfolios used for the Portfolio Journey. These are the containers you will fill with the evidence you have outlined and planned to acquire.

The Complete Traveler
An Overview of the Four Types of Portfolios

Travellers should condense their luggage as much as possible, for a passenger cannot claim more space for his hand baggage than the space in the netting overhead. All luggage should be marked with the owner's name and place of destination in full, and fastened with locks.

—Eugene Fodor (*On the Continent*, 1936)

Okay. Perhaps locks would be a bit much for student portfolios, but it would be hard to argue with the idea of labeling them with each student's name and condensing them to a convenient and portable size. Actually, the Portfolio Journey process pays a lot of attention to repacking and rearranging portfolio contents. Working with one's portfolio contents to build and arrange new portfolios is part of the process of self-assessment and self-discovery. Like train travelers "on the continent" in 1936, students can learn to be concise and efficient in their portfolio selections.

First, though, we should look at the kinds of luggage (portfolios) we will be taking with us on our journey. In previous chapters, we answered some important questions. We know why we will be keeping portfolios, and we know the purposes of the portfolios we will be keeping. We also know what themes we will be using to organize the collection process, and what sorts of souvenirs (evidence) we will be looking to collect. In this chapter, we will become acquainted with the four types of portfolios used for the Portfolio Journey. ✪

Trunks, Suitcases, Daypacks, and Kits

As has been mentioned before, there is no one *right* portfolio. Just as there is no one right kind of suitcase, or set of clothes, or collection of equipment and supplies for any journey, there is no one portfolio that will meet your students' needs in every situation.

Have you ever attended an education conference in an exciting city and taken a second suitcase that was only partially full? You were expecting to fill that empty space with souvenirs or educational materials you would acquire at the conference. You probably thought of yourself as a pretty smart traveler. Have you ever found yourself packing your most important possessions, or the things you would need to *survive*, in a separate bag to carry with you at all times? Have you ever packed a small, empty bag in your big suitcase so that you could repack and make short trips from your hotel without taking your big, bulky suitcase? Have you ever bought or borrowed special kinds of luggage to match the kind of trip you would be taking? Perhaps you needed something that could be carried comfortably, like a backpack. Maybe you needed luggage that rolled. You might have needed a bag that was waterproof, or easily "stuffable," or something that expanded. If you've ever done any of these things, it shows that you were able to think about and anticipate your journey. You were also able to modify your packing to match your needs. These are the skills you will need to help your students develop as they build and work with their portfolios.

On the Portfolio Journey, you will actually be working with four different types of portfolios for each student. Don't panic! Depending on the age and sophistication of your students, you may only be working with two of these types of portfolios. Further, you will find that your teaching situation will dictate the amount of time and energy you put into any one type of portfolio.

The four types of portfolios are the *trunk*, the *suitcase*, the *daypack*, and the *kit*. You might also call these the *working* portfolio, the *display* portfolio, the *special* portfolio, and the *project* portfolio. The types are interrelated and, at various times, will function as complements to one another. To extend the metaphor introduced above, your trunk is your archive. It is the place you store your souvenirs on a daily basis. A trunk has a lot of space, so you don't need to think too carefully about what you are saving. A trunk, or working portfolio, corresponds most directly to the documentary portfolio discussed in the previous chapter. What you live out of is your suitcase. It should be as substantial as your experiences, but it must remain portable. It will contain the portfolio items that you choose to share with others. A suitcase, or display portfolio, corresponds most directly to the presentational portfolio. A daypack is used for the short side trips you will make on your journey. It contains only what you need for the moment. Like a suitcase, a daypack, or special portfolio, corresponds to the presentational portfolio. A kit is what you use to organize or group the contents of your trunk, or working portfolio. A kit brings the exploratory element to portfolios.

Two of the types of portfolios presented here serve very different but complementary aspects in the portfolio process. They form the basis of this process. They are the working portfolio (trunk) and the display portfolio (suitcase). The first is a collection; the second is part of a presentation. The other two types of portfolios are extensions of the first two. Special portfolios (daypacks) are really display portfolios that have been edited and arranged to meet special, often short-term needs. Project portfolios (kits) are a way of focusing and organizing collections around themes or projects.

Using the terms *trunk*, *suitcase*, *daypack*, and *kit* will help students understand the different kinds of portfolios and the requirements and skills they demand.

Trunks
Working Portfolios

A trunk is a box, bag, envelope, or container that holds working portfolios. A trunk, or working portfolio, at any moment in time, may contain a large quantity of material. It is usually a holding portfolio. It is the place where students save work at the teacher's direction or by choice. Work contained in a trunk is usually unedited. A trunk may contain graded or ungraded work, work in progress, and multiple drafts of a particular piece. Everything that ends up being moved to a student's suitcase, or display portfolio, has spent some time in a trunk. Sometimes, work that is displaced from the suitcase ends up back in the trunk.

Think of a trunk as being a reservoir of evidence and samples. It will hold a lot of the souvenirs collected during your travels. It will protect things and give them a place to live until you decide whether or not they best represent your abilities.

Trunks are a starting point for building portfolios. Chapter 7 explores the creation and keeping of trunks.

Suitcases
Display Portfolios

A suitcase is what we will call a display portfolio. It is the edited version of a student's work. It may still be a collection, but it is assembled and arranged in a specific order to tell a story—the story of a student's experiences and abilities. A suitcase is created with evidence drawn from a trunk, or working portfolio. Sometimes, a suitcase will be contained within a trunk; at other times, a suitcase and a trunk will be kept separate. A suitcase may be a scrapbook, notebook, or binder, but it may also be stored digitally on a computer hard drive, diskette, or compact disc.

Additional characteristics that distinguish a suitcase from a trunk are portability and compactness. Though you could probably carry a suitcase without too much strain, carrying a trunk almost always requires assistance. A suitcase usually doesn't contain multiple drafts of a piece. It tends to contain the best examples and uses quality instead of quantity to describe a student's abilities.

A suitcase will always be a work in progress. New work that better represents a student will replace older work. The process of repacking items stored in a trunk into a suitcase is an opportunity for self-assessment and reflection. The editing process that a suitcase requires illuminates individual strengths and weaknesses, as well as opportunities: Like perusing a collection of souvenirs, sorting and organizing portfolio contents helps to remind students where they have been, the experiences they have had, and places to which they might like to return.

Suitcases are the first point of refinement for building portfolios. Suitcases introduce students to the concept of editing. Chapter 10 explores these processes in detail.

Daypacks
Special Portfolios

As its name implies, a daypack is designed to carry what you would need if you left your home, or home base, for a day. In terms of portfolios, a daypack, or special portfolio, is a collection of evidence or illustration of experience necessary for a short-term or special goal. For instance, older students might use contents from their portfolios to apply for after-school jobs, while younger students might use selected portfolio materials as acceptance requirements for special after-school programs for the arts, the sciences, athletics, or leadership. In these cases, a full suitcase, or display portfolio, might be too much information, or might not as clearly communicate a student's interest or experience in a certain area.

Creating a daypack is a way of strategically repacking a portfolio to communicate a specific story or image of a student. A suitcase is designed to be a well-rounded portrait of a student, but a daypack focuses attention on the details of a student's experiences. A suitcase shines a kind of floodlight on a student, whereas a daypack shines a spotlight on that student's most unique qualities.

As mentioned above, the age and sophistication of your students will determine how much time you spend with daypacks as a portfolio process. Typically, older students will benefit more from time spent in creating daypacks. Younger students may create daypacks from their larger portfolio collections only once or twice a year. Creating daypacks can be a productive way of interacting one-on-one with students. This can also be an engaging way for parents to work with their children.

Daypacks further refine suitcases and help students determine possible uses of their portfolios. Creating a daypack can be an empowering activity for students as they come to better understand themselves. Chapter 11 explores the creation of daypacks in greater detail.

Kits
Project Portfolios

Though a kit, or project portfolio, may stand on its own for guided self-assessment activities, it is most often considered as a way of organizing the contents of a trunk, or working portfolio. A kit is assembled to illustrate process.

Perhaps the best way to define a kit is by example. Let's assume that an important activity for the semester is an illustrated report about a foreign country. It would certainly go into a student's trunk, or working portfolio. Students may or may not have saved multiple drafts of the report in their trunk. If the report was done well and was something the student was proud of, it might be included in that student's suitcase, or display portfolio. Before being included in the suitcase, it may or may not have been retyped or rewritten to incorporate corrections. A grade may be displayed on the report, or it may not. The report might also be included in a daypack, or special portfolio, if there is reason for its inclusion. If the student was applying for an enrichment program in a foreign language or a multicultural arts program, a report on a foreign country might be very relevant to that special portfolio. If the report and its illustrations were created on a computer, and if the student was applying for a program that required such skills, such inclusion might also be relevant.

A kit for this report might have been initiated by the teacher at the outset or introduction of the project. It might be a folder or large envelope within the trunk, but it would contain plans and outlines, notes for the project, drafts and revisions, and the finished copy. Now, this is only one type of kit. Other types of kits might be organized to highlight one type of work, such as writing or drawing over a semester or school year. Or, they might contain all work done in a specific subject area, such as science or social studies. The important thing is that these portfolios, or organizing structures for portfolios, illustrate process—what a student does to reach a finished product.

Kits can help students, teachers, and parents isolate and identify problem areas and develop strategies for overcoming these problems. They also illustrate the different ways in which students view their world and approach problems. Kits help students develop a sense of continuity and progress through the work they do. Chapter 11 explores the creation of kits in greater detail. ✪

Baggage Handling

Isn't This Too Much Luggage?

Is this task beginning to seem daunting? After all, one portfolio per student is quite enough work on its own. Just remember: *All portfolios flow from the trunk, or working portfolio.* If you take your journey one step at a time, you will find that, in no time at all, your students will have healthy and dynamic working portfolios. Trunks are surprisingly easy to keep. They may even help you better organize your days. By themselves, these working portfolios are valid and valuable tools in the classroom, but without taking the next step—creating suitcases, or display portfolios—you are only experiencing a fraction of the potential of student-managed portfolios.

This next step in the Portfolio Journey does not need to happen until you are ready for it. Display portfolios are not easy to create. Your students will not finish them in an afternoon. It is a process that will take time. Like most creative endeavors, a display portfolio will require time and effort to maximize its potential. It is the very process of working on and refining display portfolios, though, that yields the most benefit.

Once your students have working and display portfolios (at least in progress), daypacks, or special portfolios, are actually rather easy to develop. Students can, in a brief time (several hours), assemble and arrange a special portfolio, for a special need, from their existing portfolios. It may also be comforting to remember that assembling these daypacks may occur infrequently and certainly needn't occur often.

Finally, kits, or project portfolios, are really not separate portfolios at all. They are actually more of a way of organizing certain kinds of portfolio documents. Project portfolios can be initiated by something as simple as assigning each student a special folder (with a large rubber band) at the beginning of a project. Because project portfolios are designed to highlight process, and because that process should be occurring anyway over the course of a project, they can be formed within working portfolios by simply providing an appropriate storage vehicle.

Setting the Mood in the Classroom

Before looking in detail at how to build trunks, or working portfolios, let's look briefly at supporting the Portfolio Journey through classroom design and arrangement.

No plane, bus, boat, train, car, or spaceship can take us as far as our imagination. With imagination primed and fueled by stories, artifacts, and imagery, we can travel the world without leaving the classroom. For some of us, all it takes is a good adventure story to set us off on an imaginary journey. For others, it might be smelling an exotic scent or tasting a new flavor. For still others, it may begin with a map, chart, or globe.

Priming the imagination for the Portfolio Journey begins with the classroom. What makes you think of travel and great voyages? How might you decorate your classroom to propel your students on their journey? Adopting and maintaining the Portfolio Journey in your classroom means reinforcing the metaphor of travel through the environment you create for your students and through the activities you use to teach. Travel is a rich metaphor and can be used to teach across the curriculum.

Some teachers may choose to allow students to create the look and feel of their classroom environment. With this approach, students are greeted each year by, essentially, a blank environment, which they organize and decorate with their work throughout the year. Other teachers may want to begin the year with a dynamic environment and then allow student-generated work to replace the teacher's decorations as the year progresses. Whichever path you choose, you may want to consider the elements of organization, imagery, props, resources, and travel games as you design your learning space.

Organization

Have you ever noticed how something so simple as rearranging students' desks can have a profound effect on their behavior and attitude? Well, if we think about how rooms in our homes can take on a totally different feeling just by rearranging the furniture, it shouldn't really surprise us that our students are affected by where they spend so much of their days.

You might consider arranging students' desks in a way that suggests traveling. First, you should consider your particular teaching style. Do you need for students to have a particular vantage point for your lectures? Do you do a lot of small-group work? What kinds of seating are available to you—individual desks or tables and chairs? Do you want to allow students to participate in the arrangement of their desks or in the selection of their preferred modes of travel? Even after you have answered these questions, you will find that you still have a lot of flexibility in modeling your classroom to reflect any of these modes of travel.

Imagery

Perhaps one of the easiest things you can do to set the mood in your classroom is to cover your walls with images that suggest travel. Pictures of far-away places are like windows onto other worlds. This kind of imagery is actually quite easy to find. Travel agencies, embassies, and cultural organizations often have free posters or graphics. Parents or libraries might donate back issues of travel magazines. With little or no expense, you can install these windows for your students.

Props

It must be admitted at the outset that props or artifacts suggesting travel are more difficult to find than imagery. They are often items highly valued by some but disregarded by most. In the beginning, you may be hard-pressed to find anything suitable. Don't rush it. As you open up to the idea of travel as a metaphor, you will find more and more objects presenting themselves to you. They will make their way into your classroom as if in search of a good home. Some things to be on the lookout for include the following:

- model trains, boats, planes, spaceships, cars, buses, and other vehicles
- globes
- working means of transport such as skates, sleds, wagons, and bicycles
- luggage
- pets
- plants
- hats and costumes

Resources

This category includes reference and activity materials that you might imagine would be found in a Portfolio Journey classroom. The following suggestions are admittedly abbreviated. There are plenty of useful and exciting travel-related resources available for educators. Some of the broad categories you might want to consider are travel and international magazines, books about travel and journeys (both real and imagined), travel-related video- and audiocassettes and computer games, and so on. Of course, nothing beats a classroom Internet connection for linking students to the world.

Travel Games

"Around the World in How Many Days?" is an activity in which students make an imaginary trip around the world during the course of a school year. By expanding this activity, you can use it to mark the passage of time, motivate attendance, teach geography or world events, encourage multicultural activities, and foster teamwork.

AROUND THE WORLD IN HOW MANY DAYS?

The Ultimate in Armchair Traveling

The first step is to acquire five or six large, black-and-white outline maps of the world—one for each student team. If this is too expensive, you might try using a simple black-and-white world map (such as the one included on p. 74) enlarged to poster size at a photocopying store. If you purchase a map instead of using the one included here, it may be necessary to add the grid lines using a black ink pen and a straight edge. The smaller the grid squares you can draw, the better.

Divide your students into cooperative learning teams. These teams will be traveling together over the course of the year. Pass out small practice maps and have each team plot a trip that will take them around the world (they should plot this trip in pencil, to allow for changes in the plan). Encourage students to think about places they would like to visit on their trip. The idea is for the trips to be adventures. Older students might develop themes for their trips. Each day of school, the team moves one square further on its trip. Movement might be traced by coloring squares with different color highlighter pens. When over water, the team moves two squares each day. Following holidays or weekends, the team moves ahead an appropriate number of squares for the days missed. If possible, the team should date the squares with a month/day number.

Encourage students by providing special treats to commemorate certain stops on their trips. For instance, each member of a team passing through China might receive a fortune cookie or almond cookie. Each member of a team passing through Hawaii might receive a spear of dried pineapple. Rice candy might represent Japan, and a square of toffee might represent England.

The only time a team would not move is when one of its members is absent. Just as on a real trip, they would stay with their sick team member until he or she recovered enough to be able to travel. To help a team get back on schedule because of absences for illness, you might issue coupons that allow a team to travel more squares than are usually allowed in a day.

These maps become fascinating documents as the course of each team's trip is colored in, one square at a time. These maps can replace some of your more generic travel decorations. They can also be used to create timelines of the year's events. Allow students to mark significant events that occur in class by adding notes or photographs to their maps. The notes or photographs might be dated and linked to the plotted course.

If the Michael Todd film of Jules Verne's *Around the World in Eighty Days* is available through your school library or a video rental service, you might arrange to show this film to the class as an introduction to this activity.

AROUND THE WORLD IN HOW MANY DAYS?

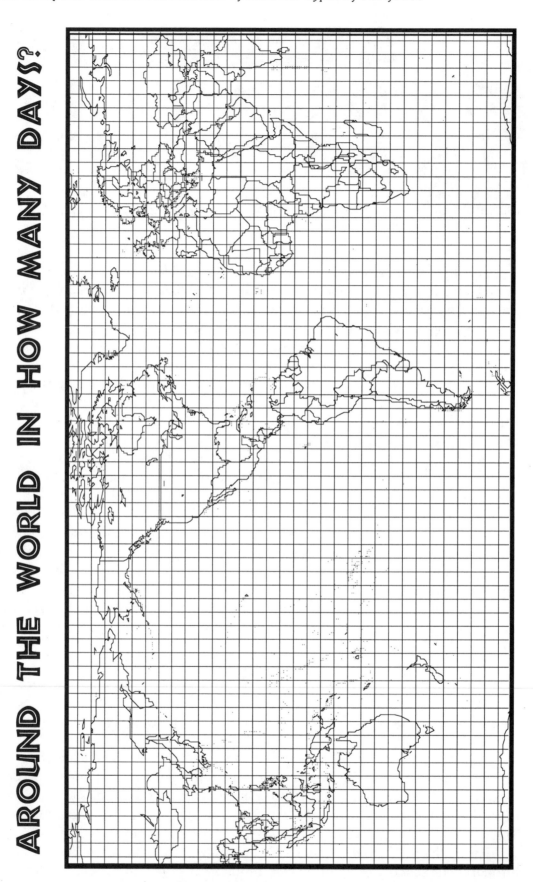

Part 3
Preparing for the Journey

The Teacher as Travel Consultant

In Part 3 of the Portfolio Journey you will:

ℰ Help your students create and manage their own trunks, or working portfolios.

ℰ Learn several strategies for labeling, annotating, and managing the contents of student portfolios.

ℰ Create student passports to introduce your students to the keeping of portfolios.

The Trunk
Building a Foundation Through Working Portfolios

The *trunk*, or working portfolio, is the foundation of the Portfolio Journey, and, though it may not need to be secured with screws to foil thieves, it will need to be sturdy and well constructed. Students will handle their trunks more than any of the other portfolios discussed in the Portfolio Journey. Because trunks are so essential, this chapter will explore in detail the establishment and management of these working portfolios. For teachers of the first through the third grades, working portfolios will be primary portfolios. If you teach at these grade levels, you may find that you work very little with display portfolios, or *suitcases*, and special portfolios, or *daypacks*. Even teachers who teach at the seventh- and eighth-grade levels, where display and special portfolios become more important, will find that these portfolios grow out of successful working portfolios.

Before we look at the logistics of creating and keeping working portfolios, though, let's revisit and expand our definition of *trunk* from chapter 6:

> *A trunk is a box, bag, envelope, or container that forms a working portfolio. A trunk, or working portfolio, at any moment in time, may contain a large quantity of material. It is usually a holding portfolio. It is the place where students save work at the teacher's direction or by choice. Work contained in a trunk is usually unedited.*

A trunk may contain graded or ungraded work, work in progress, and multiple drafts of a particular piece. Everything that ends up being moved to a student's suitcase, or display portfolio, has spent some time in a trunk. Sometimes, work that is displaced from the suitcase ends up back in the trunk.

Think of a trunk as being a reservoir of evidence and samples. It will hold a lot of the souvenirs collected during your travels. It will protect things and give them a place to live until you decide whether or not they best represent your abilities.

Trunks are, first of all, the containers into which your students will, on a daily basis, deposit samples of their work or evidence of their achievements. Second, they represent processes of selection, inclusion, and exclusion. Third, they are associated with issues of time and classroom management. This chapter addresses each of these elements of working portfolios as key questions:

1. What will students' working portfolios look like?

2. How will student work be included and excluded from their portfolios?

3. How much time will this take, and how will I manage the process? ✪

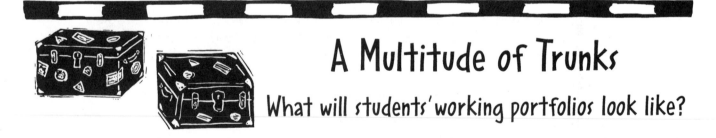

A Multitude of Trunks

What will students' working portfolios look like?

It's human nature to adapt the familiar before inventing the new. When teachers first began keeping student portfolios, they turned to what they knew best: file folders. After all, weren't portfolios similar to a student's permanent record, only filled with more stuff? Well, this worked fine—as long as *teachers* kept their students' portfolios. File folders are designed to do one thing very well: keep a collection of papers together in a filing cabinet. As soon as you remove a file folder from a drawer and give it to a student to work on, its shortcomings become apparent. In one trip across a classroom, a file folder, held at the wrong angle, can actually become a tool for distributing portfolio contents across the floor.

To address this issue, some teachers tape two sides of the portfolio to make it more like an envelope. Other teachers purchase accordion-bottomed, file-folder envelopes. The folio variation of these file-folder envelopes come' with fold-over flaps and elastic bands and can make excellent portfolio containers.

As more teachers began working with portfolios, though, they began to view the problem of portfolio containers a bit more creatively. They began to identify certain needs: Portfolio containers should be rugged enough to withstand student handling. They should be of a size that can hold a variety of media, not just written work. They should close, to prevent items from falling out. They should be able to hold three to four weeks' worth of work at a time without being edited. It would be helpful if they were easy to store, with students' names clearly identifiable from the outside. It would be helpful if students could customize them and make them their own. Oh yes—they need to be really inexpensive, too, if not free.

This may sound like a tall order, but teachers are notoriously creative. The following list includes some of the useful containers teachers have found for their working portfolios:

1. *extra-large fabric detergent boxes*
    They hold a lot of material, they are cheap, and the little handle is a plus.

2. *shopping bags with handles*
    They are inexpensive, easy to decorate and customize, and easy to carry. Their big drawbacks are that they tend to fall over and they aren't real easy to store.

3. *large plastic containers*
    These are easy to store and very efficient, but they aren't cheap (unless you can get parents to provide them for their children).

4. *three-ring binders with pocket pages*
    These tend to work better as display portfolios, but older students could use them as working portfolios.

5. *shoe boxes*
    These can be workable for young students, when folding portfolio contents is not a problem.

6. *pizza boxes*
    These are very practical containers for working portfolios, and they are the containers we will be referring to for the Portfolio Journey. They can often be acquired for free, or for a minimal amount of money, from a local pizza restaurant. Ask for the largest size available.

If possible, obtain pizza boxes before they have been folded and assembled. This will allow students to cut and paste travel-related images onto their working portfolio trunks. You might also have students color or paint their boxes. On the following pages (pp. 81 and 82), you will find a number of "travel stickers" and "ID labels" that you may photocopy and cut out for students to color and paste onto their trunks. Or, you can have students create their own stickers with computer drawing software. Photocopy the stickers and labels onto solid-colored sheets of 8½-by-11-inch adhesive label material. The stickers and labels will then be ready for students to stick them onto their trunks.

Just before folding the pizza boxes into their box shape, cover the outside with clear adhesive contact paper (available from hardware stores). This gives the portfolios a tough, durable surface that is water resistant and doesn't stain easily. Don't forget to have students leave the spine (the long, narrow edge along the "hinge" of the lid) blank for their names. If you identify the portfolios along the spine, you can store them in an upright position on a shelf, like books (as shown in the following illustration). The portfolios will take up less space, and this method of storage allows students easy access. If the lids won't stay closed, use large rubber bands or self-adhesive Velcro "buttons" to secure them.

The Portfolio Shelf

Before leaving the subject of portfolio containers, it should be noted that pizza boxes are just a suggestion. They do meet almost all the criteria established above for a working portfolio container, but other options are certainly available. One enthusiastic Portfolio Journey teacher collected actual small suitcases, which she bought at garage and yard sales for a few dollars apiece. She provided each of her students with a unique suitcase for the year to use as a working portfolio trunk. ✪

(Text continues on p. 83.)

Portfolio Stickers

OFFICAL TRAVELER

Name: _____

Teacher: _____

Grade: _____

Been There!
Done That!

My Name is

_____

Portfolio Stickers

Name Tag

PRIVATE
Ask before opening!

OFFICIAL ID

Name: _____

Teacher: _____

Grade: _____

Collecting and Clearing
How will students' work be included and exluded from their portfolios?

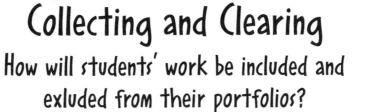

Nothing seems more daunting than the prospect of actually getting samples of student work into and out of portfolios. These processes can best be represented by the words *collecting* and *clearing*.

In the early days of student portfolios, many teachers personally took on the task of assembling and maintaining portfolios for each of their students. What a task! What a responsibility! To manage this at all, within a teacher's busy schedule, usually meant creating a file for each student and regularly depositing examples of student work into those files. While admirable in intent, this method had serious drawbacks. For one thing, it took time that could have been better spent planning, teaching, or interacting with students. The more critical shortcoming of this method was that it removed students from the process. Portfolios became another thing that was done *to them* by adults.

The best way to manage the collecting and clearing process is to facilitate student collecting and student editing. There are many ways one might achieve this goal, but the following plan has been used successfully in classrooms and is a practical way to manage working portfolios. Of course, you may want to customize this plan and adapt it for your own special needs, but the important thing is that it gives you a student-managed method for portfolio collecting and clearing that should not alter or intrude upon your classroom style.

Special Note: Savers and Trashers

Many teachers, upon hearing that their students will be empowered to edit their own portfolios, bring up a valid concern: "What do I do when some of my students are savers and some are trashers?"

"Savers" are those students who are loathe to throw out anything they have ever done. As you might imagine, this could quickly lead to a bulky and unwieldy portfolio. Never force a student to throw away work that they want to keep. For savers, you might introduce the concept of the "home portfolio." Give each of these students a portfolio box to keep at home. It is much gentler to ask a student to shift some contents from the school portfolio to the home portfolio than to ask a student to throw away work.

"Trashers" are those students who tend to throw away any and all school work. The portfolio collecting and clearing processes described below should alleviate some of the problem, but if you are still concerned (if, for example, you have mandated portfolio requirements that dictate the retention of specific items), consider this: Give students a file folder with their name on it. This is their portfolio clearing folder (a sample label for a portfolio clearing folder is included near the end of Chapter 8). When they decide to edit a piece out of their portfolios, they put it in this folder and leave it on your desk. This way, before a piece ends up in the trash, you have a chance to review what your students are discarding. Things you have specifically asked them to save can be rescued, and you will have a chance to plead for the inclusion of pieces you think are exceptional.

Step 1: Collecting

The Portfolio Collection List

Begin making a list of the specific items you want your students to include in their working portfolios. This list might be kept on a portion of the chalkboard or on a piece of poster paper tacked to a bulletin board or a wall. You needn't plan any further ahead than a day at a time. From where will this list come? It should reflect the kind of planning you did or the choices you made in Chapters 4 and 5. Refer back to the worksheets you did in these chapters. If a specific assignment meets the criteria you established for portfolio evidence, add it to the list. When you think that an assignment or a project might reflect a student's abilities, add that specific assignment to the list. You will need to allow enough space for this list to grow over a two- to three-week period of time. A portfolio collection list might look like the following illustration:

Note: You might be wondering how this method meets the criteria for a *student-managed* portfolio. After all, isn't the teacher just telling students what their portfolios should contain? At this stage, yes! By establishing a running portfolio collection list, you are ensuring that when it comes time for students to begin making decisions about the work that best represents their abilities, they will have adequate samples from which to choose. Also, you are not stopping students from deciding to save additional material. Remember that building portfolios is a skill that must be taught. Saving samples of work may not be a habit your students already have. This process makes it a habit.

The Display Portfolio Folder

The display portfolio folder is the place inside a working portfolio for evidence other than assigned work or school projects. This is the place for awards, letters of commendation, honors, evidence of extracurricular work of distinction, evidence of hobbies and other areas of interest, and so on. Just because evidence is placed in this folder does not mean that it will automatically be placed in a display portfolio at some point, but it does separate certain kinds of evidence from samples of work that will be edited according to the criteria established below (under the heading "Portfolio Clearing Day"). Students may add evidence to or remove evidence from this folder at any time. (A sample label for a display portfolio folder is included near the end of Chapter 8.)

Daily Collecting

Set aside fifteen to thirty minutes (more time may be required for more detailed processing or annotation—see Chapter 8), at least once each day, for students to retrieve their working portfolios, check their contents against the portfolio collection list, and include necessary additions. This is also the time for students to straighten and reorganize portfolio contents for neatness. Sometimes portfolio contents become shifted, bent, or wadded in portfolios because of handling. Now is the time for students to make sure that the samples are kept in such a way as to make them presentable for later inclusion in display portfolios. Students can do this themselves with little guidance from the teacher. You might choose to allow students to do this on their own time during the day. For example, students who finish an assignment early could do daily collecting for their portfolio. As a more structured activity, the end of the day might be the best time for daily collecting. This can bring a sense of closure to the day.

Students who have been absent can quickly determine from the portfolio collection list what work they need to collect from the teacher to include in their portfolios. By adding to the list in advance, teachers who must be away from the classroom can continue the collecting process through substitute teachers without fear of losing continuity. Keep in mind that although you may or may not have graded the work required in your list, you are not grading the working portfolio as a separate entity. You do not need to check working portfolios to be sure that everything on your list has been included. If students fail to do some assignments, they will already have received grades reflecting this. The fact that they also do not have these assignments in their portfolios should not be used to compound the problem. Yes, it will mean that they have less from which to choose when clearing their working portfolios, and when creating their display portfolios, but this is a matter with which students themselves should wrestle. If you can make portfolios exciting and vital to students, they will begin to care whether they have a full range of choices available to them.

Processing and Annotation

This topic will be covered in detail in the next chapter, but for now it is enough to know that you will be asking students to annotate each piece that goes into their working portfolio, at the time of inclusion. This is a simple process that will help with later organization. You may also be asking students to do some processing work for completed projects before including them in the portfolio.

Step 2: Clearing

Portfolio Clearing Day

Once every two or three weeks (this time frame could be expanded or compressed to coincide with standard reporting periods or your classroom calendar), you will need to set aside time for students to clear their working portfolios (one to two hours, depending on how long it has been since the last portfolio clearing day and how proficient students are at the process of clearing). This process begins with your most recent portfolio collection list. Based on this list, you will ask students to select their best work for retention in the portfolio. You will need to specify for students the criteria for determining their best work. If you simply say "best work," they will save the work you graded the highest. This is important to remember because you may want students to save work that they especially like even though their grade was not outstanding. Some examples of criteria that might be used for portfolio clearing include the following:

1. *Of the assignments in your working portfolio, please save three.*
   This instruction is the most open-ended way of proceeding and should be reserved for older students who have some understanding of why they are keeping portfolios.

2. *Of the assignments in your working portfolio, please save the three with the best grades.*
   This instruction should be easy to follow, but there will be students who have a number of assignments with the same grade. They will probably want additional guidance.

3. *Of the assignments in your working portfolio, please save your three favorites, regardless of what grade you received.*
   This instruction is useful when you want students to save work that is meaningful to them even if they failed to meet technical standards.

4. *Of the assignments in your working portfolio, please save the three of which you are most proud.*
   Students will probably save the three with the best grades, but sometimes their choices will be surprising.

5. *Of the assignments in your working portfolio, please save the three that, if there was no grade attached, would best show your range of talent (or ability to follow instructions, or creativity, or attention to detail, or ability to communicate, etc.).*
This instruction makes the portfolio selection process much more sophisticated and forces students to assess their work.

6. *Of the assignments in your working portfolio, you must save this piece.*
You may want to use this kind of request to meet mandated portfolio criteria or to have students include certain benchmark pieces in their portfolios. Notice that every time students do portfolio clearing, they are comparing recent work to all previous work. If you want to exempt a piece from possibly being edited out of a portfolio, you must specify this instruction each time students do clearing.

7. *Of the assignments in your working portfolio, please maintain _____ free choices.*
This guidance allows students to keep past assignments that they think still represent their abilities well.

8. *Of the assignments in your working portfolio, please select the one you intend to redo for possible inclusion in your display portfolio.*
This option allows students a chance to save work with the intention of transitioning it into a show piece for their display portfolio. Though this is usually impractical with all or even most school work, the revision process for achieving a finished product, including the incorporation of corrections and suggestions, is useful practice for life in the adult world.

Actually, your criteria for portfolio clearing will be a combination of these examples. You may have different criteria for math work than you do for writing assignments. Projects and artwork documented by annotated photographs may have different criteria than audiocassette samples of students reading aloud. You may, by your criteria, actually shape your students' working portfolios, or you may allow the portfolios to evolve under less specific criteria. The process of allowing students to clear and select their portfolio samples based on certain criteria is empowering to them. At the same time, it teaches them to make thoughtful choices.

Portfolio Clearing Teams

The best way to accomplish the clearing process is in teams. A group of students working together to help edit one another's portfolios meets several needs. For one thing, when students don't edit in teams, they tend to ask the teacher to come help them make their decisions. With teams in place, teachers can gently refer those decisions back to the team: "If you aren't sure which is your best work, ask your team members to give you their opinions, and don't forget to ask them *why* they think one of your pieces is better than another." Also, this process engages students in sharing the contents of their portfolios with their peers on a regular basis. Regular sharing of portfolios is one of the secrets to successful portfolios mentioned at the end of Chapter 2. In portfolio clearing teams, students will gain practice at explaining, defending, and elaborating upon the work that they have selected to represent themselves. ✪

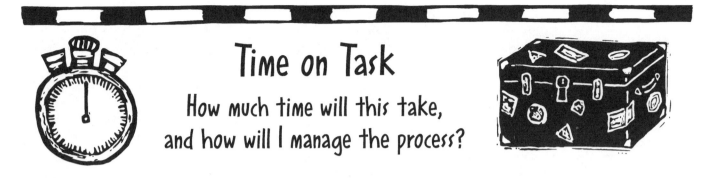

Time on Task

How much time will this take, and how will I manage the process?

You should, by now, already have an idea of about how much time it will take to maintain working portfolios: a minimum of ten to fifteen minutes each day, and one to two hours every several weeks. Of course, in the beginning, more time will be required—to create the portfolios, introduce practices, and do some of the Portfolio Journey activities described in this chapter. After the Portfolio Journey is underway, though, maintaining working portfolios does not require significant amounts of time, nor does it require a lot of preparation and planning time from teachers.

You should also have an idea of how you will manage the process of maintaining working portfolios. Students should manage most of the maintenance for their portfolios. You should not need to check or grade portfolios on a regular basis. If possible, arrange your class schedule to accommodate a time, once every two portfolio clearing days, for sitting down with students to review what is currently in their portfolios. This should be done between portfolio clearing days, not the actual days themselves. Reviewing portfolios can be a good way of organizing student/teacher conferences. Student/teacher/parent reviews can be extremely useful (this is discussed in detail in Chapter 14). ✪

Now you know how to initiate and maintain working portfolios, or trunks. As mentioned previously, if you teach young students, you may find that you go no further than establishing simple working portfolios, or that you only create display portfolios, or suitcases, at year's end. Even if you embrace the entire Portfolio Journey, though, you will still build everything from the solid foundation of the trunk.

Trunks hold the evidence that will eventually be distilled and assembled into suitcases and daypacks, or special portfolios. Trunks are less structured and can tend to become cluttered and chaotic. To maximize the value of trunks, we will need to look at some strategies for annotating and processing portfolio contents and monitoring portfolio activity. The next chapter introduces the Portfolio Journey concepts of *luggage tags*, *manifests*, and *visas* to address these issues.

Luggage Tags, Manifests, and Visas
Tools for Annotation, Processing, and Portfolio Monitoring

Like all great travellers, I have seen more than I remember, and remember more than I have seen.

—Benjamin Disraeli

Portfolios, like scrapbooks, can be useful memory aids, but we should always take care not to ask too much from either. Each piece that is saved in a portfolio has its own set of "facts": what it is, when it was created, how it was created, whose work it is. These are simple bits of information that seem almost too obvious to be concerned with at the time a given portfolio sample is new. If you doubt just how quickly these facts can fade from memory, though, go through that box of photographs you have been planning to organize and put into a scrapbook. How many dates, places, events, and names have you already forgotten? If these facts can slip away from us so easily, what of the softer data: the feelings, impressions, attitudes, intentions? How quickly will we forget these things?

The samples and evidence in portfolios mean one thing at the moment they were created and added to the portfolio. Later, one may find that these samples have different meanings. There is no way to prevent this, but we can use some techniques of annotation to help us preserve the facts that surround a particular portfolio piece. Slightly different techniques can help us preserve more of our feelings, impressions, attitudes, and intentions.

In the Portfolio Journey, these techniques are called *luggage tags*. Traditional luggage tags put essential information, such as the owner's name and address, destination, and mode of transport, on the outside of baggage. Portfolio Journey luggage tags put this kind of critical information on each piece that goes into a portfolio. This chapter will review several types of luggage tags and discuss several levels of annotation. Much of this chapter contains samples of various kinds of luggage tags for various ages of students. These may be photocopied freely for use in your classroom. If you have an interest or talent in such things, you can also create your own luggage tags (clip art and font resources used to develop the luggage tags in this book are listed in the appendix).

This chapter also introduces two additional Portfolio Journey tools: the *manifest* and the *visa*. Manifests are tables of contents, or directories, for portfolios. Visas are processes for monitoring portfolio reviews and for noting the comments of those invited to review portfolios. ✪

Luggage Tags
Methods of Annotation

Basic Luggage Tags

Each item that enters a student's portfolio should contain the following basic information:

1. *Student's Name*
   Should portfolio samples become separated from portfolios, you need an easy way of returning them to their owners.

2. *Student's Age or Grade (or Both)*
   Though it may seem unimportant now, this is the kind of information that will matter more in the future, especially with items such as awards, honors, and photographs. This kind of evidence tends to end up in display portfolios and may remain in portfolios for many years.

3. *Date*
   The date should reflect when the work was created, or when the event depicted in a photograph occurred. When documenting photographs of artwork and projects, use the date the photograph was taken (unless the creation date was much earlier than the date of the photograph). If you are using instant photography, this will be easy. If you are taking photographs and having them developed later, you may need to make notes.

4. *Descriptive Title or Caption*
   The descriptive title or caption should describe the sample in enough detail to distinguish it from other samples. For instance: *A story about two dinosaurs engaged in a battle*, or *A science research paper about predicting the weather*, or *A book report about* The Diary of Anne Frank, or *A certificate for making the honor roll after my second report card in fourth grade*. In the case of photographs, a descriptive title or caption should describe what has been photographed. In the case of video- or audiocassettes or computer diskettes, this kind of information is essential because content cannot otherwise be deduced on sight. The descriptive title or caption should include the medium of the sample (writing, painting, photograph, model, audiocassette, computer diskette, etc.) as well.

5. *Nature of the Sample (Optional)*
   You may want students to identify whether samples are graded class assignments, team projects, revisions of class assignments, or work created specifically for the portfolio.

The easiest way to ensure that such data are included for each piece is to provide students with preprinted tags that prompt them to record the information. On pages 92 and 93, you will find two variations of basic luggage tags. Select the style that seems most appropriate for your students. Photocopy and cut out the tags. Solid glue sticks, tape, or staples can be used to affix luggage tags to portfolio samples.

Luggage Tag Stamps

A variation on the idea of luggage tags is to have one of the basic luggage tags made into a rubber stamp. This way, the tag can be stamped onto the back of students' written work. This saves paper and avoids the need to attach another piece of paper to portfolio samples. If portfolio samples are coated with plastic sealer or lamination, stamp pad ink tends to smear, so consider stamping the tag onto a piece of paper and affixing the paper to the coated sample. For media such as computer diskettes and video- and audiocassettes, put the sample into an envelope and stamp the envelope.

Luggage Tags for Photographs

Though it is possible to use some of the basic luggage tags for photographs, the sample basic photo luggage tags following this section (p. 94) have been designed specifically for photographic evidence. The tags contain spaces to document information unique to this medium.

After the sample basic photo luggage tags, a full-page tag is included (p. 95). The value of photographs can be extended by using such large photo luggage tags, which prompt different kinds of written documentation. In addition to the basic information required of all portfolio samples, other types of written documentation, identification, and analysis can accompany and expound upon the photographic sample. This adds to the value of using photographs as portfolio evidence by giving students more useful activities with which to practice developing skills.

Young students should use the most basic form of written documentation for photographs: identifying colors, shapes, objects, and concepts in photographs. This documentation may take the forms of vocabulary lists, complete sentences, and brief descriptive essays. Full-page tags (see p. 95) offer more room for writing and fit nicely into display portfolios.

When photographs are used to document projects, events, and performances, they can be used in conjunction with the processing activities described under the heading "Advanced Luggage Tags" (following this section). Following the large sample photo tag is a two-page advanced luggage tag (pp. 96–97) specifically designed for use with photographs. These "Photo Project Processing" worksheets are meant to be copied onto the front and the back of the same sheet of paper.

(Text continues on p. 98.)

Basic Luggage Tags 1

_____ Portfolio Sample _____

Name:

Grade/Age:

Date:

Description of Sample:

_____ Portfolio Sample _____

Name:

Grade/Age:

Date:

Description of Sample:

Basic Luggage Tags 2

PORTFOLIO SAMPLE

Name:

Age/Grade:

Date:

Nature of Sample:

Description of Sample:

PORTFOLIO SAMPLE

Name:

Age/Grade:

Date:

Nature of Sample:

Description of Sample:

Basic Photo Luggage Tags

Photo Tag

Who took it?

Whose is it?

When was it taken?

What is it a picture of?

Photo Tag

Who took it?

Whose is it?

When was it taken?

What is it a picture of?

Photo Tag

Who took it?

Whose is it?

When was it taken?

What is it a picture of?

Photo Tag

Who took it?

Whose is it?

When was it taken?

What is it a picture of?

Name:_____

Date:_____

Photographer:_____

_____
_____
_____
_____
_____
_____
_____
_____
_____
_____
_____
_____
_____
_____

Place Photo Here

Place a photo
of your project
in this space.

Photo Project Processing
(page 1)

Name:
Date:
Photographer:

1. What was the assignment that lead to this project?

_____

_____

_____

_____

Photo Project Processing
(page 2)

2. What grade did your project receive, what grade do you think it deserved, and why do you think that?

_____

_____

_____

_____

_____

3. What would you do differently next time to improve your grade or your own sense of satisfaction with a project?

_____

_____

_____

_____

_____

_____

Advanced Luggage Tags

For most of the pieces students save in their working portfolios, basic luggage tags will be perfectly adequate. These identify the samples and provide critical information about them. In some cases, especially with older students, you may want them to take the next step: processing. It is especially useful for projects that have required more work; more thought; more research; more time; or, generally, more student energy.

Processing asks students to reflect upon finished projects before including them in portfolios. In addition to providing the basic information necessary for each portfolio sample, "Portfolio Processing" worksheets ask students to answer three important questions about a project:

1. *What assignment lead to this project?*

   This is one of the most enlightening questions a teacher can ever ask a student. Once the project has been completed, turned in, and graded, ask the students to restate the assignment to the best of their ability. If the students have this information written in their notes and they have saved them, allow the students to check their notes. If the students must do this from memory, so much the better. Do not be tempted to restate the assignment yourself. What you are trying to ascertain is how clearly the student understood the assignment.

   The answers students provide will tell you a lot. If most students understood the assignment you gave and are able to restate it after the fact, you are probably communicating well. If you receive a variety of restatements, it may indicate that the assignment was not stated clearly enough at the beginning. This is not an indictment of your abilities as a teacher. It is information for learning about how you teach. In addition, if several students obviously did not understand the assignment, look first for simple explanations, such as absences on the day the assignment was given and discussed or, if the assignment was a team project, misunderstandings coming from the same team. If you do not find a pattern there, look at individual learning styles. Is there a way you can better communicate assignments to those particular students?

2. *What grade did your project receive, what grade do you think it deserved, and why do you think that?*

   This question allows students to reflect on the grade their project received and the quality of work they did. Most of the time, you will find that students, upon reflection, will agree with the grade you gave the project. Occasionally, though, students will make a compelling case for a different grade. Be open to this possibility. It is not a sign of weakness on your part. If a student can convince you to understand a piece differently, consider changing the grade. Once students understand that you take their processing and reflection seriously enough to consider changing a grade, they will put more of their energy into it.

3. *What would you do differently next time to improve your grade or your sense of satisfaction with a project?*
    This is perhaps the most important question of all. It is the step that adds continuity to the flow of projects and assignments. Encourage students to be specific here. Before beginning the next project, have students review the processing sheets from their most recent projects. As a class, ask each student to select and commit to one "of the things" they have identified that they could do to improve their grade or their sense of satisfaction. Don't suggest that they take on all possible improvements at once. Ask for a commitment to just one. Have them write this improvement at the beginning of their notes for their next project. Sometimes, the number of improvements students would have to make to get "good" grades can seem daunting. If students focus on one improvement for *every* project, they can reach the goal of "good" grades through a series of steps. This process also helps students relate one project to another over time, allowing them to develop a sense that they are learning and gaining new skills.

The sample "Project Processing" worksheet that follows (p. 100) is similar to the "Photo Project Processing" worksheet, but without the space for a photo. Both worksheets are designed for students in grades three through the eight, though you may be able to begin this process at younger ages. Photocopy the worksheets and have them available for students. It is best if you reserve this kind of processing for selected projects because these worksheets require more time during daily collecting. Also, be careful of overusing processing. If you have students process every assignment, it can drain their enthusiasm for this kind of work. ✪

Project Processing

Date:

Name:_____

Age/Grade:_____

Project Name:_____

1. What was the assignment that lead to this project?

_____
_____
_____

2. What grade did your project receive, what grade do you think it deserved, and why do you think that?

_____
_____
_____
_____
_____
_____
_____
_____

3. What would you do differently next time to improve your grade or your own sense of satisfaction with a project?

_____
_____
_____
_____
_____
_____
_____
_____
_____
_____

Manifests

The Working Portfolio Table of Contents

A manifest is a list of cargo that a ship carries, or list of passengers and cargo for a plane, train, or ship. For the Portfolio Journey, a *manifest* is what we call a table of contents. A table of contents, or directory, is not, strictly speaking, necessary for a working portfolio, but it can help students organize and keep track of what is in their portfolios. The basic requirement for a manifest is that it have space for listing a lot of portfolio submissions. A lot of material passes through a working portfolio, and a manifest will reflect this. In addition to a column for identifying individual submissions, a manifest should have columns for the date the pieces are added to the portfolio and the date they are removed. An alternative to the column for the date removed could be simply to cross out the submission with a straight line. Another column might be used to indicate if a piece has been moved to a display or special portfolio.

Eventually, students will run out of space on their manifests. Manifests will need to be redone several times during the year, but this can be a beneficial kind of "spring cleaning" for portfolios. You may choose to have students either save or discard old manifests. Manifests are especially useful when portfolio contents are used for other purposes. Students can easily check to see if they have everything they are supposed to have.

Manifests add time to the daily collecting process, and they are most beneficial to older students. The sample that follows is designed for students in grades three through eight, though, as with the "Portfolio Processing" worksheet and the "Photo Project Processing" worksheet, you may be able to begin this process at younger ages. Photocopy the sample "Portfolio Manifest" (p. 102) onto the front and back of the same sheet of paper to provide space for more documentation. ✪

Portfolio Manifest

Manifest

Sample

	date in	date out

Visas
Monitoring Portfolio Reviews

Part of the Portfolio Journey involves sharing portfolios with others. These reviews of portfolio contents can be beneficial to students, teachers, and parents. A review is a chance for others to comment on the work in a portfolio. This is not intended as a grading process; it is intended as an interaction. It is a time for observations. An engaging way of documenting these portfolio reviews and gathering observations together in one place is by keeping portfolio visas, which have a function similar to the real-life travel documents of the same name.

The number of formal reviews any one portfolio receives in a year will be limited, so visas do not require unlimited space. They should contain enough space for nine reviews in a year, though a portfolio will not actually receive nine formal reviews in any one year. Having space for nine reviews, however, allows students to include several informal reviews of their choice. The process of reviewing will be discussed in detail in later chapters, but informal reviews might include self-assessments, peer reviews, or reviews done with visiting grandparents or relatives.

The spaces for each review should contain room for the following:

1. *Name*
   The name of the person reviewing the portfolio.

2. *Date*
   The date of the review.

3. *Title or Position*
   This could be *teacher*, *parent*, *mom*, *dad*, *brother*, *sister*, *friend*, *assistant teacher*, and so on.

4. *Comments*
   The reviewer's overall impressions of the work in the portfolio, including any observations or suggestions, framed in a positive manner.

It is important to remember that visas are not intended as a grading activity. They are designed to formalize the process of sharing portfolio contents with others. Teachers might want to find a selection of interesting rubber stamps to use for stamping the review areas after adding their comments. This makes the documents seem even more like actual visas, and students will enjoy collecting the various stamps.

The sample visa (pp. 104–5) is intended to be photocopied onto a single sheet of paper (one illustration on each side); fold the sheet of paper in half to create a visa booklet. Visa booklets printed on card stock will better withstand a year of handling. ✪

VISA

The Portfolio Journey

A Record of My Portfolio Reviews

Name:

Teacher:

Date:

Reviewed By:

Title:

Date:

Comments:

Reviewed By:

Title:

Date:

Comments:

Reviewed By:

Title:

Date:

Comments:

Reviewed By:

Date:

Title:

Comments:

Reviewed By:

Date:

Title:

Comments:

Reviewed By:

Date:

Title:

Comments:

Reviewed By:

Date:

Title:

Comments:

Reviewed By:

Date:

Title:

Comments:

Reviewed By:

Date:

Title:

Comments:

Extras
As long as you have that photocopier warmed up...

Following are a couple of additional masters that you may want to reproduce. They can be pasted or glued onto the front of file folders to create portfolio clearing folders (p. 107) and display portfolio folders (p. 108).

The portfolio clearing folder, if you choose to use it, is described in Chapter 7 under the heading "Special Note: Savers and Trashers" (p. 83). It is a holding file for work a student elects to eliminate from a working portfolio, used as an intermediate step between the working portfolio and the trash can. A portfolio clearing folder is kept in the working portfolio. It is removed and placed on the teacher's desk during portfolio cleaning. This allows teachers to review work being edited out of student portfolios and allows students a chance to reconsider their decision.

The display portfolio folder (also discussed in Chapter 7) is kept inside the working portfolio as well. It is a precursor to the display portfolio, used as a place for portfolio contents that reflect a student's experiences and abilities but that are not evaluated on portfolio clearing days along with the other materials in a portfolio. This might include certificates, honors, letters of commendation, photographs of important events, or evidence of extracurricular experiences. If your students will not be moving on to create display portfolios soon, you will need to provide them with display portfolio folders. Even if students already have display portfolios, you will find it easier if students keep potential additions to display portfolios in these separate folders until they have the time to properly integrate the new materials. ✪

Now that you have the tools you need to do a variety of types of annotation, processing, and portfolio monitoring, you are ready to begin the regular activity of daily collecting described in the last chapter. You can begin building working portfolios at any time, but at some point early in the process you should consider doing an activity that introduces students to the idea behind and importance of keeping portfolios. If this activity also reinforces the travel metaphor, so much the better. The next chapter, "Passports: A Student's Introduction to Portfolios," describes just such an activity.

Stuff I want to take out of my portfolio.

Portfolio Clearing Folder

Name:

Teacher:

Display Portfolio Folder

Stuff I will want to have in my display portfolio.

My Best Work!

Name:

Teacher:

Passports
A Student's Introduction to Portfolios

We carry within us the
wonders we seek without us.
—Sir Thomas Browne

Portfolios are engaging and useful tools. If you did not believe this, you probably would not have read this far. Part 1 of this book was devoted to convincing you of the value of student portfolios. It seems only fair that we make as compelling a case for portfolios to *our students*. Portfolios should not be a thing *done to* students. We want students to participate with enthusiasm in the creation of their portfolios. This, at any rate, should be our goal. One way of moving toward that goal is through an activity that is fun and that begins students on a journey of self-awareness. ✪

Passports
Thinking About Who We Are

When we travel to other countries, we are often required to take our passports. Passports are our capsule identities. They reduce us to what governments think is most important about us. They contain our vital statistics and the story of our travels in stamps and entries.

A passport can be an interesting metaphor for introducing self-reflective thinking to students. What if we asked our students to create their own passports—for

109

their portfolios? There is no set recipe for what information a passport must have, but it might include the following:

- *Portrait Photograph*
  The "head shot," or close-up portrait, is a traditional element of passports. This should be easy enough to accomplish whether you use 35mm, instant chemical, or digital photography. Tack a drape of light blue or green cloth onto a bulletin board. Mark an *X* with masking tape on the floor about one foot from the backdrop to indicate where the student should stand. Mark another *X* on the floor to indicate where you should stand as the photographer. Make sure the photographer's *X* is as close to the student's *X* as possible while still allowing the camera to capture the entire head and shoulders of the subject. Have your students line up and walk to the *X* in front of the backdrop. As they reach the *X*, have them turn and stop to have their picture taken, then return to their seats. In this way, you can quickly create passport photos for an entire class. Passport photos should look something like this:

My passport photo

- *Identification Information*
  This would include, of course, a student's name. It might also include a grade level and teacher's name. It might contain an address and phone number.

- *Vital Statistics*

  Vital Statistics could include anything you and your students choose. You might involve students by asking what kind of information might be really important for someone to know about them. This could include age; physical characteristics such as hair color, height, and weight (some students might be sensitive about physical characteristics, so don't force the inclusion of these); and parent or guardian information.

- *Preferences Inventory*

  A preferences inventory is a place for students to list their likes and dislikes.

- *Skills Inventory*

  A skills inventory is a place for students to list their skills. One way of setting up such an inventory would be to ask students which of their skills and abilities they would most want the people they meet in their travels to know.

- *Biography*

  A biography would be a brief personal history or life story condensed to fit into a limited space.

The portfolio passport master that follows (pp. 112–15) is intended to be reproduced on both sides of two sheets of paper, folded in half, and stapled together along the spine to form a booklet. Reproducing the cover page on card stock will make the portfolio passports more durable. As an alternative, passports, once completed, might be separated into single sheets, laminated, and restapled.

This certainly is not the only way to create student portfolio passports. You might choose to create portfolio passport masters on a computer using drawing software or by using cut-and-paste methods. You and your students might agree on an outline for what passports should contain and then have students create unique passports themselves. The size of passports is limited only by the size of the media with which you will be working. You might have student teams create their passports as if the teams themselves were different countries. Passports would then not only identify the student but identify that student's team (country) of origin as well. Passports might be handwritten, typed on a typewriter, or composed on a computer. If your students want to prepare their text using word processing software and still use the Portfolio Journey passport, have them compose text within certain size restrictions, print these pages, trim them to size, and paste them onto the appropriate pages in their passports.

Passports become a part of the working portfolio. They are, of course, documents students will want to save. You might consider creating new passports two or three times a year to help students compare and contrast their growth and development, as well as their changing preferences and skills.

Passports should be made in conjunction with and related to portfolios. Whereas passports are brief sketches of who we are, portfolios are the full stories of our lives. We keep portfolios to expand upon the claims we make in our passports. Passports are windows onto who we are; portfolios are doorways. ✪

(Text continues on p. 116.)

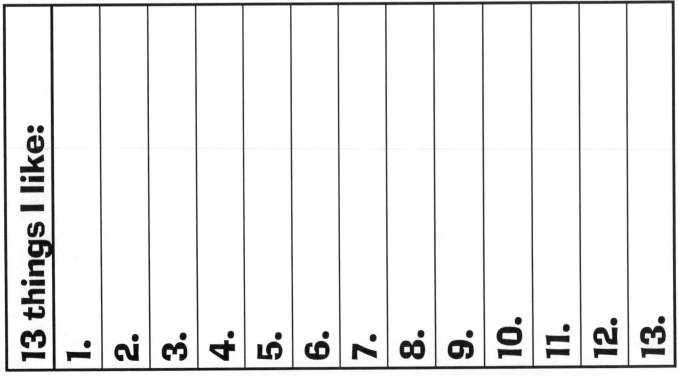

Page 6

Who I am: **Page 1**

Page 2

My Picture

Passport
Photo

My name:

My grade: My age:

My teacher:

Where I was born:

When I was born:

Page 5

I am good at these things:

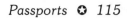

Page 4

7.

8.

9.

10.

11.

12.

13.

13 things I've done:

Page 3

1.

2.

3.

4.

5.

6.

This passport activity is a fun way to introduce students to self-reflective thinking and to portfolios in general. Now, you will be shifting roles once again: Your new role is that of Tour Guide. You will be traveling along with your students on the Portfolio Journey. You will help them repack their trunks into more compact suitcases and even more compact daypacks for the side trips they will take. You will give them a new tool for organizing their working portfolios: the kit. You will also help them analyze and assess their developing skills by implementing a rubric for the Portfolio Journey.

Part 4
On the Road

The Teacher as Tour Guide

In Part 4 of the Portfolio Journey you will:

ⓔ Help your students create their own suit-cases or display portfolios.

ⓔ Show your students how to create daypacks, or special portfolios, and introduce the idea of kits as a technique for organizing project work in portfolios.

ⓔ Help assess and evaluate students' portfolio-keeping skills with a rubric for the Portfolio Journey.

The Suitcase
Presenting Yourself Through the Display Portfolio

> It ought to be part of our patriotic feeling to
> endeavor to convey as agreeable an idea
> as possible of ourselves to those countries
> which we honour with our distinguished
> presence in our little trips.
>
> —Mrs. C. E. Humphries (*Manners for Women*, 1897)

Mrs. C. E. Humphries undoubtedly would have approved of display portfolios because their primary purpose is to help us "convey as agreeable an idea as possible of ourselves" to those individuals we meet in our travels. In the process of organizing ourselves to make the best possible impression, we may also come to learn something about ourselves.

Whereas the *trunk*, or working portfolio, is your box of photographs, programs, and ephemera, the *suitcase*, or display portfolio, is your scrapbook. It is where you gather the best of your souvenirs and organize them to tell your story: the story of who you are; where you have been; what you have done; and, by implication, of what you are capable.

A good display portfolio should suggest this story at a glance and convey the story fully in a sitting of ten to twenty minutes. This means that a display portfolio only has room for the best of you: your best writing, your most creative artwork, your most innovative projects, your most detailed efforts, and the highlights of your academic and personal achievements.

As students mature, display portfolios will evolve into real and practical tools for seeking special academic placement; after-school jobs; college admission; scholarships; summer employment; internships; and, eventually, careers. It may be premature to assemble career-track portfolios, but it is never too early to begin teaching students the skills they will need to develop such portfolios.

Display portfolios are distinguished from working portfolios by several important features:

1. *Display portfolios are bound or contained.*
   Portfolio samples might be prepared using a three-hole punch and then kept in a three-ring binder, or they might be slipped into plastic pages. They might be bound into a book or boxed in a special portfolio box, but the contents of a display portfolio are meant to remain together.

2. *Display portfolios are ordered.*
   In a display portfolio, one sample is meant to be viewed before or after another sample; in a specific order, the samples tell a specific story. The organization of a display portfolio is important to the impression it makes.

3. *Display portfolios are compact.*
   Display portfolios purposely do not contain every good example, or even several good examples, of a student's work in a certain area. Decisions and choices are made concerning the best example of a student's work. This work, this evidence of decision making, is what's on display.

4. *Display portfolios do not contain graded work.*
   If work was done for an assignment in class, the version of it that appears in a display portfolio will have been redone to include corrections (this is sort of a soft rule for display portfolios of young students, but it should become a hard rule with maturity).

5. *Display portfolios should be visually exciting.*
   A variety of kinds of evidence should be on display. Such evidence might include photographs, written work, certificates, lists, drawings, graphic devices, and so on. A display portfolio should not be boring.

6. *Display portfolios focus on product, not process.*
   Generally, display portfolios should show the outcome of process. In the rare instances when process is shown, it will usually be a condensed "highlights" version of the process, such as three photographs showing a model in different stages of construction.

7. *Display portfolios concentrate on strengths.*
   Whereas working portfolios might present a more well-rounded view of a student's strengths and weaknesses, a display portfolio focuses only on the strengths. This does not mean that display portfolios are in any way dishonest. Self-reflection and self-assessment—important skills—may be highlighted or demonstrated in a display portfolio but only in the context of documenting an ability for self-analysis. Display portfolios are about putting your best foot forward.

8. *Display portfolios are more static and evolve more gradually.*
   Display portfolios tend to reach a certain stage of development and remain set for a longer period of time than working portfolios. After a display portfolio is built, the maintenance phase involves the gradual addition or substitution of examples that better convey the impression the student hopes to communicate.

9. *Display portfolios concentrate on breadth of talent.*
   Display portfolios try to paint a general picture of an individual. They sacrifice the depth of working portfolios (as well as the focus of special portfolios) to show students as well-rounded, broadly capable people. ✪

Creating Suitcases

The process of creating suitcases, or display portfolios, includes four parts:

1. Planning: Assessing Personal Skills and Interests

2. Collecting Souvenirs: Gathering Evidence in Support of the Assessment

3. Checking the Compass: Developing a Message to Organize the Evidence

4. Packing: Creating a Document That Communicates Personality and Ability

Part 1: Planning
Assessing Personal Skills and Interests

With working portfolios, we built our containers first, collected our samples, and then tried to figure out what it all meant. Display portfolios reverse this process. For one thing, we already have a lot of our samples. With display portfolios, we first try to figure out what it all means, then we select our samples, and then we decide on the package or container.

Personal Inventory Worksheets

The first step, figuring out what it all means, involves completing personal inventory worksheets. There are three personal inventories for students to complete: interest inventory, skills inventory, and computer skills inventory. Sample personal inventory worksheets, included following this section, help students think about their interests and abilities (see pp. 123–25).

Students should not feel rushed to complete their personal inventory worksheets. They should also be allowed to add to them over time. Sometimes, it is easy to discredit or overlook a real skill or forget an interest. Students can often benefit by doing these worksheets with family members or friends. Often, those close to us can remind us of skills we may not recognize or value.

Interest Inventory

The "Interest Inventory" worksheet has two columns. The first column is for students to list their interests. The second column is for students to list evidence or documentation of their interests. These columns need not be filled in with complete sentences. Remember that this worksheet is for students' interests. They need not have skill or ability in the areas listed, only an interest. Examples might include the following:

My Interests	Evidence of My Interests
writing poetry	published work in the school newspaper
photography	a program for an art show I was in
cats	a volunteer's certificate from the SPCA,
	pictures of my three cats
Goose Bumps books	a book report on *The Green Slime,*
	vice president: R. L. Stine Fan Club

Skills Inventory

The "Skills Inventory" worksheet has three columns. The first column is for students to list the skills they think they possess. These skills need not be those they think others would appreciate but merely skills in which they have some ability. The second column is for students to list evidence or documentation of their skills. The third column is for students to rate their skills as low, average, or high in comparison to other students their age, or other students at their grade level. Examples of evidence might include the following:

My Skills	Evidence of My Skills
I play baseball	certificate for playing Little League,
	a letter from my coach,
	a picture of me playing that was in the newspaper
I am good at math	my math grades,
	certificate for being on Math Challenge team
I play chess	award from the Boys Club Chess Program
I am an inventor	certificate from Young Inventors Program,
	photos and descriptions of my inventions

Computer Skills Inventory

The "Computer Skills Inventory" worksheet is a specific list that allows students to record and rate their computer skills. If your students generally have not been exposed to computers in school or at home, you probably should not use this worksheet.

(Text continues on p. 126.)

Interest Inventory

My Interests	Evidence of My Interests

Skills Inventory

My Skills	Evidence of My Skills	Level
		☐ Low ☐ Average ☐ High
		☐ Low ☐ Average ☐ High
		☐ Low ☐ Average ☐ High
		☐ Low ☐ Average ☐ High
		☐ Low ☐ Average ☐ High
		☐ Low ☐ Average ☐ High
		☐ Low ☐ Average ☐ High
		☐ Low ☐ Average ☐ High

Computer Skills Inventory

This is a list of the software I have used and my proficiency level for each.

Computer Operating System: Mac Windows DOS

Program Type	Software	Basic proficiency	Intermediate proficiency	Advanced proficiency
Word Processing				
Spreadsheet				
Desktop Publishing				
Database				
Graphics				
Image Manipulation				
Presentation				
Multimedia Authoring				
Other				
Online Experience:				
E mail				
Newsgroups				
Gopher				
F.T.P.				
World Wide Web				
A.O.L./Compuserve/Prodigy				

Personal Inventory Option

If students find that they have a lot of skills or interests, they might choose to list each one separately on 3-by-5-inch index cards. Index cards can be easier to arrange and reorganize. They also allow students to expand their lists easily over time. For example:

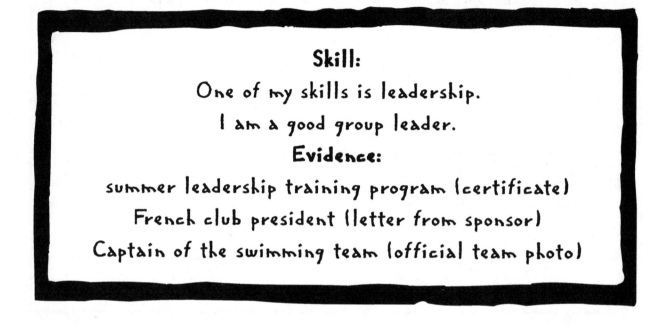

Part 2: Collecting Souvenirs
Gathering Evidence in Support of the Assessment

Filling out personal inventory worksheets should encourage students to think about what kinds of evidence they will want to have in their display portfolios. Some of this evidence may already be present in their working portfolios. If so, have students remove this work from their display portfolios and put it into their display portfolio folders which will serve as a temporary home for these pieces (see Chapters 7 and 8 for information about display portfolio folders). Other evidence must be found outside their working portfolios. Have students begin looking out for additional evidence to support their skills and interests. Often, they will find that one piece of evidence can serve multiple purposes. For instance, a report about a local environmental issue might demonstrate an interest in environmental issues, a commitment to community service, creative problem solving, and writing ability. When students find such pieces, they should place them in their display portfolio folders.

The evidence identified in the personal inventory worksheets is a natural starting point. For younger students, this might be all they need to begin building display portfolios. Older students, though, should be expected to include some basic materials in their display portfolios: writing samples; letters of recommendation; photographs; awards, certificates, press clippings, and programs; and, optionally, grades, original artwork, reading records, and travel logs.

Writing Samples

At a minimum, students need four writing samples for their display portfolios. These should be ungraded or, if they were class projects, neatly written revisions. Each of these samples will demonstrate a different ability that is essential to the skills of communicating well with written language:

1. *Outline*
   Students should include a single-page outline for a report or project. This demonstrates students' ability to organize their thoughts.

2. *Report*
   Students should include a report or paper they have written. This shows a student's ability to use language to communicate. It also shows a student's ability to follow through from the outlining phase.

3. *Business Letter*
   Students should include a one-page business letter. This demonstrates a student's ability to edit and to get to the point. Efficient writing is the sign of an effective communicator.

4. *Creative Writing*
   Students should include a short story, poem, song lyric, or dramatic speech they have written. This shows a student's creative command of the language.

Of course, students may include other writing samples, as well as evidence of other skills or interests, but these four are the basics.

Letters of Recommendation

This is a category that is less important for young students but essential for older students. The easiest way to think about this is to consider four categories of people from which it is useful for students to obtain letters: teachers, coaches or activity sponsors, employers or volunteer work supervisors, and community leaders. Students might set out to obtain one letter from each of these categories. Some tips for asking people to write letters of recommendation include the following:

1. Ask for a one-page letter (more than one page is usually too much to read for portfolio purposes).

2. Ask for the letter to be addressed to the student or "To whom it may concern."

3. Ask for the letter to be printed or typed on letterhead stationery.

4. Ask the person to briefly comment on the student's performance or abilities.

5. Ask the person to refer to specific examples that support the opinions.

6. Be sensitive to the fact that the person may be busy by giving two weeks' notice.

7. Don't solicit letters from friends and family members (unless using letters of recommendation as a practice activity for younger students).

Photographs

Photographic documentation can help create a more visually exciting portfolio and allow students to include evidence of work or experiences that might otherwise be difficult to document. Students should be on the lookout specifically for photographs from the following categories:

1. Projects—evidence that shows problem solving skills.

2. Artwork—evidence that shows creativity.

3. Performances—evidence that shows a student as being action-oriented.

4. Presentations—evidence that shows communication skills.

5. Athletics—evidence that shows motivation or team spirit.

6. Social and Extracurricular Activities—evidence that shows social skills.

Using the following "Photo-Planner Page" (pp. 130–31), have students begin to list photos they would like to acquire or create for their display portfolios. Photocopy the two pages on the front and back of the same sheet of paper.

Awards, Certificates,
Press Clippings, and Programs

If students have received any awards or certificates, even simple certificates of participation, these should be included in display portfolios. If students have received positive press coverage, this too should be included. Programs from performances are useful additions as well. These kinds of samples help convey "at a glance" an impression of talent, ambition, commitment, and promise. They also help create a more visually diverse and appealing display portfolio.

Optional Items

These items are not essential to display portfolios, but if they have not already been included under any of the other suggested categories, students might want to add the following:

1. *Grades*
   Good grades are better than no grades, but the point of a display portfolio is to create a well-rounded picture of the student. If grades are good, the student will want to show them off. If grades are mixed, they might be left out completely, or the student might list only the good grades. If grades are "middle of the road," or average, the student should make sure that the display portfolio compensates by showing a range of nonacademic areas of excellence. If the grades are all bad, they should be left out completely.

2. *Original Artwork*

   If the student has original, two-dimensional artwork that is small enough to include in a display portfolio, its presence will add visual diversity.

3. *Reading Records*

   What students read and have read can say a lot about them. Have students keep a record of the books and magazines they read to include in the display portfolio. (See "Optional Lists," later in this chapter, for a worksheet.)

4. *Travel Logs*

   If a student has traveled in this country or outside of it, or if the student speaks other languages, evidence of this, in the form of a travel log, might be included in the display portfolio. (See "Optional Lists," later in this chapter, for a worksheet.)

Part 3: Checking the Compass
Developing a Message to Organize the Evidence

The core of your students' display portfolios will be a series of statements about themselves and their abilities. These statements are what we refer to as *compass readings*—readings from the heart's compass, that part of each of us that helps us find our true direction. Have students refer to their personal inventory worksheets from this chapter and look for dominant themes or general statements that seem to apply especially well to them. These themes might include: liking to build things, working well with people, enjoying the outdoors, being creative, and so on.

Have students make a list of statements that describes their interests and abilities, then narrow this list to six to ten statements. These statements should be specific and written in complete sentences. Make six to ten copies of the "Compass Reading" worksheet on pages 132–33 for each student, or create your own variation. At the top of each worksheet, students should write one of the statements from their list.

Next, in the lined area of the worksheet, have students provide a brief written explanation of the statement, describing experiences that support the claim. Finally, have students find or take at least one photograph that supports the statement and tape it in the black area of the worksheet (see the sample "Compass Reading" worksheet that follows the master). Allow enough time for students to do their compass readings with care—they will form the core around which display portfolios are built.

After students have completed their "Compass Reading" worksheets, set them aside. It is okay to do more or to redo them later. We will return to the worksheets in the last phase of building display portfolios, but first we will look at some ways of organizing other types of portfolio evidence into efficient and effective documentation.

(Text continues on p. 134.)

Photo-Planner Page

List the photographs you want to gather, collect, or have made.

If you haven't had any experiences in a specific category, try to find photographs that might illustrate the characteristics listed for each category.

Projects:

What shows you as a problem-solver? What shows your analytical thinking ability? What shows your ability to follow through and do a good job on a project?

Artwork:

What shows you as a creative person? What would illustrate your ability to work with imagery and handle visual information? What shows your attention to detail and your ability to express yourself in a different medium?

Performances:

What shows you as being action-oriented? What would demonstrate your self-confidence? What shows your willingness to work toward perfection?

Presentations:

What shows your ability as an oral communicator? What might indicate your ability to prepare a presentation and deliver a speech?

Athletics:

What shows you as being physically active? What demonstrates your ability to work on a team? What might attest to your motivation and stamina?

Social and Extracurricular Activities:

What might illustrate your social skills? What would show your level of involvement with your community and school? What would show you as someone who gets things done? What would illustrate your level of commitment?

Compass Reading: Who I Am

Compass Reading: Who I Am (Sample)

I am a musical person.
Music is very important to me.

This is a picture of me practicing the piano with my mom. I think it represents who I am because I love music and play many instruments. I play the piano and have had two recitals. I also play the violin. I sing in the choir in church, and I play violin in the school orchestra. I love all kinds of music. I listen to classical music sometimes and rock music other times. Playing musical instruments has helped me to concentrate and work hard to learn things. It is fun, but it is also hard work. I practice a lot because I want to make my music be the best it can be.

Academics Review

Some students will place a lot of emphasis on school work. The "Academics Review" worksheet (p. 135) is a better way to present evidence of academic achievement than a simple list of grades. Also, it allows students to focus attention on the subject areas in which they excel.

Make multiple copies of the worksheet for each student, one copy for each subject area studied during a phase or period of time, such as a semester. For each period of time, have students list several of the achievements of which they are most proud for each subject. Have students describe one of these achievements in more detail. At the bottom of the worksheet is a space for students to do a self-assessment of their performance in a certain subject.

Project/Performance Records

Remember the activities for which students were to find photographic evidence? One could argue that the most complete and accurate picture of a student's abilities comes from these activities. Projects, artwork, performances, presentations, athletics, and social and extracurricular activities demonstrate interest, ability, and commitment. Photographs are one of the best, and sometimes only, ways of documenting these activities. To be useful for display portfolios, though, they must be presented attractively and annotated effectively. One strategy for achieving this is the "Project/Performance Record" worksheet that follows (see p. 136).

The large space at the top of the worksheet is for a photograph. Below this space are areas for a brief caption and a description of the photograph. In the "Caption" area, the student should briefly describe the photograph and note the date it was taken. In the "Description" area, the student should describe in more detail the event or object in the photograph. Also included on the worksheet is an area for students to describe what they learned from the event or object shown in the photograph.

Optional Lists

First of all, relax—these three lists really are optional. Your photocopier is probably smoking from all the copies you've made, but it isn't necessary to have your students include these lists in their display portfolios. You might choose to use them selectively (only for students who have the kind of information the list is designed to organize). The first is a reading list, though students might list music or films that have helped shape who they are today. The second is a travel log. If this is appropriate for any of your students, use it. The third is a list of clubs and organizations. This might be especially useful for students who are socially active.

A worksheet for each list follows (see pp. 137–39), but don't feel constrained or limited by them. Creating lists for display portfolios is easy. Just remember that they must be clear, succinct, and neat.

(Text continues on p. 140.)

Academics Review

Subject: _____

Teacher: _____

Achievements in the first half:	One achievement in detail:

Achievements in the second half:	One achievement in detail:

Self-Assessment: My performance in this subject was:

Average ☐   Above Average ☐   Exceptional ☐

📷 Project/Performance Record

Photograph

Caption:

What I learned:

Description:

My Reading List

My favorite books

Titles:	Authors:	Subjects:

Magazines I read regularly:

_____

_____

_____

_____

_____

_____

_____

_____

Travel Log

Interesting places I've been

Where:	When:

Clubs and Organizations

Club or organization name:	Purpose:	Office or role:	Dates of membership:

Part 4: Packing
Creating a Document That
Communicates Personality and Ability

In the future, we may all have our display portfolios recorded digitally. In the future, there probably will be reliable readers and monitors for this medium everywhere you look. For now, though, the most practical way to assemble a display portfolio is in book format.

The best solutions for display portfolios are prebound, slip-in, clear plastic page folders (available from office supply stores) or three-ring binders with clear plastic pages. One of the advantages of this method is flexibility—students can easily change the order and arrangement of portfolio materials. Also, portfolio contents are protected from handling and accidents by the plastic pages. Books are familiar to people (someone presented with a book-format portfolio won't need to be shown how to use it), and they have a neat and orderly appearance.

Display portfolios can be organized many ways, but the basic display portfolio layout discussed below (followed by an illustration, p. 141) is an effective beginning. Later, students might reorganize their display portfolios.

Basic Display Portfolio Layout

1. Begin with a title page. This can be as simple as a page with the student's name, age, and grade printed in large letters on an 8½-by-11-inch sheet of paper.

2. Follow with letters of recommendation (strongest recommendation first).

3. Next, add writing samples in this order: outline and report (facing each other), then business letter and creative writing (facing each other).

4. Add the "Compass Reading" worksheet that evidences the strongest ability or interest (strongest abilities and interests should appear first). Use this worksheet to build a short section focusing on that interest or ability. Draw other evidence from class work samples, "Academics Review" worksheets, awards and certificates, press clippings, and so on, to support the compass reading. Optional lists such as those for reading, travel, and club membership might be included here if they support the claim of the compass reading.

5. Repeat step 4 with each "Compass Reading" worksheet.

6. Add a list of grades, or another "Academics Review" worksheet, if appropriate.

7. Optional lists, such as reading records, travel logs, and lists of clubs and memberships, should appear last (unless they seem to fit better in one of the compass reading sections).

Basic Display Portfolio Layout

The display portfolio is a bridge to creating portfolios that communicate specific themes. Its organization is not as focused as that of a special portfolio, but it does begin to ask students to organize their portfolio samples with a purpose. This diagram gives you a general idea of how a display portfolio might be arranged. An actual display portfolio would have more samples.

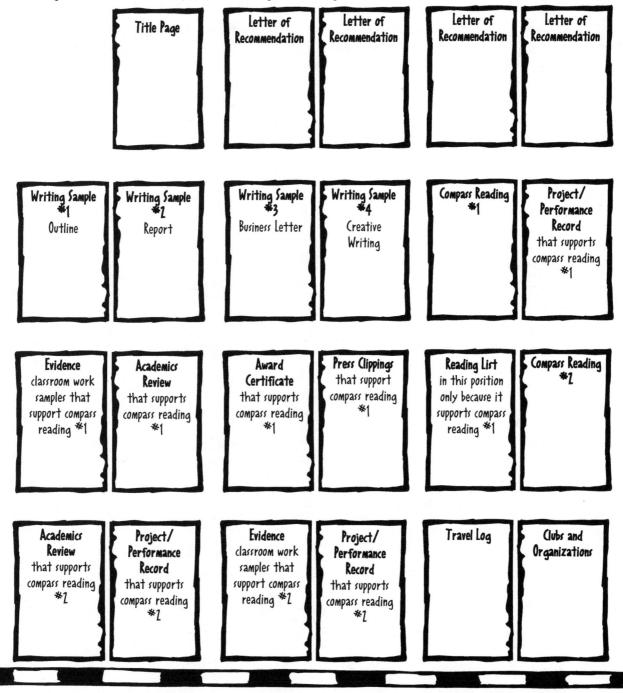

| Title Page | Letter of Recommendation | Letter of Recommendation | Letter of Recommendation | Letter of Recommendation |

| Writing Sample #1 Outline | Writing Sample #2 Report | Writing Sample #3 Business Letter | Writing Sample #4 Creative Writing | Compass Reading #1 | Project/ Performance Record that supports compass reading #1 |

| Evidence classroom work samples that support compass reading #1 | Academics Review that supports compass reading #1 | Award Certificate that supports compass reading #1 | Press Clippings that support compass reading #1 | Reading List in this position only because it supports compass reading #1 | Compass Reading #2 |

| Academics Review that supports compass reading #2 | Project/ Performance Record that supports compass reading #2 | Evidence classroom work samples that support compass reading #2 | Project/ Performance Record that supports compass reading #2 | Travel Log | Clubs and Organizations |

This process is not an afternoon's project. It will take time. Fortunately, you and your students are not in a hurry. If you begin the process of keeping working portfolios in the fall, you may not have completed display portfolios until the end of the first semester. This is okay. Work slowly. Allow students time to think about the display portfolios they are creating. This process can reveal a lot about a student. It will also generate a lot of questions. Involve parents as much as possible. Though creating a display portfolio may seem like a lot of work, the result really is worth the effort. Display portfolios help students more clearly see themselves for who they are. They help students build empowering, realistic assessments of their strengths and interests. They boost self-esteem from the most solid of grounds: individual achievement. ✪

By now, your students should have vital working portfolios and refined display portfolios—*trunks* and *suitcases*. The next chapter adds two more pieces of luggage to our traveling ensemble: the *daypack*, or special portfolio, and the *kit*, or project portfolio.

The Daypack and the Kit
Special Portfolios and Project Portfolios, for Special Needs

11

Sample Letter of Introduction

The bearer of this letter is my intimate friend. He visits your town on some important business and I have no doubt of his success, if you will have the kindness to assist him with your advice and support. When you know him, his merit will recommend him to you sufficiently: and, therefore, as I know his good qualities and the friendship you have for me, I take the liberty of recommending him warmly to your kindness, especially as my recommendations to you have never been in vain.

—Baedecker's Traveller's
Manual of Conversation in Four Languages, 1886

In many ways, your display portfolio is your "letter of introduction." It should introduce you to others in a positive and generous fashion. The work you have elected to include and the documents you have assembled should collaborate with the neatness and attractiveness of your display to recommend you effectively.

Your display portfolio is a valuable tool for making this kind of recommendation, but sometimes you may need something a little more focused and specific.

When you need your display portfolio to convey a more focused impression, this is when you adapt it into what we call a *daypack*, or special portfolio. Your daypack is the luggage you take with you for side trips and excursions. When your *trunk*, or working portfolio, would seem too big, and your *suitcase*, or display portfolio, too awkward to carry, you put your most essential items into a daypack.

Daypacks, or special portfolios, focus attention on between one and three of a student's most outstanding characteristics. They are tailored to help students apply for special programs, interview for volunteer or paid jobs and internships, or to receive special consideration. Special portfolios will be most useful to older students who are beginning to think about after-school work, taking advantage of special enrichment opportunities, or even applying to college. Even young students, though, can begin to practice interviewing and presenting themselves professionally with their portfolios.

As you and your students should already understand the distinction between working portfolios and display portfolios, the factors that differentiate a special portfolio will be easy to grasp.

1. *Special portfolios are temporary constructions.*
   Special portfolios are constructed from the materials that have been selected and prepared for display portfolios. Evidence is rearranged to accomplish a short-term objective, such as getting a job or position or making a specific, favorable impression.

2. *Special portfolios are tailored to the needs of a specific objective.*
   Whereas display portfolios cover all the bases and tend to show the full range of a student's capabilities, special portfolios only highlight those abilities and experiences germane to the objective. For instance, a student applying for a leadership program might want to highlight leadership roles, team projects, and evidence of self-motivation and personal responsibility. Though the student may have good math grades, may have won several chess competitions, and may be a prize-winning artist, evidence of such accomplishments, though perfect for inclusion in a display portfolio, would not find their way into a special portfolio created for this particular objective.

3. *Special portfolios are more compact, concise, and to-the-point than display portfolios.*
   Because of the way special portfolios are used—to make a favorable first impression—they must lead the viewer quickly through the particular academic and experiential highlights that a student wants to feature. This means that there will be less supporting evidence for the claims made. Also, there will be more emphasis on evidence that communicates graphically. A viewer may flip through a special portfolio only once. Viewers will not, most likely, read long written samples, but they may be impressed by photographic evidence, awards and press clippings, and well-presented lists.

4. *Special portfolios are organized with the viewer in mind.*
   Though display portfolios are built with an imaginary viewer in mind, that viewer tends to be general and generic. Part of the process of creating special portfolios involves students in imagining themselves in the role of a specific viewer. Sometimes, this will be easy to do; other times, it will be more difficult. Still, students must learn to analyze their portfolio selections and organization as much as possible from the perspective a specific person.

In discussing the different organizational requirements of the special portfolio, this chapter will also add a new element: the student résumé. In addition, we will also be looking at some tips for improving the visual impact and presentational quality of special portfolio samples. ✪

Creating Daypacks

Keeping Special Portfolios

The process of creating daypacks, or special portfolios, includes four parts:

1. Assessment: What Is the Objective of This Special Portfolio?

2. Planning: Developing a Student Résumé

3. Repacking: Reorganizing Evidence in Support of an Assessment

4. Aligning: Tailoring the Special Portfolio to the Presentation

Part 1: Assessment
What Is the Objective of This Special Portfolio?

Why are your students creating special portfolios? There should be either a real or imagined need for them before beginning the process. This is not to say that *every* student must be applying for a job or admission to a special program before beginning this process. Creating a special portfolio can be a valuable learning experience for any student, but to complete the first step, a specific need should be identified by or provided for students. As a teacher, you might want to designate a practice or imagined need, such as: "The purpose of your special portfolio will be to get a job as _____." Or, for something specific in which students might be interested: "Your special portfolio will help you _____." You might provide a range of options so that students can select the one for which they have the most enthusiasm.

You might find yourself in a position to provide a real purpose for students to create special portfolios. For instance, you might create six different projects around the theme of a unit and allow students the chance to apply for membership with the team doing the project in which they are most interested. They might tailor their portfolios to demonstrate the skills and experiences that would best qualify them for working on a specific project. This would give them a real purpose for creating their special portfolios, a real interview/presentation experience, and co-ownership of the project.

The important thing is for students to have a clear purpose in mind when creating their special portfolios. This purpose should be written at the top of the "Special Portfolio Research" worksheet that follows (p. 147). The purpose of this research worksheet is to help students imagine or brainstorm what kinds of portfolio samples would best support the special portfolio's purpose. More specifically, students might ask themselves what evidence they could provide in their portfolio that would best show their qualifications for the particular role, position, job, or honor. Have students complete the "Special Portfolio Research" worksheet to clarify what they should include in their special portfolios.

An engaging way for students to work on these research worksheets is with partners or in small teams. Several students, working together, can often generate more ideas or more points of view about special portfolio contents than students working alone. Students may refer to their display portfolios and working portfolios, but they should not simply flip through display portfolios and pull out materials for their special portfolios. This would limit students to only the skills or abilities they have already identified in themselves through the display portfolio process. If students do the research worksheets before looking at their display portfolios, they might gain new insights that they had previously overlooked.

After students have a solid grasp of their purpose (or "day trip") for which they will use the special portfolio, they should use the "Special Portfolio Planning" worksheet (p. 148) to begin listing the portfolio evidence they already have that would support this purpose. They might add to this list the portfolio evidence they want to acquire, advise, or improve.

Part 2: Planning
Developing a Student Résumé

Your students are now close to being able to assemble their special portfolios, but there is one more useful activity to complete before moving on to repacking. That is the creation of student résumés. Student résumés, like real résumés, condense significant experiences into a one-page document. Also, as is the case with real résumés, each should be tailored to its purpose. A person may be qualified to manage a community youth program as well as an arts organization, but the résumés used when applying for these positions, although having similarities, would highlight different accomplishments. The ability, like that of a chameleon, to change the way others perceive you in different situations is not dishonest. On the contrary, it demonstrates the kind of flexibility that will help workers of the future adapt to constant change and shifting job opportunities.

Unlike career-oriented résumés, student résumés will place more emphasis on academic and extracurricular experiences. The process of creating a résumé can help a student focus on particular strengths and abilities. It may help students see gaps in their collection of evidence and samples. More importantly, though, the student résumé will become the table of contents for the special portfolio. It will become an overview of a student's educational background and extracurricular achievements. As students move into high school, the student résumé will be adapted to include work experiences and, thereby, come to resemble the career résumé more closely.

Special Portfolio Research

Name: _____

Date: _____

What is the purpose for creating this special portfolio?

```
┌─────────────────────────────────────────────────────────────────┐
│                                                                   │
│                                                                   │
│                                                                   │
│                                                                   │
└─────────────────────────────────────────────────────────────────┘
```

List the characteristics, skills, abilities, and talents you think would be most important for meeting the purpose of the special portfolio. You may need to learn more about the purpose first.

Special Portfolio Planning

Name: _____

Date: _____

What is the purpose for creating this special portfolio?

List the portfolio evidence you already have that would support the special portfolio purpose.

What kinds of portfolio evidence might you want to acquire, revise, or improve upon?

Following the list of recommended and optional résumé information and the general résumé tips below is a "Résumé Worksheet" (p. 150) to help students create and organize their résumés.

What Student Résumés Should Have:

- *Identifying Information.* Students should be sure to include their names, addresses, and phone numbers.

- *Educational Background.* Students should list the names and addresses of the schools they have attended, including the grade levels and years of attendance for each school.

- *Extracurricular Experience.* Students should list the volunteer work they have done, the clubs and associations in which they have participated, the sports teams to which they have belonged, and the classes or lessons they have taken outside of school.

- *Honors and Awards.* Students should list the most significant awards and honors they have received.

- *References.* Students should list the names, addresses, and phone numbers of three people who can vouch for their claims. The relationship to the student of each person should be specified.

What Student Résumés Might Have:

- *Goal Statement.* Some people state the goal or the purpose of the résumé at the top of the page.

- *Photo.* If you have access to a good photocopier, you might help students incorporate small, close-up portraits (head and shoulders only) into their résumés. School portraits work well for this purpose.

General Tips for Student Résumés:

1. Limit the length of the résumé to one page.

2. Information should be listed in reverse chronological order (most recent events and experiences should appear first).

3. Remind students to ask their references for permission to be listed as references. It's the polite thing to do.

4. Have students work in pairs to check each other's spelling—twice!

5. Résumés should be typed or else composed using word processing software and then printed. Using word processing software allows one to easily customize future résumés.

6. For real interview situations, make at least two copies of a student résumé—one copy for the special portfolio, one copy for the interviewer.

Résumé Worksheet

Identifying Information:

Name:	Age:	Phone number:

Address:

Educational Background

Years attended	School name	School address

Extracurricular Experience

Experience	Date

Honors and Awards

Date of award	Award	Achievement recognized by the award

References

Name	Relationship to you	Address	Phone number

Part 3: Repacking
Reorganizing Evidence in Support of an Assessment

As mentioned previously, special portfolios must be compact. They will, therefore, be organized a little differently than display portfolios. The organizational concepts are similar: Students will still want to create two or three sections that focus on the particular attributes they have identified as supporting their purpose. However, the layout of the special portfolio will push the general and supporting evidence to the back and bring key evidence to the front. The basic special portfolio layout is discussed below (followed by a sample statement of intent, p. 152, and an illustration of the layout, p. 153).

Basic Special Portfolio Layout

1. Begin with a student résumé. It provides a general introduction that is easy for someone to scan. Also, the résumé answers many basic questions all on one page. A résumé replaces the title page of the display portfolio.

2. Follow the student résumé with a specific but brief (one short paragraph) affirmation or statement of purpose or intent. It should state clearly what the portfolio samples will evidence. If a student prepares this statement using word processing software, it should be done using a bold typeface of large size (a sample is included following this list, p. 152).

3. Next, add the "Compass Reading" worksheet that best supports the purpose identified on the "Special Portfolio Planning" worksheet. Use this worksheet to build a short section focusing on the interest or ability expressed on the "Compass Reading" worksheet. Draw other evidence from "Project/Performance Record" worksheets, class work samples, "Academics Review" worksheets, awards and certificates, press clippings, and so on, to support the compass reading. At appropriate places, include letters of recommendation that testify to the impression the student is trying to convey for this section. Optional lists may also be added at this point if they support the compass reading.

4. Repeat step 3 with a selection of the most relevant "Compass Reading" worksheets.

5. If the student has not already placed letters of recommendation, include them next (strongest recommendation first).

6. If any of the student's optional lists, such as reading records, travel logs, and lists of clubs and membership lists, would support the purpose of the portfolio, include them next (but only if they actually support the purpose).

7. Add a list of grades, or another "Academics Review" worksheet that presents additional academic information, if appropriate.

8. Next, add writing samples in this order: outline and report (facing each other), then business letter and creative writing (facing each other).

Statement of Intent

I think I am well qualified to be a counselor for summer camp. As my portfolio will demonstrate, I have four strengths that recommend me for this position:

1. I participate in many outdoor sports and activities.

2. I work well with groups and have good team spirit.

3. I am mature and have held many positions of responsibility.

4. I have a special interest in leather crafts and would be willing to help teach others.

Basic Special Portfolio Layout

The most important thing about a special portfolio is focus. If any materials don't clearly support the purpose of the portfolio, they should not be included, or they should be placed at the back of the special portfolio as supporting documents. Keep in mind that a student's actual special portfolio would have more pages than this diagram indicates.

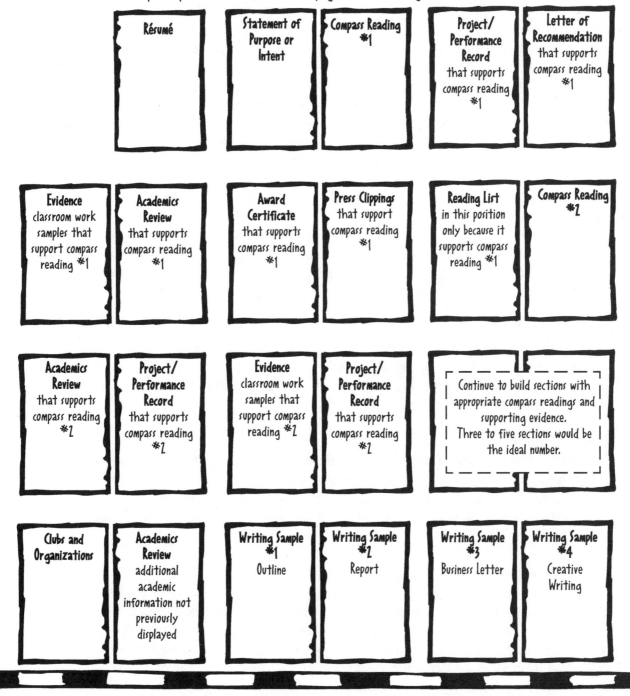

Part 4: Aligning Tailoring the Special Portfolio to the Presentation

When making a presentation with special portfolios, students will be communicating more by impression than by depth or breadth of work; therefore, it is essential that the impression made by the special portfolio be positive. One way portfolios communicate is through their organization; another way is by their condition. To make the best impression, consider the following tips:

- *Compass Readings*
  A compass reading should have a clear, sharp photograph that actively communicates the described interest or ability. Lettering should be neat (typed text or, if possible, text composed using word processing software and then printed, is preferable). Blocks of text might be typed or printed separately, trimmed to size, and glued onto new "Compass Reading" worksheets (see pp. 132–33). The new worksheets might be copied onto colorful paper stock (a compass reading will be more visually exciting if the photograph and blocks of text are glued onto colored paper).

- *Letters of Recommendation*
  A letter of recommendation should be displayed in its own clear plastic page. Three or four is a good number of letters to have in a special portfolio. They should either specifically support compass reading claims, or they should be from the most impressive sources.

- *Awards and Certificates*
  An award or certificate can be displayed as is in a clear plastic page. It would make sense to place it opposite pictures and information documenting the achievement for which the award or certificate was received. If a picture was taken of the student receiving the award, it might also be included.

- *Press Clippings*
  The best way to display a press clipping is to cut it out of the newspaper, trim it carefully, and arrange it on a sheet of 8½-by-11-inch paper. Students might use a photocopier for reducing or enlarging the clipping to fit attractively on one page. Once an attractive presentation is achieved, photocopy it onto another sheet of paper and slip this sheet into a clear plastic page.

- *Original Artwork*
  An effective way to prepare artwork is by using a black-and-white or color photocopier. Using a photocopy will save wear and tear on the original artwork. Students might use the reduction setting on photocopiers to make all artwork uniform in size. If a piece of art is smaller than the size of portfolio pages, consider centering and mounting it on black construction paper.

It is important to remember that special portfolios are temporary constructions. In many interview situations, they will not even be necessary. The display portfolio might be the perfect presentation tool for a student. If a special portfolio is created, though, it will be used to accomplish a short-term objective. After a special portfolio has been used for a specific presentation or purpose, its contents should be returned to the display portfolio or working portfolio from which they were taken. If, in the process of creating special portfolios, new materials are created, students should consider incorporating them into their display portfolios at this point. If this is not practical, students should at least save the new materials in a special portfolio folder within the working portfolio. This way, the materials can be reused later. ✪

Creating Kits

Keeping Project Portfolios

One of the most difficult balances for educators to strike is that between process and product. Our education system tends to teach process but value (i.e., grade) product. Many educational reforms that try to address this by shifting the emphasis in evaluation onto process lose sight of products. Students who endlessly practice (work on process) without realizing a product lose interest in their education. Students who generate projects without understanding process don't understand what factors they can control to improve the quality of their projects.

Portfolios, in general, place a healthy emphasis on product. For the world in which our students are coming of age, this is probably as it should be. We may, in the future, come to think differently of this, but, at present, our society judges and rewards its individuals on the basis of the products they produce. Portfolios can, however, be used to value and make students more aware of process. *Kits*, or project portfolios, are just such a tool.

We began the Portfolio Journey by constructing *trunks*, or working portfolios. These collections are intended for what might be called internal use. They are the process phase of developing portfolios, while *suitcases*, or display portfolios, and *daypacks*, or special portfolios, are the product phase. In addressing project portfolios, we are returning to process. A project portfolio is a folder within the working portfolio that contains all of the process documents for a particular project. These might include the original assignment, teacher handouts, research notes, resource notes, sketches and plans, lists, outlines, drafts, graded work, processing and self-assessments, and corrected or revised copies.

Kits are an excellent tool for actually teaching process, as well as a tool for approaching projects as an exercise in creative problem solving. They are simple enough to initiate. As a teacher, you must first decide whether you want to have your students keep informal or formal kits. Both are described below.

Informal Kits

Informal kits begin with the assignment of a project. The best projects are posed as questions to students rather than tasks. For example, rather than asking each student to make a model of a traditional Native American dwelling, you might ask students what kind of structures Native Americans traditionally built as homes and why. Effective projects also allow students to answer these questions in the way they feel best prepared to communicate. This might mean allowing some students to build models of traditional Native American dwellings while others do drawings, paintings, reports, materials collections, displays, or multimedia pieces. Such a diverse array of media is not always possible, and sometimes you will want to constrain the possible product options, but allowing students to satisfy some project requirements by capitalizing on their personal strengths is important.

To establish an informal project portfolio for a project, you will need to provide or arrange for each student to have a separate container. This container should fit physically inside the working portfolio. It might be a file folder, a 9-by-12-inch envelope, or a pocket folder. If you choose to use file folders, staple or tape one or two additional sides shut so that contents will not fall out as easily. If you discard the process materials after the project is complete, containers can be reused later for other projects. If desired, photocopy and hand out to students the informal project portfolio cover sheet that follows. Have students fill out the cover sheet and staple it to the outside of their folder or envelope. Or, the cover sheet might be placed inside the project portfolio. Ask students to save in the folder or envelope all the work they do related to the project.

Project Portfolio

Name: _____

Teacher: _____

Project Portfolio Start Date: _____

Project:

_____

This is where I keep all the work
that relates to this project.

Formal Kits

Formal kits are distinguished from informal kits in that they specify the process material to be included. Formal kits are extremely useful when teaching students research and planning skills, with a project as an outcome. Formal kits begin the same as informal kits: Propose a project, then hand out or designate project portfolio folders or envelopes, using the formal project portfolio cover sheet (following the list below, p. 160) if desired.

The next step is to decide what kinds of process documents should be included in the project portfolio. You may need to teach students how to do some of this process work as they develop their projects. Some of the process materials that might be included are the following:

- *The Original Assignment*
  If the project assignment was given in handout form, that handout might be included in the project portfolio. If the assignment was written on the chalkboard or given verbally, it is even more important that it be written down and kept with the project portfolio. In addition, if the teacher provides clarifications, alternatives, options, or additional information at a later date, these should be documented on the original assignment sheet. The original assignment can be written down or preprinted on the project portfolio cover sheet.

- *Teacher Handouts*
  Include any additional handouts or worksheets related to the project.

- *Research Notes*
  As students begin to do research for their projects, they should make notes of what they find. These notes may be handwritten, or they may be in the form of photocopies, printouts from digital reference materials, printouts from World Wide Web sites, or articles clipped from newspapers. These notes should be included in the project portfolio.

- *Resource Notes*
  You will probably want students to document the sources for the information they discover. This is best accomplished while they are doing the research, and might take the form of a bibliography or a "Resource Notes" worksheet (a sample follows the cover sheet, p. 161), which can be kept during the project and included in the project portfolio.

- *Sketches and Plans*
  If students have made rough sketches or have drawn plans for a project, these should be dated and kept. Even if the sketches represent project courses not taken, they provide interesting keys to students' thinking processes and to how they solve problems.

- *Lists and Outlines*
  If students have made lists, created outlines, done clustering or mind-mapping, or employed any creative problem solving techniques, this documentation might be saved.

- *Draft Versions*
  Drafts were once a nuisance of a process that most teachers had difficulty successfully putting into practice. Drafts implied revision, and the revision part always seemed difficult to manage. Today, however, with the advent of computers and word processing software, drafts are much easier to produce and revise. If students will be using drafts, these should be saved.

- *Graded Work*
  Projects that have been graded and returned should be saved in the project portfolio, or, if they are too large or bulky, they should be documented with photographs, annotated, and saved on "Project/Performance Record" worksheets (see p. 136).

- *Processing and Self-Assessments*
  If students have processed their work by evaluating their efforts and their success with "Photo Project Processing" worksheets or "Project Processing" worksheets (see pp. 96–97 and p. 100, respectively), include these in the project portfolio.

- *Corrected or Revised Copies*
  Finally, if students have corrected or revised their projects in response to personal, peer, or teacher feedback, this should be noted in the project portfolio as well.

Create a checklist of the process materials you expect to see in student project portfolios and hand this out to students. You might want to incorporate this checklist into the cover sheet for the project portfolio (the following sample cover sheet incorporates such a checklist).

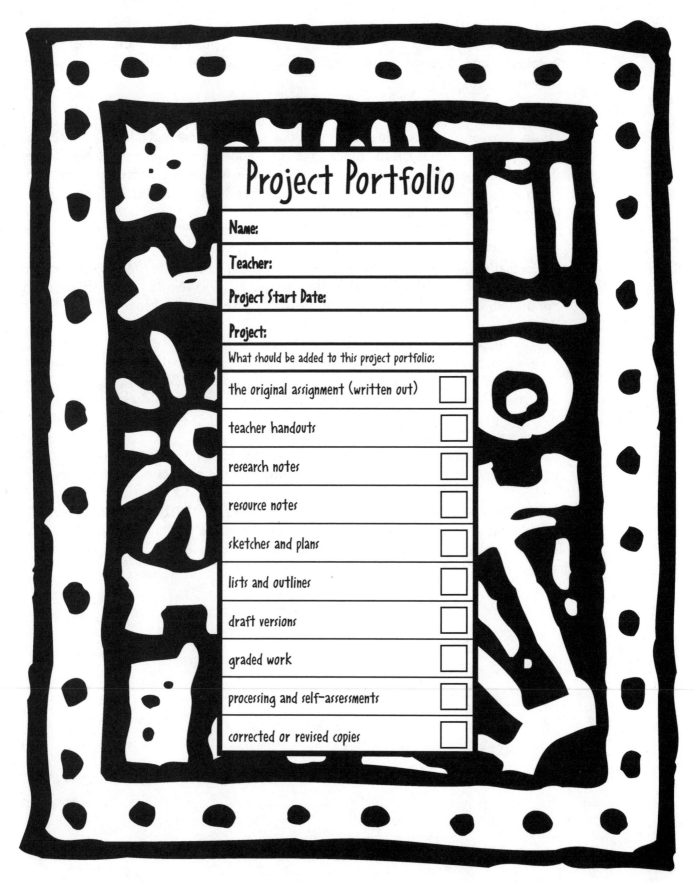

Project Portfolio

Name:

Teacher:

Project Start Date:

Project:

What should be added to this project portfolio:

the original assignment (written out) ☐

teacher handouts ☐

research notes ☐

resource notes ☐

sketches and plans ☐

lists and outlines ☐

draft versions ☐

graded work ☐

processing and self-assessments ☐

corrected or revised copies ☐

Resource Notes

Name: _____

Date: _____

Project:

_____

List all of the resources you used for this project. Resource notes are a kind of map or trail you leave so that other researchers can follow your path. Be sure to make your path clear and easy to follow by providing as much information as you can. Include titles, authors, and page numbers for books. Include article titles, authors, page numbers, magazine titles, and issue numbers when using periodicals.

Using Project Portfolios

To be effective, project portfolios, like working, display, and special portfolios, must be valued. There are two possible and not mutually exclusive strategies for valuing project portfolios. Because students have little opportunity to show off or share their project portfolios, it is easy for students to lose interest in them, especially if the teacher assigns them but then places most of the emphasis and value on the finished product. It might be necessary to grade or give credit for completing the components of or process elements for a project. Another option is to use project portfolios as the centerpiece for student/teacher reviews. These brief sessions allow teachers to assess the progress of individual students and provide assistance tailored to the needs of each student. These reviews also convey the impression that process work is important and valued by the teacher. Reviews involving student and teacher (and sometimes involving parents, too) can be used in conjunction with the grading of projects.

After a project has been completed, the project portfolio may be dismantled. The finished product, and perhaps a project processing sheet (see illustration on p. 100), might be saved in either the working or the display portfolio. Remaining contents may be discarded. Another option would be to save one or two complete project portfolios from the year for end-of-the-year reviews and progress assessments. If you (or your colleagues or your school system) have deemed that it is necessary to save more process work for each student, project portfolios make good sense. At the end of each project, they can be secured with rubber bands, labeled, and archived for the year in a box apart from students' working portfolios. This maintains the organization of the project portfolios without overburdening the holding capacity of working portfolios. ✪

With *kits*, or project portfolios, to help students attend to the process behind the work they do, and *daypacks*, or special portfolios, to help students focus the impression their portfolios convey, your students should have all the luggage they will need for their Portfolio Journey. Notice that much of the repacking and reorganizing of portfolio contents discussed in the last two chapters has occurred while you and your students are actually on the Portfolio Journey.

As a Tour Guide, helping your students repack and reorganize their portfolios while they travel is one of your most important roles. You are helping them discover and practice new skills. The next chapter will help you develop a rubric for evaluating portfolio skills. After this, your role will shift to that of Curator.

Signs of Passage
Rubrics for Travelers

The ideal traveller is temperate, with a sound
constitution, a digestion like an ostrich,
a good temper, and no race prejudices.

—William Henry Crosse, M.D.
(*Medical Hints*, 1906)

William Henry Crosse's description of the "ideal traveller" holds up as well today as it did in his time. Sometimes, it can be useful to decide what qualities we admire in others. Just as Dr. Crosse identified those characteristics for world travelers, it is possible to identify those characteristics for Portfolio Journey travelers.

It has been previously stated that although portfolio contents may or may not be graded, portfolios themselves should not be. There is a good reason for this: Portfolios, if they are kept in the true spirit of the Portfolio Journey, will be different from student to student. Though they may have similar attributes and may be organized along similar lines, their contents will reflect individuals. This quality makes portfolios very difficult to evaluate in the way we traditionally assign grades. When we grade, we almost always grade by comparison to a standard set by the teacher or a curve established by the student who comes closest to that standard. There is nothing inherently wrong with this approach, but we must be aware that it is just that: an approach.

If we look for another approach, we might be able to develop a successful rubric for evaluating portfolios—one that doesn't discourage creative portfolios and individual expression but rewards students' positive attitudes and skills. The rubric we will discuss in this chapter might be thought of more as a system of merit badges than as a system of traditional grades. Six Portfolio Journey skill levels will be posited, and with them a set of indicators. When students have achieved these indicators, they earn additional status and, perhaps, privileges to reinforce their commitment and achievement. In this way, you reward students for keeping portfolios without specifically ranking the portfolios themselves.

This chapter introduces a rubric based on six skill levels, but you are by no means limited to this rubric. If you discover additional behaviors you want to encourage, or if you want to expand the idea of having six skill levels by encouraging other kinds of (nonportfolio-related) behavior, you may add these behaviors to existing skill levels or introduce new skill levels. The Portfolio Journey rubric includes the following skill levels:

- Tourist
- Traveler
- Pathfinder
- Adventurer
- Navigator
- Explorer

We will explore the characteristics and indicators of each skill level. For each skill level, a reproducible mini-poster is included (all mini-posters follow the descriptions below) to reproduce and display in the classroom. At the end of this chapter are some ideas for supporting and extending the use of the Portfolio Journey skill levels in the classroom. ✪

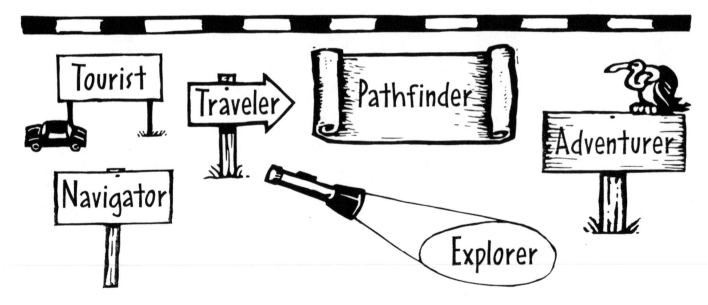

Tourist

Tourists have just begun to travel. They have learned the basics for keeping portfolios and are off to a good start. The signs of a Tourist are:

1. *Has a passport*
   This means that students have completed some sort of introductory portfolio activity, such as the activity discussed in Chapter 9, that has encouraged them to think about their identity, their personal interests and skills, and their life story to date. You may substitute any introductory activity for the passport requirement.

2. *Has a trunk, box, or container*
   This means that the student has created or modified some form of container to use as a working portfolio.

3. *Collects souvenirs according to instructions*
   This means that the student follows the instructions and guidance provided for saving samples of projects and academic work in the working portfolio.

4. *Annotates souvenirs*
   This means that the student meets the minimum standards for annotating each portfolio sample saved in the working portfolio.

5. *Has initiated a working portfolio manifest*
   This means that the student has begun keeping a table of contents for the working portfolio.

Traveler

Travelers are becoming comfortable with the idea of traveling. They are learning to be more flexible and adapt themselves to the situations they encounter. The characteristics of a Traveler are:

1. *Has a visa*
   This means that the student has and maintains some system for monitoring and documenting portfolio reviews.

2. *Has been traveling for _____ weeks*
   This means that the student has been keeping a working portfolio for a set period of time, to be determined by the classroom teacher. (Don't forget to write the amount of time in the appropriate space on the "Traveler" mini-poster.)

3. *Keeps souvenirs neat and in order*
   This means that the student makes an effort to ensure that portfolio samples are stored neatly in the working portfolio. A negative indicator would be torn, wadded, or crumpled portfolio contents.

4. *Annotates and processes souvenirs with care*
   This means that the student takes special care to ensure that annotation information is printed legibly and that project processing worksheets are filled out honestly and completely.

5. *Self-manages editing*
   This means that the student has demonstrated an ability to edit the working portfolio according to instructions and without direct supervision. Another indicator for self-management of editing is a demonstration of the student's willingness to follow-up on portfolio collecting or clearing (or both) after an absence.

Pathfinder

Pathfinders are developing the skills that make for great traveling. Pathfinders take personal responsibility for their journey. The signs a Pathfinder exhibits are:

1. *Has established a suitcase folder*
   This means that the student has a display portfolio folder in the working portfolio and is beginning to transfer into it important samples from the working portfolio.

2. *Has begun preparing a suitcase*
   This means that the student has begun to do the skills and interest inventory worksheets that are part of the display portfolio process.

3. *Has acquired additional souvenirs*
   This means that the student has begun to add samples to the portfolio beyond assigned class work. These might include awards and certificates, press clippings, documentation of extracurricular activities, and so on.

4. *Has had a student/teacher portfolio review*
   This means that the student has had at least one opportunity to sit down with the teacher for a review of the student's progress as reflected by the evidence in the portfolio.

Adventurer

Adventurers travel for the experience. They have learned how to travel safely off the beaten path. The qualities of an Adventurer are:

1. *Has kept a kit*
   This means that the student has maintained a project portfolio from the beginning to the end of a project, including all the process materials the teacher has requested.

2. *Has revised work for a suitcase*
   This means that the student has rewritten or revised assignments to reflect teacher corrections and comments, to create quality display portfolio samples.

3. *Has managed a student/parent/teacher portfolio review*
   This means that the student has successfully conducted a student/teacher/parent conference using the working portfolio as a communication tool and focal point.

Navigator

Navigators know how to get from here to there and back. They are excellent travelers with a real sense of direction. The indicators of a Navigator are:

1. *Has acquired writing souvenirs*
   This means that the student has produced and revised the writing samples necessary for the display portfolio. Though they may be updated continually, acquiring four initial samples is a big step.

2. *Has acquired photographic souvenirs*
   This means that the student has demonstrated the ability to document achievements and experiences with photography. This might include both the taking and the acquiring of photographs.

3. *Has completed a suitcase*
   This means that the student has a complete display portfolio.

4. *Has participated in a portfolio presentation*
   This means that the student has presented portfolio contents to a group in a live presentation or static display. The group should be larger than that of a student/teacher/parent conference, and the event should be more formal than participating in a portfolio clearing team (see Chapter 13 for suggestions).

Explorer

Explorers are master travelers. They travel to discover, to find new things, and to return to tell about their travels. The marks of an Explorer are:

1. *Has created a student résumé*
   This means that the student has distilled important personal information down to a single page of material and has learned how to format it professionally.

2. *Has a daypack*
   This means that the student has created a special portfolio for a specific purpose.

3. *Has participated in a portfolio interview*
   This means that the student has used a special or display portfolio in a formal interview. This may have been practice, or it may have been for some real objective.

4. *Maintains the suitcase*
   This means that the student has demonstrated the willingness and ability to regularly update the display portfolio by revising work, substituting better samples, and reviewing compass readings.

(Text continues on p. 174.)

1. Tourist

Tourists have just begun to travel. They have learned the basics for keeping portfolios and are off to a good start. The signs of a Tourist are:

☐ 1. Do you have a passport?

☐ 2. Do you have a trunk box, or working portfolio?

☐ 3. Are you collecting souvenirs (portfolio samples) according to instructions?

☐ 4. Are you annotating your souvenirs?

☐ 5. Have you initiated a manifest, or table of contents, for your working portfolio?

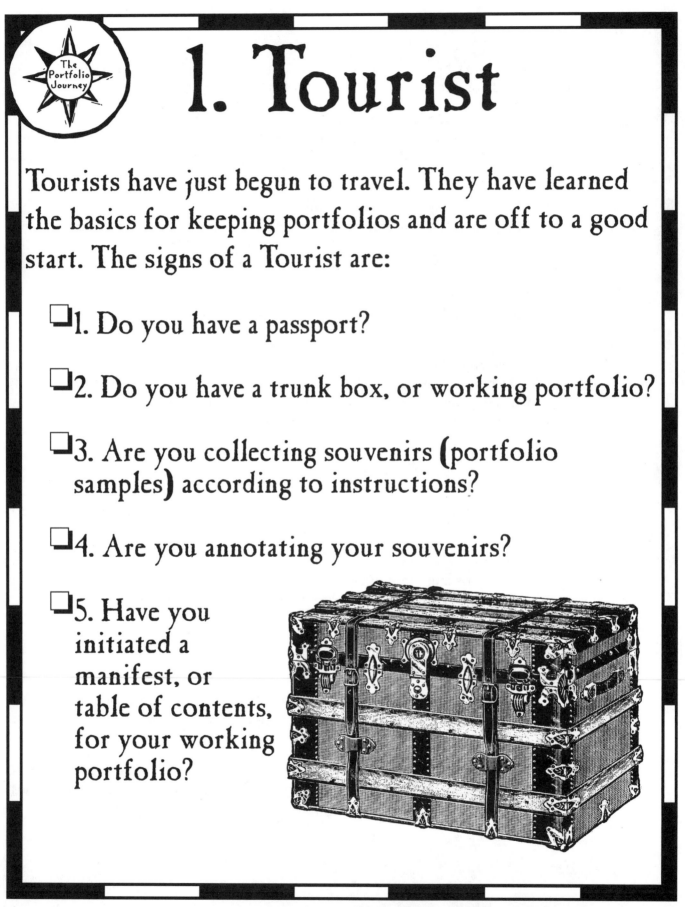

2. Traveler

Travelers are becoming comfortable with the idea of traveling. They are learning to be more flexible and adapt themselves to the situations they encounter. The characteristics of a Traveler are:

❑ 1. Do you have a visa?

❑ 2. Have you been traveling **(keeping a portfolio)** for at least ___ weeks?

❑ 3. Do you keep your souvenirs neat and in order?

❑ 4. Do you annotate and process your souvenirs with care?

❑ 5. Do you manage your own portfolio editing?

3. Pathfinder

Pathfinders are developing the skills that make for great traveling. Pathfinders take personal responsibility for their journeys. The signs a Pathfinder exhibits are:

❑ 1. Have you established a suitcase folder?

❑ 2. Have you begun preparing a suitcase or display portfolio?

❑ 3. Are you adding additional souvenirs (documenting your extracurricular activities) to your portfolio?

❑ 4. Have you had a student/ teacher portfolio review?

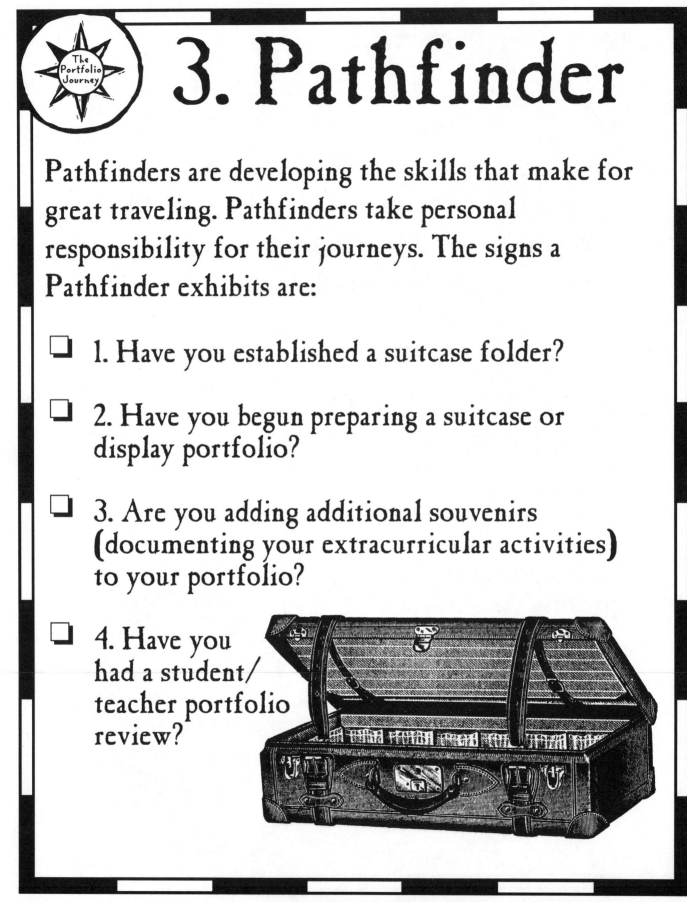

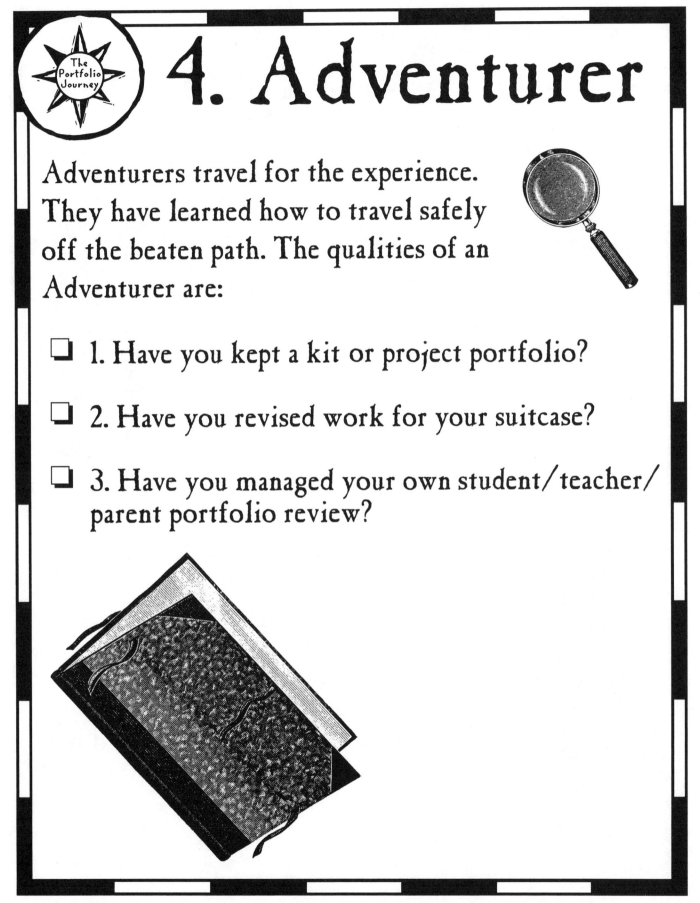

4. Adventurer

Adventurers travel for the experience. They have learned how to travel safely off the beaten path. The qualities of an Adventurer are:

❑ 1. Have you kept a kit or project portfolio?

❑ 2. Have you revised work for your suitcase?

❑ 3. Have you managed your own student/teacher/parent portfolio review?

5. Navigator

Navigators know how to get from here to there and back. They are excellent travelers with a real sense of direction. The indicators of a Navigator are:

❑ 1. Do you have the writing souvenirs you need for your suitcase?

❑ 2. Have you acquired photographic evidence for your portfolio?

❑ 3. Have you completed a suitcase?

❑ 4. Have you participated in a portfolio presentation?

6. Explorer

Explorers are master travelers. They travel for discovery, to find new things, and to return to tell about it. The marks of an Explorer are:

❏ 1. Have you created your own résumé?

❏ 2. Do you have a daypack?

❏ 3. Have you participated in a portfolio interview?

❏ 4. Are you maintaining your Suitcase regularly?

Marking the Signs of Passage

There are a number of ways you can institute and support the use of a rubric like this in the classroom. The mini-posters for the skill levels can be copied and posted in the classroom. You might consider enlarging them to poster size at a photocopy store or copying them onto brightly colored paper. Encouraging students to work toward acquiring the various skill levels might include the following strategies:

- *Rubber Stamps or Stickers*
  An illustration following this list of strategies (p. 175) has images that can be made into rubber stamps. The stamps might be used to stamp student passports and visas to signify the acquisition of new skill levels. The same images can be photocopied onto adhesive label stock to create stickers. The stickers might be affixed to working portfolios like luggage decals.

- *Credentials*
  Following this list of strategies are certificates to honor a student's portfolio achievements (see pp. 176–81). These may be photocopied and filled in with the student's name. You might consider creating a special folder or envelope within the portfolio for saving certificates. This gives the certificates a place to live, and they will seem more like real travel credentials.

- *Wall Chart*
  A poster or corner of a bulletin board might be set aside for a graph representing the levels of skill achieved by students in the class. A small chart might be used to do this by name only. A larger chart might be used to move photos of students up or across a grid as they achieve new levels.

- *Halls of Fame*
  Designate different places around the classroom as "Halls of Fame," one for each skill level. Post a photograph of each student in the appropriate Hall of Fame, mounted in cardboard frames. When a student achieves a new level of expertise, shift the photograph to the appropriate Hall of Fame.

(Text continues on p. 182.)

Rubber Stamp Images

Images that can be made into rubber stamps for marking students' progress.

Tourist

Traveler

Pathfinder

Adventurer

Navigator

Explorer

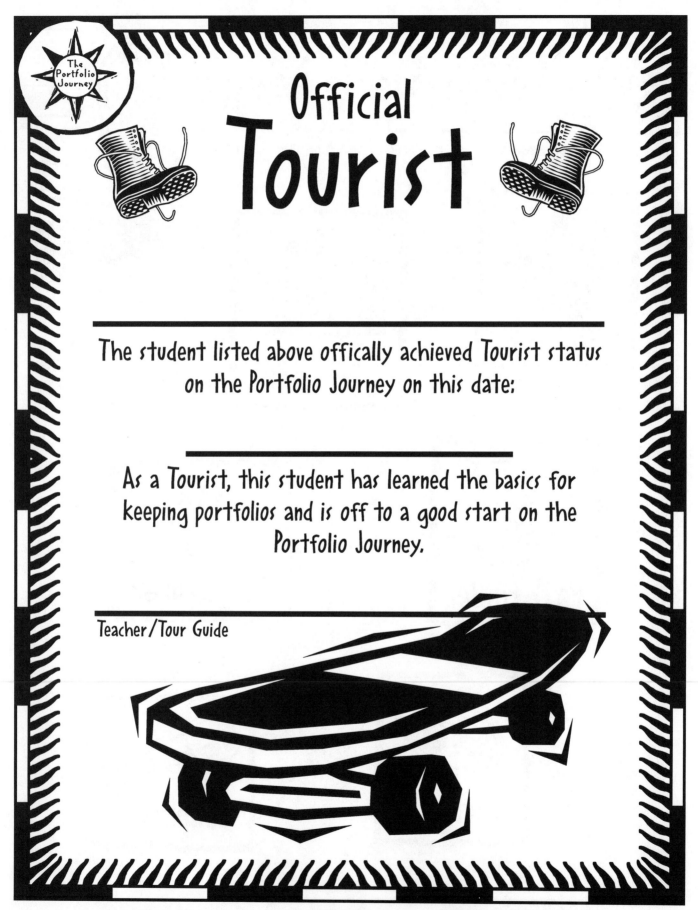

Official
Tourist

The student listed above offically achieved Tourist status on the Portfolio Journey on this date:

As a Tourist, this student has learned the basics for keeping portfolios and is off to a good start on the Portfolio Journey.

Teacher/Tour Guide

Official
Traveler

The student listed above offically achieved Traveler status on the Portfolio Journey on this date:

As a Traveler, this student is learning to be consistent in keeping portfolio materials and is making progress on the Portfolio Journey.

Teacher/Tour Guide

Official Pathfinder

The student listed above offically achieved Pathfinder status on the Portfolio Journey on this date:

As a Pathfinder, this student is demonstrating exceptional personal responsibility in keeping portfolio materials.

Teacher/Tour Guide

Official
Adventurer

The student listed above offically achieved Adventurer status on the Portfolio Journey on this date:

As an Adventurer, this student is becoming proficient in customizing and adapting portfolio materials.

Teacher/Tour Guide

Official Navigator

The student listed above offically achieved Navigator status on the Portfolio Journey on this date:

As a Navigator, this student is developing a real sense of direction and the ability to use portfolio materials to communicate.

Teacher/Tour Guide

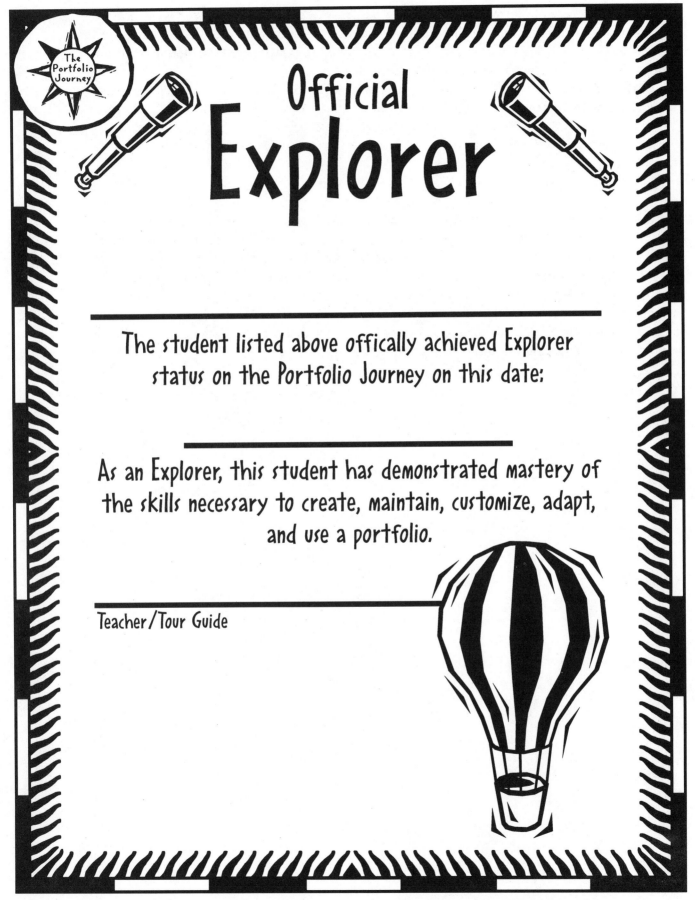

Official Explorer

The student listed above offically achieved Explorer status on the Portfolio Journey on this date:

As an Explorer, this student has demonstrated mastery of the skills necessary to create, maintain, customize, adapt, and use a portfolio.

Teacher/Tour Guide

Rewarding students for achievements is a controversial topic best left to the discretion of individual teachers. Some teachers will feel that it is sufficient motivation to reward students by publicly acknowledging their achievements; other teachers may want to institute some policy of privileges or special permissions as reward.

While a rubric system like this does not equate well with grades, it does give teachers a collection of indicators that is easy to communicate to both students and their parents. These indicators are expectations. They are within the grasp of every student. They don't so much compare students with one another as they give students landmarks by which to gauge their travels. ✪

Before we actually began the portfolio journey, we studied our terrain in Part 1 of this book. Yet the Portfolio Journey itself is made up of phases. The first phase of the journey was actually the quarter circle of planning, symbolized by the teachers as Travel Agent. The second phase was the quarter circle of preparation, with the teacher as Travel Planner. The third quarter circle, traveling with the teacher as Tour Guide, draws to a close now. The fourth phase will complete the circle by bringing us home. Part of the journey is always returning home. In Part 5, we will look at the fourth set of Portfolio Journey skills: those needed when the teacher assumes the role of Curator.

Part 5
Coming Home

The Teacher as Curator

In Part 5 of the Portfolio Journey you will:

   ℮ Create opportunities for students to share their portfolios with peers, friends, family, faculty, and the community.

   ℮ Facilitate parent involvement with their children's portfolios.

   ℮ Teach students how to use portfolios for interviews and presentations.

   ℮ Model successful portfolio behaviors and attitudes by maintaining your own professional development portfolio.

Travelogues
Ideas for Sharing Student Portfolios

13

One travels the world in search of what one
needs and returns home to find it.
—George Moore

In our case, when returning from traveling the world on our Portfolio Journey, we need look no further than our portfolios to find what we needed all along. All our best abilities should be on exhibit in our portfolios. All our secret capabilities should be revealed. Our triumphs and formative experiences should all be captured like images on postcards filed in our scrapbooks. It would be a shame, though, if all these wonderful experiences were destined to be buried away in some box or book, never to be shared or remembered.

In this chapter, we will address some strategies for sharing portfolios. As was mentioned in Chapter 2, one of the secrets of successful portfolios is student management and student ownership. The kind of work students take pride in is work that is shared with others. The more this work is shared—the greater the audience—the more students value their involvement. This has been borne out in studies of creative writing in the classroom, artwork, science fair projects, and more. Portfolios are creative projects that need to be shared to reach their fullest potential.

This will not be a long chapter. The ideas presented here are not necessarily new or revolutionary. They are intended to be a starting point. They will come to life when you add your own creative twists. As they are, they give you, the Portfolio Journey teacher as Curator, some options. These options give students the chance to share their portfolios. They range from the informal to the formal and represent an ever-expanding audience. Two specific ideas for sharing, student/teacher/parent conferences and portfolio interviews, will be addressed in subsequent chapters. ✪

Travelogues
Ideas for Sharing

Traveling Companions

Reviewing my portfolio with Diane. She really helps me make better choices for my portfolio.

Designating traveling companions is a fun way to encourage younger students who might find it easier to work on their portfolios with a partner. Traveling companions help each other gather portfolio samples, do annotation and processing, and keep track of their portfolio contents. This is a very informal kind of sharing, but it does ensure that students receive constant feedback about their portfolios. Students tend to encourage each other, and having a constant companion keeps students from quietly slipping behind in portfolio maintenance. The idea of traveling companions might be expanded to include other spheres of activity within the classroom. Traveling companions could share responsibilities and privileges while helping each other with various tasks.

Portfolio Clearing Teams

My portfolio clearing team members are Tod and Mark.

As mentioned in Chapter 7, portfolio clearing teams are extremely useful when it comes to editing student portfolios. Students often want teachers to make decisions for them about which portfolio samples to save. These decisions can be shifted back to the students by suggesting that they share their choices with their team and ask for feedback from their peers. This kind of work-oriented sharing is useful practice for students. They are provided the opportunity to share the contents of their portfolios in an informal setting without the pressure of being evaluated. Portfolio clearing teams might be the basis for classroom seating arrangements. They might be the same teams that travel together on real-life field trips or engage in simulation and role-playing games.

Portfolio Presentation Days

This was my first portfolio presentation. I was really nervous, but it went fine. Everybody said I did a good job.

Set aside one day a week and designate thirty minutes for portfolio presentations. Select six students, perhaps from the same portfolio clearing team, and give them five minutes each to present the highlights of their portfolios. This is not just a time for showing class assignments that have been saved; this should be an opportunity for encouraging students to create new documentation for extracurricular activities and special interests. For instance, if a student is very interested in ice hockey and plays on an ice hockey team after school, you might encourage this student to develop evidence that would document their interest and involvement. If students are creating display portfolios, this might be a chance to show off compass readings and other forms of documentation. This process becomes a kind of "show and tell." Students share documentation of the important experiences outside the classroom that are shaping them as individuals. This doesn't mean that students may not show examples of good school work, but if this is all that is shared, the event can quickly become boring. Use this time to highlight the kinds of documentation that will add variety and spice to student portfolios.

Videotaped Portfolio Presentations

Here is Ms. Lee about to start my videotape.

Imagine every student receiving a blank videocassette in the first grade. Now imagine them recording two, five-minute presentations on their videocassette each year through all their grade-school years (and beyond?). Twice a year, each student would have five minutes to show and explain the highlights of their portfolios. Each five-minute segment would be added to the video (as opposed to being recorded *over* the last presentation) so that students (and parents) would have a document of growing up. It would be difficult to imagine parents who wouldn't supply a videocassette for their child for a project like this, especially knowing that they would receive in turn a wonderful archive of their child's growth and development.

The easy way to tape presentations would be to check out a video camera from the media center, set it up in one spot (marked on the floor), and let it passively record students as they make their presentations to the class. Older students might be expected to script their presentations.

Students could actually learn to be better presenters from this process if they were required to view their previous presentations and improve one element of each. For instance, a first-grade student might observe that he is wandering all over the place during his presentation. His goal might be to stand in one spot. Another student might observe that she is holding her notes on big sheets of paper in front of her face the whole time she is presenting, so she might elect to do her next presentation with note cards.

Videotaped Portfolios

One of my portfolio clearing team members, Brad, helps me post my portfolio samples on the bulletin board to be videotaped.

This is a variation on video portfolios that puts more emphasis on the portfolio contents themselves. Students are asked to select their ten best portfolio pieces for inclusion in the video. They are then asked to script a thirty-second audio clip for each of the ten pieces. This should provide five minutes of narration to accompany the portfolio pieces. Students should practice their audio clips with partners, who should time them with stopwatches. Portfolio pieces might be tacked onto a bulletin board at a height convenient for the camera. The video camera is focused on a sample, the camera is turned on, and the student begins the narration. At the end of the narration, the camera would be faded out to black, stopped, shifted to the next portfolio sample, turned on, and faded in from black for the next segment of narration.

Not only is this a good opportunity for students to practice writing, reading, and dramatic speaking, but it also allows them see how a simple video presentation can be created and introduces them to the skills of video production. Students might elect to use these simple techniques to develop their own video projects. Making a videotaped portfolio also gives students a chance to review and reevaluate their portfolio samples and the work they do.

Video portfolios can become a part of working portfolios. It even would be possible for students to create their display and special portfolios in video format.

Marvelous Me Museum

These are some of the things I displayed along with my portfolio samples when I had the display case for the week.

Students might be given the use of a protected display case in the school or classroom to create a mini-museum dedicated to their talents and abilities. This can be a fun way for students to make statements about themselves. Portfolio samples may be used alongside projects and artwork that might be too bulky or awkward to store in a portfolio. Props that would never be included in a portfolio might also find their way into a Marvelous Me Museum. For instance, a chess set might graphically represent a love of the game, a skateboard might signify a real passion for the sport, or a doll collection could show an attention to detail.

Students might be allowed to keep their museums on display for one week. Don't begin the museums immediately at the beginning of the year, though. Give students a chance to collect work for at least a month. Within the classroom, every student should have had the opportunity to create a museum by the end of the school year. If you expand this idea and create Marvelous Me Museums in hallway display cases for the whole school, fewer students might get the chance to create a museum, but the prestige of doing it would be higher. Consider doing both. Teachers might nominate students and have the museums created on a rotating basis. For variety and to give students models from which to work, have a teacher create a Marvelous Me Museum every so often.

Portfolio Fairs

This was my display for our portfolio fair.

There are several ways to hold portfolio fairs, but the basic idea is a cross between a science fair and an art exhibit. Students are asked to create displays that show off the contents of their portfolios. Portfolio fairs are best held during the spring, after students have had the better part of a school year to document their achievements and create their portfolios. Portfolio fairs can also be a great way to show off a school and help build community pride in students, teachers, and faculty.

One variation on a portfolio fair is to allow graduating fifth-grade students (elementary school) or eighth-grade students (middle school) to use the cafeteria for the day. Give each student a section of cafeteria tables (marked by masking tape). This section is the student's portfolio exhibit space. Students may build backgrounds using cardboard or plywood to display samples of their school work, projects (or photos of projects they have done), honors and awards they have received, and documentation of events in which they have been involved. Students should create invitations and posters to advertise the portfolio fair, and they should be allowed to invite parents, family, friends, former teachers, faculty, and even members of the community to come see their display at the portfolio fair. On the day of the fair, students should set up their displays in the morning and remain available during the day to answer questions about their work. Teachers could schedule times during the day to bring their students to the cafeteria for a tour of the portfolio fair. This would reinforce in younger students the desire to keep their own portfolios. It would present them with peers to look up to, whose portfolios might be used as models for their own. Prizes might be given for the most inventive or creative displays (not the work itself).

A second variation of the portfolio fair would involve opening the fair up to the entire school. Displays might be created in each classroom, and the event might be treated as a spring "open house" to encourage parents to visit and review their children's progress. Again, students would be responsible for creating invitations and making sure that their guests are invited. Students would be free to tour other classrooms to see the portfolio displays of older and younger students. Hallways could be decorated with student art projects. Each class might work to decorate the doorway to their classroom, trying to make it as appealing as possible. Refreshments might be served in each classroom or at a central location.

A third variation of the portfolio fair would involve grouping students according to special theme areas they have chosen. Teachers might decide to create eight display areas around the school, each reflecting one of the multiple intelligences described in Chapters 3 and 5. Students would be allowed to select the area in which they would display evidence of their abilities. The library might be set aside for writers doing readings of their work. The playground might have displays created by student naturalists. The gym might have an ongoing program of athletic exhibitions. The auditorium might be scheduled for performances, the cafeteria for mechanical inventions, and so on. This variation would require a lot of coordination and teacher planning, but it might prove a valuable experience for students.

Portfolio Home Pages

Here I am working on my portfolio home page for the World Wide Web. It's possible that millions of people could see my portfolio.

If your school is connected to the Internet and you are beginning to experiment with creating World Wide Web sites, you might consider using portfolios as an organizing metaphor. Students might each be asked to create a home page that introduces who they are and links to three pages of samples from their portfolios. If you have access to a scanner, photographs, artwork, and even printed material can be scanned directly into the computer and posted on a Web site. You will probably want students to retype their stories directly if they choose to post them, but most work can be scanned and transformed easily. It is beyond the scope of this book to deal with the specifics of creating Web sites, but many commercial products make it as easy as creating a document with word processing or page layout software. Web sites make it possible for a portfolio to be seen by millions of people around the world. If the school has e-mail capability, students might communicate with other students who view their Web site. They can also view other students' Web sites. Already, hundreds of schools have student-created Web sites just waiting to be explored. Web sites can be created by individual students or by student partners or cooperative teams. The portfolio clearing teams described earlier in this chapter (see p. 187) would be a good basis for creating portfolio team home pages. A sample portfolio team home page follows.

Portfolio Home Pages

Sharing student portfolios is not something we do only if we have time. Portfolios are living documents; they are meant to be used. They are not scrapbooks or archives. If they are not used, then their potential goes unfulfilled. Using portfolios means showing them to others, sharing them, letting them help represent us. Sharing portfolios closes the circle that is opened when the first writing sample or photograph of a project is slipped into a portfolio box.

When students know that they will be expected to share their portfolios with peers, they become motivated to keep better portfolios. Sometimes, you may not see this in students until after the first of several sharing experiences. No matter what you say in advance, students naturally assume that the work you ask them to do is for *your* benefit. It is only after they begin to see that their work has a larger audience that they value it for themselves. ✪

The ideas for sharing in this chapter are your point of departure. You will come up with even better ways of sharing student portfolios. At least one specific kind of sharing was not covered in this chapter: sharing with parents. The next chapter, "Communiqués: Involving Parents in the Portfolio Journey," considers this challenge.

Communiqués
Involving Parents in the Portfolio Journey

Embarkation

If possible, arrange that the painful ordeal of taking leave of your friends and relations—especially those of your own sex—be got through on shore, and select a cool-headed male relation to accompany you on board.

Is this a fit time, place, and opportunity for a solemn leave-taking? Watch the expression of bewilderment on that young fellow's face; he has mislaid a portmanteau containing his stock of shirts, and, in his search for the same, he drags about the deck a weeping sister, who hysterically shampoos one of his arms, as she keeps begging him to "write soon," while, with his other arm, he supports a half-fainting mother, who stops him, at *every* third step, for "one last kiss," and the extraction of a "sacred promise" that "happen what may," he will never, *never* omit to wear flannel next to his skin. Would it not have been better, for all concerned in this little party, if they had wished each other farewell in the privacy of their own home?

—Major S. Leigh Hunt and Alexander S. Kenny
(*Tropical Trials—A Hand-Book for Women in the Tropics*, 1883)

On the kinds of journeys Major S. Leigh Hunt and Alexander S. Kenny were describing, it was certainly possible to leave family and relations behind, but on a Portfolio Journey it is essential that they be brought along. This is not always easy to accomplish. Parents are often apprehensive of new things. If they did not keep portfolios when they were in school, they may wonder why their children must. They are often most anxious that their children not become the victims of some pedagogical fad. There is only one way to overcome this kind of anxiety: communication.

Much of this chapter will be about communication—ways to involve parents in their children's portfolio building experiences. Information, exposure, and creative collaboration will be the tools we use to bring parents along on the Portfolio Journey. Actually, you will find that parents can be great partners in the process of building student portfolios. They can help you plan in your role as Travel Agent. They can become resources for supplies and materials in your role as Travel Consultant. They can become chaperones for the Portfolio Journey while you are acting as Tour Guide, and they can play a critical role in helping your students complete their journeys when you assume the role of Curator. In looking at the various ways you can integrate parents into the portfolio-building process, we will once again review the four roles of the Portfolio Journey teacher. ✪

Parents and the Travel Agent

Introduction and Involvement

Parents should be included on the Portfolio Journey from the moment you begin planning it. One of the things parents most fear about portfolios is that they will replace grades. Parents worry that, without grades, they won't understand whether their child is doing well or not. They also worry that, if a child's work is not graded, the educational experience will not be transferable. The first step you might take to reassure parents is to simply explain portfolios. There may have been a time when even you found portfolios a bit confusing and intimidating. Help parents reach your level of understanding.

Portfolio Communiqué

Begin a Portfolio Communiqué. This might be a simple parent newsletter sent home with students on a monthly basis. Following this section (see pp. 199-200) are reproducible masters for the first and successive pages of a Portfolio Communiqué (reproducibles are included throughout this chapter). The first two pages are blank. Scan or photocopy them and add your own text, or cut and paste your text into the space provided.

The first issue of the Portfolio Communiqué should contain a personal note from you. You should try to communicate in your own words why you want to encourage students to keep portfolios. Don't talk down to parents but explain your vision of student portfolios in plain and simple language. Avoid jargon and "educationese." Give parents concrete examples of what kinds of work might be saved in student portfolios. You might also include the Portfolio Communiqué page entitled "Welcome" (see p. 201). It shouldn't replace your personal introduction, but it is an engaging general introduction to portfolios.

Subsequent issues should focus on introducing new processes, portfolio news from the classroom, and stories of students creating and using their portfolios. Beyond describing what a portfolio is and why you think students should keep them, don't forget to describe the different types of portfolios students will be working with and creating over the course of the year. The Portfolio Communiqué page entitled "The Four Portfolios of the Portfolio Journey" (see p. 202), is a quick overview of the trunk (working portfolio), suitcase (display portfolio), daypack (special portfolio), and kit (project portfolio). You may go into more detail about these portfolios later, but for now, give parents a general overview.

(Text continues on p. 203.)

PORTFOLIO COMMUNIQUÉ

NEWS FLASHES FROM OUR PORTFOLIO JOURNEY

PAGE # 1

PORTFOLIO COMMUNIQUÉ

PAGE #

PORTFOLIO COMMUNIQUÉ

Welcome

The Portfolio Journey is the ultimate in fieldtrips. It is a trip we will take without leaving our classroom. This expedition will help every student build his or her own student portfolio. It is our hope that family members will make this journey with us. To make this journey together, there are a few things that we would like you to know.

1. What is a student portfolio?

A student portfolio is a collection of evidence, usually bound in some form of container, that suggests or demonstrates a student's skills or abilities.

The evidence in a portfolio might be written work such as reports, stories, essays, tests, or even worksheets. It might be annotated photographs that document projects, events, performances, or presentations. It might be work on paper or work on computer diskette. Portfolios might contain videotapes or audiotapes. The work might be finished and graded. It might even be revised. It might also be work in progress. Portfolios might include awards, certificates, letters of recommendation, and press clippings.

Students' portfolios don't replace grades or standardized testing. They supplement them. They help students develop a positive self-image linked to their achievements. They encourage students to participate in their own education and the assessment of their abilities. They respect and validate some of the very important skills and kinds of intelligence that are often overlooked or marginalized through an emphasis on grades and averages. They also help prepare students for the world in which they will work. Portfolios will be an essential tool for careers in the information age. Portfolios should also help you see growth and develpment in your child. Portfolios are a kind of communication tool. They help students communicate with peers, with teachers, with family members, and with the community.

PAGE #

PORTFOLIO COMMUNIQUÉ

The Four Portfolios of the Portfolio Journey

As we make this journey, you may hear us refer to four different kinds of luggage, or portfolios. This is a brief overview of these portfolios.

Trunks, or working portfolios

This is a holding portfolio. It is the place where students save their work at the teacher's direction or by their own choice. Everything that ends up in a student's display portfolio has spent some time in the trunk, or working portfolio.

Suitcases, or display portfolios

This is the edited version of a student's work. It is assembled and arranged to tell the story of a student's abilities and experiences. It will tend to contain a student's best work, substituting quality for quantity.

Daypacks, or special portfolios

Where a display portfolio places emphasis on a general, well-rounded portrait of a student, this is a customized version with a more specific focus. It is assembled from the display portfolio contents for a definite purpose, such as applying for admission to special programs, seeking jobs or internships, or requesting special placement.

Kits, or project portfolios

This is a way of organizing work in progress inside of a working portfolio. Kits, or project portfolios, emphasize process and continuity.

PAGE #

Alternatively, you might consider meeting with parents to present your ideas in person. The more you have to show, the better. If you have a sample portfolio, allow parents the opportunity to browse through it. If you don't have a sample portfolio, show examples of the kinds of student work that might be saved. The most productive kind of meeting you could have with parents would be one in which you ask for their help in planning. Let them know that all the decisions have not already been made, and that you are genuinely seeking their input.

Parents as Travel Agents

The easiest way to seek input from parents is around the question of appropriate souvenirs. Ask parents for their help in deciding what kinds of evidence they would like to see in their children's portfolios. In the process of explaining what a portfolio is, you will, most likely, give parents examples of what you will be encouraging students to save. Explain your reasoning. Share with parents the plan you developed in Chapter 4 for your students' portfolios. Better yet, ask parents to help shape it. What would they want their children to accomplish during the year? Share the map you made to illustrate your vision. Survey the territory with parents. Where will the challenges be? What will the indicators of success look like?

Seeking input from parents can be accomplished in a meeting with them, or some of it can be accomplished through the Portfolio Communiqué. The Portfolio Communiqué pages entitled "Portfolio Samples" (two pages—Parts 1 and 2, pp. 204–5) will allow you to list some of the samples you want students to have in their portfolios by the end of the year. Also, these pages will help you solicit ideas from parents. When listing the kinds of samples you want students to have in their portfolios, be specific. Instead of noting "a writing sample," note "a writing sample that demonstrates creative use of language," or "a writing sample that demonstrates strong organizational skills."

It is possible that some parents will find a request for input odd. After all, they might reason, you are the expert: Why are you asking them? You have to understand and anticipate their confusion. After all, how often have we asked parents for their input in what we do? Give it a try. At worst, parents won't be surprised by the portfolio process as it unfolds during the year. At best, it will help you enlist powerful allies for the Portfolio Journey. ✪

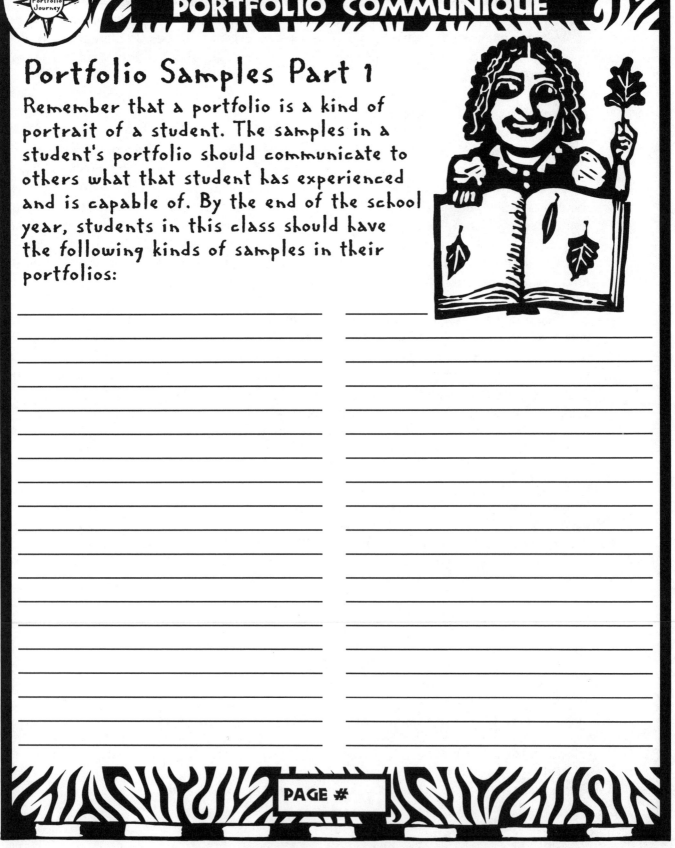

PORTFOLIO COMMUNIQUÉ

Portfolio Samples Part 1

Remember that a portfolio is a kind of portrait of a student. The samples in a student's portfolio should communicate to others what that student has experienced and is capable of. By the end of the school year, students in this class should have the following kinds of samples in their portfolios:

PAGE #

PORTFOLIO COMMUNIQUÉ

Portfolio Samples Part 2
What would you like to see?

Are there any samples you would like to see in your student's portfolio by the end of the year? You could be a big help in making sure that a student's portfolio reflects activities and interests outside of school. Please share some of your ideas with us.

PAGE #

Parents and the Travel Consultant

Powerful Allies

In mythic and heroic tales, the hero finds or develops powerful allies for the journey. Parents can be your powerful allies on the Portfolio Journey.

Parents who have been involved in the planning of portfolios, or, at the very least, have been introduced to them in a friendly, nonthreatening manner, are much more likely to help you make portfolios a reality. As a Travel Consultant, your role is to help your students prepare for their Portfolio Journeys. Setting the mood in the classroom, facilitating the creation of working portfolio containers, introducing the practice and protocols of collecting, and helping students begin their journeys with passports that create positive self-images are all part of your role as a Travel Consultant.

Don't forget parents—the powerful allies you befriended by involving them in the planning of this Portfolio Journey. You might call on them to assist you in your role as Travel Consultant in the following ways:

1. Canvas parents for things like maps, travel posters, back copies of travel magazines (the pictures can be cut and pasted for art projects), old suitcases, and travel-related models that can be rescued from attics and garages.

2. If parents want to donate materials to the class, you might ask for film for the classroom camera. When parents see how the photographs are used in their children's portfolios, they are often more than willing to donate packs of film. If you are using traditional 35mm film, consider asking parents to pay for photo processing for one roll of film during the school year. If even half the parents agreed, this would provide you with more than one roll of film each month.

3. Ask parents to be responsible for providing one travel-related resource for the class. Send home a "wish list" (the Portfolio Communiqué page that follows this list of suggestions, p. 208). Every classroom wish list will be different, but yours might include a range of such things as one-year subscriptions to age-appropriate travel-related magazines, travel-related videos and books, stories about young travelers, flags, and maps. Be specific about what you want, and, for more expensive items, consider letting parents share the expense between families.

4. Encourage parents to become resources themselves. If parents have traveled, consider asking them to do a presentation for the class about where they have been and what they have seen. Parents might also be able to teach certain travel-related skills, such as using a compass, navigating with sea charts, reading maps, surveying and mapping, and communicating in foreign languages. Keep in mind that the point is not just whether parents can teach things you cannot. You may be equally qualified to teach students how to use a compass, but inviting parents into the classroom in the role of teacher will help them feel involved in the Portfolio Journey.

5. You may find that some parents travel on a regular basis, whether for pleasure or as part of their job or career. Ask them if they would consider sending postcards to the class during their travels. This is a fun way for students to feel connected to different parts of the world. Some students may have grandparents or relatives in foreign countries or far-away places. Ask these relatives if they would consider sending decorative postcards to the class.

6. Solicit parents' help in assembling the materials to build working portfolio containers. In Chapter 7, pizza boxes were recommended as practical portfolio containers. It may be through parents that the connection is made to acquire a sufficient quantity of pizza boxes. Or, you may find that parents know of a source for even better free boxes. Bankers' boxes, packing boxes, and archiving boxes of all shapes and sizes are often available through many of the offices where parents might work. If you keep an open mind, you may benefit from these connections.

7. If you are working with younger students, you might appreciate the help of a volunteer parent on the day your students decorate and assemble their working portfolios.

8. When your students are ready to begin building display portfolios, you might need to ask parents to supply three-ring binders and plastic drop-in pages for their children's portfolios.

9. The Portfolio Journey passport activity (Chapter 9) may be the first time students have been asked to think about their interests and skills. You might have students do this activity at home with input from their parents. Parents can help students encapsulate their life stories by providing important information and details students might not recall.

10. You may find that some parents keep portfolios in connection with a job or career. Invite these parents to share their portfolios with the class. Nothing motivates students more than believing that the project they are working on is, in some way, connected with being an adult.

The point of these suggestions is to involve parents in the process, to help them feel that they are a part of the Portfolio Journey their children are making. The question should not be, "What can I manage without bothering parents?" but, "In how many ways can I involve parents?" ✪

PORTFOLIO COMMUNIQUÉ

The Portfolio Journey

Parents and family are important to the success of our Portfolio Journey. Here are some ways you can help:

PAGE #

Parents and the Tour Guide

Customs Inspectors and Chaperones

As your role on the Portfolio Journey shifts to that of Tour Guide, as your students actually begin to travel and keep their portfolios, there are new roles for parents to play in the process and new chances to involve them in the Portfolio Journey.

Parents as Customs Inspectors:
Visas and the Student/Parent Portfolio Review

As portfolios grow over the weeks, they become capsule histories of what has happened in the classroom. The portfolios themselves are an excellent tool for communicating to parents what their child has been doing in class and how well they have been doing it. Sending portfolios home with students doesn't replace a teacher's obligation to phone parents, send notes to parents, arrange for conferences, prepare interim or grade reports for parents, but it does help to ensure that these other forms of communication don't occur in a vacuum.

The Portfolio Journey visa process described in Chapter 8 is a fun and convenient way to engage parents as customs inspectors. Portfolios are sent home and parents review the contents with their children. Parents sign off and add their comments to the Portfolio Journey visa, and portfolios are returned to school. The process is easy to initiate, but the following tips will help it go more smoothly:

1. Make sure that working portfolios are secured before sending them home with students. If the portfolios don't close securely, consider fastening them with tape or string. Big rubber bands around the outside can help avoid accidental spills.

2. Make sure that manifests (directories of contents) are updated before sending working portfolios home. Parents can use the manifests to ensure that students haven't simply removed contents they don't want their parents to see.

3. Ask parents not to edit or remove any contents from the working portfolio. In addition, if parents are reviewing students' display portfolios, they should not edit contents from these documents either. Ask them to discuss the samples students have chosen to include in their portfolios. They may even make recommendations on the visa, but editing should be done in school.

4. Give parents guidelines about how to interact with their children through their portfolios (see the Portfolio Communiqué page entitled "Portfolio Reviews," p. 211). In general, parents should try to avoid evaluating the portfolios themselves. They should use questioning techniques to elicit discussion with children about the work they have done. Even if there are unsatisfactory samples of work within the portfolio, comments should always focus on positive strategies for making the work satisfactory. The discussion should have the feeling of colleagues sincerely working to improve quality. This is not an easy task, but it is possible. At the very least, parents should end the review by praising students for the work of keeping the portfolio itself.

5. If time permits, give students an opportunity to process their parent's comments in class. Discuss the kinds of suggestions their parents made. Allow students to put some of these ideas into effect.

Parents as Chaperones

It is also important to involve parents in some of the other activities their children will be working on while on their Portfolio Journeys. When your students begin doing the skills and interest inventory worksheets described in Chapter 10, have them share this work with their parents. When they begin creating the compass readings for their display portfolios, they might ask their parents for feedback. Parents can also help students arrange for letters of recommendation (though it is important that the students make the request for letters of recommendation themselves). Ask students to share their display portfolios with parents as they are working on them. Parents are almost always impressed by and proud of the documents their children create. ✪

PORTFOLIO COMMUNIQUÉ

Portfolio Reviews
Tips for effective and productive reviews

1. Set aside some quiet time without distractions to review the child's portfolio. Send the message to the child that this is important.

2. Portfolios should elicit discussion. Ask the child to walk you through the contents of their portfolio. Let them explain why each sample is in their portfolio.

3. Ask questions instead of evaluating. Instead of saying, "You can do better than this." try asking, "Do you think you can do better than this?" Questions lead to discussion. Evaluation shuts down discussion.

4. Always act as though this review was between two colleagues working together to improve the quality of a product. Ask what you can do to help the child improve.

5. Use the portfolio to understand the subjects and areas in which the child is interested.

6. Do not remove or edit contents from the portfolio. You may offer suggestions about whether a piece is the child's best work directly to the child or in writing to the teacher.

7. Always try to end a portfolio review by praising the child for the work of keeping the portfolio itself.

PAGE #

A Powerful Sharing

As a Curator, you can help guide parents through a review of their children's portfolios. How do your student/teacher/parent conferences usually occur? If you are like most teachers, they go something like this:

When parents arrive, they are somewhat anxious about the event, and you are never sure whether it is because just being in school again is such a strong emotional experience for them, or whether they are concerned about their children. Probably, it's a combination of both. Many of the parents you will encounter had traumatic experiences in school. Even if they went on to become highly successful adults, there is something about walking into a school that can send them right back to those experiences.

The students who accompany their parents are often anxious themselves. If they are bright and well appreciated and doing well in all their subjects, they may come bounding into class leading their parent or parents behind them. Most of the time, however, they have learned to be a little anxious about these conferences. There is always some skeleton they are afraid of having turn up in their closets. They may have come to associate these conferences with punishments or overreactions on the part of their parents. They may also associate these conferences as being experiences that are out of their control.

As the conference proceeds, there are several traps into which the unsuspecting participants may walk. Traps are things that subvert the best intentions of these conferences. Though it is entirely possible to conduct conferences with hidden agendas (teachers wanting to have parents discipline irritating students in ways they are not allowed to; parents wanting to find fault with everything and everyone but themselves; students wanting to preserve the delicate status quo they have established around privileges at home), let's assume that everyone is meeting with the sincere goal of helping students reach their full potential in school. If this is the case, then the following really are traps:

1. *Teachers and parents talking about students as though they were not in the room.*
   There is no quicker way to distance students from responsibility for their work and disenfranchise them from responsibility for their behavior than to talk about students as though they were not present.

2. *Teachers reviewing student progress in abstract terms.*
   Parents may understand you when you talk about curves and gradepoints and averages, but if you aren't talking about specific examples, there is no way for students to enter into the discussion. Students need to talk about specific problems as reflected in real work they have done, not about why they missed a homework assignment three weeks ago.

3. *Teachers and parents asking too many why questions.*
   Consider leaving all questions that begin with *why* outside the door of the conference room. "Why aren't you doing better?" "Why did you do that?" "Why didn't you tell me?" These are not questions that a student can answer. They end up being accusations rather than questions. Try replacing them with *how* or *what* questions: "How can I help you improve your spelling?" "How can we work together to practice your math skills?" "What can we all do to help you get your assignments in on time?"

4. *Teachers and parents saying things that embarrass or humiliate a student.*
   Be especially careful of this. This is how those parents came to be so anxious about being in these conferences in the first place. They probably remember being embarrassed themselves. They may think that this is what is supposed to happen in a conference. If parents say things that are embarrassing or hurtful to students, try to restate what was said immediately in a more positive manner. You may need to guide parents in effective and positive criticism.

Aside from just being aware of these traps, perhaps it is time to look at a new model for student/teacher/parent conferences: the Working Portfolio Review Conference. It might go something like this:

Students arrive with one or more parents in tow. Students introduce the parents to the teacher and invites them all to take a seat on one side of the conference table. Next, students get their portfolio from the shelf, open it, and carefully place preselected samples on the table in a specific order. Students discuss each piece briefly, putting them into context by explaining work the class has been doing. If good grades have been received, students might explain what led to their earning those grades. If bad grades are present among the samples, students should explain what they did or did not do that led to those grades. If bad grades or merely satisfactory grades are evident, students should also explain what they plan to do to improve those grades. If they need special help from parents or teachers, they should ask for it.

Parents and teachers may interrupt at any point to clarify statements, ask questions, probe for a better analysis, applaud good work, or make positively framed suggestions. Parents and teachers might take notes during the conference to refer to at the end. A parent or a teacher should summarize the conference at the end, restating the plans for improvement and calling for a general agreement. If parents feel the need to rearrange schedules or adjust privileges to reach the mutually agreed-upon goals, this should not be addressed as a punishment (e.g., "No more television for you until . . .") but as a plan (e.g., "We agree that you need to spend more time on homework each night, but we also know how much you like to watch certain television programs. Why don't you make a plan for me: Tell me what programs you will stop watching to add an extra hour of homework time each night.").

This kind of conference would be a win-win-win proposition. From a parent's point of view, it would be difficult to imagine a parent who would not be more comfortable with the Working Portfolio Review Conference scenario—talking about actual work, looking at real samples, and trying to solve specific problems. From a teacher's point of view, you don't have to be "the bad guy/gal" in the conference. You act as the moderator between students and parents. Letting students discuss the quality of their school work is not a loss of power for you. Students may try to frame things positively, but it isn't as if they can convey a false impression. The work will speak for itself, and the teacher can always intervene to clarify. From students' points of view, they finally regain some control. In many conferences, a student's good or acceptable work is overlooked simply because, in the limited amount of time available, teachers tend to address the problems that need correcting. In a student-managed conference based on portfolio evidence, a more balanced picture can be conveyed.

As an added benefit for students (and for the entire portfolio conference process), consider allowing them to practice their presentations in advance. Allow students to take turns in their portfolio clearing teams presenting their portfolios to their peers. Students might role-play parents and the teacher to help themselves anticipate questions. This will help them feel comfortable managing their own conferences and give them another opportunity to share their portfolios. Is this cheating? Will this give students an unfair advantage? Only if you view the process as adversarial. In real life, you have a chance to prepare for the meetings in which your performance will be discussed. If you choose to go in unprepared, that is your choice, but there is nothing preventing you from rehearsing and preparing for that evaluation. Does this give you an unfair advantage? No; it helps you feel proactive in the process. Evaluations of any sort should be something we participate in, not something *done to* us.

Working Portfolio Review Conferences are a little different than conferences that parents may have come to expect. In advance of the scheduled conference day, it might be advisable to send home an overview of what to expect in the conference itself and how the conference will be organized (see the Portfolio Communiqué page entitled "The Student/Teacher/Parent Portfolio Conference," p. 215). ✪

As you see, there are many ways you can involve parents in the Portfolio Journey. They can provide valuable support at every phase. When parents come to understand student portfolios, they usually embrace them with enthusiasm. If your students' parents are concerned that portfolios are a frill that takes time away from "serious school work," share with them the four important reasons for keeping portfolios detailed in Chapter 1. Tell them that portfolios are all about securing a positive future for children. If nothing else, knowing that children will end the school year with documentation that testifies to their particular strengths, abilities, interests, and experiences, both academic and extracurricular, is powerful motivation to support those children's Portfolio Journey.

PORTFOLIO COMMUNIQUÉ

The Working Portfolio Conference

What to Expect

Your child has been preparing for this upcoming student/teacher/parent conference and is looking forward to the chance to share their portfolio with you.

This conference might be a little different than what you are used to. For one thing, it is student centered. Your child will lead the conference by reviewing the samples in their portfolio. This review of actual work, along with teacher commentary, should give you an accurate picture of your child's progress.

These are the kinds of things we encourage:

1. Questions. Feel free to ask questions of your child or of the teacher.

2. Praise. Look for positive signs and things to praise.

3. Constructive solutions. Make suggestions of how you might help your child improve their performance. Ask for your child's opinion of what would be helpful.

4. Closure. The teacher will help establish some indicators of improvement for the next conference.

PAGE #

Crossing Borders
Using Portfolios

Journey all over the universe in a map without the expense and fatigue of travelling, without suffering the inconvenience of heat, cold, hunger, and thirst.

—Miguel de Cervantes
(*Don Quixote de la Mancha*, 1605–15)

The Portfolio Journey is both a real and an imagined journey, but the first cycle of that journey is drawing to a close now. Your students have working portfolios filled with samples of schoolwork. Their best samples are integrated into display and special portfolios. They have shared their portfolios with family, friends, peers, and the community.

In Part 5, we have looked at ways of sharing portfolios. We have looked at sharing for the sake of sharing, sharing to build self-image, and sharing to communicate academic progress. There is at least one other kind of sharing, though, that students should at least practice: sharing to achieve an end goal. Sharing to achieve an end goal includes using a portfolio for the purposes described in Chapter 11. Though students may not be in a position to actually use a portfolio to apply for a job, gain acceptance into a special program, or to enter college, students can practice the portfolio skills that they will use in the future when faced with these options. This sophisticated form of sharing may be unnecessary for or beyond the capabilities of very young students, but portfolio interview activities have been used as early as the third grade. ✪

The Portfolio Interview

The portfolio interview is an activity that asks students to apply for an imaginary job using their display or special portfolios as one of their primary communication tools. The basic idea is for students to make an appointment with an adult to interview for a job using their portfolio.

Variations on the activity should be introduced to adjust for the age and sophistication of students. Because younger children may not have special portfolios, they would use display portfolios. Older students, however, would use their special portfolios for this activity. In fact, this could be the activity that provides the motivating force behind the creation of special portfolios.

Younger students might simply make an appointment with the teacher or an assistant teacher. Older students should interview with someone other than the teacher. It provides for a fresh interaction if the adult does not already have a thorough knowledge of the student's portfolio. The participating adult should not be a parent or close family member. Another faculty member from the school would be ideal, as would parent volunteers interviewing students to whom they are not related.

The jobs younger students apply for could be the same for each child. They might interview to be part of a spaceship crew or project team. Older students could apply for very specific jobs of their choosing. Their special portfolios would be shaped to help them apply for these jobs. Let the students choose the jobs if possible. This will make the activity more exciting and more real for them.

The actual assignment might be presented like this: Each student is to make an appointment with an adult. At that appointment, students will apply for a job using their portfolio. Appointments should take between ten and twenty minutes (though enthusiastic interviewers have been known to take thirty to forty-five minutes to interview a student). No adults are *required* to play the role of interviewer, so the student's first task is to ask someone nicely and make it as easy as possible for them to say "yes." This means that students should be prepared to adjust their schedules for the convenience of the interviewer. When students find a willing adult to be the interviewer, the teacher should give a copy of "The Portfolio Interview Worksheet" to the interviewer. (A one-page sample follows, p. 219.) This sheet reminds the adult of the date and time of the appointment and describes the interview process. Finally, the worksheet asks for an answer to one question (would the interviewer hire the student for the job) and allows space for additional comments.

The Portfolio Interview Worksheet

Participating Interviewer_____.

The portfolio interview is an opportunity for students to use their portfolios in a simulation of a real-world activity: the job interview. This is also a chance for students to present themselves to others in a positive light and demonstrate an understanding of their strengths and assets. The following student, _____, has already made an appointment with you on_____ to conduct a portfolio interview. Thank you for agreeing to participate. It should take ten to twenty minutes, depending on how many questions you have. If you set aside this time and arrange to keep distractions to a minimum, it will enhance the process.

Students will bring their portfolios to the interview, and explain for what job they are applying. Your task is to allow students to use their portfolios to make a case for their qualifications for that job. In the role of the employer, your job is to listen and ask whatever questions about the student's experiences and qualifications that occur to you. There is no script for this process. Just be open to what you see and hear. Encourage the student to elaborate when you feel it is necessary. At the conclusion of the interview, complete the section below and return this sheet to_____.

Thank you again for helping us make our Portfolio Journey.

To be filled in by the participating interviewer:
- ☐ I would hire this student for this job.
- ☐ I would not hire this student for this job.

Explain your decision briefly (students will have the opportunity to read these comments).

Signature_____ Date_____

This is an excellent end-of-the-year activity. You might announce to students that it will affect their final grades, but beyond that, the less specific you are, the better. It is unfair and unnecessary to attach a pass/fail grade to getting hired. When it comes right down to it, this is not within the student's control. Still, it is appropriate to link a quiz- or test-level grade to whether the student makes the arrangements and completes the interview. If you are less than specific, students will tend to believe that getting hired is what will earn them the passing grade, and they will, therefore, tend to take this activity more seriously. By the way, this is one more activity about which you should notify parents. When parents understand the skills their children are practicing through this activity (interviewing, public speaking, presenting themselves in a positive light, making a logical argument in their favor), you will find them to be very supportive. If necessary, reassure parents of younger students that this is not an exercise designed to lock children onto some career path at an early age. Remind them that these skills are transferable to almost any career path a student chooses later in life.

To help students prepare for their interviews, suggest or discuss the following:

1. You have gone to a lot of trouble to create effective display or special portfolios. You should not forget to use them during the interview. If a portfolio is clutched in your hands during the entire interview, it will not fulfill its potential. If you simply shove it across the desk at the interviewer, it will, at best, receive only a cursory glance.

2. Does talking about yourself and showing off your portfolio feel like boasting? Get over it! You need to state your capabilities and back them up with evidence from your portfolio.

3. Several days before the interview is the time to check your portfolio. Reorganize it to match the job for which you are applying. Make sure your portfolio is neat and clean. Replace any worn plastic pages with new ones.

4. Practice what you will say during your interview. Work with a partner, each taking a turn role-playing the interviewer. Ask the questions you think the interviewer might ask. Think about which evidence in your portfolio might show that you can fulfill the requirements of the job.

5. Practice a brief opening statement to get the interview moving. You might begin by thanking the interviewer for the chance to apply for the job. You might also state clearly why you want the job and why you think you are well qualified for it.

6. What will you wear for the interview? The best advice is to dress appropriately for the job you want. You can't go wrong by dressing neatly and simply. If you are applying for a creative job like graphic artist, computer games programmer, or actor, you could be more creative in your dress.

7. Be a little early for the interview. This gives you a chance to compose yourself and rehearse one last time.

8. Sit up straight. Don't relax too much, even if you are invited to do so. Sit on the edge of your seat so that you easily point out portfolio samples.

9. Never just hand a portfolio to an interviewer. Hold onto it for a few minutes. Try to maintain control of your portfolio. If someone takes your portfolio and then doesn't even open it, it can be awkward to get it back to show examples. Remember that the purpose of having your portfolio with you is for to supply evidence to back up the things you say.

10. When you are asked questions about your experiences, try to back up what you say by referring to the evidence in your portfolio. If you are asked about a qualification that you don't have, try not to answer with, "No." Try redirecting the question to a skill you *do* have that might be compatible. For instance, if you are asked whether you have ever conducted inventory in a store, and you haven't, you might answer, "No, but my math grades are very good, I'm comfortable working with numbers, and I am good with details." You would then back up these claims with evidence from your portfolio.

11. You will never have enough time to walk someone through your entire portfolio, so don't expect to! Be prepared to point out the highlights in the limited time you do have. This means that you should know what the highlights are—and where they are.

12. After the interview, take some time to evaluate the interview process: Did you have a chance to use your portfolio? Was there anything you wished you had had that wasn't in your portfolio? Were you comfortable with the order of the samples in your portfolio? Are there new or revised portfolio samples that might better communicate your abilities next time?

Interviewers may return the worksheet to you by way of the student or directly. It is noted on the sheet, indirectly, that interviewers should not write anything they would not want the student to read. These are not secret evaluations. This is a process in which the student is a full partner. Any comments should be expressed with the idea of helping the student improve skills.

It would be helpful to discuss with students the dynamics of any interview. In an interview, two sets of needs are operating: You, the interviewee, need something from the interview (a job, an award, an admission, etc.). The interviewer also needs something (a good employee, a winner, a good student, etc.); and the faster you discover what the interviewer needs, and the quicker you appear to meet those needs, the more likely you are to meet your own personal needs. If you focus, instead, on your own needs, you will seem like most of the other candidates the interviewer has seen, or will see. Ask questions of the interviewer at the outset, try to establish the interviewer's needs, and then use your portfolio to show that you can meet these needs.

If a student feels that an interview has gone poorly, there is no reason why they could not arrange and try another one, perhaps with a different interviewer. Remember, you should not be evaluating whether or not students get hired. The purpose of this activity is for students to practice the process of interviewing. If they choose to practice more, let them. ✪

Portfolio Continuity
Where Do We Go from Here?

The interview activity brings your students' Portfolio Journey full circle. They don't end their journey. This journey never ends. Portfolio interviews will actually send students out on new Portfolio Journeys in search of new souvenirs that better reflect new directions. Working portfolios will disintegrate from wear and tear and need to be replaced. Students will want fresh photos and new information in their passports. They will want to replace their visas and update the information in their display portfolios. As this particular loop of the Portfolio Journey closes, it is appropriate to address the issue of continuity. What becomes of portfolio materials?

At the end of a school year, if you have done all or most of the activities described in the Portfolio Journey, your students should have working portfolios with samples of their work, passports, visas, manifests, one or more project portfolios, a display portfolio holding folder, and, perhaps, a portfolio clearing folder. They should also have a display portfolio book and, perhaps, a smaller special portfolio that has not yet been reintegrated into the display portfolio. What becomes of these things depends a lot on the continuity of the portfolio program in your school or school system. For the sake of discussion, let's look at some different categories of continuity.

No Continuity

This means that you alone are having your students keep portfolios. When students leave your class, they will not be expected to keep portfolios in the next grade. In this situation, consider passing the responsibility for keeping portfolios to students and parents. If they think that the process has merit, parents might take over and encourage their children to keep portfolios at home. Don't forget that students often become very attached to their portfolios; by the end of the year, they should know how to keep and manage their own portfolios. Whether or not parents and students commit to continuing their Portfolio Journeys beyond your classroom, the working, display, and special portfolios should be sent home with students at the end of the year. You might choose to have students edit out all but their best work from the working portfolios. Remember, even if there is no continuity, your students have learned valuable skills and developed remarkable documents on the Portfolio Journey you initiated.

Informal Continuity

If some teachers in your school or system are keeping portfolios, try to meet with them at the end of the school year. Share what you have been doing with portfolios and ask teachers of the grades your students will be entering how much of the evidence they would like students to have with them when they begin their new classes. Teachers may want to begin their new school year by having students create new working portfolio containers and new passports, but they might want a small sampling of what a student has done in the previous grade for the sake of a smooth transition. Sometimes, all that is necessary is the passing on of the display portfolios. This can be done by keeping the display portfolios at the school and then passing them on, or by making sure that students and parents know that the display portfolios will be needed in the following year. Display portfolios can make for engaging introductions between students and teachers.

Formal Continuity

If all teachers in your school or system are keeping portfolios, it would be valuable to have a formal meeting at the end of the school year between teachers of consecutive grade levels. Teachers might share the kinds of portfolios they have been keeping and ask what kinds of samples should be left in the working portfolios. Sometimes, teachers want students to come to class with very little of their previous year's work, but in the interest of continuity and giving students confidence, a larger sample of work, even if it is edited out on the first official portfolio clearing day, can be beneficial. If teachers of the grades your students will be entering have been keeping portfolios but have not been on the Portfolio Journey, you might take the time to introduce them to the concepts covered in this book. Additional copies of *The Portfolio Journey* are available through the publisher (see the address in the Appendix). If teachers are following a different path for maintaining student portfolios, you should be able to find common ground by explaining the idea of working and display portfolios.

Continuity Between Schools

When students move from elementary to middle school, or from middle to high school, the most important document they should take with them is the display portfolio. By the time they have completed a year in your class on the Portfolio Journey, they will know how to keep and maintain their own display portfolios. These display portfolios are tools they can continue to use, whether the school encourages portfolios or not. As students get older, their portfolios should become more and more presentational. They should be maintaining their portfolios for job applications and college admissions. The foundation you have given them will not be wasted.

Portfolios reach their fullest potential when the process is supported system-wide, from first through twelfth grade. The effect of this kind of continuity is an amplification of the power of portfolios to enhance life skills and self-esteem. It is important to remember, however, that even if the only exposure to portfolios that a student receives comes through your class, this benefit will not be lost. If the Portfolio Journey is fun and imaginative, if students learn to be proud of the evidence of their skills and abilities, if the process has truth in it (the kind of truth children instinctively sense), the journey you have made together will have been well worth the effort. ✪

Before concluding this guide to the Portfolio Journey, there is still one place we should visit. We have addressed the importance of portfolios to students. By now, you can probably list five or six excellent justifications for keeping student portfolios—without having to think much about them. Well, if this process is so helpful to students, could it be helpful to teachers? In other words, what does *your* portfolio look like?

A Teacher's Journey
Professional Development Portfolios

> The Journey is the reward.
> —Lao-tzu (*Tao Te Ching*)

What does *your* portfolio look like? This may seem like a scary question at this moment. After all, you were just getting comfortable with the work you would have to do to take your students on their Portfolio Journeys. Now someone is suggesting that you make that journey yourself. Rest assured, the suggestion is not made lightly. Portfolios can be just as valuable to teachers as they are to students. They can be a record of your teaching experiences and a resource for the future. They can help you to think and act proactively in your own professional development, and they can help motivate students to keep their own portfolios in a manner that is deep and profound.

Portfolios are the perfect place to keep documentation of all the unusual and exceptional activities you have facilitated. Many teachers regularly document bulletin boards and classroom decoration with photographs. Not only do they provide useful evidence of the kind of environment you create, but they can serve as a resource for sharing ideas with colleagues or reminding yourself what a bulletin board or display from three years ago looked like. Photographing field trips or special projects shows the diversity of methods you use to motivate and teach students. Press clippings, articles, programs, letters of thanks from parents or members of the community, letters of praise from superiors—all these things should find a home in a teacher's portfolio.

How do you prepare for professional performance reviews and evaluations? At best, an administrator might have visited your classroom two or three times in a semester or year. Their observations, no matter how penetrating, can only address the surface of what you do on a daily basis. Though you may not know when you will be observed, you usually know in advance when you are going to sit down with an administrator for a review. If you choose to go to that meeting or session unprepared, empty-handed, and passive, this is your choice—but it doesn't have to be this way.

Just as we have been trying to encourage students to become proactive in their performance reviews (student/teacher/parent conferences), portfolios can help you become proactive in your performance reviews. Before going to your next evaluation, pull out some samples from your portfolio of work done in your classroom during the previous months. You might organize this into a special portfolio, as described below, or you might just pull out loose samples from your working portfolio. Either way, it gives you the chance to answer with actual documentation the questions that arise in evaluations. Moreover, it is professional to come to a performance review prepared to participate as an equal in the process.

Using your portfolio might shift the nature of this experience for you. Remember, these evaluations are intended to be beneficial for you. To benefit truly from them, you need to be an active and equal partner in the process. These sessions should not be a lecture about your performance; they should be a discussion of it. Your portfolio samples will better prepare you to discuss your experiences. Rather than waste valuable time discussing what you may practice, but which may not have been observed, you can address your point by showing portfolio evidence, then move on to the areas where you really could improve your performance.

The very fact that you keep a portfolio sends a powerful message to students. It says that portfolios are something adults keep, not just something that teachers make students do. The reason this is such effective motivation is that it touches the secret desire of young people everywhere. Part of being young is defining who you are. What young people want more than anything is to be an adult. They want this in the most undeniable way, and they will look for any indicators they can find that signal their transition into adulthood. We all know this is true. Children and students want steps, signals, and clear demarcation of what it means to be an adult. As a culture, as a society, we often do a poor job of providing these signals. We once had rites of passage, coming-of-age ceremonies, and rituals to celebrate and signal this transition for our children. Now, with some exceptions, we leave it to chance. Just because we may not offer many clear signals, though, does not mean that our students and children don't continue to look for them. They still seek the signs of their coming-of-age, but, without positive clues, they pick up on the negative clues that are all around them. Unfortunately, what often seems to define an adult in our society (at least to outward appearances, which are sometimes all that children see) are things such as driving a car, buying and smoking cigarettes, buying and drinking alcohol, owning guns, having sexual relationships, having babies, using illegal drugs, and so on. Understanding the secret desire of children (to become adult members of the society), and understanding society's failure, oftentimes, to address these desires in a positive fashion, at least brings some sense to the stories we see all around us of young people in trouble.

The portfolio you keep as a teacher won't solve all these problems, of course, but it is a step in the right direction. It is a positive sign of adulthood for students. It says that portfolios are things adults keep to prepare them for life. Portfolios, then, might be one way for students to indicate their transition into adulthood. To get the maximum benefit from this kind of sign, make *your* display portfolio available in the classroom. Allow students the same access to your portfolio that you have to theirs. You may find that your students study and peruse your portfolio to model their own portfolios. Update your portfolio on a regular basis so that students have reason to revisit your portfolio and see how it is evolving.

It is not necessary that you go through all the processes outlined in the Portfolio Journey to keep your own portfolio, but some of the basic ideas are easily applicable to a teacher's professional development portfolio. You may find that, just like your students, it is useful to keep a trunk, a suitcase, a daypack, and an assortment of kits. ✪

The Teacher's Trunk

Your trunk, or working portfolio, will be where you put all those samples, photographs, and loose artifacts that you want to save but don't have time to organize. This may be a box, but it may also be a file cabinet drawer. If it is a file cabinet drawer, make the process easy for yourself. Don't force yourself to use agonizing filing methods just to add something to the portfolio. Allow yourself only a few big "drop" files and organize them according to easy, general categories, such as nine-week periods, subject areas, or classifications of samples (e.g., photos, student work, plans, press clippings, artifacts, etc.). You want to be able to file on the run. If you are using a box for your working portfolio, make sure that it is big enough to hold materials for two months or so. If it won't hold that much, you will need to be more disciplined about your editing process.

Categories of evidence you might want to save in your working portfolio:

1. *Evidence of an average day*
   What would show someone what an average day in your classroom is like? This evidence might include: a sample daily plan, samples of student work, photos from different standard activities (things that happen everyday), or a video of students in your class.

2. *Evidence of creative projects*
   What would show someone the kinds of creative projects you facilitate in your classroom? This evidence might include: project plans; photos of students working on their projects; photos of some or all of the finished projects, with student annotations or copies of their project processing work; photos of displays of student projects; records of feedback from parents, students, or the community about the projects; or artifacts such as programs or promotional material (if available) from the project.

3. *Evidence of how you create a nurturing teaching environment*
   What would show someone how you manipulate your classroom environment to improve learning? This evidence might include: photos of bulletin boards; photos of displays and general classroom appearance; a floor plan of classroom organization, such as the location of desks and how they are arranged and the location of workstations; or special holiday displays and transient decorations.

4. *Evidence of how you manage your classroom*
   What would show someone how you organize and manage your classroom? This evidence might include: detail photographs of storage areas, copies of classroom rules and responsibilities, or assertive discipline plans.

5. *Evidence of personal press*
   Do you save letters of appreciation or commendation from parents, peers, superiors, and the community? Do you save exceptional notes from students? Do you save press clippings from the school newspaper, community newspaper, and local newspaper?

6. *Evidence of professional development*
   Do you save documents attesting to your professional development? If you use what you have learned from developmental experiences to become a better teacher—even if you don't receive credit toward your recertification as a teacher—find a way to document the experience. Do you save certificates from classes you attend at conferences for educators? Do you save papers or photos of projects you did to improve your skills?

7. *Evidence of exceptional moments*
   Consider documenting those exceptional but often transient events that make learning in your classroom so special. This evidence might include: documentation of special visitors to your class, field trips, celebrations, and ceremonies. Whereas in category 1 you were looking for evidence of what makes your class reliable and consistent and like other classes, now you are looking for evidence of what sets your classroom apart, of what makes it unique.

8. *Evidence of student work*
   Make photocopies of exceptional student work to save in your portfolio. Photograph the best of your students' posters, artwork, projects, and constructions. Use the reduction setting on the photocopier to reduce large drawings and artwork to a more manageable size. Save representative tests, papers, homework, and school work.

9. *Evidence of the big picture*
   What kind of evidence would demonstrate your contribution to the school as a whole? Have you helped to decorate the halls, or have you taken charge of centrally located display cases? Perhaps you should document these things. If you participated in, supported, or were instrumental in the success of school-wide events such as fairs and carnivals, include adequate documentation. Are you an

informal mentor to young teachers, or are you an officially designated lead teacher? Evidence of this should be in your portfolio. Do you volunteer to accomplish projects around school? Do you work with the P.T.A./P.T.O. in your school? Do you organize dramatic or musical presentations? Do you organize extracurricular activities for students or teachers? Evidence of these things is worthy of inclusion in your portfolio.

10. *Evidence of the bigger picture*
Take the question asked in category 9 and expand its scope. Do you volunteer in your community? What might show the kind of involvement you have with causes and issues in your community? Even if you only collect money for a charity, such involvement is still worth noting. Do you do outreach work through your church or civic organization? Document it. It is an important part of who you are.

11. *Evidence of having a life*
Yes, some teachers do. It may be difficult for our students to believe, but some of us actually have lives outside the classroom. We are mothers and fathers with children of our own. We have hobbies and interests. We travel and read. We enjoy movies, plays, and concerts. Some of us have been to exotic places or have had fascinating experiences. Some of us have met extraordinary people or brushed up against celebrities. This is all information that could be shared through a portfolio. It helps round out the picture of a teacher that a portfolio creates. ✪

The Teacher's Suitcase

Your suitcase, or display portfolio, will be the basic, general-purpose overview of who you are. It will be created from the evidence you have been saving in your working portfolio (just like the process your students are using). It will change over time, and it should be flexible, but once you have put together a display portfolio, it should not require a lot of attention.

You will probably want to build your display portfolio in a two- or even three-inch thick three-ring binder with plastic drop-in pages. Use a binder with a clear plastic cover on the front so that you can create a cover for your display portfolio. You will need a binder so that you can easily change the order and nature of your samples. You will need a thick or large-capacity binder because you have had a full and rich life and there is much to document. You will need plastic drop-in pages to protect your samples because your portfolio will be handled a great deal.

To create your display portfolio, simply select some of the best examples from each of the categories of working portfolio evidence. If necessary, add annotations to explain the samples to a viewer. A page of introductory information, such as a résumé, a brief biography, or an opening statement, is an engaging touch for a display portfolio.

There is an excellent opportunity to send a message to students through a display portfolio. Remember the graduate-level education course you took for recertification or advancement? Remember the paper you had to do for that class? Are you willing to put the graded copy of it into your portfolio? If you are, you will send a powerful message to students. You are showing them that learning is a lifelong process, that they will never truly be finished with school or education. It would be difficult to imagine a more important message to convey to students. ✪

The Teacher's Daypack and Kit

These two types of portfolios can be equally useful to educators. The daypack, or special portfolio, is the customized version of the display portfolio. It is the portfolio you pull together for your performance review or evaluation. From your display portfolio, you can temporarily remove samples that might not interest an administrator or supervisor and replace them with more specific samples that reflect your classroom experiences. Though students might be fascinated with pictures of you rafting down the Grand Canyon, your supervisor will probably be more interested in the geology project you had students do with the rock samples you brought back from your trip. Remember that special portfolios are clearly defined by a purpose. This purpose might be a review of your performance as a teacher, application for a new teaching position, advancement to a supervisory position, admission into a special program, or almost anything, but your special portfolio should be molded to match the purpose.

You don't need a separate notebook for your special portfolio, but you might consider using a notebook that is thinner than the one you are using for your display portfolio. Remember that special portfolios are usually more focused than display portfolios, with fewer but stronger examples.

Kits, or project portfolios, can help you organize the samples in your working portfolio. You might, for instance, create a folder or envelope for all the evidence from a specific project done during a certain year. This will make it easy to keep all the relevant materials together; it will also make it easier to archive materials at a later date. Any way that you can think of to classify or categorize the materials you are saving into your working portfolio can potentially become the basis for a project portfolio. Just make sure that the organizational scheme you choose is fairly consistent across kits and that it doesn't end up confusing you when you are trying to find something.

Archiving is an interesting element that was not discussed with student portfolios but that becomes much more relevant to adult portfolios. There will be things you don't want to throw away but that you will not want taking up space in your working or display portfolios. This especially happens in the transition between school years. One way of dealing with this transition is to archive all or most of the samples that are still in the working portfolio at the end of the school year. These items can be put into a separate box labeled with the year and any information that would help you know what is in the box without opening it. It is highly recommended that you edit what goes into this box. Only archive what you think is really valuable or what you might want access to later. Don't save everything; save the best examples.

Keep your completed display portfolio from the previous school year to inspire and motivate students at the beginning of the new year, but replace older examples of student projects, field trips, and events with newer samples. It might be a good idea to save a photocopy of one or more student display portfolios from the previous year. This will give you an example to show students as you are explaining the Portfolio Journey to a new class. Save samples of visas, passports, and other artifacts from the previous year's Portfolio Journey as well. ✪

Making the Portfolio Journey

Now you have come full circle. If you have been putting each chapter into practice as you read it, you are already a seasoned Portfolio Journey traveler. If you have only made the Portfolio Journey in your mind, it is time to begin the real Portfolio Journey. Keeping portfolios is important work, but it can also be fun work. The strategies described in *The Portfolio Journey* are sound, but it is the metaphor of travel that makes them exciting to practice.

Do you need to use the metaphor of travel? No! As a creative teacher, you may discover metaphors that are equally rich, that capture the imaginations of your students, and that you find compelling. Feel free to experiment. Take the core activities and processes described in *The Portfolio Journey* and examine them under the lens of this new metaphor. What matters most is that you help students begin keeping portfolios. Even if you cannot imagine how you could possibly institute all the processes described in *The Portfolio Journey,* begin with the basics. Your students will benefit from whatever level of portfolio keeping you initiate.

The Portfolio Journey, in the end, is a journey like any other. While we always keep our eye upon our destination, it is important to remember that the journey itself truly is the real reward. ✪

Appendix
An Eclectic Mix of Resources
for the Portfolio Journey

Portfolio Journey Questions

As you might have gathered from the preface and introduction to this book, I do workshops, seminars, and keynote addresses on the subject of portfolios and the Portfolio Journey. I have also written a book about portfolios for secondary students that picks up where *The Portfolio Journey* leaves off. *It's About Who I Am: A Student's Guide to Portfolios* (Sayer-Burden Press: Norfolk, VA, 1996) encourages older students in a step-by-step process to build their own display portfolios. It can be used with teacher or parent mentors (or both). For more information about this book, or if you have questions, comments, or requests, please contact me:

e-mail	sayer@norfolk.infi.net
post	Tom Crockett 1220 Manchester Avenue Norfolk, VA 23508
fax	(757) 423-3198
voice	(757) 440-8092

Additional copies of *The Portfolio Journey* may be ordered by contacting Libraries Unlimited/Teacher Ideas Press at 1-800-237-6124. Or at http://www.lu.com/tip or in writing to: Teacher Ideas Press, P.O. Box 6633, Englewood, CO 80155-6633.

Portfolio Books

The following are some of the more useful books on student portfolios I have come across:

Burke, Kay, Robin Fogarty, and Susan Belgrad. *The Portfolio Connection.* Palatine, IL: IRI/Skylight, 1994.

This is a good how-to book on portfolios. It is a different approach, but an eminently practical one. You will find a lot of activities that could be incorporated into a Portfolio Journey portfolio.

Gentile, Claudia A., James Martin-Rehrmann, and John H. Kennedy. *Windows into the Classroom: NAEP's 1992 Writing Portfolio Study.* Washington, DC: Office of Educational Research and Improvement, U.S. Department of Education, 1995.

Okay, if you still need to convince someone (or yourself) of the legitimacy of portfolios, this can be your bedtime reading. It's dense, but it's filled with enough facts and statistics to impress even the most recalcitrant administrator.

Kimeldorf, Martin. *Creating Portfolios: For Success in School, Work, and Life.* Minneapolis, MN: Free Spirit, 1994.

This is a well-written book on creating portfolios. The emphasis and activities are aimed at older students and concentrate on display portfolios.

———. *A Teacher's Guide to Creating Portfolios: For Success in School, Work, and Life.* Minneapolis, MN: Free Spirit Publishing (1994)

This is the companion book to the previous title, emphasizing the teacher's role in the process of keeping portfolios.

Mundell, Susan B., and Karen DeLario. *Practical Portfolios: Reading, Writing, Math, and Life Skills.* Englewood, CO: Teacher Ideas Press, 1994.

This book is another good introduction to portfolios, with an emphasis on grades three through six.

Tierney, Robert J., Mark A. Carter, and Laura E. Desai. *Portfolio Assessment in the Reading-Writing Classroom.* Norwood, MA: Christopher Gordon, 1991.

This book is a bit more academic in approach, but there is a lot of solid, helpful information about keeping portfolios for reading and writing assessment.

Non-Portfolio Books

These are some books I highly recommend:

Bellanca, James. *The Cooperative Think Tank I.* Palatine, IL: IRI/Skylight, 1990.

A visual thinker after my own heart, Bellanca has extended the charting/graphing/mapping metaphor to teach thinking in the cooperative classroom. This is a book with about a million applications to the average classroom.

Frazee, Bruce, and William Guardia. *Helping Your Child with Maps and Globes.* Glenview, IL: Good Year Books, 1994.

This is an excellent resource of map-related activities for children in grades K–3. Many of the activities would nicely complement Portfolio Journey activities.

King, Laurie, and Dennis Stovall. *Classroom Publishing: A Practical Guide to Enhancing Student Literacy.* Hillsboro, OR: Blue Heron, 1992.

This book takes a much more in-depth (but still very practical) look at the process of student publishing.

Melton, David. *Written and Illustrated By* . . . . Kansas City, MO: Landmark Editions, 1985.

This is an excellent guide to encouraging students to write and illustrate their own books. This is such a fun book, and having students write and illustrate books about their imaginary journeys would be an engaging extension of the Portfolio Journey.

Digital/Electronic Portfolios

There are not as many digital/electronic portfolios on the market as you might think. Two of the better software products are listed below:

The Grady Profile: Portfolio Assessment
Aurbach and Associates
9378 Olive Street Road, Suite 102
St. Louis, MO 63132-3222
(1-800-774-7239)

This is the best of the formatted portfolios. It encourages student self-reflection, can be tailored to your curriculum, shares data over a network, protects confidentiality, maintains cumulative records, and handles multiple classes. It tends to be more teacher- than student-centered, but it would be a useful companion to Portfolio Journey student portfolios. It runs on the Macintosh operating system.

Scholastic's Electronic Portfolio
Scholastic Inc.
2931 East McCarty Street
Jefferson City, MO 65101
(1-800-541-5513)

> This is a more open-ended product, with versions for the Macintosh and Windows platforms, that could be customized to match the needs of the Portfolio Journey teacher. It is versatile and fairly intuitive and could be used for a student's display or special portfolios.

Fun Stuff

I am including the following resources just for the fun of it.

Cool Quotes

Brett, Simon, comp. *Take a Spare Truss: Tips for Nineteenth Century Travellers*. Elm Tree Books, 1983.

> Have you been wondering from where the cool quotes that begin each chapter of *The Portfolio Journey* come? A lot of them came from this book. It is probably out-of-print now, but you might find a copy in a used book store (that's where I found mine).

Cool Clip Art

Art Parts
Box 6547
Santa Ana, CA 92706
(1-714-834-9166)

> Ron and Joe make some of the coolest clip art around. If you want to customize, adapt, or create your own Portfolio Journey materials, or if you want them to look like the samples in this book, you gotta get some Art Parts.

Fun Fonts

A number of fonts were used in this book. The most consistently used were the following:

Smile ICG Medium

Regular Joe

SHAKA ZULU

STAMPFONT

Blox

Caslon Antique

ZORBA

Index

About the Author

Tom Crockett is a writer, an artist, and educator, with an extensive background in creativity, photography, and visual learning. Tom was an award-winning photojournalist in the United States Navy, covering events such as the first American evacuation of Beirut in 1976 and received the *Navy's Chief Information Award* in 1979. He is a summa cum laude graduate of Old Dominion University in Norfolk, Virginia, with a Bachelor of Fine Arts. His Master of Fine Arts, with an emphasis in photography is from the School of the Art Institute of Chicago.

Tom currently directs *ArtQuest*, a multicultural arts-based mentoring program at the Hermitage Foundation. He has been a secondary school teacher, teaching at Lake Taylor High School in Norfolk, Virginia. He has worked with Gifted and Talented math and science middle school students through Hampton University. Tom has also served as an adjunct professor at Old Dominion University and Tidewater Community College, designing and teaching interdisciplinary photography programs for social science majors and non-artists.

Along with his wife Meredith, Tom owns and operates a consulting service called The Visual Learning Group, which specializes in seminars and workshops on visual learning and innovative teaching strategies. They also direct the Polaroid Education Program for the southeastern United States. Tom conducts workshops in visual learning for fellow educators and students of all ages. He has designed curriculum and developed training programs in photography, portfolio development, writing, science, math, social studies, early childhood education, and self-esteem for Polaroid, Scott Foresman, and Macmillan McGraw-Hill publishing companies, and the Discovery Channel.

In addition to *The Portfolio Journey*, Tom is the author of seven other books on portfolios, writing, creativity, and self-esteem. Through the Polaroid Education Program he has co-authored books on portfolios, self-esteem, environmental issues, social studies, and science.

He lives with his wife in Norfolk Virginia with their cats Boris, Natasha, and Polaroide.

Statistics

Statistics

Concepts and Controversies

Second Edition

David S. Moore
Purdue University

W. H. Freeman and Company
New York

Library of Congress Cataloguing in Publication Data

Moore, David S.
    Statistics: concepts and controversies.
    Includes bibliographies and index.
    1. Statistics.   I. Title.
QA276.12.M66   1985   001.4′22   84–28794
ISBN 0–7167–1695–X
ISBN 0–7167–1717–4 (pbk.)

Printed in the United States of America

1 2 3 4 5 6 7 8 9 0 MP 3 2 1 0 8 9 8 9 8 7 6 5

Does not He see my ways,
 and number all my steps?
 Job

But even the hairs of your head
 are all numbered.
 Jesus

Hell is inaccurate.
 Charles Williams

Contents

To the Teacher

In Japan, October 18 is National Statistics Day. The Japanese, with their usual thoroughness, have made public and official what is quietly recognized elsewhere: that statistics, no longer satisfied to be the assistant of researchers and government planners, now forces herself into the consciousness of students of every discipline and citizens of every occupation. This book is written for those students and citizens. There are texts on statistical theory and texts on statistical methods. This is neither. It is a book on statistical ideas and their relevance in public policy and in human sciences from medicine to sociology.

I developed this material during six years of teaching students (usually freshmen and sophomores) from Purdue's School of Humanities, Social Science, and Education. The students come from many disciplines and are fulfilling a dreaded mathematical sciences requirement. Future social science majors often choose the course as preparation for later study of statistical methods; the other students may never again encounter statistics as a discipline. My intention is to make statistics accessible by teaching verbally rather than symbolically, and to bring statistics out of the technician's closet by discussing applications and issues of broad public concern. I have also used much of this material as supplementary reading in more traditional statistics courses, which usually neglect many of the concepts and issues discussed here.

So the book is popular, written for readers interested in ideas rather than technique. Yet this appellation requires several qualifications. First, readers will find genuine intellectual content, probably more than in a technique-laden methods course. I have even included several simple techniques (use of random digits for sampling and for simulation, computation of simple descriptive statistics and of index numbers) on the grounds that talking about a median without ever computing one may be empty. Second, I have been positive in my approach to statistics. I am annoyed that so many popular presentations suggest that statistics is a subcategory of lying. Third, this is a text, organized for study and provided with abundant exercises at the end of each chapter. I hope that this organization will not deter those admirable individuals who seek pleasure and learning in uncompelled reading.

I am grateful to many colleagues for comments and suggestions. Professors William Erickson of the University of Michigan and Paul Speckman of the University of Oregon used the first draft in their classes and graciously provided both their own reactions and those of their students. They will forgive me if I proved at times hard to sway. The mathematicians and statisticians who have taught from the first draft noted the challenge of teaching nonmathematical material. I have tried to provide detailed guidance for teachers in the Instructor's Manual. Here, only a few suggestions are in order. First, try to establish a "humanities course" atmosphere, with much discussion in class. Many of the exercises involve discussion and can be modified to ask "Come prepared to discuss" rather than seek written answers. There are of course techniques to be learned, but classes should not be primarily problem-oriented. Second, use the collection of readings *Statistics: A Guide to the Unknown,* by J. M. Tanur et al. (eds.), as supplementary material. It is referred to often in the text, and complements this book well.

Statistics is a subject of growing importance to general audiences, and statisticians are increasingly aware of the need to introduce their subject to a wider public. There is as yet no consensus on how this should be done. It is my opinion that words remain as effective as computer terminals. I enjoy teaching this material as much as any. The orientation toward discussion brings students and teachers closer than in a more technical course. I hope you also enjoy it.

For the second edition

I am pleased that the first edition of this book was widely read, and read by people from many disciplines and diverse backgrounds. Of the many whose comments influenced this revised edition, I must mention in particular John Bibby of the Open University (England), Robert Hogg of the University of Iowa, and Dana Quade of the University of North Carolina.

In addition to a systematic updating of the many topical examples and discussions, I have added some material in response to suggestions: An early introduction of confidence statements in Chapter 1; such newer graphical ideas as stemplots and boxplots in Chapters 4 and 5; a more extensive discussion of relations among variables, now organized into a separate Chapter 6; and in Chapter 9, a section on recipes for some common significance tests to accompany the first edition's similar section on confidence intervals. There are also a significant number of new exercises.

Most users of the book—at least most who have written me—teach students who are somewhat more quantitatively advanced than my intended audience. The added material will, I hope, satisfy them. But the purpose of the book remains unchanged: to present statistics to nonmathematical readers as an aid to clear thinking in personal and professional life.

Introduction

M ost of us associate "statistics" with the words of the play-by-play announcer at the end of the sports broadcast, "And we thank our statistician, Alan Roth. . . ." We meet the statistician as the person who compiles the batting averages or yards gained. Statisticians do indeed work with numerical facts (which we call *data*), but usually for more serious purposes. Statistics originated as *state*-istics, an accessory to governments wanting to know how many taxable farms or military-age men their realms contained. The systematic study of data has now infiltrated most areas of academic or practical endeavor. Here are some examples of statistical questions.

1. The Bureau of Labor Statistics reports that the unemployment rate last month was 7.5%. What exactly does that figure mean? How did the government obtain this information? (Neither you nor I were asked if we were employed last month.) How accurate is the unemployment rate given?

2. The Gallup Poll reports that 42% of the American public currently approve the President's performance in office. Where did that information come from? How accurate is it?

3. What kind of evidence links smoking to increased incidence of lung cancer and other health problems? You may have heard that much of this evidence is "statistical."

4. A medical researcher claims that vitamin C is not effective in reducing the incidence of colds and flu. How can an experiment be designed to prove or disprove this claim?

5. Do gun control laws reduce violent crimes? Both proponents and opponents of stricter gun legislation offer numerical arguments in favor of their position. Which of these arguments are sense and which are nonsense?

The aim of statistics is to provide insight by means of numbers. In pursuit of this aim, statistics divides the study of data into three parts:

I. Collecting data

II. Describing and presenting data

III. Drawing conclusions from data

This book is organized into three parts following this same pattern. The second of these divisions is often called *descriptive statistics*; the third is often called *statistical inference*. I hasten to add that we will not leave the interesting business of drawing conclusions to the end of the book. Collecting and organizing data usually suggest conclusions (not always correct conclusions), and we will have much to say about these informal inferences in the first two parts of our study.

Your goals in reading this book should be threefold. First, reach an understanding of statistical ideas in themselves. The basic concepts and modes of reasoning of statistics are major intellectual accomplishments (almost all developed within this century) worthy of your attention. Second, acquire the ability to deal critically with numerical arguments. Many persons are unduly credulous when numerical arguments are used; they are impressed by the solid appearance of a few numbers and do not attempt to penetrate the substance of the argument. Others are unduly cynical; they think numbers are liars by nature and never trust them. Numerical arguments are like any others. Some are good, some are bad, and some are irrelevant. A bit of quantitative sophistication will enable you to hold your own against the number-slinger. Third, gain an understanding of the impact of statistical ideas on public policy and in your primary area of academic study. The list of statistical questions given above hints at the considerable impact of statistics in areas of public policy. I will only add that the impact is sometimes aimed at your pocketbook. For example, each 1% rise in the Consumer Price Index automatically triggers a two to three billion dollar increase in government spending on such things as social security payments. You pay a share of those dollars, and you should know something about the Consumer Price Index and other creatures in the statistical zoo. The invasion of many academic areas by statistics is even more dramatic. For example, two political scientists recently compiled the percentage of articles appearing in a leading political science journal that made use of numerical data. Here are their results.[1]

1946–1948	12% of all articles used numerical data
1950–1952	16% ” ” ” ” ” ”
1963–1965	40% ” ” ” ” ” ”
1968–1970	65% ” ” ” ” ” ”

It is clear that a political scientist must now be prepared to deal with statistics.

Economists, psychologists, sociologists, and educators have long considered statistics a basic part of their tool kit. Not even historians and literary scholars can ignore statistical methods. It is now common, for example, to attempt to decide the authorship of a disputed historical or literary document by analyzing quantitative characteristics of writing style (sentence length, vocabulary counts, frequency of certain grammatical constructions, etc.). Comparing these characteristics of the disputed document with documents by known authors often leads to a decision about authorship of the disputed document. An outstanding investigation of this type concerned the authorship of 12 of the papers originally published in *The Federalist*. These papers were published anonymously in 1787–1788 to persuade the citizens of New York State to ratify the Constitution. There is general agreement as to the authors of most of those papers: John Jay wrote 5, James Madison wrote 14, and Alexander Hamilton wrote 51. The disputed 12 may belong to either Madison or Hamilton. A statistical study of the style of these papers gave good reason to think that all were written by Madison.*

I hasten to state that one need not entirely approve of the infiltration of fields such as political science and history by quantitative methods. One might well agree with the remarks of Lewis A. Coser, president of the American Sociological Association in 1975, who warned the Association's annual meeting that "if concepts and theoretical notions are weak, no measurement, however precise, will advance an explanatory science."[2] In other words, it may be misleading to attempt to measure what you don't understand. But whether we like or dislike the increasing use of statistical arguments, we must be prepared to deal with them. Even if you wish only to rebut your local statistician, this book aims to give you the conceptual tools to do so.

NOTES

1. James L. Hutter, "Statistics and Political Science," *Journal of the American Statistical Association*, Volume 67 (1972), p. 735.
2. Reported in *The New York Times*, August 30, 1975.

---

* See Frederick Mosteller and David L. Wallace, "Deciding Authorship," in J. M. Tanur et al. (eds.), *Statistics: A Guide to the Unknown* (San Francisco: Holden-Day, 1972), This book of readings contains many outstanding examples of the uses of statistics, and we shall refer to it often.

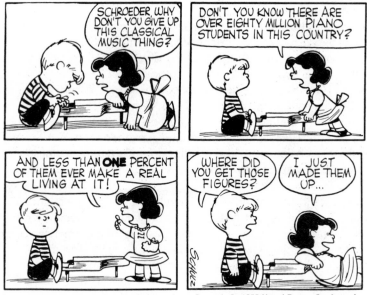

Part I

Collecting data

Before numbers can be used for good or evil, we must collect them. Of course we could make up data, a common enough practice. Leaving invention aside, many statistical studies are based on *available data*, that is, data not gathered specifically for the study at hand, but lying about in files or records kept for other reasons. Available data must be used with caution. Here is an example:

> The American Cancer Society, in a booklet called "The Hopeful Side of Cancer," claims that about one in three cancer patients is now cured, while in 1930 only one in five patients was cured. That's encouraging. But where does this encouraging estimate come from? From the state of Connecticut. Why Connecticut? Because it is the only state that kept records of cancer patients in 1930. It is a matter of available data. But Connecticut is not typical of the entire nation. It has no large cities, and few blacks. Cancer death rates are higher in large cities than in rural locations, and higher among blacks than among whites. We are left without clear knowledge of the national trend in cancer cures.

Used with proper care, available data can be invaluable. The 350,000 cases in the Connecticut Tumor Registry may not be typical of national trends. But

1

suppose we want to study the relationship between cancer and asbestos in water-supply pipes. The registry of every cancer case in Connecticut since 1930 can be matched with information about localities whose pipes contain asbestos. The registry has been used for over 200 studies of the occurrence of cancer and the effectiveness of various treatments. Not all sources of available data are so useful. Hospital records of cancer cannot tell how common the disease is, since, unlike a state registry, they have no clear geographical boundaries. "Facts" about crime based on police records are notoriously unreliable, since many crimes are never reported to the police. Good data, like other good things, are usually the fruit of systematic effort.

Historians must rely on available data. The rest of us can make an effort to obtain data that bear directly on the questions we wish to ask. Such data are obtained by either *observation* or *experimentation*. Observation is passive: The observer wishes to record data without interfering with the process being observed. Experimentation is active: The experimenter attempts to completely control the experimental situation. The difference is illustrated by the work of Tycho Brahe and Galileo at the beginning of the Scientific Revolution. Brahe devoted his life to recording precisely the positions of stars and planets and left records from which Kepler deduced his laws of planetary motion. This was observation. Galileo studied motion under the influence of gravity by rolling balls of various weights down inclined planes of various lengths and angles. This was experiment.

Neither observation nor experimentation is as simple as you might think, especially when we turn from stars and inclined planes to political opinions and the effectiveness of drugs. The first part of this book concerns the statistical ideas used to arrange observations or experiments. Statistics gives *designs* (patterns or outlines) for collecting data that can be applied in any area of study. Chapter 1 studies the design of *samples* (selecting units for observation), and Chapter 2 presents the design of *experiments*. Each chapter explores key statistical ideas, important examples of their use, and other topics, including the ethical problems of collecting data about people. Chapter 3 completes the topic of collecting data by addressing the process of *measurement* by which numbers are finally obtained.

Chapter 1

Sampling

B oswell quotes Samuel Johnson as saying, "You don't have to eat the whole ox to know that the meat is tough." That is the essential idea of sampling: to gain information about the whole by examining only a part. Here is the basic terminology used by statisticians to discuss sampling:

Population—the entire group of objects about which information is wanted.

Unit—any individual member of the population.

Sample—a part or subset of the population used to gain information about the whole.

Sampling frame—the list of units from which the sample is chosen.

Variable—a characteristic of a unit, to be measured for those units in the sample.

Notice that population is defined in terms of our desire for information. If we desire information about all U.S. college students, that is our population even if students at only one college are available for sampling. It is important to define clearly the population of interest. If you seek to discover what fraction of the American people favor a ban on private ownership of handguns, you must specify the population exactly. Are all U.S. residents included in the population, or only citizens? What minimum age will you insist on? In a similar sense, when you read a preelection poll, you should ask what the population was: all adults, registered voters only, Democrats or Republicans only?

The distinction between population and sample is basic to statistics. Some examples will illustrate this distinction and introduce some major uses of sampling. These brief descriptions also indicate the variables to be measured for each unit in the sample. They do not state the sampling frame. Ideally, the sampling frame should be a list of all units in the population. But, as we shall see, obtaining such a list is one of the practical difficulties in sampling.

Example 1. *Public opinion polls,* such as those conducted by the Gallup and Harris organizations, are designed to determine public opinion on a variety of issues. The specific variables measured are responses to questions about public issues. Though most noticed at election time, these polls are conducted on a regular basis throughout the year. For the Gallup Poll,

Population: U.S. residents 18 years of age and over.
Sample: About 1500 persons interviewed weekly.

Example 2. *Market research* is designed to discover consumer preferences and usage of products. Among the better-known examples of market research are the television-rating services. One of these services uses as its sampling frame households having telephones. Note that a unit here is a household, not an individual person.

Population: All U.S. households.
Sample: About 1200 households weekly that agree to keep a "TV diary" when contacted by phone.

Example 3. *The decennial census** is required by the constitution. An attempt is made to collect basic information (number of occupants, age, race, sex, family relationship, etc.) from each household in the country. Much other information is collected, but only from a sample of households.

Population: All U.S. households.
Sample: The entire population (as far as possible) for basic information; only 20% of the population for other information.

Example 4. *Acceptance sampling* is the selection and careful inspection of a sample from a large lot of a product shipped by a supplier. On the

---

* *Decennial* means every 10 years. A census has been taken every 10 years since 1790. For more information on sampling by the Bureau of the Census, see Morris H. Hansen, "How to Count Better: Using Statistics to Improve the Census," in J. M. Tanur et al. (eds.), *Statistics: A Guide to the Unknown.* (San Francisco: Holden-Day, 1972.)

basis of this, a decision is made whether to accept or reject the entire lot. The exact acceptance-sampling procedure to be followed is usually stated in the contract between the purchaser and the supplier.

Population: A lot of items shipped by the supplier.
Sample: A portion of the lot that the purchaser chooses for inspection.

Example 5. *Sampling of accounting data* is a widely accepted accounting procedure. It is quite expensive and time-consuming to verify each of a large number of invoices, accounts receivable, spare parts in inventory, and so forth. Accountants therefore use a sample of invoices or accounts receivable in auditing a firm's records, and the firm itself counts its inventory of spare parts by taking a sample of it. A good example of this business use of sampling is the procedure for settling accounts among airlines for interline tickets. The passenger who takes a trip involving two or more carriers pays the first carrier, which then owes the other carriers a portion of the ticket cost. It is too expensive for the airlines to calculate exactly how much they owe each other, so only a sample of tickets is examined and accounts are settled on that basis.

Population: All interline air tickets purchased in a given month.
Sample: About 10% of these tickets used to settle accounts among airlines.

There are many more uses of sampling, some bordering on the bizarre. For example, a radio station that plays a song owes the song's composer a royalty. The organization of composers (called ASCAP) collects these royalties for all its members by charging stations a license fee for the right to play members' songs. But how should this income be distributed among the 20,000 members of ASCAP? By sampling: ASCAP tapes about 60,000 hours of local radio programs across the country each year. The tapes are shipped to New York, where ASCAP employs monitors (professional trivia experts who recognize nearly every song ever written) to record how often each song was played. This sample count is used to split royalty income among composers, depending on how often their music was played. Sampling is a pervasive, though usually hidden, aspect of modern life.

1. The need for sampling design

A *census* is a sample consisting of the entire population. If information is desired about a population, why not take a census? The first reason should be clear from the examples we have given: If the population is large, it is too expensive and time-consuming to take a census. Even the federal government, which can afford a census, uses samples to collect data on prices, employment, and many other variables. Attempting to take a census would result in this month's unemployment rate becoming available next year rather than next month.

There are also less obvious reasons for preferring a sample to a census. In some cases, such as acceptance sampling of fuses or ammunition, the units in the sample are destroyed. In other cases a relatively small sample yields more accurate data than a census. This is true in developing nations that lack adequate trained personnel for a census. Even when personnel are available, a careful sample of an inventory of spare parts will almost certainly give more accurate results than asking the clerks to count all 500,000 parts in the warehouse. Bored people do not count accurately. The experience of the Census Bureau itself reminds us that a more careful definition of a census is "an *attempt* to sample the entire population." The bureau estimates that the 1970 census missed 2.5% of the American population. These missing persons include an estimated 7.7% of the black population, largely in inner cities. In 1980, the Census Bureau reduced, at considerable cost, the undercount to less than 1% of the population. Nonetheless, a number of cities sued the bureau, alleging that their minority population had been undercounted. So a census is not foolproof, even with the legal and financial resources of the government behind it.

Nevertheless, only a census can give detailed information about every small area of the population. For example, block-by-block population figures are required to create election districts with equal population. It is the main function of the decennial census to provide this local information.

So sample we must. Selecting a sample from the units available often seems simple enough, but this simplicity is misleading. If I were a supplier of oranges who sold your company several crates per week, you would be wise to examine a sample of oranges in each crate to determine the quality of the oranges supplied. You find it convenient to inspect a few oranges from the top of each crate. But these oranges may not be representative of the entire crate if, for example, those on the bottom are damaged more often in shipment. Your method of sampling might even tempt me to be sure that the rotten oranges are packed on the bottom with some good ones on top for you to inspect. Selection of whichever units of the population are easily accessible is called *convenience sampling.* Samples obtained in this way are often not representative of the population and lead to misleading conclusions about the population.

Convenience sampling occurs in situations less obvious than squeezing the oranges on the top of the crate. Suppose that we obtain a sample of public opinion by hiring interviewers and sending them to street corners and shopping centers to interview the public. The typical interviewer is a white, middle-class female. She is unlikely to interview many working-class males, blacks, or others who are unlike her. Even if we assign the interviewer quotas by race, age, and sex, she will tend to select the best-dressed and least threatening members of each group. The result will be a sample that systematically overrepresents some parts of the population (persons of middle-class appearance) and underrepresents others. The opinions of such a convenience sample may be very different from those of the population as a whole. When a sampling method produces results that consistently and repeatedly differ from the truth about the population in the same direction, we say that the sampling method is *biased*. Convenience samples are often biased. Here are other examples of convenience sampling:

> **Example 6.** *Voluntary response* to a mail or television questionnaire elicits the opinions of those who feel strongly enough to respond. The opinions of this group are often systematically different from those of the population as a whole. For example, in 1972 a local television station asked viewers to send postcards indicating whether they favored or opposed President Nixon's decision to mine Haiphong harbor. Of those who responded, 5157 agreed with the decision and 1158 disagreed. It later developed that Nixon campaign workers had mailed about 2000 responses agreeing with his decision. "That type of voluntary poll is the most stackable thing," the Associated Press quoted a campaign spokesman as saying. "When you're involved in an election, you do what you can."[1]

> **Example 7.** The spacecraft Mariners 4, 6, and 7 flew past Mars in 1965 and 1969, photographing about 10% of that planet's surface. On the basis of this sample of its surface, Mars appeared to be a dead planet similar to the moon. Then, in 1971–1972, Mariner 9 orbited Mars and photographed 85% of its surface. Mars was revealed as a varied world with natural features that appear to have been shaped by water. The earlier Mariner observations had been concentrated in an area of Mars not representative of the entire planet.

2. Simple random sampling

A remedy for the "favoritism" usually caused by a convenience sample is to take a *simple random sample*. The essential idea is to give each unit in the sampling frame the same chance to be chosen for the sample as any other unit. For reasons to be explained later, the precise definition is slightly more complicated.

A *simple random sample* of size n is a sample of n units chosen in such a way that every collection of n units from the sampling frame has the same chance of being chosen.

We will abbreviate simple random sample as *SRS*. Notice that the definition concerns a property of the method for choosing the sample: An SRS is obtained by a method that gives *every* possible sample of size *n* the same chance of being the sample actually chosen. An SRS has a clear advantage over a convenience sample: It is fair, or *unbiased*. No part of the sampling frame has any advantage over any other in obtaining representation in the sample. The definition of an SRS is designed to correct the overrepresentation of one part of the population often produced by convenience sampling.

Very well then, if an SRS is so useful a commodity, how do we actually obtain one? One way is to use *physical mixing*: Identify each unit in the sampling frame on an identical tag, mix the tags thoroughly in a box, then draw one blindly. If the mixing is truly complete, every tag in the box has the same chance of being chosen. The unit identified on the tag drawn is the first unit in our SRS. Now draw another tag without replacing the first. Again, if the mixing is thorough, every remaining tag has the same chance of being drawn. So every pair of tags has the same chance of being the pair we have now drawn; we have an SRS of size 2. To obtain an SRS of size *n*, we continue drawing until we have *n* tags corresponding to *n* units in the sampling frame. Those *n* units are an SRS of size *n*.

Physical mixing and drawing convey clearly the idea of an SRS. You should now grasp what it means to give each unit and each possible set of *n* units the same chance of being chosen. Physical mixing is even practiced on some occasions. But it is surprisingly difficult to achieve a really thorough mixing, as those who spend their evenings shuffling cards know. Physical mixing is also awkward and time-consuming. There is a better way.

Picture a wheel (such as a roulette wheel) rotating on a smooth bearing so that it does not favor any particular orientation when coming to rest. Divide the circumference of the wheel into 10 equal sectors and label them 0, 1, 2, 3, 4, 5, 6, 7, 8, and 9. Fix a stationary pointer at the wheel's rim and spin the wheel.

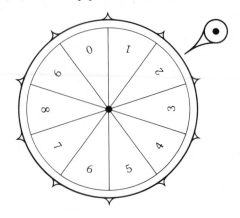

Slowly and smoothly it comes to rest. Sector number 2, say, is opposite the pointer. Spin the wheel again. It comes to rest with, say, sector number 9 opposite the pointer. If we continue this process, we will produce a string of the digits 0, 1, . . . , and 9 in some order. On any one spin, the wheel has the same chance of producing each of these 10 digits. And because the wheel has no memory, the outcome of any one spin has no effect on the outcome of any other. We are producing a table of random digits.

A *table of random digits* is a list of the 10 digits 0, 1, 2, 3, 4, 5, 6, 7, 8, and 9 having the following properties:

1. The digit in any position in the list has the same chance of being any one of 0, 1, 2, 3, 4, 5, 6, 7, 8, and 9; and

2. The digits in different positions are independent in the sense that the value of one has no influence on the value of any other.

Table A on page 344 is a table of random digits. The division into groups of five digits and into numbered rows makes the table easier to read and use but has no meaning. The table is just a long list of digits having properties 1 and 2. The table of random digits was produced by a very careful physical mixing process, much more elaborate than the wheel I used to illustrate random digits.

We can think of random digits as the result of someone else's careful physical mixing; our goal is to use their work in choosing an SRS rather than doing our own physical mixing. To use the table, we need the following facts about random digits, which are consequences of the basic properties 1 and 2:

3. Any *pair* of digits in the table has the same chance of being any of the 100 possible pairs, 00, 01, 02, . . . , 98, and 99;

4. Any *triple* of digits in the table has the same chance of being any of the 1000 possible triples, 000, 001, 002, . . . , 998, and 999;

5. And so on for groups of four or more digits from the table.

How to use Table A to choose an SRS is best illustrated by a sequence of examples.

Example 8. A dairy products manufacturer must select an SRS of size 5 from 100 lots of yogurt to check for bacterial contamination. We proceed as follows:

(a) Label the 100 lots 00, 01, 02, . . . , 99, in any order.

(b) Enter Table A in any place and read systematically through it. We choose to enter the line 111 and read across:

> 81486   69487   60513   09297. . . .

(c) Read groups of two digits. Each group chooses a label attached to a lot of yogurt. Our SRS consists of the lots having the labels

> 81, 48, 66, 94, 87.

This example illustrates the basic technique: Give the units in the sampling frame numerical labels and use Table A to choose an SRS of these labels. *It is essential that each label consist of the same number of digits.* In the example, each label consists of two digits. By Property 3 of random digits, each pair of digits in Table A is then equally likely to choose any label. Two-digit labels are adequate for a sampling frame containing between 11 and 100 units. (If no more than 10 units must be labeled, one-digit labels can be used. If 101 to 1000 units must be labeled, three-digit labels are needed.) *Always use as few digits as possible in labels.* That is why we labeled the first lot of yogurt 00 instead of 01; there are 100 labels 00, 01, . . . , and 99, so 100 units can be labeled with two digits if we start with 00. It is good practice to begin at zero rather than one even when all labels are not needed.

Suppose that the line of Table A used in the example had read

> 81486   68186   60513   09297. . . .

The first three lots chosen are those with labels 81, 48, and 66, as before. The next pair of digits in the table is 81. Because lot 81 is already in the sample, we *ignore repeated groups of digits* and go on to choose lots 86 and 60 to complete an SRS of size 5. You are now ready for a more difficult example.

Example 9. An SRS of size 5 must be chosen from a group of 300 convicts who have volunteered to take part in a medical experiment. We proceed as follows:

(a) List the convicts in some order, such as alphabetically. This list is the sampling frame.

(b) Label the convicts 000, 001, . . . , 299.

(c) Enter Table A at, say, line 116 and read across in three-digit groups. Each three-digit group 000 to 299 chooses a convict; each three-digit group 300 to 999 is not a label and is ignored. The result is

> 144   592 ignore
> 605 ignore   631 ignore

424 ignore   803 ignore
716 ignore   510 ignore
362 ignore   253
and so on.

This example illustrates the fact that we must *ignore unused labels*. But we examined 10 three-digit groups and succeeded in choosing only 2 convicts. It is much more efficient to give several labels to each unit in the sampling frame, being sure to give each unit the same number of labels. Let us redo the last example.

Example 10. An SRS of size 5 must be chosen from a group of 300 convicts who have volunteered to take part in a medical experiment. We proceed as follows:

(a) List the convicts in some order.

(b) Label the first convict 000, 300, and 600.
Label the second convict 001, 301, and 601.
⋮
Label the last convict 299, 599, and 899.

(c) Enter Table A at line 116 and read across in three-digit groups. Choose a convict for the sample if any of his labels occur. The result is

144   convict 144 is in the sample
592   convict 292 is in the sample
605   convict 005 is in the sample
631   convict 031 is in the sample
424   convict 124 is in the sample.

Notice that the three labels given each convict in Example 10 are

1. The original label, between 000 and 299;

2. The original label plus 300 (the number of units in the sampling frame); and

3. The original label plus 600.

So label 592 is the same as label 592 − 300 = 292, and label 605 is the same as label 605 − 600 = 005. The labels 900 to 999 are not used and are ignored if we come upon them in Table A.

"Hey, Pops, what was that letter you sent off to Ann Landers yesterday?"

3. Population information from a sample

Ann Landers once asked her readers, "If you had it to do over again, would you have children?" She received nearly 10,000 responses, almost 70% saying "NO!" Now this is an egregious example of voluntary response. How egregious was suggested by a professional nationwide random sample commissioned by *Newsday*. That sample polled 1373 parents and found that 91% would have children again, to which a newspaper reporter responded, "Far be it from us to question the validity of any statistic that we read in the papers, but in 1974 there were 54,917,000 families in America. This means we are talking somewhere in the neighborhood of a 1-in-50,000 sampling."[2] Leaving aside the reporter's poor arithmetic (1373 out of 54,917,000 families is 1 in 40,000, not 1 in 50,000), he has raised a perceptive question. We know why convenience sampling is unreliable, but why is an SRS reliable, especially when so small a fraction of the population is sampled?

Well, an SRS has no bias. In this case, the *Newsday* poll gave all parents the same chance of responding, rather than favoring those who were mad enough at their children to write Ann Landers. But lack of favoritism alone is not enough when we are asked to draw conclusions about 55 million families from results on only 1400 of them. We need to think more carefully about the process of gaining information about a population from a sample, starting with some new vocabulary.

The conclusions we wish to draw from a sample usually concern some numerical characteristic of the population, such as the fraction of American parents who would have children again, the average lifetime of General Electric 40-watt standard light bulbs, or the fraction of Princeton alumni who approve of co-education. As always, we must distinguish between population and sample.

A *parameter* is a numerical characteristic of the *population*. It is a fixed number, but we usually do not know its value.

A *statistic* is a numerical characteristic of the *sample*. The value of a statistic is known when we have taken a sample, but it changes from sample to sample.

Put simply, parameter is to population as statistic is to sample. Both parameters and statistics are numbers. The distinction lies entirely in whether the number describes the population (then it is a parameter) or a sample (then it is a statistic). The fraction of all American parents who would have children again is a parameter describing the population of parents. Call it p. Alas, we do not know the numerical value of p. We usually use a sample statistic to estimate the unknown value of a population parameter. *Newsday*, in an attempt to estimate p, took a sample of 1373 parents. The fraction (call it $\hat{p}$) of the sample who would have children again is a statistic. If 1249 of this sample of size 1373 would do it again, then

$$\hat{p} = \frac{1249}{1373} = 0.91 .$$

It is reasonable to use the sample proportion $\hat{p} = 0.91$ as an estimate of the unknown population proportion p, and that is exactly what *Newsday* did. But if *Newsday* took a second sample of size 1373, it is almost certain that there would *not* be exactly 1249 positive responses. So the value of $\hat{p}$ will vary from sample to sample. This is called *sampling variability*.

Aha! So what is to prevent one random sample from finding that 91% of parents would have children again and a second random sample from finding that 70% would not? After all, we just admitted that the statistic $\hat{p}$ wanders about from sample to sample. We are saved by a second property of random sampling, a property even more important than lack of bias: A sample statistic from an SRS has a predictable pattern of values in repeated sampling. This pattern is called the *sampling distribution* of the statistic. Knowledge of the sampling distribution allows us to make statements about how far the sample proportion $\hat{p}$ is likely to wander from the population proportion p owing to sampling variability.

To illustrate a sampling distribution, let us do an experiment. We will assume for now that the sampling frame contains every unit in the population. I have a box containing a large number of round beads, identical except for color.

These beads are a population. The fraction of dark beads in the box is

$$p = 0.20$$

and this number is a parameter describing this population of beads. I also have a paddle with 25 bead-sized indentations in it, so when I thrust it into the beads in the box, it selects a sample of 25 beads. If the beads in the box are well mixed, this is an SRS of size 25. Ask yourself a few questions about this SRS of size 25 from a population containing 20% dark beads.

- How many dark beads do you expect to appear in the sample?
- If you take several SRSs, do you expect to find a sample with 25 dark beads? One with no dark beads? One with as many as 15 dark beads?

You might reasonably expect about 20% of the beads in the sample to be dark, that is, about 5 dark beads among the 25 beads in the sample. But we will not always get exactly 5 dark beads. If we get, say, 4 dark beads, then the statistic

$$\hat{p} = \frac{4}{25} = 0.16$$

is still a good estimate of the parameter $p = 0.20$. But if we draw a sample with 15 dark beads, then

$$\hat{p} = \frac{15}{25} = 0.60$$

is a very bad estimate of p. How often will we get such poor estimates from an SRS?

I carried out this bead-sampling experiment 200 times and recorded the number of dark beads in each sample. (I was careful to return the sample to the population and stir the population after each repetition.) The results are shown in a table and pictorially in Figure 1-1. None of the 200 samples contained more than 9 dark beads. The sample proportion $\hat{p}$ did indeed vary from sample to sample: It ranged from 0 (no dark beads) to 0.36 (9 dark beads) when all 200 samples were examined. But estimates as bad as $\hat{p} = 0$ or $\hat{p} = 0.36$ (remember that the true p is 0.20 for this population) did not occur often. Of the 200 samples, 56% had either 4, 5, or 6 dark beads ($\hat{p}$ of 0.16, 0.20, or 0.24) and 83% had 3, 4, 5, 6, or 7 dark beads ($\hat{p}$ between 0.12 and 0.28).

In our experiment, we knew p. If p were not known, the same facts would

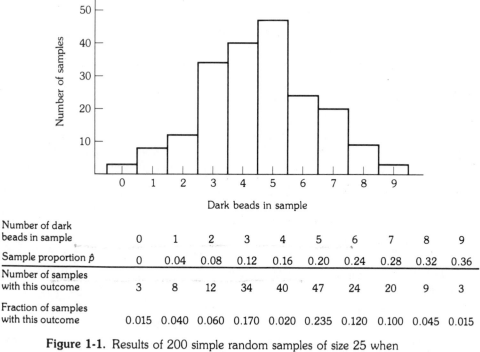

Number of dark beads in sample	0	1	2	3	4	5	6	7	8	9
Sample proportion $\hat{p}$	0	0.04	0.08	0.12	0.16	0.20	0.24	0.28	0.32	0.36
Number of samples with this outcome	3	8	12	34	40	47	24	20	9	3
Fraction of samples with this outcome	0.015	0.040	0.060	0.170	0.020	0.235	0.120	0.100	0.045	0.015

Figure 1-1. Results of 200 simple random samples of size 25 when $p = 0.20$.

hold. We could not guarantee that the sample statistic $\hat{p}$ is close to the unknown p (because of sampling variability), but we could be confident that it is close (because most of the time an SRS gives a $\hat{p}$ close to p). So the results of an SRS not only show no favoritism but tend to be repeatable from sample to sample. We need a final bit of vocabulary to describe the fact that lack of repeatability (the sample result wanders all over the barnyard) is as serious a flaw in a sampling method as is favoritism.

Because a sample is selected for the purpose of gaining information about a population, by error in a sample we mean an incorrect estimate of a population parameter by a sample statistic. Two basic types of error are associated with any method of collecting sample data.

Bias is consistent, repeated divergence of the sample statistic from the population parameter in the same direction.

Lack of precision means that in repeated sampling the values of the sample statistic are spread out or scattered; the result of sampling is not repeatable.

A common misunderstanding is to confuse bias in a sampling method with a strong trend in the population itself, especially if that trend is a reflection of prejudice or bias in the ordinary sense of that word. If, for example, 93% of a population of corporate personnel directors are opposed to the federal government's affirmative action hiring program, this is *not* bias in the statistical sense. It is simply a fact about this population.

We can think of the true value of the population parameter as the bull's-eye on a target, and of the sample statistic as a bullet fired at the bull's-eye. *Bias* means that our sight is misaligned and we shoot consistently off the bull's-eye in one direction. Our sample values do not center about the population value. *Lack of precision* means that repeated shots are widely scattered on the target; that is, repeated samples do not give similar results but differ widely among themselves.

This target illustration of the results of repeated sampling is shown in Figure 1-2. Notice that high precision (repeated shots are close together) can accompany high bias (the shots are consistently away from the bull's-eye in one direction). Notice also that low bias (the shots center on the bull's-eye) can accompany low precision (repeated shots are widely scattered). A good sampling scheme, like a good shooter, must have both low bias and high precision.

The sampling distribution of a statistic describes both its bias and its precision. For example, the precision of $\hat{p}$ as an estimator of p in Figure 1-1 can be expressed by a statement such as "56% of SRSs of size 25 have a value of $\hat{p}$ within $\pm$ 0.04 of the true value of p." The shape of the distribution of values shown in Figure 1-1 is typical of an SRS. These distributions can be studied mathematically to save us the work of experimentation. As you might guess, such studies (and experiments as well) show that *increasing the size of the sample increases the precision of sample statistics*. If in our experiment we had used samples of size 100, about 74% of these samples would have sample proportions $\hat{p}$ within $\pm$ 0.04 of p.

Only one other fact about precision is needed to apply the coup de grâce to that newspaper reporter's skepticism about 1-in-40,000 samples: *The precision of a sample statistic does not depend on the size of the population as long as the population is much larger than the sample*. In other words, the pattern of results from repeatedly thrusting my 25-bead paddle into a large box of beads does not depend on whether the box contains 1000 beads (as it did in my experiment) or 10,000 beads. The precision does depend on how many beads the paddle selects (sample size) and, to a lesser extent, on the fraction p of dark beads in the population.

This is good news for *Newsday*. Their sample of size 1373 has high precision because the sample size is large. That only 1-in-40,000 in the population were sampled is irrelevant. It is almost certain—Ann Landers to the contrary—that

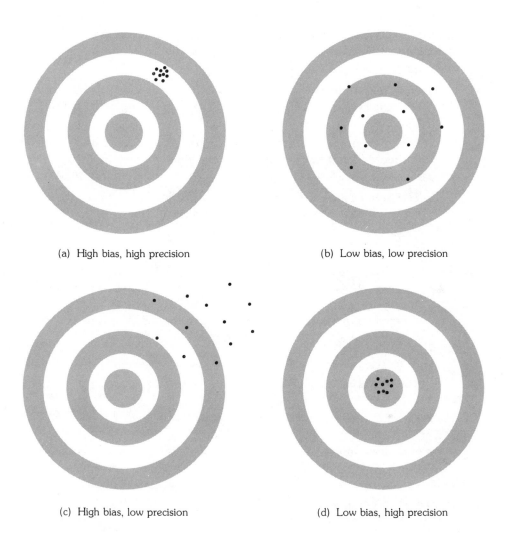

(a) High bias, high precision

(b) Low bias, low precision

(c) High bias, low precision

(d) Low bias, high precision

Figure 1-2. Bias and lack of precision in sample results.

close to 91% of American parents would have children again. But the fact that the precision of a sample statistic depends on the size of the sample and not on the size of the population is bad news for anyone planning an opinion poll in a university or small city. For example, it takes just as large an SRS to estimate the proportion of Purdue University students who favor legalizing marijuana as to estimate with the same precision the proportion of all U.S. residents 18 and over who favor legalization. That there are about 30,000 Purdue students and about 175 million U.S. residents 18 and over does *not* mean that equally precise results can be obtained by taking a smaller SRS at Purdue.

The facts acquired here are the foundation for an understanding of the uses of sampling. In review, those facts are as follows:

1. **Despite the *sampling variability* of statistics from an SRS, the values of those statistics have a *known distribution* in repeated sampling.**

2. **When the sampling frame lists the entire population, simple random sampling produces *unbiased* estimates—the values of a statistic computed from an SRS neither consistently overestimate nor consistently underestimate the value of the population parameter.**

3. **The *precision* of a statistic from an SRS depends on the size of the sample and can be made as high as desired by taking a large-enough sample.**

I have a closing confession to make: *Newsday* did not use an SRS to refute Ann Landers. Opinion polls use more complicated sampling methods—just how complicated will be seen in Section 6 of this chapter. But these sampling methods are based on random selection and so share the three basic properties listed. Our conclusions about the *Newsday* poll stand.

4.   Confidence statements

The results of an SRS are *random* in the special sense in which statisticians use that word: The outcome of a single sample is unpredictable, but there is a definite pattern of results in the long run. The results of tossing a coin are also random, as are the sexes of human or animal offspring. Random phenomena are described by the laws of probability, which allow us to calculate how often each outcome will occur in the long run. Statisticians use probability to calculate the sampling distributions of statistics. That's much faster than the actual repeated sampling of beads that we did in Section 3. The most important reason for the deliberate use of chance in collecting data is that we can then apply the laws of probability to draw conclusions from the data.

We will have much to say about probability later (Chapter 8), and we will even give the recipes for some methods of statistical inference based on probability (Chapter 9). But one form of statement based on probability is so commonly used to describe the accuracy of opinion polls and other samples that any reader of the press should be familiar with it. Often the statement is casual. For example, a news report on the shifts in public attitudes in response to a presidential speech said,

The poll, conducted by Gordon Black Associates of Rochester, N.Y., is based on 714 interviews with adults randomly selected from across the

USA. Results before the speech have a margin of error of 5.5 percent. Post-speech results have a 5 percent margin of error. *

That "5 percent margin of error" describes the accuracy of the poll, but it leaves much unsaid. As connoisseurs of data, we want to know the whole story.

A sample statistic is *unbiased* if, on the average over many samples, the statistic is a correct estimate of the population parameter of interest. Simple random sampling produces unbiased statistics, and so do the more complex sampling designs used by polling organizations. So the values of the statistic, though they vary in repeated sampling, have a sampling distribution that is centered on the parameter value. The shape of the sampling distribution depends on the exact sample design and on the size of the sample, but can be calculated using the laws of probability. This sampling distribution permits a statement of the precision of the statistic.

> **Example 11.** On July 30, 1982, the Gallup Poll asked 1514 adults, "Do you approve of the way Ronald Reagan is handling his job as president?" Here the parameter of interest is the proportion p of all U.S. adults who approve of the president's handling of his job. In the sample, 621 answered "Yes." The statistic used to estimate p is therefore
>
> $$\hat{p} = \frac{621}{1514} = 0.41.$$
>
> Gallup Poll statisticians, from their knowledge of the sampling distribution of $\hat{p}$, describe the precision of the statistic as follows: *In 95% of all possible samples, the statistic $\hat{p}$ will take a value within $\pm$ 0.03 of the parameter p.*

We made similar statements about the bead-sampling experiment on the basis of the sampling distribution in Figure 1-1 on page 15. If, for example, $p = 0.43$ were the true proportion of U.S. adults approving of the president, then 95 out of 100 Gallup Poll samples would produce sample proportions in the range 0.43 ± 0.03, or 0.40 to 0.46. The Gallup Poll will miss the truth by more than 0.03 in only 5% (1 in 20) of their samples.

This statement of precision has two parts: a *level of confidence* (95%) and a *margin of error* ($\pm$ 0.03). The level of confidence says how often in the long run the margin of error will be met. We could demand higher confidence (99%), or settle for lower confidence (90%). But we cannot achieve 100% confidence for any margin of error that does not allow $\hat{p}$ to range all the way from 0 to 1.

---

* *USA TODAY*, November 1, 1983.

There is always some chance—a very small chance, to be sure—that 1514 persons chosen at random will all be avid fans of the president ($\hat{p} = 1$) or all bitterly hostile to him ($\hat{p} = 0$). The *USA TODAY* report left out the level of confidence that should accompany its margin of error. A naive reader might imagine that the postspeech $\hat{p}$ is *certain* to be within ± 0.05 (5%) of the true p. The connoisseur knows that polling organizations almost always make 95% confidence statements, and fills in the missing confidence level.

The margin of error that is met 95% of the time is a direct measure of precision. A Gallup $\hat{p}$ that is within ± 0.03 of the truth with 95% confidence is more precise than a *USA TODAY* $\hat{p}$ that is within only ± 0.05 with 95% confidence. *The smaller the margin of error at 95% confidence, the greater the precision.* The greater size of Gallup's sample (1514 versus 714 for *USA TODAY*) accounts for its smaller margin of error. Table 1-1 gives the margins of error of $\hat{p}$ in 95% confidence statements for the Gallup Poll's sampling procedure. Since Gallup's sampling methods are typical of those used by modern opinion polls, you can use the table to judge the precision of most poll results appearing in the press, provided that the size of the sample is reported.

One last step: Saying that $\hat{p}$ falls within ± 0.03 of p 95% of the time is the same as saying that p (which is unknown) is within ± 0.03 of $\hat{p}$ (which is known) 95% of the time. Not knowing the true p, we cannot say whether the Gallup Poll of July 30, 1982 was one of the 95% that hit or one of the 5% that miss. But, since 95% of all such polls do hit within ± 0.03 of the true p, we say that

Table 1-1 Precision of the sampling procedure used by the Gallup Poll as of 1972*

Population percentage	Sample size						
	100	200	400	600	750	1000	1500
Near 10	7	5	4	3	3	2	2
Near 20	9	7	5	4	4	3	2
Near 30	10	8	6	4	4	4	3
Near 40	11	8	6	5	4	4	3
Near 50	11	8	6	5	4	4	3
Near 60	11	8	6	5	4	4	3
Near 70	10	8	6	4	4	4	3
Near 80	9	7	5	4	4	3	2
Near 90	7	5	4	3	3	2	2

SOURCE: George Gallup, *The Sophisticated Poll Watcher's Guide* (Princeton Opinion Press, 1972), p. 228.
* The table shows the range, plus or minus, within which the sample percentage $\hat{p}$ falls in 95% of all samples. This margin of error depends on the size of the sample and on the population percentage p. For example, when p is near 60%, 95% of all samples of size 1000 will have $\hat{p}$ between 56% and 64%, because the margin of error is $\pm$ 4%.

we are *95% confident* that between 0.38 and 0.44 of all adults approve of the president's handling of his job. (Check that: The sample gave $\hat{p} = 0.41$, and the margin of error was $\pm$ 0.03. So we are confident that p falls between 0.41 − 0.03 and 0.41 + 0.03.)

A *confidence statement* turns a long-run fact about the sampling distribution of a statistic into a statement of our confidence in the result of a single sample. The usual form of a 95% confidence statement about a parameter estimated by an unbiased statistic is

With 95% confidence, the parameter lies in the range *statistic* $\pm$ *margin of error*.

This is shorthand for

> **The sampling distribution of the statistic is such that in 95% of all possible samples, *the statistic falls within* $\pm$ *margin of error* of the true parameter value.**

> **Example 12.** If the Gallup Poll interviews 986 people and finds that 53% of them oppose a longer school year, what confidence statement can we make?
>
> Table 1-1 shows that the margin of error for a sample of size 1000 never exceeds 4 percentage points (± 0.04). Since the margin of error changes slowly with sample size, we can use this value for a sample of 986 people. We are 95% confident that between 49% and 57% of adult Americans oppose lengthening the school year.

Table 1-1 shows that the margin of error, although it does not depend on the size of the population, does depend a bit on the parameter p. You can either use the largest margin of error given in the column or use $\hat{p}$ to estimate about what p must be. Remember that Table 1-1 is for a complex national sample. The margins of error for simple random samples are a bit *smaller* than those in Table 1-1. The details are in Chapter 9, should you actually have to produce confidence statements. But you are already a sophisticated consumer.

5. Sampling can go wrong

The conclusions of the last two sections seem too good to be true. Most of us are aware of times when samples led to erroneous results, as when opinion polls predicted that Thomas Dewey would defeat Harry Truman in the 1948 presidential election. Alas, the glowing conclusions of the last two sections say only that errors from one source can be made small by properly conducted random sampling. These are *random sampling errors*, the deviations between sample statistic and population parameter caused by chance in selecting a random sample. When we are sampling beads or ball bearings or laboratory rats, random sampling error is our main problem, and it is an *easy* problem to deal with. That was the good news of Section 3. But, when we turn from sampling beads to sampling public opinion, consumer preferences, or personal habits, other sources of error become more serious than random sampling error in all but the smallest samples.

Sampling errors are errors caused by the act of taking a sample. They cause sample results to be different from the results of a census.

Nonsampling errors are errors not related to the act of selecting a sample from the population and that might be present even in a census.

Random sampling error is one kind of sampling error. *Nonrandom sampling errors* arise from improper sampling and have nothing to do with the chance selection in an SRS. One source of nonrandom sampling error is a biased sampling method, such as convenience sampling. Another common source of nonrandom sampling error is a sampling frame that differs systematically from the population. Even an SRS from such a frame will give biased conclusions about the population. Here are some examples of improper sampling:

Example 13. *Telephone directories.* Until recently, the two principal television-rating services selected their sample households at random from telephone directories. This sampling frame omits households having no telephones and those with unlisted numbers. Households without phones continue to be excluded by the random-digit-dialing equipment now in use. Roger Rice, a San Francisco television station operator, charged in 1974 that television ratings are biased: They underestimate the audience for programs of special interest to minorities because the sampling system underrepresents the poor.[3] Rice noted that in the San Francisco–Oakland area, about 62% of households had listed telephones, 25% had unlisted phones, and 13% had no telephone service. Census data reported that about 57% of the population was white, but the sample for one of the rating services was 78% white. Hispanics made up 14% of the population but only 1.2% of the rating-service sample.

Example 14. *Volunteer subjects.* Much behavioral research, especially in areas such as sexual habits, can use only subjects who volunteer to discuss their behavior or otherwise participate in the research. Although it is naturally hard to study persons who refuse to volunteer, there is evidence that the behavior of volunteers and nonvolunteers is quite different in many respects. Conclusions about a population that are based on a sample of persons in the population willing to volunteer may therefore be biased.[4]

Nonsampling errors, those which plague even a census, are often rooted in the perversity and complexity of human behavior. I will mention four types of nonsampling error: missing data, response errors, processing errors, and the effect of the data-collection procedure.

Missing data are due to inability to contact a subject or to the subject's refusal to respond. If subjects who cannot be contacted or who refuse to respond differ from the rest of the population, bias will result. For example, a survey conducted entirely during ordinary working hours will fail to contact households in which all adults work. Refusal to respond to survey questions is becoming more common. Though estimates vary, it appears that about 15% of persons sampled refuse to respond to nongovernmental surveys. In large cities the refusal rate is higher, probably 20–25%. This growing emphasis on privacy is in many ways praiseworthy, but it threatens even random samples with the same bias caused by use of volunteer subjects.

Response errors concern the subject's own response. The subject may lie about her age or income. Or he may remember incorrectly when asked how many packs of cigarettes he smoked last week. Or a subject who cannot understand a question may give a faulty response out of fear of showing ignorance.

Processing errors are mistakes in such mechanical tasks as doing arithmetic, entering responses on a computer terminal, or coding the data (that is, assigning numerical values to responses for data-processing purposes). These can be minimized by rechecking every mechanical task.

The effect of the method used to collect data can be large. Sometimes this effect clearly leads to errors in conclusions drawn about the population—as when black subjects speak less openly about their views on race relations to a white interviewer than they would to a black interviewer. The timing of a survey often affects its results: The Department of Agriculture, to the great frustration of almost everyone, collects data on farm labor only in December. As a result, the typical "seasonal farm worker" is a white, male college student who can be located in December to answer questions about his summer job. Hundreds of thousands of Mexican farmworkers, many in the United States illegally, seem to disappear.[5]

One important decision about the method of collecting data once a sample is chosen concerns the exact wording of questions. It is surprisingly difficult to word questions that are completely clear. (A survey that asked about "ownership

"Do I own any stock, Ma'am? Why, I've got 10,000 head out there."

of stock" found that most Texas ranchers owned stock, though probably not the kind traded on the New York Stock Exchange.) What is more, small changes in the wording of questions can significantly change the responses received. In fact, it is easy to introduce a definite bias into a sample survey by slanting the questions. A favorite trick is to ask if the subject favors some policy as a means to a desirable end: "Do you favor banning private ownership of handguns in order to reduce the rate of violent crime?" and "Do you favor restoring capital punishment in order to reduce the rate of violent crime?" are loaded questions that draw positive responses from persons worried about crime.

Finally, a survey taker must decide whether to use mail, telephone, or personal interviews to contact subjects. Mail surveys often have low response rates. Because people with strong feelings on an issue are most likely to respond, a serious bias can result; more people will express strongly negative opinions or "socially unacceptable" opinions by mail. Telephone surveys are fast, and the development of random-digit-dialing equipment during the past decade has made it possible to automatically dial a random sample of residential telephones, including those with unlisted numbers. But 8% of American households have no telephone. Moreover, the response rate for telephone surveys is about 10% less than for face-to-face contact. Personal interviews allow a skillful interviewer to establish rapport with the subject; this results in a higher response rate and clearer communication of the questions and probably introduces less bias than other methods of collecting data. But personal contact is very expensive, and it is harder to keep the questioning the same for all subjects than it is in a telephone interview.* Telephone interviewing is now used by almost all opinion polls. Personal contact is the choice of the Gallup Poll, government agencies collecting such information as unemployment rates, and most university survey workers.

Here are some examples of nonsampling errors:

> **Example 15.** *Race of interviewer.* In 1968, one year after a major racial disturbance in Detroit, a sample of black residents were asked:
>
> "Do you personally feel that you can trust most white people, some white people, or none at all?"
>
> Of those interviewed by whites, 35% answered "Most," while only 7% of those interviewed by blacks gave this answer. (Many questions were asked in this experiment. Only on some topics, particularly black—white trust or hostility, did the race of the interviewer have a strong effect on the answers given. Most sample surveys try to match the race of the interviewer to that of the subject.)[6]

> **Example 16.** *Wording of questions.* In 1980, the New York Times/CBS News Poll asked a random sample of Americans about abortion. When asked "Do you think there should be an amendment to the Constitution prohibiting abortions, or shouldn't there be such an amendment?" 29% were in favor and 62% were opposed. (The rest were uncertain.) The same people were later asked a different question: "Do you believe there should be an amendment to the Constitution protecting the life of the unborn child, or shouldn't there be such an amendment?" Now 50% were in favor and only 39% were opposed.[7]

> **Example 17.** *Telling the truth?* Official vote counts show that 86.5 million people voted in the 1980 presidential election. But a Census Bureau survey of 64,000 households a few weeks later asked about voting and estimated

---

* There is a surprising variation in the responses obtained by different interviewers. For an account of this interviewer effect on responses to the decennial census, see Morris H. Hansen, "How to Count Better: Using Statistics to Improve the Census," in *Statistics: A Guide to the Unknown.*

from the response that 93.1 million people voted. Some people were ashamed to admit that they failed to vote.

Example 18. *Processing error.* The initial release of 1980 census data on income showed Stumpy Point, N.C., (pop. 205) to be a haven of the rich, with an average household income of $84,413. Stumpy Point has no doctors and no lawyers, and only half of the adults finished high school. Sure enough, the Census Bureau soon corrected the average income to $22,773. What happened? The incomes reported on census forms are coded in tens of dollars for entry into the computer. That is, an $8000 income is entered as 0800. Whoever coded Stumpy Point slipped up and entered $8000 as 8000 in many cases. The computer, following instructions, read this as $80,000 and declared Stumpy Point wealthy.[8]

The moral of this presentation of possible errors in conclusions drawn from samples is not that sampling is unreliable and untrustworthy. The moral is that great care is required in sampling human subjects and that the statistical idea of using an SRS is not the cure for all possible ills. (It *is* an essential part of the cure, and for sampling ball bearings or accounting data it is most of the cure.) When you read or write an account of a sample survey, be sure that answers to the following questions are included:

- What was the *population*? That is, whose opinions were being sought?
- How was the sample *selected*? Look for mention of random sampling or probability sampling.
- What was the *size* of the sample? It is even better to give a measure of precision, such as the margin of error within which 95% of all samples drawn as this one was would fall.
- How were the subjects *contacted*?
- *When* was the survey conducted? Was it just after some event which might have influenced opinion?
- What were the *exact questions* asked?

The code of ethics of the American Association for Public Opinion Research (AAPOR) requires disclosure of this information. The major opinion polls always answer these questions in their press releases when announcing the results of a poll. But newspaper editors have the bad habit of cutting out the paragraphs containing these facts and printing only the lead paragraphs announcing the sample results. Worse, new methods for conducting telephone surveys have brought a proliferation of state or regional polls run by newspapers or broadcasting stations. CBS News counted 147 of these in 1980 and found that fewer than half used reliable methods. If a politician, an advertiser, or your local newspaper announces the results of a poll without complete information, be skeptical.

6. More on sampling design

By now you have absorbed the message that a reliable sample survey depends both on statistical ideas (random sampling) and on practical skills (wording questions, skillful interviewing, etc.). When our goal is to sample a large human population, using an SRS is good statistics but bad practice. First, a sampling frame is rarely available. Second, if we choose an SRS of 1600 U.S. residents for a public opinion poll, it would be a bit expensive to send interviewers off to Beetle, Kentucky and Searchlight, Nevada to find the lucky persons chosen. The solution to these practical difficulties is to use a sampling design more complicated than an SRS and "to sample not people but the map."[9] Thus an opinion poll or market researcher or government office usually proceeds somewhat as follows:

First, select a sample of counties, then a sample of townships or wards within each county chosen. There is no difficulty in obtaining lists of counties and wards to serve as sampling frames for these two steps. Now, using a map or aerial photograph as the sampling frame, select a sample of small areas (such as city blocks) within each ward chosen earlier. Finally, select a sample of households in each small area chosen. This can be done by sending interviewers to the area to compile a list of households if none is available. Interview one adult from each household selected.

Such a *multistage sampling design* overcomes the practical drawbacks of an SRS. We do not need a list of all U.S. households, only a list of households in the small areas arrived at by sampling counties, then wards, then areas within wards. Moreover, all the households in the sample are *clustered* within these few small areas, thus making it much cheaper to collect the data.

The sample selected at each stage of a multistage design may be an SRS, but other types of random samples are also used. Households in a block or telephone numbers in an exchange are often selected by a *systematic random sample*. A starting point is chosen at random, then every third or tenth unit in geographical or numerical order is selected. See Exercise 6 (Section 6) for details. Systematic samples are fast, require no frame, and make geographical spread certain if the units are in geographical order. But there are pitfalls. A colleague of mine, working as an interviewer, was once instructed to visit every third address in a Chicago neighborhood. The block contained three-story walk-up apartments, so all the addresses visited were on the third floor. These households are poorer than those on the lower floors.

The earlier stages in a multistage sample often select a *stratified random sample* of counties or telephone exchanges. To obtain a stratified random sample, proceed as follows:

> **Step 1. Divide the sampling frame into groups, called *strata*, of units. The strata are chosen because we have a special interest in these groups within the population or because the units in each stratum resemble each other.**
>
> **Step 2. Take a separate SRS in each stratum and combine these to make up the stratified random sample.**

In a stratified random sample, units need not have equal chances to be chosen. Some strata may be deliberately overrepresented in the sample. For example, if a poll of student opinion at a Big Ten university used an SRS of moderate size, there would probably be too few blacks in the sample to draw separate conclusions about black student opinion. By stratifying, we can take an SRS of black students and a separate SRS of other students and then combine them to make up the overall sample. If the university has 30,000 students, of which 3,000 are black, we would expect an SRS of 500 students to contain only about 50 blacks. (Because 10% of the population is black, we expect about 10% of an SRS to be black. Remember those beads in Section 3?) So we might instead take a stratified random sample of 200 blacks and 300 other students. The 200 blacks allow us to study black opinion with fair precision. You know how to choose the sample if you remember how to take an SRS: Use Table A on page 344 to select an SRS of 200 of the 3000 blacks; then use Table A a second time to select an SRS of 300 of the other 27,000 students. Because 200 of the 3000 black students are selected, the chance that any one black student is chosen is

$$\frac{200}{3000}, \quad \text{or} \quad \frac{1}{15}.$$

The chance that any one nonblack student is selected is

$$\frac{300}{27,000}, \quad \text{or} \quad \frac{1}{90}.$$

Each student has a known chance to be chosen, but that chance is different for blacks and others. This is a probability sample, but not an SRS.

Stratified samples have two advantages. First, they allow us to gather separate information about each stratum. Second, if the units in each stratum are more alike in the variable measured than is the population as a whole, estimates from a stratified sample will be more precise than from an SRS of the same size. To grasp this, think about the extreme case in which all the units in each stratum are exactly alike. Then a stratified sample of only one unit from each stratum would completely describe the population, but an SRS of the same size would have very low precision. Because of these advantages, stratified samples are widely used.

Opinion polls and the Census Bureau surveys that collect national economic and social data employ multistage designs with stratification in the early stages. Counties, for example, may be stratified by population and geographical location. Another common use of stratification is in sampling economic units. Because the largest corporations, or farms, or bills payable are especially important, economic surveys usually stratify by size and sample a higher proportion of the larger units. Sometimes *all* the large units are chosen and only a sample of the smaller ones. This is a stratified sample where a census is taken in one stratum.*

Simple, systematic, and stratified random samples all use chance to select units from the population, as do multistage samples constructed from these building blocks. The details of complex sampling designs should be left to experts. (Strike a blow against poverty—hire a statistician.) But all fit the general statistical framework of *probability sampling*.

> A *probability sample* is a sample chosen in such a way that we know what samples are possible (not all need be possible) and what chance, or probability, each possible sample has (not all need be equally probable).

In an SRS of size 500, every group of 500 units from the population is a possible sample, and all are equally likely to be chosen. But in our stratified sample of 500 students, the only possible samples have exactly 200 black students. The laws of probability apply to any probability sample. But haven't we defeated the first aim of an SRS, which was to eliminate bias in sampling? A stratified sample, for example, may deliberately overrepresent blacks in a survey of student opinion, or larger corporations in a survey of business practices. True. Fortunately, the fact that probabilities of selection are known allows us to correct for overrepresentation when we analyze the data. When this is done, statistics from any probability sample share the essential characteristics of statistics based on an SRS. The sampling distribution is known, and confidence statements can

---

* See John Neter, "How Accountants Save Money by Sampling," in *Statistics: A Guide to the Unknown*, for an example of the use of such a sampling design by the Chesapeake and Ohio Railroad.

be made without bias and with increasing precision as the size of the sample increases.

The details of estimating a population parameter from sample data depend on the sampling design and can be quite complicated. Example 19 illustrates estimation from a stratified sample. The details of confidence statements are yet more complicated, so we will leave them to the experts. The major point even of Example 19 is, not the technique, but the lesson that we can analyze data correctly only when we know how they were collected.

Example 19. The Internal Revenue Service is said to use a stratified sampling design to choose income tax returns to be audited. (This is in addition to the auditing of suspicious returns.) The strata are groups of returns showing similar adjusted gross incomes. Suppose that a district IRS office has 1000 returns divided into three strata as follows:

Stratum	Size of stratum	Size of sample	Returns in sample showing fraud
1. Under $15,000	800	8	1
2. $15,000–50,000	190	7	1
3. Over $50,000	10	5	3
	1000	20	5

As the table shows, a stratified sample is selected by taking an SRS of 8 of the 800 returns in stratum 1, an SRS of 7 of the 190 returns in stratum 2, and an SRS of 5 of the 10 returns in stratum 3. In all, 20 of the 1000 returns are chosen. The last column in the table shows that five fraudulent returns were found in the audit of this sample.

It is foolish to estimate that because 5/20, or 25%, of the returns in the sample showed fraud, therefore about 25% of all 1000 returns show fraud. This is biased upward because we did not use an SRS but deliberately overrepresented the high-income returns, which appear to have a higher incidence of fraud. Instead, we analyze these data as follows:

1. Estimate the proportion of fraud in each stratum separately by using the SRS for that stratum.

$$\text{Stratum 1: Estimate } \hat{p} = 1/8 \,.$$

$$\text{Stratum 2: Estimate } \hat{p} = 1/7 \,.$$

$$\text{Stratum 3: Estimate } \hat{p} = 3/5 \,.$$

2. Now estimate the *number* of fraudulent returns in each stratum by multiplying the estimated fraction of fraudulent returns by the size of

the stratum. Add these together to estimate the *total number* of fraudulent returns in the population.

Stratum 1: Estimate (800) (1/8) = 100 bad returns.

Stratum 2: Estimate (190) (1/7) = 27.1 bad returns.

Stratum 3: Estimate (10) (3/5) = 6 bad returns.

Total estimate is 100 + 27.1 + 6 = 133.1 bad returns. (We round this off to 133 returns.)

3. Now the estimated *proportion* of fraudulent returns in the population is

$$\hat{p} = \frac{133}{1000}, \quad \text{or} \quad 13.3\%.$$

This is much lower than the incorrect estimate of 25%, because we corrected for the overrepresentation of high-income returns in the sample. This method of estimation is *unbiased*—it will be correct on the average in many samples.

It may be that you will never have the good fortune to participate in the design of a sample survey. But if you work in sociology, politics, advertising, or marketing or you use government economic and social data, you will surely have to use the results of surveys. We can summarize our study in an outline of the steps in designing a sample survey.

Step 1. *Determine the population*, both its extent and the basic unit. If you are interested in buyers of new cars, your unit could be new-car registrations, new-car owners (individuals), or households that purchased new cars. You must also be specific about the geographic area and date of purchase needed to qualify a unit for this population.

Step 2. *Specify the variables to be measured*, and prepare the questionnaires or other instruments you will use to measure them. Your decisions here are related to those made at Step 1. If you seek information about the income of households buying new cars (so household income is your variable), then the unit must be a household rather than an individual or a new car.

Step 3. *Set up the sampling frame*. This also is related to Step 1. If you use a list of new-car registrations as a sampling frame (because this list is easy to obtain), households who bought several new cars will appear several times on the list. So an SRS of registrations will not be an SRS of households. (I bought a new car in 1974. The retiring president of General Motors, to express his confidence in the industry in a year of poor sales, bought *five* new GM cars that year. His household is five times as likely as mine to appear in an SRS of 1974 new-car registrations.)

Step 4. *Do the statistical design* of the sample, specifying how large the sample will be and how it will be chosen from the sampling frame.

Step 5. *Attend to details*, such as training interviewers and arranging the timing of the survey.

Much more might be said about each of these steps. A good deal is known about how to word questions, how to train interviewers, how to increase response in a mail survey, and so on. Much of this is interesting, and some is slightly amusing; for example, colorful commemorative stamps on the outer and return envelopes greatly increase the response rate in a mail survey. But a sample survey would show that you already know more about sampling than 99.9% of U.S. residents aged 18 or over. Enough is enough.

7.   Opinion polls and the political process

Public opinion polls, especially preelection "For-whom-would-you-vote?" polls, are the most visible example of survey sampling. They are also one of the most controversial. Most people are happy that sampling methods make employment and unemployment information rapidly available, and few people are upset when marketers survey consumer buying intentions. But the sampling of opinion on candidates or issues is sometimes strongly attacked as well as strongly praised. We will briefly explore three aspects of polls and politics: first, polls of opinion on public issues; second, polls as a tool used by candidates seeking nomination or election; and third, preelection polls for public consumption, designed to satisfy our curiosity as to who's ahead and by how much.

Polls on public issues (e.g., defense spending, gun control, legalization of marijuana) are praised as the only way our representatives can know what the people think. You now have the background to understand why other means (such as mail for and against) are unreliable, and why surveys such as the Gallup Poll give accurate information about public opinion. Legislators are constantly under pressure by special-interest groups who back their interests with lobbyists and campaign contributions. Opinion polls give the general public a chance to offset this pressure. As George Gallup says, "The modern poll can beam a bright and devastating light on the gap which too often exists between the will of the people and the translation of this will into law by legislators."[*] Not only that,

---

[*] George Gallup, "Opinion Polling in a Democracy," in *Statistics: A Guide to the Unknown.*

*"Seventy-three percent are in favor of one through five,
forty-one percent find six unfair, thirteen percent are opposed
to seven, sixty-two percent applauded eight, thirty-seven percent . . ."*

but such open-ended questions as "What do you consider to be the most urgent problems facing our country today?" can reveal areas of public concern that otherwise would be only vaguely sensed. In short, public opinion is an essential part of democratic government. Polls express this opinion accurately; the alternative is vague impressions and the loud voices of special interests.

Intelligent arguments against polling do not dispute that modern sampling methods guarantee that the polls will give results close to the results we would get if we put the poll questions to the entire population. Some would argue against opinion polls on the ground that we elect representatives to use their best judgment, not to slavishly follow public opinion. This seems to be no argument against polls; they only inform our governors what the opinion of the governed is and cannot force them to follow it.

More thoughtful critics ask what the opinions revealed by the polls are worth. Leo Bogart has written a provocative book that raises this very question.[10] He points out that many citizens will not have thought about an issue until a poller questions them. Unwilling to appear ignorant or uncaring, they will give hasty and uninformed answers. A question put by an interviewer who appears at the door as you were planning supper, a question with no responsibility attached to answering it, will get a low-quality opinion. As Bogart says, "We are likely to answer questions differently when we know the decision is really up to us." He doubts that the 62% of Americans who favored using atomic artillery shells against the Chinese Communists in a 1954 Gallup Poll would give the same answer if seriously faced with starting a nuclear war. If not all opinions are of equal weight, because some are uninformed and some are flippant, then "public opinion" is not the sum of individual opinions reported by the polls.

What is more, public opinions and attitudes are complex, not easily gauged by a few questions. Because of this (and because some of our answers to a poll lack serious thought), polls sometimes produce contradictory answers to related questions. Bogart points out that in 1969, over half of one sample favored President Nixon's anti-ballistic missile program, but over half of a second sample thought the money could be better spent on education, health, and other needs. What *is* public opinion, anyway? That's a question worth pondering.

Opinion polls conducted privately by candidates are now a common tool of campaign strategy. This is the second area of impact of polls on politics. The purpose of these polls is information for more effective campaigning. In what areas and with what groups of voters is the candidate weak? Where are large numbers of uncommitted voters to be found? Which of the opponent's views are liabilities to be exploited? What arguments are most effective in advocating the candidate's views? You might argue that campaigners have always sought such information and that sampling methods only replace vague impressions and intuition by reliable estimates.

Yet polls are sometimes viewed as part of the transformation of campaigns into exercises in marketing—selling the candidate to the consumers. By market research (sample surveys), the campaign manager discovers what the voters want and then, using all the devices of advertising and sales promotion, cleverly presents the candidate as satisfying those wants.

Most political professionals feel that attempting to present the candidate in a false light to fit voter preferences will fail. It is better politics to use poll results as guides in presenting the candidate's real views and concerns most effectively. If this is true, we as voters need not be alarmed by survey sampling as a campaign tool. As with any tool, it can be used unethically, but the ethical problem is the user rather than the tool. With attention, we should be able to accurately judge the candidate's programs and intentions.

Polls as election predictors are the third—and most dubious—political use of polls. I speak here of the results that fill the news before each election, informing us that Senator So-and-so is the choice of 58% of Ohio voters. Such polls are certainly popular, as they speak to our wish to know the future. The public is entitled to have its wants satisfied (within reasonable limits), so preelection polls will probably always be with us. Notice also that election polls do not have the drawbacks of opinion research. In an election poll, as in the voting booth, we are presented with a clear choice in an area where the decision is really up to us.

But election forecasts are somewhat shaky statistically, and some people think they have undesirable political effects. Let us examine both of these problems.

The key question asked in preelection polls takes the form "If the election were held today, would you vote for X or Y?" Here is the exact question from the Gallup Poll presidential election questionnaire:

Suppose you were voting TODAY for President and Vice President of the United States. Here is a Gallup Poll Secret Ballot listing the candidates for these offices. Will you please MARK that secret ballot for the candidates you favor today—and then drop the folded ballot into the box.

"Suppose you were voting today. . . ." Modern sampling methods give us great confidence that the sample result of the Lou Harris poll of November 2 and 3, 1984 (55% would vote for Reagan, 43% for Mondale, and 2% were undecided) was close to the truth about the population on that date. But the election is not being held today, and minds may change between the poll and the election. What is more, some of those who said for whom they would vote today will not take the trouble to vote for *anyone* on election day. Gallup and other pollsters make great efforts to determine how strongly their respondents hold their preferences and how likely they are to vote. For example, the Gallup Poll questionnaire included such questions as

- Where do people who live in this neighborhood go to vote?
- Are you NOW registered so that you can vote in the election this November?
- Do you, yourself, plan to vote in the election this November, or not?

But the problems of changing opinions and low voter turnout cannot be entirely avoided, especially in primary elections. Election forecasting is one of the less satisfactory uses of sampling.

Changing opinions were a major cause of the polls' famous failure in the 1948 Dewey–Truman election. The last poll was conducted three weeks before the election. It is likely (as the polls indicated) that Dewey was leading at the time, but Truman was gaining fast and continued to gain, winning an extremely close election. The other major cause of error was the sampling method. Interviewers were given quotas of voters by age, race, sex, and economic status, but selection of individual subjects was left to the interviewer. Such quota samples are far better than "straw polls" that depend on voluntary response, but they are not probability samples. We saw in Section 1 that such quotas favor the well dressed and prosperous. In political terms, such a poll has a Republican bias. Gallup and others overestimated the Republican vote in every election from 1936 to 1948, and in the close 1948 election this bias caused an incorrect forecast of a Republican victory.

The opinion polls switched to probability samples after 1948, and computers now enable the final poll to be taken three days rather than three weeks before the election. Despite the problem of failure to vote, election forecasts are now quite accurate. In the seven presidential elections from 1956 to 1980, the average error of Gallup's final preelection poll in predicting the winner's percentage of the popular vote was only 1.7%. Yet rapidly changing voter attitudes caught the polls again in 1980. Gallup underestimated Reagan's percent of the popular vote by 3.8%, and other polls had similar errors.

The political effects of election forecasts are much debated. Nobody maintains that they have any major beneficial effects. Here are some of the alleged disadvantages. Voters may decide to stay home if the polls predict a landslide (why bother to vote if the result is a foregone conclusion?). There is little evidence for this claim. But there is clear evidence that contributions dry up when the polls show that a candidate is weak. In particular, polls taken far in advance can make it difficult for a little-known candidate to gather resources for primary election campaigns. Such a candidate may do well if, despite the polls, resources are found for an effective campaign that captures the attention of the voters. The charge is that the effect of polls on both candidates and contributors may be to encourage them to act on practical calculations rather than on their convictions.

In reply, note that voters and contributors are likely to react only when the polls show a one-sided contest—a state of affairs that is clear even without polls. Potential contributors surely know that an unknown candidate is unknown. Mondale or Goldwater supporters surely knew that they were the minority. I see no substantial reason to fret over the effects of election forecasts. What is your opinion?

8.   Random selection as public policy

On January 23, 1976, the draft died, remembered but not mourned by the 50 million men who had been registered since selective service was initiated in 1948. Of these 50 million men, less than 5 million were inducted into the armed forces between 1948 and the end of inductions in 1972. Because only about 1 in 10 were actually drafted, how should the choice be made? For many years, an involved system of deferments, exemptions, and quotas was followed, with final decisions lying in the hands of local draft boards. But beginning in 1970, a draft lottery was introduced to choose draftees by random selection.

The idea of random selection is that of drawing lots—or of taking an SRS. The goal is to treat everyone identically by giving all the same chance to be selected. Random selection for military service was used during parts of World Wars I and II, and lotteries have been employed or proposed for other public policy purposes. A panel of the National Heart and Lung Institute predicted in 1973 that artificial hearts might be available within 10 years. Because as many as 50,000 patients a year might be helped by such a device (at enormous cost), the demand will exceed the supply. Who should receive them? The panel recommended that recipients be selected randomly from the pool of persons meeting similar medical criteria. Random selection has been used already to allot space in public housing to eligible applicants when there are more applicants than available housing units.

When should random selection decide public issues? I claim that this is a policy question, not a statistical question. Random selection does treat everyone identically; it is fair or unbiased in that sense. If a policy of identical treatment is desired, random selection is the tool that will implement that policy. Debate over random selection should concentrate on whether or not distinctions among persons are desirable in a certain situation. With the draft, Congress felt that distinctions ought not to be made, and so requested random selection. In the case of alloting public housing, a federal court has ruled that random selection is allowed only when applicants are equally needy. Distinctions *are* to be made among different degrees of need, so random selection is inappropriate for the entire pool of eligible applicants.

How is random selection carried out? In principle, the same way that an SRS is selected: Label everyone in the pool and use a table of random digits to select at random as many persons from the pool as are needed. In practice, random digits are not used. Instead, physical mixing and drawing of labels is used, for public relations reasons. Because few people understand random digits, the draft lottery looks fairer if a dignitary chooses capsules from a glass bowl in front of the TV cameras. This also prevents cheating; no one can check the table of random digits in advance to see how cousin Joe will make out in the selection.

Physical mixing *looks* random, but you may recall from Section 2 that it is devilishly hard to achieve a mixing that *is* random. There is no better illustration of this than the 1970 draft lottery. Because an SRS of all eligible men would be hopelessly awkward, the draft lottery aimed to select birth dates in a random order. Men born on the date chosen first would be drafted first, then those born on date number 2, and so on. Because all men ages 19 to 25 were included in the first lottery, 366 birth dates were to be drawn. Here is an account of the 1970 lottery:

They started out with 366 cylindrical capsules, one and a half inches long and one inch in diameter. The caps at the end were round.

The men counted out 31 capsules and inserted in them slips of paper with the January dates. The January capsules were then placed in a large square wooden box and pushed to one side with a cardboard divider, leaving part of the box empty.

The 29 February capsules were then poured into the empty portion of the box, counted again, and then scraped with the divider into the January capsules. Thus, according to Captain Pascoe, the January and February capsules were thoroughly mixed.

The same process was followed with each subsequent month, counting the capsules into the empty side of the box and then pushing them with the divider into the capsules of the previous months.

Thus, the January capsules were mixed with the other capsules 11 times, the February capsules 10 times and so on with the November capsules intermingled with others only twice and the December ones only once.

The box was then shut, and Colonel Fox shook it several times. He then carried it up three flights of stairs, a process that Captain Pascoe says further mixed the capsules.

The box was carried down the three flights shortly before the drawing began. In public view, the capsules were poured from the black box into the two-foot deep bowl.[11]

You can guess what happened. Dates in January tended to be on the bottom, while birth dates in December were put in last and tended to be on top. Newspaper reporters noticed at once that men born later in the year seemed to receive lower draft numbers, and statisticians soon showed that this trend was so strong that it would occur less than once in a thousand years of truly random lotteries. An inquiry was made, which produced the account quoted.

What's done is done, and off to Vietnam went too many men born in December. But for 1971, the captain and the colonel were given other duties, and

"So you were born in December too, eh?"

statisticians from the National Bureau of Standards were asked to design the lottery. Their design was worthy of Rube Goldberg. The numbers 1 to 365 (no leap year in 1951) were placed in capsules in a random order determined by a table of random digits. The dates of the year were placed in another set of capsules in a random order determined again by the random digit table. Then the date capsules were put into a drum in random order determined by a third use of the table of random digits. And the number capsules went into a second drum, again in random order. The drums were rotated for an hour. The TV cameras were turned on, and the dignitary reached into the date drum: Out came September 16. He reached into the number drum: Out came 139. So men born on September 16 received draft number 139. Back to both drums: Out came April 27 and draft number 235. And so on. It's awful, but it's random.[12] You can now rejoice that in choosing samples we have Table A to do the randomization for us.

9. Some ethical questions

Whenever our activities impinge on others (as they usually do), those activities should be carried on with sensitivity to their effects. Sampling of human populations is therefore a possible source of ethical problems. In general, the ethical problems posed by sample surveys are much less severe than those arising in experimentation with human subjects. This is because an experiment imposes some treatment (such as a new drug for a medical symptom), while a sample survey only seeks information or opinion from the respondents. Many ethical problems of survey work concern *deceiving respondents*; very rarely is any physical harm possible.

At one extreme of deceit is the use of false pretenses, as when encyclopedia salespersons pretend to be taking a survey in order to gain access to homes. This fraud has little to do with actual survey work and is detested by users of sample surveys because it increases resistance to genuine polling. Another extreme is covert collection of information. Covert operations are not limited to spy rings. Social psychologists, for example, have gathered data by "infiltrating" small religious groups under the pretense of sincere membership. Spies and researchers both give the same rationale for violation of privacy: The information they desire cannot be obtained by other methods. The moral problem is to decide when the information sought justifies such deceit.

Some withholding of information from subjects is often essential to avoid bias. A political poll sponsored by a candidate cannot tell subjects who is paying, for knowing that a representative of the Senator X Committee stood before us would influence our answers. Academic survey workers sometimes cannot tell subjects the full purpose of their research for the same reason. This withholding of information does not amount to active deceit, but certain safeguards are called for. The political poll representative should provide subjects with the name, address, and telephone number of the polling organization so that the subject has an avenue of recourse if the poll or its taker are offensive. (The polling organization must have a neutral name to avoid bias. This is easy if the candidate has hired a professional pollster; it is otherwise accomplished by setting up a polling office separate from the campaign office.) The academic researcher can inform subjects of the full purpose (and sometimes the results) of the research after the fact, thus providing the information that could not be given in advance. In any case, potential respondents always must be told how much time the interview will require, what kinds of information are wanted, and how widely this information will circulate with or without personal identification. Only then can the subject make an informed decision to participate or not.

A second area of ethical problems in sampling work is *anonymity and confidentiality*. These are not identical. Anonymity means that the respondent is anonymous; his or her name is not known even to the sampler. Anonymity causes severe problems because it is then not known who responded to a poll and who did not. This means that no follow-up work can be done to increase the response rate. And, of course, anonymity is usually possible only in mail surveys, where responses can be mailed in without any identification.

Confidentiality means that each individual response will be kept confidential, that only sample statistics from the entire sample or parts of it will be made public. Confidentiality is a basic requirement of most survey work, and any breach of confidentiality is a serious violation of professional standards. The best practice is to separate the identity of the respondent from the rest of the data at once and use the identification only to check on who did or did not respond.

Some common practices, however, seem to promise anonymity while actually delivering only confidentiality. Market researchers often use mail surveys that do not ask the respondent's identity but contain hidden codes on the questionnaire that do identify the respondent. Invisible ink coding and code numbers hidden under the flap of the return envelope are the usual techniques. A false claim of anonymity is clearly unethical; but if only confidentiality is promised, is it also unethical to hide the identifying code, thus perhaps causing respondents to believe their replies are anonymous? Here is a story to frame the question.

In 1975, the *National Observer* hired a survey firm to mail a detailed questionnaire to a sample of that newspaper's subscribers. The paper desired information about the tastes and lifestyles of its audience to aid its planning and advertising. The survey form was headed "A confidential survey" and was accompanied by a letter from the editor, Henry Gemmill, stating: "Each individual reply will be kept confidential, of course, but when your reply is combined with others from all over this land, we'll have a composite picture of our subscribers." Confidentiality was promised and observed. But because name and address were not requested, an impression of anonymity was created. One member of the sample, an optics professor, used ultraviolet light to detect an invisible ink code and wrote Gemmill a letter of complaint. Gemmill did not know that a hidden code had been used, and he reacted with outrage. He called it "slick trickery" in an article apologizing to subscribers. Gemmill also discovered that most market researchers felt that hidden codes were ethical as long as confidentiality was promised and observed. University survey researchers felt that hidden identification was not ethical and that open identification of respondents should be used to make follow-up possible. Some of the market researchers felt that this would reduce the response rate. What do you think?[13]

The *use of information* is the final area I wish to question. A rigorous standard would require public availability of all poll results. Otherwise, the possessors of poll results can use the information gained to their own advantage. This may involve acting on the information, releasing only selected parts of it, or timing the release for best effect. Private polls taken for political candidates are often used in these ways. Is it unrealistic to ask complete disclosure of poll results?

Whatever our response to this question, some aspects of disclosure are agreed upon. The information about the sampling process required by the AAPOR code of ethics (examined at the end of Section 5) should be revealed whenever a sample result is announced. In addition, the AAPOR code requires disclosure

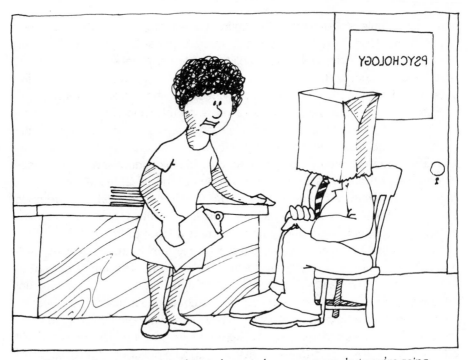

"I realize the participants in this study are to be anonymous, but you're going to have to expose your eyes."

of the identity of the sponsor of the survey. After all, we might more carefully inspect a poll paid for by a political party or other interest group than a poll sponsored by a news organization or other neutral party.

Finally, statisticians have an obligation to speak out when their work is misused by those who paid for it. The AAPOR code of ethics recognizes this responsibility in strong terms: "When we become aware of the appearance in public of serious distortions of our research we shall publicly disclose what is required to correct the distortions."

Potential abuses certainly exist in sampling, and we shall meet more difficult ethical problems in studying statistically designed experiments. These abuses and problems should not blind us to the fact that decisions based on incorrect information surely cause far more hardship. Because the statistical ideas we have met reduce the chance of incorrect information being used by decision makers, their overall ethical impact seems to me to be positive.

NOTES

1. Associated Press dispatch appearing in the *Lafayette* (Indiana) *Journal and Courier* of April 26, 1973.
2. From an article by Michael Kernan of the *Washington Post*, printed in the *Lafayette Journal and Courier* of August 19, 1976.

3. Rice's speech reported in the *New York Times* of February 19, 1974.

4. The evidence on this issue is discussed at length in Robert Rosenthal and Ralph L. Rosnow, *The Volunteer Subject* (New York: Wiley, 1975).

5. See the detailed discussion by Philip L. Martin, "Labor-Intensive Agriculture," *Scientific American*, October 1983, pp. 54–59.

6. Reported in *Public Opinion Quarterly*, Volume 35 (1971–1972), p. 54.

7. From the *New York Times* of August 18, 1980.

8. From a Gannett News Service dispatch appearing in the *Lafayette Journal and Courier* of November 24, 1983.

9. These are the words of John B. Lansing and James N. Morgan, *Economic Survey Sampling* (Institute for Social Research, The University of Michigan, 1971). This book is an excellent source of practical advice on carrying out sample surveys.

10. Leo Bogart, *Silent Politics: Polls and the Awareness of Public Opinion* (New York: Wiley-Interscience, 1972).

11. From the *New York Times* of January 4, 1970. Quoted with extensive discussion by Stephen E. Fienberg, "Randomization and Social Affairs: The 1970 Draft Lottery," *Science*, Volume 171 (1971), pp. 255–261.

12. It's even a little more complicated than I've described. For all the details, see Joan R. Rosenblatt and James J. Filliben, "Randomization and the Draft Lottery," *Science*, Volume 171 (1971), pp. 306–308.

13. The details in the text are taken from Henry Gemmill, "The Invisible Ink Caper," in the *National Observer* of November 1, 1975.

Exercises

Section 1

In each of Exercises 1–4, briefly identify the *population* (what is the basic unit and which units fall in the population?), the *variables* measured (what is the information desired?), and the *sample*. If the situation is not described in enough detail to completely identify the population, complete the description of the population in a reasonable way. Be sure that from your description it is possible to tell exactly when a unit is in the population and when it is not.

Moreover, each sampling situation described in Exercises 1–4 contains a serious source of probable bias. In each case, discuss the *reason* you suspect that bias will occur and also the *direction* of the likely bias. (That is, in what way will the sample conclusions probably differ from the truth about the population?)

1. A national newspaper wanted Iowa's reaction to President Reagan's agricultural policy in early 1984. A reporter interviewed the first 50 persons willing to give their views, all in a single voting precinct. The headline on the resulting article read "Reagan Policies Disenchant Iowa," and the reporter wrote that Reagan would lose an election in Iowa if one were held then.

2. A Congressman is interested in whether his constituents favor a proposed gun control bill. His staff reports that letters on the bill have been received from 361 constituents and that 283 of these oppose the bill.

3. A flour company wants to know what fraction of Minneapolis households bake some or all of their own bread. A sample of 500 residential addresses is taken, and interviewers are sent to these addresses. The interviewers are employed during regular working hours on weekdays and interview only during those hours.

4. The Chicago Police Department wants to know how black residents of Chicago feel about police service. A questionnaire with several questions about the police is prepared. A sample of 300 mailing addresses in predominantly black neighborhoods is chosen, and a police officer is sent to each address to administer the questionnaire to an adult living there.

5. You have probably seen the printer's filler ETAOINSHRDLU resulting from running a finger across a linotype keyboard. These are said to be the most frequently occurring letters in English. How do English and German differ in the frequency with which these letters occur? Open a book of English prose and a book of German prose haphazardly. Record how often each of these 12 letters occurs in the first 100 letters on the page you open to in each book.

   What is the population in this sampling exercise? What is the sample? What are the variables measured? Does the sampling method contain any serious sources of bias?

6. Advice columnist Ann Landers was once asked by a young couple whether having children was worth the problems involved. She asked her readers, "If you had it to do over again, would you have children?" A few weeks later, her column was headlined "70% OF PARENTS SAY KIDS NOT WORTH IT," for indeed 70 percent of the parents who wrote said they would not have children if they could make the choice again. (From the *Lafayette Journal and Courier* of January 23, 1976.) Do you think that this sample is biased? Why, and in what direction?

Section 2

1. Use Table A (Random Digits, p. 344) to select an SRS of 3 of the following 25 volunteers for a drug test. Be sure to say where you entered the table and how you used it.

Agarwal	Garcia	Petrucelli
Andrews	Healy	Reda
Baer	Hixson	Roberts
Berger	Lee	Shen
Brockman	Lynch	Smith

Casella	Milhalko	Sundheim
Frank	Moser	Wilson
Fuest	Musselman	
Fuhrmann	Pavnica	

2. A food processor has 50 large lots of canned mushrooms ready for shipment, each labeled with one of the lot numbers below.

A1109	A2056	A2219	A2381	B0001
A1123	A2083	A2336	A2382	B0012
A1186	A2084	A2337	A2383	B0046
A1197	A2100	A2338	A2384	B0123
A1198	A2108	A2339	A2385	B0124
A2016	A2113	A2340	A2390	B0125
A2017	A2119	A2351	A2396	B0138
A2020	A2124	A2352	A2410	B0139
A2029	A2125	A2367	A2411	B0145
A2032	A2130	A2372	A2500	B0151

An SRS of 5 lots must be chosen for inspection. Use Table A to do this, beginning at line 139.

3. An SRS of 25 of 440 voting precincts in a metropolitan region must be chosen for special voting-fraud surveillance on election day. Explain clearly how you would label the precincts. Then use Table A to choose the SRS, and list the precincts you selected. Enter Table A at line 117.

4. The following page contains a population of 80 circles. (They might represent fish in a pond or tumors removed in surgery.) Do a sampling experiment as follows:

   (a) Label the circles 00, 01, . . . , 79 in any order, and use Table A to draw an SRS of size 4.

   (b) Measure the diameter of each circle in your sample. (All of the circles have diameters that are multiples of 1/8 inch for convenience, so record the diameters as 1/8, 2/8, 3/8, etc.) Now compute the *mean* diameter of the four circles in your sample. (The mean of the diameters d_1, d_2, d_3, d_4 is the ordinary average

$$\frac{d_1 + d_2 + d_3 + d_4}{4}.$$

Because (4)(8) = 32, it is easiest to record the mean in 1/32s of an inch.)

   (c) Now repeat steps (a) and (b) three more times (four times in all) by using different parts of Table A. Was any circle chosen more than once in your four SRSs? How different were the mean diameters for the four samples?

(d) Now draw an SRS of size 16 from this population by taking a part of Table A not yet used in this exercise. Measure the diameters of the 16 circles in your sample and find the mean (average) diameter. (Because (16) (8) = 128, it is easiest to record this mean in 1/128s of an inch.)

Your results for SRSs of size 4 and 16 can be combined with those of the rest of the class to produce two pictures like the one in Figure 1-1. These pictures show less sampling variability for means of samples with size 16 than for samples with size 4.

5. Another way to sample the population of circles in Exercise 4 is to close your eyes and drop your pencil point at random onto the page. Mark the circle that you hit. Do this until you have hit 4 circles.
   (a) Is this (at least approximately) an SRS of size 4? Why or why not?
   (b) Think of these circles as cross sections of trees at breast height above the ground. Foresters who want to estimate the total volume of wood in a woodlot use a sampling method that has the same effect as dropping a pencil point into the circles. Explain why this is done.

6. Figure 1-3 is map of a census tract in Cedar Rapids, Iowa. [I took this map from *A Student's Workbook on the 1970 Census* (U.S. Department of Commerce, 1975). Statistics buffs will find this and the *1980 Census User's Guide* interesting.] Census tracts are small, homogenous areas averaging 4000 in population. An SRS of blocks from a census tract is often the penultimate stage in a sample survey. Use Table A beginning at line 125 to choose an SRS of 5 blocks from this tract. Note that each block has a Census Bureau identification number on the map.

7. Want to sample public opinion instantly and cheaply? AT&T will set up "900" telephone numbers that record how many calls are made to each number. Announce your question on TV, give a 900 number for "Yes" and another for "No," and wait. No word is needed from respondents; they just dial a number. AT&T will add a small charge to the phone bills of those who call. ABC-TV did this following the Reagan–Carter preelection debate in October 1980. The call-in poll proclaimed that Reagan had won the debate by a 2 to 1 margin. But a random survey by CBS News showed only a 44% to 36% margin for Reagan. Why are call-in polls likely to be biased? Can you suggest why this bias might have favored Reagan over Carter?

8. How bad is crime? It depends on whose statistics you look at. The annual FBI publication *Crime in the United States* says that the rate of rape rose by 38% between 1976 and 1980. The FBI data list crimes that are reported to law enforcement agencies. But the Census Bureau, as part of its monthly sample of about 60,000 households, asks people if they have been victims of a crime. This "victimization survey" usually shows over three times as many thefts as the FBI data but reports a smaller (12%) increase in the rate

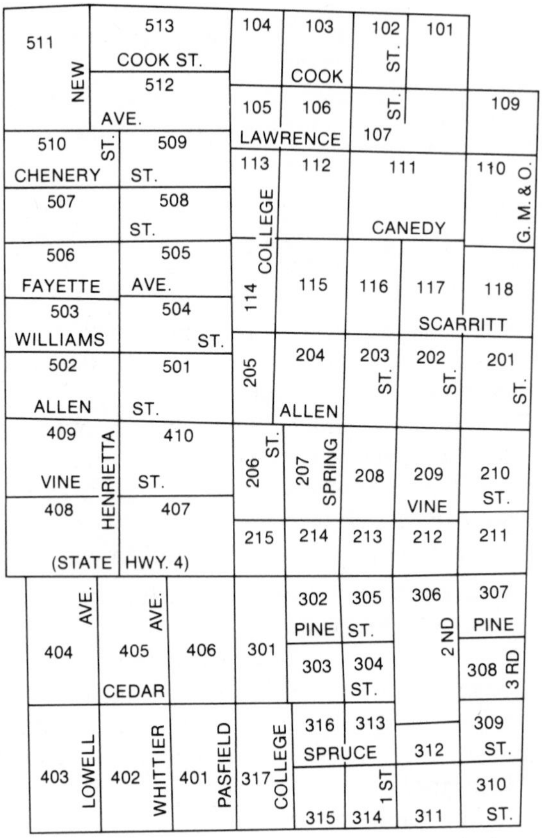

Figure 1-3.

of rape from 1976 to 1980. These two sets of data appear almost side by side in the *Statistical Abstract of the United States.*

Why does the Census Bureau survey report a higher theft rate than the FBI? Can you suggest reasons why the survey shows a smaller increase in rape than the FBI? Which source probably gives a more accurate picture of the amount of crime in the United States?

Section 3

Each boldface number in Exercises 1–3 is the value of either a *parameter* or a *statistic*. In each case, state which it is.

1. The Bureau of Labor Statistics announces that last month it interviewed a sample of 60,000 members of the labor force, of which **6.5%** were unemployed.

2. A carload lot of ball bearings has an average diameter of **2.503** cm. This is within the specifications for acceptance of the lot by the purchaser. But the acceptance sampling procedure happens to inspect 100 bearings from the lot with an average diameter of **2.515** cm. This is outside the specified limits, so the lot is mistakenly rejected.

3. A telephone sales outfit in Los Angeles uses a device that dials residential phone numbers in that city at random. Of the first 100 numbers dialed, **23** are unlisted numbers. This is not surprising, because **38%** of all Los Angeles residential phones are unlisted.

4. Figure 1-1 is a graph of the values of a sample statistic in 200 samples when the population parameter has the same value. Bias and lack of precision can be seen pictorially in such a graph of the sampling distribution as well as in the target illustration of Figure 1-2. Label each of the sampling distributions in Figure 1-4 as high or low bias and as high or low precision.

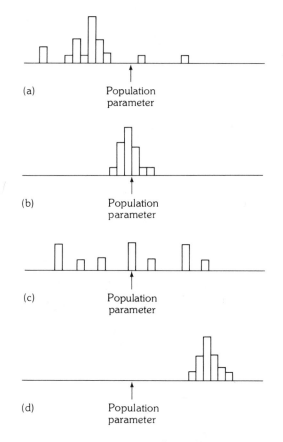

Figure 1-4.

5. I confess with some feelings of guilt that Figure 1-1 shows that my sampling procedure has a tendency to underestimate the true proportion, *p*, of dark beads in the population. How is this visible in the graph? Give a numerical measure of this bias by counting the number of samples that underestimated *p* and the number that overestimated it. (I don't know the cause of this bias. I suspected that the dark and light beads were of slightly different sizes, but not even with a micrometer could I verify this. Well, I *said* it is hard to get a true SRS by physical mixing and drawing.)

6. An agency of the federal government plans to take an SRS of residents in each state to estimate the proportion of owners of real estate in each state's population. States range from California (over 24 million) to Wyoming (under 500,000) in number of inhabitants.

   (a) Will the precision of the sample proportion change from state to state if an SRS of size 2000 is taken in each state? Explain your answer.

   (b) Will the precision of the sample proportion change from state to state if an SRS of 1/10 of 1% (0.001) of the state's population is taken in each state? Explain your answer.

7. The *New York Times*/CBS News Poll contacted 705 adults on September 14, 1983. Forty-six percent of this sample approved of how Mr. Reagan was handling his job as president. The *New York Times* publishes complete descriptions of its polling methods. Here is part of the description for this poll:

"In theory, in 19 cases out of 20 the results based on the entire sample will differ by no more than 4 percentage points in either direction from what would have been obtained by interviewing all adult Americans. The error for smaller subgroups is larger. For example, the margin of sampling error for men or women is plus or minus 5 percentage points." (From the *New York Times* of September 16, 1983.)

About half the sample consisted of women. But about half of adult Americans are women. Explain why in these circumstances the margin of error is larger for women alone than for all adults.

8. Not every household fills out the same form in the decennial census of the United States. Basic questions about the number of people in the household and their age, sex, race, and so on appear on all the forms. Other questions appear on only a sample of 20% of the forms. The Census Bureau publishes summary statistics for various geographic areas. For the questions that appear on all forms, these statistics are published for areas with as few as 100 households. But for questions appearing on the 20% sample, the bureau does not publish statistics for areas with fewer than about 2000 households. Can you think of possible reasons for this policy?

Section 4

1. A news article on a Gallup Poll noted that "28 percent of the 1548 adults questioned felt that those who were able to work should be taken off welfare."

The article also said, "The margin of error for a sample size of 1548 is plus or minus three percentage points." (From the *New York Times* of June 20, 1977.) Explain to someone who knows no statistics what "margin of error" means here.

2. A poll of 1000 voters uses the Gallup Poll's sampling design. Although 52% of the sample say they will vote for Ms. Caucus, the polling organization announces that the election is too close to call. Why is this the proper conclusion?

3. You ask a random sample of 1493 adults, chosen by the Gallup Poll's sampling method, "Are you afraid to go out at night within a mile of your home because of crime?" Of your sample, 672 say "Yes." Make a 95%-confidence statement about the percent of all adult Americans who fear to go out at night because of crime.

4. A national poll of 1433 adults find that 46% feel that the country's future will be better than the present. No margin of error is given in the news account you read. If the poll used a method much like Gallup's (and most do), what confidence statement can you make based on the information given?

5. A news report says, "The latest Harris survey on crime in America indicates that 26% of Americans feel less safe on the streets than they did a year ago." Can you make a confidence statement about this result? If so, make one. If not, explain why you cannot.

6. The final Gallup Poll prior to the 1980 presidential election interviewed 3509 people. This is a larger sample size than appears in Table 1-1. Is the margin of error of the result (46% would vote for Reagan) more or less than 3 percentage points? Why?

7. Though opinion polls usually make 95%-confidence statements, other confidence levels are in common use. The monthly unemployment rate, for example, is based on a Census Bureau survey of about 60,000 households. The margin of error in the announced unemployment rate is ±0.0019 (that is, 0.19%) with 90% confidence. Would you expect the margin of error for 95% confidence to be smaller or larger? Why?

Section 5

1. On the next page is a newspaper report of a public opinion poll, reprinted from the *New York Times* of June 2, 1977. At the end of Section 5 (p. 26) are some questions that should be answered by a careful account of a sample survey. Which of these questions does this newspaper report answer, and which not? Give the answers whenever the article contains them.

2. Read in *Statistics: A Guide to the Unknown* the articles by Hansen, "How to Count Better," and Taeuber, "Information for the Nation from a Sample Survey." Both articles describe a use of sampling and mention several prac-

---

Only About Half of Public Knows U.S. Has to Import Oil, Gallup Survey Shows

Only a little more than half of the American public is aware that the United States must import oil to meet its energy needs, according to the latest Gallup Poll.

Thirty-three percent of 1,506 adults interviewed April 29 through May 1 in more than 300 communities indicated they believed the country was self-sufficient in oil while 15 percent said they would not venture a guess.

Of those who were aware of the need to import oil, the Gallup organization reported, about a third (9 percent of all adults) knew that the amount shipped into the United States last year was 42 percent.

In the poll, Gallup found that residents of the Northeast and Midwest were more aware of the need to import oil than were people living in the warmer climates of the South and West.

Gallup said that the poll indicated that those who were best informed on the oil situation appeared to be most receptive to the call from President Carter for energy conservation and sacrifice.

For example, the polling organization said, among those who believe that Mr. Carter's proposals call for too many sacrifices on the part of the public 41 percent think "we have enough oil in this country."

Responding to the question, "From what you have heard or read, do you think we produce enough oil in this country to meet our present energy needs or do we have to import some oil from other countries," 52 percent replied "must import," 33 percent replied "produce enough" and 15 percent said "don't know."

---

tical difficulties and possible sources of error in the sampling application described. Describe in one sentence each such difficulty you find mentioned. Are there any that were not mentioned in the text?

3. Market research is sometimes based on samples chosen from telephone directories and contacted by telephone. The sampling frame therefore omits households having unlisted numbers and those without phones.
   (a) What groups of people do you think will be underrepresented by such a sampling procedure?
   (b) Can you think of any way to include in the sample households with unlisted telephone numbers?
   (c) Can you think of any way to include in the sample households without telephones?

4. We have seen that the method of collecting the data can influence the accuracy of sample results. The following methods have been used to collect data on television viewing in a sample household:
   (a) *The diary method.* The household is asked to keep a diary of all programs watched and who watched them for a week, then mail in the diary at the end of the week.
   (b) *The roster-recall method.* An interviewer shows the subject a list of programs for the preceding week and asks which programs were seen.
   (c) *The telephone-coincidental method.* The household is telephoned at a specific time and asked if the television is on, which program is being watched, and who is watching it.

(d) *The automatic recorder method.* A device attached to the set records what hours the set is on and which channel it is tuned to. At the end of the week, this record is removed from the recorder.

For each method, discuss its advantages and disadvantages, especially any possible sources of error associated with each method. Method (a) is the most commonly used. Do you agree with that choice? Explain. (Do not discuss choosing the sample, just collecting data once the sample is chosen.)

5. You wish to determine whether students at your school think that faculty are sufficiently available to students outside the classroom. You will select an SRS of 800 students.
   (a) Specify the exact population. (Will you include part-time students? Graduate students?)
   (b) How will you obtain a sampling frame?
   (c) How will you contact subjects? (Is door-to-door interviewing allowed in campus residence halls?)
   (d) What specific question or questions will you ask?

6. The monthly unemployment rate is estimated from the Current Population Survey (CPS), a probability sample of about 65,000 households each month conducted by the Bureau of the Census. It would be cheaper to choose one probability sample and reinterview the adults in the chosen households each month for a year or more. This is called using a *panel.* Because we are interested most of all in changes over time for employment and unemployment, a panel also has the advantage of following these changes for a group of people over time. Can you think of any disadvantages of the panel method?

7. The CPS uses a modified panel method. The sample is changed *every* month, but not completely. Once chosen, a household stays in the sample for four months, drops out for eight months, then returns for four more months before finally dropping from the sample. Which of the disadvantages that you listed in Exercise 6 will be partly overcome by this rotation system?

8. We have seen that the exact wording of questions can influence sample survey results. Two basic types of questions are *closed questions* and *open questions.* A closed question asks the subject for one or more of a fixed set of responses. An open question allows the subject to answer in his or her own words; the responses are written down verbatim by the interviewer and sorted later. For example, here are an open and a closed question on the same issue, both asked by the Gallup Poll within a few years of each other [Recorded in *Public Opinion Quarterly.* Volume 38 (1974–1975), pp. 492–493]:

OPEN: In recent years there has been a sharp increase in the nation's crime rate. What steps do you think should be taken to reduce crime?

CLOSED: Which two or three of the approaches listed on this card do you think would be the best ways to reduce crime?

Cleaning up social and economic conditions in our slums and ghettos that tend to breed drug addicts and criminals.

Putting more policemen on the job to prevent crimes and arrest more criminals.

Getting parents to exert stricter discipline over their children.

Improving conditions in our jails and prisons so that more people convicted of crimes will be rehabilitated and not go back to a life of crime.

Really cracking down on criminals by giving them longer prison terms to be served under the toughest possible conditions.

Reforming our courts so that persons charged with crimes can get fairer and speedier justice.

What are the advantages and disadvantages of open and closed questions? Use the example just given in your discussion.

9. Comment on each of the following as potential sample survey questions. If any are unclear or slanted, restate the question in better words.
    (a) Does your family use food stamps?
    (b) Which of these best represents your opinion on gun control?
        (1) The government should confiscate our guns.
        (2) We have the right to keep and bear arms.
    (c) In view of escalating environmental degradation and predictions of serious resource depletion, would you favor economic incentives for recycling of resource-intensive consumer goods?

10. Response to a proposal often varies with its source. Try the following: Tell several of your friends (don't burden yourself with selecting an SRS) that you are collecting opinions for a course. Ask some,

    Thomas Jefferson said, "I hold that a little rebellion, now and then, is a good thing, and as necessary in the political world as storms are in the physical." Do you generally agree or generally disagree with this statement?

    Ask others the same question, but replace "Thomas Jefferson said" with "Lenin said." (Be sure to ask each privately. To avoid bias, randomize the question you ask each person by tossing a coin.) Record the opinions you obtain and be prepared to discuss your results.

11. The noted scientist Dr. Iconu wanted to investigate attitudes toward television advertising among American college students. He decided to use a sample of 100 students. Students in freshman psychology (PSY 001) are required to serve as subjects for experimental work. Dr. Iconu obtained a class list for PSY 001 and chose a simple random sample of 100 of the 340 students on the list. He asked each of the 100 students in the sample the following question:

Do you agree or disagree that having commercials on TV is a fair price to pay for being able to watch it?

Of the 100 students in the sample, 82 marked "Agree." Dr. Iconu announced the result of his investigation by saying, "82% of American college students are in favor of TV commercials."

(a) What is the population in this example?

(b) What is the sampling frame in this example?

(c) Explain briefly why the sampling frame is or is not suitable.

(d) Discuss briefly the question Dr. Iconu asked. Is it a slanted question?

(e) Discuss briefly why Dr. Iconu's announced result is misleading.

(f) Dr. Iconu defended himself against criticism by pointing out that he had carefully selected a simple random sample from his sampling frame. Is this defense relevant?

Section 6

1. A university employs 2000 male and 500 female faculty members. The equal employment opportunity officer polls a stratified random sample of 200 male and 200 female faculty members.

(a) What is the chance that a particular female faculty member will be polled?

(b) What is the chance that a particular male faculty member will be polled?

(c) Explain why this is a probability sample.

(d) Each member of the sample is asked, "In your opinion, are female faculty members in general paid less than males with similar positions and qualifications?"

> 180 of the 200 females (90%) say "Yes."
> 60 of the 200 males (30%) say "Yes."

So 240 of the sample of 400 (60%) answered "Yes," and the officer therefore reports that "based on a sample, we can conclude that 60% of the total faculty feel that female members are underpaid relative to males." Explain why this conclusion is wrong.

(e) If we took a stratified random sample of 200 male and 50 female faculty members at this university, each member of the faculty would have the same chance of being chosen. What is that chance? Is this an SRS? Explain.

2. A club contains 25 students, named

Abel	Fisher	Huber	Moran	Reinmann
Carson	Golomb	Jack	Moskowitz	Silvers
Cryer	Griswold	Jones	Neyman	Sobar
David	Hein	Kiefer	O'Brien	Thompson
Elashoff	Holland	Lamb	Potter	Vlasic

and 10 faculty members, named

Andrews	Fischang	Knoll	Moore	Rabinowitz
Besicovitch	Gupta	Lightman	Phillips	Vincent

The club can send 4 students and 2 faculty members to a convention and decides to choose those who will go by random selection. Use Table A to choose a stratified random sample of 4 students and 2 faculty members. (There are two strata here, faculty and students. A stratified random sample can be taken only when the strata are chosen in advance and you can identify the members of each stratum.)

3. You have alphabetized lists of the 2000 male faculty and of the 500 female faculty at the university described in Exercise 1. Explain how you would assign labels and use Table A to choose a stratified random sample of 200 female and 200 male faculty members. What are the labels of the first 5 males and the first 5 females in your sample?

4. Using the information in Part (d) of Exercise 1, give an unbiased estimate of the proportion of the total faculty who feel that females are underpaid.

5. A city contains 33 supermarkets. A health inspector wants to check compliance with a new city ordinance on meat storage. Because of the time required, he can inspect only 10 markets. He decides to choose a stratified random sample and stratifies the markets by sales volume. Stratum A consists of 3 large chain stores; the inspector decides to inspect all 3. Stratum B consists of 10 smaller chain stores; 4 out of the 10 will be inspected. Stratum C consists of 20 locally owned small stores; 3 of these 20 will be inspected.

Let "Yes" mean that the store is in compliance and "No" mean that it is not. The population is as follows (unknown to the inspector, of course):

Stratum A			Stratum B			Stratum C				
Store	1	Yes	Store	1	No	Store	1	Yes	11	Yes
	2	Yes		2	Yes		2	Yes	12	Yes
	3	No		3	No		3	No	13	No
				4	No		4	Yes	14	Yes
				5	Yes		5	No	15	Yes
				6	No		6	No	16	No
				7	Yes		7	No	17	No
				8	No		8	Yes	18	No
				9	No		9	No	19	Yes
				10	Yes		10	No	20	Yes

(a) Use Table A to choose a stratified random sample of size 10 allotted among the strata as described above.

(b) Use your sample results to estimate the proportion of the entire population of stores in compliance with the ordinance.

(c) Use the description of the population given above to find the true proportion of stores in compliance. How accurate is the estimate from Part (b)?

6. Suppose that the final area chosen in a multistage sampling design contains 500 addresses, of which 5 must be selected. A systematic random sample is chosen as follows:

Step 1. Choose one of the first 100 addresses on the list at random. (Label them 00, 01, . . . , 99 and use a pair of digits from Table A to make the choice.)

Step 2. The sample consists of the address from Step 1 and the addresses 100, 200, 300, and 400 positions down the list from it.

For example, if 71 is chosen at random in Step 1, the systematic random sample consists of the addresses numbered 71, 171, 271, 371, and 471.

(a) Use Table A to choose a systematic random sample of 5 from a list of 500 addresses. Enter the table at line 130.

(b) What is the chance that a certain address will be chosen? Explain your answer.

(c) Is this an SRS? Explain your answer.

7. A group of librarians once wanted to estimate what fraction of books in large libraries falls in each of several size (height-and-width) categories. This information would help them plan shelving. To obtain it, they measured all of the several hundred thousand books in a library. Describe a sampling design that would have saved them time and money. That is, outline steps 1–4 at the end of Section 6 for a sampling design (simple or complicated) you would suggest to the librarians.

8. A labor organization wishes to study the attitudes of college faculty members toward collective bargaining. These attitudes appear to be different at different types of colleges. The American Association of University Professors classifies colleges as follows:

Class I	Offer the doctorate, and award at least 15 per year.
Class IIA	Award degrees above the bachelor's, but are not in Class I.
Class IIB	Award only bachelor's degrees.
Class III	Two-year colleges.

Describe a sampling design that would gather information for each class separately as well as overall information about faculty attitudes.

9. An important government sample survey is the monthly Current Population Survey (CPS), from which employment and unemployment statistics are produced. The sampling design of the CPS is described in the *BLS Hand-*

book of Methods (Bureau of Labor Statistics, 1982). Obtain the handbook from the library, and write a brief description of the multistage sample design used in the CPS.

10. Many nationwide surveys "sample the map"; that is, the sampling frame consists of identifiable geographic units rather than of a list of people or places. The Statistical Reporting Service of the U.S. Department of Agriculture makes extensive use of such "area frames" in its surveys of crops, farm economics, and so forth.
    (a) What are the general advantages and disadvantages of an area frame as opposed to a list of farms or mailing addresses? [Part (b) may help you here.]
    (b) The Agriculture Department finds that an area frame is preferred for surveys of the acreage planted in each crop, but a list frame is superior for surveys of farm income. Can you explain why?

11. One topic of this section has been estimation of population parameters from sample statistics in a variety of sampling designs. Estimation is much harder when a neat sampling design is not possible. As an example, read the essay by Douglas G. Chapman, "The Plight of the Whales," in *Statistics: A Guide to the Unknown.* Chapman describes three methods for estimating the size of an animal population, methods widely used in ecological studies. Which method would you use to estimate the total number of lake trout in Lake Winnebago, Wisconsin? Explain your answer.

Section 7

1. Never since the beginnings of opinion polls over 40 years ago have less than two-thirds of those sampled favored stronger controls on firearms. Specific gun control proposals have often been favored by 80% to 85% of respondents. Yet little national gun control legislation has passed, and no major national restrictions on firearms exist.

    Why do you think this has occurred? Does this mean that opinion polls on issues do not really offer the public a means of offsetting special-interest groups?

2. To see whether people often give responses on subjects they are entirely ignorant about, ask several persons (we won't ask for an SRS) the following questions:
    (a) Have you ever heard of the Taft-Johnson-Pepper bill on veteran's housing?
    (b) Have you ever heard of *Midwestern Life* magazine?

    (In a study of a few years ago, 53% said yes to (a) and 25% to (b) even though neither the bill nor the magazine ever existed. The study is cited by Dennis Trewin, "Non-sampling Errors in Sample Surveys," *CSIRO Division of Mathematics and Statistics Newsletter,* June 1977.)

3. Bogart (see Sourcenote 10) reports that during the 1968 campaign George Wallace accused the polls of favoring Eastern moneyed interests and neglecting the common people. He would ask crowds at his rallies, "Have any of you-all ever been asked about this here election by Mr. Harris or Mr. Gallup?" and receive shouts of "No" and "Never" in reply. (*Silent Politics*, p. 39).

If 170 million U.S. residents are of age 18 and over, and a poll selects 1700 at random, what is the chance that you will be interviewed? Suppose that the major polling organizations conduct 20 surveys during a presidential campaign. What is the chance that you will be interviewed at least once? (Being interviewed by an opinion poll is an unlikely event, and no accusations of bias are needed to explain why you haven't been chosen.)

4. A committee of the British Parliament suggested in 1966 that no poll results should be published during the three days before an election. Do you feel that this is a good idea? Explain.

5. Election-night television coverage features a sampling design that often allows quite precise predictions of the outcome before the polls have closed in parts of the country. (For a brief description, read Richard F. Link, "Election Night on Television," in *Statistics: A Guide to the Unknown*.) It is sometimes charged that late voters may stay home if the networks say that the national election is decided. Therefore, predictions based on samples of actual votes should not be allowed until the polls have closed *everywhere* in the country. Do you agree with this proposal? Explain your opinion.

6. The 1980 Gallup Poll election questionnaire cited in the text used a "secret ballot" arrangement. Why do you think this arrangement was used?

7. In the text we briefly examined the pros and cons of public opinion polls on issues. For more background, read Gallup's essay in *Statistics: A Guide to the Unknown* and the chapter "Polling and the Concept of Public Opinion" in Bogart's book. Come to class prepared to discuss using public opinion (as reported by polls) in government.

Section 8

1. Discuss the recommendation of the National Heart and Lung Institute panel that artificial hearts be allotted at random among patients of similar medical condition. Do you favor random selection? If not, how should recipients be chosen? By ability to pay? By value to society (as assessed by whom)? By age and family responsibilities?

2. Give an example of a situation where you definitely would *approve* random selection. Give an example of a situation where you would definitely *disapprove* random selection.

3. A basketball arena has 8000 student seats, but 18,000 students would like to watch basketball games. Design a system of allotting tickets that seems fair to you. (All students can see some of the 12 home games if you use a rotation system. Will you give upperclassmen some preference? How many tickets may an individual buy? Will you use random allotment, and how? If your school actually does use a random drawing to allot seats, describe the details of the official system and discuss any changes you favor.)

4. In 1975, the Dutch government adopted random selection for admissions to university programs in medicine, dentistry, and veterinary medicine. Applicants for these programs are much more numerous than available places. The random selection is stratified so that students with higher grades have a greater chance of being chosen. Do you favor such a system? Why?

Section 9

1. In what circumstances is collecting personal information without the subject's consent permitted? Consider the following cases in your discussion:
    (a) A government agency takes a random sample of income tax returns to obtain information on the average income of persons in different occupations. Only the incomes and occupations are recorded from the returns, not the names.
    (b) A psychologist asks a random sample of students to fill out a questionnaire; he explains that their responses will be used to measure several personality traits so that he can study how these traits are related. The psychologist does not inform the students that one trait measured by the test is how prejudiced they are toward other races.
    (c) A social psychologist attends public meetings of a religious sect to study the behavior patterns of members.
    (d) The social psychologist pretends to be converted to membership in a religious sect and attends private meetings to study and report the behavior patterns of members.

2. A researcher suspects that orthodox religious beliefs tend to be associated with an authoritarian personality. A questionnaire is prepared to measure authoritarian tendencies and also ask many religious questions. Write a description of the purpose of this research to be read to potential respondents. You must balance the conflicting goals of not deceiving respondents as to what the questionnaire will tell about them and of not biasing the sample by scaring off certain types of people.

3. Does having an abortion affect the health of mother or child in any future live births? To study this question, the New York State Health Department traced the reproductive histories of 21,000 women who had abortions in New York in 1970–1971 and compared them with 27,000 women who gave birth to living children in the same period. The comparison was carried out entirely with Health Department records, beginning in 1970 and tracing any later maternity records for these 48,000 women through 1977.

Do you consider this study an invasion of privacy? If you do, do you think the information to be gained and the difficulties in asking consent justify the study anyway?

4. The federal government, unlike opinion polls or academic researchers, has the legal power to compel response to survey questions. The long form, given to 20% of all households in the 1980 census, contained the following question:

H25. How many bathrooms do you have?

A _complete_ bathroom is a room with flush toilet, bathtub or shower, and _wash basin_ with piped water.

A _half_ bathroom has at least a flush toilet _or_ bathtub or shower, but does _not_ have all the facilities for a complete bathroom.

- ○ No bathroom, or only a half bathroom
- ○ 1 complete bathroom
- ○ 1 complete bathroom, plus half bath(s)
- ○ 2 or more complete bathrooms

(This is reproduced from an informational copy of the 1980 census form provided by the Census Bureau.)

Some members of Congress felt that this was an invasion of privacy and that the Census Bureau should be prohibited from asking such questions. The bureau replied that, as with all census data, no individual information would be released, only averages for various regions. Moreover, lack of plumbing is the best single measure of substandard housing, and the government needs this information to plan housing programs.

Do you feel that this question is proper? If not, when do you think that the government's need for information outweighs a citizen's wish to withhold personal facts? If you do think the plumbing question is proper, where does the citizen's right to withhold information begin?

5. If only confidentiality is promised and confidentiality is carefully observed, are hidden codes that identify respondents ethical? Do you agree with Mr. Gemmill that this is "trickery" or with those who claim that this practice serves a necessary purpose and does not violate the assurances given respondents?

6. Discuss how anonymity can be preserved while still recording who did and who did not respond to a survey. (See Exercise 6 in Section 7 for one idea.)

7. A radical critique of polling is given by Herbert I. Schiller, "Polls are Prostitutes for the Establishment," *Psychology Today,* July 1972, p. 20. His arguments, which apply to almost any sample survey, are
   (a) The poller exercises power over the respondent by wording questions and restricting alternatives in answering.

(b) Polls provide information about the respondent to the poller with no reciprocal flow of information in the other direction. They give power to the poller by allowing him to choose the uses of this information.

Thus Schiller feels that polls are an instrument of manipulation, enabling the poller to manipulate respondents. (Read his article, if possible.) Discuss Schiller's position and give your reasons for agreeing or disagreeing.

8. Do you favor requiring complete disclosure of the methods, sponsorship, and results (sample statistics only, never individual responses) of all sample surveys? In your discussion, you must balance any benefits of this policy against the cost of carrying it out and the resulting restriction on your ability to ask questions of other people.

9. One of the best discussions of the ethics of sampling is by Lester R. Frankel, "Statistics and People—the Statistician's Responsibilities," *Journal of the American Statistical Association*, Volume 71 (1976), pp. 9–16. Mr. Frankel was then president of the American Statistical Association and works for a firm specializing in sample surveys.

Read this article as an example of the ethical standards that survey statisticians currently hold. Make a list of the areas in which Frankel suggests guidelines for the behavior of survey takers.

Chapter 2

Experimentation

Experimentation differs from sample surveys (and other forms of observation) in that an experimenter controls or manipulates the environment of the units. In an experiment, researchers actively intervene by administering a treatment in order to study its effects. The great advantage of experimentation is that we can study the effects of the specific treatments that interest us, rather than simply observe units as they occur "in nature." Imagine the frustration of a researcher trying to study the effects of prolonged sleeplessness on reaction time by finding persons who just happen to have been awake for at least 48 hours. Instead, she performs the experiment of keeping volunteer subjects awake for 48 hours and then measuring their reaction time. She can even keep the subjects awake for 36, 48, 60, and 72 hours and measure their reaction times for each duration of sleeplessness. This kind of experimentation makes conclusions about the effect of sleeplessness on reaction time possible.

The intent of most experiments is to study the effect of changes in one variable (such as hours without sleep) on another variable (such as reaction time). We distinguish response, or *dependent*, variables from *independent* variables that the experimenter manipulates. Experiments often have several of each kind of variable. We might, for example, wish to study the effect of hours awake (independent variable A) and noise level (independent variable B) on reaction time (dependent variable 1) and score on a test of manual dexterity (dependent variable 2). The idea behind this terminology is that the dependent variables depend on the independent variables.

A sample survey may also study the effect of some variables (which thus become independent variables) on others (the dependent variables). A survey of natural deaths, for example, might study the relationship between the smoking habits of the deceased and the cause of death. It is clear that a sample survey may show a relationship between smoking and death from lung cancer, but it cannot show that smoking causes lung cancer. In principle, experiments can establish causation: If we change the value of an independent variable with no other changes in the experimental conditions, any resulting changes in a dependent variable must be caused by the changing independent variable. This ideal is not often achieved in real experiments. It is devilishly hard to arrange an experiment so that nothing affects the dependent variables except changes in the independent variables. Nonetheless, experimentation is far better than observation when we wish to conclude that one variable really does explain another. Sample surveys, on the other hand, are better suited for describing a population. Here is a summary of the vocabulary of experimentation:

Units—the basic objects on which the experiment is done. When the units are human beings, they are called *subjects*.

Variable—a measured characteristic of a unit.

Dependent variable—a variable whose changes we wish to study; a response variable.

Independent variable—a variable whose effect on the dependent variables we wish to study. An independent variable in an experiment is called a *factor*.

Treatment—any specific experimental condition applied to the units. A treatment is usually a combination of specific values (called *levels*) of each of the experimental factors.

Here is an example that illustrates our terminology:

Example 1. A fabrics researcher is studying the durability of a fabric under repeated washings. Because the durability may depend on the water temperature and the type of cleansing agent used, the researcher decides to investigate the effect of these two factors on durability. Factor A is water temperature and has three levels: hot (145°F), warm (100°F), and cold (50°F). Factor B is the cleansing agent and also has three levels: regular Tide, low-phosphate Tide, and Ivory Liquid. A treatment consists of washing a piece of the fabric (a unit) 50 times in a home automatic washer with a specific combination of water temperature and cleansing agent. The dependent variable is strength after 50 washes, measured by a fabric-testing machine that forces a steel ball through the fabric and records the fabric's resistance to breaking.

In this example there are 9 possible treatments (combinations of a temperature and a cleansing agent). By using them all, the researcher obtains a wealth of information on how temperature alone, washing agent alone, and the two in combination affect the durability of the fabric. For example, water temperature may have no effect on the strength of the fabric when regular Tide is used, but after 50 washings in low-phosphate Tide the fabric may be weaker when cold water is used instead of hot water. This kind of combination effect is called an *interaction* between cleansing agent and water temperature. Interactions can be important, as when a drug that ordinarily has no unpleasant side effects interacts with alcohol to knock out the patient who drinks a martini. Because an experiment can combine levels of several factors, interactions between the factors can be observed.

So experiments allow us to study factors of interest to us, either individually or in combination. And, an experiment can show that these factors actually cause certain effects. For these reasons, experimentation is the favored method of collecting data whenever our goal is to study the effects of variables rather than simply to describe a population. Experiments are universal in the physical and life sciences. They are carried out whenever possible in the social sciences (that's quite often in psychology, but less often in sociology or economics). Some experiments influence the lives of all of us. For example, the safety of food additives and the safety and effectiveness of drugs must be demonstrated by experiment before public use is allowed.

In this chapter we are concerned with the statistical ideas of experimental design. The *design of an experiment* is the pattern or outline according to which treatments are applied to units. The basic concepts of experimental design apply to experiments in all areas, whether they study agricultural fertilizers, vaccines, or teaching methods.

1.   The need for experimental design

Laboratory experiments often have a simple design, such as

(1)   Treatment → Observation

in which a treatment is applied (often to several units) and its effect is observed.

If before-and-after measurements are made, the design is

(2)   Observation 1 → Treatment → Observation 2

Statistical ideas are not used in the design of such simple experiments. (These experiments are "simple" in their design or pattern, even though the treatment may be quite complex.) When experiments are conducted outside the controlled environment of a laboratory, simple designs such as (1) and (2) often yield *invalid* data; we cannot tell whether the treatment had an effect on the units. The same sad tale must often be told of observational studies, such as sample surveys. Some examples will show what can go wrong.

> **Example 2.** In 1940, a psychologist conducted a study of the effect of propaganda on attitude toward a foreign government. He devised a test of attitude toward the German government and administered it to a group of American students. After reading German propaganda material for several months, the students were tested again to see if their attitudes had changed. This experiment had a design of the form (2), namely,
>
> Test of attitude → Reading of propaganda → Retest of attitude
>
> Unfortunately, Germany attacked and conquered France while the experiment was in progress. There was a profound change of attitude toward the German government between the test and the retest, but we shall never know how much of this change was due to the independent variable (reading propaganda) and how much to the historical events of that time. The data are invalid; they give no information about the effect of reading propaganda.

> **Example 3.** A high school Latin teacher wished to demonstrate the favorable effect of studying Latin on mastery of English. She therefore obtained from the school records the scores of all seniors on a standard English-proficiency examination. The average score for seniors who had studied Latin was much higher than the average score for those who had not. The Latin teacher concluded that "the study of Latin greatly improves one's command of English." But students elect whether or not to study Latin. Those who elect Latin are probably (on the average) both smarter and more interested in language than those who do not. This self-selected group would have a higher average English-proficiency score whether or not they studied Latin. Whether studying Latin raised their English scores yet more we cannot tell; the data are invalid for this purpose. (This is a census of the school's seniors, not an experiment. But it is similar to Example 2 in that the effect of the independent variable on the dependent variable cannot be ascertained.)

No valid conclusion can be drawn in either of these examples because the effect of the independent variable cannot be distinguished from the effect of influences outside the study. Variables not of interest in a study that nonetheless influence the dependent variable are *extraneous variables*. In Example 2, reading propaganda is the experimental factor (the independent variable), and the events of current history are an extraneous variable. In Example 3, study of Latin is the independent variable and the innate ability of the students is an extraneous variable.

The effects of two variables (independent variables or extraneous variables) on a dependent variable are said to be *confounded* when they cannot be distinguished from one another.

In Example 2, the effect of reading propaganda was confounded with the effect of historical events; the influences of these two variables on attitude toward Germany cannot be separated. In Example 3, the effect of studying Latin was confounded with the ability of the students; both influence English-proficiency scores, and their influences cannot be separated.

Confounding of different variables (mixing up of their effects) often obscures the true effect of independent variables on a dependent variable. Here are some additional examples:

Example 4. An article in a women's magazine reported that women who nurse their babies feel warmer and more receptive toward the infants than mothers who bottle-feed. The author concluded that nursing has desirable effects on the mother's attitude toward the child. But women choose whether to nurse or bottle-feed, and it is possible that those who already feel receptive toward the child choose to nurse, while those to whom the baby is a nuisance choose the bottle. The effect on the mother's attitude of the method of feeding is confounded with the already existing attitude of the mother toward the child. Observational studies of cause and effect, such as this one, rarely lead to clear conclusions because confounding with extraneous variables almost always occurs.

Example 5. A particularly important example of confounding occurs in clinical trials of drugs and other medical treatments. Many patients respond positively to *any* treatment, even a dummy medication such as a sugar pill. This is presumably a reaction to receiving personal attention and especially to the authority of the doctor who administers the treatment. Dummy medications are called *placebos*, and the response of patients to any treatment in which they have confidence is called the *placebo effect*. Many studies have shown, for example, that placebos relieve pain in 30% to 40% of patients, even those recovering from surgery.

The placebo effect is not confined to the patient's imagination. Not only subjective effects (''My pain is less'') but objectively measured responses often occur. In a clinical trial of the effectiveness of vitamin C in preventing colds, patients who were given a placebo that they thought was vitamin C actually had fewer colds than patients given vitamin C who thought it was a placebo! There is no doubt that faith healing works (sometimes).

Experiments of the designs (1) and (2), therefore, are often useless in testing drugs or other medical treatments. The placebo effect is confounded with the effect of the treatment; the patients might have responded as well to a sugar pill as they did to the drug being tested.

So both observation and simple experiments often yield invalid data owing to confounding with extraneous variables. This situation is difficult to remedy when only observation is possible. Experiments offer the possibility of escaping the effects of confounding in ways not possible by observation alone. The first goal of experimental design is to make possible valid conclusions—to enable us to say how the independent variables affected the dependent variables. It is now clear that some new ideas are needed to reach this goal.

''I want to make one thing perfectly clear, Mr. Smith. The medication I prescribe will cure that run-down feeling.''

2.   First steps in statistical design of experiments

The central idea in avoiding confounding of experimental with extraneous variables is _comparative experimentation_. If we can set up two equivalent groups of units, then give the treatment to only one group (the experimental group) while treating the other group (the control group) exactly the same in every way except that it does not receive the treatment, then any differences between the groups at the end of the experiment must be due to the effect of the treatment. Any extraneous variables influence _both_ groups, while the experimental treatment influences only one; so by comparing the two groups, the effect of the treatment can be discovered. If two treatments (two drugs, or two fertilizers, for example) are to be compared, we can give one to each of two equivalent groups, and no control group is needed.

Comparative studies need not be experiments. We might, for example, assess the safety of various surgical anesthetics by analyzing hospital records to compare death rates during surgery when the different anesthetics are used. But the groups being compared are not equivalent, for some anesthetics tend to be used in serious operations, or on patients who are old or in poor physical condition, while others are used in less risky situations. A high death rate may mean only that this anesthetic is used in high-risk operations.* If comparison is to eliminate such confounding, we must have equivalent groups of subjects. Arranging for equivalent groups to receive the treatments is the kind of active intervention that distinguishes experiments from other types of studies.

Comparative experimentation was first used in earnest in agricultural research, beginning in the nineteenth century. Agronomists tried to obtain equivalent groups of units (small plots of land) by carefully matching plots in fertility, soil type, and other variables. It is difficult to match units in all important extraneous variables—especially because the experimenter may not think of them all ahead of time! What is more, experimenter judgment in assigning units to groups opens the door to bias. A medical researcher may unconsciously tend to assign more seriously ill patients to the standard treatment and leave less serious cases to the new and untried treatment. The moral is clear: If comparative experimentation is to be effective, we need a better way of assigning units to groups.

The better way was provided in the 1920s by R. A. Fisher, a statistician

---

* An account of the most important study of this problem appears in Lincoln E. Moses and Frederick Mosteller, "Safety of Anesthetics," in _Statistics: A Guide to the Unknown._ Because the hospital records contained information on the kind of surgery and type of patient, it was possible to correct for the effects of these extraneous variables.

working for an English agricultural experiment station.* Fisher realized that equivalent groups for experimental use can be obtained by *randomly assigning* units to groups. Just as a simple random sample is likely to be representative of the population, so a random selection of, say, half the units available is likely to create two groups (the one selected and the one left behind) similar in *every* respect. We have now reached the simplest statistically designed experiment:

(3)

$$\text{Random allocation} \nearrow \begin{array}{l} \text{Group 1} \rightarrow \text{Treatment} \rightarrow \text{Observation} \\ \\ \text{Group 2} \rightarrow \begin{array}{c} \text{No treatment} \\ \text{or alternative} \\ \text{treatment} \end{array} \rightarrow \text{Observation} \end{array}$$

This is the replacement for design (1), which involved no comparison. If before-and-after observations are made, as in design (2), we simply make them on each group:

(4)

$$\text{Random allocation} \nearrow \begin{array}{l} \text{Observation 1} \rightarrow \text{Treatment} \rightarrow \text{Observation 2} \\ \\ \text{Observation 1} \rightarrow \begin{array}{c} \text{No treatment} \\ \text{or alternative} \\ \text{treatment} \end{array} \rightarrow \text{Observation 2} \end{array}$$

Let us study some examples of simple designed experiments.

> **Example 6.** Suppose that we wish to give an experimental design for the propaganda study (Example 2 on p. 66) that will allow conclusions to be drawn. There are 100 subjects available. We first choose an SRS of 50 subjects in the usual way: Label the subjects 00, 01, . . . , 99 and use the table of random digits to choose 50. If we enter the table in line 136, we obtain
>
> Group 1
>
> | | | | | | | | | | |
> |----|----|----|----|----|----|----|----|----|----|
> | 08 | 42 | 14 | 47 | 53 | 77 | 37 | 72 | 87 | 44 |
> | 75 | 59 | 20 | 85 | 63 | 79 | 09 | 24 | 54 | 64 |
> | 56 | 68 | 12 | 61 | 78 | 36 | 60 | 91 | 73 | 98 |
> | 48 | 11 | 45 | 92 | 66 | 83 | 16 | 89 | 40 | 22 |
> | 15 | 58 | 13 | 35 | 86 | 17 | 70 | 69 | 28 | 55 |

---

* Sir Ronald Aylmer Fisher (1890–1962) was one of the century's greatest scientists in two fields, genetics and statistics. He invented statistical design of experiments and much else besides.

Group 2 consists of the 50 remaining subjects. All 100 subjects are tested for attitude toward the German government. The 50 subjects in Group 1 then read German propaganda regularly for several months, while the 50 subjects in Group 2 are instructed not to read German propaganda; otherwise, both groups go about their normal lives. Then all 100 subjects are retested. This experiment has the design (4):

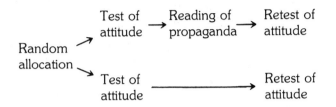

If Group 1 shows a more positive (or less negative) change in attitude toward Germany between test and retest, we can attribute this difference to the effect of reading propaganda.

Some comments on Example 6 are in order. First, notice that "random allocation" to Groups 1 and 2 is done by selecting an SRS from the available units to be Group 1. (Please check the use of the table of random digits in Example 6 if you are unsure of how to do this.) The purpose of randomization is to create groups that are equivalent prior to the experiment. Many variables (e.g., sex, age, race, religion, political opinion) may influence a subject's reaction to German propaganda. Random allocation should "average out" the effects of these extraneous variables by dividing them evenly between the groups. Moreover, random allocation will average out the effects of extraneous variables we have not thought of, as well as those we have listed.

Second, notice how randomization and *control* ensure that valid conclusions can be drawn. The control group shares the experiences of the experimental group except for propaganda reading. The fall of France, for example, influences the attitudes of both groups. The groups were equivalent prior to the experiment (we can check this by comparing their average scores on the first test), and the groups were identically treated except that Group 1 read propaganda while Group 2 did not. So any difference in the average change in the attitudes of the two groups must be due to the effect of the propaganda. It might happen, for example, that the attitude of both groups becomes much more negative after the fall of France, but the attitude of Group 1 changes less in the negative direction than does the attitude of Group 2. This would show the effect of the propaganda read by Group 1 but not by Group 2.

Example 7. It has been claimed, most notably by the two-time Nobel laureate Linus Pauling, that large doses of vitamin C will prevent colds. An experiment to test this claim was performed in Toronto in the winter of 1971–1972. About 500 volunteer subjects were randomly allocated to each of two groups. Group 1 received 1 gram per day of vitamin C and 4 grams per day at the first sign of a cold. (This is a large amount of vitamin C; the recommended daily allowance of this vitamin for adults is only 60 milligrams, or 60/1000 of a gram.) Group 2 served as a control group, receiving a placebo pill identical in appearance to the vitamin C capsules. Both groups were regularly checked for illness during the winter. The experimental design is (3):

Random allocation
Group 1 ⟶ Vitamin C ⟶ Health checked
Group 2 ⟶ Placebo ⟶ Health checked

Some of the subjects dropped out of the experiment for various reasons, but 818 completed at least two months. Groups 1 and 2 remained well matched in age, occupation, smoking habits, and other extraneous variables. At the end of the winter, 26% of the subjects in Group 1 had not had a cold, compared with 18% in Group 2. Thus vitamin C does appear to prevent colds better than a placebo—but not much better.[1]

Again, in Example 7, confounding has been avoided, so the effect of the treatment can be separated from the effects of extraneous variables, including the placebo effect. If Group 2 had received nothing, the effect of vitamin C would still have been confounded with the placebo effect, because Group 1 might be responding to being given any treatment at all. As it is, *both* groups receive pills, and both were equivalent before the experiment began, so the chemical effect of vitamin C is the only difference between the groups. So we should be able to draw valid conclusions as to whether vitamin C prevents colds better than a placebo does.

Examples 6 and 7 show how valid data can be obtained in the settings of Examples 2 and 5 by a simple experimental design. Examples 3 and 4 are observational studies. Simple experiments also would yield valid data in those settings. But such experiments would mean randomly assigning students to study or avoid Latin, and women to nurse or bottle-feed their children. These treatments cannot be imposed, for practical and moral reasons. It is only when experimentation is not possible that we try (often without success) to study cause and effect by observation alone.

Randomization in an experiment is the analog of probability sampling in a sample survey and serves the same purposes. Randomization is a fair or unbiased way of assigning units to experimental groups, just as an SRS is a fair or unbiased way of selecting units from a population. As in sampling, randomization in experimental design has a less obvious but equally important function. Recall that probability sampling produces sample statistics having a known sampling distribution, so we know how likely the statistic is to fall within any given distance of the population parameter. In a similar sense, if experimental units are randomly allocated to treatments, we know how likely is any degree of difference among the groups. For example, in the Toronto vitamin C experiment, a difference between the groups of 26% versus 18% illness-free was observed. Because of the use of randomization, we can say that if the two treatments (viz.,vitamin C and placebo) have the same effect, a difference at least this large would occur in less than 1% of a large number of experiments. We therefore can be confident that the difference is due to the differing effects of the treatments. Randomization as the basis for drawing conclusions will receive much attention in Chapter 9. At this point, we concentrate instead on randomization as a means of eliminating possible bias by averaging extraneous variables and creating equivalent groups that allow valid comparison of treatments.

Increasing the number of units assigned to each group has the same effect as increasing the size of a sample. In both cases, a greater number of observations produces less variable (more precise) results. That is, we can be more confident that a repetition of the experiment would give results that differ little from those we obtained. Thus we can be more confident that our experimental results reflect the effect of the treatments and are not just an accident arising from bad luck in the random assignment of units to groups. Let us sum up the analogy between random sampling and randomized experiments.

1. **Random sampling has no bias; it favors no part of the population in choosing a sample. Random allocation of experimental units to groups has no bias; units with special properties are not favored in choosing any group.**

2. **The sample obtained by random sampling varies in repeated sampling and may be unrepresentative of the population. The experimental groups obtained by randomization vary in repeated trials and may fail to be closely equivalent.**

3. **Using larger random samples decreases the variability of the result and increases our confidence that the sample is representative of the population. Using larger randomly chosen groups of experimental units decreases the variability of the result and increases our confidence that the groups are equivalent before treatments are applied.**

How well does randomization work in practice? Here is an example in which this question was investigated:

> **Example 8.** When the University Group Diabetes Program, a major medical experiment on treatments for diabetes, produced evidence that the drug tolbutamide was ineffective and perhaps unsafe, the design of the experiment was questioned. In response, statistician Jerome Cornfield wrote a detailed account of the conduct of the study that includes a look at the effectiveness of the randomization.[2]
>
> Subjects were randomly assigned to four treatments. The tolbutamide group showed higher cardiovascular mortality (i.e., more subjects died of heart attacks) than the other groups. Could this have happened because the tolbutamide group contained higher-risk subjects? Cornfield examined how patients with each of eight "risk factors" that increase the chance of a heart attack were distributed among the groups. These risk factors were age 55 or older, high blood pressure, history of digitalis use, history of chest pains, abnormal electrocardiogram, high cholesterol level, overweight, and calcification of the arteries. The results appear in Table 2-1. The groups do appear quite equivalent in these risk factors. For example, 84.9% of the patients assigned to placebo had one or more risk factors, compared with 86.8% of those assigned to tolbutamide. "All in all," Cornfield commented, "the luck of the draw does not seem to have been too

Table 2-1. Number of subjects in the University Group Diabetes Program having each number of risk factors*

Number of risk factors	Group 1 (placebo)	Group 2 (tolbutamide)	Group 3 (insulin standard)	Group 4 (insulin variable)
0	28	25	22	15
1	60	50	62	76
2	59	58	60	57
3	26	34	34	30
4	10	17	8	4
5	2	4	8	4
6	0	1	1	1
Total number of subjects	185	189	195	187

SOURCE: Jerome Comfield, "The University Group Diabetes Program," *Journal of the American Medical Association*, September 20, 1971, pp. 1676–1687. Copyright 1971, American Medical Association.
* This table covers the 756 subjects (out of a total of 823) for which information on all eight risk factors was available.

bad." He reminded his medical readers that randomization achieves groups also comparable in other extraneous variables, such as a patient's smoking history, for which information was not available.

The simplest kind of randomization allocates experimental units at random among *all* treatments. Such experimental designs are called *completely randomized designs*. They correspond to the SRS in sampling. The designs (3) and (4) are completely randomized designs with two groups. If more treatments are to be compared, we can randomly divide the units into more groups. It is not necessary to allot the same number of units to each group, but the data are easier to use when this is done. The University Group Diabetes Study (Example 8) was a completely randomized design with four groups. This design is illustrated in the following figure:

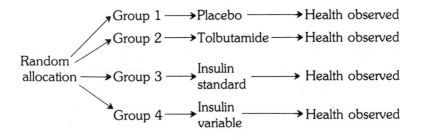

3. Difficulties in experimentation

Just as probability sampling does not ensure accurate results from a sample survey, so statistically designed experiments are not a total solution to the problem of obtaining valid experimental data. In this section, we increase our understanding of experimentation by looking at some common difficulties in drawing valid conclusions.

Difficulty 1: To what population do the conclusions apply?

If you've seen one alpha particle, you've seen them all. So experimental conclusions about alpha particles reached in Denmark in 1923 remain true in Berkeley in 1983. The physical sciences often work with essentially identical experimental units. This has two heavenly consequences: Random assignment is not needed to create equivalent groups when all units are identical, and conclusions about one set of units generalize to the population of all such units. In other areas of study, the units are often highly variable. This may be due to variation in the units themselves or to the effects of extraneous variables. We know that random assignment can, on the average, create equivalent groups from variable units. Now we must ask how widely one can apply the conclusions from such an experiment. An example will convey the difficulty.

> **Example 9.** A psychologist selects as experimental subjects students enrolled in freshman psychology, PSY 001, at Upper Wabash University. Because two treatments are being compared, the students are assigned at random to two groups; that is, design (3) of Section 2 is used. There is a large difference in the average response of the two groups, too large to be reasonably due to the accidents of random assignment. The psychologist therefore concludes that the effects of the two treatments on the units differ.

For what population is this conclusion valid? In a strict sense, only for the group of students who served as subjects. If they are not representative of some larger population, the experimental conclusions are not valid for any larger population. The situation is quite similar to taking an SRS from a sampling frame that is not representative of the population. To take an extreme example, an experiment on psychological reactions to a pain-relieving drug, however well designed, will not give valid conclusions about adults in general if the subjects are mental patients.

What shall we do? the ideal solution is clear: Take an SRS from the population of interest to obtain the experimental subjects, and then apply the random assignment needed for the experiment. This ensures (or at least makes it very likely) that the experimental subjects are representative of the larger population. Such an ideal solution is almost never possible in practice. What *is* possible is to use an SRS from the pool of available subjects. The psychologist, for instance, should draw an SRS of PSY 001 students rather than allow students to choose which of a list of experiments they will participate in. If, for example, his experiment concerns the effect of watching pornographic movies, the reactions of students who choose to watch may differ sharply from the reactions of randomly selected students. (Of course, telling randomly selected students they must watch pornography is morally objectionable, so student choice of experiments rather than random selection is often necessary. It's enough to make psychologists envy physicists.)

If the experimental subjects are an SRS of a pool of available units, the experimental results are surely valid for that pool. Our psychologist can now draw conclusions about the population of students in PSY 001 this semester.

No doubt he had grander things in mind. So he must start being persuasive: He must persuade us that his experimental subjects are representative of some larger population. Here he draws on his understanding of his subject matter, not on statistics. If the experiment involved eye movements in response to visual stimuli, the experimenter can probably persuade us that the conclusions are valid for all persons with normal vision. If the experiment involved response to pornographic films, it is not clear that conclusions drawn from student subjects can be generalized to executives. If the subjects were volunteers, this limits still more the population to which the conclusions apply.

Difficulty 2: Lack of realism

Our psychologist, let us say, is interested in response to frustration. His experiment requires the subjects to play a game rigged against them. The game demands team cooperation, and the experimenter will observe the relations among team members as they repeatedly lose. This is an artificial situation, and the PSY 001 students know it's "only an experiment," even if they don't know that the game is rigged. Do their reactions in this situation give information about their response to genuine frustration outside the laboratory? As with Difficulty 1, the question involves how much the experimental conclusions can be generalized. But the barrier to general conclusions here is the lack of realism of the experimental treatment. Once again the experimenter must try to persuade us. And once again the eye-movements expert has a better case than the student of pornography or frustration. Inability to apply realistic treatments is a serious barrier to effective experimentation in many areas of the social sciences.

Lack of realism in experiments is an issue that touches our health and prosperity more than do the frustrations of social scientists. Food additives are required, not unreasonably, to be safe. The Food and Drug Administration (FDA) is charged with seeing that they are safe. The FDA's exercise of judgment is restricted by laws, in particular by the famous Delaney Amendment of 1958, an all-or-nothing statement that outlaws additives found to cause cancer in

---

THE DELANEY AMENDMENT

Sec. 409 (c) (3) (A). No additive shall be deemed to be safe if it is found to induce cancer when ingested by man or animal, or if it is found, after tests which are appropriate for the evaluation of the safety of food additives, to induce cancer in man or animal.
—*Federal Food, Drug and Cosmetic Act, 1958*

human *or animal*. A typical trial of a food additive involves adding large amounts of the substance to the diet of laboratory rats. If significantly more tumors appear in this experimental group than in the control group of rats fed an additive-free diet, the additive is found guilty and must be banned.

Now, such an experiment can provide strong evidence that large doses of an additive over a short period do (or don't) induce cancer in rats. We would really like to know whether small doses over a long period induce cancer in people. As the list of condemned additives grows (cyclamates, the food color Red 2, saccharin, . . .), so does the grumbling. Part of the grumbling is about the all-or-nothing character of the law. Surely, some say, if so useful a substance as saccharin causes just a little cancer, we ought to allow it in our colas, cookies, and cakes. That's a policy question, not a scientific question, and I leave you to choose your own poison. But part of the grumbling concerns the realism of rat experiments as indicators of human health hazards.

Informed opinion holds that the rats can be trusted in general. But every species has its peculiarities, and the case of the universally used sweetener saccharin may ride on a peculiarity of rats. Saccharin caused bladder tumors in rat trials, and the bladders of rats are special. Rats concentrate their urine very highly before excreting it. Saccharin is not metabolized but is excreted unchanged. So the saccharin sits there in the rat bladders for a long time, in raw form and in high concentration, waiting for the rat to get around to urinating. Some respectable scientists think that all that saccharin could cause tumors by physically irritating the bladder—only in rats, of course, not in people.

Can we check this hypothesis that saccharin does not cause bladder cancer in humans? Not easily. Such experiments on people are frowned on. We might try to see if bladder-cancer patients tend to be heavy users of saccharin. Several such observational studies have shown no link, but these studies are not sensitive enough to detect the small increase in cancer predicted by the animal experiments. Saccharin remains on the market by special decree of Congress, despite the scientific consensus that it probably does cause just a little cancer.[3]

This—and many another—example points to a clear principle: Rarely does a single experiment definitely establish that A causes B; there is almost always some flaw. (What flaws there might be is the subject of this section.) Repeated experiments, perhaps combined with other kinds of studies, are usually needed to found a conclusion on rock rather than sand.

Difficulty 3: Avoiding hidden bias

Many of our warnings about sources of bias in sample surveys concerned the need for care in areas other than the statistical design. There is an art to wording questions; there are special techniques to increase the response rate. In experimentation, there are also special techniques and precautions that go beyond the statistical design. We will mention two common precautions: the double-blind technique and randomization for purposes other than assigning units to treatments.

> **Example 10.** *Double-blind experiments.* In the vitamin C trial (Example 7 on p. 72), the health of the subjects was checked regularly and a judgment was made as to whether each was illness-free. These judgments are necessarily somewhat subjective, especially because the experiment concerned mild illnesses such as the common cold. The physician making the judgment may be unconsciously influenced by knowledge of what treatment the subject received, especially if he or she knows that the treatment was a placebo and so "ought" to have no effect. (Keep in mind that this is not a deliberate bias but simply an unconscious influence similar to the placebo effect in patients.) Therefore, the diagnosing physician is kept ignorant of which treatment each subject received, so the diagnosis cannot

"Dr. Burns, are you sure this is what the statisticians call a double blind experiment?"

be different for subjects in the two groups. This is called the *double-blind technique*. If only the subjects are ignorant of which treatment they are given, we have a single-blind experiment. When, as here, both the subjects and those who evaluate the outcome are ignorant of which treatment was given, we have a double-blind experiment. Only the director of the experiment knows which patients received vitamin C pills and which received sugar pills.

The double-blind procedure is used whenever possible in medical trials, because experience has shown that even careful investigators can be influenced by knowledge of the treatments used. Such ideas ought to be used in other experimental settings whenever they are appropriate. For example, in a common ESP (extrasensory perception) experiment, the experimenter looks at cards printed with various shapes (star, square, circle, etc.) invisible to the subject. The subject guesses the shapes, and the experimenter records whether the guesses are correct. It was noticed that the experimenter often recorded some incorrect guesses as correct. This does not necessarily show deliberate distortion but may be a result of the experimenter's desire to discover ESP. The remedy is to have the subject's guesses recorded by a third party who cannot see the cards and does not know whether a guess is right or wrong. The written record of guesses is later compared with a written record (made before the experiment) of the shape of each card in the shuffled deck used. Failure to use blind experimentation often invalidates "experiments" set up to prove a point.

Example 11. *More randomization.* In experiments on nutrition, it is common to use newly weaned male white rats as experimental units. Rats are randomly assigned to the diets to be compared, thus assuring that the stronger rats are not somehow assigned to one diet. Weight gain over a several-week period is observed. Now it turns out that rats placed in top cages gain weight somewhat faster than rats housed in bottom cages.* If rats fed diet A were placed in the bottom row, those fed diet B in the row above, and those fed diet C in the top row, the effects of diet and cage location would be confounded. The remedy is to assign rats to cages at random. Note that this is not the same as the random assignment to diets used in the experimental design. It is quite common to use additional randomization somewhere in carrying out an experiment.

---

* See Example 14 in this chapter for a more detailed study of this example, which is based on Elisabeth Street and Mavis B. Carroll, "Preliminary Evaluation of a New Food Product," in *Statistics: A Guide to the Unknown*. This fact about rats appears on p. 222 of that book.

The design of the ESP experiment also can be improved by an additional randomization. Instead of using a deck of cards, we might place cards bearing different shapes on a table in front of the "sender," with a light next to each. The lights are lit in an order determined by a table of random digits. The sender concentrates on the card whose light is on. The subject being tested for ESP sits in another room with the shapes in front of him and pushes a button under the shape he thinks the sender is concentrating on. Score is kept automatically by an electronic device that sees whether the button pushed by the subject matches the sender's light. The use of a table of random digits prevents the subject from picking up patterns in a reshuffled deck and keeps the sender "blind." The entire format is designed to prevent communication between sender and subject.

No precaution is too elaborate in such an experiment, for many professional "psychics" are clever frauds, and many "researchers" on psychic phenomena want so badly to find paranormal effects that they unconsciously collaborate with the psychic. It is not surprising that the most publicized "scientific experiments" on psychic phenomena have been arranged by physicists, who are naive where human subjects are concerned. As one skeptic put it, "Electrons and rats don't cheat. Professional psychics do."[4] Anyone planning to test the powers of psychics should have at least a psychologist, and preferably a professional magician who knows the tricks of the trade, present. (Houdini made a regular practice of exposing phony spiritualist "mediums," and contemporary magicians perform like services.)

Difficulty 4: Attention to detail

Even when your subjects are not so slippery as psychics, no data-collection design can survive lack of attention to detail. It is surprising how often sloppiness infects even important experiments. In 1976, the FDA banned Red 2, the food color most widely used in the United States, as a potential cause of cancer. Here is a quote from an account of the experiment that led to the ban:

> **Example 12.** The study involved feeding Red 2 to four different groups of rats, each at a diifferent dosage level, and then comparing the health of these treated groups with the health of a control group. There were 500 rats in all—seemingly enough for a solid evaluation. But the study was left unsupervised for a long period of time after a scientist was transferred, and it developed two serious flaws. To begin with, the animal handlers managed to put some of the rats back in the wrong cages part way through the experiment, so that an undetermined number of rats were shifted among the control group and the four treated groups. Second, the

animal handlers were lackadaisical about retrieving dead rats from their cages and rushing them off to the pathologist for examination. As a result, virtually all of the rats that died during the course of the experiment were so badly decomposed as to be of little use for evaluation. Only those rats that survived to the end of the experiment and were killed—some 96 in all—were available for detailed histopathological examination, "It was the lousiest experiment I've seen in my life," commented one scientist who reviewed the data.[5]

A decision had to be made, and a clever statistician managed to rescue some information. But careless supervision prevented the kind of clear conclusion that properly designed experiments are intended to produce. The detailed statement of exactly how the experiment is to be conducted is called (especially in clinical trials) the *protocol* of the experiment. Writing a careful protocol and making certain that it is followed is part of an experimenter's job.

4. More on experimental design

The basic ideas of statistical design of experiments are *randomization* and *control*.

> **Randomization** is the random allocation of experimental units among treatments, most simply by assigning an SRS of units to each treatment.
>
> **Control** is taking account of extraneous variables in the experimental design, most simply by the use of equivalent groups for comparison.

Completely randomized designs use both randomization and control in their simplest form, allocating the units at random among all the treatments. The examples in Section 2 were particularly simple in that the treatments were levels of a single factor, such as "drug administered" in the University Group Diabetes Program. Many experiments have more than one factor, so interactions among the factors can be studied. Here is an example with two factors and six treatments:

> **Example 13.** A food products company is preparing a new cake mix for marketing. It is important that the taste of the cake not be changed by small variations in baking time or temperature. An experiment is done in which batches of batter are baked at 300, 320, and 340°F, and for 1 hour

and 1 hour and 15 minutes. All possible combinations are used, resulting in six treatments that can be outlined as follows:

| | Factor A (temperature) | | |
	300°F	320°F	340°F
1hr	1	2	3
1¼ hr	4	5	6

Sixty batches of batter—ten for each treatment—will be prepared from the mix and baked. The batches should be assigned at random to the treatments. This can be done by rolling a fair die repeatedly. If the first roll gives a 4, the first cake prepared is baked under treatment 4 (300° for 1¼ hours), and so on until 10 cakes have been baked under each treatment. It is also possible to choose an SRS of size 10 from the numbers 01 to 60 to obtain the positions in which cakes will receive Treatment 1 on baking, then an SRS of the remaining 50 numbers to obtain the baking positions for Treatment 2, and so on. After baking, each cake will be scored for taste and texture by a panel of tasters. These scores are the dependent variables.

It would be a serious mistake in this example to first prepare 10 batches of batter to bake under Treatment 1, then 10 under Treatment 2, and so on. Any variable changing systematically over time, as room humidity might, would be confounded with the experimental treatments. Notice that there are two experimental factors (baking time and oven temperature). Each treatment is a combination of a particular level of each factor. This design is somewhat more complex than those with only one experimental factor, but it is completely randomized because the 60 units (batches of batter) are assigned completely at random to the six treatments.

Control appears in completely randomized designs only in the basic idea of comparative experimentation. Much of the advanced study of experimental design concentrates on more elaborate ways of controlling extraneous variables. We will introduce only one additional experimental design to illustrate the use of control in experiments.

Example 14. It is common in nutrition studies to compare diets by feeding them to newly weaned male rats and measuring the weight gained by the rats over a 28-day period.* If 30 such rats are available and three diets

---

* For more information on this example, see Elisabeth Street and Mavis B. Carroll, "Preliminary Evaluation of a New Food Product," in *Statistics: A Guide to the Unknown*.

are to be compared, each diet will be fed to 10 rats. Random assignment of rats to diets will average the effect of extraneous variables, such as the health of the rats. It is nonetheless wise to take additional steps to produce equivalent groups of rats for each diet. For example, standard strains of laboratory rats are available; this minimizes hereditary differences among the rats.

We can also redesign the experiment. The initial weight of the rats is an extraneous variable that is especially important as an influence on weight gain. Rather than randomly assign 10 rats to each diet, we therefore first divide the animals into 10 groups of three rats each based on weight. The three lightest rats form the first group, the next lightest three form the second group, and so on, with the tenth group consisting of the three heaviest rats. These groups of rats of similar weight are called *blocks*. Now we randomly assign one rat from each block to each diet. The blocks help to create equivalent groups of 10 rats to be fed each diet, because the rats in each block are approximately equal in weight and one of them is assigned to each diet.

In Example 14, we did *not* use the completely randomized design described by:

Random allocation →
Group 1 → Diet A → Record weight gain
Group 2 → Diet B → Record weight gain
Group 3 → Diet C → Record weight gain

A completely randomized design handles all extraneous variables by randomization. If the weight gained by individual rats varies a lot from rat to rat, the groups fed diets A, B, and C will have quite different average weight gains just because of this individual variation. Thus it will be hard to detect the systematic effect of the diets. One remedy is to add more rats to each group to obtain less variable average results. That's expensive. Another remedy is to take account of the worrisome extraneous variable in the layout of the experiment, that is, to control for the effect of initial weight directly rather than simply relying on randomization to average the effect. This was done in Example 14. First divide the rats into blocks consisting of rats of about the same weight. This is *not* random but is based on a particular extraneous variable: the initial weight of the rats. Then randomize, but only within the blocks, by randomly assigning one of the three rats in each block to each diet. This is called a *randomized complete block design*. It has the pattern shown in Figure 2-1.

There are still three experimental groups of 10 rats each, one fed each of diets A, B, and C. Each group contains one rat from each of the 10 blocks, so

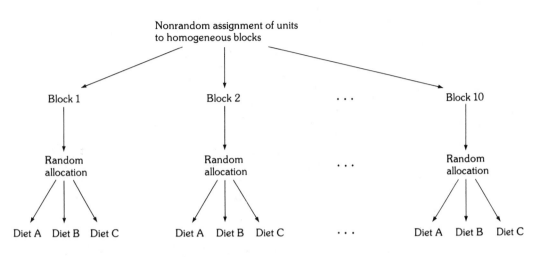

Figure 2-1. Randomized complete block design. In such a design, judgment is used to form blocks of similar units, and randomization is applied within each block separately.

the initial weights of the rats in the three groups closely match. This matching greatly reduces the variation in average weight gain among the groups owing to different initial weights. It is now much easier to detect any difference in weight gain resulting from the different diets. Each block in a randomized complete block design contains exactly as many experimental units as there are treatments. Each treatment is then applied once within each block. Other designs may use larger blocks so that each treatment is assigned to several units within each block. Still other designs use incomplete blocks having fewer units than there are treatments.

Blocking in experimental design is similar to stratification in sampling. Both require judgment to classify units into groups (blocks or strata) in such a way that units within a group show less variability than the entire population of units. Randomization is then used only within each block or stratum; that is, the randomization no longer is "complete" as in a completely randomized design but is restricted to each block separately.

The definition of *control* as taking account of extraneous variables in the experimental design is now clearer. The blocks in a randomized block design are groups of units that agree in some extraneous variable important to the outcome of the experiment. The term "block" originated in agricultural experimentation, where it refers to a compact plot of land with little variation in soil type, fertility, and so forth. In experiments on fertilizers or cultivation methods, we are not interested in such extraneous variables as soil type and fertility. Random assignment of treatments (fertilizers or whatever) to small plots of ground (experimental units) within the same block gives equivalent units for comparison of treatments. Several blocks give a larger number of observations and also provide data on more than one soil type and fertility. In Example 14, a block consisted of animals of approximately equal weight. We are interested in the effect of diet, not of initial weight. Because animals within a block have the same initial weight, it should be easier to detect the effect of diet when these animals are fed different diets. We use several blocks to obtain more observations; data on three rats would not be precise even if all had the same initial weight. In summary, blocks are a way of holding fixed an extraneous variable that would otherwise cause large variations in the experimental results. A randomized block design therefore will give more precise (more repeatable) results than a completely randomized design with the same number of units.

Completely randomized designs and simple random samples employ random selection from the entire available set of units. Randomized block designs and stratified random samples restrict random selection to predetermined blocks or strata that are less variable than the entire population. More elaborate experimental designs further restrict the groups of units within which random selection is made. Because these groups often are formed by taking account of extraneous variables, restrictions on randomization frequently are associated with control of extraneous influences.

Extraneous variables can be dealt with by either randomization or control. Completely randomized experiments rely exclusively on the averaging effects of randomization, while randomized block experiments include an extraneous variable directly in forming blocks. Elaborate experimental designs often deal with many variables by control. In a general sense, variables with a large influence on the outcome should be controlled. Others can be randomized. Using a completely randomized design in place of a randomized block design is not wrong in the sense of producing invalid results. But it is inefficient; that is, the more elaborate design requires fewer experimental units to give equally precise results. In Section 1, I stated that the first goal of experimental design was to obtain valid results, to discover the true effects of the treatments. The second goal is to do this as efficiently as possible, to use as few units as possible for a given degree of precision. The randomized block design hints at how this second goal is pursued.

5.   Social experiments

The effectiveness of a new fertilizer or a new drug is always tested by a controlled and randomized experiment—and for good reason: A well-designed experiment can provide clearer answers than any other method of study. What about testing the effectiveness of a new welfare program or health care system or preschool education program? Public policy decisions in these areas have usually been based on much supposition and little knowledge. It is tempting to try an experiment in the hope of finding clear answers. Such *social experiments* have been done in recent years. I will describe one such experiment and comment on this method of testing social programs.

Many proposals for change in the present welfare system have been made. Supporters of these changes argue that new welfare programs would provide stronger incentives for welfare families to seek work and for families to stay together. Opponents argue that the new programs would be expensive and of doubtful effectiveness. In response to these arguments, the federal government has sponsored five experiments to test alternative welfare policies. One of these, the New Jersey Income-Maintenance Experiment, was conducted in four urban areas in New Jersey and Pennsylvania, beginning in 1968.[6]

The policy tested in this experiment comprised a guaranteed annual income and a negative income tax that the government pays to (rather than collects from) low-income families. Just as the ordinary income tax rises by some percentage of earned income, the payment made under the negative income tax drops by some percentage of earned income. There are two factors in this scheme: the guarantee level and the tax rate. The guarantee is the amount the government pays a family having no earned income. The tax rate states how fast the welfare payments fall as earned income increases. Suppose, for example, that the guarantee is $3000 and the tax rate is 30%. A family with no earned income receives $3000 (the guarantee) in welfare payments. If the family earns $2000, the welfare payment decreases by 30% of this, or $600. Now the family receives $2400 in welfare ($3000 less $600) plus the $2000 it earned, or $4400 in all. Figure 2-2 shows that as the family earns more, the welfare payments decrease but total income always increases. Under the present system, payments end abruptly at a certain income level, so taking a job may lower a recipient's income. The negative income tax is intended to provide an incentive for welfare recipients to find jobs.

This social experiment had nine treatments, including the current welfare system as a control. The eight experimental treatments are shown in Table 2-2. The guarantee is expressed as a percent of the poverty lines established by the Social Security Administration. The actual dollar amounts guaranteed depended on the size of the family and were raised during the four years of the study as rising prices pushed up the poverty line. (Notice that not all possible combinations of the two factors were used as treatments.)

The population from which units for the experiment were selected consisted of low-income households containing at least two persons, one of them a healthy male between 18 and 58 years old. This requirement eliminates many poverty-stricken families in which no employable male is present. This population was chosen because of special interest in the effects of the new welfare system on

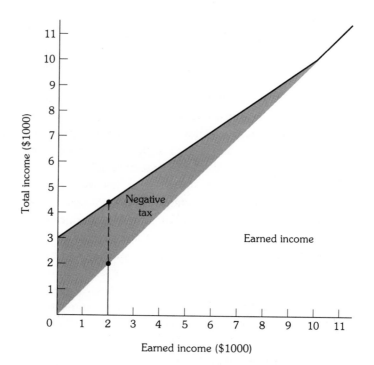

Figure 2-2. The negative income tax. As a family's earned income grows, the negative tax (shaded region) decreases but total income increases. A family earning $2000 (solid line) also receives $2400 in negative tax payments (broken line), for a total income of $4400. The graph assumes a $3000 base and a 30% tax rate.

working-age males, an interest aroused not so much by sexism as by the fact that working-age males generally cannot collect welfare under the present system and so might have less incentive to work under a new system that would provide welfare benefits to them. None of the four income-maintenance experiments

Table 2-2. Experimental treatments for the New Jersey Income-Maintenance Experiment

		Factor A (guarantee as percentage of poverty line)			
		50	75	100	125
Factor B (tax rate in percent)	30	x	x		
	50	x	x	x	x
	70		x	x	

funded by the federal government in other parts of the country required that a male worker be present.

As recommended in Section 3, experimental units were chosen from the population by sampling. Poverty areas in four cities were selected from census data and on-site inspection. Then blocks were selected at random within these areas, and field workers were sent out to make lists of all dwelling units in each block selected. From these, a sample of households was chosen. Interviewers visited these households to see if they belonged to the target population and to explain the experiment. Now came the fun—dark stairwells, vicious dogs, hostile local politicians, and militant community groups. These were dealt with. But 10% of the dwelling units were empty. Of the remaining households, 19% were never at home (in five tries), and 18% refused to speak to the interviewer in four visits. The initial sample of 48,000 households yielded 27,000 that were interviewed. Of these, only 3124 were eligible to participate in the experiment; low income families with able-bodied men present are not common in urban areas. Another 425 families had vanished by the time interviewers returned to invite them to join the experiment. The life of an experimenter out there in the real world has its frustrations. But at last 1357 families were chosen, and agreed, to participate.

You might well ask if this sample is representative of the population, after all those refusals and never-at-homes. Comparing characteristics of the sample with characteristics of all families in their neighborhoods (courtesy of the 1970 census) suggests, amazingly enough, that the sample is quite representative in income, family composition, and so on. Whether the noncooperators and never-at-homes are different in less tangible ways that would affect their reaction to a negative income tax remains unanswered.

Now for the random assignment of units to treatments. Well, not quite yet. First the sample households were divided into three blocks of 400 to 500 families each, depending on their normal income. Random assignment to the nine treatments took place separately within each block. The use of blocks was due to a reason not mentioned in Section 4: The experiment could not afford to assign too many of the lowest-income families to the most expensive (high guarantee and low tax rate) treatments. It would simply cost too much, because the gap between these families' normal earned income and that promised by the new welfare scheme was so great. So the randomization did not make all treatments equally likely. Indeed, the chance of being assigned to a specific treatment was different in each of the three blocks. But each family had a known chance of being assigned to each treatment, and these chances were the same for every family in a block. It was a complicated bit of randomization, much akin to moving from an SRS to a general probability sample.

This experimental design is more involved than any we met earlier, in three ways: First, it makes use of blocks in a two-factor experiment; second, not all of the possible combinations of the two factors were used; and third, different randomization patterns, none of them giving a household the same chance of landing in all nine groups, were employed in each block. You would call a statistician before entering such a jungle, but a glimpse of this statistical jungle is one motive for the tale I have told in this section. A second motive is to remind you once again of how much harder experiments are in the slums of Trenton than on the statistician's desk. The third, and most important, of my motives is to instill the idea of using statistically designed experiments to answer questions about public policy.

The advantages of social experimentation are clear: There is a real possibility that experiments will give a better picture of the effects of a new welfare policy than any amount of debate. The new welfare system tested in the New Jersey experiment succeeded in increasing the income of poverty-level families without reducing the employment rate of the husbands. But the new system did lower the employment of their wives; the wives in the experimental groups worked 23% fewer hours per week than the controls. (Because these families had an average of four children, the wives were working hard at home.) These and other effects of the negative income tax are illuminated by the experiment.

The disadvantages of social experiments are also clear: They take a long time and are expensive. The New Jersey experiment lasted four years, cost $8 million, and the detailed results did not appear until 1977. Often problems of validity arise; for example, participating in an experiment may change the behavior of welfare families. Moreover, conditions may so change between the planning of an experiment and the release of first results nine years later that the answers given by the experiment no longer respond to the right questions.

Public policy decisions affect us all, either directly or indirectly by changing our society and spending our taxes. Experimentation is a powerful tool for gathering information on the effects of treatments. Such a tool should certainly help to guide policy decisions. Social experimentation, used carefully, is an idea whose time has come.

6. Ethics and experimentation

Carrying out experiments on human subjects raises serious ethical problems. Medical experiments (often called *clinical trials*) have been particularly controversial because the giving or withholding of medical treatment can result in direct danger to a patient. Yet comparative experiments are necessary if life-saving medical knowledge is to be obtained. Some treatments—"magic bullets" like penicillin—have effects so dramatic that properly designed experiments are not needed to detect them. But this is rare. Medicine usually advances in smaller steps: The death rate from the new operation is 10% lower than for the old one; patients given the new drug live 5% longer than those given the old. The dilemma is that medical experiments often are potentially harmful to some of the subjects yet are needed to obtain valuable knowledge. The potential for harm must be balanced against the value of the knowledge.

All agree that medical experiments must be guided by the first principle of medical ethics, expressed in the ancient Latin motto *"Primum non nocere,"* or "First of all, do no harm"; that is, exposing patients to treatments *known* to be harmful is clearly unethical. Latin mottos lack teeth, however, and experimenters have only recently become sufficiently sensitive to their subjects' welfare. Here are two examples of blatant abuse of subjects:

> **Example 15.** In the early 1960s, two cancer researchers injected live cancer cells into geriatric patients without the informed consent of the patients. Their intent was to study the possibility of "infection" with cancer.

> **Example 16.** Syphilis progresses slowly, so it is difficult to study the development of the disease. From 1932 to 1972, researchers observed two groups of subjects in Tuskegee, Alabama, one with and one without the disease. (This was an observational study with a control group, not an experiment.) In 1945, the first effective treatment for syphilis (penicillin) became known. The researchers did not treat their subjects with penicillin but continued observing the progress of their syphilis.[7]

The second ethical standard for clinical trials requires that the *informed consent* of the subjects be obtained. Subjects are told that they will be part of a research study, that is, that something beyond treating their illness is going on. The nature of the study and the possible risks and benefits are explained, and the patients are asked to agree to participate and to consent to random assignment to a treatment. Those who refuse are not included in the experiment and usually receive the standard therapy. (Why cannot these patients be used as part of the control group, even though they receive the standard therapy?) Many individuals are willing to participate in random clinical trials for the future benefit of all. But many patients find the idea of being subjects in an experiment hard to accept, and the idea that their treatment will be chosen by the toss of a coin even harder to accept. In studies of serious conditions such as cancer, as many as 80% or 90% of the subjects approached sometimes refuse to participate. The strict rules on disclosure and informed consent now enforced in clinical trials cause considerable grumbling among medical researchers.

Informed consent is somewhat difficult to achieve, especially when the subjects are a dependent group rather than paying consumers of medical care. It is probably not accidental that the subjects in Example 15 were aged and institutionalized, while those in Example 16 were poor and black. Groups such as prisoners have often been volunteer subjects for medical experiments. We might doubt whether prisoners requested to "volunteer" are really free to refuse. In early 1976, the Federal Bureau of Prisons announced that medical experimentation on federal prisoners no longer would be permitted. The *New York Times* commented in an editorial (March 8, 1976),

> *Truly voluntary consent is virtually impossible to achieve in prison and there is a large temptation to undervalue prisoners' interests during the course of such research. The new Federal policy is clearly the appropriate response to these problems and it should serve as an example to the states which still permit experiments to be conducted in their prisons.*

What all of this adds up to is that medical experimentation in the United States is subject to tight rules for the protection of subjects, rules drawn up by the federal agencies that pay for (and hence can control) almost all medical studies. Some doctors and statisticians say that as a result we will never learn the answers to some medical questions. That is true enough, yet it has always been true that some valuable experiments were forbidden by ethical constraints. Here is an example:

> **Example 17.** People who smoke are more likely to contract lung cancer (and many other diseases) than those who do not, and the disease is more common among long-term heavy smokers than among those who have smoked less. This may happen because smoking is a cause of lung cancer. But because people choose whether or not to smoke, some variable, such as heredity, might cause cancer-prone persons to choose to smoke in greater numbers than others. An experiment to settle this question is easy to imagine. Choose young subjects (say age 10) who have not smoked. Assign them at random to groups. Group 1 will begin to smoke at age 18 and smoke two packs of cigarettes a day for life. Group 2 will not smoke at all. Other groups will smoke less, or for shorter periods. All subjects will be observed for life. Such an experiment is morally impossible; we are not willing to force some subjects to smoke and others not to.

There is no easy answer to the problem of balancing the growth of knowledge and the protection of patients. I think it is fair to say that the present rules restore that balance after a period in which medical researchers were largely free to follow their natural bias in favor of gaining knowledge.

Clinical trials also present a more subtle class of moral problems: those arising from random assignment of subjects to different treatments. Here are two examples:

Example 18. There is at present no vaccine for a serious viral disease. A vaccine is developed and appears effective in animal trials. Only a comparative experiment with human subjects in which a control group receives a placebo can determine the true worth of the vaccine. Is it ethical to give some subjects the placebo, which cannot protect them against the disease? (Of course, the vaccine may have undesirable side effects. It may even give a few patients the disease it is designed to protect against. So a risk accompanies the chance of protection.)

Example 19. The standard surgical treatment for breast cancer has long been radical mastectomy, an operation to remove the infected breast, underlying chest muscles, and lymph nodes in the armpits. This operation is quite disfiguring, and many women would prefer a simple mastectomy (removal of the breast only) or even removal of the tumor only. But these operations cannot be more effective than a radical mastectomy and may be less effective, because they often leave cancer cells behind. The effectiveness of these operations can be compared only by a clinical trial. But is it ethical to randomly assign women to a treatment that cannot be more effective than the radical surgery? The other treatments should be used if they equal the effectiveness of radical surgery, since they are less disfiguring. But we cannot know whether they are equally effective without a trial.

In each case, one group of patients will receive an inferior therapy. I think that experimentation is ethical in such situations, for two reasons: First, it is not known which of the treatments is superior; if that were certain, all patients would be given the better therapy. No one is deliberately deprived of the best therapy, even though because of our ignorance one group will receive an inferior treatment. Second, I remind you again that controlled and randomized experiments are the only method of discovering which therapy is superior. Refusing to experiment is therefore not a solution to these ethical problems. The natural reluctance to "use human beings as guinea pigs" cannot be justified. For refusing to experiment would not only leave *all* present patients with an inferior treatment if the new is better, but it would deprive all future patients of the better treatments, which can be found only by experimentation. Dr. Bernard Fisher, director of a study of breast cancer treatments now in progress, was quoted in the *New York Times* (October 2, 1974) as follows:

[Dr. Fisher said] that random clinical trials were "ethical" and the only way to answer women's questions about breast cancer surgery. Without such trials, the current state of uncertainty will persist indefinitely, Dr. Fisher insisted, and women will continue either to be disfigured unnecessarily or to receive less than the best therapy.

Events appear to have vindicated Dr. Fisher. The 1700 women in his study have shown no significant differences in survival between radical and simple mastectomy a decade after surgery. This and other experimental results, and the concern of women's groups about the physical and emotional trauma of breast surgery, are changing the medical treatment of breast cancer.

When we move from medicine to the behavioral sciences, the direct risks to experimental subjects are less clear. But so is the value of the knowledge gained. Consider, for example, the experiments conducted by psychologists in their study of human behavior.

> **Example 20.** Stanley Milgram of Yale conducted the following experiment "to see if a person will perform acts under group pressure that he would not have performed in the absence of social inducement."[8] The subject arrives with three others who (unknown to the subject) are confederates of the experimenter. The experimenter explains that he is studying the effects of punishment on learning. The Learner (one of the confederates) is strapped into an electric chair, mentioning in passing that he has a mild heart condition. The subject and the other two confederates are Teachers. They sit in front of a panel with switches with labels ranging from "Slight Shock" to "Danger: Severe Shock" and are told that they must shock the Learner whenever he fails in a memory learning task. How badly the Learner is shocked is up to the Teachers and will be the *lowest* level suggested by any Teacher on that trial.
>
> All is rigged. The Learner answers incorrectly on 30 of the 40 trials. The two Teacher-confederates call for a higher shock level at each failure. As the shocks increase, the Learner protests, asks to be let out, shouts, complains of heart trouble, and finally screams in pain. (The "shocks" are phony and the Learner is an actor; but the subject doesn't know this.) What will the subject do? He can keep the shock at the lowest level, but the two Teacher-stooges are pressuring him to torture the Learner more for each failure.
>
> What the subject most often does is give in to the pressure. "While the experiment yields wide variation in performance, a substantial number of subjects submitted readily to pressure applied to them by the confederates." Milgram noted that in questioning after the experiment, the subjects often admit that they acted against their own principles and are upset by what they did. "The subject was then dehoaxed carefully and had a friendly reconciliation with the victim."[9]

Even though this experiment offends most people, we must agree that the potential harm to the subjects is not so clear as in some medical experiments. That sick feeling of knowing that you were tricked into acts you consider des-

picable doesn't put Dr. Milgram in the class of those who in Example 15 injected
live cancer cells into aged patients. But then neither is knowledge of the behavior
of individuals under group pressure so clearly valuable as knowledge of whether
or not cancer can be infectious.

Social scientists, like medical researchers, have steadily tightened their standards of conduct. A report on a 1979 conference on ethics in social research
said of Milgram's work: "A decade ago it was hailed as a brilliant if disturbing
experiment. Now it is regarded as raising serious ethical questions; the dominant
view is that to conduct such a study is wrong."[10] All universities and research
institutions now have review committees that screen all research with human
subjects for potentially harmful treatments. Experiments with possibly negative
emotional effects much less severe than those in Milgram's studies are regularly
vetoed by the review committee at Purdue (where I teach) and presumably
elsewhere. The committe system serves as a check on the consciences of individual researchers. Yet many experiments in the social sciences include treatments in the gray area where "possible emotional harm" shades into "attacks

*"I'm doing a little study on the effects of emotional stress. Now, just take the
axe from my assistant."*

human dignity" or merely into the slippery category of "in bad taste." Solomon himself could not make decisions acceptable to all in so foggy a situation.

In addition to the question of what constitutes "possible harm to the subject," Milgram's work illustrates another problem common to studies of human behavior. The informed consent required by medical ethics is simply not possible. If the subject were aware of the true purpose of the experiment, the experiment would not be valid. So subjects are usually asked to consent to participation without being given a detailed description of the experiment and its purpose. Do such experiments amount to unjustified manipulation of the subjects, bringing out aspects of their behavior that they would prefer not to reveal to scrutiny? Or are the experiments justified by the knowledge gained, by uninformed consent, and by the fact that the treatments are not harmful? Exercises 1 and 2 afford an opportunity for you to make this judgment in some specific cases.

Experimentation is necessary for the advance of knowledge, and, at least with medical trials, few would deny that the knowledge gained serves the general good. Nevertheless, experimenters are often tempted to place their search for knowledge ahead of the welfare of their subjects. It is fortunate that interest in the welfare of subjects has greatly increased in recent years. Yet citizens would do well not to rely entirely on review committees and other expressions of the collective conscience of researchers. The record of experimenters on human subjects is not good enough to justify complacency.

NOTES

1. Read "Is Vitamin C Really Good for Colds?" in *Consumer Reports*, February 1976, pp. 68–70, for a discussion of this conclusion. The article also reviews the need for controlled experiments and the Toronto study.

2. Jerome Cornfield, "The University Group Diabetes Program," *Journal of the American Medical Association*, Volume 217 (1971), pp. 1676–1687.

3. The saccharin question is discussed in detail in the "News and Comment" section of *Science*, Volume 196 (1977), pp. 1179–1183, and Volume 208 (1980), pp. 154–156. Details of the data from the rat experiment that led to FDA action appear in a letter to the editor in *Science*, Volume 197 (1977), p. 320.

4. Martin Gardner, "Supergull," *New York Review of Books*, March 17, 1977. This review of two books on psychic researchers illustrates nicely the naive experiments and vague and deceptive accounts that pervade this field.

5. From Philip M. Boffey, "Color Additives: Botched Experiment Leads to Banning of Red Dye No. 2," *Science*, Volume 191 (1976), p. 450.

6. For a full account of this social experiment, see David Kershaw and Jerilyn Fair, *The New Jersey Income-Maintenance Experiment, Volume I* (New York: Academic Press, 1976). All of the specific information about that experiment cited in this section is taken from that book.

7. Both cases are reported in Bernard Barber, "The Ethics of Experimentation with Human Subjects," *Scientific American*, February 1976, pp. 25–31.

8. Stanley Milgram, "Group Pressure and Action Against a Person," *Journal of Abnormal and Social Psychology*, Volume 69 (1964), pp. 137–143.

9. Postexperimental attitudes and the final quotation are in Stanley Milgram, "Liberating Effects of Group Pressure," *Journal of Personality and Social Psychology*, Volume 1 (1965), pp. 127–134.

10. Quoted from Constance Holden, "Ethics in Social Science Research," *Science*, Volume 206 (1979), pp. 537–540.

Exercises

Section 1

1. A study of the effect of living in public housing on family stability and other variables in poverty-level households was carried out as follows: A list of applicants accepted for public housing was obtained, together with a list of families who applied but were rejected by the housing authorities. A random sample was drawn from each list, and the two groups were observed for several years.
   (a) Is this an experiment? Why or why not?
   (b) What are the independent and dependent variables?
   (c) Does this study contain confounding that may prevent valid conclusions on the effects of living in public housing? Explain.

2. An educator wants to compare the effectiveness of a "reading machine" with that of a standard reading curriculum. She tests the reading ability of each student in a class of fourth graders, then divides them into two groups. One group uses only the machine, while the other studies a standard curriculum. At the end of the year, all students are retested, and the two groups are compared for increase in reading ability.
   (a) Is this an experiment? Why or why not?
   (b) What are the independent and dependent variables?

3. In each of the situations that follow, confounding is present. Explain briefly what variables are confounded and why the conclusions drawn about the effect of the independent variable on the dependent variable are not valid.
   (a) Last year only 10% of a group of adult men did not have a cold at some time during the winter. This year all the men in the group took 1 gram of vitamin C each day, and 20% had no colds. This shows that vitamin C helps prevent colds.
   (b) The educator in Exercise 2 asked for teachers who would volunteer to use the teaching machines. One group of students was taught by teachers who volunteered to use the machines, while the control group was taught by teachers who did not volunteer. At the end of the year, the machine group had improved their reading scores somewhat more than the nonmachine group.

(c) It was suspected that a daily vitamin supplement might improve the health of nursing home patients. The patients in a large nursing home were divided into two groups. One group was given a vitamin supplement each day, while the other group received no treatment. After six months, the first group had fewer days ill than the second.

4. In 1976, Pepsi-Cola ran a television advertising campaign that featured an experiment. Regular drinkers of Coca-Cola were given a glass of Coke, marked only as "Q," and a glass of Pepsi, marked only as "M." More than half of the subjects said brand "M" tasted better.

Coca-Cola said (in less technical language) that this experiment was invalid owing to confounding of the brand of cola with an extraneous variable. Can you see where the confounding lies?

5. A chemical engineer is designing the production process for a new drug. The drug will be manufactured in batches, which may have a higher or lower yield depending on the temperature and pressure at which the batch is processed. The engineer decides to try three temperatures and two pressures in a search for the combination having the highest yield. She processes four batches at each temperature–pressure combination and measures the percent yield of the drug in each batch.
   (a) What are the experimental units and the dependent variable in this experiment?
   (b) How many factors are there? How many treatments?
   (c) How many experimental units are required for the experiment?

6. A survey of physicians in 1979 found that some doctors give a placebo to a patient who complains of pain for which the physician can find no cause. If the patient's pain improves, these doctors conclude that it had no physical basis. The medical school researchers who conducted the survey claimed that these doctors do not understand the placebo effect. Why?

7. Read the article "Safety of Anesthetics" by Lincoln E. Moses and Frederick Mosteller in *Statistics: A Guide to the Unknown*. Identify the independent variables, the dependent variables, and the extraneous variables confounded with the independent variable. Why is it that the data in Table 1 "cannot be trusted"?

8. After the July 1976 convention of the American Legion in Philadelphia, 29 convention-goers died of a mysterious "Legionnaires' disease." It was at first suspected that the disease might be a variety of influenza. To check this theory, laboratory experimenters injected material from dead and sick Legionnaires into chick embryos and watched to see if influenza virus grew in the embryo. (The presence of small numbers of virus in the material injected would go undetected. But if they grew into many, they could be detected.) No influenza virus was found. A Yale Medical School virologist commented that these results were not quite convincing. He said that a known dose of

influenza virus should have been injected into other chick embryos as a "positive control."

Can you see the virologist's point and explain his objection in more detail?

Section 2

1. A vaccine for use against a dangerous virus has been developed. You have available 10 rats (named below), which will be exposed to the virus. Unprotected rats usually die when infected. Design an experiment to test the effectiveness of the vaccine. Use line 140 of Table A to carry out the random assignment.

Alfie	Bernie	Chuck	David	Frank
Harry	Lyman	Mercedes	Polyphemus	Zaffo

2. A group of 200 first graders is available to compare the effectiveness of method A and method B for teaching reading.

  (a) Design an experiment to make this comparison.

  (b) Explain carefully how you would carry out the random assignment called for in your design. Use Table A, beginning at line 137, to assign five students as a demonstration of your randomization.

3. You wish to compare three treatments for effectiveness in preventing flu: (1) a flu vaccine, (2) 1 gram of vitamin C per day, (3) a placebo taken daily. Describe how you would use 600 volunteer subjects in a designed experiment to compare these treatments. (Do not actually do any randomization, but do include a diagram showing your design.)

4. To demonstrate how randomization elminates confounding, consider the following situation: A nutrition experimenter intends to compare the weight gain of newly weaned male rats fed diet A with that of rats fed diet B. To do this she will feed each diet to 10 rats. She has available 10 rats of genetic strain 1 and 10 of strain 2. Strain 1 is more vigorous, so if the 10 rats of strain 1 were fed diet A, the effects of strain and diet would be confounded, and the experiment would be biased in favor of diet A.

Label the rats 00, 01, . . . , 19 (use repeated labels if you wish). Use Table A to assign 10 rats to diet A. Do this four times, using different parts of the table, and write down the four experimental groups you obtained.

Suppose that the strain 1 rats are numbers 00, 02, 04, 06, 08, 10, 12, 14, 16, and 18. How many of these rats were in each of the four diet-A groups that you generated? What was the average number of strain-1 rats assigned to diet A?

5. Comparison alone does not make a study an experiment. Examples 3 and 4 in Section 1 are observational studies that compare two groups, but they are not experiments. Describe clearly the difference between a comparative observational study and a comparative experiment. What advantages do comparative experiments have over comparative observational studies?

6. Read "The Biggest Public Health Experiment Ever," by Paul Meier, in *Statistics: A Guide to the Unknown*. Describe the experimental design used in the Salk vaccine trials. What extraneous variables would have been confounded with the treatment if the "observed control" approach had been used?

7. Makers of competing pain relievers sometimes claim that their pills dissolve faster and illustrate this claim with pictures of pills dissolving in a glass of water. You are to compare the dissolving time of Anacin and aspirin.
   (a) Give the statistical design of an experiment to make this comparison.
   (b) Discuss any nonstatistical aspects of the experiment that may be important to your conclusion. (For example, what do you mean by "aspirin"?)

8. Think of a simple question of interest to you that might be settled by an experiment. Discuss in detail the design of an appropriate experiment. (If you plan to carry out the experiment, show the design to your instructor first.)

9. The following article by the Associated Press appeared in the *New York Times* of October 16, 1975. Describe in detail how you think the experiment was designed. Does the news report omit any important information about the design? Are there any inconsistencies in the details given?

Marijuana Is Called An Effective Relief In Cancer Therapy

BOSTON, Oct. 15 (AP)—Marijuana is far more effective than any other drug in relieving the vomiting and nausea that plagues thousands of cancer patients undergoing chemical therapy, researchers say.

Clinical trials with cancer patients using a marijuana derivative have been so successful that the drug should be considered seriously as a treatment for the chemical therapy side effects, they add.

In a report to be published tomorrow in the New England Journal of Medicine, Harvard Medical School researchers at the Sidney Farber Cancer Center say they tested the effectiveness of the marijuana drug against a dummy drug in 22 patients with a variety of cancers.

For patients who completed the study, 12 of 15 cases involving marijuana drug treatments resulted in at least a 50 per cent reduction in vomiting and nausea after cancer therapy. And in five of these treatments, the patients suffered no nausea at all, the report added.

There was no decrease in nausea or vomiting in 14 cases in which placebo, or dummy treatment, was used, the researchers said. In the "double-blind" experiment, neither patients nor doctors knew in advance who got the real or dummy drugs.

Dr. Stephen E. Salan said in an interview that about 75 per cent of the thousands of patients getting chemotherapy for cancer suffered moderate to extreme nausea and vomiting.

And of this group, 90 per cent get no relief from conventional antinausea drugs, he added.

Dr. Salan said he and his colleagues in the study, Dr. Norman E. Zinberg and Dr. Emil Frei 30, did not know specifically why marijauna worked to decrease nausea.

10. The following Associated Press dispatch appeared in the *Lafayette Journal and Courier* of November 30, 1974:
    (a) What important information about the experiment design is given in the article?
    (b) Is any important information omitted?
    (c) Do you consider the results of the experiment convincing? Why or why not?

Praying to soybeans aids in higher yields

By GEORGE CORNELL

With county officials measuring the results, experimenters on an Ohio farm say they found that portions of a field that had been the object of loving prayers yielded the biggest crop.

The case offered an unusual instance of recent stepped-up interest in psychic phenomena, viewed by many with keen skepticism.

"Somehow God's creative energy of growth can be channeled through us even to plants," says Gus Alexander of Wright State University, who holds a doctorate in communications research and who set up the project.

It was carried out on a soybean field near Jamestown, Ohio, east of Dayton, with daily prayerful attention of a church group focused on six designated plots, but not on six adjoining control plots.

Alexander says the yield of soybeans receiving the special attention was increased by 4 percent over the comparable control plot, even though the experiment had extended over only a third of the growing season.

In checking results of the experiment late in October, the Greene county agent's technical assistant, Donald H. Tate, was on hand to weigh the yields from the six experimental and six control plots.

According to the figures, five of the experimental strips had produced heavier yields than had adjacent control strips, while in the sixth case the control strip had a slightly greater yield.

In the experiment, a group of 10 people at Dayton's Church of the Golden Key, supplied with diagrams of the soybean plots, took on the task of "sending love" to the experimental areas each night at 11:30 p.m. for about 40 days.

Reprinted by permission of The Associated Press.

Section 3

1. For what population do you think the experimental conclusions are valid in each of the following cases? (We cannot be definite about this question without expert knowledge, so our answers will be partly guesses.)
    (a) The vitamin C study of Example 7 on page 72.
    (b) The propaganda study of Example 6 on page 70.
    (c) The dissolving-time study of Exercise 7 on page 100.

2. Fizz Laboratories, a pharmaceutical company, has developed a new pain-relief medication. Sixty patients suffering from arthritis and needing pain relief are available. Each patient will be treated and asked an hour later, "About what percentage of pain relief did you experience?"

(a) Why should Fizz not simply administer the new drug and record the patients' responses?

(b) Design an experiment to compare the drug's effectiveness with that of aspirin and of a placebo.

(c) Should patients be told which drug they are receiving? How would this knowledge probably affect their reactions?

(d) If patients are not told which treatment they are receiving, the experiment is single-blind. Should this experiment be double-blind also? Explain.

3. An experiment that was publicized as showing that a meditation technique lowered the anxiety level of subjects was conducted as follows: The experimenter interviewed the subjects and assessed their levels of anxiety. The subjects then learned how to meditate and did so regularly for a month. The experimenter re-interviewed them at the end of the month and assessed whether their anxiety levels had decreased or not.

(a) There was no control group in this experiment. Why is this a blunder? What extraneous variables may be confounded with the effect of meditation?

(b) The experimenter who diagnosed the effect of the treatment knew that the subjects had been meditating. Explain how this knowledge could bias the experimental conclusions.

(c) Briefly discuss a proper experimental design, with controls and blind diagnosis, to assess the effect of meditation on anxiety level.

4. Additional randomization will improve the Coke-versus-Pepsi taste experiment described in Exercise 4 on page 98. Explain what randomization is needed, and why.

5. Experiments with human subjects that continue over a long period of time face the problem of "dropouts" (subjects who quit the experiment) and "nonadherers" (subjects who stay in but don't follow the experimental protocol). In his account of the University Group Diabetes Program (Example 8 on p. 74), Dr. Cornfield makes the following statement:

> For this complex problem, the UGDP has followed the generally accepted practice of comparing the mortality experience of the originally randomized groups, and of not eliminating dropouts or nonadherers from the analysis. This practice is conservative in that it dilutes whatever treatment effects, beneficial or adverse, are present.

Explain why not counting dropouts and nonadherers in the final results might exaggerate differences between groups.

6. One of the most significant clinical trials of recent years demonstrated convincingly that lowering the level of cholesterol in the blood can reduce the risk of heart attacks. An accessible account is Gina Kolata, "Lowered Cho-

lesterol Decreases Heart Disease," *Science*, Volume 223 (1984), pp. 381–382. Read this article as an example of the size and complexity of a major medical experiment. Describe the statistical design of the experiment (which was quite simple). Describe the serious practical difficulties that had to be overcome.

Section 4

1. Since 1974, most cars have been equipped with catalytic converters to reduce harmful emissions. The Corning Glass Company is a manufacturer of the ceramic used to make the converters. The ceramic must be baked to a certain hardness. Corning had to decide which of three temperatures (500°F, 750°F, and 1000°F) was best. But they also found that it mattered where the converter was placed in the oven (front, middle, or back). So there are two experimental factors: temperature and placement.
   (a) Design a completely randomized experiment with five units in each group.
   (b) Using Table A, beginning with line 101, do the randomization required by your design.

2. A drug is suspected of affecting the coordination of subjects. The drug can be administered in three ways: orally, by injection under the skin, or by injection into a vein. The potency of the drug probably depends on the method of administration as well as on the dosage administered. A researcher therefore wishes to study the effects of the two factors, dosage at two levels and method of administration by the three methods mentioned. The response variable is the score of the subjects on a standard test of coordination. Ninety subjects are available.
   (a) Describe an appropriate completely randomized design. (Just give the design; don't do any randomization.)
   (b) The researcher could study the effect of dosage in an experiment comparing two dosage levels for one method of administration. He then could separately study the effect of administration by comparing the three methods for one dosage level. What advantages does the two-factor experiment you designed in (a) have over these two one-factor experiments together?

3. There is good evidence that physical stress—even someone stroking the leaves of a plant for a minute a day—inhibits plant growth. Some claim (without good evidence) that speaking kindly to plants encourages growth. We are going to investigate the effects of physical contact, talking to plants, or both, on growth. Our experimental units are young tomato seedlings that have just developed their first pairs of true leaves. Discuss the design of such an experiment. You must carefully describe the treatments and other aspects of the protocol as well as the statistical design.

4. The batches to be processed in the drug-making experiment of Exercise 5 in Section 1 are mixed and processed one at a time. Label the first batch processed 01, the second 02, and so on. Use Table A to do the randomization required for a completely randomized design. Which batches did you assign to each treatment?

5. Twenty overweight females agree to participate in a study of the effectiveness of four reducing regimens. The researcher first compares each subject's weight with her "ideal weight" and then calculates how many pounds overweight each is. The subjects and their excess poundage are

Birnbaum	35	Hernandez	25	Moses	25	Smith	29
Brown	34	Jackson	33	Nevesky	39	Stall	33
Brunk	30	Kendall	28	Obrach	30	Suggs	35
Dixon	34	Loren	32	Rakov	30	Wilansky	42
Festinger	24	Mann	28	Siegel	27	Williams	22

The subjects are grouped into five blocks of four subjects each by excess weight, and the four regimens A, B, C, and D are assigned at random, each to one subject in each block. This is a randomized complete block design. After eight weeks the researcher measures each subject's weight loss.

(a) How many experimental units are there? How many factors? How many treatments?

(b) Arrange the subjects in order of increasing excess weight, then group the four least overweight, the next four, and so on. These groups are blocks.

(c) Use Table A to do the required random assignment of subjects to treatments separately within each block. Explain carefully how you used the table.

6. In Exercise 4 of Section 2, a nutritionist had 10 rats of each of two genetic strains. The effect of genetic strain can be controlled by treating the strains as blocks and randomly assigning five rats of each strain to diet A. Use Table A, beginning at line 111, to do the randomization. This is a randomized block design but not a randomized complete block design. Why not?

7. An agronomist wishes to compare the yield of five corn varieties. The field in which the experiment will be carried out increases in fertility from north to south. The agronomist therefore divides the field into 30 plots of equal size, arranged in six east–west rows of five plots each, and employs a randomized complete block design.

Identify the experimental units, the treatments, and the blocks. Describe the arrangement of the randomized complete block design, but do not actually do the randomization.

8. Hearing loss is much more common among premature infants than among full-term babies. It has long been thought that this is a physical effect of premature birth. Recently it has been suggested that hearing loss develops in infants who spend long periods in incubators, because of the high noise level in standard incubators. (You see that the effect of being premature is confounded with the effect of spending a long period in an incubator, because usually only premature babies spend time in incubators.)

Design an experiment to decide which explanation is true. (Ignore practical and moral problems. You can get more or less information out of a correct experiment here, depending on how elaborate you want to make it.)

9. Can aspirin help prevent heart attacks? A large clinical trial called Aspirin Myocardial Infarction Study (AMIS) addressed this question. AMIS involved 4524 cardiac patients and cost $17 million, but it found no evidence that aspirin prevents further heart attacks. The subjects were randomly divided into experimental and control groups, with patients in the experimental group receiving 1 gram of aspirin per day. Critics of AMIS claim that it was poorly designed. There is evidence that as little as 180 milligrams (180/1000 gram) of aspirin each day has the chemical effect needed to prevent heart attacks. The larger dose used in AMIS may have other chemical effects that make this amount ineffective for heart attack prevention.

Discuss the design of an experiment to study the effect of different dosages of aspirin on heart attacks. Be sure to state what treatment you would give each group [AMIS is discussed in *Science*, Volume 196 (1977), p. 1075, and Volume 207 (1980), pp. 859–860.]

Section 5

1. Two reports of social experiments are S. J. Press, "Police Manpower Versus Crime," and F. A. Haight, "Do Speed Limits Reduce Traffic Accidents?" both in *Statistics: A Guide to the Unknown.*
   (a) Neither the New York experiment of Press's article nor the Scandinavian experiment discussed by Haight use statistical design to the extent of the New Jersey Income-Maintenance Experiment. What aspects of design (control, randomization, repetition on many units) are present and which are absent in each case?
   (b) Describe briefly the practical barriers to social experiments mentioned in these essays. (Many potential social experiments remain undone for similar reasons.)

2. Another of the experimental trials of the negative income tax was conducted in Gary, Indiana. Unlike the New Jersey experiment, households both with and without working-age males present were included. The statistical design of the Gary experiment divided families into two blocks, those with and those without an employable adult male. Families were randomly assigned to treatments separately within each block.

Explain why blocking was used in this social experiment.

3. Would requiring cars to keep their headlights on during daylight hours reduce traffic accidents? Discuss the statistical design of an experiment to investigate this question.

4. Choose an issue of public policy that you feel might be clarified by a social experiment. Briefly discuss the statistical design of the experiment you are recommending. What are the treatments? Should blocking be used?

Section 6

There are no "right" answers to these exercises. Thoughtful persons are found on both sides of the dilemmas presented. I wish mainly to invite you to think about the ethics of experimentation.

1. (*Deception of subjects*) A psychologist conducts the following experiment: A team of subjects plays a game of skill against a computer for money rewards. Unknown to the subjects, one team member is a stooge whose stupidity causes the team to lose regularly. The experimenter observes the subjects through one-way glass. Her intent is to study the behavior of the subjects toward the stupid team member.

   This experiment involves no risk to the subject and is intended simply to create the kind of situation that might occur in any pickup basketball game. To create the situation, the subjects are deceived. Is this deception morally objectionable? Explain your position.

2. (*Enticement of subjects*) A psychologist conducted the following experiment: She measured the attitude of subjects toward cheating, then had them play a game rigged so that winning without cheating was impossible. Unknown to them, the subjects were watched through one-way glass, and a record was kept of who cheated and who did not. Then a second test of attitude was given.

   Subjects who cheated tended to change their attitudes to find cheating more acceptable. Those who resisted the temptation to cheat tended to condemn cheating more strongly on the second test of attitude. These results confirmed the psychologist's theory.

   Unlike the experiment of Exercise 1, this experiment entices subjects to engage in behavior (cheating) that probably contradicts their own standards of behavior. And the subjects are led to believe that they can cheat secretly when in fact they are observed. Is this experiment morally objectionable? Explain your position.

3. (*Morality, good taste, and public money*) In 1976 the House of Representatives deleted from an appropriations bill funding for an experiment to study the effect of marijuana on sexual response. Like all government-supported research, the proposed study had been reviewed by a panel of scientists,

both for scientific value and for risk to the subjects. *Science* [Volume 192 (1976), p. 1086] reported,

> *Dr. Harris B. Rubin and his colleagues at the Southern Illinois Medical School proposed to exhibit pornographic films to people who had smoked marihuana and to measure the response with sensors attached to the penis.*
>
> *Marihuana, sex, pornographic films—all in one package, priced at $120,000. The senators smothered the hot potato with a ketchup of colorful oratory and mixed metaphors.*
>
> *"I am firmly convinced we can do without this combination of red ink, 'blue' movies, and Acapulco 'gold,'" Senator John McClellan of Arkansas opined in a persiflage of purple prose. . . .*
>
> *The research community is up in arms because of political interference with the integrity of the peer review process.*

Two questions arise here:

- **(a)** Assume that no physical or psychological harm can come to the volunteer subjects. I might still object to the experiment on grounds of "decency" or "good taste." If you were a member of a review panel, would you veto the experiment on such grounds? Explain.
- **(b)** Suppose we concede that any legal experiment with volunteer subjects should be permitted in a free society. It is a further step to say that any such experiment is entitled to government funding if the usual review procedure finds it scientifically worthwhile. If you were a member of Congress, would you ever refuse to pay for an experiment on grounds of "decency" or "good taste"?

4. (*Informed consent*) The information given to potential subjects in a clinical trial before asking them to decide whether or not to participate might include
- **(a)** The basic statement that an experiment is being conducted—that is, something beyond simply treating your medical problem occurs in your therapy.
- **(b)** A statement of any potential risks from any of the experimental treatments.
- **(c)** An explanation that random assignment will be used to decide which treatment you get.
- **(d)** An explanation that one "treatment" is a placebo and a statement of the probability that you will receive the placebo.

Do you feel that all of this information is ethically required? Discuss.

5. (*Informed consent*) The subjects in the New Jersey Income-Maintenance Experiment (Section 5) were given a complete explanation of the purpose of the study and of the workings of the treatment to which they were assigned.

They were *not* told that there were other treatments that would have paid them more (or less), nor that the luck of randomization had determined the income they would receive. Do you agree or disagree that the information given is adequate for informed consent?

6. (*Prison experiments*) The decision to ban medical experiments on federal prisoners followed uncovering of experiments in the 1960s that exposed prisoners to serious harm. But experiments such as the vitamin C test of Example 7 in Section 2 are also banned from federal prisons. Is it necessary to ban experiments in which all treatments appear harmless because of the difficulty of obtaining truly voluntary consent in a prison? What is your overall opinion of this ban on experimentation?

7. (*Dependent subjects*) Students in PSY 001 are required to serve as experimental subjects. Students in PSY 002 are not required to serve, but they are given extra credit if they do so. Students in PSY 003 are required either to sign up as subjects or to write a term paper.

Do you object to any of these policies? Which ones, and why?

8. (*Popular pressure*) The substance Laetrile received abundant publicity in 1977 as a treatment for cancer. Like hundreds of thousands of other chemical compounds, Laetrile had earlier been tested to see if it showed antitumor activity in animals. It didn't. Because no known drug fights cancer in people but not in animals, the medical community branded Laetrile as worthless. Advocates of Laetrile wanted the FDA to conduct a clinical trial on human cancer patients.

It is usually considered unethical to use a drug on people without some promise based on animal trials that it is safe and effective. What is more, Laetrile may have toxic side effects. Do the popular interest in Laetrile and the fervor of its advocates justify a clinical trial?

9. (*Equal treatment*) A group of researchers on aging proposed to investigate the effect of supplemental health services on the quality of life of older persons. Eligible patients on the rolls of a large medical clinic were to be randomly assigned to treatment and control groups. The treatment group would be offered hearing aids, dentures, transportation, and other services not available without charge to the control group. A review committee felt that providing these services to some but not other persons in the same institution raised ethical questions. Do you agree?

10. (*Animal welfare*) Many people are concerned about the ethics of experimentation with living animals. Some go so far as to regard any animal experiments as unethical, regardless of the benefits to human beings. Briefly discuss each of the following examples:

   (a) Military doctors use goats that have been deliberately shot (while completely anesthetized) to study and teach the treatment of combat wounds. There is no equally effective way to prepare doctors to treat human wounds.

(b) Several states are considering legislation that would end the practice of using cats and dogs from pounds in medical research. Instead, the animals will be killed at the pounds.

(c) The cancer-causing potential of chemicals is assessed by exposing lab rats to high concentrations. The rats are bred for this specific purpose. (Would your opinion differ if dogs or monkeys were used?)

Chapter 3

Measurement

Professor Nous is interested in how much the intelligence of a child is influenced by the environment in which the child is raised. Children raised in the same environment still differ in intelligence because of heredity and other factors, so a comparative study is needed.

Professor Nous daydreams about randomized comparative experiments in which newborn babies are snatched from their mothers and assigned to various environments. Alas, in this instance she must be content with an observational study. A brilliant idea strikes: Why not look at the variation in intelligence between identical twins who for some reason have been raised in separate homes since birth? Because identical twins have the same heredity, differences in their intelligence must reflect the effect of environment. A careful search turns up 20 pairs of separated twins. Professor Nous feels that her troubles are over.

Not so. Once the units for study (the twins) are chosen, it remains to collect data by measuring the properties of each unit that interest the good professor. In particular, she must measure the intelligence of each child. Because intelligence, unlike sex or age, is not directly observable, Professor Nous is faced with a serious problem.

In Chapters 1 and 2, we thought about designing a study by choosing or assigning the units of study. Professor Nous has successfully completed this task. Now we must think about measurement, for the final step in collecting data is to measure some property of the units. Measurement produces numbers. You always thought that statistics concerns numbers, but I have not allowed them to encroach on you until this chapter. The real point of thinking about measurement is to help you become more comfortable with numbers. We will ask when numbers are meaningful (Section 1), inquire about their accuracy (Section 2), and learn that not all numbers are equally informative (Section 3). All you have learned will be applied, in Section 4, to the art of looking at numbers intelligently.

1. First steps in measurement: Validity

In Chapters 1 and 2, we defined a *variable* as a measured characteristic of a unit. Variables result from measuring properties of units. To be useful, a variable must be exactly defined. And to use data intelligently, we must know the definitions of the variables whose values are reported. What, for example, does it mean when the Bureau of Labor Statistics (BLS for short) announces that last month's unemployment rate was 7.3%? This statistic comes from the Current Population Survey, a monthly probability sample of about 65,000 households conducted by the Census Bureau. So its numerical value is quite accurate. In fact, the bureau's statisticians will happily tell us that

(a) There is a small bias, mainly because the survey can't find perhaps 5% or 6% of the population. We guess that these persons are more likely to be unemployed than the rest of us. Fortunately, this small bias is probably about the same from month to month, so *changes* in the unemployment rate (that's what economists and politicians really watch) have little bias.

(b) The precision of the sampling process is such that 90% of all samples drawn will give an unemployment rate within $\pm 0.2\%$ (that's ± 0.002) of the rate a census would produce.

Fine. That's a review of Chapter 1. But we don't understand the monthly unemployment rate until we know the definition of "unemployed." Is a full-time student who holds no job unemployed? Is a worker on strike unemployed? And when the unemployment rate is 7.3%, that's 7.3% of what group? You can see that changing the definition could change the announced unemployment rate a great deal.

Here is the BLS definition: You are *employed* if you did any paid work in the last week, or worked at least 15 hours in a family business, or were on leave from a regular job. You are *unemployed* if you were not employed last week *and* were available for work and looking for work. If you were not both available and looking, you were *not in the labor force*. So a full-time student who chooses not to seek a paying job is neither unemployed nor employed; he is not in the labor force. The unemployment rate is the percent unemployed among civilians over 16 years of age who are in the labor force.

"Unemployed? Not me, I'm out of the labor force."

That definition took a paragraph yet is still not detailed enough so that you or I could say exactly who is unemployed. But it is a great help in assessing the meaning of a 7.3% unemployment rate. In particular, you can appreciate the argument of labor leaders that this announced rate always underestimates the seriousness of unemployment. If you hold a part-time job but want a full-time job and can't find one, you are "employed." If you are without a job and so discouraged that you stop looking for one, you are "out of the labor force" and therefore no longer unemployed! Definitions can accomplish wondrous things.

The interviewers employed by the Current Population Survey are engaged in measuring employment status. They measure the employment status of the persons in the sample by asking them questions spelled out on the interview form, then classifying them according to the BLS definitions of employment status. I want to go one step further by insisting that the result of measurement be a number.

To *measure* a property means to assign numbers to units as a way of representing that property.

Note that we measure properties of things, not the things themselves. You can measure my weight, or my intelligence, or my employment status, but you can't measure me. And note that measurement is always an operation that produces a number. Specifying the details of that operation is as important as specifying the protocol of an experiment. Height can be measured with a tape measure. My height is 182 centimeters; that's the number resulting from measurement. Dr. Nous might decide to measure intelligence by the Wechsler Adult Intelligence Scale, the most common "IQ test." I won't tell you my IQ, but it's a number determined by that specific process. My employment status is measured by classifying me according to the BLS definitions. I'm employed. That's not a number, you say. True enough, but to run my employment status through the computer, we must assign a numerical code to each employment status. Let's use 0 for "not in the labor force," 1 for "unemployed," and 2 for "employed." Now my employment status is 2. Any measurement *must* result in a number. (That's the *definition* of measurement; we too can play the definition game.)

It is possible to talk about "classifying" or "categorizing" separately from measurement because classifying persons by sex or race or employment status does not naturally produce numbers. I prefer to lump classifying in with measurement by insisting that we assign numbers to the classes. As we saw with employment status, that's no hardship. In Chapters 1 and 2, variables could have values such as "agree" or "disagree" (as when an opinion poll asks your reaction to a statement). Now we insist that variables have numerical values.

Statistics deals with variables, that is, with numbers resulting from measurement. Beware of the easy passage from a property of units to a variable that claims to represent the property. The variable must be clearly and exactly defined. The property may be vague, inexact, and not directly observable. In this situation, the variable is rarely a complete representation of the property.

> **Example 1.** The BLS definition of "unemployed" may not agree in detail with your vague idea of what it means to be unemployed. Labor says this variable understates unemployment by insisting that only persons actively seeking work can be unemployed. On the other hand, management argues that the BLS overstates unemployment because some persons who are looking for work may refuse to accept a job unless it is exactly right for them. Many married women and teenagers, secure because the household already has one steady wage earner, shop around for the right job. By the BLS definition, these persons are unemployed. (I pass over in silence the claim of the National Association of Manufacturers, recorded on the front page of the *Wall Street Journal* on September 13, 1976, that the official employment rate is inflated because "criminal elements" are included in the labor force.)

Though both management and labor would prefer slightly different definitions of "unemployed," neither accuses the BLS of having a completely inappropriate definition. The official unemployment rate is a useful indicator of the state of the economy. That is, the BLS produces a *valid* measure of employment and unemployment.

A variable is a *valid* measure of a property if it is relevant or appropriate as a representation of that property.

Validity of a measurement process is a simple but slippery idea. Does the process measure what you want it to? That is the question of validity. If I measured your height in inches and recorded you as "employed" if your height exceeds 65 inches, that is an invalid measure of your employment status. The BLS uses a valid measure—not a perfect measure of employment (whatever that might mean), not the whole story about employment status, not the only variable that might measure employment status, but an appropriate and relevant variable,

It is easy for persons who are not experienced with numbers to fall into the trap of using an invalid measure. A common case is the use of absolute numbers when rates are appropriate. Here is an example:

> **Example 2.** If customers returned 36 coats to Sears and only 12 to La Boutique Classique next door, this does not mean that Sears' customers were less satisfied. Sears sold 1100 coats that season, while La Boutique sold 200. So Sears' return rate was
>
> $$\frac{36}{1100} = 0.033, \quad \text{or} \quad 3.3\%,$$
>
> while the return rate at La Boutique was
>
> $$\frac{12}{200} = 0.06, \quad \text{or} \quad 6\%.$$
>
> This return rate, or percentage of coats returned, is a more valid measure of dissatisfaction than the number of returns.

It is easy to decide if a variable is a valid measure of a property when we understand the property well. That's true of physical properties, such as length. Employment status and customer satisfaction (Examples 1 and 2) are a bit less clear, but we still have a good idea of what we want to measure. But it sometimes happens that the property to be measured is so fuzzy that reasonable persons can disagree on the validity of a variable as a measure of that property. This situation is not uncommon in the social and behavioral sciences. Psychologists wish to measure such things as intelligence, or authoritarian personality, or mathematical aptitude. The variables are typically scores on a test—an IQ test for intelligence, the mathematics part of the Scholastic Aptitude Test (the "college boards") for mathematical aptitude, and so on. The validity of these variables is exceedingly controversial.

Example 3. The Scholastic Aptitude Tests (SATs) are taken each year by about a million high school seniors seeking admission to colleges and universities. There are two SATs, testing verbal and mathematical aptitude. Scores range from 200 to 800. These tests have been attacked because black and Hispanic students score considerably lower, on the average, than do whites. In 1982, the College Board released the following information:[1]

	Average SAT score		Parents' average income
	Verbal	Math	
Asian	397	513	$21,500
Black	332	362	$12,500
White	442	483	$26,300

What can we say about the validity of SAT scores?

To discuss the issue sensibly, we must ask validity *for what purpose?* and validity *for what population?* Critics of the SATs, for example, complain that these tests measure only cognitive ability, ignoring emotional and physical abilities that are just as important. That is much like criticizing a yardstick for not giving the time of day, because the SATs do not claim to measure such other abilities. But it is also difficult to claim that SATs measure some innate cognitive ability. "Scholastic aptitude" probably has many components and cannot be measured by two multiple-choice exams. And SAT scores can be improved by intensive coaching courses, which surely could not change a student's innate ability. In short, "scholastic aptitude" is so poorly understood in itself that we cannot say that SAT scores are a valid measure of this vague concept.

What can be said is that SAT scores are valid for predicting academic success in college. Success in college is a clear concept, and there is an observed connection between high SAT scores and high grades in college. This is predictive validity. *A measurement of a property has predictive validity if it can be used to predict success on tasks that are related to the property to be measured,* as success in college is related to scholastic aptitude. Predictive validity is much less vague than our original definition. It is often the most useful answer to "validity for what?"

There remains the question of "validity for whom?" The most common criticism of SATs is that they are *culturally biased*—that they are valid for the white middle class but not for other groups. This is certainly plausible if SATs are taken to measure scholastic ability. Asians, for example, have the highest math SAT scores of any group, but their verbal scores are less than the white average. This may reflect the fact that many Asians are not native speakers of English. Similarly, the family income of blacks taking the SATs is less than half that of whites. The lower SAT scores of blacks are certainly influenced by the great disparity between the social and economic status of blacks and whites in America.

But when the SATs are considered as measures not of ability but of future academic success, they appear to be innocent of cultural bias. SAT scores predict future grades for minorities at least as well as for whites. Success in college depends on exposure to middle-class education and habits as well as on innate ability. White, middle-class students have an advantage on the SATs, but they have the same advantage in college.

Much of the controversy over standardized tests such as the SATs arises because some users ignore the limitations on the validity of the tests. The SATs are valid predictors of future academic success, but they are quite imperfect predictors. Many factors not measured by such tests also influence a student's success in college. It is not appropriate to base college admissions decisions on test scores alone. It *is* appropriate to regard low SAT scores as a danger signal, to look for other abilities that will help the student overcome them, or even to plan special compensatory training for such students. Like a sharp knife, a standardized test can be used wisely by the wise or foolishly by the foolish. Those who call for an end to such tests finally base their case on the judgment that the foolish so outnumber the wise that sharp knives ought to be confiscated.

The example of standardized tests illustrates the care needed in discussing the validity of measures of fuzzy concepts. It also illustrates the way social and behavioral scientists often deal with this problem: They try to show a connection between the measuring variable and other variables that ought to be connected with the original fuzzy idea. Persons of high mental ability ought to do better in school than those of low ability. Persons with high IQ or SAT scores do tend to do better in school than those with low scores. The final step is to replace the vague idea with the precise variable that seems to be connected with the same behavior. That is, for statistical purposes, *the best way to define a property is to give a rule for measuring it.* The saying that "intelligence is whatever it is that IQ measures" is an example of such a definition. IQ measures some combination of innate ability, learned knowledge, and exposure to mainstream culture. This is a clearly defined property of people because it is established by the Wechsler Adult Intelligence Scale. It is an interesting variable because it is related to success in school and other interesting dependent variables. But IQ is not the same as our everyday idea of intelligence. Our old friend Professor Nous should probably decide to use her sample of separated twins to study the effect of environment on IQ. To study "intelligence" is beyond her reach.

Statistics can deal only with measured properties. "Intelligence" and "maturity" cannot be studied statistically, though variables such as IQ can be. Beware of the arrogance that says that everything can be measured or that only things we can measure are important. The world contains much that is beyond the grasp of statistics.

2.   Accuracy in measurement

Even the most exact laboratory measurements are not perfectly accurate. Physicists and chemists, who make little use of statistical ideas in data collection, use statistics heavily in analyzing errors in their measurements. When a measurement is made as accurately as the instrument allows, repeated measurements do not always give the same result. (Try Exercises 1 and 2 to see that for yourself.) Accuracy in measurement has two aspects: lack of bias and reliability.

> A measurement process is *unbiased* if it does not systematically overstate or understate the true value of the variable.

> A measurement process is *reliable* if repeated measurements on the same unit give the same (or approximately the same) results.

Lack of bias and reliability in measurement carry the same meanings as do unbiasedness and precision in data collection. (In fact, it is common in the physical sciences and engineering to use the word "precision" instead of "reliability" to describe the repeatability of the results of measurement.) Unbiased means correct on the average; reliable means repeatable. The difference is that these meanings now apply to the process of measuring a property of a unit, not to the process of choosing units to be measured. If an egg scale always weighs 10 grams heavy, it is biased. If the scale has dust in its pivot and gives widely different weights when the same egg is weighed several times, it is unreliable.

The analogy between repeated measurement and repeated sampling extends further. The results of repeated measurement are *random* in the same sense that the results of repeated sampling are random. That is, individual results vary, but there is a definite *distribution* of results when many trials are made. The average of several measurements is less variable (more reliable) than a single measurement, just as a sample statistic becomes more precise in larger samples. That is why laboratory instructors in physics or chemistry suggest that you repeat your measurements several times and use the average value. It is a pleasing instance of the harmony of thought that measurement error and sampling error can be studied and overcome by the same ideas.

> **Example 4.** If you want to know how much something weighs, you use a scale. If an analytical chemist wants to know how much a specimen weighs, he uses a better scale. His scale is less biased and more reliable than yours, and he calibrates it regularly by weighing a "standard weight" whose mass is accurately known. The mass of standard weights is accurately known because they have been compared with superstandard weights kept by the National Bureau of Standards (NBS) in Washington, D.C. And the mass of *these* weights is known very accurately because they have been compared with the International Prototype Kilogram, which lives in a guarded vault in Paris and indirectly determines all weights in the world.

These National Bureau of Standards mass standards provide the basis for measuring weight in the United States, whether by a laboratory balance or your bathroom scale. [Photo courtesy of Mass and Volume Section, National Bureau of Standards.]

The NBS standard weight called NB 10, for example, weighs 9.999596 grams. (It is supposed to weigh 10 grams but is light by about the mass of a grain of salt.) Because the NBS knows that the results of repeated measurements are random, it repeatedly weighs standards such as NB 10 to determine the reliability of the weighing process. Then, when the analytical chemist sends in his standard weight for calibration, the NBS can tell him the reliability of their answer, just as the Gallup Poll can state the precision of their conclusions. Here are the results of 11 determinations of the mass (in grams) of NB 10, made in May 1963 with all the care the NBS can apply:[2]

9.9995992	9.9995985
9.9995947	9.9996008
9.9995978	9.9996027
9.9995925	9.9995929
9.9996006	9.9995988
9.9996014	

You see that the 11 measurements do vary. There is no such thing as an absolutely accurate measurement. The average (mean) of these measurements is 9.9995982 grams, which is a more reliable estimate of the true mass than a single measurement. In fact, the NBS says it is 95% confident that this average is within ±0.0000023 gram of the truth. Such reliability statements also apply to unknown masses, such as that of the analytical chemist's standard weight.

I hope that this excursion into the world ruled by the International Prototype Kilogram has reminded you that even physicists and chemists don't get "the right answer" on every measurement. If you have spent part of your youth in laboratories, you need no reminder. I well remember the dark midnight when, after hours of failing to get the same answer twice in an optics lab, I faced the alternative of smashing the wretched interferometer or choosing a major other than physics. Because the interferometer was expensive, I got out of physics.

As usual, things are tougher yet outside the laboratory. Measuring unemployment is also "measurement," and the concepts of bias and reliability apply here just as they do to measuring the mass of NB 10. The sampling process from which the unemployment rate is obtained has a high but not perfect precision, which can be clearly stated because probability sampling is used. The measurement of employment status is also not perfectly repeatable—not perfectly reliable. The BLS checks the reliability of its measurements by having supervisors reinterview about 5% of the sample. This is repeated measurement on the same unit, just as when NB 10 is weighed several times. It turns out that interviewers and supervisors almost always agree on who is not in the labor force and who has a full-time job. These measurements are extremely reliable. But supervisors and interviewers disagree on the status of about 10% of the "unemployed." The distinctions between "unemployed," "temporarily laid off," and "underemployed" are a bit subjective. The measurement of unemployment is therefore somewhat unreliable. To sum up: The precision of sampling refers to the repeatability of sample statistics in *different* samples. The reliability of measurement refers to repeatability of measured values on the *same* units.

Bias has the same meaning in measuring unemployment as in measuring mass: systematic deviation of the measured result from the "true value" that perfect measurement would produce. The "true value" isn't exactly known even for a mass, but the idea of a biased scale that systematically weighs high or low is clear enough. For unemployment, the "true employment status" of a person might be his status by the BLS definitions when classified by the Commissioner of Labor Statistics herself. Other interviewers will sometimes disagree with the commissioner (the reliability of measurement is not perfect), but there is no bias unless, for example, the interviewers systematically call "unemployed" persons the commissioner would say are "not in the labor force." There appears to be little bias in measuring unemployment.

Take note of one detail: If the definition of unemployment from the BLS understates the "unemployment problem," this is not bias in measurement. It is instead a question of the validity of the BLS definition as a measure of unemployment. Bias in a measurement process means that the process gives measurements on a variable that are systematically higher or lower than the true value of that variable. Whether the variable is a valid measure of a property such as intelligence or employment status is a different—and harder—question.

Example 5. Data on college enrollments are collected by the federal government's National Center for Education Statistics. The preliminary data for the fall of 1976 showed that the number of first-time students in public universities had grown by 4%. But the questionnaire for collecting preliminary data contained confused wording that led many colleges to include new graduate students in the category of first-time students, a category meant to include only students with no previous higher education. The final figures showed that the number of new students in public institutions was *down* 9%, not up 4%, compared with a year earlier.

This is an example of measurement bias. The badly worded form produced values of the variable "number of first-time students" that were systematically higher than the true value.

Reliability of weighings or of employment status classifications is checked by making repeated measurements on the same units. Reliability of IQ tests or the SATs cannot be checked this way because subjects taking a test the second time have an advantage over their first try. Even with different but (one hopes) equivalent forms of the test, this learning effect rules out assessing reliability from many repeated measurements. Behavioral scientists must fall back on less direct and more complicated ways of checking reliability, though the basic ideas we have covered still apply. Here is yet another way in which psychology is a more complicated subject than physics.

3. Scales of measurement

Measurement of a property means assigning a number to represent it. Having designed our data-collection process and stated what measurements are to be made on the units, we can cheerfully amass our data—a pile of numbers resulting from the measurements we made. The next step is usually to find averages or prepare some other summary of these data. Before plunging ahead, it is wise to ask how much information our numbers carry. Consider, for example, my employment status. We agreed to represent this by the variable having value 0 if I'm not in the labor force, value 1 if I'm unemployed, and value 2 if I'm employed. Now, 2 is twice as much as 1. And 2 inches is twice as much as 1 inch. But an employment status of 2 is *not* twice an employment status of 1. That's obvious, but sneaky. The numbers used to code employment status are just category labels disguised as numbers. We could have used the labels A, B, and C, except that to include categorization as part of measurement we insisted on numbers. So not all numbers resulting from measurement carry information, such as "twice as much," that we naturally associate with numbers. What we can do with data depends on how much information the numbers carry.

We speak of the kind of information a measurement carries by saying in what kind of *scale* the measurement is made. Here are the kind of scales:

A measurement of a property has a *nominal scale* if the measurement tells only *what class* a unit falls in with respect to the property.

The measurement has an *ordinal scale* if it also tells when one unit has *more of* the property than does another unit.

The measurement has an *interval scale* if it also tells us that one unit *differs by a certain amount* of the property from another unit.

The measurement has a *ratio scale* if it tells us that one unit has *so many times as much* of the property as does another unit.

Measurements in a *nominal scale* place units in categories—nothing more. Such properties as race, sex, and employment status are measured in a nominal scale. We can code the sex of a subject by

> 0—female
> 1—male

or by

> 0—male
> 1—female.

Which numbers we assign makes no difference; the value of this variable indicates only what the sex of the subject is.

In an *ordinal scale*, the order of numbers is meaningful. If a committee ranks 10 fellowship candidates from 1 (weakest) to 10 (strongest), the candidate ranked 8 is better than the candidate ranked 6—not just different (as a nominal scale would tell us), but better. But the usual arithmetic is not meaningful: 8 is not twice as good as 4, and the difference in quality between 8 and 6 need not be the same as between 6 and 4. Only the order of the values is meaningful. Ordinal scales are important when social scientists measure properties such as "authoritarian personality" by giving a test on which a subject can score, say, between 0 and 100 points. If the test is valid as a measure of this property, then Esther who scores 80 is more authoritarian than Lydia who scores 60. But if Jane scores 40, we can probably not conclude that Esther is "twice as authoritarian" as Jane. Nor can we say that "the difference in authoritarianism between Esther and Lydia is the same as between Lydia and Jane" just because their scores differ by 20 in each case. Whether a particular test has an ordinal scale or actually does carry information about differences and ratios we leave for psychologists to discuss. Many tests have ordinal scales.

With *interval and ratio scales* we reach the kind of measurement familiar to us. These are *measurements made on a scale of equal units,* such as height in centimeters, reaction time in seconds, or temperature in degrees Celsius. Arithmetic such as finding differences is meaningful when these scales are used. A cockroach 4 centimeters long is 2 centimeters longer than one 2 centimeters long. There is a rather fine distinction between interval and ratio scales. A cockroach 4 centimeters long is twice as long as one 2 centimeters long; length in centimeters has a ratio scale. But when the temperature is 40°C it is not twice as hot as when it is 20°C. Temperature in degrees Celsius has an interval, not a ratio, scale. Another way of expressing the difference is that ratio scales have a meaningful zero. A length of 0 centimeters is "no length," a time of 0 seconds is "no time." But a temperature of 0°C is just the freezing point of water, not "no heat." (There is a temperature scale, the absolute or Kelvin scale, with 0°

at "absolute zero," the temperature at which molecules stop moving, and there is literally "no heat." This is a ratio scale.)

We will not pay attention to the distinction between interval and ratio scales. But it is important (and usually easy) to notice whether a variable has a nominal scale (objects are put into categories), an ordinal scale (objects are ordered in some way), or an interval/ratio scale (measurements are made on a scale marked off in units).

One concluding fine point: The scale of a measurement depends mainly on the method of measurement, not on the property measured. The weight of a carton of eggs measured in grams has an interval/ratio scale. But if I label the carton as one of small, medium, large, or extra large, I have measured the weight in an ordinal scale. If a standard test of authoritarian personality has an ordinal scale, this does not mean that it is impossible to measure authoritarian personality on an interval/ratio scale, only that this test does not do so.

4. Looking at data intelligently

Political rhetoric, advertising claims, debate on public issues—we are assailed daily by numbers employed to prove a point or to buttress an argument. Asking a few preliminary questions of such data will help us to distinguish sense from nonsense.

What is the source of the data?

Knowledge of the source helps us decide whether to trust the data. Knowing the source of data also allows us to check whether it was quoted correctly and to use the knowledge gained in Chapters 1 and 2 to assess the quality of the data. Here are some examples:

> **Example 6.** In a climate of increased concern over the risks of exposure to radiation, veterans' groups collected instances of multiple myeloma (a form of cancer) among veterans of the Hiroshima and Nagasaki occupation forces. They claimed that the number of cases was unusual and called for government study and compensation. This is *anecdotal evidence*, based on a few cases without systematic comparison or data collection. A committee of the National Research Council found no evidence that the rate of multiple myeloma for the atomic veterans was higher than that in other similar populations. Anecdotal data may be an incentive to more careful investigation, but in themselves they reflect rumor and emotion as often as fact.

> **Example 7.** "Charles D. Masters of the United States Geological Survey told oil industry officials that the world's supply of crude oil would run out in about the year 2046 if used at the current rate." Here we have an *expert opinion*. We cannot sample yet-to-be-discovered oil supplies, so any conclusion must be based on past data and informed judgment about the future. We must ask ourselves if we trust the expert. Is his statement a careful estimate or a shot in the dark? Is he speaking under political pressure or in support of a pet project? Does his judgment agree with that of other experts? Is it supported by a reasonable reading of past data?

> **Example 8.** "So we went to 21 major cities and asked 550 drinkers to compare white rum with the leading brands of gin and vodka. 24.2% preferred gin. 34.4% preferred vodka. And 41.4% preferred white rum." This statement in a rum advertisement by the Commonwealth of Puerto Rico describes a comparative taste test, but it says little about the design of the experiment. Government regulations require that claims such as "more drinkers prefer rum than either gin or vodka" be based on actual studies and that the details of such studies be available on request. We can write the advertiser if we wish to assess the claim.

Anecdotal evidence (Example 6) should be given little credence until substantiated by systematically collected data. We are well equipped to assess data from sample surveys or experiments (Example 8) if only we are given the details

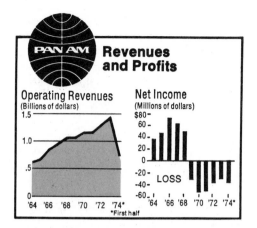

Figure 3-1. Extrapolation is risky. [Copyright © 1974 by the New York Times Company. Reprinted by permission.]

we need. Example 7 lies in the murky middle ground between these cases. Informed opinion is a common source of data in public issues concerning future trends. While potentially more trustworthy than anecdotal accounts, no informed judgment is as reliable as a properly designed survey or experiment. Whenever surveys or experiments are possible, informed judgment is a second-rate source of data. The rapid adoption of random sampling by experienced political campaign managers is one of many examples of the replacement of expert judgment by statistical methods.

As for future trends, extrapolation is always dangerous. Extrapolation means projecting the trend of past data to future results. The future can differ from past trends, as we all learned at the gas pump after the 1973 oil embargo and the 1978 Iranian revolution. Figure 3-1 provides another example. The unwary investor looking at Pan Am's net income from 1964 to 1968 might have been rather more optimistic about the future than was justified. Experts are not exempt from the risks of extrapolation. Nor are they immune to outside pressure or without private prejudices. Reaching a clear conclusion when extrapolation is necessary and political and economic special interests are strong is extraordinarily difficult. Unfortunately, crucial issues such as future energy supply fall in this category.

Do the data make sense?

You would not accept verbal nonsense in a discussion. Don't accept numerical nonsense either.

Example 9. "The mayor said that 90% of the police force had never taken a bribe. These honest men should not be tarnished by the misdeeds of a few." That "90%" is a *meaningless number*. The mayor has no idea what percent of the police have never taken a bribe. He wants to say that "a great majority" or "all but a few" have not. We can (and do) ignore his "90%."

Example 10. "True cigarettes have 5 milligrams less tar." This is a *meaningless comparison*. Five milligrams less tar than what?

A more serious aspect of asking whether data make sense is to examine them for *internal consistency*. Do the numbers fit together in a way that makes sense? A little thought here will do wonders. Here is part of an article dealing with a cancer researcher at the Sloan-Kettering Institute who was accused of committing the ultimate scientific sin, falsifying data:

Example 11. "One thing he did manage to finish was a summary paper dealing with the Minnesota mouse experiments. . . . That paper, cleared at SKI and accepted by the *Journal of Experimental Medicine*, contains a statistical table that is erroneous in such an elementary way that a bright grammar school pupil could catch the flaw. It lists 6 sets of 20 animals each, with the percentages of successful takes. Although any percentage of 20 has to be a multiple of 5, the percentages that Summerlin recorded were 53, 58, 63, 46, 48, and 67."[3]

In Example 11, lack of internal consistency led to the suspicion that the data were phony. *Too much precision or regularity* can lead to the same suspicion, as when a student's lab report contains data that are exactly as the theory predicts. The laboratory instructor knows that the accuracy of the equipment and the student's laboratory technique are not good enough to give such perfect results. He suspects that the student made them up. Here is another example of phony precision:

Example 12. If you asked the Alabama Development Office in 1973 how many new industrial jobs were created in the state in the past year, you would get an answer: 42,878. And in the past 25 years, 422,657 new industrial jobs had been created. This is spurious (phony) precision. The Development Office simply adds up company announcements of new jobs without checking how many jobs were actually created. It cannot know the number of new jobs to the last digit and probably does not know the number even to the nearest thousand.[4]

Careful statistical writers avoid the appearance of more precision than the data warrant. In technical writing, a confidence statement can be made. In nontechnical writing, the degree of precision is indicated by rounding off. The Alabama Department of Industrial Relations, in cooperation with the Bureau of Labor Statistics, counts industrial workers in the state. They recorded a gain of 103,000 instead of the Development Office's 422,657. We can surmise that the gain of 103,000 is accurate to about the nearest thousand. Aside from spurious precision, the great difference between the two numbers is a matter of definition of variables. The Development Office does not bother to subtract jobs eliminated, so the actual number of jobs might even be decreasing. The department reports the actual change in number of industrial jobs. The latter is surely a more valid measure of employment trends in Alabama.

The final part of asking if the data make sense is to *ask if they are plausible*. Numbers are easily misquoted, and the result is often wildly too high or too low. A little knowledge and common sense will detect many unbelievable numbers. For example, *Organic Gardening* magazine (July 1983) says that "the U.S. Interstate Highway System spans 3.9 million miles and is wearing out 50% faster than it can be fixed. Continuous road deterioration adds $7 billion yearly in fuel costs to motorists." Now, 3.9 million miles of pavement would build 1300 separate highways across the 3000 miles separating the east and west coasts. Sure enough, the *Statistical Abstract of the United States* gives a more plausible 41,000 miles of interstate highways. *Organic Gardening* probably meant 39,000 rather than 3.9 million. I will leave you to assess that $7 billion per year in extra fuel costs. Here is another example:

> **Example 13.** A writer in *Science* [Volume 192 (1976), p. 1081] stated that "people over 65, now numbering 10 million, will number 30 million by the year 2000, and will constitute an unprecedented 25 percent of the population." Such explosive growth of the elderly—tripling in a quarter century to become a fourth of the population—would profoundly change any society. But wait. Thirty million is 25% of 120 million, and the U.S. population is already much higher than that. Something is wrong with the writer's figures. Thus alerted, we can check reliable sources such as census reports to learn the truth. A reader of *Science* did so [letter to the editor, Volume 193 (1976)] and noted that in 1975 there were 22.4 million persons over 65, not 10 million. The projection of 30 million by the year 2000 is correct, but that is only 11% or 12% of the projected population for that year. The explosive growth of the elderly vanishes in the light cast by accurate statistics.

I hope that reading this book will help you form the habit of looking at numbers closely. Your reward will be the reputation for brillance that accrues to those who point out that a number being honored by everyone else is clearly nonsense.

Is the information complete?

A subtle way of using data in support of dubious conclusions is giving only part of the relevant information. This is perhaps the single most common trick employed by those who use numbers to make an impression rather than to tell the whole truth. Here are some typical examples:

> **Example 14.** A television advertisement by the Investment Company Institute (the mutual fund trade association) said that a $10,000 investment made in 1950 in an average common stock mutual fund would have increased to $113,500 by the end of 1972. That's true. The *Wall Street Journal* (June 7, 1972) pointed out that the ad had omitted that the same investment spread over all the stocks making up the New York Stock Exchange Composite Index would have grown to $151,427; that is, mutual funds performed worse than the stock market as a whole.

> **Example 15.** Anacin was long advertised as containing "more of the ingredient doctors recommend most." The ad did not mention that the ingredient is aspirin. Another over-the-counter pain reliever claimed that "doctors specify Bufferin most" over other "leading brands." Bufferin also consists primarily of aspirin and was specified most only because doctors rarely recommend a particular brand of pure aspirin. Both advertising claims were literally true; the Federal Trade Commission found them both misleading.

> **Example 16.** A television commercial for Schick Super Chromium razor blades showed a group of barbers shaving with the same blade, one after another. The twelfth, thirteenth, fifteenth, and seventeenth men to use the blade were interviewed. All said the shave was satisfactory. Consumers Union repeated this experiment with 18 men. The seventeenth and eighteenth to shave with the same blade were satisfied, but the seventh, eighth, ninth, and tenth all said the blade needed changing. Did all 17 users in the commercial get good shaves, or was the interviewing selective? Were the barbers chosen at random? Was their judgment biased by the knowledge that Schick was sponsoring the test and that they might appear on TV?[5]

Examples 14, 15, and 16 illustrate the misleading effect of giving true information out of context. The truth without the *whole* truth can lie.

Even complete and accurate data may mislead us if we are not aware of changes in the process of measuring and collecting the data. This too is part of the background information needed to interpret data intelligently. The reported size of a university's faculty changed when postdoctoral researchers, who had been listed as faculty members, were dropped from the list. This is a change of definition. The number of petty larcenies reported in Chicago more than doubled between 1959 and 1960 because a new police commissioner had introduced an improved reporting system. The new system gave a much better count of crimes committed, so the number of crimes reported rose. This is a change in data-collection procedure. Almost all series of numbers covering many years are affected by changing definitions and collection methods. Often these changes are pointed to by sudden jumps in the series of numbers (lack of internal consistency), but not always. Alertness and care are needed to avoid false conclusions.

> **Example 17.** Data collected by the General Electric Company once showed that a component of a major appliance was failing at ever higher rates as the appliance became older. Preparations began for the manufacture of a more reliable component. Then a statistician noted that the rate of failure was roughly constant for the first year of service, turned up sharply at exactly 12 months, was roughly constant at this higher rate during the second year of service, and turned up again at exactly 24

"Sure your patients have 50% fewer cavities. That's because they have 50% fewer teeth!"

months. No appliances in the sample had been in service more than 29 months.

Alerted by this suspicious regularity, the statistician checked into the source of the data. For the first 12 months, all appliances were sampled because all had a one-year warranty. Data for the second 12 months referred only to appliances whose owners had bought a service contract for the second year. Data beyond 24 months were collected only for appliances on a renewed service contract. Because a service contract provides free service, appliances covered by contracts are serviced more often. And owners of troublesome appliances are more likely to buy and renew a service contract. So the higher failure rates in the second and third years were not representative of the entire population of appliances. GE did not have to develop a new component. (I hope they paid part of the savings to their statistician.)[6]

Is the arithmetic crooked?

Conclusions that are wrong or just incomprehensible are often the result of plain old-fashioned blunders. Rates and percentages are the most common causes of crooked arithmetic. Sometimes the matter can be straightened out by some numerical detective work. Here is an example:

Example 18. The BLS report on employment and unemployment for August 1977 noted that the unemployment rate was 6.1% for whites and 14.5% for blacks. The *New York Times* (September 3, 1977) included the following paragraph in its article on this report:

> The bureau also reported that the ratio of black to white jobless rates "continued its recent updrift to the unusually high level of 2.4 to 1 in August," meaning that 2.4 black workers were without jobs for every unemployed white worker.

Now 14.5% is 2.4 times as great as 6.1%, so the BLS is correct in stating that the ratio of black to white jobless rates was 2.4 to 1. But the *Times'* interpretation is completely wrong. Because blacks make up only a small part of the labor force, there are fewer jobless blacks than whites even though the percent of blacks who are unemployed is higher than the percent of whites who are without jobs. The *Times* confused percent unemployed with actual counts of the number of unemployed workers.

I concede that percents are a bit mysterious, but if you are going to write on statistical subjects you will have to get such things straight. Most subjects these days are statistical subjects.

Data that enlighten

The aim of statistics is to provide insight by means of numbers. To achieve this aim, we must first collect numbers that are *valid* in the sense of being both correct and relevant to the issue at hand. Since we most often have data on only some people or things from a larger population, we distinguish between *internal validity* and *external validity*. Internal validity refers to the particular people or things that we have measured. External validity concerns generalizability of our conclusions to a wider population.

Valid measurement is part of internal validity. Scores on an employment test that is unrelated to the job to be done are of no value in judging those who took the test, let alone for broader conclusions. Confounding with extraneous variables can also destroy internal validity, as can arithmetic mistakes or incomplete information.

Convenience samples are a common threat to external validity. Even though we have accurate information about the sample (internal validity), the data say little about any wider population. Unrealistic experimental treatments or unrepresentative experimental subjects can also make correct numbers useless for broad conclusions.

A naked number, without source or context, can easily mislead. But the many examples of misleading numbers in this section should reinforce rather than weaken our resolution to master the statistical ideas that produce clear, precise, and valid data.

NOTES

1. Reported in the *Chronicle of Higher Education* of October 11, 1982.
2. These data appear in Harry H. Ku, "Statistical Concepts in Metrology," in Harry H. Ku, ed., *Precision Measurement and Calibration* (National Bureau of Standards Special Publication 300, 1969), p. 319.
3. Quoted from Barbara Yuncker, "The Strange Case of the Painted Mice," *Saturday Review/World*, November 30, 1974, p. 53.
4. From Roy Reed, "Statistics on Rise in Jobs are Disputed in Alabama," *New York Times*, August 20, 1973.
5. *Consumer Reports*, October 1971, pp. 584–586.
6. This example appears in Wayne B. Nelson, "Data Analysis with Simple Plots," General Electric Technical Information Series, April 1975.

Exercises

Section 1

1. One of the preliminary problems in the negative income tax social experiments (Section 5 of Chapter 2) was to give a definition of the "income" of a family. This was important because the welfare "negative tax" payments decrease as income rises. Write an exact definition of "income" for this purpose. A short essay may be needed. For example, will you include nonmoney income, such as the value of food stamps or of subsidized housing? Will you allow deductions for the cost of child care needed to permit the parent to work?

2. The essay by Brian J. L. Berry, "Measuring Racial Integration Potentials," in *Statistics: A Guide to the Unknown* describes an attempt to define a variable that measures a complex and somewhat vague concept. Read the essay and explain clearly what was to be measured.

3. The number of persons killed in bicycle accidents rose from about 600 in 1967 to over 1100 in 1973. Does this indicate that bicycle riding is becoming less safe? Let us put this question more specifically.
    (a) Is this total number of fatalities per year a valid measure of the danger of bicycle riding? Why or why not?
    (b) If you question the validity of total deaths as a measure of danger, suggest a variable that is a more valid measure. Explain your suggestion.

4. Congress wants the medical establishment to show that progress is being made in fighting cancer. Some variables that might be used are
    (a) Death rates—what percent of all Americans die from cancer of various kinds? (These death rates are rising steadily.)
    (b) Survival rates among cancer patients—what percent of cancer patients survive for five years from the time it was discovered that they had the disease? (These rates are rising slowly for all cancer, though the survival rate has improved greatly for a few kinds of cancer.)
    Discuss the validity of each of these variables as a measure of the effectiveness of cancer treatment.

5. "Domestic automakers led foreign manufacturers in the number of vehicles recalled in the United States because of safety problems in the first half of 1983, the National Highway Traffic Safety Administration says." That is the lead sentence in an Associated Press dispatch, which my local paper (*Lafayette Journal and Courier*) of July 3, 1983, headlined "U.S. AUTOMAKERS RECALL MORE THAN COMPETITION." The article goes on to state that domestic companies recalled 2,047,400 cars and trucks, while foreign manufacturers recalled 903,100. Both the article and the headline suggest that domestic vehicles had a more serious safety-recall problem than imports. This is quite wrong: The imports suffered worse. Explain how an invalid measure led to this incorrect conclusion.

6. You wish to study the effect of violent television programs on antisocial behavior in children.
    (a) Define (that is, tell how to measure) the independent and dependent variables. You have many possible choices of variables—just be sure that the ones you choose are valid and clearly defined.

(b) Do you think that an experiment is practically and morally possible? If so, briefly describe the design of an experiment for this study.

(c) If you were unable or unwilling to do an experiment, briefly discuss the design of a sample study. Will confounding with other variables threaten the validity of your conclusions about the effect of TV violence on child behavior?

7. "Standardized tests" are so called because a certain score—say 500 on the SAT verbal test— represents the same level of ability independent of whether it was measured in 1963 or 1983. The 1963 test form cannot be used in 1983, for by then the questions would have leaked out and students could prepare for them. To see how tests are kept standardized, read William H. Angoff, "Calibrating College Board Scores," in *Statistics: A Guide to the Unknown*. Discuss briefly the "equating" of scores on different forms of a standardized test.

Section 2

1. Use a ruler to mark off a piece of stiff paper in inches (mark only full inches— no fractions) about as shown here:

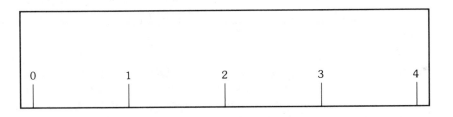

Measure the line below with your instrument, recording your answer to a hundredth of an inch (such as 2.23 inches or 2.39 inches).

To make this measurement, you must estimate what portion of the distance between the 2- and 3-inch marks the line extends. Careful measurements usually involve an uncertainty such as this; we have only magnified it by using an instrument divided into inches only.

(a) What is the result of your first measurement?

(b) Measure the line 5 times and record your results. What margin of error do you think a measurement with your instrument has? (That is, how reliable is it?)

(c) Suppose that someone measures the line by placing its left end at the end of the instrument instead of at the 0 mark. This causes bias. Explain why. Is the reliability of the measurement also affected, or not?

Comment: Your work in part (b) may not be a good indication of variability in measurement because your trials are not independent. You remember the answer you gave in part (a), and this may affect your later measurements. A better picture of the degree of reliability here is obtained by collecting the answers of the entire class to part (a). Doing this will produce a graph similar to that in Figure 1-1 in Chapter 1.

2. Take a 1-foot ruler and measure the length of one wall of a room to the nearest inch. Do this five times, recording your answers in feet and inches. What is your average result? If possible, now use a tape measure at least as long as the wall to get a more accurate measurement. Did your ruler measurements show bias? (For example, were they almost all too long?)

3. A news article reported a study of preemployment job performance tests and subsequent job performance for 1400 government technicians. Such tests are often accused of being biased against minority groups. A psychologist for the Educational Testing Service commenting on the results of the study said, "Six years later, we found that belief wrong, if you define bias as meaning the scores are unrealistically low in relation to performance on the job." (*New York Times,* July 27, 1973.)

   Is "bias" in the everyday sense used in this news article the same as "measurement bias" in the technical sense of this chapter? Why or why not?

4. Give an example of a measurement process that is valid but has large bias. Then give an example of a measurement process that is invalid but highly reliable.

5. In the mid-nineteenth century, craniometry was a respectible scientific endeavor. It was thought that measuring the volume of a human skull would measure the intelligence of the skull's owner. It was difficult to measure a skull's volume accurately, but at last Paul Broca, a professor of surgery, perfected a method of filling the skull with lead shot that gave nearly the same answer in repeated measurements. Alas, cranial capacity has turned out to have no visible relation to achievement or intelligence. Were Broca's measurements of intelligence by skull volume reliable? Were they valid? Explain your answer.

Section 3

1. Identify the scale of each of the following variables as nominal, ordinal, or interval/ratio:
   (a) The concentration of DDT in a sample of milk, in milligrams per liter.
   (b) The species of each insect found in a sample plot of cropland.
   (c) The reaction time of a subject, in milliseconds, after exposure to a stimulus.
   (d) A subject's response to the following personality test question:

"It is natural for people of one race to want to live away from people of other races.

> Strongly agree
> Agree
> Undecided
> Disagree
> Strongly disagree"

(e) The ZIP code of a respondent to a mail questionnaire.

(f) The position of the New York Mets in the National League Eastern Division Standings (1st, 2nd, 3rd, 4th, 5th, or 6th).

(g) The pressure in pounds per square inch required to crack a specimen of copper tubing.

2. Here is an article from the *New York Times* of July 8, 1976:

Candidates Stir Voter Less Now Than in Recent Past, Poll Finds

---

None of the three leading Presidential candidates today engenders the personal enthusiasm of voters that other leading contenders for the office since 1960 did, the Gallup Poll reported yesterday.

In the current survey, the expected Democratic candidate, Jimmy Carter, was given a "highly favorable" rating by 25 percent of voters nationwide, while President Ford and Ronald Reagan each received a "highly favorable" rating by 2 percent.

By comparison, Gen. Dwight D. Eisenhower was rated "highly favorable" by 47 percent and 65 percent of voters in his successful Presidential campaigns in 1952 and 1956. John J. Kennedy had a 41 percent high rating in 1960; President Johnson had a 59 percent high rating in 1964; Richard M. Nixon had 28 and 40 percent high rating in 1968 and 1972, respectively.

In all of those election years, their challengers scored better than the current candidates, with the exception of Barry Goldwater, who had a high rating of 15 percent in 1964. George McGovern had a high raitng of 23 in 1972.

The polling organization says that while the current ratings fall below most of the leading Presidential candidates of the past elections, the ratings of the candidates tend to improve following the nominating conventions.

The results reported yesterday are based on personal interviews with 1,543 adults, 18 years of age and older, in more than 300 scientifically selected localities during the period of May 21 to 24.

To measure the personality factor, respondents are asked to indicate on a 10-point scale how highly they regard a candidate. These ratings are measurements of the appeal of a candidate as a person, the Gallup group noted, and should not be confused with hypothetical election results.

(a) What type of scale was used to measure the personal enthusiasm of a voter toward a candidate? Explain your answer.

(b) On page 26 in Chapter 1 is a list of questions for which any account of a sample survey should give answers. Find answers to these questions in the article, or state that the article does not give the answer. What is the most serious omission in the article?

3. (a) What type of scale is illustrated by the numbers on the shirts of a basketball team?

(b) What type of scale is illustrated by house address numbers along a typical city street?

4. The 1980 census long form, given to a sample of 20% of all households, asks, "In what State or foreign country was this person born?" At the bottom of the page, marked "For census use only," is a grid of digits in which census workers code the written answer to the question as a string of 3 digits, 000 to 999. The answer is read by the computer in this coded form. Another question asks "If this person is a female—How many babies has she ever had, not counting stillbirths?" What type of measurement scale is used in each of these two questions?

Section 4

1. The following quotation appears in a book review in *Science,* Volume 189 (1975), p. 373:

". . . a set of 20 studies with 57 percent reporting significant results, of which 42 percent agree on one conclusion while the remaining 15 percent favor another conclusion, often the opposite one."

Do the numbers given in this quotation make sense? Can you decide how many of the 20 studies agreed on "one conclusion," how many favored another conclusion, and how many did not report significant results?

2. The following excerpts and graph are from a United Press International dispatch that appeared in the Middletown, N.Y., *Times Herald Record* of June 7, 1975:

Unemployment hit a 34-year high of 9.2 percent in May, the government reported Friday, but a labor analyst insisted there are new signs the recession may be over.

The Bureau of Labor Statistics said the number of unemployed rose 362,000 in May to a total of 8,538,000 – 9.2 percent of the labor force compared to 8.9 percent in April.

It was the first time the rate exceeded 9 percent since the final Depression year of 1941 when the 12-month average was 9.9 percent.

• • •

The report showed unemployment in construction trades hit an all-time high of 21.8 percent in May.

Reprinted with permission of U.P.I.

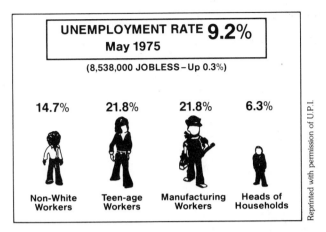

(a) Is the source of the data given, and is that source trustworthy?

(b) Because of suspicious regularity, I do not believe that 21.8% of man-ufacturing workers were unemployed, as the graph claims. Explain why I'm suspicious and how you think this apparent error came about.

3. The late English psychologist Cyril Burt is famous for studies of the IQ scores of identical twins who were raised apart. The high correlation between the IQs of separated twins in Burt's studies pointed to heredity as a major factor in IQ. ("Correlation" is a measure of the connection or association between two variables. We will become better acquainted with it in Chapter 6.) Burt wrote several accounts of his work, each reporting on more pairs of twins. Here are his reported correlations as he published them:

Date of publication	Twins reared apart	Twins reared together
1955	0.771 (21 pairs)	0.944 (83 pairs)
1958	0.771 ("over 30" pairs)	0.944 (no count)
1966	0.771 (53 pairs)	0.944 (95 pairs)

What is suspicious here? (Further investigation made it almost certain that Burt fabricated his data.)

4. A series of measurements of weights in grams is recorded as

| 11.25 | 13.75 | 12.00 | 13.25 | 10.75 |
| 12.50 | 12.25 | 11.00 | 13.25 | 11.75 |

Because two decimal places are given, we might conclude that the mea-surements are precise to two decimal places, that is, are rounded to the nearest 0.01 gram. A closer look at the data suggests that they are much less precise than this. How precise do you think these data are? Why?

5. Here are some citations containing numbers that may not be plausible. In each case, identify the data that seem implausible. Try to decide if the numbers are actually right. (Not all of them are wrong!)

   (a) From the *New York Times,* May 8, 1976, p. 25: "Altogether, in some 30 associations and groups of independents, there are almost 80 million Baptists in the nation. They are outnumbered only by the Roman Catholics."

   (b) From *Audubon,* May 1976, p. 28, writing of Alaska: "Throughout the state each year, hunters harvest upward of 10,000 moose, skin them out, pack them out, and dress them out—five, six million pounds of meat in their freezers. . . ."

   (c) The *Statistical Abstract of the United States,* 1973 edition, p. 83, reports that on December 31, 1971, there were 82,294 narcotics addicts in the United States.

6. An advertisement for the pain reliever Tylenol was headlined: "Why Doctors Recommend Tylenol More Than All Leading Aspirin Brands Combined." A counteradvertisement by the makers of Bayer Aspirin, headlined "Makers of Tylenol, Shame On You!" accused Tylenol of misleading by giving the truth but not the whole truth. You be the detective again: How is Tylenol's claim misleading even if true?

7. An article on adding organic matter to soil in *Organic Gardening,* March 1983, said, "Since a 6-inch layer of mineral soil in a 100-square-foot plot weighs about 45,000 pounds, adding 230 pounds of compost will give you an instant 5% organic matter." What percent of 45,000 is 230? Does the error lie in the arithmetic, or is that 45,000 pounds too heavy?

8. The newspaper article on marijuana reprinted on page 100 contains numbers that appear to be inconsistent. Find the inconsistency.

9. Data on accidents in recreational boating in the *Statistical Abstract* show that the number of deaths remained steady between 1970 and 1980 (1418 deaths in 1970; 1360 in 1980). But the number of injuries reported jumped from 780 in 1970 to 2650 in 1980. Why do you think the injury count rose when deaths did not? Why are there so few injuries in these government data relative to the number of deaths? Which count (deaths or injuries) is probably more accurate?

10. The question-and-answer column of the Purdue campus newspaper was asked what percent of the campus was "Greek." The answer given was that "the figures for the fall semester are approximately 13 percent for the girls and 15–18 percent for the guys, which produces a 'Greek' figure of approximately 28–31 percent of the undergraduates at Purdue" (*Purdue Exponent,* September 21, 1977). Discuss the campus newspaper's arithmetic.

11. A newspaper story on housing costs (*Lafayette Journal and Courier,* September 21, 1977) noted that in 1975 the median price of a new house was

$39,300 and the median family income was $13,991. (The median income is the amount that half of all families earn less than and half earn more than. We become better acquainted with the median in Chapter 5.) The writer then claimed that "the ratio of housing prices to income is much lower today than it was in 1900 (2.8 percent in 1975 vs. 9.8 percent in 1900)."

I do wish that I could buy a new house for 2.8% of my income. Where did that 2.8 come from? What is the correct expression for $39,300 as a percent of $13,991?

12. Below is a table from a 1971 report of the British Royal College of Physicians, *Smoking and Health Now.* It shows the number and percent of deaths among men age 35 and over from the chief diseases related to smoking. One of the entries in the table is incorrect, and an erratum slip was inserted to correct it. Which entry is wrong, and what is the correct value?

	Lung cancer	Chronic bronchitis	Coronary heart disease	All causes
Number	26,973	24,976	85,892	312,537
Percent	8.6%	8.0%	2.75%	100%

13. The January 1982 issue of *Playboy* magazine contained a 133-question survey on sexual habits. A total of 80,324 usable responses (65,396 men and 14,928 women) were mailed in. The results showed that women claimed to be sexually active earlier than men: Of the respondents under age 21, 58% of the women and 38% of the men claimed intercourse before age 16. Discuss the internal and external validity of these results.

14. Find in a newspaper or magazine an example of one of the following; explain in detail the statistical shortcomings of your example:

> Meaningless numbers or comparisons
> Lack of internal consistency
> Spurious precision
> Implausible numbers
> Omission of essential information
> Faulty arithmetic

"Tonight, we're going to let the statistics speak for themselves."

Part **II**

Organizing data

Data, like words, speak clearly only when they are organized. Also like words, data speak more effectively when well organized than when poorly organized. Again like words, data can obscure a subject by their quantity, requiring a brief summary to highlight essential facts. The second of statistics' three domains is the organizing, summarizing, and presenting of data.

Data are produced in many forms: completed questionnaires, laboratory notebooks, electronically stored readings from recording instruments. A completed set of data is usually stored as a table, either in printed form or on a computer-readable magnetic tape. Our task is to digest such sets of raw data, to organize and summarize them for human use. Raw data can often be greatly compressed by a summary table or effectively presented in a graph. These are the subject of Chapter 4. A few statistics can often sum up aspects of a whole data set. In Chapter 5 we shall meet means, medians, variances, and other such summary statistics, as well as the family of normal distributions that approximately describe many data sets. Relationships among several variables deserve separate treatment, which Chapter 6 provides. Chapter 7 considers data that are collected regularly over time and focuses on understanding some of the economic and social statistics that attract such attention in difficult times.

Summarizing and presenting a large body of facts offers to ignorance or malice ample opportunity for distortion. This is no less (but also no more) the case when the facts to be summarized are numbers rather than words. We shall therefore take due note of the traps that the ignorant fall into and the tools of duplicity that the malicious use. Those who picture statistics as primarily a piece of the liar's art concentrate on the part of statistics that deals with summarizing and presenting data. I claim that misleading summaries and selective presentations go back to that after-the-apple conversation between Adam, Eve, and God. Don't blame statistics. But do remember the saying "Figures don't lie, but liars figure," and beware.

Chapter 4

Tables, graphs, and distributions

What mental picture does the word *statistics* call to mind in most people? Very likely a picture of tables crowded with numbers. And close behind tables come graphs, zigging up or zagging down. Now, tables do lack sex appeal, and you may have exhausted your interest in graphs when you mastered pie charts in grade school. But tables remain the first step in organizing data, and data are most vividly presented in graphs. I promise to be brief in presenting tables and graphs and not to mention pie charts again.

Yet there is an art to presenting complex data clearly, an art best learned by example. One of the best ways to decide how to make a table or graph of a set of data is to look for similar examples in the *Statistical Abstract of the United States*. This yearly compilation of data contains tables of every sort, and many graphs as well, that are models of clear presentation. Any library will have copies of the *Statistical Abstract*. Two principles apply to all tables and graphs: First, always *label* the graph or table clearly; second, always give the *source* of the data. These principles, some educated common sense, and the *Statistical Abstract* will carry you most of the way through these subjects. Sections 1 and 2 of this chapter will educate your common sense.

It is no accident that we met our first table and an accompanying graph in discussing the sampling distribution of statistics computed from an SRS in Chapter 1. Distributions are central to statistics. They therefore receive VIP treatment in Section 3.

1.   Frequency tables

One of our first acts in organizing a set of data is usually to count how often each value occurs. After completing a sample survey of 1537 students that included the question "Do you agree or disagree that possession of small amounts of marijuana should not be a crime?" we are eager to tabulate the answers and learn that 928 agreed, 543 disagreed, and 66 had no opinion. (Check that 928 + 543 + 66 = 1537, so all the answers are accounted for. That's a check for internal consistency.) Because rates or proportions are often more useful than totals, we go on to compute that

$$\frac{928}{1537} = 0.60, \text{ or } 60\%, \text{ agreed,}$$

$$\frac{543}{1537} = 0.35, \text{ or } 35\%, \text{ disagreed, and}$$

$$\frac{66}{1537} = 0.04, \text{ or } 4\%, \text{ had no opinion.}$$

Again you should check for internal consistency. There should be 100% in all. We got 60% + 35% + 4% = 99%. What happened? The arithmetic is right, but when we rounded the fractions off to two decimal places, a little precision was lost, and the results do not quite add up to 100%. Such *roundoff errors* will be with us from now on as we do more arithmetic.

Totals and percentages of this kind occur so often that they deserve formal names:

The *frequency* of any value of a variable is the number of times that value occurs in the data; that is, a frequency is a count.

The *relative frequency* of any value is the proportion or fraction or percent of all observations that have that value.

In the sample survey, the frequency of students in the sample who agreed that marijuana possession should be legalized was 928. The relative frequency was 0.60. Relative frequencies are usually expressed in this decimal form, but we can just as correctly say that the relative frequency was 60%. Remember that 1% is 1/100 or 0.01. A number in decimal form can be changed to a percent by moving the decimal point two places to the right. So 0.60 is 60%.

Frequencies and relative frequencies are a common way of summarizing data

Table 4-1. Farms by size (1978)

Size of farm (acres)	Number of farms (thousands)	Percent of farms
Under 10	215	8.7
10–49	475	19.2
50–99	387	15.6
100–179	428	17.3
180–259	242	9.8
260–499	354	14.3
500–999	215	8.7
1000–1999	99	4.0
2000 and over	64	2.6
Total	2,479	100.2

SOURCE: *Statistical Abstract of the United States*, 1982–1983, Table 1142. From the 1978 U.S. Census of Agriculture.

when a nominal scale is used. Even when an interval/ratio scale is used and the variable has numerous possible values, we often summarize data by giving frequencies or relative frequencies for groups of values. Such a summary is conveniently presented in a table. Table 4-1 is an example. From this table we can learn much about the size of American farms. For example, the most common size category in 1978 was 100–179 acres. There were 428,000 farms in that size range. (Did you read the heading carefully enough to see that the number of farms is given in *thousands*?) This was 17.3% of all U.S. farms. The "number" column gives frequencies, while the "percent" column gives relative frequencies; it is good practice to follow the *Statistical Abstract* in *not* using the technical terms so that the table is easier for untrained persons to read. Finally, it is important that the source is given. Remembering how essential it is to know the definitions of variables, we should ask what the definition of a "farm" is. Without knowing what makes a piece of land a farm, we don't know what is being counted in Table 4-1. The source cited gives the exact definition: A farm is any place from which $1000 or more of agricultural products are normally sold in a year.

Frequency tables become more interesting when more than one variable is measured on each unit. We have already noted many examples in which several variables are measured, sometimes as independent and dependent variables when causation is at issue, and sometimes just for descriptive purposes. It is time to learn the proper vocabulary here:

"8.7% of American farms are under 10 acres."

Data are *univariate* when only one variable is measured on each unit.

Data are *bivariate* when two variables are measured on each unit.

Data are *multivariate* when more than one variable is measured on each unit.

If both the height and the weight of each pupil in a schoolroom are measured, we have a set of bivariate data. These data carry much more information than do the two sets of univariate data (heights alone and weights alone). Knowing which height and which weight go together (come from the same pupil) lets us study the connection or association between height and weight.

To see how much information bivariate data contain, look at Table 4-2, a *bivariate frequency table*. The entries are numbers of earned degrees, categorized by two nominal variables: the level of the degree and the sex of the recipient. For example, 9677 doctorate degrees were earned by women in 1980. Here are some questions we might ask of this table:

Table 4-2. Earned degrees, by level and sex (1980)

	Bachelor's	Master's	Doctorates
Male	477,450	151,369	23,081
Female	461,986	148,123	9,677
Totals	939,436	299,492	32,758

SOURCE: National Center for Education Statistics.

1. What fraction of all degrees were doctorates earned by women?

2. What fraction of all doctorate degrees were earned by women?

3. What fraction of all degrees earned by women were doctorates?

These questions sound alike, but they are not. Recognizing which question we want to ask in a given situation and learning how to answer all of them from the table is part of developing statistical skill. Each question asks for the relative frequency of doctorate degrees earned by women. In a bivariate frequency table, an entry has *three* relative frequencies, which differ in the total of which the entry is a fraction. Question 1 asks the relative frequency of doctorates earned by women among all degrees. The table does not give the total number of degrees awarded, so we must compute it by adding the totals for each level.

$$939,436 + 299,492 + 32,758 = 1,271,686.$$

So the answer to Question 1 is

$$\frac{\text{entry}}{\text{table total}} = \frac{9677}{1,271,686} = 0.0076.$$

Only eight-tenths of 1% of degrees awarded fell in this category.

Question 2 says: Look only at the "Doctorates" column in the table; what is the relative frequency of women among the degrees in this column? The answer is

$$\frac{\text{entry}}{\text{column total}} = \frac{9677}{32,758} = 0.2954.$$

About 29.5% of all doctorate degrees were earned by women. This is sometimes called a *conditional* relative frequency, because it is the relative frequency of female degree-earners given the condition that only doctorate degrees are considered.

Question 3 says: Look only at the "Female" row in the table, and find the relative frequency of doctorates among the degrees in this row. The table does not give the total number of degrees earned by women. This row total is

$$461,986 + 148,123 + 9677 = 619,786.$$

The answer to Question 3 is then

$$\frac{\text{entry}}{\text{row total}} = \frac{9677}{619,786} = 0.0156.$$

Table 4-3. Earned degrees, by level and sex (1980)

	Bachelor's	Master's	Doctorates	Total
Male	477,450	151,369	23,081	651,900
Female	461,986	148,123	9,677	619,786
Totals	939,436	299,492	32,758	1,271,686

SOURCE: National Center For Education Statistics.

About 1.6% of all degrees earned by women were doctorates. This is another conditional relative frequency; now the given condition is that only degrees earned by women are considered.

Answering these questions was mainly a matter of straight thinking, complicated a bit because the table did not give all of the totals we needed. We might well have begun the study of our data by putting the row totals at the right of the table, and the grand total of our degrees in the lower right corner. Table 4-2 then becomes Table 4-3. The column totals (bottom row) are a univariate frequency table of degrees by level. The row totals (right column) are a univariate frequency table of degrees by sex of the recipient. Both of these univariate tables can be obtained from the bivariate table (the six entries in the body of the table), but the bivariate table *cannot* be obtained from the two univariate tables. The entries in these univariate tables are sometimes called *marginal* frequencies because they appear at the margins of the table.

2.   Graphs

The purpose of a graph is to provide a visual summary of data. A good graph frequently reveals facts about the data that would require careful study to detect in a table. What is more, the immediate visual impression of a graph is stronger than the impression made by data in numerical form—so strong, in fact, that we must guard against false impressions. Let us look now at the use and abuse of several common types of graphs.

Line graphs

Line graphs show the behavior of a variable over time. Time is marked on the horizontal axis, and the variable being plotted is marked on the vertical axis. Figure 4-1 is an example. The variable here is the average retail price of fresh oranges, collected monthly from a probability sample of 2300 food outlets as part of the government's effort to measure consumer prices. From this line graph, we can see at once that

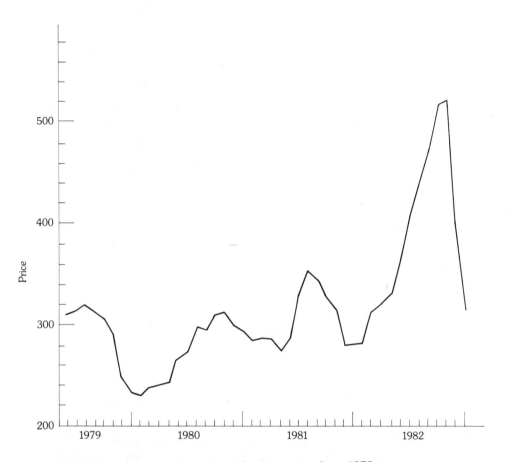

Figure 4-1. Average retail price of fresh oranges, June 1979 to December 1982. The prices are given as a percent of the 1967 average price. [From Bureau of Labor Statistics, *CPI Detailed Reports*, 1979–1982.]

- The price of oranges is highest in late summer and early fall, and lowest early in the year. This is *seasonal variation*.

- Prices were generally increasing in the 1979–1982 period, once the seasonal variation is ignored. This is a long-term *trend*.

Just because graphs speak so strongly, they can mislead the unwary. The intelligent reader of a line graph looks closely at the *scales* marked off on both axes. In Figure 4-2, one can transform the left-hand graph into the right-hand graph by stretching the vertical axis, compressing the horizontal axis, and cutting off the vertical axis at a value above zero. Now you know the trick of giving an exaggerated impression with a line graph. Because there is no one "right" scale

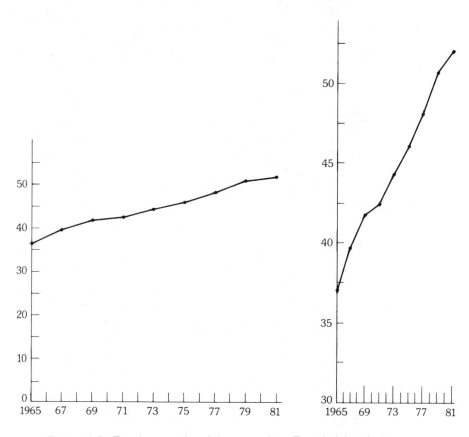

Figure 4-2. Two line graphs of the same data. Female labor force as percent of female population age 16 and over. [From *Statistical Abstract of the United States*, 1973 and 1982–1983.]

for a line graph, perfectly honest sources can give somewhat different impressions by their choices of scale. Figure 4-3 contains line graphs of the same data that appeared on the same day in the nation's two leading financial newspapers. The *New York Times* drew a larger vertical scale than did the *Wall Street Journal*, cut it off at 125 instead of 90, and used a shorter time period on the horizontal scale. As a result, the *Times'* graph suggests a steeper rise than does the *Journal's*. Moral: Look at the scales.

Once in a while you may encounter a more barbarous line graph. Figure 4-4 is the least civilized I have seen. Note first that time is on the vertical axis. So when the graph goes straight up (1940–1946), this means that taxes were not increasing at all. And when the graph is quite flat (1965–1972), this means that taxes were thundering upward. The graph gives an impression exactly the reverse of the truth. That's why time always belongs on the horizontal axis. Second, the time scale does not have equal units; equal lengths on the vertical axis

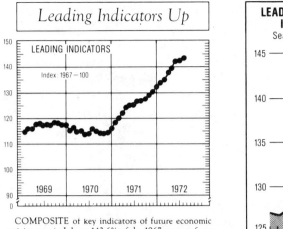

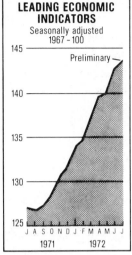

COMPOSITE of key indicators of future economic activity rose in July to 143.6% of the 1967 average from a revised 142.6% in June, the Commerce Department reports.

Figure 4-3. Two line graphs of the same data. [Graph on left from the *Wall Street Journal*, August 29, 1972. Reprinted with permission of the Wall Street Journal. Copyright © Dow Jones & Company, Inc. 1972. All rights reserved. Right graph from the *New York Times*, August 29, 1972. Copyright © 1972 by the New York Times Company. Reprinted by permission.]

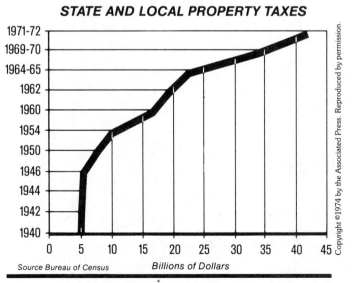

Chart indicates rise in state and local property taxes over 12 years

Figure 4-4.

represent first two years, then four years, then two years again, then whatever the interval between 1962 and 1964–1965 is, and so on. The graph is stretched and squeezed haphazardly by the changing time scale, so the rise in taxes in different time periods cannot be compared by looking at the steepness of the graph. These barbarisms were perpetrated by the Associated Press (not by the Census Bureau, which was only the source of the data). The newspaper then provided the caption below the chart, which no doubt refers to the "12 years" from 1940 to 1972.

Bar graphs

Bar graphs compare the values of several variables. Often the values compared are frequencies or relative frequencies of outcomes of a nominal variable. For example, Figure 4-5 is a bar graph of the data in Table 4-2. This is actually three bar graphs drawn together, showing the number of degrees awarded to men and women separately for each of the three types of degree.

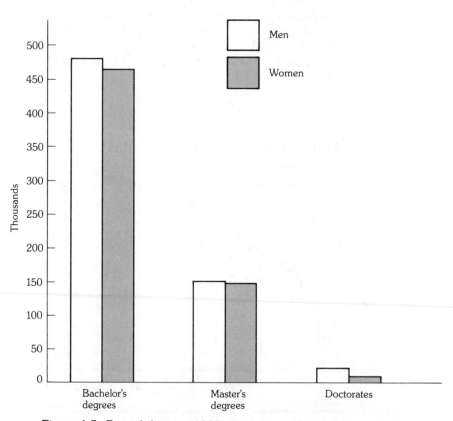

Figure 4-5. Earned degrees, 1980. [From National Center for Education Statistics.]

The bars in a bar chart may be vertical (as in Figure 4-5) or horizontal. They may touch each other (as in Figure 4-5) or be separated. But all bars must have the same width, for our eyes respond to the *area* of the bars. When the bars have the same width and a height that varies with the variable being graphed, then the area (height times width) also varies with the variable and our eyes receive the correct impression. The most common abuse of bar graphs is to replace the bars by pictures and to change both the width and the height of the picture as the variable graphed changes. Figure 4-6, an advertisement placed

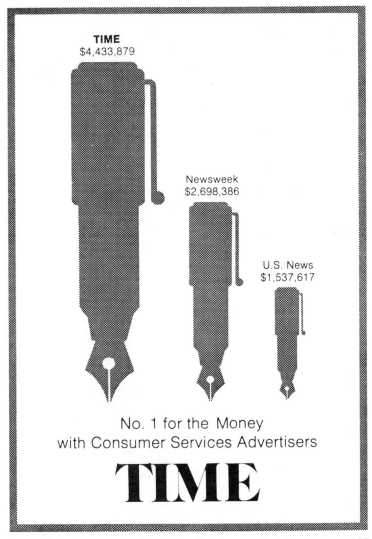

Figure 4-6. An attractive but misleading bar graph. [Copyright © 1971 by Time, Inc. Reproduced by permission.]

by *Time* magazine in the commercial section of the *New York Times*, illustrates this. *Time* enjoys a lead of less than two to one over *Newsweek* in dollar value of consumer-services advertising (the dollar amounts appear over the pictures). But because *both* the height and width of the pen representing *Time* are almost double those of *Newsweek*'s pen, the area of *Time*'s pen is almost four times

Figure 4-7. An attractive and accurate bar graph. [Copyright © 1972 by Time, Inc. Reproduced by permission.]

that of *Newsweek*'s. Our eyes receive the misleading impression that *Time* has a four-to-one, rather than a two-to-one, edge.

In case you are wondering if graphic attractiveness must always be sacrificed to accuracy, I present Figure 4-7. This is another *Time* ad making the same point as Figure 4-6, and it is at least as attractive as Figure 4-6. Unlike Figure 4-6, the graph in Figure 4-7 is accurate. Congratulations to the designer who managed to combine accuracy with graphic impact.

Scatterplots

Scatterplots graph bivariate data when both variables are measured in an interval/ratio or ordinal scale. Units for one variable are marked on the horizontal axis and units for the other variable on the vertical axis. The independent variable should always go on the horizontal axis when one of the variables is an independent and one a dependent variable. Each bivariate observation is represented by a point with a horizontal coordinate equal to the value of the first variable and a vertical coordinate equal to the value of the second.

Figure 4-8 is a scatterplot of data from an agricultural experiment. The independent variable was planting rate for corn (in thousands of plants per acre) and the dependent variable was yield (in bushels per acre). The scatterplot shows observations on 13 plots of land. One plot received 12,000 plants per acre and yielded 130.5 bushels per acre. This is indicated by the circled dot on the scatterplot at 12 on the horizontal scale and 130.5 on the vertical scale. The association between planting rate and yield is clear from Figure 4-8: Yield increases with planting rate until about 24,000 plants per acre are planted, then drops off. (This was irrigated corn. The conclusions may differ if irrigation is not used.)

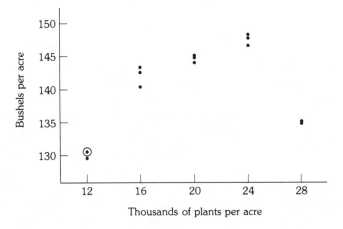

Figure 4-8. Corn planting rate versus yield, a scatterplot.

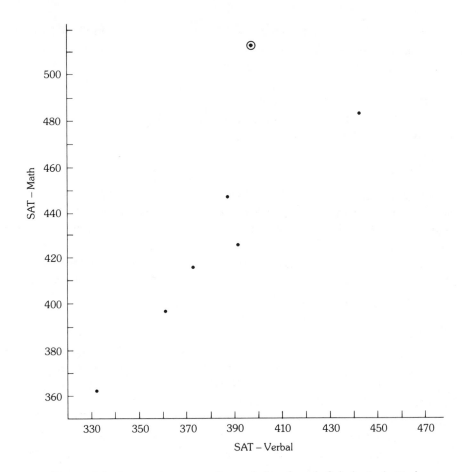

Figure 4-9. Average scores on the verbal and math Scholastic Aptitude Tests for students in seven groups. [From College Board, 1982.]

Scatterplots not only display the relationship between variables but also highlight individual observations which deviate from the overall relationship. These observations appear as *outliers*, data points that stand apart from the rest. Figure 4-9 is a scatterplot of average scores on the math and verbal Scholastic Aptitude Tests for seven groups of students, including the three for which data were given on page 115. We suspect that these scores will rise and fall together. The scatterplot confirms this suspicion and even shows that there is an approximate straight-line pattern of relationship, since six of the seven points fall in a rough line from lower left to upper right. However, the circled point is an outlier. This point represents the average scores of Asian students. These students score lower on the verbal SAT, or higher on the math SAT, than would be expected from the pattern formed by the other six groups. It is often helpful in describing data to look first for an overall pattern and then for deviations from that pattern. When the data concern relationships between two variables, scatterplots can reveal both patterns and outliers.

3.   Distributions

The sampling distribution of a statistic describes the frequency or relative frequency with which the statistic takes each possible value in repeated sampling. The idea of a distribution of values is not confined to sample statistics but is useful whenever our data are values of a variable measured in an interval/ratio scale. The distribution of a variable can be displayed by a table of frequencies of each value or, if these are numerous, of groups of possible values of the variable. Table 4-1 on page 145 shows the distribution of sizes of American farms. There are several effective ways of displaying distributions graphically.

Histograms

Frequency or relative frequency distributions are most commonly displayed by *histograms*. Table 4-4 presents the distribution of two economic variables by state. Figure 4-10 is a histogram of one of these variables: 1982 per capita income. To draw the histogram, the incomes were divided into classes $1000 wide. The base of each bar covers one such class. The height of the bar is the frequency (count) of states with average incomes falling in that class. A frequency table containing this information is below the graph. The histogram is a lot more vivid. We can see at once the overall pattern of incomes, with most states falling between $8000 and $13,000. There is one poorer state, a few richer states, and one outlier at $16,257. Copying errors often produce outliers, so we should check this figure for accuracy. It is in fact the correct per capita income for Alaska, where extremes of climate and distance raise both costs and incomes.

Histograms look like bar graphs, but they differ from bar graphs in several respects. First, the bars in a histogram are always vertical, and the base scale is marked off in equal units; there is no base scale in a bar graph (such as Figure 4-5). Second, the width of the bars in a histogram has meaning: The base of each bar covers a class of values of the variable, the class whose frequency is the height of that bar; the width of the bars in a bar graph has no meaning. Third, the bars in a histogram touch each other (unless some class has frequency zero), because their bases must cover the entire range of observed values of the variable, with no gaps. Even when the possible values of a variable have gaps between them, we extend the bases of the bars to meet halfway between

Table 4-4. Median rent (1980) and per capita income (1982), by state

State	Median rent	Per capita income	State	Median rent	Per capita income
Alabama	119	8,649	Missouri	153	10,170
Alaska	340	16,257	Montana	165	9,580
Arizona	227	10,173	Nebraska	170	10,683
Arkansas	127	8,479	Nevada	268	11,981
California	253	12,567	New Hampshire	205	10,729
Colorado	223	12,302	New Jersey	226	13,089
Connecticut	203	13,748	New Mexico	177	9,190
Delaware	202	11,731	New York	210	12,314
District			North Carolina	134	9,044
of Columbia	207	14,550	North Dakota	175	10,876
Florida	208	10,978	Ohio	167	10,677
Georgia	153	9,583	Oklahoma	164	11,370
Hawaii	271	11,652	Oregon	212	10,335
Idaho	171	9,029	Pennsylvania	173	10,955
Illinois	201	12,100	Rhode Island	158	10,723
Indiana	166	10,021	South Carolina	130	8,502
Iowa	175	10,791	South Dakota	148	9,666
Kansas	168	11,765	Tennessee	148	8,906
Kentucky	151	8,934	Texas	213	11,419
Louisiana	156	10,231	Utah	187	8,875
Maine	172	9,042	Vermont	174	9,507
Maryland	222	12,238	Virginia	207	11,095
Massachusetts	197	12,088	Washington	219	11,560
Michigan	196	10,956	West Virginia	136	8,769
Minnesota	212	11,175	Wisconsin	185	10,774
Mississippi	109	7,778	Wyoming	217	12,372

SOURCE: 1980 Census for rents; Current Population Survey for incomes.

two adjacent possible values. For example, in a histogram of the ages of university faculty, the bars representing 25–29 years and 30–34 years would meet at 29.5.

Just as with bar graphs, our eyes respond to the area of the bars in a histogram. If the heights are frequencies, the widths of all bars must be equal in order to avoid false impressions. So in dividing a set of data into classes, you should

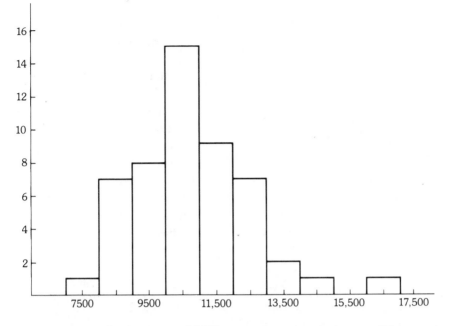

Figure 4-10. Histogram of 1982 per capita personal incomes of the states. [From Current Population Survey.]

usually choose classes of equal width if you wish to draw a histogram. There is no single correct choice of class width. The goal is to display the distribution effectively. Avoid either cramming all the observations into a few big classes or sprinkling one or two observations into each of many tiny classes. We did not make a histogram of the farm data in Table 4-1 because the classes are of unequal width and the top class (2000 acres or more) has no upper end point. Making an accurate graph of the distribution in such a case is a more complicated affair than I want to deal with.

Stemplots

For small data sets, say less than 100 observations, a different graphical portrayal of the distribution is quicker to make and retains more information than a histogram. This is the *stemplot*. I will illustrate the making of a stemplot by asking how long American presidents live. Table 4-5 lists the ages at death of the presidents. To make a stemplot, we use the first digit of the age as the *stem*. Write the stems vertically, with a vertical line to their right. Then proceed through Table 4-5 writing the second digit of each age as a *leaf* to the right of the proper stem. The first entry made, for George Washington's death at age 67, is a 7

Table 4-5. Age at death of U.S. presidents

Washington	67	Fillmore	74	Roosevelt	60
Adams	90	Pierce	64	Taft	72
Jefferson	83	Buchanan	77	Wilson	67
Madison	85	Lincoln	56	Harding	57
Monroe	73	Johnson	66	Coolidge	60
Adams	80	Grant	63	Hoover	90
Jackson	78	Hayes	70	Roosevelt	63
Van Buren	79	Garfield	49	Truman	88
Harrison	68	Arthur	56	Eisenhower	78
Tyler	71	Cleveland	71	Kennedy	46
Polk	53	Harrison	67	Johnson	64
Taylor	65	McKinley	58		

following the stem 6. The plot at Step 2 of Figure 4-11 results. The final step is to arrange the leaves following each stem in increasing order from left to right. The final stemplot appears as Step 3 in Figure 4-11.

As a display of the shape of a distribution, a stemplot looks like a histogram turned on its side. The chief advantage of a stemplot is that it retains the actual values of the observations. We can see, as we could not from a histogram, that the earliest death of a president occurred at age 46 and that two are tied for the latest death at age 90. The stemplot is also faster to draw, as long as we are willing to use the one or more uppermost digits as stems. This amounts to an automatic choice of classes and can give a poor picture of the distribution. It is possible to split these stems to approach the flexibility of the classes in a histogram, but we will not pursue this. Stemplots do not work well with large data sets, since the natural stems then have too many leaves.

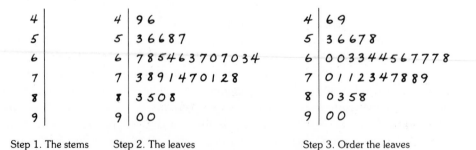

| Step 1. The stems | Step 2. The leaves | Step 3. Order the leaves |

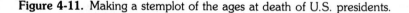

Figure 4-11. Making a stemplot of the ages at death of U.S. presidents.

Distributions

Both histograms and stemplots display the overall shape of a distribution of values. A distribution is *symmetric* if its two sides are approximately mirror images of each other about a center line. The distribution of ages at death in Figure 4-11 is quite symmetric. The distribution of state per capita incomes in Figure 4-10 on the other hand is *skewed to the right;* that is, the right tail extends farther than the left. This is typical of distributions of incomes (whether of individuals, firms, or nations), which tend to have many middling values and a few very high values. Although we did not graph the farm-size data of Table 4-1, you can see that this distribution is also strongly skewed to the right.

The shape of a histogram is the same whether it is frequencies or relative frequencies that we plot—this choice only changes the vertical scale. Histograms of relative frequencies are convenient for comparing the distributions of two data sets of different sizes, since we can use the same vertical scale for both graphs. Relative-frequency histograms are also used to portray the sampling distributions of statistics in a more general way than we have done thus far.

Figure 1-1 on page 15, our first histogram, showed the distribution of the sample proportion $\hat{p}$ in 200 SRSs drawn independently from the same population. It is a frequency histogram of the sampling distribution of $\hat{p}$. Its shape is characteristic of the sampling method and allows us to evaluate the precision of the statistic as an estimate of the corresponding population parameter. But in a strict sense, the sampling distribution of $\hat{p}$ is, not a specific observed distribution, but the ideal distribution that is approached as more and more samples are taken. This distribution can be found by long experiments or, much more quickly, by mathematics. It must be presented in terms of relative frequencies since it does not refer to any specific number of trials.

Figure 4-12 redraws the results of the 200 SRSs of Chapter 1 as relative frequencies (the dashed bars) and also presents the theoretical sampling distribution (solid bars) for comparison. The sampling distribution is similar to the distribution observed in 200 trials, but it differs in several respects. In particular, the sampling distribution is more symmetric than the observed distribution. Some of the deviation between the observed and theoretical distributions is caused by the chance outcome of the particular 200 trials made. But some of the deviation occurs also because the theoretical sampling distribution describes truly random sampling, while the scoop gives only approximately random samples of beads. If we use a table of random digits to select the samples, the observed distribution of values of $\hat{p}$ will always approach the sampling distribution as more and more samples are drawn.

The shape of the sampling distribution in Figure 4-12 depends on three facts about the bead-sampling experiment: First, simple random sampling was em-

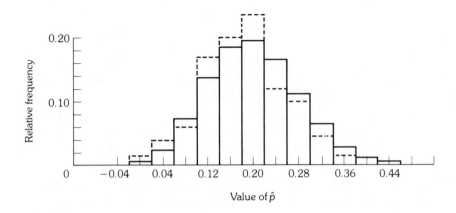

Figure 4-12. Sampling distribution for a sample proportion, observed (broken bars) and theoretical (solid bars).

ployed. Second, the sample size was 25. Third, the population contained 20% dark beads. This characteristic shape appears even more clearly in Figure 4-13. This is a *frequency polygon*, drawn by placing a dot in the center of the top of each bar of the histogram, then drawing straight lines between the dots. As a final approximation, used to convey quickly the shape of a distribution, we can replace the frequency polygon by a smooth curve. It is a remarkable fact that the sampling distribution of $\hat{p}$ from random sampling can always be approximated by a smooth curve of a certain kind. These are the *normal curves*, which we will study further in the next chapter. Figure 4-14 is the normal curve of the sampling distribution of $\hat{p}$ that was described earlier by a histogram in Figure 4-12 and a polygon in Figure 4-13. Such a curve provides a mathematical description of the distribution. It does not depend on either a particular number of trials or a particular grouping of observations into classes. The symmetry

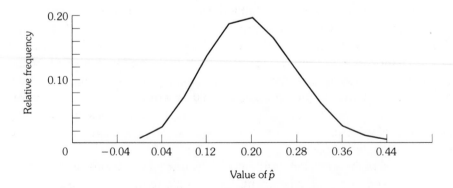

Figure 4-13. A frequency polygon.

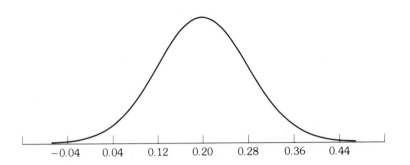

Figure 4-14. A normal curve.

of the sampling distribution, for example, is portrayed clearly and exactly. With distribution curves, we have completed our discussion of graphical methods of presenting distributions.

Exercises

Section 1

1. Answer the following questions about Table 4-1 (p. 145):
 (a) What percent of all American farms in 1978 were at least 500 acres in size?
 (b) How many farms were there in 1978? About how precise is this figure (nearest 1, nearest 100, or nearest 1000)?
 (c) Why do the percents in the last column sum to 100.2% rather than to 100%?

2. The U.S. Office for Civil Rights has among its jobs the investigation of possible sex discrimination in university hiring. The office wants to know if women are hired for the faculty in the same proportion as their availability in the pool of potential employees. If new university faculty in 1980 were recruited almost entirely from new doctorate degree recipients, which of the three questions about Table 4-2 on page 146 is useful to the office? Why?

3. From Table 4-2, find the percent of degrees at each level (bachelor's, master's, doctorate) earned by women. What do you conclude about the relative educational patterns of men and women in 1980?

4. Here are the marginal entries of a bivariate frequency table with two rows and two columns:

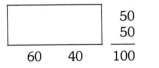

Find *two different* sets of entries in the body of the table that give these same marginal totals. This shows that the bivariate frequencies cannot be obtained from the univariate (marginal) frequencies alone.

5. Look up the table of earned degrees conferred in any recent *Statistical Abstract*. From that table, make a properly labeled frequency table of earned degrees *in mathematical subjects*, categorized by the level of the degree and the sex of the recipient.

6. Here is a bivariate frequency table:

Persons below poverty level, by age and race (1981, thousands)

	White	Black	Other
Under 16 years	7009	3777	437
16 to 21 years	2477	1242	148
22 to 44 years	6154	2251	349
45 to 64 years	2934	1083	108
65 years and over	2978	820	55

SOURCE: *Statistical Abstract of the United States, 1982–1983*, Table 729.

Answer the following questions from this table:
(a) To understand these data, you need an essential definition that is given in the source. What definition?
(b) How many persons below the poverty level were there in 1981?
(c) What percent of persons below the poverty level were 65 or older?
(d) What percent of persons below the poverty level were black?
(e) Of all whites below the poverty level, what percent were 65 or older?
(f) Of all children under 16 below the poverty level, what percent were black?
(g) You want to know what percent of all people 65 and older were below the poverty level. Can you learn the answer from this table?

7. Here is a pleasant little bivariate frequency table:

Suicides, by sex and method (1979)

	Male	Female
Poison	2974	2754
Hanging	2783	742
Firearms	12,919	2639
Other	1580	815

SOURCE: *Statistical Abstract of the United States, 1982–1983*, Table 121.

Answer the following questions from this table:
(a) How many suicides were reported in 1979?
(b) Give a univariate frequency table of suicides by method. What method was most commonly used, and what percent of all suicides were committed by this method?

(c) What percent of all women who committed suicide used poison?

(d) Describe the chief differences between men and women in their choice of suicide methods, referring to the table to support your statement.

Section 2

1. The rate of deaths from cancer in the United States has increased since 1930 as follows:

Cancer deaths per 100,000 population

Year	1930	1935	1940	1945	1950	1955	1960	1965	1970	1975	1980
Death rate	97.4	108.2	120.3	134.0	139.8	146.5	149.2	153.5	162.8	169.7	183.9

SOURCE: *Historical Statistics of the United States,* Part I, p. 58, and *Statistical Abstract of the United States,* 1984, Table 110.

(a) Draw a line graph of these data designed to emphasize the rise in the cancer death rates. (Imagine you are trying to persuade Congress to appropriate more money to fight cancer.)

(b) Draw another line graph of the same data designed to show only a moderate increase in the death rate.

2. Use Figure 4-4 to make an approximate table of the total amount of state and local property taxes in the years 1940, 1942, 1944, 1946, 1950, 1954, 1960, 1962, 1964, 1969, and 1971. Then draw a line graph from your table to see what a correct version of Figure 4-4 would look like.

3. Figure 4-15 shows a graph that appeared in the Lexington, Kentucky, *Herald-Leader* of October 5, 1975. Discuss the correctness of this graph.

Figure 4-15.

4. The table below shows the trend of U.S. imports of crude oil (in millions of barrels) from 1965 to 1982. These data appear in Table 991 of the 1984 *Statistical Abstract*. Present them in a clear, well-labeled graph.

Year	1965	1968	1970	1972	1974	1976	1978	1980	1982
Oil imports	452	472	483	811	1269	1935	2320	1926	1263

5. Plotting two line graphs on the same axes is a useful way of comparing two time series. Here are the death rates per 100,000 population for women age 45 to 54 from the two types of cancer that kill the most women, breast cancer and respiratory/intrathoracic (mainly lung) cancer. Plot the two together.

Year	1940	1950	1960	1970	1975	1980
Breast	47.5	46.9	51.4	52.6	50.4	48.9
Respiratory	6.2	6.7	10.1	22.2	28.0	34.8

SOURCE: *Statistical Abstract of the United States*, 1984, Table 114.

Now extrapolate your plots (this is risky) to estimate when lung cancer will pass breast cancer as the leading killer of women.

6. Here are data on the percent of females among people earning doctorates in 1980 in several fields of study (from data compiled by the National Center for Education Statistics). Present these data in a well-labeled bar graph.

All fields	29.5%
Biological sciences	26.0%
Education	44.2%
Engineering	3.8%
Physical sciences	12.5%
Psychology	41.7%

7. In Exercise 2 on page 137 there is a newspaper graph of unemployment rates for several groups of workers. Comment on the correctness of the graph as a presentation of the numbers given. (We already saw that some of those numbers are probably incorrect.)

8. Figure 4-16 is a full-page advertisement for *Fortune* magazine. It contains eight separate graphic presentations of data. Comment briefly on the correctness of each one.

9. Figure 4-17 is a scatterplot of the heights of the mothers and the fathers in a sample of parents. Answer the following questions from this graph:
   (a) What is the smallest height of any mother in the sample? How many women had that particular height? What were the heights of the husbands of these women?
   (b) What is the greatest height of any father in the sample? How many men had that height, and what were the heights of their wives?

We asked America's top businessmen about business magazines. This is what they said.

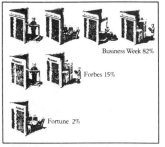

Which one contains the best writing?

Which one best keeps its readers up to date on business events?

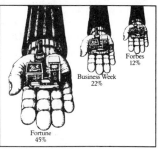

Which one has the most persuasive advertising?

Which one carries the most interesting advertising?

Which one is easiest to read?

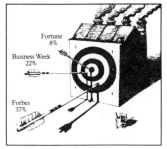

Which one is least accurate?

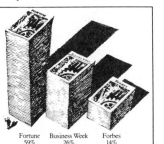

In which one would you like to see a major story on your company?

Erdos and Morgan recently asked officers of the top one thousand companies—chairmen, presidents, vice presidents, treasurers, secretaries and controllers—for their opinions of Business Week, Forbes and Fortune. 999 executives responded.

You can see the results for yourself. In nearly every instance, Fortune was the winner. Not just by a hair—but overwhelmingly.

Most authoritative? Best writing? Where would they most like to see their company story? Of course they named Fortune. You'd expect them to.

But why did they see the advertising in Fortune as more persuasive and more interesting—when the same advertising often runs in all three magazines?

Obviously, the Fortune climate makes something happen to advertising that doesn't happen anyplace else. It's a valuable edge.

Business leaders get more involved with Fortune, so they get more involved with the advertising. They respond to Fortune, so they respond to the advertising. The survey proves it.

The conclusion is clear and simple: dollar for dollar, your advertising investment gets more impact in Fortune.

You get more than mere advertising exposure in Fortune. You get real communication with the people who can *act* on your business or consumer message. Isn't that what advertising is all about?

FORTUNE

Nobody takes you to the top like Fortune.

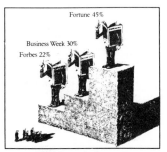

Which one is the most authoritative?

Figure 4-16.

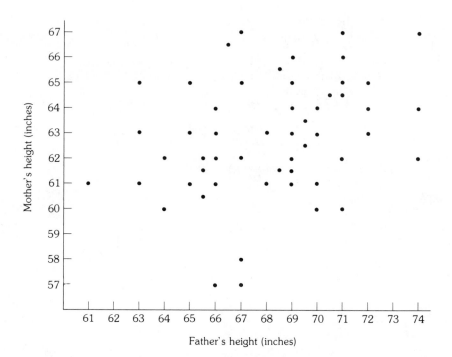

Father's height (inches)

Figure 4-17. Data for an SRS of 53 pairs of parents from a group of 1079 pairs whose heights are recorded in Table XIII of Karl Pearson and Alice Lee, "On the laws of inheritance in man," *Biometrika*, November 1903, p. 408.

(c) Does the scatterplot show any connection between the heights of mothers and fathers? (For example, do tall women tend to marry short men?)

10. A homeowner is interested in how demand for heating in cold weather affects the amount of natural gas his home consumes. Demand for heating is often measured in "degree-days." (To find the number of degree-days for a certain day, record the high and low temperature on that day and find the temperature midway between the high and low. If this temperature is less than 65°F, there is one degree-day for every degree below 65°F.)

The homeowner recorded his natural gas consumption in cubic feet per day, and also the average number of degree-days per day, for nine consecutive months. Here are the data:

Degree-days per day	15.6	26.8	37.8	36.4	35.5	18.6	15.3	7.9	0
Cubic feet of gas per day	5.2	6.1	8.7	8.5	8.8	4.9	4.5	2.5	1.1

(a) Make a scatterplot of these data. (Which is the independent variable?)

(b) From the scatterplot, give a rough estimate of gas consumption on a day with 20 degree-days.

11. The Wheat Industry Council surveyed 3368 people, asking them to estimate the number of calories in several common foods. Here is a table of the average estimated calorie level and the correct number of calories.

Food	Estimated calories	Correct calories
8 oz. whole milk	196	159
5 oz. spaghetti with tomato sauce	394	163
5 oz. macaroni and cheese	350	269
One slice wheat bread	117	61
One slice white bread	136	76
2-oz. candy bar	364	260
Saltine cracker	74	12
Medium-size apple	107	80
Medium-size potato	160	88
Cream-filled snack cake	419	160

SOURCE: *USA TODAY*, October 20, 1983.

Make a scatterplot of estimated versus correct calories. Is there an approximate straight-line relationship that fits most of the points? Are there any outliers from this pattern?

Section 3

1. A study of bacterial contamination in milk counted the number of coliform organisms (fecal bacteria) per milliliter in 100 specimens of milk purchased in East Coast groceries. The U.S. Public Health Service recommends no more than 10 coliform bacteria per milliliter. Here are the data:

```
5  8  6  7  8  3  2  4  7  8  6  4  4  8  8  8  6 10  6  5
6  6  6  6  4  3  7  7  5  7  4  5  6  7  4  4  4  3  5  7
7  5  8  3  9  7  3  4  6  6  8  7  4  8  5  7  9  4  4  7
8  8  7  5  4 10  7  6  6  7  8  6  6  6  0  4  5 10  4  5
7  9  8  9  5  6  3  6  3  7  1  6  9  6  8  5  2  8  5  3
```

(a) Make a table of the frequencies of each of the values 0 to 10 in this set of 100 observations.

(b) Draw a frequency histogram of these data. (Graph paper makes this easier.)

(c) On the histogram you have drawn, put a second vertical scale, labeled in relative frequency rather than frequency. Because there are 100 observations, relative frequency = frequency/100. Your histogram is now a relative-frequency histogram.

(d) Make a frequency polygon similar to Figure 4-13 by connecting the centers of the tops of the bars in your histogram.

(e) Describe the shape of the distribution. Are the data symmetric? If so, approximately where is the center about which they are symmetric? Are the data strongly skewed? If so, in which direction? Are there any outliers? Is the distribution approximately normal in shape?

2. Table 4-4 lists the median rent paid for housing units in each state and the District of Columbia, according to the 1980 Census.

(a) Make a stemplot of these data, using the first two digits of the monthly rent as stems.

(b) Are there any outliers? Neglecting the outliers, is the distribution of rents approximately symmetric or skewed?

3. To make a stemplot of the per capita incomes in Table 4-4, it is convenient to *truncate* the data by ignoring the last two digits. Then, use the first two digits as stems and the third digits as leaves. The resulting stemplot is essentially the same as the histogram of Figure 4-10. Make this stemplot.

4. Agronomists have developed varieties of corn that have increased amounts of the essential amino acid lysine. In a test of the protein quality of this corn, an experimental group of 20 one-day-old male chicks was fed a corn–soybean ration containing high-lysine corn. A control group of another 20 chicks was fed the same diet except that normal corn was used. The weight gains (in grams) after 21 days are recorded below.

Control group				Experimental group			
380	321	366	356	361	447	401	375
283	349	402	462	434	403	393	426
356	410	329	399	406	318	467	407
350	384	316	272	427	420	477	392
345	455	360	431	430	339	410	326

(a) This experiment was designed using the principles of Chapter 2. Briefly discuss the proper design of this experiment.

(b) To compare the two distributions of weight gains, make a *back-to-back stemplot*: Draw a single column of stems with vertical lines on both sides of it. Now add leaves to these stems on both sides, the experimental group on the right and the control group on the left. Then, order the leaves so that they increase as you move away from the stem.

(c) What does your plot show about the effect of high-lysine corn on weight gain?

5. Although the stemplot of Exercise 4 is effective for comparing the two weight-gain distributions, the natural stems divide the data into too many classes to clearly show the shape of the distributions.

(a) Make separate frequency tables for the weight gains in the experimental group and the control group. Use the classes 270–299, 300–329, 330–359, and so on.

(b) Draw separate histograms for the two groups. For easy comparison, draw them one above the other, with the scales on the horizontal axes aligned. What does this plot show about the effect of high-lysine corn on weight gain?

(c) Are the distributions of weight gains symmetric or skewed? Are they approximately normal in shape or not?

6. Draw a frequency curve for a distribution that is skewed to the left.

7. Another graphical means of presenting a distribution is the *segmented bar graph*. This is particularly useful when the variable is measured in a nominal scale or when the classes are few in number or unequal in size. Here is a segmented bar graph of degrees awarded by level, computed from the bottom row of Table 4-3 on page 148:

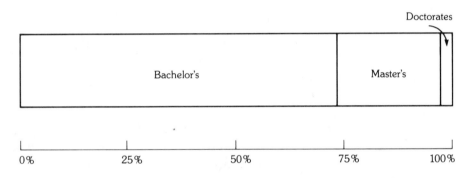

A segmented bar graph can be either vertical or horizontal. If vertical, it amounts to stacking the bars of an ordinary bar graph one atop the other. Make segmented bar graphs of the following data:

(a) The Bureau of Labor Statistics reports that in June 1982, 57.2% of the noninstitutional population were employed, 6.0% were unemployed, 1.3% were in the armed forces, and 35.5% were not in the labor force.

(b) The relative frequency distribution of farms by size, from Table 4-1 on page 145.

8. The entries in the table of random digits have the property that each value 0, 1, 2, 3, 4, 5, 6, 7, 8, and 9 occurs equally often in the long run.

(a) Make a frequency table and draw a frequency histogram for the entries in the first three rows of Table A (120 digits in all).

(b) Is this distribution approximately normal? How does it deviate from normality?

(c) Is this distribution approximately symmetric?

(d) Draw a frequency curve representing the distribution of values in a very large number of observations from a table of random digits.

Chapter 5

Descriptive statistics: Few numbers in place of many

T ables organize data, and graphs present a vivid overall picture. But more specific aspects of data such as their average and their variability are most succinctly summarized by a few well-chosen numbers. We often read or hear such statements as "The median income of households covered by Medicaid was $6900, less than one-third the median for all households." The median is one of the numerical measures called *descriptive statistics* that summarize specific features of a data set. Descriptive statistics are as important in your statistical vocabulary as random samples and line graphs. We have already met counts (frequencies) and rates or proportions (relative frequencies). This chapter lengthens the list of descriptive statistics we can claim as acquaintances, if not as friends. Our task here is to describe the distribution of a single variable. Wider acquaintance with descriptive statistics will introduce as to new graphical descriptions as well and, finally, to the important family of normal distributions.

1. Measuring center or average

Almost any presentation of data uses averages—average gas mileage, average income, average score on the exam, average absolutely refractory period of the tibial nerves of rats fed DDT. (I am quoting that last one from a report on the effects of persistent pesticides—don't blame me for it.) Everyone has heard that statistics features the mean, the median, and the mode. Those are in fact the three "averages" we will study. But do remember that you absorbed four solid chapters of statistics before meeting this famous trio. Our subject has other (and more interesting) parts, but to be statistically literate we must add the mean, the median, and the mode to our vocabulary. Here are brief definitions, followed in turn by a discussion of each measure of center:

> The *mean* of a set of *n* observations is the arithmetic *average;* it is the sum of the observations divided by the number of observations, *n.*
>
> The *median* is the *typical value;* it is the midpoint of the observations when they are arranged in increasing order.
>
> The *mode* is the *most frequent value;* it is any value having the highest frequency among the observations.

Note that we have defined these measures for any set of *n* observations. The mean, the median, and the mode are statistics if these observations are a sample; they are parameters if the observations form an entire population.

The *mean* is the usual arithmetic average. Add the observations and divide by the number of them. The mean of the 10 observations

$$4, 6, 10, 3, 7, 6, 6, 8, 5, 9$$

is

$$\frac{4 + 6 + 10 + 3 + 7 + 6 + 6 + 8 + 5 + 9}{10} = \frac{64}{10} = 6.4.$$

When someone says "average," it is usually the mean that is intended. Now that we know the proper vocabulary, be sure to say "mean" and not "average." Means are so common that a compact notation is useful. Remember the idea from algebra of letting letters stand for numbers so recipes applicable to any set of numbers can be given? We will do this. A set of *n* observations is denoted by

$$x_1, x_2, \ldots, x_n$$

and the mean of this set of observations is

$$\bar{x} = \frac{x_1 + x_2 + \ldots + x_n}{n}.$$

That is read "x bar" and is such common notation that in reading literature in psychology, sociology, biology, and other fields you can assume that an $\bar{x}$ or $\bar{y}$ or $\bar{z}$ used without explanation is a mean.

The *median* is the midpoint of the observations when they are arranged in increasing order of magnitude. To find the median of the numbers

$$8, 4, 9, 1, 3,$$

arrange them in increasing order as

$$1, 3, 4, 8, 9.$$

The median is 4, because it is the midpoint; two observations fall below 4 and two fall above it. Whenever the number of observations is odd, the middle observation is the median. If the number of observations is even, there is no one middle observation. But there is a middle pair, and we take the median to be the mean of this middle pair, the point halfway between them. So the median of

$$8, 4, 1, 9, 1, 3$$

is found by arranging these numbers in increasing order:

$$1, 1, 3, 4, 8, 9$$

$$\text{median} = \frac{3 + 4}{2} = 3.5.$$

Note that three observations fall below 3.5 and three fall above.

Some words to the wise about finding medians are needed: First, never fail to arrange the observations in increasing order; the middle value in the haphazard order in which the numbers come to you is not the median. Second, never fail to write down all the observations, even if some have the same value. The median of

$$4, 5, 5, 6, 6, 6, 8, 9$$

is 6 because both of the middle pair of numbers have the value 6. Third, a recipe can save you from trying to locate the middle one of 471 observations or the middle pair of 232 observations by counting in from both ends. Here it is:

If there are *n* observations in all, find the number (*n* + 1)/2. Arrange the observations from smallest to largest, and count (*n* + 1)/2 observations

up from the bottom. **This gives the** *location* **of the median in the list of observations.**

Returning to the examples, the set of data 1, 3, 4, 8, 9 has $n = 5$ observations. Because $(n + 1)/2 = (5 + 1)/2 = 3$, the median is the third number in the list, which is 4. The data set 4, 5, 5, 6, 6, 6, 8, 9 has $n = 8$ observations. So $(n + 1)/2 = (8 + 1)/2 = 4.5$. This means that the median has location "four and a half," or midway between the fourth and fifth numbers in the list. (Note that 4.5 is not the median but merely its location in the list.) The median of a set of 232 numbers has location $(232 + 1)/2 = 116.5$, or midway between the 116th and 117th numbers when arranged from smallest to largest. The median of 471 observations is the 236th in order of magnitude, because

$$\frac{471 + 1}{2} = \frac{472}{2} = 236.$$

The *mode* is any value occurring most frequently in the set of observations. It is convenient to arrange observations in increasing order as an aid to seeing how often each value occurs. The mode of

$$4, 5, 5, 6, 6, 6, 8, 9$$

is 6 because this value occurs three times and no other value appears more than twice. What about

$$1, 4, 5, 5, 5, 6, 8, 9, 9, 9, 12?$$

Both 5 and 9 are modes, because both are "most frequent" in this data set. Such a data set is called *bimodal*. When no value occurs more than once, we could say that all are modes; that's not very helpful, so we prefer to say that such a set of data has no mode.

Having made the acquaintance of mean, median, and mode, we now ought to inquire how they do their job of describing a set of observations. Certainly "most frequent value," "midpoint," and "arithmetic average" are quite different notions with different uses. Here is a survey of their use.

The *mode* is little used, because it records only the most frequent value, and this may be far from the center of the distribution of values. We have also seen that there may be several modes, or none. The chief advantage of the mode is that, of our three measures, it alone makes sense for variables measured in a nominal scale. It is nonsense to speak of the median sex or mean race of United States ambassadors, but the most frequent (modal) sex is male and the modal race is white.

The *median* uses only order information in the data. (How many observations are above a point? How many are below?) The median therefore makes sense for ordinal variables as well as for interval/ratio variables. The median does not employ the actual numerical value of the observations; it is not affected by how far above or below it the observations fall but only requires that equal numbers of observations fall above and below. The *mean* alone of our measures of center does use the actual numerical values of the observations. Thus the mean utilizes more of the information in the data than either the mode or the median. For this reason, the mean is the most common measure of center. In a strict sense, the mean makes sense only for interval/ratio data, because it requires adding the observations. But in practice, means are frequently computed for ordinal variables as well.

Some occasions when the median is a better description of the center of a distribution of values than is the mean are determined by the fact that the median does *not* respond to actual numerical values. An example will show how this insensitivity can be a virtue.

Example 1. A professional basketball team has 4 players earning $80,000 per year, 5 who earn $200,000, and a superstar who earns $1,100,000. The mean salary for the team's 10 players is therefore

$$\frac{(4)(80,000) + (5)(200,000) + 1,100,000}{10} = \frac{2,420,000}{10} = \$242,000.$$

You see that the superstar's salary has pulled the mean well above the amount paid to any other player. The mean is quite sensitive to a few extreme observations. The median, though, is $200,000 and does not change even if the superstar earns $5 million; his salary is just one number falling above the midpoint. Lest you think that extreme differences between the median and the mean are confined to artificial examples, consider jury awards made in Chicago civil cases (personal injury, product liability, etc.) in 1983: The median award was $8000, the mean $69,000. Because income data often have a few extremely high observations, descriptions of income distributions usually use the median— "half earned more than this, and half earned less." Medians are prominent in the income data in the *Statistical Abstract,* for example. This is not to say that the median always should be used for data containing extreme observations. If you were interested in the total income of a group, the median income would be uninformative, while the mean would tell you what you want to know, because it is computed from the sum of the incomes. Always ask which of "most frequent value," "midpoint," or "arithmetic average" best represents the data for your intended use.

"Should we scare the opposition by announcing our mean height or lull them by announcing our median height?"

The different response of the mean and the median to extreme values can be pictured by using the frequency curve for a set of data. The mode is the value where the curve peaks. The median is the value such that half the area under the curve lies below it and half above it. These facts are true because the frequency curve is a smooth version of the frequency histogram. So it is highest at the most frequent value, or mode. And because areas in a histogram represent frequencies, equal areas lie above and below the median. Figure 5-1 illustrates these facts.

It is not so clear where to place the mean on a frequency curve or histogram. But these are the facts: If we think of the curve as cut out of solid material, the mean is the point where the shape would balance. Figure 5-2 illustrates this.

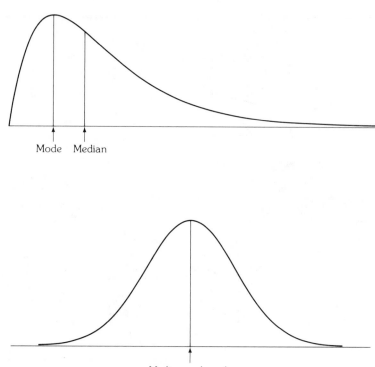

Figure 5-1 The mode and median of a frequency distribution. The mode is the point at which the frequency curve attains its highest value. The median is the point that divides the area under the curve into two equal parts to the left and to the right of it. The median is the center point of any symmetric frequency curve. This normal curve is highest at the center, so the center point is also the mode.

Now, if a frequency curve is symmetric, the "balance point" and the "equal areas" point are the same. The mean and median are the same for symmetric distributions. This is one reason that mean scores are often reported for standardized tests even though the scores have an ordinal scale. The distribution of such scores is often roughly normal, and therefore symmetric, so the mean and median all fall close together. If one tail of a frequency curve is stretched to correspond to a few extreme observations on one side, the frequency curve becomes skewed. A little weight far out in one direction moves the balance point quite a bit in that direction. So the mean moves farther toward the long tail than does the median. We saw a numerical example earlier, and Figure 5.3 gives a pictorial view.

Now you are an expert on mean, median, and mode. I hope they have lived

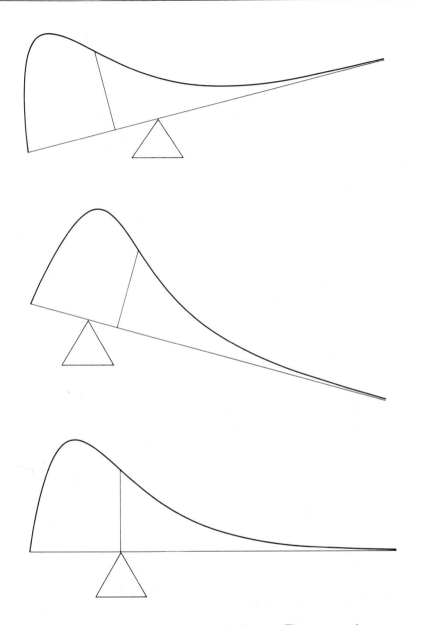

Figure 5-2 The mean of a frequency distribution. The mean is the center of gravity of the frequency curve, the point about which the curve would balance on a pivot placed beneath it.

up to your expectations. Be warned, however, that averages of all kinds can play tricks if you are not alert. Some examples of these tricks appear in the exercises. Arithmetic is never a substitute for understanding.

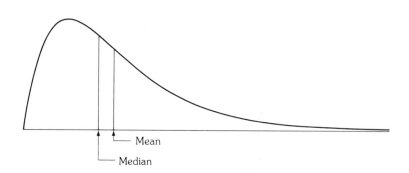

Figure 5-3 The mean and median of a skewed distribution. The mean is located farther toward the long tail of a skewed frequency curve than is the median.

2.   Measuring spread or variability

Useful as the measures of center are, they are usually incomplete and often misleading without some accompanying indication of how spread out or dispersed the data are. The median family income of $23,433 in 1982 masks the fact that 6.0% of all families received less than $5000 and 10.9% had incomes above $50,000. The distribution of family incomes is skewed to the right and very spread out. Knowing the median alone gives us an inadequate description of the distribution of incomes for American families. Similarly, the mean potency of a drug may be exactly what the doctor ordered, but if the potency of the lot varies too much, many doses will be ineffective owing to low potency or perhaps dangerous owing to high potency. The simplest adequate summary of a univariate distribution usually requires both a measure of center and a measure of variability.

   Beware of falling prey to partial information in the form of an average without a measure of variability. Has the press overstated the harm done by rising food prices? In 1973, Secretary of Agriculture Earl Butz thought so, and he gave an argument based on an average.

   In his speech, Dr. Butz said that food costs were now under 16 percent of Americans' spendable personal income, indicating he felt that the press gave too little attention to this figure.

   However, many economic experts believe that that figure is itself misleading.

   "Whenever they use it like this, it makes us shudder," one official said. "The trouble is, it lumps the Rockefellers in with the welfare cases." [1]

That's the weakness of an average alone: It lumps the Rockefellers in with the welfare cases.

Percentiles

When the median is used to measure center, both the variability and general shape of a distribution can be described by giving several percentiles.

> The *cth percentile* of a set of numbers is a value such that *c* percent of the numbers fall below it and the rest fall above.

You have met percentiles if after taking a standardized test such as the SAT you received a report of the result in the form "Raw score 590, percentile 81." You scored 590, but more informative is the fact that 81% of those taking the exam had scores lower than yours.

The median is the 50th percentile. Some other percentiles are important enough to have individual names.

> The *lower quartile* is the 25th percentile.

> The *upper quartile* is the 75th percentile.

A convenient way of indicating the spread of a data set is to give the quartiles along with the median. Often we also give the extremes (the smallest and largest individual observations). Median, quartiles, and extremes offer a reasonably complete *five-number summary* of a data set. An example will illustrate the details.

> **Example 2.** Table 5-1 shows the Nielsen ratings of all 68 national prime-time television shows for a week in 1982. The ratings are already arranged in numerical order, so the median is midway between the 34th and 35th in that order. The median is
>
> $$\frac{16.0 + 16.2}{2} = \frac{32.2}{2} = 16.1.$$
>
> *To find the lower quartile, compute the median of all observations falling below the location of the overall median.* There are 34 ratings below 16.1. By our usual rule for the median of 34 observations, the median of these ratings is halfway between the 17th and 18th ratings from the bottom of the list. So the lower quartile is
>
> $$\frac{13.8 + 13.9}{2} = \frac{27.7}{2} = 13.85.$$

Table 5-1. Nielsen television ratings, April 12–18, 1982

Program	Network	Rating	Program	Network	Rating
1. MASH	CBS	23.7	35. "My Body, My Child"	ABC	16.0
2. 60 Minutes	CBS	23.5	36. Flamingo Road	NBC	16.0
3. The Jeffersons	CBS	23.5	37. 9 to 5	ABC	15.8
4. Alice	CBS	22.5	38. 20/20	ABC	15.6
5. Three's Company	ABC	22.3	39. Greatest American Hero	ABC	15.4
6. Dallas	CBS	22.0	40. Fame	NBC	15.4
7. Joanie Loves Chachi	ABC	21.8	41. Lou Grant	NBC	15.2
8. Trapper John, M.D.	CBS	21.5	42. Quincy, M.E.	NBC	14.5
9. Falcon Crest	CBS	21.4	43. "Yanks"	ABC	14.5
10. The Love Boat	ABC	21.1	44. "Thou Shalt Not Kill"	NBC	14.4
11. Too Close for Comfort	ABC	20.9	45. Taxi	ABC	14.3
12. Dynasty	ABC	20.8	46. Phoenix	ABC	14.2
13. Dukes of Hazzard	CBS	20.6	47. Benson	ABC	14.1
14. Magnum, P.I.	CBS	20.6	48. Barney Miller	ABC	14.1
15. The Facts of Life	NBC	20.2	49. "Dean Martin—Animal Park"	NBC	14.1
16. Hart to Hart	ABC	20.0	50. Strike Force	ABC	13.9
17. Making the Grade	CBS	19.6	51. Little House on the Prairie	NBC	13.9
18. Happy Days	ABC	19.5	52. "Same Time Next Year"	CBS	13.8
19. Fall Guy	ABC	19.1	53. Herbie, the Love Bug	CBS	13.5
20. One Day at a Time	CBS	19.1	54. No Soap, Radio	ABC	13.4
21. Gimme a Break	NBC	18.9	55. "Loretta Lynn—Lady/Legend"	NBC	12.7
22. Fantasy Island	ABC	18.2	56. "Dukes of Hazzard Special"	CBS	12.5
23. Real People	NBC	18.2	57. Mork and Mindy	ABC	12.2
24. CHIPs	NBC	18.2	58. Walt Disney	CBS	11.8
25. Private Benjamin	CBS	18.1	59. "The Last Song"	CBS	11.5
26. Archie Bunker's Place	CBS	17.9	60. Father Murphy	NBC	10.4
27. Report to Murphy	CBS	17.9	61. Shape of Things	NBC	10.2
28. Different Strokes	NBC	17.7	62. Barbara Mandrell	NBC	9.6
29. Simon & Simon	CBS	17.1	63. Q.E.D.	CBS	9.6
30. That's Incredible	ABC	16.7	64. Harper Valley	NBC	9.0
31. Teachers Only	NBC	16.5	65. One of the Boys	NBC	8.8
32. Hill Street Blues	NBC	16.3	66. Chicago Story	NBC	7.9
33. Knots Landing	CBS	16.2	67. Inside America	ABC	7.3
34. Bret Maverick	NBC	16.2	68. "Protection for Sale"	NBC	6.4

SOURCE: A. C. Nielsen Co. Published by permission. A program's rating is the estimated percent of households with television sets that watched the program.

Similarly, *the upper quartile is the median of all observations falling above the location of the overall median.* Check that this is

$$\frac{19.6 + 19.5}{2} = \frac{39.1}{2} = 19.55.$$

The extreme ratings are 6.4 and 23.7. The five-number summary of the distribution of ratings is therefore 6.4, 13.85, 16.1, 19.55, 23.7.

When several observations are tied, be sure to pay attention to the *location* of the overall median, as given by the rule on page 174, when computing quartiles. For example, the median of the 12 observations

$$2 \quad 4 \quad 7 \quad 11 \quad 11 \quad 11 \ \bigg| \ 11 \quad 14 \quad 16 \quad 16 \quad 24 \quad 29$$

is located as marked, between the 6th and 7th observations from the bottom of the ordered list. The value of the median is 11. The lower quartile is the median of the six observations falling below the location of the overall median, not of the three observations with values less than 11. The lower quartile of these data is 9, and the upper quartile is 16.

The extremes indicate the overall spread of the data but are sensitive to outliers. The quartiles and the median (which is the middle quartile) divide the data into quarters. The lower and upper quartiles show the spread of the middle half of the data and are a good description of the variability of a distribution. The spacing of the quartiles about the median also gives an indication of the symmetry or skewness of the distribution. In a symmetric distribution, the lower and upper quartiles are equally distant from the median. But the upper quartile will be farther above the median than the lower quartile is below it in most distributions that are skewed to the right. Figure 5-4 illustrates these facts.

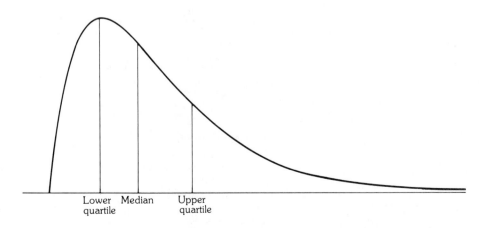

Lower   Median   Upper
quartile   quartile

Figure 5-4

The extremes of a large set of data may be very far from the median and not descriptive of any but outlying observations. In such cases we can replace the extremes by the lower and upper *deciles* in the five-number summary. The lower decile is the 10th percentile, and the upper decile is the 90th percentile. We will not give precise rules for computing the deciles and other percentiles but will be satisfied with approximate answers. For example, to find the upper decile of the 68 Nielsen ratings in Table 5-1, note that 90% of 68 is

$$(0.90)(68) = 61.2.$$

This rounds off to 61, so we will take the 61st rating (in increasing order) as the upper decile. That rating is the 21.5 earned by "Trapper John, M.D."

Boxplots

The five-number summary of a distribution lends itself to a graphical portrayal that is particularly helpful in comparing two or more distributions. This is the *boxplot*. Figure 5-5 gives boxplots for the distributions of Nielsen ratings for the three networks. Each central box has its ends at the quartiles, and the median of the distribution is marked by the line within the box. The "whiskers" at either

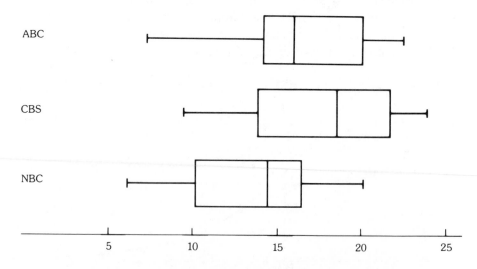

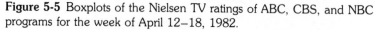

Figure 5-5 Boxplots of the Nielsen TV ratings of ABC, CBS, and NBC programs for the week of April 12–18, 1982.

end extend to the extremes. For example, the 23 CBS programs rated have the five-number summary 9.6, 13.8, 18.1, 21.5, 23.7. These numbers determine the CBS boxplot in Figure 5-5.

Figure 5-5 allows immediate comparison of the popularity of the three networks' shows. CBS won the ratings war that week, while NBC's highest-rated show falls short of CBS's upper quartile. NBC's rating distribution is skewed to the left, indicating many unpopular programs. ABC's median rating is not much better than NBC's, but ABC's distribution is skewed to the right, with the upper quartile well above that of NBC. Figure 5-5 is another example of the effectiveness of graphs in conveying information.

There are many variations of the boxplot idea. Sometimes the ends of the box are at the extremes, with the median and quartiles marked by three lines within the box. Sometimes the whiskers extend only to the lower and upper deciles rather than to the extremes. When you meet a boxplot, be sure to check which variation has been chosen.

Standard deviation

Though the five-number summary is the most generally useful description of spread or variability, it is not the most common. That distinction belongs to the *standard deviation*. The standard deviation and its close relaative, the *variance*, measure spread about the mean as center. They should be used only in the company of the mean.

> The *variance* **is the mean of the squares of the deviations of the observations from their mean.**
>
> The *standard deviation* **is the positive square root of the variance.**

These definitions require an example to see what they say, and then some commentary to see why they say it. Here is the example:

> **Example 3.** Find the variance and standard deviation of the 5 observations
>
> $$6, 7, 5, 3, 4.$$
>
> (a) First compute the mean.
>
> $$\bar{x} = (6 + 7 + 5 + 3 + 4)/5 = 25/5 = 5.$$

(b) The deviation of any observation x from the mean is the difference $x - \bar{x}$, which may be either positive or negative. Use this arrangement to compute the variance:

Observation x	Deviation $x - \bar{x}$	Squared deviation $(x - \bar{x})^2$
6	$6 - 5 = 1$	$(1)^2 = 1$
7	$7 - 5 = 2$	$(2)^2 = 4$
5	$5 - 5 = 0$	$(0)^2 = 0$
3	$3 - 5 = -2$	$(-2)^2 = 4$
4	$4 - 5 = -1$	$(-1)^2 = 1$
		Sum $= 10$

The sum of the squares of the deviations from the mean is 10. The variance is therefore

$$\text{variance} = \frac{\text{sum of squared deviations}}{\text{number of observations}} = \frac{10}{5} = 2.$$

(c) The standard deviation is the square root of the variance.

$$\sqrt{2} = 1.4.$$

A calculator with a $\sqrt{}$ key makes square roots easy.

In the language of algebra, the recipe for the standard deviation is as follows:

Observations $\qquad\qquad x_1, x_2, \ldots, x_n$

Mean $\qquad\qquad\qquad \bar{x} = \dfrac{x_1 + x_2 + \ldots + x_n}{n}$

Variance $\qquad\qquad s^2 = \dfrac{(x_1 - \bar{x})^2 + (x_2 - \bar{x})^2 + \ldots + (x_n - \bar{x})^2}{n}$

Standard deviation $\quad s = \sqrt{s^2}$

If you have difficulty following this algebraic recipe, look back at the example for guidance.*

Some comments on the standard deviation will help you to interpret it.

1. s makes sense as a measure of spread or variability. It is a kind of average deviation of the observations from their mean. If the observations are spread out, they will tend to be far from the mean, both above and below. Some deviations will be large positive numbers, and some will be large negative numbers. But the squared deviations will all be large and positive, so both s^2 and s will be large when the data are spread out. And s^2 and s will be small when all the data are close together. (The deviations from the mean will always be both positive and negative and will always have sum zero. Look back at the example to check that the sum of the "Deviation" column is zero. This helps you check your arithmetic. Remember that the square of a negative number is positive, so squared deviations are never negative.)

2. s is always zero or positive. It can be zero only if all the squared deviations are zero, which means that every observation x_i has the same value as $\bar{x}$, and so all observations x_i are the same. *Standard deviation zero means no spread at all; otherwise the standard deviation is positive and increases as the spread of the data increases.*

3. When the observations x_i are measured in some units (seconds, centimeters, grams), their variance s^2 is measured in the square of those units because it is an average squared deviation. The standard deviation s has the same units as the original observations. This is one reason why s is used more often than s^2. (Another reason appears in Section 3.)

4. Like the mean, the variance and standard deviation are heavily influenced by outliers. If, for example, the largest value in Example 3 were 17 instead of 7, the mean would increase to $\bar{x} = 7$, and the variance would increase to $s^2 = 26$. Even the standard deviation increases from 1.4 to $s = 5.1$. If a few outliers make $\bar{x}$ and s seem inappropriate, you can use the five-number summary, or you can recompute $\bar{x}$ and s without the outliers. There is no rule for such decisions. It is a matter of judgment in describing data.

5. To allow more meaningful comparisons of the variability of different distributions, the *coefficient of variation* is often used. This is just the standard deviation expressed as a percent of the mean: $CV = s/\bar{x}$ converted to percent. An appendix in the *Statistical Abstract* gives CVs among other information for

---

* There is a complication that you should be aware of if you study more statistics. When the observations form an SRS of size n, s^2 is usually found by dividing the sum of the squared deviations by $n - 1$ rather than n. There are arguments in favor of both n and $n - 1$. Since the difference is quite small when n is of moderate size, we use n for simplicity.

many government sample surveys. For example, the CV is only 0.2% for annual average size of the labor force from the Current Population Survey but is 4% for the count of personal robberies from the National Crime Survey. CVs are preferable to standard deviations for comparing the accuracy of these surveys because the surveys are measuring variables that differ in both kind and size. A raw standard deviation that is small when measuring the labor force (over 110 million persons) would be large when counting personal robberies (about 1.5 million). Comparison of variability requires some care.

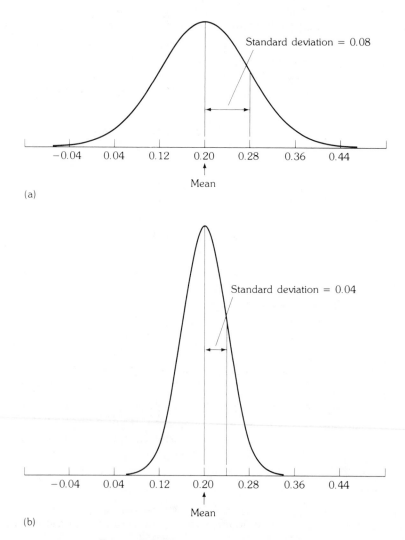

(a)

(b)

Figure 5-6 Two normal distribution curves.

3.   The normal distributions

Frequency curves offer a means of quickly describing the shape of a distribution. The normal curves are particularly important in statistics because the sampling distributions of many statistics (including the proportion $\hat{p}$ and the mean $\bar{x}$) are described well by normal curves for moderate and large sample sizes. There is an entire family of normal curves, two of which are shown in Figure 5-6. All normal curves share several characteristics: They are symmetric. They are bell-shaped. Their tails drop off quickly, so that a set of normally distributed data will have few outliers.

Because normal distributions are symmetric, the mean and median lie together at the center of the curve. This is also the peak of the curve, so the mean, median, and mode of a normal distribution are all identical.

The standard deviation of a normal distribution also can be located on the normal curve. Notice that near its center, a normal curve falls ever more steeply as we move away from the center, like this:

But in either tail, the curve falls ever less steeply as we move away from the center, like this:

The points at which the curvature changes from the first type illustrated to the second are located one standard deviation on either side of the mean. With a bit of practice, you can learn to find these points by running a pencil along the curve and feeling where the curvature changes. So both the mean and the standard deviation (but not the variance) of a normal frequency distribution are visible on the normal curve. Because normal curves are common, here is another reason why the standard deviation is often preferred to the variance.

Figure 5-6 presents two normal curves with the means and standard deviations marked. Study those curves. The shape of a normal curve is completely determined by its mean and standard deviation; there is only one normal curve with mean 0.2 and standard deviation 0.08, for example, and it appears in Figure 5-6(a). The mean fixes the center of the curve, while the standard deviation determines its shape. Changing the mean of a normal distribution does not change its shape, only its location on the axis. Changing the standard deviation does change the shape of a normal curve, as Figure 5-6 illustrates. The distribution with the smaller standard deviation is less spread out and more sharply peaked. But in both cases almost the entire distribution of values described by the curve lies within three standard deviations on either side of the mean. This is true of any normal curve, no matter what mean and standard deviation it has.

The normal curves in Figure 5-6 in fact describe sampling distributions. The first describes the distribution of the sample proportion $\hat{p}$ in SRSs of size 25 from the bead population of Chapter 1 with $p = 0.20$ as the population proportion of colored beads. This is seen by looking again at the progression from histogram to polygon to normal curve in Figures 4-12, 4-13, and 4-14 on pages 162–163. The bottom curve in Figure 5-6 describes the sampling distribution of $\hat{p}$ in SRSs of size 100 from this same population. In both cases, the mean (and also the median and the mode) of the sampling distribution of $\hat{p}$ falls at 0.20, the true value of the parameter being estimated. So $\hat{p}$ is as likely to fall below p as above it—there is no systematic tendency to overestimate or underestimate the parameter. This is our final version of lack of bias. *When the sampling distribution of a statistic is normal, the statistic has no bias when the mean of the distribution is equal to the parameter being estimated.* If the population of beads had $p = 0.10$ or $p = 0.30$, the center of the curves in Figure 5-6 would move to those values.

The spread or dispersion of a normal curve is completely described by its standard deviation. Figure 5-6(a), for sample size 25, has standard deviation 0.08. Figure 5-6(b), for sample size 100, has standard deviation 0.04. The smaller spread of the second curve about its mean reflects the greater precision of the statistic $\hat{p}$ for the larger sample size. *When the sampling distribution of a statistic is normal, the precision can be described by giving the standard deviation of its sampling distribution.* So when a sampling distribution is normal, the mean and standard deviation together describe both bias and precision. News releases of sample results usually give precision by way of a confidence statement, but accounts in professional publications often report the standard deviation (sometimes called the "standard error" in this context) of the sample statistic.

In addition to sampling distributions, many types of data have distributions whose shape is approximately described by a normal curve. One kind of data that are often normal is physical measurements of many members of a biological population. As an example, Figure 5-7 presents 2000 Hungarian skulls. The results of repeated careful measurements of the same quantity also tend to follow a normal distribution. (Recall that the results of repeated sampling and measurement were said in Chapter 3 to have similar properties!) This tendency was discovered by the great mathematician Carl Friedrich Gauss (1777–1855), who used normal distributions for errors in astronomical measurements. (You will

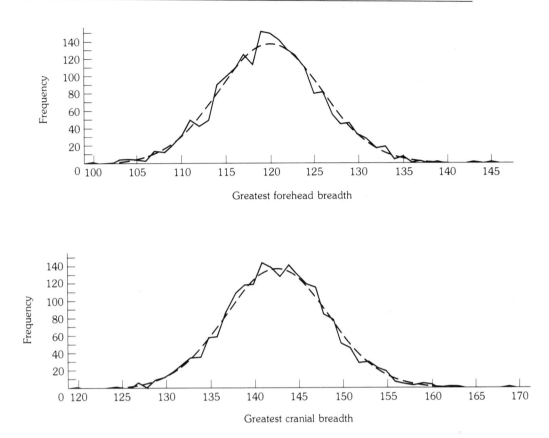

Figure 5-7 2000 Hungarian skulls. The distribution of each of two measurements on a large sample of male skulls is approximately normal. The solid line is the actual frequency curve, and the broken line is a normal curve that approximates the distribution. [From Karl Pearson, "Craniological notes," *Biometrika,* June 1903, p. 344. Reproduced by permission of the Biometrika Trustees.]

sometimes see normal distributions labeled "Gaussian" in his honor. That is a small honor for a man who made major contributions to astronomy, surveying, and several fields of physics in addition to being one of the supreme mathematicians.) Finally, it can be proved mathematically that any variable that is the sum of many small independent effects will have a distribution of values that is close to normal. So scores on long multiple-choice examinations such as SAT tests come close to following a normal curve. You should again ponder the harmony of creation—that distributions derived from a mathematical study of random sampling should be also useful in describing the real world.

HOWEVER . . . even though many sets of data follow a normal distribution, many do not. Income distributions are skewed to the right and hence are not normal. Nonnormal data, like nonnormal people, meet us quite often and are sometimes more interesting than their normal counterparts.

More detail

To make explicit the connection between standard deviation and spread or variability, here are some facts about the normal distributions:

1. **In any normal distribution, 68% of the observations fall within one standard deviation of the mean. Half of these (34%) fall within one standard deviation above the mean and the other half within one standard deviation below the mean.**
2. **Another 27% of the observations fall between one and two standard deviations away from the mean. So 95% (68% plus 27%) fall within two standard deviations of the mean.**
3. **In all, 99.7% of the observations fall within three standard deviations of the mean.**

The third fact makes precise the earlier comment that any normal curve is about six standard deviations wide. The second fact states that when a statistic with a normal sampling distribution has no bias, 95% of all samples will give values of the statistic falling within two standard deviations of the true parameter value. The sample proportion from an SRS, for example, has a normal sampling distribution and is an unbiased estimate of the true proportion in the population. So

The sample proportion has a standard error of 1.5 points

implies our former statement of precision

In repeated sampling, 95% of all samples have sample proportions falling within 3 points (two standard deviations) of the true parameter value.

Figure 5-8 illustrates all three facts. Let's call them the "68-95-99.7 rule." This rule describes the shape of normal curves more exactly than the description "bell-shaped." When using the normal curves to describe the shape of data sets, remember that no set of data is exactly described by a normal curve. The 68-95-99.7 rule will be only approximately true for SAT scores or the forehead breadth of 2000 Hungarian skulls.

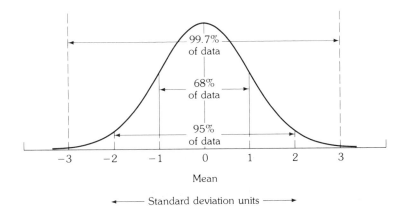

Figure 5-8 The 68-95-99.7 rule for normal distributions.

The 68-95-99.7 rule shows just how the standard deviation measures the spread or variability for normal distributions. Because any normal distribution satisfies the rule, the point one standard deviation above the mean is always the 84th percentile (because 50% of the observations fall below the mean and another 34% within one standard deviation above the mean, as Figure 5-9 shows). Similarly, one standard deviation below the mean is always the 16th percentile, and the point two standard deviations above the mean is the 97.5th percentile. Pictures similar to Figure 5-9 will help you solve problems like the following examples:

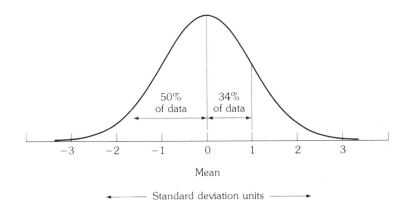

Figure 5-9 The 84th percentile of a normal distribution lies one standard deviation above the mean.

Example 4. The heights of adult American women are approximately normally distributed with mean 64 inches and standard deviation 2.5 inches. What heights contain the central 95% of this population?

Since 95% of all women have heights within two standard deviations of the mean, the central 95% of women's heights lie between 59 inches and 69 inches.

Example 5. Twenty percent of a large corporation's clerical staff are males. Of the last 100 workers chosen for promotion to administrative positions, 32 were males. How likely is it that 32 or more men would be chosen if the 100 workers promoted were drawn at random?

Here $p = 0.20$ and we want to know how often $\hat{p}$ for an SRS of size 100 will exceed 0.32. The sampling distribution of $\hat{p}$ [Figure 5-6(b)] is approximately normal with mean 0.20 and standard deviation 0.04. So 0.32 is three standard deviations above the mean. Since 99.7% of all SRSs would have $\hat{p}$ closer to the mean, and only half of the remaining 0.3% would fall on the high side, only 0.15% (that's 0.0015) of all possible SRSs would produce 32 or more men. Men are being favored for promotion, either because of discrimination or because the male clerical workers are more highly qualified.

The standard deviation is the natural unit of measurement for normal distributions. Observations from a normal distribution are often reduced to *standard scores* expressed in standard deviation units about the mean. The recipe is

$$\text{standard score} = \frac{\text{observation} - \text{mean}}{\text{standard deviation}}.$$

A standard score of 1 is always at the 84th percentile, as Figure 5-9 shows. In fact, every standard score translates into a specific percentile, which is the same no matter what the mean and standard deviation of the original normal distribution are. Table B on page 345 lists the percentiles corresponding to various standard scores. This table enables us to do calculations in greater detail than the 68-95-99.7 rule.

Example 6. Matt scores 590 on the verbal part of the SAT. Scores on the SAT follow a normal distribution with mean 500 and standard deviation 100.* Matt's standard score is therefore

---

* This is an oversimplification that is true only for a standardization population used to set up the original scale of SAT scores. The group of students who took the same form of the test as did Matt may have had a mean score higher or lower than 500, depending on their ability. For an account of how the tests are calibrated so that reported scores have the same meaning no matter when the test was taken, see William H. Angoff, "Calibrating College Board Scores" in *Statistics: A Guide to the Unknown*. Notice the normal curves on p. 242 of that essay.

$$\frac{590 - 500}{100} = \frac{90}{100} = 0.9.$$

Table B shows that this is the 81.59 percentile of the distribution of scores. In plain language, Matt did better than 81% of students who take the test.

Because a standard score translates into the same percentile for all normal distributions, standard scores allow direct comparison of scores from different normal distributions. Do remember that standard scores can be used to compare observations from different distributions only when both distributions are approximately normal. This condition is not always fulfilled.

NOTES

1. From an article by William Robbins in the *New York Times* of February 23, 1973.

Exercises

Section 1

1. Compute the mean, the median, and the mode for each of the following sets of numbers:
   (a) 4, 15, 2, 8, 4, 6, 10
   (b) 4, 2, 2, 6, 4, 4, 15, 8, 2, 17, 10, 4, 2, 6
   (c) 6, −3, 0, −11, 7, 120, −3

2. Return to the sample of 100 counts of coliform bacteria in milk given in Exercise 1 on page 169. You drew a frequency histogram for the data as part of that exercise.
   (a) Compute the mean and the median of the data.
   (b) Explain in terms of the shape of the frequency distribution why these measures of center fall as they do (close together or apart).

3. Here is a sample of 100 reaction times of a subject to a stimulus, in milliseconds:

   10, 14, 11, 15, 7, 7, 20, 10, 14, 9, 8, 6, 12, 12, 10, 14, 11, 13, 9, 12
   13, 11, 12, 10, 8, 9, 14, 18, 12, 10, 10, 11, 7, 17, 12, 9, 9, 11, 7, 10
   14, 12, 12, 10, 9, 7, 11, 9, 18, 6, 12, 12, 10, 8, 14, 15, 12, 11, 9, 9
   11, 8, 11, 10, 13, 8, 11, 11, 13, 20, 6, 13, 13, 8, 9, 16, 15, 11, 10, 11
   20, 8, 17, 12, 19, 14, 17, 12, 18, 16, 15, 16, 10, 20, 11, 19, 20, 13, 11, 20

   (a) Compute the mean and the median of these data.
   (b) Find the frequency of each outcome 6, 7, 8, . . . , 20, and draw a frequency histogram for these data.
   (c) Explain in terms of the shape of the frequency distribution why these measures of center fall as they do (close together or apart).

4. Identify which measure of center (mean, median, or mode) is the appropriate "average" in each of the following situations:
   (a) Someone declares, "The average American is a white female."
   (b) Middletown is considering imposing an income tax on its citizens. The city government wants to know the average income of citizens so that it can estimate the total tax base.
   (c) In an attempt to study the standard of living of typical families in Middletown, a sociologist estimates the average family income in that city.

5. As part of its twenty-fifth reunion celebration, the Class of '60 of Central New Jersey University mails a questionnaire to its members. One of the questions asks the respondent to give his or her total income last year. Of the 820 members of the Class of '60, the university alumni office has addresses for 583. Of these, 421 return the questionnaire. The reunion committee computes the mean income given in the responses and announces, "The members of '60 have enjoyed resounding success. The average income of class members is $80,000!".

   This result exaggerates the income of the members of the Class of '60 for (at least) three reasons. What are these reasons?

6. According to the Department of Commerce, the mean and median prices of new houses sold in the United States in 1982 were $69,300 and $83,900. Which of these numbers is the mean, and which is the median? Explain your answer.

7. The mean age of 5 persons in a room is 30 years. A 36-year-old person walks in. What is now the mean age of the persons in the room?

8. You wish to measure the average speed of vehicles on the interstate highway on which you are driving, so you adjust your speed until the number of vehicles passing you equals the number you are passing. Have you found the mean speed, the median speed, or the modal speed of vehicles on the highway?

9. Figure 5-10 presents three frequency curves, each with several points marked on them. At which of these points on each curve do the mean, the median, and the mode fall? (More than one measure of center may fall at one point.)

10. Make up a list of numbers of which only 10% are "above the average" (that is, above the mean). What percent of the numbers in your list fall above the median?

11. Which of the mean, median, and mode of a list of numbers must always appear as one of the numbers in the list?

12. In computing the median income of any group, federal agencies omit all members of the group who had zero income. Give an example to show how the median income of a group (as reported by the federal government) can go *down* when the group becomes better off economically.

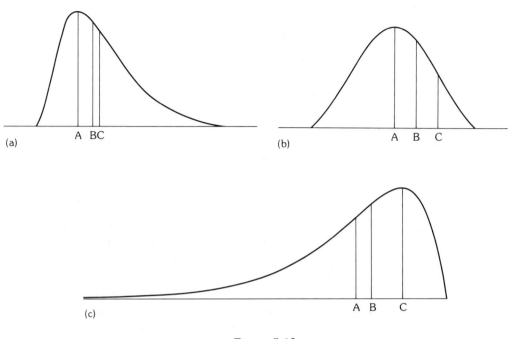

(a) A BC

(b) A B C

(c) A B C

Figure 5-10

13. The mean age of members of the class of '24 at their fiftieth reunion was 71.9 years. At their fifty-first reunion the next year, the mean age was 71.5 years. How can the mean age decrease when all the class members are a year older?

14. You drive 5 miles at 30 miles per hour, then 5 more miles at 50 miles per hour. Have you driven at an average speed of 40 miles per hour? (Your average speed is total miles driven divided by the time you took to drive it.)

15. The following paragraph contains three major statistical blunders. Describe them in one sentence each.

"In response to protests over the firing of coach Rockne, the university administration released the results of a questionnaire mailed to all 90,000 living alumni. Of the 8000 responses, 65% favored firing the coach, showing that the alumni want Rockne to go. And these alumni are supporters of the athletic program—the mean gift of those responding was over $200 last year, including James Barkadiddy's handsome gift of $1 million for a new scoreboard. What is more, 25% of the faculty want Rockne fired, so that when faculty and alumni are considered together, an overwhelming 90% want a new coach."

Section 2

1. Calculate the five-number summary of the Nielsen ratings for the 23 ABC programs in Table 5-1. Verify your answers by comparison with the boxplot in Figure 5-5.

2. Calculate five-number summaries for each of the following sets of data, and make a boxplot of each distribution. What does the boxplot show about the shape of the distribution?
   (a) The coliform bacteria counts in Exercise 1 on page 169.
   (b) The reaction times in Exercise 3 on page 195.
   (c) The state per capita incomes in Table 4-4 on page 158.

3. Compute five-number summaries for the weight gains of the experimental and control groups in the chicken-nutrition experiment of Exercise 4 on page 170. By how much does the weight gain of a typical chick fed high-lysine corn exceed that of a typical chick fed normal corn?
   Draw boxplots for the two groups with a common scale, as in Figure 5-5. Describe the conclusions that can be drawn from your plot. (Are the distributions symmetric? Skewed? Do they differ in variability?)

4. Here are five-number summaries of the distributions of weekly earnings (in pounds sterling) of full-time male and female workers in Britain as of 1982. (The data are from the annual New Earnings Survey, which reports similar information for many occupational and age groups. U.S. income data are collected by the Current Population Survey, but the United States does not yet use the convenient five-number summary.)

	Lower decile	Lower quartile	Median	Upper quartile	Upper decile
Men	89.7	109.9	139.1	180.5	233.8
Women	60.2	71.7	90.0	116.5	152.0

   (a) Why does the New Earnings Survey report deciles rather than extremes in its summaries?
   (b) Make boxplots of these two distributions on a common scale. Write a brief description of the differences between the distributions of earnings of men and women workers in Britain.
   (c) The median weekly earnings of full-time American workers were $370 for men and $240 for women in 1982. Based on these limited data, are the male/female differences in income comparable in the United States and Britain? Explain your answer.

5. The detailed price data collected for the Bureau of Labor Statistics includes prices of about 400 different items at many thousands of retail outlets each month. Would a five-number summary be appropriate to summarize these data for a year? Explain your answer.

6. Calculate the mean, the variance, and the standard deviation of each of the following sets of numbers:

   (a) 4, 0, 1, 4, 3, 6

   (b) 5, 3, 1, 3, 4, 2

   Which of the sets is more spread out? Draw a histogram of set (a) and one of set (b) to see how the set with the larger variance is more spread out.

7. Suppose that we add 2 to each of the numbers in the first set in Exercise 6. That gives us

$$6, 2, 3, 6, 5, 8.$$

   (a) Find the mean and the standard deviation of this set of numbers.

   (b) Compare your answers with those for set (a) in Exercise 6. How did adding 2 to each number change the mean? How did it change the standard deviation?

   (c) Can you guess, without doing the arithmetic, what will happen to the mean and standard deviation of set (a) in Exercise 6 if we add 10 to each number in that set?

   This exercise should help you see that the standard deviation (or variance) measures only spread about the mean and ignores changes in where the data are centered.

8. This is a variance contest. You must give a list of 6 numbers chosen from the whole numbers 0, 1, 2, 3, 4, 5, 6, 7, 8, and 9, with repeats allowed.

   (a) Give a list of 6 numbers with the largest variance such a list can possibly have.

   (b) Give a list of 6 numbers with the smallest variance such a list can possibly have.

   (c) Does either part (a) or part (b) have more than one correct answer?

9. Scores on the Stanford-Binet IQ test are approximately normally distributed with mean 100 and standard deviation 15. What is the variance of scores on this test?

10. If two distributions have exactly the same mean and standard deviation, must their frequency curves look exactly alike? If they have the same five-number summary, must their frequency curves be identical? Explain.

11. A school system employs teachers at salaries between $16,000 and $31,000. The teachers' union and the school board are negotiating the form of next year's increase in the salary schedule.

   (a) If every teacher is given a flat $1000 raise, what will this do to the mean salary? To the median salary? To the extremes and quartiles of the salary distribution?

   (b) What would a flat $1000 raise do to the standard deviation of teachers' salaries? (Do Exercise 7 if you need help.)

(c) If, instead, each teacher receives a 5% raise, the amount of the raise will vary from $800 to $1550, depending on the present salary. What will this do to the mean salary? To the median salary?

(d) A flat raise would not increase the spread of the salary distribution. What about a 5% raise? Specifically, will a 5% raise increase the distance of the quartiles from the median? Will it increase the standard deviation?

12. Another measure of the spread of a set of data is the *range*, which is the difference between the largest and smallest observations.

(a) Find the range of the reaction times in Exercise 3 of Section 1.

(b) The range is rarely used for any but very small samples. Can you explain why?

(c) Can you give an example in which the range is the most appropriate measure of spread?

Section 3

1. Figure 5-11 is a normal frequency curve. What are the mean and the standard deviation of this distribution?

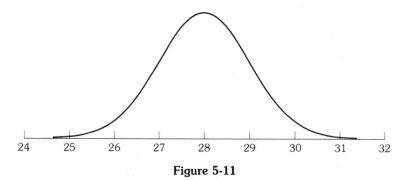

Figure 5-11

2. Figure 5-7 on page 191 records two frequency distributions for measurements on 2000 Hungarian skulls. Both are approximately normal. Estimate the mean and the standard deviation of each set of data.

3. Return once more to the coliform counts of Exercise 1 on page 169. You found the mean of these data in Exercise 2 of Section 1. The standard deviation can be calculated to be 2.02. What percent of the observations fall within one, two, and three standard deviations of the mean? Do you still feel that the distribution of coliform counts is approximately normal?

4. Explain, by using curves like those in Figures 5-8 and 5-9, why the point one standard deviation below the mean in a normal distribution is always the 16th percentile. Explain why the point two standard deviations above the means is the 97.5th percentile.

5. The heights of women ages 18 to 24 are approximately normally distributed with mean 64 inches and standard deviation 2.5 inches.
   (a) Draw a frequency curve for this distribution, with the scale on the horizontal axis correctly marked.
   (b) What percent of women in this age group are taller than 64 inches? Taller than 66.5 inches? Shorter than 59 inches?

6. Scores on the Wechsler Adult Intelligence Scale for the 20–34 age group are approximately normally distributed with mean 110 and standard deviation 25. About what percent of people in this age group have scores
   (a) above 110?
   (b) above 160?
   (c) below 85?

7. Elanor scores 700 on the mathematics part of the SAT. Scores on the SAT follow the normal distribution with mean 500 and standard deviation 100. Gerald takes the American College Testing Program test of mathematical ability, which has approximately mean 18 and standard deviation 6. He scores 24. If both tests measure the same kind of ability, who has the higher score?

8. Scores on the Wechsler Adult Intelligence Scale for the 60–64 age group are approximately normally distributed with mean 90 and standard deviation 25.
   (a) Sarah, who is 30, scores 135 on this test. Use the information of Exercise 6 to restate this score as a standard score.
   (b) Sarah's mother, who is 60, also takes the test and scores 120. Express this as a standard score by using the information given in this exercise.
   (c) Who scored higher relative to her age group, Sarah or her mother? Who has the higher absolute level of the variable measured by the test?

9. Scores on the Wechsler Adult Intelligence Scale for Air Force flyers ages 20 to 34 are approximately normal with mean 122 and standard deviation 7. The mean and standard deviation for this group are quite different from those given in Exercise 6 for all Americans in this age group. Can you give a plausible reason for the difference?

10. The mean height of men ages 18 to 24 is about 69 inches, while women that age have a mean height of 64 inches. Do you think that the distribution of heights for all Americans ages 18 to 24 is approximately normal? Explain your answer.

11. Example 4 on page 118 reported 11 measurements of the mass standard NB10 conducted by the National Bureau of Standards (NBS). I said there that the NBS is 95% confident that the mean of these measurements is within 0.0000023 of the true mass of NB10. Actually, the NBS gave the standard error of the mean measurement, from which I got this statement

of precision by assuming (as is roughly true) that the sample mean has a normal distribution. What value of the standard error did the NBS give?

The following exercises, unlike the preceding ones, require Table B on page 345.

12. The Wechsler Intelligence Scale for Children is used (in several languages) in the United States and Europe. Scores in each case are approximately normally distributed with mean 100 and standard deviation 15. When the test was standardized in Japan, the mean was 111. To what percentile of the American–European distribution of scores does the Japanese mean correspond?

13. The IQ scores on the Wechsler Adult Intelligence Scale for the 20–34 age group are approximately normal with mean 110 and standard deviation 25.
    (a) What percent of persons ages 20 to 34 have IQs below 100? What percent have IQs 100 or above?
    (b) What percent of persons ages 20 to 34 have IQs above 150?
    (c) If only 1% of persons ages 20 to 34 have IQs higher than Elanor's, what is Elanor's IQ? (Use the entry in Table B that comes closest to the point with 1% of the observations above it.)

14. SAT scores are approximately normal with mean 500 and standard deviation 100. Scores of 800 or higher are reported as 800. (So an SAT score of 800 does not, as you may have thought, imply a perfect performance.) What percent of scores are 800 or higher?

15. Suppose that the proportion of all adult Americans who are afraid to go out at night because of crime is $p = 0.45$. The distribution of the sample proportion $\hat{p}$ in a Gallup Poll probability sample of size 1500 is then approximately normal with mean 0.45 and standard deviation 0.015.
    (a) What percent of all Gallup Poll samples would give a $\hat{p}$ of 0.43 or lower? Of 0.47 or higher?
    (b) What percent of all Gallup Poll samples would give a $\hat{p}$ that misses the true p by two percentage points (± 0.02) or more?
    (c) In approximately what margin of error about $p = 0.45$ can we be 80% confident that $\hat{p}$ will fall? In what margin of error can we be 90% confident that $\hat{p}$ will fall?

Chapter **6**

Understanding relationships

A set of univariate data can be summarized by a measure of center and a measure of spread. Such a summary is far from a complete description of the data but does provide basic information. In contrast, even the briefest summary of bivariate data requires more than measures of center and spread for each of the two variables. We are usually also interested in the relationship between the variables. In a large group of people, the taller people also tend to be heavier. And those who smoke more cigarettes per day tend not to live as long as those who smoke fewer. We say that pairs of variables such as height and weight or smoking and life expectancy are *associated*.

Association in bivariate data means that certain values of one variable tend to occur more often with some values of the second variable than with other values of that variable.

Association between variables is easiest to understand in the physical sciences, where values of one variable are often connected to values of another by a "law." For example, one of the laws of motion states that if you drop a ball from a height, the downward speed of the ball is directly proportional to the time it has been falling. After four seconds it is moving twice as fast as after two seconds. This association can be graphed as a perfect straight-line relation between time and velocity.

Statistics is less concerned with ironclad relationships of the kind expressed by "physical laws" than with relationships that hold "on the average." There is an association between the height and the weight of individuals because, on the average, tall people are heavier than shorter people. There is an association between the sex of workers and their pay, because, on the average, women earn less than do men. Yet many individual women earn more than do many individual men, just as many individual short people are heavier than many individual taller people.

Our first goal is to describe association, keeping in mind its "on-the-average" character. When both variables are nominal (or their values are grouped into classes), a bivariate frequency table displays the association between them. This case occupies Section 1 of this chapter. When both variables have an interval/ratio scale, a scatterplot displays the association. Sometimes this association is very close—look back at the scatterplot on page 155 of corn yield versus planting rate, for example. The simplest such relationship between two variables is a straight line. There is an important descriptive statistic, the correlation coefficient, that describes the strength of straight-line association. Correlation is discussed in Section 2.

Once a strong association is discovered, it is natural to seek an explanation. There is an association between cigarette smoking and early death from several causes, an association so strong that the U.S. surgeon general states that cigarette smoking is "the largest avoidable cause of death and disability in the United States."[1] But does this association really reflect a cause-and-effect relationship, as the surgeon general suggests? There are many possible relationships between variables other than cause and effect that can explain an observed association. The most intense controversies in which statistics is involved center on explaining observed associations: Does smoking cause lung cancer? Does discrimination against women account for the fact that women earn much less than men on the average? An understanding of relationships is essential for the statistical sophisticate. This topic is addressed in Section 1 and then in more detail in Section 3, where the tie between smoking and lung cancer serves as a suitably controversial example.

Another way of stating that two variables are associated is that knowledge of one helps to predict the other. Since nonsmokers live (on the average, of course) longer than do smokers, many life insurance firms charge lower rates for nonsmokers. In doing so, the firms use one variable (smoking) to help predict a second (life expectancy). This prediction is useful whether or not the two variables are linked by cause and effect. Prediction, with emphasis on straight-line relationships between two variables, is discussed in Section 4.

1. Cross-classified data

Frequency tables are one of the most common and most useful forms of data display. Such a table shows how many members of a sample or a population fall into each of several groups. Each group is determined by the values of one or more variables, and the frequency table grows more complex as the number of variables used to define each group increases. A univariate frequency table classifies data according to the value of a single variable. Table 4-1 on page 145 classifies farms according to their size in acres. A bivariate frequency table classifies the data according to the values of two variables. Table 4-2 on page 146 classifies earned degrees by level and the sex of the recipient. Because one variable is arranged vertically and the other horizontally, a bivariate frequency table is an example of *cross-classified data*. More elaborate sets of cross-classified data group the observations according to the values of three or more variables.

When cross-classified data on two or more variables are at hand, we can display and investigate association between the variables. Here is an example:

Example 1. A university offers only two degree programs, one in electrical engineering and one in English. Admission to these programs is competitive, and the women's caucus suspects discrimination against women in the admissions process. The caucus obtains the following data from the university, a two-way classification of all applicants by sex and admission decision:

	Male	Female
Admit	35	20
Deny	45	40

The data in Example 1 do show an association between the sex of applicants and their success in obtaining admission. To describe this association more precisely, we compute some percents from the data.

$$\text{Percent of male applicants admitted} = \frac{35}{80} = 44\%$$

$$\text{Percent of female applicants admitted} = \frac{20}{60} = 33\%$$

Aha! Almost half the males but only one-third of the females who applied were admitted.

The university replies that although the observed association is correct, it is not due to discrimination. In its defense, the university produces a *three-way* table that classifies applicants by sex, admission decision, *and* the program to which they applied. Such a three-way table is conveniently presented as several two-way tables side-by-side, one for each value of the third variable. In this case there are two two-way tables, one for each program.

Engineering	Male	Female
Admit	30	10
Deny	30	10

English	Male	Female
Admit	5	10
Deny	15	30

Check that these entries do add to the entries in the two-way table. The university has simply broken that table down by department. We now see that engineering admitted exactly half of all applicants, both male and female, while English admitted one-fourth of both males and females. There is *no association* between sex and admission decision in either program.

How can no association in either program produce strong association when the two are combined? Easily: English is hard to get into, and mainly females applied to that program, while electrical engineering is *easy* to get into and attracted mainly male applicants. Look at the three-way table, and you will see this clearly. English had 40 female and 20 male applicants, while engineering had 60 male and only 20 female applicants.

The discussion of Example 1 illustrates two useful skills: reporting association in a two-way table by computing well-chosen percents, and displaying a three-way table as several two-way tables. But the point of the example is to demonstrate that an observed association between two variables can be misleading when there is another variable that interacts strongly with both variables but was not reported. Example 1 demonstrates *Simpson's Paradox*: Classify two groups with respect to the incidence of some attribute, such as admission in Example 1; if the groups are then separated into several categories, the group with the higher overall incidence can have lower incidence within each category.

Although Example 1 was artificial for the sake of simplicity, the effect of other variables on an observed association is at the heart of most controversies over alleged discrimination. Women earn (on the average) only about 60 percent as much as men. But women also (on the average) differ from male workers in age, years of schooling, labor force experience, and so on. In particular, many women have spent time outside the labor force for family reasons. Since pay rises with experience, the average pay of men would exceed that of women even in the absence of discrimination. The differing characteristics of male and female workers appear to explain about half of the earnings gap. Much (but not all) of the remaining gap exists because women tend to hold jobs in lower-paying industries and professions (textiles rather than steel, nursing rather than accounting). It is difficult to measure the extent of discrimination, even with the aid of advanced statistical methods.[2] In complex situations when many variables affect an outcome, you should be slow to jump to a conclusion suggested by a strong association alone.

Cross-product ratios*

A frequency table, like that in Example 1, that classifies observations according to two variables, each of which has only two classes, is called a 2×2 (read "two-by-two") table. A variety of descriptive statistics are used to describe association in a 2×2 table. When one variable (sex in Example 1) is thought of as an independent variable that may explain the other variable, comparisons of the two conditional relative frequencies given the values of the independent variable work well. We made such a comparison to reveal the male–female gap in Example 1. But the most common measure of association for 2×2 tables does not distinguish between the two variables.

The *cross-product ratio* for a 2×2 table with entries

$$
\begin{array}{cc}
r & s \\
t & u
\end{array}
$$

is

$$
c = \frac{r \times u}{s \times t}.
$$

Why does the cross-product ratio measure association? Return to Example 1. Since 35 males were admitted and 45 denied, the "odds" that a male is admitted are 35 to 45, or 35/45 as a ratio. For females, the odds are 20/40. If we compare these odds by taking their ratio, we get

$$
\frac{35/45}{20/40} = \frac{(35)(40)}{(20)(45)} = 1.56
$$

which is the cross-product ratio! If we had instead compared the odds that an admitted applicant is male (35/20) to the odds that one denied admission is male (45/40), we obtain the same cross-product ratio.

When there is *no* association, the odds are equal and the cross-product ratio is 1. The 2×2 table for applicants to English on page 206, for example, has cross-product ratio

$$
\frac{(5)(30)}{(15)(10)} = \frac{150}{150} = 1.
$$

*This is an optional topic not required for understanding later sections.

Values other than 1 show association. The cross-product ratio in Example 1 is 1.56. If the order of the columns were reversed (Exercise 8), the cross-product ratio would be the reciprocal of this value, $1/1.56$, or 0.64. So cross-product ratios c and $1/c$ show the same degree of association. As the association grows stronger, the cross product ratio moves away from 1, either increasing without bound or decreasing to zero.

Cross-product ratios form the basis for more elaborate measures of association in general two-way tables and in three- and higher-way tables. They are the most common descriptive statistics for association in grouped or nominal data, just as correlations (Section 2) are for interval/ratio data. Though correlations appear more often in texts and in general discussions, a statistical sophisticate should also be aware of cross-product ratios.

2.   Correlation

When both of two associated variables are measured in ordinal or interval/ratio scales, the association between the variables has a direction:

> **Two variables are *positively associated* when larger values of one tend to be accompanied by larger values of the other. The variables are *negatively associated* when larger values of one tend to be accompanied by smaller values of the other.**

There is a positive association between height and weight in a group of people and a negative association between number of cigarettes smoked per day and life expectancy.

Association can be described in many ways. We will give only a single numerical measure of association, the *correlation coefficient*. By a strict interpretation of the theory of scales of measurement, this measure requires that both variables have an interval/ratio scale. Just as with the mean and standard deviation, however, the correlation coefficient is often used with ordinal scales as well. Correlation is almost as common as mean and standard deviation in summaries of data.

The correlation coefficient is the algebraic high point of this book. Be of good courage: In mastering this, you have passed the worst. The notation of algebra is essential for a brief definition of correlation. Here is the definition:

> **Given n bivariate observations on variables x and y,**
>
> $$x_1, x_2, \ldots, x_n$$
>
> $$y_1, y_2, \ldots, y_n$$

"He says we've ruined his positive association between height and weight."

compute the correlation coefficient as follows:

(1) **Find the mean $\bar{x}$ and standard deviation s_x of the values x_1, x_2, . . . , x_n of the first variable.**

(2) **Find the mean $\bar{y}$ and standard deviation s_y of the values y_1, y_2, . . . , y_n of the second variable.**

(3) **The *correlation coefficient* (r) is**

$$r = \frac{\dfrac{1}{n}\left[(x_1 - \bar{x})(y_1 - \bar{y}) + \cdots + (x_n - \bar{x})(y_n - \bar{y})\right]}{s_x s_y}.$$

This definition deserves a short explanation, then an example to show what it says, and then a commentary on exactly what r measures. First, the explanation of the definition. The data are bivariate, so x_1 goes with y_1 ("my height and my weight"), x_2 goes with y_2 ("your height and your weight"), and so on. The numerator in r is the mean of the products of the deviations of each x and the corresponding y from their means. The denominator in r is the product of the standard deviation of the xs alone and the standard deviation of the ys alone.

Because both numerator and denominator are built up from deviations from the mean, there is a convenient arrangement for putting the definition into practice. The following example illustrates the arithmetic:

Example 2. Suppose that the data are

$$
\begin{array}{ccccc}
x & 6 & 2 & 2 & -2 \\
y & 5 & 5 & -3 & -3
\end{array}
$$

A scatterplot (Figure 6-1) shows positive association as a trend from lower left (both x and y small) to upper right (both x and y large). The means are

$$\bar{x} = (6 + 2 + 2 - 2)/4 = 8/4 = 2$$
$$\bar{y} = (5 + 5 - 3 - 3)/4 = 4/4 = 1$$

Now make the following table:

(1) x	(2) y	(3) $x - \bar{x}$	(4) $y - \bar{y}$	(5) $(x - \bar{x})(y - \bar{y})$	(6) $(x - \bar{x})^2$	(7) $(y - \bar{y})^2$
6	5	4	4	16	16	16
2	5	0	4	0	0	16
2	-3	0	-4	0	0	16
-2	-3	-4	-4	16	16	16
		0	0	32	32	64

Columns (3) and (4) are the deviations from the mean for the xs and ys obtained from columns (1) and (2) by subtracting the proper mean. Note that the sum of each set of deviations is 0, as is always the case. Columns (6) and (7) are the squares of these deviations. If we divide the sums of these columns by the number of observations, 4, the variances of x and y are

$$s_x^2 = 32/4 = 8$$
$$s_y^2 = 64/4 = 16$$

and the standard deviations are

$$s_x = \sqrt{8} = 2.8$$
$$s_y = \sqrt{16} = 4.$$

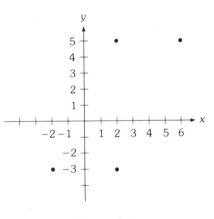

Figure 6-1

Column (5) contains the product of each entry in column (3) and the corresponding entry in column (4). Be careful of the signs here! Both positive and negative products may occur. The sum of the entries in column (5) is the sum in the numerator of r. We need only divide by the number of observations $n = 4$ (*not* $n = 8$, because n is the number of *bivariate* observations). So, finally

$$r = \frac{32/4}{(2.8)(4)} = \frac{8}{(2.8)(4)} = \frac{2}{2.8} = 0.71.$$

The primary purpose of Example 2 is not to show you how to calculate r. (You will no doubt use a computer or a special statistical calculator if you must do such calculations for any but the smallest sets of data.) Rather, we have shown by example what the recipe for the correlation coefficient r says. Be sure that you now understand the definition of r. I won't blame you if the thought of computing the correlation of IQ and grade index for 1200 college freshmen makes you a bit ill. Let a machine do that. But when the result is $r = 0.38$, we need to know what this means. And to know that, we first must know what r is. Now we know, so let's relax and interpret r. There are five points to be made.

1. *The correlation coefficient r makes sense as a measure of association; it is positive when the association is positive, and negative when the association is negative.* To understand how r measures association, look at the sum of products of deviations in the numerator of r. When x and y are positively associated, above-average values of x tend to go with above-average values of y, and below-average values of both variables also tend to occur together. So the deviations $x - \bar{x}$ and $y - \bar{y}$ are usually both positive or both negative. In

either case, the product $(x - \bar{x})(y - \bar{y})$ is positive, and it is large whenever both x and y are far from their means in the same direction. So "on the average" for all observations (that's what the numerator of r does), we get a large positive result when the association is strong. If, though, the association between x and y is negative, corresponding values of x and y tend to be on opposite sides of their means; when one is large, the other is small. The numerator of r is then negative, and more negative if large xs go with small ys and vice versa. So the numerator of r does seem to measure association. What about the denominator of r, which we have been ignoring? That brings us to the second point.

2. *The correlation coefficient r always has a value between -1 and $+1$.* It turns out that the standard deviations in the denominator standardize r in this way. That's why they are there. Can you see that the units in both numerator and denominator of r are the same? If x is height in centimeters and y is weight in grams, both numerator and denominator have the units "centimeters times grams." Therefore r itself has no units; it is a "pure number" between -1 and 1. And r does not depend on the choice of units for x and y. If x were measured in inches (not centimeters) and y in ounces (not grams), the correlation between height and weight would be unchanged so long as the same set of objects were being measured.

3. *The extreme values $r = -1$ and $r = +1$ indicate perfect straight-line association.* In particular, $r = -1$ means that all of the data points fall exactly on a straight line having negative slope (that is, when x increases, y decreases). And $r = +1$ means that all of the data points fall exactly on a straight line with positive slope (as x increases, y also increases).

4. *The correlation coefficient r measures how tightly the points on a scatterplot cluster about a straight line.* That is, r does not measure association in general but only straight-line association. Correlations near either $+1$ or -1 indicate that the points fall close to a straight line. When $r > 0$, the scatterplot shows a trend from lower left to upper right, and the line about which the points cluster has positive slope. For $r < 0$, the trend is from upper left to lower right, and the slope is negative. The scatterplots in Figure 6-2 illustrate how r measures straight-line association. Study them carefully. (These scatterplots are arranged so that the two variables have the same standard deviation in all six cases. It is not so easy to guess r from a scatterplot as these examples suggest, because changing the standard deviations can change the appearance of the scatterplots quite a bit.)

5. There is a specific way in which r measures straight-line association: *The square r^2 of the correlation coefficient is the proportion of the variance of one variable that can be explained by straight-line dependence on the other variable.* Notice that r^2 always falls between 0 and 1, so it can be interpreted as a proportion. To understand the meaning of the italicized fact, think about a case of

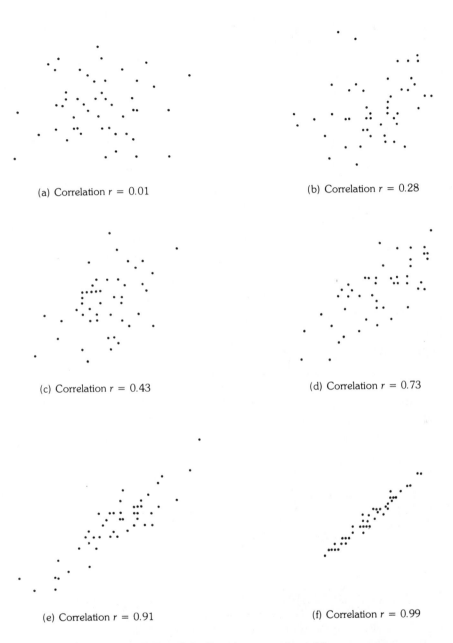

(a) Correlation $r = 0.01$

(b) Correlation $r = 0.28$

(c) Correlation $r = 0.43$

(d) Correlation $r = 0.73$

(e) Correlation $r = 0.91$

(f) Correlation $r = 0.99$

Figure 6-2. Correlation made visible.

perfect straight-line association with $r = -1$, such as in Figure 6-3(a). The variable y is completely tied to x; when x changes, y moves, so the point (x, y) moves along the line. Now, the eight values of y in Figure 6-3(a) have a fairly large variance. But that variance is entirely due to different x values occurring,

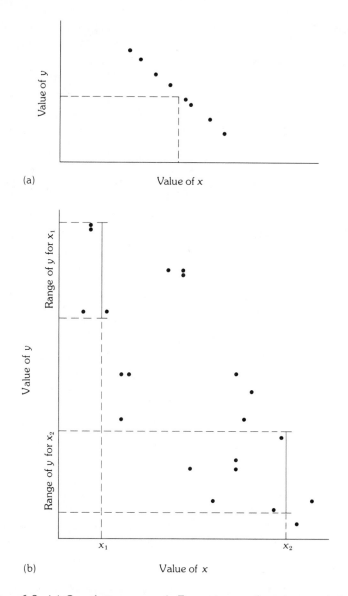

(a)   Value of x

(b)   Value of x

Figure 6-3. (a) Correlation $r = -1$. For a given x, there is no variation in y, hence y is perfectly predictable from x. (b) Correlation $r = -0.7$. For a given x, y takes on a range of values, hence y is only approximately predictable from x. Because the range of values of y does change with x (compare x_1 and x_2), x is of some use in predicting y.

bringing with them different y values. For a fixed x, there is *no* variation in y, because the data points all fall on the line. Straight-line dependence on x accounts for *all* of the variability in y, and $r^2 = 1$. The y values in Figure 6-3(b) also show a large variance. Some of this variance can be explained again by the fact that changing x brings with it (on the average) a change in y. This is shown by the quite different values of y that accompany the two different x values in Figure 6-3(b). But in this case r is not ± 1, and the association between x and y explains only part of the variability in y. Even when x remains fixed, y still varies. It is possible by mathematics to separate out the part of the variance of y that is explained by straight-line dependence on x. This is the fraction r^2 of the variance of the y values. In Figure 6-3(b), for example, $r = -0.7$ and so $r^2 = 0.49$. The straight-line dependence of the ys on the xs accounts for 49% of the variance of the ys in that figure. Because r^2 has this specific interpretation, it is used almost as much as is r itself. Of course, r^2 only measures the *strength* of the association, not whether it is positive or negative.

6. *Like the mean and the standard deviation, the correlation coefficient is heavily influenced by outliers.* If in Example 2 the value $y = 5$ in the first data point were mistakenly entered as $y = 50$, the correlation would increase from $r = 0.71$ to $r = 0.86$. This is a substantial increase, for the proportion of variance explained rises from $r^2 = (0.71)^2 = 0.50$ to $r^2 = (0.86)^2 = 0.74$.

3. Association and causation

There is a strong association between cigarette smoking and death rate from lung cancer. A study of British doctors found that smokers had 20 times the risk of nonsmokers, and a large study of American men ages 40 to 79 found 11 times higher death rates among smokers (see Figure 6-4). Does this mean that cigarette smoking causes lung cancer?

We are asking whether a specific association is due to changes in one variable (lung cancer) being caused by changes in another variable (smoking). Some observed associations are due to cause and effect. But others are not. Here are some examples of different relationships among variables that can explain an observed association:

Example 3. In the Australian state of Victoria, a law compelling motorists to wear seat belts went into effect in December 1970. As time passed, an increasing percentage of motorists complied. A study found high positive correlation between the percent of motorists wearing belts and the percent reduction in injuries from the 1970 level (see Figure 6-5). This is a clear instance of cause and effect: Seat belts prevent injuries when an accident occurs, so an increase in their use causes a drop in injuries. The top diagram in Figure 6-6 outlines this relationship between two variables.

Example 4. A moderate correlation exists between the Scholastic Aptitude Test (SAT) scores of high school students and their grade index later as

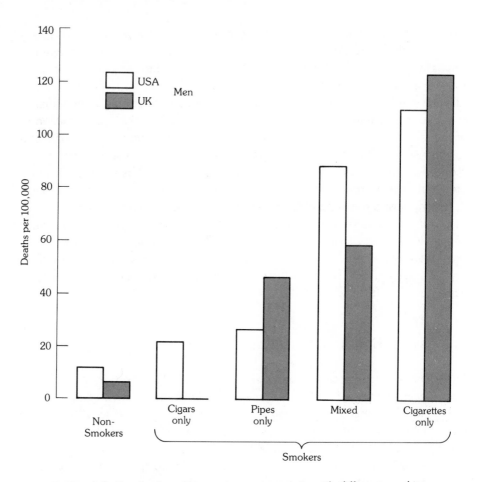

Figure 6-4. Deaths from lung cancer among men with different smoking habits. From two large studies, one of British doctors, one of American men. [From Royal College of Physicians, *Smoking and Health Now* (London: Pitman Medical Publishing, 1971), p. 5.]

freshmen in college. Surely high SAT scores do not cause high freshman grades. Rather, the same combination of ability and knowledge shows itself in both high SAT scores and high grades. Both of the observed variables are responding to the same unobserved variable, and this is the reason for the correlation between them. The middle diagram in Figure 6-6 illustrates this type of relationship.

Example 5. A study once showed a *negative* association between the starting salary of persons with a degree in economics and the level of the degree; that is, persons with a master's degree earned less on the average

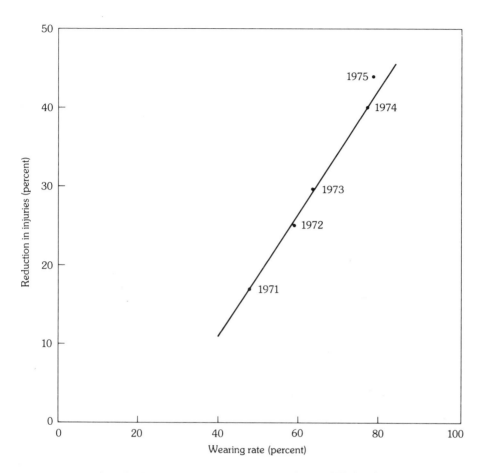

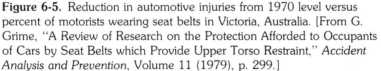

Figure 6-5. Reduction in automotive injuries from 1970 level versus percent of motorists wearing seat belts in Victoria, Australia. [From G. Grime, "A Review of Research on the Protection Afforded to Occupants of Cars by Seat Belts which Provide Upper Torso Restraint," *Accident Analysis and Prevention*, Volume 11 (1979), p. 299.]

than those with a bachelor's degree, and Ph.D.s earned less than holders of a master's. So much for the rewards of learning. But wait. Further detective work revealed that there was a *positive* association between starting salary and degree level among economists who went to work for private industry. There was also a positive association among economists working in government. And if only economists who took teaching jobs were considered, there was again a positive association between salary and degree level. So within every class of job, holders of higher degrees were better paid.

What happened? Simply another version of Simpson's Paradox. Teach-

CAUSATION – Changes in A cause changes in B.

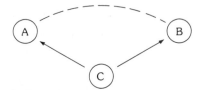

COMMON RESPONSE – Changes in both A and B
are caused by changes in a third variable, C.

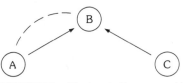

CONFOUNDING – Changes in B are caused both by
changes in A and by changes in third variable C.

Figure 6-6. Some causes of association. Variables A and B show a
strong association, indicated by the broken line. This association may
result from any of several types of causal relationships, indicated by solid
arrows.

ing salaries were much lower than those in government and industry. Few
holders of bachelor's degrees in economics chose teaching, but many holders of advanced degrees did. So average salaries for advanced degree
holders were lower, even though each employer paid them more than
B.A. employees. The negative association between salary and level of
degree did not mean that more education depressed salaries; it was due
to the effect of another variable (type of employer) on salaries. This third
variable was confounded with the degree held. The bottom diagram in
Figure 6-6 displays this relationship schematically.

So association may be due to (in the language of Figure 6-6) either *common
response* or *confounding* as well as *causation*. The tobacco industry has argued
that the association between smoking and lung cancer may be an instance of
common response. Perhaps there is a genetic factor that predisposes people
both to nicotine addiction and to lung cancer. Then smoking and lung cancer
would be positively associated even if smoking had no direct effect on health.

How can we detect causation? Here are some general words of wisdom: First, *causation is not a simple idea*. Rarely is A "the cause" of B. Smoking is at most a *contributory cause* of lung cancer. It is one of several circumstances that make lung cancer more likely. Exposure to asbestos and breathing polluted air may be other contributory causes. Second, as I stressed in Chapter 2, *properly de-signed experiments are the best means of settling questions of causation*. You should be able to imagine a randomized controlled experiment with human subjects that would determine beyond doubt whether cigarette smoking causes lung cancer. But such an experiment is morally and practically impossible. So the evidence for causation in this case, while very strong, must always fall short of the strongest statistical evidence, which comes from experimentation.

Third, in the absence of an experiment, *to conclude that association is due to causation requires evidence and judgment beyond what statistics can provide.* The case for the claim that variable A causes changes in variable B is strength-ened if

- the association between A and B recurs in different circumstances, thus reducing the chance that it is due to confounding;
- a plausible explanation is available showing how A could cause changes in B; and
- no equally plausible third factor exists that could cause changes in A and B together.

The case for the conclusion that smoking causes lung cancer meets these criteria. A strong association has been observed in studies of many groups of people in many places and over long periods of time. The risk of death from lung cancer is related to the number of cigarettes smoked and to the age at which smoking began. The number of men dying of lung cancer has risen in parallel to the prevalence of smoking, with a lag of about 30 years. Lung cancer now kills more men than any other form of cancer. As smoking by women has increased, lung cancer among women (once rare) has risen with the same 30-year lag. Lung cancer will soon pass breast cancer as the leading cause of cancer death among women. Thus unusually good evidence suggests that the asso-ciation between smoking and lung cancer is not due to confounding or other defects in producing the data.

Second, cigarette smoke contains tars that have been shown by experiment to cause tumors on the skin of mice and rabbits when applied in sufficient quantity. So it is plausible that these tars, applied in smaller quantities over many years, can cause tumors in human lungs. Finally, such suggested third factors as a "genetic predisposition" are only hypothetical. The genetic hypothesis in particular cannot explain the different patterns in the rise of lung cancer in the two sexes or the fact that giving up smoking reduces the risk of cancer. People who once smoked but who have stopped for 10 years have no higher risk of lung cancer than those who never smoked. The evidence that smoking is a cause of lung cancer is about as convincing as nonexperimental evidence can be. And so it is that we read

> Warning: The Surgeon General Has Determined That Cigarette Smoking Is Dangerous to Your Health.

4. Prediction

A strong relationship between two variables can be used to predict the value of one when the value of the other is known. From Figure 4-8 on page 155 you could predict the yield of corn when 26,000 plants per acre are planted under the same conditions as the experimental data. From Figure 6-5 on page 217 you could predict the percent reduction in injuries from 1970 if 75% of motorists in Victoria wore seat belts. In these two cases, the relationship is so close that it can be called "lawlike." Nonetheless, the relation between the variables is not exact, and so predictions based on the relationship will also not be exactly correct.

The usefulness for prediction of an observed relationship depends on the strength of the association. In the case of a straight-line association, r^2 measures how strong the association is. Look back at Figure 6-3 on page 214. Figure 6-3(a) shows perfect straight-line association ($r^2 = 1$); in this case, y is perfectly predictable from x. Figure 6-3(b) shows an association with $r^2 = 0.49$. When a value of x (say x_1 in the figure) is given in this case, y still varies quite a bit, so only approximate prediction is possible.

But the usefulness of an observed association in predicting y given the value of x does *not* depend on a cause-and-effect relation between x and y. An employer who uses an aptitude test to screen potential employees does not think that high test scores cause good job performance after the person is hired. Rather, the test attempts to measure abilities that will usually result in good performance. It is a matter of common response. If there is a relationship between the test results and later performance on the job, then, in the language of Chapter 4, the test has predictive validity.

To predict one variable from another based on a scatterplot that displays the observed relationship, we must draw a curve through the points of the scatterplot. The simplest curve is a straight line, and this is the case we shall consider. Of course, it would be foolish to draw a straight line through the corn yield versus planting rate scatterplot. The data must show a roughly linear trend, as, for example, the injury reduction versus seat belt usage data do. Let us see how to do prediction from straight-line data.

> **Example 6.** Exercise 10 on page 168 presents a set of data on natural gas consumption (y) versus heating degree-days (x). The scatterplot of these data in Figure 6-7 shows a close straight-line relationship. In fact, r^2 = 0.98, so the points are tightly clustered about a line. To fit a line, just stretch a black thread through the points. Since we wish to predict y from x, fiddle the line about until the distances from the line to the points in the *vertical* (y) direction seem smallest. The resulting line is drawn in Figure 6-7. Now for prediction. How much gas can the homeowner expect to use in a month that averages 24 degree-days per day? Find the point on the fitted line directly above x = 24 degree-days. Then move horizontally over to the y axis and find that the corresponding y value is about 6 cubic feet of gas per day. That is our prediction.

The line used for predicting y from x is often called the *regression line of y on x*. This is not a very descriptive term, but you will meet it often. There are many recipes that you (or a computer working for you) can use to compute a regression line. Such recipes are more objective than stretching a thread. But

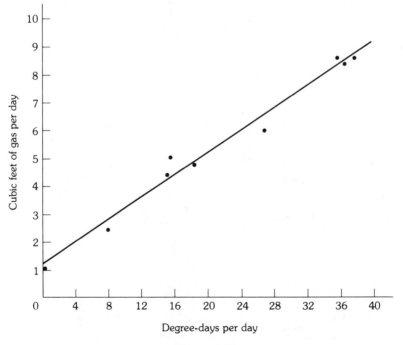

Figure 6-7.

when r^2 is large, any method will give about the same line. And when r^2 is small, the methods can differ so much that choosing a specific recipe is as subjective as using the thread.

You will discover that how large an r^2—and hence how precise a prediction—you can expect depends on the variables you are interested in. In many fields outside the physical sciences, high correlations are rare. American law schools, for example, use the Law School Admission Test (LSAT) to help predict performance and aid in admissions decisions.[3] Yet the correlation between LSAT scores and the first-year grades in law school of admitted applicants is only about $r = 0.36$. This is discouraging, for such a correlation means that only 13% of the variance in law school grades is accounted for. But LSAT scores are a better predictor than are the applicants' undergraduate grades, which have a correlation of only about $r = 0.25$ with later grades in law school.

When no single explanatory variable has a high correlation with a dependent variable, several explanatory variables together can be used for prediction. This is called *multiple regression*. We can no longer fit a relationship among the variables by stretching a thread. A recipe that a computer can follow is essential. Fortunately, the computer will produce a *multiple correlation coefficient* (also called r) between the dependent variable and all the explanatory variables at

"How did I get into this business? Well, I couldn't understand multiple regression and correlation in college, so I settled for this instead."

once. The square r^2 of the multiple correlation coefficient has the same inter-pretation as in the one-explanatory-variable case. For example, when both LSAT scores and undergraduate grades are used to predict law school grades, the multiple correlation coefficient is about $r = 0.45$. So straight-line dependence on both explanatory variables together accounts for $(0.45)^2$, or about 20%, of the variability in first-year law school grades.

I hope that our tour of association, causation, and prediction has left you with that slightly winded feeling that follows a good workout. Overconfidence in interpreting association is the root of many a statistical sin. Most users of statistics have learned that "correlation does not imply causation." Some go to the other extreme and label all correlations not due to causation as "nonsense correlations." That label is inspired by examples such as the alleged strong positive correlation between teachers' salaries and liquor sales, both of which have steadily increased over time as a result of general prosperity. But this correlation is perfectly real and not at all nonsensical; what is nonsense is the interpretation that teachers are spending their salaries on booze. With sufficient skill and enough information, most associations can be usefully interpreted, even though (as in Example 5) the obvious interpretation may be seriously misleading.

It has been, you may feel, a long, dry journey through the desert of descriptive statistics from $\bar{x}$ to r^2. True enough; but we have managed to mine some valuable resources on the way. In the Introduction, I mentioned a study of political science journals as an example of the invasion of new fields by statistics. That study also lists the numerical measures most often used in a sample of 576 articles in political science journals.[4] They are, in order of use,

1. Relative frequency
2. Frequency
3. Mean
4. Correlation coefficient r
5. Index numbers
6. r^2
7. Standard deviation and variance

We have encountered six of these top seven statistics already, and the other (index numbers) will be treated in Chapter 7. You now can deal with much of the statistics you will meet in discussions of public policy and in many academic areas. That knowledge is worth the effort you put into gaining it.

NOTES

1. From *The Health Consequences of Smoking: 1983,* U.S. Public Health Service.
2. A good review is given by the Commissioner of Labor Statistics herself in Janet L. Norwood, *The Male-Female Earnings Gap: A Review of Employment and Earnings Issues* (Bureau of Labor Statistics Report 673, 1982).

3. The information on the LSAT, along with much useful information about the alleged cultural bias of such tests, is found in David Kaye, "Searching for the Truth About Testing," *The Yale Law Journal,* Volume 90 (1980), pp. 431-457.
4. James L. Hutter, "Statistics and Political Science," *Journal of the American Statistical Association,* Volume 67 (1972), p. 741.

Exercises

Section 1

1. Do seat belts and other restraints prevent injuries in automobile accidents? Figure 6-5 gives one piece of evidence. Another comes from a study of reported crashes of 1967 and later-model cars in North Carolina in 1973–1974. There were 26,971 passengers under the age of 15 in these cars. Here are data on their conditions. [Adapted from data of Williams and Zador in *Accident Analysis and Prevention,* Volume 9 (1977), pp. 69–76.]

	Restrained	Unrestrained
Injured	197	3844
Uninjured	1749	21,181

   (a) What percent of these 26,971 young passengers were wearing seat belts or were otherwise restrained?
   (b) Compute appropriate percents to show the association between wearing restraints and escaping uninjured.

2. The study in Exercise 1 also looked at where the passengers were seated. Here is a three-way table of passengers by seat location, restraint, and condition.

	Front seat		Back seat	
	Restrained	Not	Restrained	Not
Injured	121	2125	76	1719
Uninjured	981	9679	768	11,502

   Unlike Example 1, the third variable here does *not* greatly change the observed association between the first two. Compute appropriate percents to demonstrate this.

3. (a) Compute the cross-product ratio for the 2×2 table in Exercise 1. (Use a calculator!)
   (b) Now compute the cross-product ratios for each of the two 2×2 tables in Exercise 2. The values are both close to that in (a), indicating that the association is about the same for front- and rear-seat passengers.

(c) Is the association between injury and restraint stronger for front-seat passengers or for rear-seat passengers?

4. Here is a three-way table classifying all persons employed in the United States in 1981 by sex, race, and age:

Employed persons (1981, thousands)

	Male		Female	
	White	Other	White	Other
16–19	3469	346	3119	291
20–34	21,050	2721	15,979	2554
35–64	25,134	2866	17,284	2641
65 and over	1662	149	1013	120

SOURCE: *Statistical Abstract of the United States, 1982–1983*, Table 629.

(a) How many white females ages 16 to 19 were employed in 1981?

(b) What proportion of all employed persons ages 20 to 34 were females?

(c) From this three-way table, construct a two-way table of employed persons by sex (horizontal) and race (vertical).

(d) "White" and "other" races differ in male versus female employment. Describe the difference in words, and compute appropriate percents to describe this association between race and sex among employed persons.

5. Cross-product ratios can help ferret out rather complex associations between several variables. Here is an example:

(a) Compute the cross-product ratio for the 2×2 table you obtained in Exercise 4(c).

(b) Each row of the three-way table of Exercise 4 is in effect a 2×2 table of employed persons by sex and race within a certain age group. Write these four tables in the format of Exercise 4(c), and compute the cross-product ratio for each one.

(c) The cross-product ratios show that the 16–19 age group differs from all others in the pattern of sex–race association, since its cross-product ratio is less than 1 while the others are all greater than 1 and similar in size. Compute for the 16–19 age group the same percents you computed for all employed persons in Exercise 4(d). Discuss how this age group differs from the others in sex versus race employment patterns.

6. The National Science Foundation publication *Science Indicators 1980* contains the results of a survey showing that women scientists and engineers earned, on the average, only 77% as much as male scientists and engineers. But when we look at the results for separate fields of science and engineering, we find that women earned at least 92% as much as men in every field. Explain how this apparent paradox can happen.

7. A study of the effect of parents' smoking habits on the smoking habits of students in eight Arizona high schools produced the following counts. [From S. V. Zagona (ed.), *Studies and Issues in Smoking Behavior* (Tucson: University of Arizona Press, 1967), pp. 157–180.]

	Student smokes	Student does not smoke
Both parents smoke	400	1380
One parent smokes	416	1823
Neither parent smokes	188	1168

Describe in words the association between the smoking habits of parents and children, and compute appropriate descriptive statistics to back up your statements.

8. Return to Example 1 on page 205, and rewrite the 2×2 table there with the order of the columns reversed.

	Female	Male
Admit	20	35
Deny	40	45

Verify that the cross-product ratio is the reciprocal of that for the original table. Then reverse the order of the rows and find the cross-product ratio with both orders of the columns. In all cases, the degree of association and the direction (males are admitted more often than females) are the same.

Section 2

1. For each of the following sets of data,
- draw a scatterplot.
- compute the mean, the variance, and the standard deviation of each variable x and y separately.
- compute the correlation coefficient r, and also r^2.

(a) x	4	4	-4	-4
y	-4	4	4	-4

(b) x	4	3	0	-3	-4
y	-4	-2	0	2	4

(c) x	4	2	-2	-4
y	4	-2	2	-4

For your own instruction, compare the values of r^2 and the closeness of the points in the scatterplots to a line.

2. Make a scatterplot of the following data:

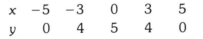

$$
\begin{array}{cccccc}
x & -5 & -3 & 0 & 3 & 5 \\
y & 0 & 4 & 5 & 4 & 0
\end{array}
$$

   Show that the correlation coefficient is zero. (You can do this by showing that the *numerator* of r is zero. You need not compute any standard deviations.) The scatterplot shows a tight connection between x and y. Explain how it can happen that $r = 0$ in this case.

3. Figure 6-8 shows four scatterplots. Which (if any) of these have the same r? Which (if any) have the same r^2?

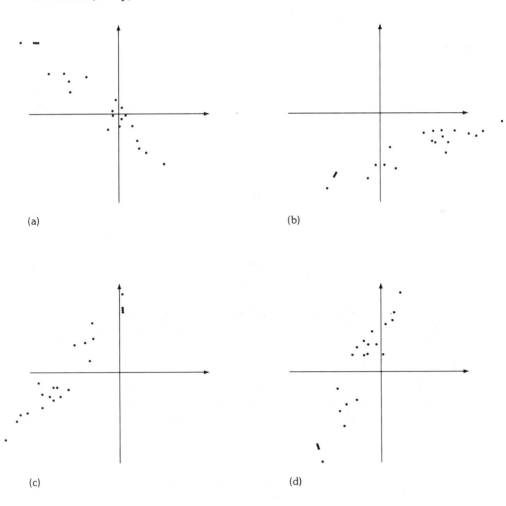

(a)

(b)

(c)

(d)

Figure 6-8. Recognizing r and r^2.

4. Make a scatterplot of the following data:

x	1	2	3	4	10	10
y	1	3	3	5	1	11

Show that the correlation is about 0.5. What feature of the data is responsible for reducing the correlation to this value despite a strong straight-line association between x and y in most of the observations?

5. Figure 6-9 contains five scatterplots. Match each to the r below that best describes it. (Some rs will be left over.)

$$r = -0.9 \qquad r = 0 \qquad r = 0.9$$
$$r = -0.7 \qquad r = 0.3$$
$$r = -0.3 \qquad r = 0.7$$

6. Your data consist of bivariate observations on the age of the subject (measured in years) and the reaction time of the subject (measured in seconds). In what units are each of the following descriptive statistics measured?

(a) The mean age of the subjects.
(b) The variance of the subjects' reaction times.
(c) The standard deviation of the subjects' reaction times.
(d) The correlation coefficient between age and reaction time.
(e) The median age of the subjects.

7. A psychologist speaking to a meeting of the American Association of University Professors recently said, "The evidence suggests that there is nearly correlation zero between teaching ability of a faculty member and his or her research productivity." The student newspaper reported this as: "Professor McDaniel said that good teachers tend to be poor researchers and good researchers tend to be poor teachers."

Explain what (if anything) is wrong with the newspaper's report. If the report is not accurate, write your own plain-language account of what the speaker meant.

8. Measurements in large samples show that the correlation

(a) between father's height and son's adult height is about _____ .
(b) between husband's height and wife's height is about _____ .
(c) between a male's height at age 4 and his height at age 18 is about _____ .

The answers (in scrambled order) are

$$r = 0.25, \ r = 0.5, \ r = 0.8.$$

Match the answers to the statements and explain your choice.

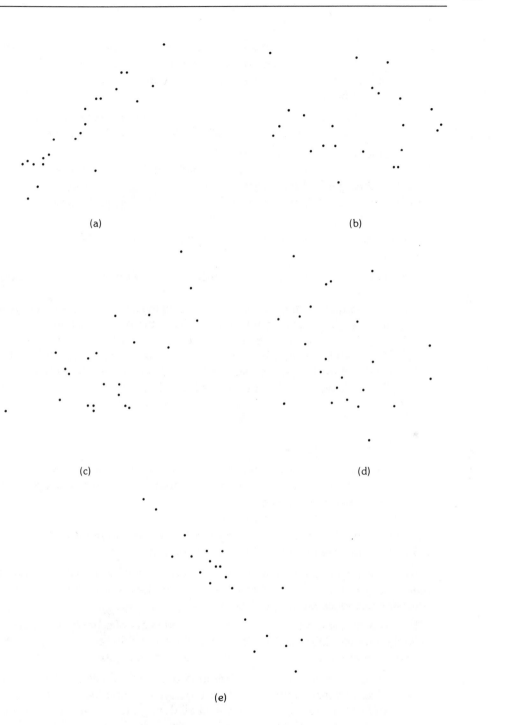

Figure 6-9. Match the correlation.

9. If women always married men who were 2 years older than themselves, what would be the correlation between the ages of husband and wife? (*Hint:* Draw a scatterplot for the ages of husband and wife when the wife is 20, 30, 40, and 50 years old.)

10. For each of the following pairs of variables, would you expect a substantial negative correlation, a substantial positive correlation, or a small correlation?

   (a) The age of a second-hand car and its price.
   (b) The weight of a new car and its overall miles-per-gallon rating.
   (c) The height and the weight of a person.
   (d) The height of a person and the height of his or her father.
   (e) The height and the IQ of a person.

11. Each of the following statements contains a blunder. Explain in each case what is wrong.

   (a) There is a high correlation between the sex and income of American workers.
   (b) Since student ratings of professors' teaching and colleagues' ratings of their research have correlation $r = 1.21$, the better teachers also tend to be the better researchers.
   (c) The correlation between pounds of nitrogen fertilizer applied to the field and the bushels per acre of corn harvested was $r = 0.63$ bushels. So applying more fertilizer increases yields.

Section 3

Each of Exercises 1–6 reports an observed association. In each case, discuss possible explanations for the association. Note that more than one explanation may contribute to a single association.

1. A study of grade-school children ages 6 to 11 years found a high positive correlation between reading ability and shoe size.

2. There is a negative correlation between the number of flu cases reported each week through the year and the amount of ice cream sold that week. Perhaps eating ice cream prevents flu.

3. There is a strong positive correlation between years of schooling completed and lifetime earnings for American men. One possible reason for this association is that more education leads to higher-paying jobs.

4. A public health survey of 7000 California males found little correlation between alcohol consumption and chance of dying during the $5\frac{1}{2}$ years of the study. In fact, men who did not drink at all during these years had a slightly higher death rate than did light drinkers. This lack of correlation was somewhat surprising.

5. Another public health study using statistics from 41 states found a positive correlation between per capita beer consumption and death rates from cancer of the large intestine and rectum. The states with the highest rectal cancer death rates were Rhode Island and New York. The beer consumption in those states was 80 quarts per capita. South Carolina, Alabama, and Arkansas drank only 26 quarts of beer per capita and had rectal cancer death rates less than one-third of those in Rhode Island and New York. (This study was reported in a Gannett News Service dispatch appearing in the *Lafayette Journal and Courier* of November 20, 1974.)

List some variables possibly influencing state cancer death rates that appear to be confounded with beer consumption. For a clue, look at the high- and low-consumption states given above.

6. A study of London double-decker bus drivers and conductors found that drivers had twice the death rate from heart disease as conductors. Because drivers sit while conductors climb up and down stairs all day, it was first thought that this association reflected the effect of type of job on heart disease. Then a look at bus company records showed that drivers were issued consistently larger-size uniforms when hired than were conductors. This fact suggested an alternative explanation of the observed association between job type and deaths. What is it?

7. Draw a diagram like one of those in Figure 6-6 on page 218 for each of the following examples. Variables A and B are given in each case. Be sure to identify the variable or variables that play the role of C in Figure 6-6.

(a) Smoking (A) is strongly associated with risk of death from lung cancer (B).

(b) Saccharin in a diet (A) may cause bladder cancer (B) in rats by a biochemical mechanism that would also operate in humans. (See pp. 77–78.)

(c) There is a substantial positive correlation between a father's height (A) and the height of his adult son (B).

Section 4

1. Use the regression line in Figure 6-5 on page 217 to predict the percent reduction from the 1970 injury level that would occur if 75% of motorists wore seat belts.

2. Exercise 11 on page 169 presents data on estimated versus true calorie content for 10 foods. You wish to predict what calorie count people will guess for a food that has 150 calories.

(a) Make a scatterplot of the data. (Which is the independent variable?)

(b) You decide to ignore the two outliers for which the people sampled guessed much too high. The other foods form a straight-line pattern.

Use a thread to fit a line to this pattern, and draw the line on your scatterplot.

(c) Use your line to predict the calories guessed for a food that has 150 calories.

(d) A computer regression routine using all 10 points predicts about 253 calories for the guess. Your value should be lower. Why?

3. Here are several years' freight tonnage and net income (or loss) for Conrail, the government-owned railroad formed from six bankrupt rail lines in 1976:

	Freight (million tons)	Income ($ million)
1977	266.7	−412
1978	262.7	−430
1979	268.8	−221
1980	238.4	−244
1981	219.4	39.2
1982	177.4	174.2

(a) Draw a scatterplot. There is a strong straight-line association between income and freight tonnage. In fact, $r = -0.91$.

(b) What percent of the variability in Conrail's income during this period can be accounted for by the association of income with freight tonnage?

(c) We wish to predict Conrail's 1983 income, having been told that 160 million tons of freight were hauled that year. Use a thread to fit a line to the data, draw the line on your scatterplot, and give a prediction.

(d) This prediction is quite risky. Why?

4. We might expect per capita income and median rent in the states to be positively correlated. In fact, these variables as presented in Table 4-4 on page 158 have $r = 0.82$. (I omitted the District of Columbia, since it is a city and not comparable to the 50 states.) We wish to predict rent from income.

(a) Make a scatterplot of Table 4-4. Is the District of Columbia an outlier?

(b) Use a thread to fit a regression line and draw it on your scatterplot.

(c) Use your line to predict the median rent in a state with per capita income $10,000. (These points have a smaller r^2 than those in Figure 6-7. The lines and predictions made by different people therefore will vary more in this case.)

5. Regression programs for computers usually give you the regression line as an equation that you can then use for prediction. The most common method for computing regression lines (called the "least squares" method) produces the line

$$y = 1.2 + 0.2x$$

for the gas-consumption example of Figure 6-7. To use this result for pre-diction, substitute x = degree-days per day. The result y is the predicted gas usage in cubic feet per day.

Use this equation to predict gas usage when x = 24 degree-days and when x = 40 degree-days.

6. Suppose that Figure 6-10 represents data on the number of slices of pizza consumed by pledges at a fraternity party (the independent variable x) and the number of laps around the block the pledges could run immediately afterward (the dependent variable y). The line on the scatterplot is the regression line computed from these points and used to predict y from x.

   (a) At the next party, a pledge eats 6 slices of pizza before running. How many laps do you predict he will complete?

   (b) Another pledge eats 9 pieces of pizza. Predict how many laps he will complete.

   (c) A third pledge shows off by eating 25 pieces of pizza. You should refuse to predict his performance from the scatterplot and regression line. Explain why.

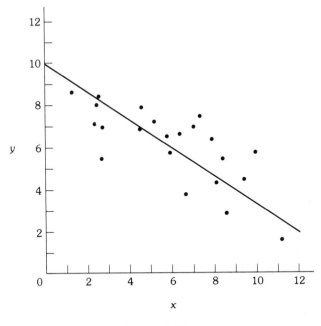

Figure 6-10.

7. "When r = 0.7, this means that y can be predicted from x for 70% of the individuals in the sample." Is this statement true or false? Would it be true if r^2 = 0.7? Explain your answers.

Chapter 7

The Consumer Price Index and its neighbors

C oncern over the state of the economy rises as economic health declines, but such concern is never far from the front pages of the newspapers. Much of the news that arouses comment and expressions of official concern is veiled in the language of statistics: "The Consumer Price Index rose 0.6% in August. . . ." "Senator Bean called for increased stimulation of the economy, pointing out that the Composite Index of Leading Indicators had leveled off following six months of growth. . . ." "In his speech, the President expressed satisfaction that the Producer Price Index had increased at only a 4% annual rate during the past quarter. . . ." The data that alarm or soothe the politicians are collected by sample surveys. We are therefore well equipped to understand their basic trustworthiness as well as the occasional comment that last month's rise of 0.1% in the unemployment rate should not be taken seriously since such a change is within the margin of sampling error. In some cases, such as the measurement of unemployment, we have looked at these government economic statistics in more detail. But what is meant by the Consumer Price *Index*, the *index* of leading indicators, the Producer Price *Index*? These are *index numbers*, the only one of the top seven statistics (p. 223) that we have not yet met. This chapter introduces index numbers and their uses (Section 1), looks in more

"Yes sir, I know that we have to know where the economy is going. But do we have to publish the statistics so that everyone else does too?"

detail at the most famous index, the Consumer Price Index (Section 2), then gives a brief overview of the government's economic indicators and the proposal that official social indicators also be compiled (Section 3).

1. Index numbers

An index number measures the value of a variable relative to its value at a base period. Thus the essential idea of an index number is to give a picture of changes in a variable much like that drawn by saying "The price of hospital rooms rose 11% in 1983." Such a statement measures change without giving the actual numerical values of the variable. The recipe for an index number is

$$\text{index number} = \frac{\text{value}}{\text{base value}} \times 100.$$

Here is an example:

> **Example 1.** A pound of apples that cost 28 cents in 1973 cost 70 cents in 1982. The apple price index in 1982 with 1973 as base is
>
> $$\frac{70}{28} \times 100 = 250.$$
>
> The apple price index for the base period, 1973, is
>
> $$\frac{28}{28} \times 100 = 100.$$

Example 1 illustrates some important points. The choice of base is a crucial part of any index number and must always be stated. The index number for the base period is always 100, so it is usual to identify the base period as 1973 by writing "1973 = 100." You will notice in press articles concerning the Consumer Price Index the notation "1967 = 100." This mysterious equation simply means that 1967 is the base period for the index.

> **Example 2.** A Toyota Corolla that cost $2800 in 1973 cost $7000 in 1982. The corresponding index number (1973 = 100) for 1982 is
>
> $$\frac{7000}{2800} \times 100 = 250.$$

Comparing Examples 1 and 2 makes it clear that an index number measures only change relative to the base value. The apple price index and the Toyota price index for 1982 are both 250. That apples rose from 28 cents to 70 cents and the Toyota from $2800 to $7000 is irrelevant. Both rose to 250% of the base value, so both index numbers are 250.

Index numbers can be interpreted in plain terms as giving the value of a variable as a percent of the base value. An index of 140 means 140% of the base value, or a 40% increase from the base value. An index of 80 means that the current value is 80% of the base, a 20% decrease. Be sure to notice that index numbers can be read as percents only relative to the base value. Do not confuse an increase of so many *points* with an increase of so many *percent* in news accounts of an index.

> **Example 3.** The Consumer Price Index increased from 276.5 in August 1981 to 292.8 in August 1982. This is an increase of 16.3 points, because
>
> $$292.8 - 276.5 = 16.3.$$

But to find the *percent* increase in that one-year period, we express the 16.3-point increase as a percent of the value at the beginning of the period, which was 276.5. Since

$$\frac{16.3}{276.5} = 0.059,$$

the Consumer Price Index rose by 5.9% during that year.

Thus far it may seem that the fancy terminology of index numbers is little more than a plot to disguise simple statements in complicated language. Why say "The Consumer Price Index (1967 = 100) stood at 292.8 by August 1982" instead of "Consumer prices rose 192.8% between 1967 and August 1982?" In fact, the term *index number* usually means more than a measure of change relative to a base; it also tells us the kind of quantity whose change we measure. That quantity is a weighted average of several variables, with fixed weights. This idea is best illustrated by an example of a simple price index.

Example 4. A homesteader striving for self-sufficiency purchases only salt, kerosene, and the services of a professional welder. In 1975 the quantities purchased and total costs were as follows (the cost of an item is the price per unit multiplied by the number of units purchased):

Good or service	1975 quantity	1975 price	1975 cost
Salt	100 pounds	0.07/pound	$ 7.00
Kerosene	50 gallons	0.50/gallons	25.00
Welding	10 hours	10.00/hour	100.00
			$132.00

The total cost of this collection of goods and services in 1975 was $132. To find the "homesteader price index" for 1983, we compute the 1983 cost of this same collection of goods and services. Suppose that in 1983 we have the following:

Good or service	1975 quantity	1983 price	1983 cost
Salt	100 pounds	0.05/pound	$ 5.00
Kerosene	50 gallons	1.30/gallon	65.00
Welding	10 hours	14.00/hour	140.00
			$210.00

The same goods and services that cost \$132 in 1975 cost \$210 in 1983. So the homesteader price index (1975 = 100) for 1983 is

$$\frac{210}{132} \times 100 = 159.1.$$

When prices of a collection of goods and services are being measured (as in Example 4 and also in the Consumer Price Index and the government's Producer Price Index for wholesale prices), the kind of index number illustrated in Example 4 is called a *fixed market basket price index*. The variable for which an index is found is the total cost of a "fixed market basket" of goods and services. The makeup of the market basket is determined in the base year; in Example 4, the basket contained 100 pounds of salt, 50 gallons of kerosene, and 10 hours of welder's services. By 1983 the homesteader may have changed his purchases, but no matter. The price index measures the relative change in the cost of the *same* market basket from 1975 to 1983.

The basic idea of a fixed market basket price index is that the weight given to each component (salt, kerosene, welding) remains fixed over time. This basic idea can be extended (we won't go into the details) to produce the general idea of an "aggregative weighted index number with fixed weights." The index numbers published by the federal government and featured in our economic news are almost all of this type. Thus the term *index number* carries two ideas.

- It is a measure of the change of a variable relative to a base value.
- The variable is an average of many quantities, with the weight given to each quantity remaining fixed over time.

2.   The Consumer Price Index

The Consumer Price Index (forever after abbreviated CPI), published monthly by the Bureau of Labor Statistics, is a fixed market basket index measuring changes in the prices of consumer goods and services. The CPI is the most important of all index numbers. Not only does the CPI make headlines as the most popular measure of inflation (the declining buying power of the dollar), but it directly affects the income of almost half of all Americans. This is so because many sources of income are "indexed"; that is, they are tied to the CPI and automatically increase when the CPI increases. (The last year in which the CPI decreased was 1955, so we can ignore that pleasant but unlikely possibility.) Since the United Auto Workers first won a "cost of living escalator clause" in 1948, indexing has become a standard feature of union contracts. Over 8.5 million workers now have such contracts. Social Security payments are indexed, and so are federal civil service and military pension payments. Even food stamp allowances are indexed. When dependents are included, the CPI influences the income of half the population. This state of affairs may well be economically foolish, for *every* rise in the CPI generates more inflation by driving up labor and pension costs. But it certainly focuses attention on the Consumer Price Index.[1]

What does the CPI measure? It is a fixed market basket index covering the cost of a collection of over 400 goods and services. The CPI is computed just as in Example 4, though the arithmetic is a bit longer with 400 items. Prior to 1978, there was a single CPI, officially called the Consumer Price Index for Urban Wage Earners and Clerical Workers. The 400 items in the market basket, and their weights in the index, were chosen to represent the spending habits of families of city wage earners and clerical workers. The market basket did *not* represent the spending habits of rural families, or of professional and self-employed workers, or of the unemployed, or of people not in the labor force. So if you were a farmer, a teacher, a medical doctor, or unemployed, the CPI did not describe the change in prices of the goods and services typically consumed by people like you. Only about 45% of the population was covered by the pre-1978 CPI.

Because of the great importance of the CPI, the Bureau of Labor Statistics (BLS) decided to update and enlarge the market basket, choosing items and weights to represent the average purchases of all nonfarm households living in metropolitan areas. About 80% of the population live in such households. ("Metropolitan areas" as officially defined include most suburban regions and a good many rural regions in addition to cities.) The teacher, medical doctor, and unemployed are now included, but not the farmer. Labor leaders were unhappy with this idea because the old CPI described changes in the price of a market basket typical of union households and was embedded in many labor contracts. As a result of their protests, the BLS decided to publish *two* CPIs beginning in 1978. One directly continues the old CPI for urban wage earners and clerical workers, while the other is the new "Consumer Price Index for All Urban Consumers." The new index is the one usually reported and the one on which we shall concentrate. But the old, narrower index is still used to index union wages and Social Security payments.

How is the market basket arrived at? By an exercise in probability sampling. The Bureau of the Census, under a contract with the BLS, conducts a Consumer Expenditure Survey (CES) in which about 4800 households keep diaries of all expenses for a week during the year and another 4800 households are interviewed about major purchases each quarter. The Consumer Expenditure Survey is a multistage probability sample like those you met in Section 6 of Chapter 1. It provides detailed information on how Americans spend their money. Because the CPI is a fixed market basket index, the market basket changes only infrequently. (The next revision is planned for 1987.) The present market basket is based on consumer expenditures in 1972–1973.

These expenditures were classified into groups, such as "Fruits and Vegetables," "Women's and Girls' Apparel," and "Fuel and Utilities." Then a stratified probability sample was taken to choose individual items to represent each group. These items make up the market basket. The weight given to each item in computing the index depends on the share of spending its group received in the Consumer Expenditure Survey.

How are the data for the monthly CPI collected? By another exercise in probability sampling. The CES also asks *where* the sample households bought each item, so a sample of retail outlets can be chosen that gives proper weight to drug stores, department stores, discount stores, and so forth. Prices are collected each month in 85 metropolitan areas. These 85 areas are a probability sample of all the nation's metropolitan areas—a stratified sample consisting of 28 large metropolitan areas specified in advance and a probability sample of 57 others. (Recall from Chapter 1 that stratified samples automatically including all the largest units are common in economic sampling.) Then prices are obtained from a probability sample of over 18,000 retail outlets each month, distributed over the 85 metropolitan areas. It's a big job.

The result of all this sampling is the monthly CPI, both the two national CPIs and separate CPIs for the largest metropolitan areas. Probability sampling produces results with little bias and quite high precision. Because the published CPI is rounded off to one decimal point (such as 305.3), a change of 0.1 may be due to rounding off. But a change of 0.2 in the CPI almost certainly reflects a real change in the price of the market basket.

Does the CPI have shortcomings? Indeed it does.[2] The CPI is computed with great statistical expertise, but we have seen again and again that statistics is not a cure-all. The CPI is a fixed market basket price index, and all such indices have some problems with validity of measurement (recall Chapter 3). It is not really possible to keep the market basket fixed year after year. After all, a 1985 car is not the same as a 1975 car, so the "new car" item in the market basket changes each year. The BLS then must decide the issue of *changes in quality*. How much of the yearly rise in passenger car prices is due to the better quality of the product, and how much is a genuine price hike? In 1982, for example, manufacturer's wholesale prices for passenger cars rose an average of $463.61. The Bureau decided that $104.70 of this increase paid for higher quality, primarily improved fuel economy. So only the remaining $358.91 counted as a price increase in computing the Producer Price Index and the CPI. (There were *no* increases in auto prices in the CPI between 1959 and 1970.)

A related difficulty with a fixed market basket is *changing buying habits*. "Men's business shirts" in 1960 were white and 100% cotton. But men soon shifted to permanent-press shirts made of blends of synthetic fibers, and color became acceptable in business shirts. The BLS is slow to change the market basket as items become outdated, because this is contrary to the fixed market basket idea. Shirts of synthetic fibers entered the market basket in 1966, but colored business shirts were kept out until 1971.

Adjustment for quality and replacement of outdated items are carefully made and generally can be ignored in interpreting the CPI. More important is the question of the *costs of owning a home.* The CPI long treated housing as just another consumer expense, and mortgage costs, property taxes, and other expenses of purchasing and financing a home made up about 26% of the entire CPI. But people buy homes as an investment as well as to live in. During inflationary times the prospect of a fat profit on resale makes buyers willing to pay higher prices and interest rates in order to own a home. A better measure of the cost of shelter stripped of its investment aspects is the cost of renting houses or condominiums that are similar to those that are owned. Beginning in 1983, the BLS switched to this "rental equivalence" method. Homeowners' costs dropped from 26% to 14% of the CPI. Until this was done, the CPI consistently overstated the rise in prices during the inflation that began in the late 1960s.

Finally, a fixed market basket index *does not measure changes in the cost of living.* Our buying habits are directly affected by changing prices. We can keep our cost of living down by switching to substitutes when one item rises in price. If beef prices skyrocket, we eat less beef and more chicken. Or even more beans. The CPI measures price changes, not changes in the cost of living. It probably slightly overstates rises in the cost of living by ignoring our ability to change our buying habits. As evidence of this, we might note that from September 1972 to September 1973, the CPI food component increased 21.5%, but total sales at grocery stores rose only 12.5%. Consumers were changing their choice of food items, especially switching away from expensive prepared foods. Thus the cost of the food they actually bought rose more slowly than the price of the CPI's fixed market basket of food.

How is the CPI used to adjust for the effects of inflation? A dollar in 1985 is not the same as a dollar in 1960, for the decrepit 1985 dollar could buy much less than the more robust 1960 dollar. Especially in times of rapid inflation, we can understand changes in our financial picture over time only by using "constant dollars" rather than "current dollars." Constant dollars are dollars of constant buying power, usually equal to the buying power of actual dollars in the base period of the CPI. The recipe for converting a current dollar amount into constant 1967 dollars is

$$\textbf{constant dollars} = \frac{\textbf{current dollars}}{\textbf{current CPI}} \times \textbf{100.}$$

Here is an example:

> **Example 5.** A worker earned $10,000 in 1967 and $24,000 in 1982. The average CPI (1967 = 100) for 1982 was 288.6. So an income of $24,000 in 1982 dollars was worth only
>
> $$\frac{\$24,000}{288.6} \times 100 = \$8316$$
>
> in 1967 dollars. The worker's real income, measured in terms of buying power, has dropped since 1967, because raises did not keep pace with inflation. A worker must earn $28,860 in 1982 to have the same buying power that $10,000 had in 1967.

The value in constant 1967 dollars of amounts in dollars of earlier years can be found from the CPI (1967 = 100) for those years. Table 7-1 gives the CPI values needed.

Table 7-1. Annual average CPI (1967 = 100)

Year	CPI	Year	CPI	Year	CPI
1800	51	1940	42.0	1970	116.3
1825	34	1945	53.9	1971	121.3
1850	25	1950	72.1	1972	125.3
1860	27	1955	80.2	1973	133.1
1870	38	1960	88.7	1974	147.7
1880	29	1961	89.6	1975	161.2
1890	27	1962	90.6	1976	170.5
1900	25	1963	91.7	1977	181.5
1910	28	1964	92.9	1978	195.3
1915	30.4	1965	94.5	1979	217.6
1920	60.0	1966	97.2	1980	247.0
1925	52.5	1967	100.0	1981	272.3
1930	50.6	1968	104.2	1982	288.6
1935	41.1	1969	109.8	1983	297.4

SOURCES: *Handbook of Labor Statistics 1975*, and current issues of the *Monthly Labor Review*. Pre-1917 values are estimates made by the BLS. Post-1917 values come from previous versions of the CPI updated to 1967 = 100.

Example 6. In 1920, the median earnings of full-time manufacturing workers were $1532 per year. What is the value of that income in 1967 dollars? The CPI (1967 = 100) for 1920 was 60.0. So the 1967 buying power of $1532 in 1920 is

$$\frac{\$1532}{60.0} \times 100 = \$2553.$$

What is the value of that $1532 in 1920 in terms of, say, 1982 dollars instead of 1967 dollars? The answer requires another formula, one that actually includes the "constant dollars" recipe as a special case.

To convert an amount in current dollars at time A to the amount with the same buying power at time B,

$$\textbf{Dollars at time B = Dollars at time A} \times \frac{\textbf{CPI at time B}}{\textbf{CPI at time A}}.$$

Example 7. The average manufacturing worker's 1920 income of $1532 is equal in buying power to a 1982 income of

$$\$1532 \times \frac{288.6}{60.0} = \$7369.$$

because the CPI (1967 = 100) was 60.0 in 1920 and 288.6 in 1982. The average manufacturing worker of 1920 didn't earn very much. Remember that when you next feel a yearning for the "good old days."

An advantage of the last recipe is that it is not affected by base changes for the CPI. So long as the same base is used for time A and time B, the recipe always gives the same answer. Because the CPI (1967 = 100) passed 300 in 1983 and would have passed 350 if the previous base (1957–1959 = 100) had continued in use, politicians prefer to have the base changed now and then to keep the index below the clouds. The base for the CPI was changed in 1935, 1953, 1961, and 1972. Another change should be along shortly.

Don't go away unhappy at the steep climb of the CPI in recent years. The German wholesale price index (1914 = 100) reached 234 when World War I ended in November 1918, hit 3490 by December 1921, and finally 126,160,000,000,000 in December 1923. Now *that's* inflation.

"Now this here's a genuine 1950 dollar. They don't make 'em like that anymore."

3. Economic and social indicators

The monthly Consumer Price Index, the monthly unemployment rate, and most other newsmaking government statistics are produced at regular time intervals. Indeed, frequently the *change* in prices or unemployment from month to month is the center of attention rather than the actual value of the CPI or the unemployment rate.

> **A sequence of measurements of the same variable made at different times is called a *time series*. Usually (but not always) the variable is measured at regular intervals of time, such as monthly.**

The variable measured in a time series may be any of the many kinds we have studied—counts (such as the number of persons employed), rates (such as the unemployment rate), index numbers (such as the CPI), and other kinds of variables as well. The key idea of a time series is that each observation records both the value of the variable and the time when the observation was made.

An especially important set of time series are the *national economic indicators*. These time series, compiled by agencies of the federal government, are designed to indicate the state of the economy. They are chosen for their importance according to economic theory, their validity as measures of significant economic facts, and their consistent behavior over time when compared with the behavior of the economy. We have already met important economic indicators in discussing the CPI and the unemployment rate.* Until quite recently, the national economic indicators were of interest primarily to academicians and to government officials as a guide for economic policy. Now, however, legislation ties large transfers of money to the economic indicators. A one-point rise in the CPI, for example, triggers a $2-billion increase in federal spending. The national economic indicators have moved from the business section of the newspaper to the front page.

The best-publicized economic indicators are those which, like the CPI and the unemployment rate, measure the present state of the economy. These are called *coincident indicators*, because their movements coincide with those of the economy as a whole. Less known to the public, but critical to business and government policy makers, are the *leading indicators*. These are economic time series whose movements tend to lead (occur before) movements of the overall economy; thus they can help to forecast future economic conditions.

There are 12 major leading economic indicators. In addition to fulfilling the criteria used to select all economic indicators, the leading indicators are chosen for their past success in changing direction ahead of turning points in overall economic activity. Most of the leading economic indicators are measures of *demand* for various kinds of economic output. Some are direct measures of demand, such as the number of new building permits issued for residential houses or the dollar value of new orders for industrial plants and equipment (in 1967 dollars, of course). Others are indirect measures of demand, such as the average work week of manufacturing workers. (This is a leading indicator because manufacturers increase or reduce overtime quickly when demand for their products changes. They hire or lay off workers more slowly; measures of employment and unemployment are coincident indicators.)

The Department of Commerce has spared us from trying to make sense of 12 different time series at once by publishing the *Composite Index of Leading Indicators* (CLI) each month. This is a fixed-weight index number of the kind we have seen already. It is a weighted average of the 12 leading indicators. Since combining several leading indicators usually results in better forecasts of the future, the CLI is not far behind the CPI in the attention it gets from the media. In Figure 4-3 on page 151, for example, we compared two graphs of the CLI that appeared in different newspapers on the same day.

---

* More detail on economic indicators can be found in Geoffrey H. Moore and Julius Shiskin, "Early Warning Signals for the Economy," in *Statistics: A Guide to the Unknown.*

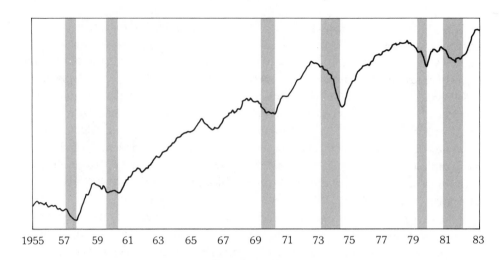

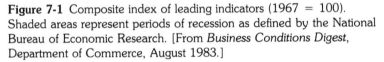

Figure 7-1 Composite index of leading indicators (1967 = 100). Shaded areas represent periods of recession as defined by the National Bureau of Economic Research. [From *Business Conditions Digest*, Department of Commerce, August 1983.]

How well does the CLI predict future economic activity? Take the change in the CLI over a quarter (three-month period) as the independent variable. Let the percent change in the Gross National Product for the following quarter be the dependent variable. (The Gross National Product is the total value of all goods and services produced in the economy. It is the usual measure of overall economic activity.) For the period 1953 to 1970, these variables had $r^2 = 0.37$. That's pretty good by social science standards.[3] Another picture is given by Figure 7-1. Notice that the CLI turns down *before* a recession (shaded areas) and then turns up *during* the recession and before economic recovery. That's what "leading" means.

A question should now occur to any properly greedy reader: Can I use the CLI to forecast what will happen to the stock market and make a killing? Sorry. Stock prices are one of the 12 leading indicators in the CLI; they tend to move before the economy as a whole.

Social indicators

The national economic indicators are well established with the government, the media, and the public. Social scientists have urged the adoption of a similarly authoritative series of *social indicators*. Social indicators are time series intended to provide statistical measures of social values and well-being. Such indicators might provide information for policy makers and for the public similar to the official economic information already available. The government has shown some interest in this idea. The Census Bureau published volumes entitled *Social Indicators* in 1973, 1976, and 1980.

Many statistical measures of health, housing, crime, and other social concerns already are published by the government. But these are far less carefully collected than are our economic indicators. Economic statistics are more precise, are compiled more regularly, and are published with a shorter time lag. (*Social Indicators 1976* appeared in December of 1977!) It is noteworthy that economic indicators such as the unemployment rate are based on regular large sample surveys of citizens. No comparable effort is expended on social statistics. Official social indicators would treat social variables with the level of statistical care now reserved for economic variables.

The suggestion that social indicators be added to economic indicators seems to bring up one new idea and several difficulties. The new idea is to add "subjective" or "opinion" information to improved versions of the "objective" social statistics now available. This is an attractive idea. It would be interesting to follow changes in the values Americans hold, their degree of satisfaction with their jobs,

"Have you ever thought of adding an indicator of how people feel about having their opinions asked every other day?"

how much they are afraid of crime, and so on. Politicians and others now operate on hearsay in these areas. A well-designed sample survey, regularly repeated, would provide fascinating data.

Some of the difficulties in the proposal for official social indicators are directly related to the inclusion of subjective responses. Measuring even so objective a factor as "unemployment" is not entirely easy. How then shall we measure "satisfaction with the quality of life?" Any measure placed on an official list of social indicators will receive much attention and so should be well chosen. To measure a factor, you recall, we must have a clear concept of what the factor is. For example, economists have a clear concept and definition of "money supply." They agree that money supply has an important influence on the economy. So money supply is regularly measured and is one of the leading economic indicators. Social scientists have no such agreement over the concept of "quality of life." Many different measures of the quality of life, both objective and subjective, have been proposed, none of which commands the kind of respect that "money supply" has among economists. The measurement and conceptualization problems so common in the social sciences appear once again. It is probably necessary to begin with many measures of the quality of life, with the hope that regular data collection will clarify which are most useful. Certainly there is interesting information to be gained. One-time surveys suggest, for example, that satisfaction with the quality of life goes *down* as level of education increases. Has this dissatisfaction grown in recent years? Is there really a turning away from material things to things of the spirit as sources of satisfaction? I'd like to know.

Social indicators have problems other than conceptualization and measurement. The economic indicators serve as a basis for making short-term economic policy and for transferring large sums in government payments. That justifies the expense needed to compile the indicators at frequent intervals. Social indicators do not appear to have the same direct relation to policy making by either public or private bodies. I'd like to know if more Americans are looking for satisfaction in things of the spirit this year than last, but I'm not sure my curiosity justifies the kind of massive effort described for the CPI in Section 2. A considerable effort would be required to collect accurate social indicators. At least this would employ more statisticians. But perhaps by now you feel that there are statisticians enough already.

4. Interpreting time series

And so the CLI, the CPI, and other time series run on toward the future, providing us each month with new data. The goal of this machinery is in part to tell us where we are but also to suggest where are going. Predicting the future

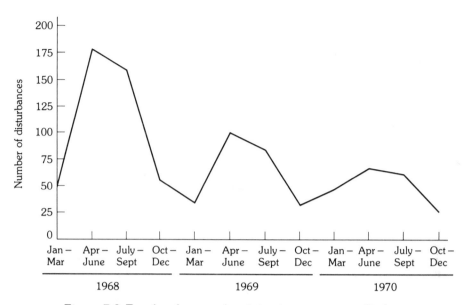

Figure 7-2 Trend and seasonal variation in a time series. Civil disturbances, 1968 to 1970. [From *Statistical Abstract of the United States*, 1971, p. 139.]

is always a risky business, and statistical time series do not remove the risk. The interpretation of time series is complicated by the fact that several types of movement are going on together. Let us look at each type separately.

Seasonal variations are regular changes that recur in periods of less than a year. Figure 7-2 shows a large seasonal variation in the frequency of civil disturbances, which regularly increase in the summer and decrease in winter. We must remove the effect of seasonal variation to see the underlying trend in the time series. In Figure 7-2 we can do this visually, and we find that underneath the seasonal variation the frequency of civil disturbances was decreasing during these years. In the case of many official statistics, a calculation is made to adjust for the expected seasonal variation and to allow month-to-month comparisons. A rise in unemployment in January, for example, need not mean that the economy is in trouble. Rising unemployment is expected in January as Christmas employees are laid off and construction employment drops owing to bad weather. A "seasonally adjusted" unemployment rate for January takes this expected increase into account and can be compared directly to December's rate. If no seasonal adjustment is made, we must be aware of the seasonal variation and take it into account in interpreting the published data.

Example 8. President Reagan, eager to publicize an upturn in the economic cycle, claimed in an April 1982 speech that unemployment had fallen by 88,000 in March. But the Bureau of Labor Statistics had just announced an *increase* of 98,000 in the number of persons out of work. The President used unadjusted figures, while the Bureau's unemployment data were seasonally adjusted to take account of the fact that employment usually increases from February to March. "The statisticians in Washington have funny ways of counting," said Mr. Reagan.

Trend and cycles are long-term features of a time series. A trend is a persistent long-term rise or fall, while cycles are up-and-down movements of irregular strength and duration. The terms are not precise, since a trend may be part of a cycle when the time series is followed for a longer period. For example, the level of prices has been generally increasing since about 1940, a trend that has affected most people. But in the longer view, this inflationary period may be followed by a deflationary period and so take its place as one cycle (though the strongest to date) in the rise and fall of prices over several centuries past. Over the short term, Figure 7-1 shows a continuing trend upward in the level of the

"Isn't it fascinating that you were ruined by a business cycle, while I was ruined by an erratic fluctuation?"

CLI, on which are superimposed up-and-down cycles whose major bottoms occur in the shaded periods of economic recession.

The goal of analysis of a time series is usually the study of trend, cycles, or both. The upward trend in the CLI is probably a result of inflation and is of no particular interest. The cycles, however, reflect the up-and-down business cycles of the economy as a whole (in advance, since the CLI is composed of leading indicators). Analysis of the CLI therefore seeks to decide where we are in the current business cycle so that proper economic policies can be adopted. Even with seasonal variation removed, this is not easy to do. First, business cycles are irregular in length and strength, so they cannot be systematically predicted as seasonal variation can be. Even isolating *past* business cycles in Figure 7-1 is quite subjective. Second, superimposed on trend, cycles, and seasonal variations in a time series are movements of a final type: *erratic fluctuations*. Storms, strikes, oil embargoes, and other chance occurrences large and small affect the economy and the CLI. It is extremely difficult to tell if a three-month flat spot in the CLI means that the business cycle has peaked and is about to turn down. Perhaps it is only a "pause" (to quote the president's chief economic advisor on one such occasion) caused by lack of rain in Nebraska, a strike at Ford Motor Company, and an upcoming presidential election. We cannot see the future clearly, even with the aid of a statistical record of the past.

NOTES

1. Detailed information about the CPI and the surveys that sustain it, as well as about the Current Population Survey and other important data sources, can be found in the Bureau of Labor Statistics' *Handbook of Methods* (Bulletin 2134, 1982).

2. More information on these topics can be found in P. Cagan and G. H. Moore, "Some Proposals to Improve the Consumer Price Index," *Monthly Labor Review*, September 1981, pp. 20–25. The *Monthly Labor Review*, published by the BLS, is a source of current information on many of the topics in this chapter.

3. This result is from Maury N. Harris and Deborah Jamroz, "Evaluating the Leading Indicators," *Federal Reserve Bank of New York Monthly Review*, June 1976, p. 170.

Exercises

Section 1

1. Home heating oil has increased in price as follows:

1976	40¢ per gallon
1979	66¢ per gallon
1982	120¢ per gallon

Give the oil price index numbers (1976 = 100) for 1976, 1979, and 1982.

2. The average price farmers received for a bushel of corn fluctuated as follows:

1978	$2.25
1979	$2.50
1980	$3.10
1981	$2.45

Give a corn price index (1979 = 100) for all four years.

3. In Exercise 2,
  (a) How many points did the corn price index rise from 1979 to 1980? What percent increase was this?
  (b) How many points did the corn price index rise from 1978 to 1980? What percent increase was this?

4. The Consumer Price Index (1967 = 100) stood at 170.1 in June 1976 and at 181.8 in June 1977.
  (a) How many points did the index gain between 1967 and June 1977? What percent increase was this?
  (b) How many points did the index gain between June 1976 and June 1977? What percent increase was this?

5. The Bureau of Labor Statistics publishes separate price indexes for major metropolitan areas in addition to the national index. The values of two of these indexes (1967 = 100) in September 1982 were

296.4 for Los Angeles
324.0 for Houston.

Can you conclude that prices were higher in Houston than in Los Angeles? Why or why not?

6. A bicycle racer must purchase a bicycle, helmet, riding shorts, and riding shoes with cleats to equip himself. His 1980 purchases and their prices in both 1980 and 1985 are given below:

Commodity	1980 quantity	1980 price	1985 price
Bicycle	2	$300 each	$350 each
Helmet	1	$30 each	$35 each
Shorts	3	$10 each	$10 each
Shoes (pair)	2	$20/pair	$25/pair

Compute a fixed market basket price index (1980 = 100) for 1985 by using these data.

7. A certain guru must purchase for his sustenance only olive oil, loincloths, and copies of the *Atharva Veda*, from which to select mantras for his disciples. Here are the quantities and prices of his purchases in 1975 and 1985:

Commodity	1975 quantity	1975 price	1985 quantity	1985 price
Olive oil	20 pints	$0.50/pint	18 pints	$1.00/pint
Loincloth	2	$0.75 each	3	$0.80 each
Atharva Veda	1	$8.50	1	$8.40

From these data, find the Guru Price Index (1975 = 100) for 1985.

Section 2

1. Tuition for Indiana residents at Purdue University has increased as follows:

Year	1967	1969	1971	1973	1975	1977	1979	1981	1983
Tuition	$400	$700	$700	$700	$750	$820	$933	$1158	$1432

Use the annual average CPIs given in Table 7-1 to restate the tuition in constant 1967 dollars. Make two line graphs on the same axes, one showing current dollar tuition for these years and the other showing constant dollar tuition.

2. Few prices have had more influence on the world's economic condition than the benchmark price of crude oil set by the Organization of Petroleum Exporting Countries (OPEC). Here are OPEC benchmark prices (dollars per barrel) at year end:

Year	1971	1973	1975	1977	1979	1981	1983
Oil price	$2.18	$2.59	$10.46	$12.09	$14.54	$32.00	$29.00

Use the annual average CPIs given in Table 7-1 to restate OPEC's price in constant 1967 dollars. Make two line graphs on the same axes, one showing current dollar oil prices and the other showing constant dollar prices.

3. A Chevrolet Malibu Classic cost $3773 in 1973. The same model cost $9011 in 1982. Express the 1982 cost in 1973 dollars. Did the price of a Chevy increase more or less rapidly than inflation in the period 1973–1982?

4. The median income of U.S. families in 1975 was $14,094. How much is this in 1982 dollars? The median family income in 1982 was $23,433. Did a typical family gain or lose buying power between 1975 and 1982?

5. Much has been made of the inability of middle-class families to buy houses at the high prices of recent years. Here are the median prices of new single-family homes sold in each of three years:

1972	$27,600
1977	$48,800
1982	$69,300

Express the 1972 and 1977 prices in 1982 dollars. What has happened to real housing costs in the years 1972–1982?

6. The Ford Model T sold for $950 in 1910 and for $290 in 1925. Obtain the current value of the CPI, and use it to restate these costs in current dollars.

7. In 1956, Yankee outfielder Mickey Mantle hit .353 with 52 home runs and was paid $50,000. In 1981, Yankee outfielder Dave Winfield hit .294 with 13 home runs and was paid $1.5 million. How do these salaries compare in purchasing power? (Use the 1955 CPI in Table 7-1 for Mantle's salary.)

8. What would the CPI be in 1980 if the base period were 1940? [You can find this by changing $100 in 1940 dollars into 1980 dollars. The resulting number of 1980 dollars is the 1980 price index (1940 = 100).] What would the current CPI be if the base period were 1940?

9. Here are some examples of how the CPI is often said to overestimate price increases. Comment on each example. In particular, which can be corrected by a new consumer survey because the overestimates are due to out-of-date information?
    (a) Exterior house-paint prices in the CPI are up, but buyers have switched from the oil paints of 1960 to latex water-base paints, a different product.
    (b) Exterior house-paint prices are up, but new paints cover better so that less paint is needed to paint a house once. New paints also last longer, so we need to buy them less often.
    (c) Exterior house-paint prices are up, but buyers have switched from small hardware stores (higher prices) to discount stores (lower prices). So the price actually paid is not up as much as the hardware store price.
    (d) Exterior house-paint prices are up, but new paints are much more convenient; they are easier to use and to clean up. This convenience has no direct money value, but it means we get greater satisfaction and would be willing to pay more than for less-convenient paints.

10. Now that there is more than one CPI, political pressure may lead to creation of a whole family of price indices, each with a market basket tailored to a specific group. In particular, some congressmen want to set up an index for the aged, to be used in place of the general CPI to adjust Social Security payments. Briefly discuss the pros and cons of this proposal, and express your opinion.

Section 3

1. Choose one of the following economic indicators. Write a short essay describing what the indicator measures, why it is economically important, and what statistical procedures are used to compile the indicator. (To help you locate material in the library, the government agency responsible for each

index is listed. Each agency publishes material describing the indicators for which it is responsible.)

(a) Producer Price Indices (Bureau of Labor Statistics, U.S. Department of Labor).

(b) Gross National Product (Office of Business Economics, U.S. Department of Commerce).

(c) Index of Industrial Production (Federal Reserve Board).

2. We wish to include as part of a set of social indicators measures of the amount of crime and of the impact of crime on people's attitudes and activities. Suggest some possible indicators in each of the following categories:

(a) Statistics to be compiled from official sources.

(b) "Objective" information to be collected by a sample survey of citizens.

(c) "Subjective" information on opinions and attitudes to be collected by sample survey.

3. The two primary collections of official statistics on crime in America are the FBI's annual *Crime in the United States* and the U.S. Law Enforcement Administration's annual *Criminal Victimization in the United States*. You can find selected data from both sources in the *Statistical Abstract*. Describe these sources in a short essay. What kinds of data do they contain? How are the data collected? How frequently are they collected? (Basic information is given in the appendix of the *Statistical Abstract*. If possible, look at the two publications themselves.)

Section 4

1. The price of fresh oranges is collected monthly as part of the data for the CPI. Figure 4-1 on page 149 displays this time series over a period of $3\frac{1}{2}$ years. What causes can you think of that might account for the erratic fluctuations, seasonal variation, and trend that the data display?

2. The sales at your new gift shop in December are double the November value. Should you conclude that your shop is growing more popular and will soon make you rich? Explain your answer.

3. The BLS publishes the CPI both unadjusted and seasonally adjusted. There is some seasonal variation owing to weather (food prices), holidays, and so forth, so the two versions of the CPI often will be slightly different.

(a) If you want to follow general price trends in the economy, would you use the seasonally adjusted or unadjusted version of the CPI? Why?

(b) If you have a labor contract with an escalation clause tied to the CPI, you want your wages to keep pace with the actual prices you must pay. Which version of the CPI would you use for this purpose, and why?

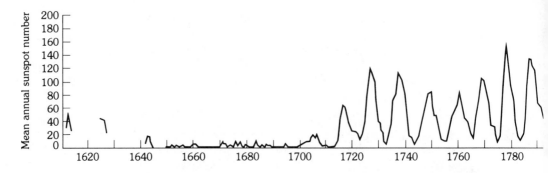

4. Figure 7-3 is a plot of the "mean annual sunspot number" from 1610 to 1976. Since the superstitious think that sunspots influence all manner of earthly happenings, study of this time series should be interesting.

    (a) The sunspot cycle is the most obvious feature of this time series. About how long is the sunspot cycle from maximum to maximum? Does the length of the cycle remain constant over time, or are there significant variations in the length?

    (b) By tracing the curve of the sunspot maxima over many cycles, I think I can see a longer cycle superimposed on the sunspot cycle. Comment on this suggestion.

    (c) Does this time series show any striking noncyclical phenomena? Describe any you notice.

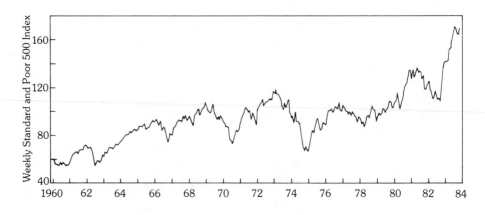

Figure 7-4 The Standard and Poor's 500 Stock Index, 1960–1983.

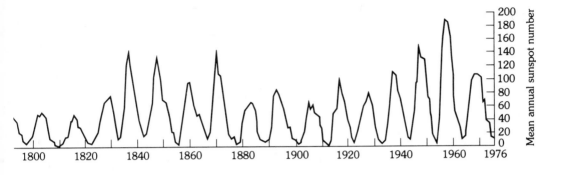

5. Few time series are watched more closely than stock market averages. One of the most popular is the Standard and Poor's 500, an index of the prices of 500 major stocks weighted by their total market value. Figure 7-4 is a plot of the S&P 500 from 1960 to June 1983.

   (a) Describe the trend of stock market prices over this period.

   (b) Do you see any evidence of cycles that tend to recur at regular periods? If so, can you think of a possible explanation for the timing of the cycles?

Part III

Drawing conclusions
from data

The experiment was designed, the protocol tested, the subjects assembled, the myriad details dealt with, double-blind enforced, the diagnoses completed. The raw data have been graphed and tabled, averaged and correlated. And now you must state a conclusion that will stand the scrutiny of nitpicking journal editors and jealous rivals.

Sir Peter Medawar, a Nobel laureate, wrote that

*It is a truism to say that a "good" experiment is precisely that which spares us the exertion of thinking: the better it is, the less we have to worry about its interpretation, about what it "really" means.**

In recognition of this wisdom, your experiment was carefully controlled and randomized, so that any effect that appears must be due to your treatment. But wait. You assigned subjects to treatments at random, and while this eliminates

---

* Sir Peter Medawar, *Induction and Intuition in Scientific Thought* (Philadelphia: American Philosophical Society, 1969), p. 15.

259

systematic bias, there will still be differences between the groups due to the luck of the draw. Will someone charge that the good performance of your favored treatment is just an accidental result of the randomization? Alas, it isn't true that any effect that appears must be due to the treatment. In even the best experiment, the effect might be due to an unlucky randomization that happened to produce very unlike groups of subjects. You need still more statistics to argue convincingly that your effects really are due to the treatment. The methods of statistical inference are designed to draw conclusions taking into account the effects of randomization.

We must study these effects of randomization in more detail. The study of randomness is called *probability theory*, a subject of interest to those who wish to understand such worldly pursuits as roulette and state lotteries as well as to students of the lofty subject of statistics. Probability is the subject of Chapter 8. Since randomization is the foundation of statistical designs for collecting data, probability is the foundation of statistical methods for drawing conclusions from data. Chapter 9 presents some of the concepts behind statistical inference. The methods of inference are largely left to more traditional introductions to statistics, which usually begin where I leave off.

Probability: The study of randomness

E ven the rules of football agree that tossing a coin avoids favoritism. Favoritism in choosing subjects for a sample survey or allotting patients to treatment and placebo groups is as undesirable as it is in awarding first possession of the ball in football. Statisticians therefore recommend probability samples and randomized experiments, which are fancy-dress versions of tossing a coin. The central idea of statistical data collection is the deliberate introduction of randomness into the choice or assignment of units. Both tossing a coin and choosing an SRS are *random* in the sense that

- the exact outcome is not predictable in advance;
- nonetheless, a predictable long-term pattern exists and can be expressed by a relative frequency distribution of the outcomes after many trials.

The inventors of probability samples and randomized experiments in this century were not the first to notice that some phenomena are random in this sense. They were drawing upon a long history of the study of randomness and applying the results of that study to statistics.

Randomness is most easily noticed in many repetitions of games of chance—rolling dice, dealing shuffled cards, spinning a roulette wheel. Chance devices similar to these have been used from remote antiquity to discover the will of the gods. The most common method of randomization was "rolling the bones," tossing several *astragali*. The astragalus is a solid, quite regular bone from the heel of animals that, when thrown, will come to rest on any of four sides. (The other two sides are rounded.) Cubical dice, made of pottery or bone, came later, but even dice existed before 2000 B.C. Gambling on the throw of astragali or dice is, in contrast to divination, almost a modern development; there is no clear record of this vice before about 300 B.C. Gambling reached flood tide in Roman times, then temporarily receded (along with divination) in the face of Christian displeasure. Clearly unpredictable outcomes have been noticed and used from the beginning of recorded time.[1]

But none of the great mathematicians of antiquity considered that the outcomes of throwing bones or dice have a clear pattern in many trials. Perhaps this is because astragali and most ancient dice were so irregular that each had a different pattern of outcomes. Or perhaps the reasons lie deeper, in the classical reluctance to engage in systematic experimentation. Professional gamblers, not so inhibited as philosophers and mathematicians, must have long known something of the regular pattern of outcomes of dice or cards and adjusted their bets to the "odds" of success. These odds the gamblers often could not guess correctly from experience alone. The systematic study of randomness began (I oversimplify, but not too much) when seventeenth-century French gamblers asked French mathematicians for help. The mathematical study of randomness, *probability theory*, originated with Pierre de Fermat and Blaise Pascal in the seventeenth century and was well developed by the time statisticians took it over in the twentieth century. In this chapter we examine probability, but without

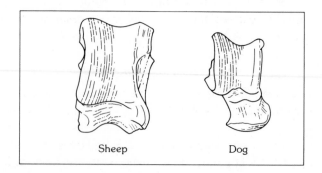

Animal astragali, actual size. [Reproduced by permission of the publishers, Charles Griffin & Company, Ltd., of London and High Wycombe. From F. N. David, *Games, Gods, and Gambling*, 1962.]

mention of the actual mathematics that has grown from the first attempts of the French mathematicians to aid their gambler friends.

Probability is now important for many reasons having little to do with either gambling or collecting data. Many natural and artificial phenomena are random in the sense that they are not predictable in advance but have long-term patterns. For example, the science of genetics is based on Gregor Mendel's observation that for given parents the characteristics of offspring are random with long-run patterns that he began to uncover. And the emission of particles from a radioactive source occurs randomly over time, with a pattern that helped to suggest the cause of radioactivity. Probability theory is used to describe phenomena ("construct models" is the fashionable terminology) in genetics, physics, and many other fields of study. Although we will not meet such applications here, the ideas of this chapter shed light on these fields as well.

1.   What is probability?

Probability begins with the observed fact that some phenomena are random. We do not know whether a pair of dice will give 8 as their sum on the next roll, but by observation we can discover that an 8 will occur on about 14% of a long series of rolls. That 14% is part of the predictable pattern that emerges after many rolls. Since an 8 will appear in 14%, or in fraction form 14/100, of many rolls of two dice, we think of "14 in 100" as the chance of getting an 8 on any one roll. In more formal language, the probability of an 8 when two dice are rolled is 14/100, or in decimal form 0.14. Here is the vocabulary we will use:

> **Event—any specific collection of the possible outcomes of a random phenomenon.**
>
> **Frequency of an event—the number of times the event occurs in a sequence of repetitions of the random phenomenon.**
>
> **Relative frequency of an event—the fraction or proportion of repetitions on which the event occurs. A relative frequency is always a number between 0 and 1.**
>
> **Probability of an event—If in a long sequence of repetitions the relative frequency of an event approaches a fixed number, that number is the probability of the event. A probability is always a number between 0 (the event never occurs) and 1 (the event always occurs).**

We have met frequency and relative frequency before. *Probability* is succinctly defined as long-term relative frequency. Return once more to the bead-sampling experiment summarized in Figure 1-1 on page 15. This experiment consisted

"What kind of childish nonsense are you working on now?"

of 200 trials of the random phenomenon of drawing an SRS of size 25 from a large box of beads, 20% of which were dark. The outcome "5 dark beads in the sample" had frequency 47 and relative frequency 47/200 = 0.24. The *event* "4, 5, or 6 dark beads in the sample" had frequency 111 and relative frequency 111/200 = 0.56 because on 111 of the 200 trials one of the outcomes 4, 5, or 6 occurred. The number 0.56 is not quite the probability of the event "4, 5, or 6 dark beads," but it is quite close because it is the relative frequency in 200 trials. Making more and more trials would give a relative frequency even closer to the probability. The first three exercises for this section are intended to give you some experience with the somewhat mysterious phenomenon of randomness.

Our "definition" of probability is not intended to satisfy either the mathematician or the philosopher. It merely builds on the observation that long-term relative frequencies often do settle down to fixed numbers, and it provides the terminology to describe this situation. I do not know why the world is made so that randomness exists, but it is an observed fact that it is so made. You should note that not all phenomena are random in our sense. Some (such as dropping a coin from a fixed height and measuring the time it takes to fall) are predictable; that is, repetitions give the same result time after time. Such phenomena we call *deterministic*. They are the subject of much of the older physical sciences. Other phenomena are unpredictable but display no long-term pattern. If, for example, the operator of a roulette wheel has a brake that he can apply at will, he can prevent the relative frequency of "red" from settling down to a fixed probability in the long run.

If an unpredictable phenomenon is to show a long-term pattern, it must at least be true that the *same* phenomenon is repeated, and repetitions are *independent* in the sense that the outcome of one repetition has no effect on the outcome of any other repetition. Both of these conditions are violated if the operator of a roulette wheel can apply a brake to it.

Here are some examples to help you think about probability as long-term relative frequency:

Example 1. If the same (or identical) pennies are tossed repeatedly, the conditions for making statements about probability are present: The *same* coin is being tossed, and since the coin has no memory, the repetitions cannot influence each other. Experience shows that the probability of a head is very close to 1/2. For example, the eighteenth-century French naturalist Comte de Buffon tossed a coin 4040 times and got 2048 heads. That's a relative frequency of 0.507. The statistician Karl Pearson spent some time at the turn of the century making 24,000 tosses. He got 12,012 heads, for a relative frequency of 0.501.

You may feel that it is obvious from the balance of the coin that the probability of a head is about 1/2. Such opinions are not always correct. You are invited to take a penny and, instead of tossing it, hold it on end on a hard surface with the index finger of one hand and snap it with the other index finger. The coin will spin for several seconds and then fall with either heads or tails showing. A long series of trials reveals that the probability of a head in this random experiment is not at all close to 1/2. Moral: We defined probability *empirically* (that is, in terms of observations), and only by observation can we be sure of the approximate value of the probability of an event.

Example 2. Insurance is based on the idea of probability. If, for instance, all males in the United States are observed during their twenty-first year, some will die during that year. Whether a certain 21-year-old male will die is not predictable, but observation of several million such men shows that about 0.18% of them (that's 0.0018 in decimal form) die each year. So if an insurance company sells many policies to 21-year-old men, it knows that it will have to pay off on about 0.18% of them and sets the premium high enough to cover this cost. The number 0.0018 is the *probability* that an American male will die in his twenty-first year.

The probability of an event is a measure of how likely the event is to occur, but does not make sense unless we can at least imagine many independent repetitions of the random phenomenon. When we say that a coin has probability 1/2 of coming up heads *on this toss*, we are applying to a single toss a measure of the chance of a head based on what would happen in a long series of tosses.

The idea of probability is a bit subtle. Here are some fine points to set you thinking:

The "Law of Averages." If in tossing a fair coin we get 10 straight heads, is tails more likely on the next toss? Because the probability of tails is 1/2, many people think that the "Law of Averages" demands that some tails now appear to balance the 10 heads. Are they right?

No. The coin has no memory, so it does not know that it has come up heads 10 straight times. Put more formally, because tosses are independent, the probability of a tail on the next toss is still 1/2.

That answer is correct but not satisfying. It can be checked empirically if you have several years to waste: Toss a penny many times. Every time you get 10 straight heads, record whether the next toss gives heads or tails. In the long run you will find tails occurring about half the time after 10 heads. A better tactic is to seek to understand how the long-run relative frequency of tails can be 1/2

"So the law of averages doesn't guarantee me a girl after seven straight boys, but can't I at least get a group discount on the delivery fee?"

without making up for the 10 straight heads with some extra tails. To understand this, let us suppose that the next 10,000 tosses are evenly divided, giving 5000 heads and 5000 tails. Then the relative frequency of tails after 10,010 tosses is

$$\frac{5000}{10,010} = 0.4995.$$

This is very close to 1/2. The 10 straight heads are swamped by later tosses and need not be made up for by extra tails. (Of course, the next 10,000 tosses will not yield exactly 5000 tails, but the point is that if the fraction of tails in the long run is about 1/2, 10 straight heads will not affect this at all.)

Belief in this phony "Law of Averages" can lead to consequences close to disastrous, and not only for gamblers. A few years ago, "Dear Abby" published in her advice column a letter from a distraught mother of eight girls. It seems that she and her husband had planned to limit their family to four children. But when all four were girls, they tried again. And again, and again. After seven straight girls, even her doctor had assured her that "the law of averages was in our favor 100 to one." Unfortunately for this couple, having children is like tossing coins: Eight girls in a row is highly unlikely, but once seven girls have been born it is not at all unlikely that the next child will be a girl. And it was.

What Probability Doesn't Say. There is, you may think, little difference between the statements

(a) "In many tosses of a fair coin, the fraction of heads will be close to one-half" and

(b) "In many tosses of a fair coin, the number of heads will be close to one-half the number of tosses."

Alas, Statement (a) is true and is what we mean by saying that the probability of a head is 1/2. Statement (b) is false; in many tosses of a fair coin, the number of heads is certain to deviate more and more from one-half the number of tosses. This is, as Pooh would say, mystigious. To see why it is true, consider the following example:

Number of tosses	Number of heads	Fraction of heads	Difference between number of heads and 1/2 number of tosses
100	51	0.51	1
1000	510	0.51	10
10,000	5100	0.51	100
100,000	51,000	0.51	1000

There it is: The *fraction* of heads stays close to 1/2 while the *number* of heads departs more and more from one-half the number of tosses. (Again, this exact outcome is unlikely, but it is typical of what happens in many repetitions.)

Probability versus Odds. Probability was born in a gambling hall, from whence it climbed to more respectable status. Back in the gambling hall, the chance of an event often is stated in terms of "odds" rather than probability. At the risk of encouraging you to misapply your knowledge of probability, let us learn to translate odds into probabilities.

> **Example 3.** You are rolling two dice, a common way of losing money. You would very much like to roll a 7, and you have heard that the odds against this are 5 to 1. What's the probability of a 7? Odds of 5 to 1 means that failing to roll a 7 happens five times as often as success. In the long run, then, five of every six tries will fail, and one will succeed in rolling a 7. The probability of a 7 is now clear. It is one out of six, or
>
> $$\frac{1}{6} = 0.167.$$
>
> Notice that odds of 5 to 1 are not the same as "1 in 5." The latter means probability 1/5, while the former gives the probability as 1/6.

The recipe illustrated in Example 3 is

Odds of A to B against an outcome means that the probability of that outcome is $B/(A + B)$.

Thus if the odds against the favorite in a horse race are 3 to 2, this is equivalent to that horse having probability 2/5 of winning.

Enough of conceptualizing about probability. In practice, we often wish to describe a random phenomenon by assigning probabilities to its various outcomes. This is called giving a *probability model* for the phenomenon. Such a probability model is often based partly on observation and partly on our feeling about what the probability of the outcomes should be. These models are useful for thinking about random phenomena and for computing the probabilities of complicated events from probabilities of simple events. We shall soon meet some examples. But the correctness of the model must always be judged by comparing it with observations of the random phenomenon it is supposed to describe, because probabilities are defined empirically.

The mathematics of probability begins by describing properties of all legitimate probability models. We need only two such properties.

A. **The probability of any event must be a number between 0 and 1.**

B. **If we assign a probability to every possible outcome of a random phenomenon, the sum of these probabilities must be 1.**

Properties A and B of any probability model follow from our understanding of probability as long-run relative frequency. Any relative frequency is a number between 0 and 1, and this is Property A. Because some outcome must occur on each repetition, the sum of the relative frequencies of all possible outcomes must be 1, and this is Property B. Here are some simple examples of probability models:

> **Example 4.** On the basis of several thousand repetitions of the experiment of randomly selecting a voter on November 2, 1980, the Harris polling organization gave the following probability model for voter presidential preferences:
>
> | Outcome | Probability |
> | --- | --- |
> | Would vote for Reagan | 0.46 |
> | Would vote for Carter | 0.41 |
> | Would vote for Anderson | 0.09 |
> | Others or undecided | 0.04 |
>
> This example would be described more naturally as "relative frequencies in a sample." Instead we have thought of it as giving (from sample observations) a model for the random phenomenon of choosing an adult American at random on November 2, 1980, and asking for whom he or she would vote. Notice that all four outcomes have probabilities between 0 and 1 (Property A), and that these probabilities add to 1 (Property B).

> **Example 5.** You are about to begin gambling with a die. (That's the singular of "dice." The study of "house/houses," "mouse/mice," "die/dice," and so on must set speakers of simpler languages muttering.) On inspection, you feel that the die is "fair," and so you assign each of the six faces the same probability of coming up. This is a legitimate probability model, because it satisfies properties A and B. It is also correct for many dice. Whether or not it is correct for your die can be decided only by tossing the die many times and checking whether the long-term relative frequencies are close to 1/6 for each face

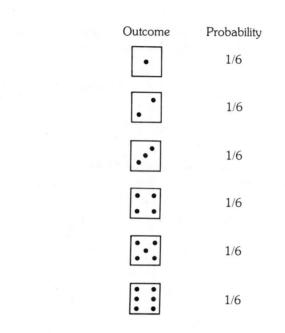

Summing up: What is probability?

I have stressed that long-term stability of relative frequencies is an observed fact in some circumstances. This observation provided a way to think about probability in detail, coming at last to properties A and B, which characterize all legitimate probability models. But long-term relative frequency is not the only important interpretation of what probability is. We could instead define the probability of an event as a number between 0 and 1 that represents my personal assessment of the chance that the event will occur. ("I think Dallas has a 30% chance of going to the Super Bowl this year.") Probabilities interpreted this way are called *personal probabilities* or *subjective probabilities*, because they express personal opinion. Your personal probability for the event that Dallas will play in this year's Super Bowl is no doubt not the same as mine.

Personal probability has several advantages over the relative-frequency interpretation. The probability that Dallas will go to the Super Bowl this year, or the probability that my firm's bid will be high enough to win a certain contract, cannot be thought of as long-term relative frequencies because these probabilities refer to a single, unrepeatable chance phenomenon. So personal probability has a wider scope than long-term relative frequency. The other advantage of a subjective interpretation of probability is that it provides a meaningful definition of probability, not just a way of thinking about randomness. Long-term relative frequency is not truly a definition of probability; we can never watch an endless series of trials to be certain that the relative frequency settles down to a probability. So "long-term relative frequency" refers to an ideal never quite attained. Personal probability, on the other hand, is exactly what it pretends to be: a subjective assessment of chance.

The disadvantage of personal probability is that it is personal. When long-term relative frequencies do exist, my personal assignment of probabilities may bear no relation to the pattern of outcomes actually observed. Which interpretation of probability is favored in applications varies with the weight accorded to these advantages and disadvantages. Personal probability predominates when the insight and partial information of a decision maker are important, as in business decisions and gambling on horses. Frequency ideas rule when repeatable events are in question, as in quality control of mass-produced items and gambling on roulette wheels.

I prefer to keep the frequency interpretation of probability foremost in your mind, partly because of my own view of the relative usefulness of frequency versus subjective interpretations and partly for pedagogic reasons. But we will meet both interpretations, not always sharply distinguished, through the rest of this book. The clash of interpretations can be played down because any assignment of probabilities must have properties A and B, whether interpreted as personal assessment of chance or as long-term relative frequency. The users of probability in science, business, gambling, and statistics begin by assigning probabilities to outcomes. However you interpret the notion of probability, the rules describing legitimate assignments of probabilities to outcomes stand forever firm.

2.   Finding probabilities by simulation

Suppose that a couple plans to have children until they have a girl or until they have four children, whichever comes first. What is the probability that they will have a girl among their children? To answer probability questions such as this, we first construct a probability model. In this case, it seems reasonable to assume that

(a) Each child has probability 1/2 of being a girl and 1/2 of being a boy; and

(b) The sexes of successive children are independent.

But how can we compute the probability of a somewhat complex event (having a girl in four tries) from this simple model?

There are two ways of finding the probability of complex events from known probabilities of simple events. One is to master the mathematics of probability theory, a worthwhile endeavor that we wish to avoid. The other is to *simulate* (imitate or run a small scale model of) the random phenomenon by using our trusty companion, the table of random digits. The idea is to imitate the probability model by using the properties of random digits, then use the table to simulate many repetitions of the phenomenon. The relative frequency of any event eventually will be close to its probability, so that many repetitions give a good estimate of probability.

We will simulate the child-bearing strategy of the couple discussed above.

Example 6. Step 1. A single random digit simulates the sex of a single child as follows:

0, 1, 2, 3, 4	the child is a girl
5, 6, 7, 8, 9	the child is a boy

Step 2. To simulate one repetition of the child-bearing experiment, use successive random digits until either a girl or four children are obtained. Using line 130 of Table A, we find

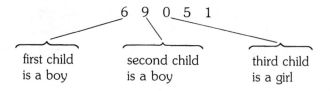

and the couple stops at three children, having obtained a girl.

Step 3. Simulate many repetitions and use the relative frequency of the event "the couple has a girl" to estimate its probability. Here is the result of using line 130. To interpret the digits, we have written G for girl and B for boy under them, have drawn vertical lines between repetitions, and under each repetition have written " + " if a girl was born and " − " if not.

690	51	64	81	7871	74	0	951	784	53	4	0	64	8987
BBG	BG	BG	BG	BBBG	BG	G	BBG	BBG	BG	G	G	BG	BBBB
+	+	+	+	+	+	+	+	+	+	+	+	+	−

In 14 repetitions, a girl was born 13 times. So our estimate of the probability that this strategy will produce a girl is

$$\frac{13}{14} = 0.93.$$

"I've had it! Simulated wood, simulated leather, simulated coffee, and now simulated probabilities!"

This example of simulation deserves careful discussion. Step 1 simulates part (a) of the probability model because we assigned 5 of the 10 possible digits to the outcome "girl." Because all 10 are equally likely to occur at any point in the table, any one table entry has probability 5/10 or 1/2 of indicating "girl." Here are further examples of this idea:

Example 7. Simulate an event that has probability 3/10 as follows:

       0, 1, 2   the event occurs

       3, 4, 5, 6, 7, 8, 9   the event does not occur

Example 8. To simulate an event that has probability 0.33, use *two* digits to simulate one repetition, with

      00, 01, 02, . . . , 31, 32   the event occurs

      33, 34, 35, . . . , 98, 99   the event does not occur

Example 9. Simulate a random trial having *three* possible outcomes with probabilities 2/10, 3/10, and 5/10 as follows:

           0, 1   outcome A occurs

           2, 3, 4   outcome B occurs

           5, 6, 7, 8, 9   outcome C occurs

Step 2 in Example 6 simulates one repetiton of the child-bearing process, because successive random digits are independent and therefore simulate successive independent births. In Step 3, 14 repetitions were made, and the relative frequency of bearing a girl was found. The relative frequency 0.93 is not a very precise estimate of the probability, because only 14 repetitions were made. With mathematics we could show that if the probability model given is correct, then the true probability of having a girl is 0.938. Our simulated answer came quite close.

Now that we have seen a first illustration of the mechanics of simulation, let's pause for a long look at some of the ideas.

The probability model is the foundation of any computation of probability, whether by simulation or by mathematics. It may appear a bit shady to begin the process of finding a probability by assuming that we already know some other probabilities, but not even mathematics can give you something for nothing. The idea is to state the basic structure of the random phenomenon and then use simulation to move from the basics to the probabilities of more complicated events. The model is based on opinion and past experience; if it does not correctly describe the random phenomenon, the probabilities derived from it by simulation also will be incorrect. So will the probabilities a mathematician might obtain by his black arts, like that 0.938 in the childbearing example. That is the "true" probability of a girl only if the sexes of successive children are independent and each child is equally likely to be male or female.

The probability models we will meet have two parts.

(a) A simple random phenomenon with a small number of possible outcomes. These are assigned probabilities with properties A and B as discussed in Section 1.

(b) Independent trials of phenomena such as part (a) describes, sometimes repetitions of the same random phenomenon (like the successive children in Example 6), and sometimes independent trials of different random phenomena.

The random digits play their usual role as substitutes for physical randomization. We could physically simulate the behavior of our probability model. The childbearing strategy might be simulated by an urn* with a number of balls, half red and half white. Red balls are female children and white balls are males. Draw a ball to represent the sex of the first child; you are equally likely to get

---

* I would like to call this container a pot, but protocol forbids. Pots full of balls of varying colors are officially called "urn models" in probability theory.

To find the probability of an event by simulation

(a) Specify a probability model for the random phenomenon by assigning probabilities to individual outcomes and assuming independence where appropriate.

(b) Decide how to simulate the basic outcomes of the phenomenon, using assignments of digits to match the assignment of probabilities (Step 1).

(c) Decide how to simulate a single repetition of the random phenomenon by combining simulations of the basic outcomes (Step 2).

(d) Estimate the probability of an event by the relative frequency of the event in many repetitions of the simulated phenomenon (Step 3).

---

a female or a male. Replace the ball (to maintain the half red and half white mixture), stir the urn well, and draw again; that's the second child. And so on. Urns and balls could always be used to do our simulations. But random digits have the same advantages in simulation as in random sampling; they are faster and more accurate than physical randomization. Thinking of physical models like urns full of balls does help to take the mystery out of random digits in simulation. Both the urn and the random digits make a manageable copy of the random phenomenon under study.

The precision of a simulation for estimating probabilities increases as more repetitions are used. This is simply a restatement of the "definition" of probability as long-term relative frequency. But there is a close connection with the precision of sample statistics from probability samples. Both statistics from large samples and probabilities simulated from many trials are highly precise in the sense that repeating the whole process would give nearly the same answer. Indeed, estimating an unknown probability p by a relative frequency $\hat{p}$ is substantially the same as estimating a population proportion p by a sample proportion $\hat{p}$.

More extensive simulations

Simulation is a common procedure for finding probabilities too difficult to compute, even for those who know probability theory. Such simulation is always done by a computer, which can be programmed to do thousands of repetitions in a short time. Large numbers of repetitions give very precise results, but the ideas remain those we have met. Simulations in science and engineering are usually accompanied by a statement of precision in the form of the standard deviation of the relative frequency used to estimate the unknown probability.

Recall from Section 3 of Chapter 5 that the standard deviation of the sample statistic is a common way of stating precision in sampling as well. The next example illustrates the close connection between sampling and simulation by asking a probability question about a sampling procedure.

> **Example 10.** Suppose that 80% of all consumers prefer Brand A instant coffee to Brand B. If an SRS of 10 consumers is chosen, what is the probability that 7 or more of them prefer Brand A? (This is a question about the long-term pattern of results of an SRS. That long-term pattern, which has been with us since Chapter 1, can be described now in terms of the probability of various outcomes.)
>
> We first need a probability model. Here is the model we will simulate:
>
> **(a)** Each consumer has probability 8/10 of preferring Brand A.
>
> **(b)** The preferences of successive consumers are independent.
>
> This is a good model for an SRS of size 10 from a population of which 80% (8/10) favor Brand A *if* the population is large.* Now for the simulation.
>
> Step 1. One digit simulates one consumer's preference.
>
> > 0, 1, 2, 3, 4, 5, 6, 7   Brand A
> >
> > 8, 9   Brand B
>
> Step 2. To simulate one repetition of the experiment, use 10 random digits. Count how many of these digits are 0, 1, . . . , 7. This is the number of consumers in a sample of size 10 who prefer Brand A.
>
> Step 3. We do this 10 times, starting at line 110 of Table A. Here are the 10 repetitions:
>
> > 38448   48789   5 prefer Brand A
> > ABAAB   ABABB

---

* That's a fine point. Think of an urn filled with 80% red balls (Brand A) and 20% white balls (Brand B). We begin to draw our SRS, and the first ball is red. Now the urn contains *less* than 80% red balls. So the preferences of the 10 consumers in our SRS are *not* independent, because each consumer drawn changes the makeup of the remaining population. When the population is large, the dependence is so small we can neglect it: Drawing a red ball from an urn containing 80,000 reds and 20,000 whites does not noticeably change the chance of a red on the second draw.

18338	24697	7 prefer Brand A
ABAAB	AAABA	
39364	42006	9 prefer Brand A
ABAAA	AAAAA	
76688	08708	6 prefer Brand A
AAABB	ABAAB	
81486	69487	6 prefer Brand A
BAABA	ABABA	
60513	09297	8 prefer Brand A
AAAAA	ABABA	
00412	71238	9 prefer Brand A
AAAAA	AAAAB	
27649	39950	7 prefer Brand A
AAAAB	ABBAA	
59636	88804	6 prefer Brand A
ABAAA	BBBAA	
04634	71197	9 prefer Brand A
AAAAA	AAABA	

The event "7 or more prefer Brand A" occurs in 6 of the 10 repetitions, so we estimate its probability to be

$$\frac{6}{10} = 0.6.$$

Ten repetitions gives quite poor precision. By mathematics or more extensive simulation we can find that the true probability that 7 or more of an SRS of 10 consumers prefer Brand A is 0.88. I did a set of 50 trials and got a relative frequency of 41/50 = 0.82, which is closer to home.

The probability we estimated by simulation in Example 10 depends on the assumption that 80% of the population prefer Brand A. If that population proportion is different, the probabilities of various outcomes in the SRS are different. A complete study of probabilities for an SRS would include a description of how these probabilities change when the population proportion changes.

The building and simulation of random models is a powerful tool of contemporary science, yet a tool that can be understood in substance without advanced mathematics. What is more, several attempts to simulate simple random phenomena will increase your understanding of probability more than many pages of my prose. Having in mind these two goals of understanding simulation for itself and understanding simulation to understand probability, let us study a more extensive example.

Example 11. We are studying the Asian Stochastic Beetle,[2] and we observe that females of this insect have the following pattern of reproduction:

> 20% of females die without female offspring
>
> 30% have one female offspring
>
> 50% have two female offspring

What will happen to the population of Asian Stochastic Beetles: Will they increase rapidly, barely hold their own, or die out? (Notice that we can ignore the male beetles in studying reproduction, as long as there are some around for certain essential purposes. Notice also that we are studying only a single population. It is common for ecologists to use probability models and simulation in their study of the interaction of several populations, such as predators and prey.)

The reproduction of a single female is simulated as follows:

> 0, 1   dies without female offspring
>
> 2, 3, 4,   has one female offspring
>
> 5, 6, 7, 8, 9   has two female offspring

Moreover, we will assume that female beetles reproduce independently of each other.

To answer the question "What is the future of the Asian Stochastic Beetle?" we will simulate the female descendents of several female beetles until they either die out or reach the fifth generation. Beginning at line 122 of the table of random digits.

> 13873   81598   95052   90908   73592

the first beetle dies without offspring (1). The second has one female offspring (3); she in turn has two female offspring (8); the first of these has two (7) and the second has one (3) female offspring. So the fourth generation of this family contains three female beetles.

We need a better way to record this simulation. Figure 8-1 records the female descendents of seven female Asian Stochastic Beetles. Each family is followed to the fifth generation. The two families on the left are those we just met, and the random digits beside each beetle in these families remind you how line 122 was used "from left to right in each generation

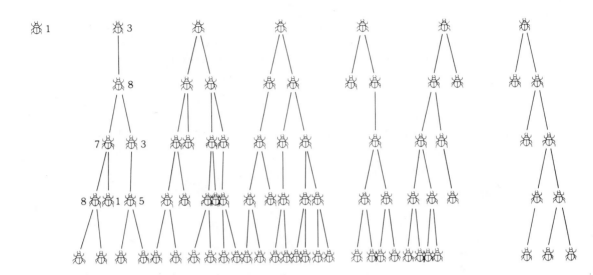

Figure 8-1. Simulation of the descendants of seven female Asian Stochastic Beetles. 20% die without female offspring; 30% have one female offspring; 50% have two female offspring.

of offspring." The fifth generation has 29 female beetles from the original 7. It is clear that the population of Asian Stochastic Beetles will increase rapidly until crowding, shortage of food, or increased predator populations change the reproductive pattern we have simulated.

3.   State lotteries and expected values

In 1964, the conservative state of New Hampshire caused a furor by introducing state-run gambling in the form of a lottery to raise public revenue without raising taxes. The furor subsided quickly as larger states adopted the idea, until more than a third of the states now sponsor lotteries. A lottery uses random selection to distribute prizes among those who have bought tickets. How can we measure the value of a lottery ticket or compare the return we can expect from buying lottery tickets with that from gambling in Las Vegas? It is not enough to know the probability of winning. The amount won is also important, because one lottery might offer many small prizes and another might award a few large prizes. The larger prizes might compensate for the lower probability of winning, making the second lottery a better bet. We need a way to take into account both the probability of winning and the amount won to compute the *expected value* of a lottery.

State lotteries have introduced ever more gimmicks and special prizes in an attempt to keep public interest high, and these make computation of the expected value of a ticket difficult. So let us go back a few years and study the original, uncluttered New York State Lottery.

> **Example 12.** The New York State Lottery awarded, for each one million tickets sold,
>
> > 1 $50,000 prize
> >
> > 9 $5000 prizes
> >
> > 90 $500 prizes
> >
> > 900 $50 prizes
>
> The winning tickets were drawn at random from those sold. The total value of these prizes is
>
> ($50,000) + (9)($5000) + (90)($500) + (900)($50) = $185,000
>
> Since this amount is divided among 1,000,000 tickets, the average winnings per ticket is
>
> $$\frac{\$185,000}{1,000,000} = \$0.185$$
>
> or $18\frac{1}{2}$ cents. This is the *expected value* of a ticket—the average value of an individual ticket.

Because lottery tickets cost 50 cents, New York State paid out a bit less than 40% ($18\frac{1}{2}$ over 50 is 0.37, or 37%) of the amount wagered by ticket buyers and kept over 60%. Competition has since sweetened the pot, and most state lotteries now pay out about one-half of their take. By way of comparison, casinos in Las Vegas or Atlantic City pay out 85% to 92% of the amount wagered, depending on which game you choose. State lotteries are a poor bet. Professional gamblers avoid them, not wanting to waste money on so bad a bargain. Politicians avoid them for reasons nicely put by Nelson Rockefeller when he was Governor of New York: "I'm afraid I might win." Almost everyone else in lottery states plays. Surveys usually show that about 80% of the adult residents have purchased at least one lottery ticket. Why is such a poor bet so popular? Lack of knowledge of how poor the bet is plays a role. So does skillful advertising by the state. But the major attraction is probably the lure of possible wealth, no

"I think the lottery is a great idea. If they raised taxes instead, we'd have to pay them."

matter how unlikely the jackpot is. Many people find 50 cents a week a fair price for the entertainment value of imagining themselves rich. As one Carmen Brutto of Harrisburg, Pa., said in a newspaper interview, "My chances of winning a million are better than my chances of earning a million."[3]

There is another way of calculating the expected value of a New York State lottery ticket that can be applied more generally than the method of Example 12. (It gives the same answer; I just wish to organize the arithmetic differently.)

Example 13. Buying a ticket in the New York State Lottery and observing how much you win is a random phenomenon. Because winning tickets are drawn at random, each ticket has 1 chance in 1,000,000 to win $50,000, 9 chances in 1,000,000 to win $5000, and so on. Here is a probability model for the amount won by one ticket:

Amount	Probability
$50,000	1/1,000,000
$5000	9/1,000,000
$500	90/1,000,000
$50	900/1,000,000
$0	999,000/1,000,000

The total probability of winning anything is 1/1000; that is, 1000 out of 1,000,000 tickets win something. The expected value can be found by multiplying each possible outcome by its probability and summing.

$$(\$50{,}000)\left(\frac{1}{1{,}000{,}000}\right) + (\$5000)\left(\frac{9}{1{,}000{,}000}\right)$$

$$+ (\$500)\left(\frac{90}{1{,}000{,}000}\right) + (\$50)\left(\frac{900}{1{,}000{,}000}\right) + (\$0)\left(\frac{999{,}000}{1{,}000{,}000}\right)$$

$$= \$0.185 \text{ (just as before)}$$

We have arrived at the following definition:

> **If a random phenomenon has numerical outcomes $a_1, a_2, \ldots, a_k$ that have probabilities $p_1, p_2, \ldots, p_k$, the _expected value_ is found by multiplying each outcome by its probability and then summing over all possible outcomes. In symbols,**

$$\textbf{Expected value} = a_1 p_1 + a_2 p_2 + \cdots + a_k p_k.$$

The expected value is an average of the possible outcomes, but an average in which outcomes with higher probability count more. The expected value is the average outcome in another sense as well: _If the random phenomenon is repeated many times independently, the mean value of the outcomes approaches the expected value._ Statisticians call this fact the _law of large numbers._ Because of this law, the "house" in a gambling operation is not gambling at all. The average winnings of a large number of customers will be quite close to the expected value. The house has calculated the expected value ahead of time and knows what its take will be in the long run.

The law of large numbers is closely related to our definition of probability: In many independent repetitions, the relative frequencies of the possible outcomes will be close to their probabilities, and the average outcome obtained will be close to the expected value. Expected values, since they give the "average outcome" in two senses, are widely used. Some nongambling examples are given in the exercises. Here is another gambling example:

Example 14. The numbers racket is a well-entrenched illegal gambling operation in the poorer areas of most large cities. The New York City version works as follows: You choose any one of the 1000 three-digit numbers 000 to 999 and pay your friendly local numbers runner 50 cents to enter your bet. Each day, one three-digit number is chosen at random and pays off $300.

Amount	Probability
$300	1/1000
$0	999/1000

$$\text{Expected value} = (\$300)\left(\frac{1}{1000}\right) + (\$0)\left(\frac{999}{1000}\right) = \$0.30$$

Notice that this 30-cent expected value is considerably higher than the $18\frac{1}{2}$-cent expected value of a 50-cent New York State Lottery ticket. Crime pays.

Because the criminal organization receives many thousands of bets through its runners each day, by the law of large numbers it will have to pay out very close to 30 cents per ticket. The rest is profit. This guaranteed profit might be endangered if bets were dependent, that is, if many customers chose to bet on the same number. Some numbers (such as 333) are so popular that they are "cut numbers"; a bet on such a number pays off less than $300 if it is the winning number. For a time in the good old days, Willie Mays' batting average was a cut number. The cut numbers protect the racket against very large payouts when a popular number wins.

You might trust the state lottery to conduct an honest random drawing, but perhaps you would not trust the local branch of organized crime.* How, then, does the numbers racket choose a three-digit number each day in a way its customers can trust? The winning number is the last three digits of a large number published every day in the newspaper. In New York, this number is the total amount bet at a local race track. If $1,454,123 was bet at the track, 123 is the winning number. The race track handle is printed in newspapers, so the winning number is publicly available. And the last three digits of a large number such as this are close to being random digits. (Can you see why the first three digits are not close to random?) There was a time when the numbers racket in Jersey City, New Jersey, paid off on the winning New York State Lottery number. That's adding insult to the injury of a higher payout. In Cleveland, Pittsburgh, and Indianapolis the numbers-game payoff is based on certain stock market

---

* Maybe you shouldn't trust anyone. The New York State Lottery was closed down for almost a year in 1975 and 1976 after it was discovered that ticket holders were being cheated by the inclusion of unsold ticket numbers in the prize drawings.

tables printed in the regional edition of the *Wall Street Journal*. This edition is printed in Cleveland, and gamblers appear at the printing plant at midnight to learn the winning number. A *Journal* official told a reporter, "The cars line up bumper to bumper. You should see some of them—they're solid chrome." [4] Those, I suppose, are the racketeers, not the players. The law of large numbers guarantees the house a steady income and regular players a steady deficit.

As with probability, it is worth exploring a few fine points about expected values and the law of large numbers.

How large is a large number? The law of large numbers says that the empirical average of many trials will be close to the expected value; it doesn't say how many trials are needed to achieve this. That depends on the *variability* of the random phenomenon. Gambles with extremely variable outcomes (like state lotteries) require very large numbers of trials to ensure that the average outcome is close to the expected value. In 1977, Tom and Philomena Drake set out to invest $20,000 in lottery tickets in the hope of winning big. That would buy 40,000 tickets in the old New York lottery of Example 12. Even 40,000 tickets is not enough to be confident that their average winnings will be close to the expected value of $18\frac{1}{2}$ cents. They might well either lose everything or make a profit.* Much of the psychological allure of gambling is its unpredictability for the player; the business of gambling rests on the fact that the result is not unpredictable for the house. Though most forms of gambling are less variable than state lotteries, the layman's answer to the applicability of the law of large numbers is usually that the house plays often enough to rely on it, but you don't.

Is there a winning system? Serious gamblers often follow a system of betting in which the amount bet on each play depends on the outcome of previous plays. You might, for example, double your bet on each spin of the roulette wheel until you win—or, of course, until your fortune is exhausted. Such a system tries to take advantage of the fact that you have a memory even though the roulette wheel doesn't. Can you beat the odds with a system? No. Mathematicians have established a stronger version of the law of large numbers that says that your average winnings (the expected value) remains the same so long as successive trials of the game (such as spins of the roulette wheel) are independent and you do not have an infinite fortune to gamble with. Sorry.

How can I find expected values? You know the mathematical recipe, but that

---

* The Drakes actually invested in the Pennsylvania lottery, which like most present state lotteries has highly improbable "millionnaire drawings" that make them even more variable than the older versions. I learned about the Drakes in an Associated Press dispatch appearing in the *Lafayette Journal and Courier* of May 26, 1977.

requires that you know the probability of each outcome. Expected values too difficult to compute in this way can be found by simulation. The procedure is as before: Give a probability model and simulate many repetitions. By the law of large numbers, the average outcome of these repetitions will be close to the expected value.

Example 15. If a fair coin is tossed repeatedly, what is the expected number of trials required to obtain the first head? (Here is the same question in a different guise: What is the expected number of children a couple must have in order to have a girl?) Each random digit simulates one toss, with odd meaning head and even meaning tail. One repetition is simulated by as many digits as are required to obtain the first odd digit. Here are simulated trials using line 131 of the table of random digits, with vertical bars dividing the repetitions:

05|007| 1|663|2   81|1|9|4   1|487|3| 041|9|7|

There are 13 trials, which required the following numbers of tosses to the first head:

2, 3, 1, 3, 3, 1, 1, 2, 3, 1, 3, 1, 1

The average number of tosses required was

$$(2 + 3 + 1 + \cdots + 1)/13 = 25/13 = 1.9.$$

and this is our estimate of the expected value. (It is a good estimate; the true expected value is 2.)

A summing up

Probability and expected values give us a language to describe randomness. Random phenomena are not haphazard or chaotic any more than random sampling is haphazard. Randomness is instead a kind of order in the world, a long-run regularity as opposed to either chaos or a determinism that fixes events in advance. When randomness is present, probability answers the question "How often in the long run?" and expected value answers the question "How much in the long run?" The two answers are tied together by the definition of expected value in terms of probabilities.

It appears more and more that randomness is embedded in the way the world is made. Albert Einstein reacted to the growing emphasis on randomness in physics by saying "I cannot believe that God plays dice with the universe." Lest you have similar qualms, I remind you again that randomness is not chaos but a kind of order. Our immediate concern, however, is man-made randomness—not God's dice, but Reno's. In particular, statistical designs for data collection are founded on deliberate randomizing. The order thus introduced into the data is the basis for statistical inference, as we have noticed repeatedly and will study more thoroughly in the next chapter. If you understand probability, statistical inference is stripped of mystery. That may console you as you contemplate the remark of the great economist John Maynard Keynes on long-term orderliness: "In the long run, we are all dead."

NOTES

1. More detail can be found in the opening chapters of Florence N. David, *Games, Gods and Gambling* (London: Charles Griffin and Co., 1962). The historical information given here comes from this excellent and entertaining book.
2. Stochastic Beetles are well known in the folklore of simulation, if not in entomology. They are said to be the invention of Arthur Engle of the School Mathematics Study Group.
3. Quoted in an article by Frank J. Prial in the *New York Times* of February 17, 1976.
4. Quoted in an Associated Press dispatch appearing in the *Lafayette Journal and Courier* of March 7, 1976.

Exercises

Section 1

1. Hold a penny on edge on a flat surface with the index finger of one hand and snap it with your other index finger so that it spins rapidly until finally falling with either heads or tails upward. Repeat this 50 times and record the number of heads. What is your estimate of the probability of a head in this random experiment? (In doing this experiment, disregard any trial in which the penny does not spin for several seconds or in which it hits an obstacle.)

2. Suppose that we toss a penny. Experience shows that the probability (long-term relative frequency) of a head is close to 1/2. Suppose, then, that we toss the penny repeatedly until we get a head. What is the probability that the first head comes up in an *odd* number of tosses (1, 3, 5, and so on)? To find out, repeat this experiment 50 times, and keep a record of the number of tosses needed to get a head on each of your 50 trials.
   (a) From your experiment, estimate the probability of a head on the first toss. What value should we expect this probability to have?
   (b) Use your empirical results to estimate the probability that the first head appears on an odd-numbered toss.

3. Roll a pair of dice 100 times and record the sum of the dots on the upward faces in each trial. What is the relative frequency of 8 among these 100 trials? (It is said in the text that in the long run this relative frequency will settle down to the probability of an 8, which is about 0.14.)

4. Probability is a measure of how likely an event is to occur. Match one of the probabilities that follow with each statement of likelihood given. (The probability is usually a much more exact measure of likelihood than is the verbal statement.)

$$0, 0.01, 0.3, 0.6, 0.99, 1$$

   (a) This event is impossible. It can never occur.
   (b) This event is certain; it will occur on every trial of the random phenomenon.
   (c) This event is very unlikely, but it will occur once in a while in a long sequence of trials.
   (d) This event will occur more often than not.

5. (a) A gambler knows that red and black are equally likely to occur on each spin of a roulette wheel. He observes five consecutive reds occur and bets heavily on black at the next spin. Asked why, he explains that black is "due by the law of averages." Explain to the gambler what is wrong with this reasoning.
    (b) After hearing you explain why red and black are still equally likely after five reds on the roulette wheel, the gambler moves to a poker game. He is dealt five straight red cards. He remembers what you said, and assumes that the next card dealt in the same hand is equally likely to be red or black. Is the gambler right or wrong, and why?

6. The odds against being dealt three of a kind in a five-card poker hand are about 49-to-1. What is the probability of being dealt three of a kind?

7. An American roulette wheel contains compartments numbered 1 through 36 plus 0 and 00. Of the 38 compartments, 0 and 00 are colored green, 18 of the others are red, and 18 are black. A ball is spun in the direction opposite to the wheel's motion, and bets are made on the number where the ball comes to rest. A simple wager is *red-or-black*, in which you bet that the ball will stop in, say, a red compartment. If the wheel is fair, all 38 compartments are equally likely.
   (a) What is the probability of a red?
   (b) What are the odds against a red?

8. On page 288 are four assignments of probability to the outcomes of rolling a die. Which, if any, is *correct* for this die can be discovered only by rolling the die. But some of the models are not *legitimate* assignments of probability. Which are legitimate and which are not, and why?

		Probability		
Outcome	Model 1	Model 2	Model 3	Model 4
⚀	1/7	1/3	1/3	1
⚁	1/7	1/6	1/6	1
⚂	1/7	1/6	1/6	2
⚃	1/7	0	1/6	1
⚄	1/7	1/6	1/6	1
⚅	1/7	1/6	1/6	2

9. Make an assignment of probabilities to outcomes in each of the following cases. Be sure that your assignment has properties A and B (see p. 269).

   (a) A coin is tossed and lands heads or tails. (Assume that the coin is balanced so that either face is equally likely to come up. Probability models are often based on assuming balance or symmetry. In this case, observation supports the assumption.)

   (b) A coin is spun and lands heads or tails. (Use the result of Exercise 1 to construct a probability model that is approximately correct.)

   (c) Two coins are tossed, the four possible outcomes being (head, head), (head, tail), (tail, head), and (tail, tail). (There are many legitimate models here, that is, assignments of probability satisfying properties A and B of the text. Try to assign approximately correct probabilities. Experiment if necessary.)

10. Using the understanding of probability as long-run relative frequency, explain carefully why the following rule is true in any legitimate probability model:

    "The probability that an event does not occur is one minus the probability that the event does occur."

11. You are gambling with a fair coin, which has probability 1/2 of coming up heads on each toss. You are allowed to choose either 10 or 100 tosses.

    (a) On the first bet, you win if the relative frequency of heads is between 0.4 and 0.6. Should you choose 10 tosses or 100 tosses?

(b) On the second bet, you win if exactly half of the tosses are heads. Should you choose 10 tosses or 100 tosses?

Section 2

1. An opinion poll selects Americans over 18 at random and asks them, "If the election were held today, would you vote for Demo or Public?" Explain carefully how you would use Table A (Random Digits) to simulate the response of one voter in each of the following situations:
   (a) Of all Americans over 18, 50% would vote for Demo and 50% for Public.
   (b) Of all Americans over 18, 60% would vote for Demo and 40% for Public.
   (c) Of all Americans over 18, 40% would vote for Demo, 40% would vote for Public, and 20% are undecided.
   (d) Of all Americans over 18, 53% would vote for Demo and 47% for Public.

2. Use Table A to simulate the responses of 10 independently chosen Americans over 18 in each of the four situations of Exercise 1.
   For situation (a), use line 110.
   For situation (b), use line 111.
   For situation (c), use line 112.
   For situation (d), use line 113.

3. A student is enrolled in a self-paced course that allows three attempts to take an examination on the material. To pass the course, the student must pass the examination. The student does not study and has probability 2/10 of passing on any one attempt by luck. What is the probability of passing on at least one of the three attempts? (Assume the attempts are independent because the student is given a different examination on each attempt.)
   (a) Explain how you would simulate the student's three tries by using random digits.
   (b) Simulate this experiment 50 times by using Table A beginning at line 120. What is your estimate of the student's probability of passing the course?
   (c) Do you think the assumption that the probability of passing is the same on each trial is realistic? Why or why not?

4. A wildcat oil driller estimates that the probability of finding a producing well when he drills a hole is 0.1. If he drills 10 holes without finding oil, he will be broke. What is the probability that he will go broke? Answer this question as follows:
   (a) State a simple probability model for drilling 10 holes.
   (b) Explain how you will use random digits to simulate drilling 1 hole and then explain how to simulate drilling 10 holes.

(c) Use Table A beginning at line 140 to simulate 20 repetitions of drilling 10 holes. Estimate from this simulation the probability that the wildcatter will go broke.

5. Tossing four astragali was the most popular game of chance in Roman times. The scoring for the four possible outcomes of a single bone was

broad convex side of bone	4
broad concave side of bone	3
narrow flat side of bone	1
narrow hollow side of bone	6

Many throws of a present-day sheep's astragalus show that the approximate probability distribution for these scores is

Score	Probability
1	1/10
3	4/10
4	4/10
6	1/10

The best throw of four astragali was the "Venus," when all the four uppermost sides were different. [From Florence N. David, *Games, Gods and Gambling* (London: Charles Griffin and Co., 1962), p. 7.]

(a) Explain how to simulate the throw of a single astragalus and of four independent astragali.

(b) Simulate 25 throws of four astragali. Estimate the probability of throwing a "Venus."

6. The Pennsylvania State Lottery (in 1974 and neglecting a few gimmicks) worked as follows: Each lottery ticket bears a six-digit number. Suppose that you have ticket 123456. A weekly winning number is drawn at random, so every six-digit number has the same chance to be drawn. You win

$50,000 if the winning number is 123456

$2000 if the winning number is X23456 or 12345X

$200 if the winning number is XX3456 or 1234XX

$40 if the winning number is XXX456 or 123XXX

where X stands for any nonmatching number.

(a) Explain how to simulate one play of this lottery by using Table A to draw the weekly winning number.

(b) Simulate 20 plays of the lottery and record the weekly winning numbers drawn.

(c) On which plays did your ticket 123456 win a prize, and what were the values of the prizes won?

(d) Based on your 20 trials, what is your estimate of the probability of winning a prize if you hold one ticket in this lottery?

7. From your experience with random digits, you can find the exact value of the probability of winning the Pennsylvania lottery as it is given in Exercise 6.

(a) How many different six-digit numbers are there?

(b) How many of these will pay you each of

$$\$50,000 \qquad \$2000 \qquad \$200 \qquad \$40$$

if drawn as the weekly winning number?

(c) Now find the total number of winning numbers that will pay you a prize. From this and part (a), find the probability of winning a prize.

8. Females of the Benign Boiler Beetle have the following reproductive pattern:

> 40% die without female offspring
>
> 40% have one female offspring
>
> 20% have two female offspring

(a) Explain how you would use random digits to simulate the number of offspring of a single female Benign Boiler Beetle.

(b) Simulate the family trees to the fifth generation of enough of these beetles to decide whether the population will definitely die out, will definitely grow rapidly, or appears to barely hold its own. (Simulate the offspring of at least five beetles.)

9. A nuclear reactor is equipped with two independent automatic shutdown systems to shut down the reactor when the core temperature reaches the danger level. Neither system is perfect: System A shuts down the reactor 90% of the time when the danger level is reached; system B does so 80% of the time. The reactor is shut down if *either* system works.

(a) Explain how to simulate the response of system A to a dangerous temperature level.

(b) Explain how to simulate the response of system B to a dangerous temperature level.

(c) Both systems are in operation simultaneously. Combine your answers to (a) and (b) to simulate the response of both systems to a dangerous temperature level. Explain why you cannot use the same random digit to simulate both responses.

(d) Now simulate 100 trials of the reactor's response to an emergency of this kind. Estimate the probability that it will shut down.

10. The game of craps is played with two dice. The player rolls both dice and

wins immediately if the outcome (the sum of the faces) is 7 or 11. If the outcome is 2, 3, or 12, the player loses immediately. If he rolls any other outcome, he continues to throw the dice until he either wins by repeating the first outcome or loses by rolling a 7.

(a) Explain how to simulate the roll of a single fair die. (It is easiest to use one digit and skip those not needed to represent outcomes.) Then explain how to simulate a roll of two fair dice.

(b) Use Table A beginning at line 114 to simulate three plays of craps. Explain at each throw of the dice what the result was.

(c) Now that you understand craps, simulate 25 plays and estimate the probability that the player wins.

11. A famous example in probability theory shows that the probability that at least two people in a room have the same birthday is already greater than 1/2 when 23 people are in the room. The probability model for this situation is

(a) The birth date of a randomly chosen person is equally likely to be any of the 365 dates of the year.

(b) The birth dates of different people in the room are independent.

Explain carefully how you would simulate the birth dates of 23 people to see if any two have the same birthday. Do the simulation *once* by using line 139 of Table A. [*Comment:* This simulation is most easily done by letting three-digit groups stand for the birth dates of successive people. Some groups must be skipped in doing this. The simulation is too lengthy to ask you to repeat it many times, but in principle you can find the probability of matching birthdays by routine repetition. This birthday problem is too hard for most of your math-major friends to solve, so it shows the power of simulation.]

12. In Example 10, I commented that the responses of successive units drawn in an SRS are not truly independent but that the dependence is negligible if the population is large. Let's examine this comment.

(a) An urn contains 10 balls, of which 8 are red and 2 are white. One ball is drawn at random. What is the probability that it is red? That it is white?

(b) The first ball is the first unit in our SRS from this population of 10 balls. We set it aside, and draw a second ball from the urn at random. If the first ball was red, what is the probability that the second is red? (*Hint:* What are the colors of the 9 balls left in the urn?)

(c) If the first ball was white, what is the probability that the second is red?

Because the probability that the second ball drawn is red when we know the color of the first ball drawn changes with the color of the first ball, the first and second responses in our SRS are *not* independent.

(d) Now answer the questions of parts (a), (b), and (c) again, this time for an urn containing 100,000 balls, of which 80,000 are red and 20,000 white.

The probability of a red on the second draw still changes with the color of the first draw. But the difference is now so small that we can ignore it. That leaves us with the probability model of Example 10. No probability model exactly describes a real-world random phenomenon, so we are satisfied with this one.

Section 3

1. The Connecticut State Lottery (in its original simple form and ignoring some gimmicks that raise the payout slightly) awarded at random, for each 100,000 50-cent tickets sold,

1	$5000 prize
18	$200 prizes
120	$25 prizes
270	$20 prizes

What is the expected value of the winnings of one ticket in this lottery?

2. Green Mountain Numbers, the Vermont state lottery, offers a choice of several bets. In each case, the player chooses a three-digit number. The lottery commission announces the winning number, chosen at random, at the end of the day. Find the expected winnings for a $1 bet for each of the following options in this lottery:
   (a) The "triple" pays $500 if your chosen number exactly matches the winning number.
   (b) The "box" pays $83.33 if your chosen number has the same digits as the winning number, in any order. (Assume that you chose a number having three distinct digits.)

3.   (a) What is the expected number of female offspring produced by a female Asian Stochastic Beetle? (See Example 11 of Section 2 for this insect's reproductive pattern.)
   (b) What is the expected number of female offspring produced by a female Benign Boiler Beetle? (See Exercise 8 of Section 2.)
   (c) Use the law of large numbers to explain why the population should grow if the expected number of female offspring is greater than 1 and die out if this expected value is less than 1. Do your expected values in parts (a) and (b) confirm the results of the simulations of these populations done in Section 2?

4. An insurance company sells a term life insurance policy that pays $10,000 if the insured dies within the next five years. The insured is a 21-year-old

male, and the probability that he will die in each of the next five years can be found in *mortality tables* that record what fraction of men die at each age. Since the company collects a premium of $50 per year, the net payout if the insured dies is $10,000 less the premiums collected. Here is the table containing this information:

Outcome	Probability	Payout
Insured dies at 21	0.0018	$9950
Insured dies at 22	0.0018	$9900
Insured dies at 23	0.0019	$9850
Insured dies at 24	0.0019	$9800
Insured dies at 25	0.0020	$9750
Insured lives past 25	0.9906	0

What is the expected value of the payout on this policy?

5. Grocery store games are required by law to disclose the available prizes and the odds of winning each prize. From this information you can compute the expected value of the game. Here is the prize disclosure for one such game:

Prize disclosure

Prize values	Number of prizes	Odds of winning With 1 card	With 13 cards
$1000	26	1 in 120, 000	1 in 9231
$100	130	1 in 24,000	1 in 1847
$10	650	1 in 4800	1 in 370
$2	2600	1 in 1200	1 in 93
$1	49,400	1 in 64	1 in 5

A customer receives one card on each visit to the store.
   (a) What is the expected value of one card?
   (b) What is the expected value of 13 cards?

6. We play a game by reading a pair of random digits from Table A. If the two digits are the same (for example, 2 and 2), you win $10. If they differ by one (for example, 1 and 0, 7 and 8, or 9 and 0—note that we say 0 and 9 differ by one), you win $5. Otherwise, you lose $3. What is your expected outcome in this game?

7. A "psychic" runs the following ad in a magazine:

Expecting a baby? Renowned psychic will tell you the sex of the unborn child from any photograph of the mother. Cost $10. Money-back guarantee.

This may be a profitable con game. Suppose that the psychic simply replies "girl" to each inquiry. In the worst case, everyone who has a boy will ask for her money back. Find the expected value of the psychic's profit by filling in the table below.

Sex of child	Probability	Profit in this case
Male		
Female		

8. Use the probability distribution of prizes for the Pennsylvania State Lottery (Exercise 7 in Section 2) to compute the expected value of the winnings from one ticket in this lottery.

9. Simulate the offspring (one generation only) of 100 female Asian Stochastic Beetles. What is your estimate of the expected number of offspring of one such beetle, based on this simulation? Compare the simulated value with the exact expected value you found in Exercise 3(a). Explain how your results illustrate the law of large numbers.

10. Section 2 opened with a discussion of a couple who plan to have children until they have either a girl or four children. What is the expected number of children that such a couple will have? (We don't know enough mathematics to find this expected value from the definition, so we must use simulation. Do the simulation as outlined in Section 2, and make 30 repetitions.)

11. If your state has a lottery, find out what percent of the money bet is returned to the bettors in the form of prizes. What percent of the money bet is used by the state to pay lottery expenses, and what percent is net revenue to the state that can be used for other purposes?

12. Write a brief essay giving arguments for and against state-run lotteries as a means of financing state governments. Conclude the essay by explaining why you support or oppose such lotteries.

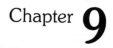

Formal statistical reasoning

How shall we come to sound conclusions from empirical evidence? How shall we decide, for example, whether large doses of vitamin C reduce the incidence of colds and flu? Or how shall we decide whether the 1970 draft lottery was biased in favor of men born early in the year? It may happen that the evidence is so clear that no reasonable person would argue with our conclusion. If in a randomized and controlled experiment 80% of the placebo group caught colds during the winter while only 30% of the vitamin C group did so, who would hesitate to recommend vitamin C? If in 1970 the 31 birthdates in December had all got draft numbers less than 50, the unfairness of the lottery would have been obvious. So it may happen that simply describing the data by graphs or descriptive statistics points to the conclusion. But it happens at least as often that the data only hint at the proper conclusion. In the Toronto vitamin C trial (Example 7 on p. 72), 18% of the placebo group and 26% of the vitamin C group were free of illness. Is this good evidence that vitamin C prevents colds and flu? Or is the difference (26% versus 18%) so small that we should instead conclude that vitamin C is not noticeably more effective than a placebo? Common sense is not enough to answer such questions. We need systematic methods for drawing conclusions from data. Such methods make up the subject of *statistical inference*.

Drawing conclusions in pure mathematics is a matter of starting from a hypothesis and using accepted methods of logical argument to prove without doubt that the conclusion follows. Empirical science argues in almost the reverse order.

If vitamin C prevents colds, we would expect the vitamin C group to have fewer colds than the placebo group; the vitamin C group did have fewer colds, so this is evidence in favor of vitamin C's effect. This is an *inductive argument* (from consequences back to a hypothesis) as opposed to the *deductive arguments* of pure mathematics (from hypothesis to consequences). Inductive arguments do not produce proof. The good health of the vitamin C group *might* be due to something other than the vitamin C they took. You have no doubt heard that "statistics cannot prove anything." True enough. Neither can any other kind of inductive argument. Outside mathematics there is no proof. But inductive arguments can be quite convincing, and statistical arguments are sometimes among the most convincing.

In Chapter 8 I side-stepped the heated philosophical argument over "What is probability?" by explaining probability theory simply as the vocabulary used to describe the observed phenomenon of randomness. Now we again face an area of controversy—controversy that this time we cannot quite ignore. Since inductive arguments seem in general harder to grasp than deductive arguments, it is not surprising that statisticians disagree over the proper kind of reasoning for drawing conclusions from data. I have chosen to give most of this chapter over to the kinds of statistical reasoning most favored by users of statistics. Even theoreticians who believe that the users have poor taste cannot fault me for a choice solidly based on such empirical grounds. The final section of the chapter will bring to light some of the controversies surrounding statistical inference by introducing a way of thinking about the subject quite different from those appearing in earlier sections.

One principle is agreed upon by all sides in the discussion about statistical inference: *Formal statistical reasoning is based on the laws of probability.* The views of statistics presented in this chapter are based on the approach to probability emphasized in Chapter 8. Probability there was long-term relative frequency.* So formal statistical reasoning is based on considering what would happen in many repetitions of the experiment or survey. This entire chapter is a working out of that idea.

Here is a distinction that you first met in Chapter 1 and that you absolutely must keep in mind when thinking about statistical inference:

> A *parameter* is a number describing the population. For example, the proportion of the population with some special property is a parameter that we call p. In a statistical inference problem, the population parameters are fixed numbers, but we do not know their values.

---

* Another school of thought holds that statistical reasoning should begin with the "personal" or "subjective" idea of probability as a personal assessment of chance. Of this I will say nothing.

A *statistic* is a number describing the sample data. For example, the proportion of the sample with some special property is a statistic that we call $\hat{p}$. Statistics change from sample to sample. We use the observed statistics to get information about the unknown parameters.

1.   Estimating with confidence

Senator Bean wants very much to know what fraction of the voters in his state plan to vote for him in the election, now only a month away. (This unknown proportion of the population of voters is a *parameter p*.) He therefore commissions a poll. Being rich, he can afford a genuine SRS of 1000 registered voters. Of these voters, 570 say that they plan to vote for Bean. That's a reassuring 57% of those polled. (This observed proportion of the sample is a

"It was a numbers explosion."

statistic, $\hat{p}$ = 0.57.) But wait. Bean and his pollster know very well that a different sample of 1000 voters would no doubt have produced a different response— perhaps 59% or 55%. Or perhaps even 51% or (horrors) 49%. How should the senator interpret the 57% sample result?

If you advised the senator to demand a confidence statement, you may join the chorus of the wise. A confidence statement will attach a margin of error to that 57% estimate and also state how confident we can be that the true fraction of voters who favor Bean falls within the margin of error. Confidence statements are based on the distribution of values of the sample proportion $\hat{p}$ that would occur if many independent SRSs were taken from the same population. This is the *sampling distribution* of the statistic $\hat{p}$. Armed with the language of probability, we now see that the sampling distribution is the *probability distribution* of $\hat{p}$: It gives the probability of each possible outcome for $\hat{p}$.

A probability distribution is interpreted exactly like a relative frequency distribution. Instead of describing a particular set of data, it describes the distribution that would arise after many, many repetitions. For example (to return to the senator), suppose that in fact 55% of the several million voters in Bean's state plan to vote for him. What would be the pattern (probability distribution) of the sample proportion $\hat{p}$ favoring Bean in many, many independent SRSs of size 1000?

We could discover this pattern by a very long simulation. Fortunately, it is also possible to discover the pattern by mathematics, and I will tell you the answer. The probability distribution of the sample proportion $\hat{p}$ favoring Bean in an SRS of size 1000 when 55% of the population favor Bean is very close to the normal distribution with mean 0.55 and standard deviation 0.015. If you don't believe me, go and simulate several thousand SRSs of size 1000 from such a population and make a histogram of the several thousand values of $\hat{p}$ you get. That histogram will look very much like the normal curve with mean 0.55 and standard deviation 0.015. (Because $\hat{p}$ is unbiased, you could guess that the mean of the distribution of $\hat{p}$ is 0.55 when the true p is 0.55.) We did a similar "simulation" in the bead-sampling experiment of Chapter 1, with results that appear in Figures 4-12, 4-13, and 4-14 of Chapter 4. That the probability distribution of a sample proportion $\hat{p}$ is close to normal is not news to you.

Figure 9-1 shows the probability distribution of the sample proportion $\hat{p}$ in Senator Bean's case. This distribution shares the properties of all normal curves, which were described in Section 3 of Chapter 5. But now we can use the language of probability instead of relative frequency. The 68-95-99.7 rule can be stated for Figure 9-1 as follows:

- The probability is 0.68 that an SRS of size 1000 from this population will have a $\hat{p}$ between 0.535 and 0.565 (because 0.535 is one standard deviation below the mean and 0.565 is one standard deviation above).

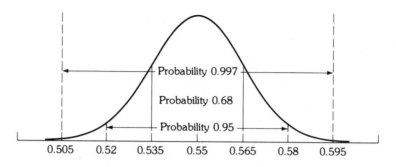

Figure 9-1. The probability distribution of a statistic. The sample proportion $\hat{p}$ of an SRS of size 1000 drawn from a population in which the population proportion is $p = 0.55$ has the normal probability distribution shown. The probability is 0.95 that $\hat{p}$ will fall within two standard deviations of p.

- The probability is 0.95 that an SRS of size 1000 from this population will have a $\hat{p}$ between 0.52 and 0.58, that is, within two standard deviations of the mean.

- The probability is 0.997 (almost certainty) that an SRS of size 1000 from this population will have a $\hat{p}$ between 0.505 and 0.595.

Senator Bean is becoming impatient. We are telling him how $\hat{p}$ behaves for a known population proportion p. He wants to know what he can say about p (the *unknown* fraction of voters who are for him) once he has taken a sample and observed $\hat{p} = 0.57$. Patience, senator. We're coming to that. Chew on this line of argument.

A. When an SRS of size 1000 is chosen from a large population of which a proportion p favor Bean, the proportion $\hat{p}$ of the sample who favor Bean has approximately the normal distribution with mean equal to p and standard deviation 0.015.*

B. By the 68-95-99.7 rule, the probability is 0.95 that $\hat{p}$ will be within 0.03 (two standard deviations) of its mean p.

C. That's exactly the same as saying that the probability is 0.95 that the unknown p is within 0.03 of the observed $\hat{p}$.

---

* Actually, the standard deviation changes when p changes. But for p anywhere between $p = 0.3$ and $p = 0.7$, the standard deviation of $\hat{p}$ is within 0.001 of 0.015. You can find more detailed information in Section 2.

Aha! We see that 95% of all such SRSs produce a $\hat{p}$ within 0.03 of the true p. Bean's SRS had $\hat{p}$ = 0.57. So he can be quite confident that the true proportion of voters who favor him lies in the interval between

$$\hat{p} - 0.03 = 0.57 - 0.03 = 0.54$$

and

$$\hat{p} + 0.03 = 0.57 + 0.03 = 0.60.$$

Bean can be confident that he's favored by between 54% and 60% of the population.

Be sure you understand the ground of his confidence. There are only two possibilities. *Either* the true p lies between 0.54 and 0.60, *or* Bean's SRS was one of the few samples for which $\hat{p}$ is not within 0.03 of the true p. Only 5% of all samples give such inaccurate results, because of the 95% rule. It is not impossible that Bean had the bad luck to draw a sample for which $\hat{p}$ misses p by more than 0.03, but over many drawings this will happen only 5% of the time (probability 0.05). We say that Bean is "95% confident" that he is favored by between 54% and 60% of the voters.

Bean is a cautious man, and a method that will be right 95% of the time and wrong 5% of the time is not good enough for him. Very well, let's use the 99.7% rule. The probability is 0.997 that $\hat{p}$ falls within 0.045 (three standard deviations) of its mean p. So Bean can be 99.7% confident that the true p falls between

$$\hat{p} - 0.045 = 0.57 - 0.045 = 0.525$$

and

$$\hat{p} + 0.045 = 0.57 + 0.045 = 0.615.$$

Now he's smiling. A method that is correct 997 times in 1000 in the long run (probability 0.997) estimates that he is safely ahead.

You have just followed one of the most common lines of reasoning in formal statistical inference. Here it is in general terms:

> **A. A statistic computed from a sample survey or a randomized experiment has a probability distribution (a regular long-term pattern of outcomes) because of the randomization used to collect the data.**

> **B. This probability distribution changes when the population parameter changes. That is, the behavior of the sample statistic reflects the truth about the population.**

C. **Knowing this probability distribution, we can give a recipe for finding from the sample statistic an interval that has probability γ of covering the unknown true parameter value. This is called a *confidence interval* with confidence level γ.**

Step C is the definition of a confidence interval. (γ is the Greek letter gamma, the symbol commonly used in statistics to denote the confidence level.) Steps A and B show how confidence intervals are based on a knowledge of the probability distributions of sample statistics. This knowledge is obtained by mathematics and provides recipes for confidence intervals in many different settings. We saw two such recipes, and some of their background, in the case of Senator Bean. In our new vocabulary, if an SRS of size 1000 gives a sample proportion $\hat{p}$, we can make the following statements:

- A 95% confidence interval for the population proportion p is the interval from $\hat{p} - 0.03$ to $\hat{p} + 0.03$.

- A 99.7% confidence interval for the population proportion p is the interval from $\hat{p} - 0.045$ to $\hat{p} + 0.045$.

The key idea of a 95% confidence interval is that the recipe gives a correct answer (an interval that covers the true parameter value) 95% of the time in the long run. A 90% confidence interval is right 90% of the time, and a 99.7% confidence interval is right 99.7% of the time. Figure 9-2 shows the results of simulating 25 trials of the 95% confidence interval $\hat{p} \pm 0.03$ based on an SRS of size 1000 from a population with $p = 0.55$. The normal curve at the top of the figure is the probability distribution of the sample proportion $\hat{p}$, in this case having a mean equal to 0.55 (the true value of p) and standard deviation 0.015. Below are the confidence intervals resulting from 25 SRSs. The dot in the center of each interval is the observed value of $\hat{p}$ for that sample. The intervals shift from sample to sample, but only one of the 25 fails to cover the true p, represented by the vertical line. In the long run, the interval from $\hat{p} - 0.03$ to $\hat{p} + 0.03$ would cover the true p in 95% of all the samples drawn. This is the essential idea; as always, some fine points should be pondered. To these we now turn.

What confidence does not mean. For Senator Bean's poll, a method with probability 95% of being right estimated that he was favored by between 0.54 and 0.60 of the voters in his state. Be careful: We *cannot* say that the probability is 95% that the true p falls between 0.54 and 0.60. It either does or does not; we don't know which. No randomness is left after we draw a particular sample and get from it a particular interval, 0.54 to 0.60. So it makes no sense to give a probability. All we can say is that the interval 0.54 to 0.60 was obtained by

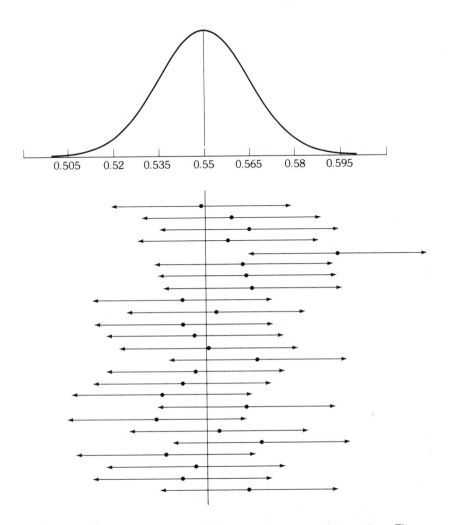

Figure 9-2. Behavior of confidence intervals in repeated sampling. The intervals above are 95% confidence intervals for p computed from 25 independent SRSs of size 1000 drawn from a population in which p = 0.55. The intervals vary from sample to sample, but all except one contain the true value of p.

a method that covers the true p in 95% of all possible samples. That's what we mean in saying we are 95% confident that p lies between 0.54 and 0.60.

High confidence is not free. Why would anyone use a 95% confidence interval when 99.7% confidence is available? Look again at Senator Bean. His 95% confidence interval was $\hat{p} \pm 0.03$, while 99.7% confidence required a wider interval, $\hat{p} \pm 0.045$. It is true in general that there is a tradeoff between the confidence level and the width of the interval. To obtain higher confidence from the same sample, you must be willing to accept a larger margin of error (wider interval). The way to get higher confidence and still have a short interval is to take a larger sample. The precision of a sample statistic increases as the sample size increases. That means that for a fixed level of confidence, the confidence interval grows ever shorter as the sample size increases. Or, if you prefer, the confidence level for an interval of the same length grows ever higher as the sample size increases.

It's a poor cook who uses the same recipe in every meal. The Gallup Poll's probability sampling method is such that when a sample of size 1000 is taken, we can be 95% confident that the announced sample proportion is within 4 points of the true population proportion. (Table 1-1 on page 20 gives this information in more detail. That table shows that the confidence statement I just made holds whenever the true population p falls between 0.3 and 0.7. Otherwise the margin of error is even smaller.) In more formal language, a 95% confidence interval for the population proportion p based on a sample of size 1000 drawn by Gallup's probability sampling method is the interval from $\hat{p} - 0.04$ to $\hat{p} + 0.04$.

Now the 95% confidence interval for an SRS of size 1000 was $\hat{p} - 0.03$ to $\hat{p} + 0.03$. That recipe is wrong for the Gallup Poll because Gallup does not use an SRS. The recipe for a confidence interval depends on how the data were collected. Section 2 gives some more-detailed recipes for use when you have an SRS. To use them when the data are not an SRS is tantamount to pouring catsup into your egg-drop soup.

You might notice that Gallup's sampling method is less precise (has a wider 95% confidence interval) than an SRS of the same size. That is the price paid for the convenience of cluster sampling.

Confidence intervals are used whenever statistical methods are applied, and some of the recipes are complicated indeed. But the idea of 95% confidence is always the same: The recipe employed catches the true parameter value 95% of the time when used repeatedly.

2. Confidence intervals for proportions and means*

Although the idea of a confidence interval remains ever the same, the specific recipes vary greatly. The form of a confidence interval depends first on the parameter you wish to estimate—a population proportion, or mean, or variance, or whatever. The second influence is the design of the sample or experiment; estimating a population proportion from a stratified sample requires a different

---

* This section is optional. It contains material more technical than the rest of the book.

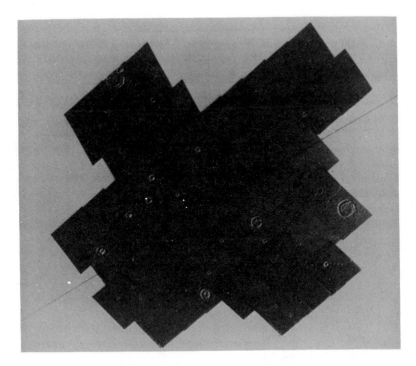

Confidence regions for a Mars landing. Predicting the landing site of an unmanned spacecraft is an exercise in estimation. The ellipses drawn on this photomosaic of the Chryse Planitia region of Mars represent NASA's before-the-act estimation of the landing site of the 1976 Viking 1 mission. The outer ellipse is a 99% confidence region; the probability was 50% that touchdown would occur within the inner ellipse. [Photo courtesy of NASA.]

recipe than if the data come from an SRS. The sampling design and the parameter to be estimated usually determine the form of the confidence interval. The final details depend on the sample size and the confidence level you choose. The two recipes in this section are quite useful, but in comparison with the statistician's full array of confidence intervals for all occasions, these two resemble a tool kit containing only a chisel and a roofing square. These are useful tools, but only sometimes.

Confidence intervals for a population proportion

When a large SRS is selected from a population, the sampling distribution of the sample proportion $\hat{p}$ is close to a normal distribution. This normal sampling distribution has mean equal to the population proportion p because $\hat{p}$ is unbiased as an estimator of p. When the sample size n is 1000 and p is between 0.3 and

0.7, the standard deviation of $\hat{p}$ is close to 0.015. So by the 68-95-99.7 rule, $\hat{p} \pm (2)(0.015)$ is a 95% confidence interval for p. The same reasoning leads to the conclusion that whenever we know the standard deviation of the sampling distribution of $\hat{p}$, a 95% confidence interval for p is

$$\hat{p} \pm (2)(\text{standard deviation of } \hat{p})$$

because 95% of the probability in the normal distribution of $\hat{p}$ falls within 2 standard deviations of the mean p.

By mathematics we can discover the standard deviation of the normal sampling distribution of $\hat{p}$. Here is the full story:

Sampling distribution of a sample proportion

Suppose that an SRS of size n is drawn from a population in which the proportion p of the units have some special property. The proportion of units in the sample having this property is the statistic $\hat{p}$. When n is large, the sampling distribution $\hat{p}$ is approximately normal with mean p and standard deviation

$$\sqrt{\frac{p(1 - p)}{n}}.$$

Figure 9-3 illustrates this sampling distribution. The standard deviation of $\hat{p}$ depends on the true p and on the sample size n. For example, when $n = 1000$ and $p = 0.5$, the standard deviation of $\hat{p}$ is

$$\sqrt{\frac{(0.5)(0.5)}{1000}} = (0.00025)^{1/2} = 0.0158$$

And when $p = 0.3$ (or 0.7), the standard deviation is

$$\sqrt{\frac{(0.3)(0.7)}{1000}} = (0.00021)^{1/2} = 0.0145.$$

These more exact results lie behind the statement in Section 1 that for p between 0.3 and 0.7, the standard error of $\hat{p}$ in an SRS of size 1000 is close to 0.015.

We now know that a more accurate recipe for a 95% confidence interval for p, taking p and n into account, is

$$\hat{p} \pm 2 \sqrt{\frac{p(1 - p)}{n}}.$$

But this formula is unusable because we don't know p. (If we did know p, we would not need to settle for 95% confidence!) When n is large, $\hat{p}$ is quite close

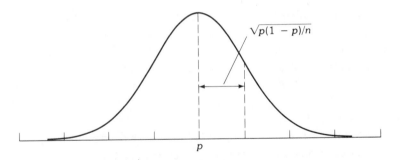

Figure 9-3. The distribution of $\hat{p}$ in a large SRS. The probability distribution of $\hat{p}$ is approximately normal with mean equal to the population proportion p. The standard deviation is $\sqrt{p(1-p)/n}$, which decreases as larger sample sizes n are chosen.

to p. So at the cost of a further approximation, the estimated standard deviation formed by replacing p by $\hat{p}$ can be employed in the recipe. So the final version of a 95% confidence interval for p is

$$\hat{p} \pm 2\sqrt{\frac{\hat{p}(1-\hat{p})}{n}} \, .$$

All of this started with the fact that in any normal distribution there is probability 0.95 within 2 standard deviations of the mean. What if we want a 90% confidence interval, or a 75% confidence interval? For any number γ between 0 and 1 ($0 < \gamma < 1$), there is a number z^* such that any normal distribution has probability γ within z^* standard deviations of the mean. Figure 9-4 illustrates

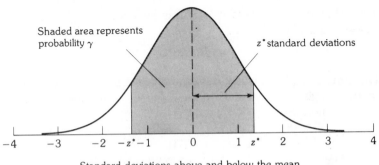

Standard deviations above and below the mean

Figure 9-4. Critical points of the normal distributions. The critical point z^* is the number such that any normal distribution assigns probability γ to the interval from z^* standard deviations below the mean to z^* standard deviations above it.

the situation, and Table C-1 in the back of the book lists the numbers z^* for various choices of γ. These numbers are often called *critical values* for the normal distributions. For example, any normal distribution has probability 0.90 within ± 1.64 standard deviations of its mean. And any normal distribution has probability 0.95 within ± 1.96 standard deviations of its mean. (The number $z^* = 1.96$ was rounded off to 2 in giving the 68-95-99.7 rule.)

Now for the final assault on p. With probability γ, the sample proportion $\hat{p}$ is within z^* standard deviations of p. Otherwise said, the unknown p is within z^* standard deviations of the observed $\hat{p}$ with probability γ. Using the estimated standard deviation of $\hat{p}$ produces at last the following recipe:

> **Confidence interval for a population proportion**
>
> **Suppose that an SRS of size n is drawn from a population of units of which proportion p have some special characteristic. When n is large, an approximate level γ confidence interval for p is**
>
> $$\hat{p} \pm z^* \sqrt{\frac{\hat{p}(1 - \hat{p})}{n}}$$
>
> **where z^* is the two-sided critical value for γ.**

Please note that this recipe is valid only when an SRS is chosen. Even then it is only approximately correct, for two reasons. First, the sampling distribution of $\hat{p}$ is only approximately normal. Second, the estimated standard deviation of $\hat{p}$ is only approximately equal to the exact standard deviation $\sqrt{p(1 - p)/n}$. Both of these approximations improve as the sample size n increases. For samples of size 100 and larger, the recipe given is quite accurate. It is often used for sample sizes as small as 25 or 30. If you have a small sample, or if your sample is not an SRS, please visit your friendly local statistician for advice. Now for some examples.

> **Example 1.** Senator Bean, our acquaintance from Section 1, took an SRS of 1000 registered voters. Of these, 570 supported the Senator in his bid for reelection. So
>
> $$\hat{p} = \frac{570}{1000} = 0.57$$
>
> and the estimated standard deviation of $\hat{p}$ is
>
> $$\sqrt{\frac{\hat{p}(1 - \hat{p})}{n}} = \sqrt{\frac{(0.57)(0.43)}{1000}} = 0.0157.$$

A 95% confidence interval for the proportion p of all registered voters who support Bean is therefore

$$\hat{p} \pm z^* \sqrt{\frac{\hat{p}(1 - \hat{p})}{n}}$$

$$= 0.57 \pm (1.96)(0.0157)$$

$$= 0.57 \pm 0.031$$

or 0.54 to 0.60. This is the same result we found in Section 1. If Bean insists on 99% confidence, the interval is

$$\hat{p} \pm z^* \sqrt{\frac{\hat{p}(1 - \hat{p})}{n}}$$

$$= 0.57 \pm (2.58)(0.0157)$$

$$= 0.57 \pm 0.041$$

or 0.53 to 0.61. As usual, higher confidence exacts its price in the form of a larger margin of error.

Example 2. On page 52, a news article reports a Gallup Poll of 1506 adults. Thirty-three percent of these believed (incorrectly) that the United States is self-sufficient in oil. If Gallup had used an SRS, a 95% confidence interval for the proportion of American adults who share the delusion that we need not import oil would be

$$\hat{p} \pm z^* \sqrt{\frac{\hat{p}(1 - \hat{p})}{n}}$$

$$= 0.33 \pm (1.96) \sqrt{\frac{(0.33)(0.67)}{1506}}$$

$$= 0.33 \pm 0.024.$$

(In fact, Gallup does not use an SRS, so this recipe is not appropriate. See Exercise 3 of Section 1 for Gallup's 95% confidence interval.)

Confidence intervals for a population mean

Like the sample proportion $\hat{p}$, the sample mean $\bar{x}$ from a large SRS has a sampling distribution that is close to normal. Since the sample mean of an SRS is an unbiased estimator of the mean of the population, usually denoted by μ (the Greek letter mu), μ is the mean of the sampling distribution of $\bar{x}$. The standard deviation of $\bar{x}$ depends on the standard deviation of the population, which is usually denoted by σ (the Greek letter sigma). By mathematics we can discover the following fact:

Sampling distribution of the sample mean

Suppose that an SRS of size n is drawn from a population having mean μ and standard deviation σ. The mean of the sample is the statistic $\bar{x}$. When n is large, the sampling distribution of $\bar{x}$ is approximately normal with mean μ and standard deviation $\sigma/\sqrt{n}$.

The standard deviation of $\bar{x}$ depends on both σ and the sample size n. We know n, but not σ. But when n is large, the sample standard deviation s is close to σ and can be used to estimate it. So the estimated standard deviation of $\bar{x}$ is $s/\sqrt{n}$. Now confidence intervals for μ can be found just as with p:

Confidence interval for a population mean

Suppose that an SRS of size n is drawn from a population of units having mean μ. When n is large, an approximate level γ confidence interval for μ is

$$\bar{x} \pm z^* \frac{s}{\sqrt{n}}.$$

where z^* is the two-sided critical value for probability γ.

The cautions cited in estimating p apply here as well: The recipe is valid only when an SRS is drawn and the sample size n is reasonably large.

> **Example 3.** In Exercise 1 on page 169 there appears the count of coliform bacteria per milliliter in each of 100 specimens of milk. Suppose that these specimens can be assumed to be an SRS of the milk sold in a certain region. Give a 90% confidence interval for the mean coliform count of all milk sold in that region.
>
> We first compute the sample mean and standard deviation for this set of data. The results are
>
> $$\bar{x} = 5.88 \quad s = 2.02$$
>
> so the 90% confidence interval is
>
> $$\bar{x} \pm z^* \frac{s}{\sqrt{n}}$$

$$= 5.88 \pm (1.64) \frac{2.02}{\sqrt{100}}$$

$$= 5.88 \pm 0.33.$$

We are 90% confident that the mean coliform count in the population falls between 5.55 and 6.21 per milliliter.

3. Statistical significance

Confidence intervals are one of the two most common types of statistical inference. They are appropriate when our goal is to estimate a population parameter. The second common type of inference is directed at a quite different goal: to assess the evidence provided by the data in favor of a statement. An example will illustrate the reasoning used.

Example 4. When the correlation coefficient between birth date (1 to 366) and draft number (1 to 366) for the 1970 draft lottery is calculated, we get $r = -0.226$. Is this correlation good evidence that the lottery was not random?

Formal Question: Suppose for the sake of argument that the lottery were truly random. What is the probability that a random lottery would produce an r at least as far from 0 as the observed $r = -0.226$?

Answer (from mathematics or simulation): The probability that a random draft lottery will have an r this far from 0 is less than 0.001 (one in a thousand).

Conclusion: Since an r as far from 0 as that observed in 1970 would almost never occur in a random lottery, we have strong evidence that the 1970 draft lottery was not random.

In a random assignment of draft numbers to birth dates, we would expect the correlation to be close to 0. The correlation for the 1970 lottery was -0.226, showing that men born later in the year tended to get lower draft numbers. This is not a large correlation. The scatterplot (Figure 9-5) shows little association. Common sense is not enough to decide if $r = -0.226$ means the lottery was not random. After all, the correlation will almost never be exactly 0, and perhaps $r = -0.226$ is within the range that a random lottery would be expected to produce. So as an aid to answering the informal question "Is this good evidence of a nonrandom lottery?" we stated a formal question about probabilities. We asked just how often a random lottery would produce an r as far from 0 as the r observed in 1970. The answer could be obtained by many simulations of a random lottery, but I obtained it by mathematics. If a random draft lottery were

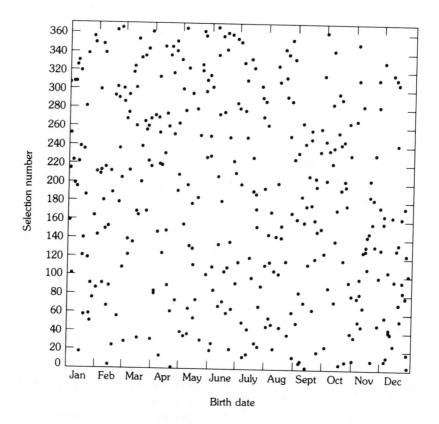

Figure 9-5. The 1970 draft lottery. The scatterplot shows the association between birth dates and draft numbers in the 1970 draft lottery. When birth dates are labeled from 1 (January 1, 1952) to 366 (December 31, 1952), their correlation with draft numbers 1 to 366 is $r = -0.226$.

run each year, a correlation as strong as that observed in 1970 would occur less than once in a thousand years! This convinces us that the 1970 lottery was biased.

Be sure you understand why this evidence is convincing. There are two possible explanations of that notorious $r = -0.226$.

(a) The lottery was random, and by bad luck a very unlikely outcome occurred.

(b) The lottery was biased, so the outcome is about what would be expected from such a lottery.

We cannot be certain that explanation (a) is untrue. The 1970 results *could* be due to chance alone. But the probability that such results would occur by chance in a random lottery is so small (0.001) that we are quite confident that explanation (b) is right. Here is a second example of this reasoning:

> **Example 5.** The Toronto vitamin C experiment (Example 7 on p. 72) was a randomized double-blind experiment with about 400 subjects in each of two groups. In this study, 26% of the vitamin C group and 18% of the placebo group were free of illness through the winter. Is this good evidence that vitamin C prevents illness better than a placebo?
>
> *Formal Question:* Suppose for the sake of argument that there is no difference between the effects of vitamin C and the placebo. That is, suppose that the only difference between the two groups of volunteers is due to the random allocation in the experimental design. What is the probability of observing an outcome favoring vitamin C by 26% versus 18% or more?
>
> *Answer:* The probability that a difference this large would occur because of the random allocation alone is less than 0.01 (one in a hundred).
>
> *Conclusion:* Since a difference as large as the one actually observed would occur only one time in a hundred if vitamin C has no more effect than a placebo, there is good evidence that vitamin C is more effective than a placebo.

The reasoning used in these examples is codified in *tests of significance*. In both examples, we hoped to show that an effect was present—that the draft lottery was biased in Example 4, and that vitamin C outperformed the placebo in Example 5. To do this, we began by supposing for the sake of argument that the effect we sought was not present. In Example 4, we supposed that the lottery was random, not biased. In Example 5, we supposed that a volunteer given vitamin C was no more likely to be free of illness than one given a placebo. We then looked for evidence against the supposition we made. Such evidence is also evidence in favor of the effect we hoped to find. But the first step in tests of significance is to state a claim that we will try to find evidence against.

> **The statement being tested in a test of significance is called the *null hypothesis*. The test of significance is designed to assess the strength of the evidence against the null hypothesis. Usually the null hypothesis is a statement of "no difference" or "no effect."**

The term "null hypothesis" is abbreviated as H_0, which is read "H-nought." It is usually stated in terms of some population parameter or parameters. For example, suppose that p_1 is the proportion of the whole population of North American males who would have been illness-free in 1971 if they had taken a gram of vitamin C each day, and let p_2 stand for the illness-free proportion if a placebo were given instead. Then the null hypothesis of Example 5 is

$$H_0: p_1 = p_2$$

because this says that vitamin C has the same effectiveness as a placebo. It is useful to give a name to the statement we hope or suspect is true instead of H_0. This is called the *alternative hypothesis* and is abbreviated by H_1. In Example 5, the alternative hypothesis is that vitamin C is more effective than a placebo. In terms of population parameters this is

$$H_1\colon p_1 > p_2.$$

A test of significance assesses the strength of the evidence against the null hypothesis in terms of probability. If the observed outcome is unlikely under the supposition that the null hypothesis is true, but is more probable if the alternative hypothesis is true, that outcome is evidence against H_0 in favor of H_1. The less probable the outcome is, the stronger is the evidence that H_0 is false. Now, usually any individual outcome has low probability. It is unlikely that a random draft lottery would give exactly $r = 0$, but if we observed $r = 0$ we would certainly not have evidence against the null hypothesis that the lottery is random. Our procedure is therefore to say what kinds of outcomes would count as evidence against H_0 and in favor of H_1. In the draft lottery case, correlations r away from 0 (either positive or negative) count against the hypothesis of a random lottery. The farther from 0 the observed r is, the stronger the evidence. The probability that measures the strength of the evidence that the 1970 lottery is nonrandom is therefore the probability that a random lottery would produce an r *at least as far from* 0 as the 1970 lottery did.

In general, we find the probability of getting an outcome at least as far as the actually observed outcome from what we would expect when H_0 is true. What counts as "far from what we would expect" depends on H_1 as well as H_0. In Example 4, an observed r away from 0 *in either direction* is evidence of a nonrandom lottery. In Example 5, we wanted to know if vitamin C was more effective than a placebo (that's H_1). So evidence against H_0 is measured by the probability that the percent illness-free in the vitamin C group *exceeds* that percent in the placebo group by as much as 26% versus 18%.

> **The probability of getting an outcome at least as far from what we would expect if H_0 were true as was the actually observed outcome is called the *P-value*. The smaller the P-value is, the stronger is the evidence against H_0 provided by the data.**

One final step is sometimes taken in assessing the evidence against H_0. We can compare the evidence we obtained with a fixed level of evidence that we regard as decisive. Because the strength of the evidence provided by the data is measured by the P-value, we need only say how small a P-vlaue we insist on. This decisive value is called the *significance level*. It is always denoted by α, the Greek letter alpha. If we take $\alpha = 0.05$, we are requiring that the data give evidence against H_0 so strong that it would happen no more than 5% of the time (one time in twenty) when H_0 is really true. If we take $\alpha = 0.01$, we are insisting on stronger evidence against H_0, evidence so strong that it would appear only 1% of the time (one time in a hundred) if H_0 is really true. If the P-value is as small or smaller than α, we say that the data are *statistically significant at level* α. This is just a way of saying that the evidence against the null hypothesis reached the standard set by the level α. A common abbreviation for significance at, say, level 0.01 is "The results were significant ($P < 0.01$)." Here P stands for the P-value.

A recipe for testing the significance of the evidence against a null hypothesis H_0 is called a *test of significance* (or a *test of hypotheses*, but I will save that language for a slightly different kind of reasoning, which we will meet in Section 5). Courses on statistical methods teach many such recipes for different hypotheses H_0 and H_1, for different significance levels α, and for different data-collection designs. An outline of what such a recipe must include appears in the boxed section below. We are concerned not with any specific recipe but rather with the reasoning that lies behind all such recipes. You are now well prepared to understand the meaning of conclusions stated in terms of statistical significance. "The results of the Toronto vitamin C experiment were significant at level $\alpha = 0.01$" summarizes in one sentence the long chain of reasoning we followed in discussing Example 5. It means that the experimental evidence favoring vitamin C was so strong that it would appear in less than 1% of a long series of experiments if the only difference between the experimental and control groups is due to random allocation of subjects.

Steps in a test of significance

(a) Choose the *null hypothesis* H_0 and the *alternative hypothesis* H_1. The test is designed to assess the strength of the evidence against H_0. H_1 is a statement of the alternative we will accept if the evidence enables us to reject H_0.

(b) (Optional) Choose the *significance level* α. This states how much evidence against H_0 we will accept as decisive.

(c) Choose the *test statistic* on which the test will be based. This is a statistic which measures how well the data conform to H_0. In Example 4, the correlation coefficient was used because in a random lottery there should be little or no correlation between birth date and draft number.

(d) Find the *P-value* for the observed data. This is the probability that the test statistic would weigh against H_0 at least as strongly as it does for these data if H_0 were in fact true. If the P-value is less than or equal to α, the test was *statistically significant at level* α.

To review and solidify this introduction to tests of significance, here is a concluding example:

> **Example 6.** Is a new method of teaching reading to first graders (method B) more effective than the method now in use (method A)? An experiment is called for. We will use a *paired-sample experimental design:* 20 pairs of first graders are available, with the two children in each pair carefully matched in IQ, socioeconomic status, reading-readiness score, and other variables that may influence their reading performance. One student from each pair is randomly assigned to method A, while the other student in the pair is taught by method B. At the end of first grade, all the children take a test of reading skill.
>
> (a) We want to know if the new method B is superior to the old method A. So the null hypothesis is that method B and method A are equally effective. We will examine the experimental evidence against this H_0 in favor of the alternative that method B is more effective. To state H_0 and H_1 in terms of parameters, and later to do the necessary simulation, we must give a probability model for the experiment. The children in each pair are (as closely as possible) exactly identical as reading students. So if the two teaching methods are equally effective, each child has the same chance to score higher on the test. Let p stand for the proportion of all possible matched pairs of children for which the child taught by method B will have the higher score. The null hypothesis is
>
> $$H_0: p = 1/2$$
>
> and the alternative is
>
> $$H_1: p > 1/2.$$
>
> We can think of p as the probability that the method-B child in any one pair will do better.
>
> (b) We choose $\alpha = 0.10$. That is, we are willing to say that method B is better if it shows a superiority in the experiment that would occur no more than 10% of the time if the two methods were equally effective.
>
> (c) The test statistic is the number of pairs out of 20 in which the child taught by method B has a higher score. The larger this number is, the stronger is the evidence that method B is better.
>
> (d) Now we take a year off to do the experiment. The result is that method B gave the higher score in 12 of the 20 groups. The *P*-value for these data is the probability that 12 *or more* pairs out of 20 favor method B when H_0 is true. This is exactly the same as the probability of 12 or more heads in 20 tosses of a coin with heads and tails equally likely. We find this probability by simulation as follows:
>
> Step 1. Each random digit simulates one pair of students.
>
> | odd | method A scores higher |
> |------|------------------------|
> | even | method B scores higher |

Step 2. One repetition requires 20 digits representing 20 pairs of students.

Step 3. Begin simulating at line 110 of Table A, recording for each repetition how many times B scored higher.

38448	48789	18338	24697	
ABBBB	BBABA	ABAAB	BBBAA	12 Bs
39364	42006	76688	08708	
AAABB	BBBBB	ABBBB	BBABB	15 Bs
81486	69487	60513	09297	
BABBB	BABBA	BBAAA	BABAA	11 Bs
00412	71238	27649	39950	
BBBAB	AABAB	BABBA	AAAAB	10 Bs

and so on. In these four trials the relative frequency of 12 or more Bs was 1/2. Many more trials are needed to estimate the probability precisely. When they are made, the probability of 12 or more Bs in 20 pairs of students is 0.25. This is the P-value. The P-value did not reach the required level of significance. The experimental results were not statistically significant at the $\alpha = 0.10$ level. We do not have adequate evidence that method B is superior to Method A.

4. Significance tests for proportions and means*

As is the case for confidence intervals, statisticians have developed tests of significance for use in many different circumstances. The recipes for carrying out these tests generally have two parts: a statistic that measures the effect being sought and a probability distribution for the statistic that gives the corresponding P-value. Tests are now often implemented by computer routines that compute the test statistic and its P-value starting from the raw data. The computer will not explain to you what statistical significance means, however. Your understanding of the reasoning common to all tests is therefore more valuable than knowledge of the specific procedures discussed in this section.

Tests for a population proportion

Inspired by Senator Bean's use of polls and statistics, his colleague Senator Caucus commissions an SRS of 1200 registered voters in her state. The poll finds that 53% of the sample plan to vote for Caucus. We know how to use this sample result $\hat{p} = 0.53$ to give a confidence interval for the unknown proportion p of all voters who favor Caucus. But the senator just wants to know

---

* This section is optional. It contains material more technical than the rest of the book.

if she's ahead. Does the sample provide strong evidence that a majority of the population plan to vote for Caucus? We wish to test the null hypothesis

$$H_0: p = 0.5$$

against the alternative hypothesis

$$H_1: p > 0.5.$$

As usual, H_1 states that the effect we seek (a majority for Caucus) is present, and H_0 that the effect is absent.

The statistic is $\hat{p}$. We recorded the sampling distribution of $\hat{p}$ on page 306. One point to emphasize is that for computing the P-value we must use the sampling distribution *assuming that the null hypothesis is true*. Since H_0 states that $p = 0.5$, the distribution of $\hat{p}$ is then approximately normal with mean 0.5 and standard deviation

$$\sqrt{\frac{p(1 - p)}{n}} = \sqrt{\frac{(0.5)(0.5)}{1200}} = 0.0144.$$

The P-value is the probability that a statistic having this distribution will take a value at least as large as 0.53, the actual observed value of $\hat{p}$. Figure 9-6 illustrates this probability as an area under a normal curve.

To find this probability, recall again that all normal distributions are the same when measured in standard deviation units from the mean. So convert $\hat{p} = 0.53$ to a standard score.

$$z = \frac{0.53 - 0.5}{0.0144} = 2.1.$$

Table B shows that a standard score of 2.1 corresponds to the 98.2 percentile. The P-value is therefore $P = 0.018$, since if 98.2% of the distribution lies below 2.1, the remaining 1.8% lies above. Senator Caucus is pleased. If the race were even, there is only probability 0.018 that the poll would show her as far ahead as it did. This is good evidence that she actually is ahead.

If a particular degree of evidence, stated as a significance level α, is required, the test procedure is simpler. Compute the standard score as before, and compare it with the number z^* such that any normal distribution has probability α falling more than z^* standard deviations above the mean. If the standard score is greater than z^*, the observed $\hat{p}$ is statistically significant at level α. The numbers z^* are *one-sided critical values* for the normal distribution. They are not the same as the two-sided critical values used in Section 2. Table C-2 at the back

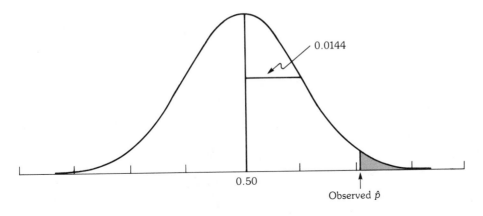

Figure 9-6. The P-value for Senator Caucus's poll. The normal curve is the sampling distribution of $\hat{p}$ assuming that the null hypothesis is true. The shaded area represents the P-value.

of the book lists the numbers z^* for various choices of α. We can now give the following recipe:

> **Suppose that an SRS of size n is drawn from a population of units of which proportion p have some special characteristic. When n is large, a test of**

$$H_0\!: p = p_0 \text{ vs. } H_1\!: p > p_0$$

> **for a specified value p_0 is obtained by computing the standard score**

$$z = \frac{\hat{p} - p_0}{\sqrt{\dfrac{p_0(1 - p_0)}{n}}}.$$

> **The test result is significant at level α if $z \geq z^*$, where z^* is the one-sided critical value for α.**

I recommend that you give the P-value rather than simply stating "Significant at $\alpha = 0.05$." To do this, just use Table B to find the normal probability lying above z.

The same reasoning that led to this recipe shows how to test $H_0\!: p = p_0$ against other alternatives.

To test

$$H_0: p = p_0 \text{ vs. } H_1: p < p_0$$

compute z and declare the result significant at level α if $z \leq - z^*$, where z^* is the one-sided critical value for α.

To test

$$H_0: p = p_0 \text{ vs. } H_1: p \neq p_0$$

compute z and declare the result significant at level α if $z \geq z^*$ or $z \leq - z^*$, where z^* is the two-sided critical point for $\gamma = 1 - \alpha$.

In all three cases, the direction of the alternative hypothesis H_1 determines which deviations of z from zero count as evidence against H_0. If H_1 is two-sided, so that deviations in either direction count against H_0, we use two-sided critical points. That table is arranged for confidence intervals, but entering it with $\gamma = 1 - \alpha$ finds the z^* with probability γ within z^* of the mean and therefore probability α more than z^* from the mean.

Example 7. We suspect that spinning a penny, unlike tossing it, does not give heads and tails equal probabilities. I spun a penny 200 times and got 83 heads. How significant is this evidence against equal probabilities?

We can think of this as an SRS of size $n = 200$ from the population of all spins of the penny. If p is the probability of a head, we must test

$$H_0: p = 0.5 \text{ vs. } H_1: p \neq 0.5$$

since we are seeking evidence of imbalance in either direction. The sample gave $\hat{p} = 83/200 = 0.415$, so

$$z = \frac{0.415 - 0.5}{\sqrt{\dfrac{(0.5)(0.5)}{200}}} = -2.40.$$

Comparing z with two-sided critical values in Table C-1 shows that this result is significant at $\alpha = 0.05$ (since $2.40 > 1.96$, the table entry for $\gamma = 0.95$), but not significant at $\alpha = 0.01$ (since $2.40 < 2.58$).

We now know that $0.01 < P < 0.05$. If we need the exact P-value, we must use Table B and think a bit. The standard score -2.40 is the 0.82 percentile. So probability 0.0082 lies below -2.40 and another 0.0082 above 2.40. Adding these, $P = 0.0164$ is the probability that z takes a value farther from zero in either direction than that observed.

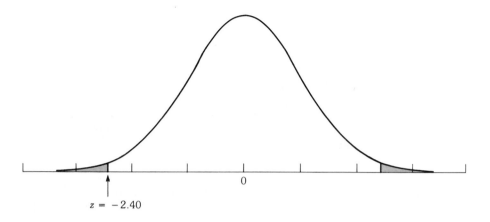

Figure 9-7. The *P*-value for Example 7. The standard normal curve that is the sampling distribution of the standard score *z* is pictured. The shaded area represents the *P*-value. This area is two-tailed because H_1 is two-sided.

Tests for a population mean

The reasoning that led us to the test statistic *z* for a population proportion is remarkably general. It applies without change whenever a parameter is estimated by a statistic having a normal distribution with known standard deviation when the null hypothesis is true. When we wish to test a hypothesis about the mean μ of a population, the natural statistic is the sample mean $\bar{x}$. When the sample size *n* is large and the population has standard deviation σ, we know (from p. 310) that $\bar{x}$ is approximately normal with mean μ and standard deviation $\sigma/\sqrt{n}$. This leads to tests for hypotheses about μ:

> **Suppose that an SRS of size *n* is drawn from a population with unknown mean μ and known standard deviation σ. When *n* is large, a test of**
>
> $$H_0: \mu = \mu_0 \text{ vs. } H_1: \mu > \mu_0$$
>
> **is obtained by computing the standard score**
>
> $$z = \frac{\bar{x} - \mu_0}{\sigma/\sqrt{n}}.$$
>
> **The test result is significant at level α if $z \geq z^*$, where z^* is the one-sided critical value for α.**

The variations for the other one-sided alternative $H_1: \mu < \mu_0$ and the two-sided alternative $H_1: \mu \neq \mu_0$ are the same as in the case of proportions. So too is the process of finding the P-value. The common notation z for a standard score emphasizes the similarity of these tests.

> **Example 8.** A camera company buys a machined metal part from a supplier. The length of a slot in the part is supposed to be 0.550″. No manufacturing process is perfectly precise, so the actual lengths vary according to a distribution with $\sigma = 0.001″$. This standard deviation measures the precision of the supplier's work and is known from long experience. But the mean μ of the current shipment of 80,000 parts may have moved away from the desired value $\mu_0 = 0.550″$ because of improper adjustment, tool wear, or other reasons. The camera company measures a sample of $n = 80$ parts and finds that the mean slot length is $\bar{x} = 0.5501$. Is the mean of the shipment correct or not?
>
> We must test against a two-sided alternative, since slot lengths either too short or too long are undesirable. The hypotheses are
>
> $$H_0:\ \mu = 0.550″ \text{ vs. } H_1:\ \mu \neq 0.550″.$$
>
> The test statistic is
>
> $$z = \frac{0.5501 - 0.550}{0.001/\sqrt{80}} = 0.89.$$
>
> Comparing z with the two-sided critical values in Table C-1, we see that this result is significant at $\alpha = 0.40$ but not at $\alpha = 0.35$. (In fact, we can compute from Table B that $P = 0.37$.) So over 35% of all samples would have an $\bar{x}$ at least this far from 0.550 even if μ were exactly equal to 0.550. There is no suspicion that μ is incorrect, and the lot should be accepted.

If the population standard deviation σ is unknown, we can estimate it by the sample standard deviation s and replace σ by s in the formula for z. When n is large, the test remains approximately correct with this substitution. Small samples (say n less than 30) are a more complex matter. Now the distribution of z depends on the distribution of the population, and replacing σ by s changes the critical values of z. Tables B and C may not be accurate in this case.

5.   Use and abuse of tests of significance

Tests of statistical significance are routinely used to assess the results of research in agriculture, medicine, education, psychology, and sociology and increasingly in other fields as well. Any tool used routinely is often used unthinkingly. This section therefore offers some comments for the thinking researcher on the use and abuse of this tool. Thinking consumers of research findings (such as students) might also ponder these comments.

1. *Choosing a level of significance.* The spirit of a test of significance is to give a clear statement of the degree of evidence against the null hypothesis obtained from the sample. This is best done by the P-value. But sometimes some action will be taken if the evidence reaches a certain standard. Such a standard is set by giving a level of significance α. Perhaps you will announce a new scientific finding if your data are significant at the $\alpha = 0.05$ level. Or perhaps you will recommend using a new method of teaching reading if the evidence of its superiority is significant at the $\alpha = 0.01$ level. When α serves as a standard of evidence, we speak of *rejecting H_0 at level α* if the data are significant at that level.

The idea of using α as a criterion for taking some decision or action goes beyond the idea of a test of significance. But when you want to give such a rule, α is chosen by deciding how much evidence is required to reject H_0. This depends first on how plausible H_0 is. If H_0 represents an assumption that everyone in your field has believed for years, strong evidence (small α) will be needed to reject it. Second, the level of evidence required to reject H_0 depends on the consequences of such a decision. If rejecting H_0 in favor of H_1 means making an expensive changeover from one medical therapy or instructional method to another, strong evidence is needed. Both the plausibility of H_0 and H_1 and the consequences of any action that rejection may lead to are somewhat subjective. Different persons may feel that different levels of significance are appropriate. When this is the case, it is better to report the P-value, which leaves each of us to decide individually if the evidence is sufficiently strong.

When you really must make a decision with well-defined consequences, you should abandon the idea of testing significance and think about rules for making decisions. This approach to statistical inference is discussed in Section 6. It is different in spirit from testing significance, though the two are usually mixed in textbooks and are often mixed in practice. Choosing a level α in advance makes sense if you must make a decision, but not if you wish only to describe the strength of your evidence. In short: When a test of significance is what you want, don't set α in advance and do always report the P-value. This advice is easy to follow, since the computer programs used for most statistical arithmetic automatically print out the P-value. It is acceptable to use "significant at level $\alpha = 0.01$" or the shorthand "$P < 0.01$" to describe your results, but the actual P-value is more informative.

Textbooks commonly stress certain standard levels of significance, such as 10%, 5%, and 1%. The 5% level ($\alpha = 0.05$) is particularly common. Significance at that level is still a widely accepted criterion for meaningful evidence in research work. Now there is no sharp border between "significant" and "insignificant," only increasingly strong evidence as the *P*-value decreases. It makes no sense to treat $\alpha = 0.05$ as a universal rule for what is significant. There is a reason for the common use of $\alpha = 0.05$—the great influence of Sir R. A. Fisher.* Fisher's ideas on statistical inference agreed with the reasoning behind tests of significance. Here is his opinion on level of significance:

> . . . *it is convenient to draw the line at about the level at which we can say: "Either there is something in the treatment, or a coincidence has occurred such as does not occur more than once in twenty trials. . . ."*
> *If one in twenty does not seem high enough odds, we may, if we prefer it, draw the line at one in fifty (the 2 percent point), or one in a hundred (the 1 percent point). Personally, the writer prefers to set a low standard of significance at the 5 percent point, and ignore entirely all results which fail to reach that level. A scientific fact should be regarded as experimentally established only if a properly designed experiment* rarely fails *to give this level of significance.*[1]

There you have it. Fisher thought 5% was about right, and who was to disagree with the master?

2. *What statistical significance doesn't mean.* When a null hypothesis ("no effect" or "no difference") can be rejected at the usual levels, $\alpha = 0.05$ or $\alpha = 0.01$, there is good evidence that an effect is present. But that effect may be extremely small. When large samples are available, statistical tests are very sensitive and will detect even tiny deviations from the null hypothesis. For example, suppose that we are testing the hypothesis of no correlation between two variables. With 1000 observations, an observed correlation of only $r = 0.08$ is significant evidence at the $\alpha = 0.01$ level that the correlation in the population is not zero but positive. The low significance level does not mean there is a strong association, only that there is strong evidence of some association. The true population correlation is probably quite close to the observed sample value, $r = 0.08$. We might well conclude that for practical purposes there is no association between these variables, even though we are confident (at the 1% level) that this is not literally true.

---

* We met the great British statistician R. A. Fisher in Chapter 2 as the father of randomized experimental design. He was the father of much else in modern statistics as well, including the general use of regression (Chapter 6) and the mathematical derivation of the probability distributions of common test statistics. Fisher did not originate tests of significance. But since his writings organized statistics, especially as a tool of scientific research, his views on tests were enormously influential.

Remember the wise saying: *Statistical significance is not the same thing as practical significance.* I am tempted to interpret the results of the Toronto vitamin C experiment in this light. Since the observed difference (that 26% versus 18% again) was significant at the $\alpha = 0.01$ level, it does appear that vitamin C prevented colds better than a placebo. But not much better. The difference between an 18% chance of avoiding colds and a 26% chance is nothing to fuss about.

The remedy for attaching too much importance to statistical significance is to pay attention to the actual experimental results as well as to the *P*-value. It is usually wise to give a confidence interval for the population parameter you are interested in. Confidence intervals are not used as often as they should be, while tests of significance are perhaps overused.

3. *Don't ignore lack of significance.* Researchers typically have in mind the research hypothesis that some effect exists. Following the peculiar logic of tests of significance, they set up as H_0 the null hypothesis that no such effect exists and try their best to get evidence against H_0. Now a perverse legacy of Fisher's opinion on $\alpha = 0.05$ is that research in some fields has rarely been published unless significance at that level is attained. A survey of four journals of the American Psychological Association published in 1959 showed that of 294 articles using statistical tests, only 8 did not attain the 5% significance level.[2]

Such a publication policy impedes the spread of knowledge. If a researcher has good reason to suspect that an effect is present and then fails to find significant evidence of it, that may be interesting news—perhaps more interesting than if evidence in favor of the effect at the 5% level had been found. If you follow the history of science, you will recall examples such as the famous Michelson–Morley experiment, which changed the course of physics by *not* detecting a change in the speed of light that they expected to find. (Of course, an experiment that fails only causes a stir if it is clear that the experiment would have detected the effect if it were really there. Such experiments are much rarer in psychology than in physics.) Keeping silent about negative results may condemn other researchers to repeat the attempt to find an effect that isn't there. Witness this parable.

. . . There's this desert prison, see, with an old prisoner, resigned to his life, and a young one just arrived. The young one talks constantly of escape, and, after a few months, he makes a break. He's gone a week, and then he's brought back by the guards. He's half dead, crazy with hunger and thirst. He describes how awful it was to the old prisoner. The endless stretches of sand, no oasis, no signs of life anywhere. The old prisoner listens for a while, then says, "Yep. I know. I tried to escape myself, twenty years ago." The young prisoner says, "You did? Why

didn't you tell me, all these months I was planning my escape? Why didn't you let me know it was impossible?" And the old prisoner shrugs, and says, "So who publishes negative results?"[3]

4. *Statistical inference is not valid for all sets of data.* We learned long ago that badly designed surveys or experiments often produce invalid results. Formal statistical inference cannot correct basic flaws in the design. There is no doubt a significant difference in English vocabulary scores between high school seniors who have studied Latin and those who have not. (Recall Example 3 on p. 66.) But so long as the *effect* of actually studying Latin is confounded with the differences between students who choose Latin and those who do not, this statistical significance has little meaning. It does indicate that the difference in English scores is greater than would often arise by chance alone. That leaves unsettled the issue of *what* other than chance caused the difference.

Both tests of significance and confidence intervals are based on the laws of probability. Randomization in sampling or experimentation assures that these laws apply. When these statistical strategies for collecting data cannot be used, statistical inference from the data obtained should be done only with extreme caution. Many data in the social sciences by necessity are collected without randomization. It is universal practice to use tests of significance on such data. It can be argued that significance at least points to the presence of an effect greater than would be likely by chance. But that indication alone is little evidence against H_0 and in favor of the research hypothesis H_1. Do not allow the wonders of this chapter to obscure the common sense of Chapters 1 and 2.

5. *Beware of searching for significance.* Statistical significance is a commodity much sought after by researchers. It means (or ought to mean) that you have found something you were looking for. The reasoning behind statistical significance works well if you decide what effect you are seeking, design an experiment or sample to search for it, and use a test of significance to weigh the evidence you get. But because a successful search for a new scientific phenomenon often ends with statistical significance, it is all too easy to make significance itself the object of the search. There are several ways to do this, none of them acceptable in polite scientific society.

A common tactic is to make many tests on the same data. The story is told of three psychiatrists who studied a sample of schizophrenic persons in comparison with a sample of nonschizophrenic persons. They measured 77 variables for each subject—religion, family background, childhood experiences, and so on. Their goal was to discover what distinguishes persons who later become schizophrenic. Having measured 77 variables, they made 77 separate tests of the significance of the differences between the two groups of subjects. Now pause for a moment of reflection. If you made 77 tests at the 5% level, you would expect a few of them to be significant by chance alone, right? After all, results significant at the 5% level do occur five times in a hundred in the long run even when H_0 is true. Well, our psychiatrists found 2 of their 77 tests significant at the 5% level and immediately published this exciting news.[4] Running one test and reaching the $\alpha = 0.05$ level is reasonably good evidence that you have found something; running 77 tests and reaching that level only twice is not.

The case of the 77 tests happened long ago, and such crimes are rarer now— or at least better concealed, for some common practices are not very different. The computer has freed us from the labor of doing arithmetic, and this is surely a blessing in statistics, where the arithmetic can be long and complicated indeed. All computing centers maintain "libraries" of statistical programs, so a few simple commands will set the machine to work performing all manner of complicated tests and operations on your data. The result can be much like the 77 tests of old. I will state it as a law that any large set of data—even several pages of a table of random numbers—contains some unusual pattern. Sufficient computer time will discover that pattern, and when you test specifically for the pattern that turned up, the test will be significant. It also will mean exactly nothing.

One lesson here is not to be overawed by the computer. It is a wondrous tool that makes possible statistical analysis of large data sets and allows ever more complicated and sensitive statistical procedures to be used. The computer has greatly extended the range of statistical inference. But it has changed the logic of inference not one bit. Doing 77 tests and finding 2 significant at the $\alpha = 0.05$ level was not evidence of a real discovery. Neither is doing multiple regression analysis followed by principal components analysis followed by factor analysis and at last discovering a pattern in the data. Fancy words, and fancy computer programs, but still bad scientific logic. It is convincing to hypothesize that an effect or pattern will be present, design a study to look for it, and find it at a low significance level. It is not convincing to search for any effect or pattern whatever and find one.

Now I do not mean that searching data for suggestive patterns is not proper scientific work. It certainly is. Many important discoveries have been made by accident rather than by design. New computer-based methods of searching through data are important in statistics. I do mean that the usual reasoning of statistical inference does not apply when the search is successful. You cannot legitimately test a hypothesis on the same data that first suggested that hypothesis. After all, any data set has some peculiarity, and you may have found only the peculiarity of this one set of data. The remedy is clear. Now that you have a hypothesis, design a study to search specifically for the effect you now think is there. If the result of this study is statistically significant, you have real evidence at last.

6.   Inference as decision

Tests of significance were presented in Section 3 as methods for assessing the strength of evidence against the null hypothesis. This assessment is made by the P-value, which is a probability computed under the assumption that the null hypothesis is true. The alternative hypothesis (the statement we seek evidence for) enters the test only to help us see what outcomes count against the null hypothesis. Such is the theory of tests of significance as advocated by Fisher and as practiced by many users of statistics.

But already in Section 5, signs of another way of thinking were present. A level of significance α chosen in advance points to the outcome of the test as a *decision*. If the P-value is less than α, we reject H_0 in favor of H_1, otherwise we fail to reject H_0. The transition from measuring the strength of evidence to making a decision is not a small step. It can be argued (and is argued by followers of Fisher) that making decisions is too grand a goal, especially in scientific inference. A decision is reached only after the evidence of many experiments is weighed, and indeed the goal of research is not "decision" but a gradually evolving understanding. Better that statistical inference should content itself with confidence intervals and tests of significance. Many users of statistics are content with such methods. It is rare (outside textbooks) to set up a level α in advance as a rule for making a decision in a scientific problem. More commonly, users think of significance at level 0.05 as a description of good evidence. This is made clearer by talking about P-values, and this newer language is spreading.

Yet there are circumstances in which a decision or action is called for as the end result of inference. *Acceptance sampling* (Example 4 on p. 4) is one such circumstance. The supplier of bearings and the consumer of the bearings agree that each carload lot shall meet certain quality standards. When a carload arrives, the consumer chooses a sample of bearings to be inspected. On the basis of the sample outcome, the consumer will either accept or reject the carload. Fisher agreed that this is a genuine decision problem. But he insisted that acceptance sampling is completely different from scientific inference. Other eminent statisticians have argued that if "decision" is given a broad meaning, almost all problems of statistical inference can be posed as problems of making decisions in the presence of uncertainty. I am not going to venture further into the arguments over how we ought to think about inference. I do want to show how a different concept—inference as decision—changes the ways of reasoning used in tests of significance.

Tests of significance fasten attention on H_0, the null hypothesis. If a decision is called for, however, there is no reason to single out H_0. There are simply two alternatives, and we must accept one and reject the other. It is convenient to call the two alternatives H_0 and H_1, but H_0 no longer has the special status (the statement we try to find evidence against) that it had in tests of significance. In the acceptance sampling problem, we must decide between

H_0:   the lot of bearings meets standards

H_1:   the lot does not meet standards

on the basis of a sample of bearings. There is no reason to put the burden of proof on the consumer by accepting H_0 unless we have strong evidence against it. It is equally sensible to put the burden of proof on the producer by accepting H_1 unless we have strong evidence that the lot meets standards. Producer and consumer must agree on where to place the burden of proof, but neither H_0 nor H_1 has any special status.

In a decision problem, we must give a *decision rule*—a recipe based on the sample that tells us what decision to make. Decision rules are expressed in terms of sample statistics, usually the same statistics we would use in a test of significance. In fact, we have seen already that a test of significance becomes a decision rule if we reject H_0 (accept H_1) when the sample statistic is statistically significant at level α and otherwise accept H_0 (reject H_1).

Suppose, then, that we use statistical significance at level α as our criterion for decision. And suppose that the null hypothesis H_0 is really true. Then sample outcomes significant at level α will occur with probability α. (That's the definition of "significant at level α"; outcomes weighing this strongly against H_0 occur with probability α when H_0 is really true.) But now we make a *wrong decision* in all such outcomes, by rejecting H_0 when it is really true. That is, the significance level α now can be understood as the probability of a certain type of wrong decision.

Now H_1 requires equal attention. Just as rejecting H_0 (accepting H_1) when H_0 is really true is an error, so is accepting H_0 (rejecting H_1) when H_1 is really true. We can make two kinds of errors.

If we reject H_0 (accept H_1) when in fact H_0 is true, this is a *Type I error*.

If we accept H_0 (reject H_1) when in fact H_1 is true, this is a *Type II error*.

The possibilities are summed up in Figure 9-8. If H_0 is true, our decision is either correct (if we accept H_0) or is a Type I error. Only one error is possible at one time. Figure 9-9 applies these ideas to the acceptance sampling example.

So the significance level α is the probability of a Type I error. In acceptance sampling, this is the probability that a good lot will be rejected. The probability of a Type II error is the probability that a bad lot will be accepted. A Type I error hurts the producer, while a Type II error hurts the consumer. *Any decision*

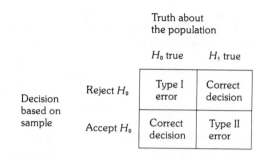

Figure 9-8. Possible outcomes of a two-action decision problem.

rule is assessed in terms of the probabilities of the two types of error. This is in keeping with the idea that statistical inference is based on probability. We cannot (short of inspecting the whole lot) guarantee that good lots will never be rejected and bad lots never be accepted. But by random sampling and the laws of probability, we can say what the probabilities of both kinds of error are. Because we can find out the monetary cost of accepting bad lots and of rejecting good ones, we can determine how much loss the producer and consumer each will suffer in the long run from wrong decisions.

Advocates of decision theory argue that the kind of "economic" thinking natural in acceptance sampling applies to all inference problems. Even a scientific researcher decides whether to announce results, or to do another experiment, or to give up the research as unproductive. Wrong decisions carry costs, though these costs are not always measured in dollars. A scientist suffers by announcing a false effect and also by failing to detect a true effect. Decision theorists maintain that the scientist should try to give numerical weights (called *utilities*) to the consequences of the two types of wrong decision. Then he can choose a decision rule with error probabilities that reflect how serious the two kinds of error are. This argument has won favor where utilities are easily expressed in money.

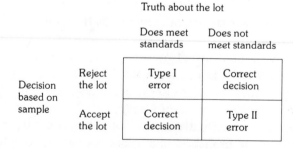

Figure 9-9. Possible outcomes of an acceptance sampling decision.

Decision theory is widely used by business in making capital investment decisions, for example. But scientific researchers have been reluctant to take this approach to statistical inference.

To sum up, in a test of significance we focus on a single hypothesis (H_0) and a single probability (the P-value). The goal is to measure the strength of the sample evidence against H_0. If the same inference problem is thought of as a decision problem, we focus on two hypotheses and give a rule for deciding between them based on the sample evidence. We therefore must focus on two probabilities, the probabilities of the two types of error.

Such a clear distinction between the two ways of thinking is helpful for understanding. In practice, the two approaches often merge, to the dismay of partisans of one or the other. We continued to call one of the hypotheses in a decision problem H_0. In the common practice of *testing hypotheses*, we mix significance tests and decision rules as follows:

(a) Choose H_0 just as in a test of significance.

(b) Think of the problem as a decision problem, so the probabilities of Type I and Type II error are relevant.

(c) Because of Step (a), Type I errors are more serious. So choose an α (significance level) and consider only tests with probability of Type I error no greater than α.

(d) Among these tests, select one that makes the probability of a Type II error as small as possible. If this probability is too large, you will have to take a larger sample to reduce the chance of an error.

Testing hypotheses may seem to be a hybrid approach, or maybe a bastard approach. It was, historically, the effective beginning of decision-oriented ideas in statistics. Hypothesis testing was developed by Jerzy Neyman and Egon S. Pearson from 1928 to 1938.* The decision theory approach came later (1940s) and grew out of the Neyman–Pearson ideas. Because decision theory in its pure form leaves you with two error probabilities and no simple rule on how to balance them, it has been used less often than tests of significance. Decision theory ideas have been applied in testing problems mainly by way of the Neyman–Pearson theory. That theory asks you first to choose α, and the influence of Fisher often has led users of hypothesis testing comfortably back to $\alpha = 0.05$ or $\alpha = 0.01$ (and also back to the warnings of Section 5 about this state of affairs). Fisher,

---

* Neyman was born in 1894 and was active until his death in 1981. In addition to developing the decision-oriented approach to testing, Neyman was also the chief architect of the theory of confidence intervals.

who was exceedingly argumentative, violently attacked the Neyman–Pearson decision-oriented ideas, and the argument still continues.

The reasoning in statistical inference is subtle, and the principles at issue are complex. I have (believe it or not) oversimplified the ideas of all the viewpoints mentioned and omitted several other viewpoints altogether. If you are feeling that you do not fully grasp all of the ideas in this chapter, you are in excellent company. Nonetheless, any user of statistics should make a serious effort to grasp the conflicting views on the nature of statistical inference. More than most other kinds of intellectual exercise, statistical inference can be done automatically, by recipe or by computer. These valuable shortcuts are of no worth without understanding. What Euclid said of his own science to King Ptolemy of Egypt long ago remains true of all knowledge: "There is no royal road to geometry."

NOTES

1. R. A. Fisher, "The Arrangement of Field Experiments," *Journal of the Ministry of Agriculture of Great Britain*, Volume 33 (1926), p. 504. Quoted in Leonard J. Savage, "On Rereading R. A. Fisher," *The Annals of Statistics*, Volume 4 (1976), p. 471.

2. Theodore D. Sterling, "Publication Decisions and their Possible Effects on Inferences Drawn from Tests of Significance—or Vice Versa," *Journal of the American Statistical Association*, Volume 54 (1959), pp. 30–34.

3. From Jeffrey Hudson, *A Case of Need* (New York: New American Library, 1968). Quoted in G. William Walster and T. Anne Cleary, "A Proposal for a New Editorial Policy in the Social Sciences," *The American Statistician*, April 1970, p. 16.

4. This example is cited by William Feller, "Are Life Scientists Overawed by Statistics?" *Scientific Research*, February 3, 1969, p. 26.

Exercises

Section 1

1. Suppose that Senator Bean's SRS of size 1000 produced 520 voters who plan to vote for Bean.
   - (a) What is the 95% confidence interval for the population proportion p who plan to vote for Bean?
   - (b) What is the 99.7% confidence interval for p?
   - (c) Based on the sample results, can Bean be confident that he is leading the race?

2. An SRS of 1000 graduates of a university showed that 54% earned at least $30,000 a year. Give a 95% confidence interval for the proportion of all graduates of that university who earn at least $30,000 a year.

3. Table 1-1 on page 20 is a table of margins of error for samples of several sizes drawn by the Gallup Poll's probability sampling procedure. We now can use that table to give 95% confidence intervals.

Exercise 1 on page 51 reports a 1977 Gallup Poll of 1506 American adults, of whom 33% thought (incorrectly) that the United States is self-sufficient in oil. Give a 95% confidence interval for the proportion of all American adults who believed this.

4. If Senator Bean took an SRS of only 25 voters, the probability distribution of the sample proportion $\hat{p}$ who favor him would be (very roughly) normal with mean equal to the population proportion p and standard deviation 0.1.

   (a) What property of this distribution shows that $\hat{p}$ is an unbiased estimate of p?

   (b) A sample of size 25 gives less precision than a sample of size 1000. How is this reflected in the distributions of $\hat{p}$ for the two sample sizes?

   (c) For the SRS of size 25, what is the number m such that the interval from $\hat{p} - m$ to $\hat{p} + m$ is a 95% confidence interval for p? Explain your answer.

   (d) If Senator Bean found 17 of 25 voters in an SRS favoring him, give a 95% confidence interval for the proportion of all voters who favor Bean.

5. In Senator Bean's SRS of 1000 voters, what is the number m such that the interval from $\hat{p} - m$ to $\hat{p} + m$ is a 68% confidence interval for p? Explain your answer.

6. We are going to simulate the performance of a 68% confidence interval for p based on an SRS of size 25.

   (a) Using the information given in Exercise 4, explain why the interval from $\hat{p} - 0.1$ to $\hat{p} + 0.1$ is a 68% confidence interval for p.

   (b) Suppose that in fact $p = 0.6$ (that is, 60% of all the voters favor Bean). Explain how to use Table A to simulate drawing an SRS of size 25.

   (c) Starting at line 101 of Table A, simulate drawing 10 SRSs of size 25 from this population. For each sample, compute the sample proportion $\hat{p}$ who favor Bean. Then compute the 68% confidence interval $\hat{p} - 0.1$ to $\hat{p} + 0.1$ for each sample. How many of the intervals covered the true $p = 0.6$? How many failed to cover p?

7. The recipes for confidence intervals depend on the probability distribution of the sample statistic used. In the text we considered only $\hat{p}$, the sample proportion. Here is a fact about the probability distribution of the sample mean, $\bar{x}$:

   If an SRS of size 100 is chosen from a population that has standard deviation 1 but unknown mean μ, the sample mean $\bar{x}$ has approximately the normal distribution with mean μ and standard deviation 0.1.

   From this fact, follow the argument given in the text for $\hat{p}$ step by step to derive the recipe for a 95% confidence interval for the unknown population mean μ.

8. A scientist measures the length in microns of a small object. (A micron is one-millionth of a meter.) Her measuring procedure is not perfectly accurate. In fact, repeated measurements follow the normal distribution with mean equal to the unknown true length μ (the measurement process is unbiased). The standard deviation of the distribution of measurements is 1 micron. (This is a statement of the reliability of the measuring process.)

   (a) The results of 100 independent measurements can be thought of as an SRS of size 100 from the population of all possible measurements. If the mean of 100 measurements of the object is $\bar{x} = 21.3$ microns, use the result of Exercise 7 to give a 95% confidence interval for the true length μ.

   (b) Suppose that only one measurement were taken and gave the result $x = 21.3$ microns. Give a 95% confidence interval for μ based on this single observation.

9. A poll taken immediately before the 1976 presidential election showed that 51% of the sample intended to vote for Carter. The polling organization announced that they were 95% confident that the sample result was within ± 2 points of the true percent of all voters who favored Carter.

   (a) Explain in plain language to someone who knows no statistics what "95% confident" means in this announcement.

   (b) The poll showed Carter leading. Yet the polling organization said the election was too close to call. Explain why.

10. On hearing of the poll mentioned in Exercise 9, a nervous politician asked, "What is the probability that over half the voters prefer Carter?" A statistician said in reply that this question not only can't be answered from the poll results, it doesn't even make sense to talk about such a probability. Can you explain why?

Section 2

1. You are the polling consultant to a member of Congress. An SRS of 500 registered voters showed that 28% listed "energy problems" as the most important issue facing the nation. Give a 90% confidence interval for the proportion of all voters who hold this opinion.

2. In the setting of Exercise 1,

   (a) Give a 75% confidence interval and a 99% confidence interval. Note how the confidence level affects the width of the interval.

   (b) Suppose that the sample result $\hat{p} = 0.28$ had come from an SRS of 100 persons or an SRS of 4000 persons. Give a 90% confidence interval in both cases. Note how the sample size affects the width of the interval.

3. The congressman receives 1310 pieces of mail on pending gun control

legislation. Of these, 86% oppose the legislation. Having learned from you about estimating with confidence, he asks you for an analysis of these opinions. What will you tell him?

4. An agricultural extension agent is concerned about hornworms infesting the tomatoes in the home gardens of her district. She checks a sample of 128 hornworms and is pleased to find 67 of them being parasitized by wasp larvae. Assuming these 128 can be regarded as an SRS, give an 80% confidence interval for the proportion of hornworms in her district that are parasitized.

5. Some people use mayonnaise jars rather than specially made canning jars, to can garden vegetables. *Organic Gardening* magazine (August 1983, p. 86) used mayonnaise jars for canning to estimate how likely they are to break in such use. Said the magazine, "The mayonnaise jars didn't do badly—only three out of 100 broke. Statistically this means you'd expect between 0 and 6.4% to break." Can you verify this confidence interval and give the confidence level used by the magazine?

6. The sampling distribution of $\hat{p}$ (the estimated proportion) for the Gallup Poll's probability sampling procedure is normal with mean equal to the population proportion p. But the standard deviation is *not* given by the SRS recipe $\sqrt{p(1 - p)/n}$. Be clever: Using Table 1-1 on page 20 and your knowledge of normal distributions, find the standard deviation of $\hat{p}$ in a Gallup Poll sample of 1000 persons when the true p is 0.5. Compare your result with the standard deviation of $\hat{p}$ from an SRS of size 1000 from a population with $p = 0.5$.

7. The congressman you advise knows from preliminary polls that about half the registered voters in his district favor his reelection. He wants to commission a poll that will estimate this proportion accurately. You, as his polling consultant, decide to take an SRS lage enough to get a 95% confidence interval with margin of error ± 0.02. How large a sample must you take? (*Hint:* The margin of error is $\pm z^*\sqrt{p(1 - p)/n}$, and p is close to 0.5.)

8. An SRS of 120 farmers in north-central Indiana is selected and asked their corn yield last year. The sample mean of the replies is $\bar{x} = 125$ bushels per acre, and the sample standard deviation is $s = 11$ bushels per acre. Give a 90% confidence interval for the mean corn yield of all north-central Indiana farmers.

9. Family income was one of the items included on only 20% of the forms in the 1980 census. Suppose (alas, it is too simple to be true) that the families who answer this question are an SRS of the families in each district. In Middletown, a city of 65,000 persons, 2621 families were asked their income. The mean of the responses was $\bar{x} = \$23,453$ and the standard deviation was $\$8721$. Give a 99% confidence interval for the 1980 mean family income in Middletown.

10. A laboratory scale is known to have errors of measurement normally distributed with mean 0 and standard deviation $\sigma = 0.0001$ gram. So repeated measurements of the same quantity are normally distributed with mean equal to the true weight and standard deviation $\sigma = 0.0001$ gram. A series of 25 weighings gives $\bar{x} = 2.3214$ grams and sample standard deviation $s = 0.00013$ gram.

   (a) Give a recipe for a level γ confidence interval for the mean μ of a population having *known* standard deviation σ. Explain why you should use σ and ignore the sample standard deviation s.

   (b) Use your recipe to give a 75% confidence interval for the true weight of the quantity weighed 25 times above.

11. The estimated standard deviation of a statistic is often called a *standard error*. For example, the standard error of $\bar{x}$ from an SRS of size n is $s/\sqrt{n}$. When the standard error is given, you can compute confidence intervals for means and proportions from complex sample designs without knowing the formula that led to the standard error.

   A report based on the Current Population Survey gives the 1981 mean household income as \$22,787 with a standard error of \$83. Give a 99% confidence interval for the mean 1981 income of all U.S. households.

Section 3

1. In Exercise 10 on page 101, an experiment was reported which used a paired-sample design like that of Example 3. Out of six pairs of plots, the experimental plot had a higher yield in five cases. We will assess the significance of this evidence against the null hypothesis that each plot in a pair is equally likely to have the higher yield. (This null hypothesis says that the experimental treatment—praying to the soybeans—had no effect.)

   (a) Supposing that the null hypothesis is true, explain how to simulate for one pair whether the experimental or control plot has higher yield. Then explain how to simulate one repetition of the experiment with six independent pairs of plots.

   (b) Simulate 20 repetitions of the experiment; begin at line 113 of Table A.

   (c) The P-value is the probability that five or more (that is, either five or six) out of six pairs favor the experimental plot. Estimate the P-value from your simulation. (Of course, 20 trials will not give a precise estimate.)

   (d) About how low would the P-value have to be for you to conclude that prayer does increase yields? That is, what level of significance would you insist on to believe the result suggested by the experiment? Were the experimental results significant at that level?

2. For each of the following situations, state in words the proper null hypothesis H_0 and alternative hypothesis H_1:

(a) A sociologist asks a large sample of high school students which academic subject is their favorite. She suspects that a lower percentage of females than of males will say that mathematics is their favorite subject.

(b) An educational researcher randomly divides sixth-grade students into two groups for gym class. He teaches both groups basketball skills with the same methods of instruction. He encourages Group A with compliments and other positive behavior but acts cool and neutral toward Group B. He hopes to show that Group A does better (on the average) than Group B on a test of basketball skills at the end of the instructional unit.

(c) A political scientist hypothesizes that among registered voters there is a negative correlation between age and the percent who actually vote. To test this, she draws a random sample from public records on registration and voting.

3. The classic experiment to detect ESP uses a shuffled deck of cards containing five suits (waves, stars, circles, squares, and crosses). As the experimenter turns over each card and concentrates on it, the subject guesses the suit of the card. If the subject has no ESP, he has probability 1/5 of being right by luck on each guess. If he does have ESP, he will be right more often. A subject is right in 5 of 10 tries. (Actual experiments naturally use much longer series of guesses so that weak ESP could be spotted. No one has ever been right half the time in a long experiment!)

    (a) Give H_0 and H_1 for a test to see if this result is significant evidence that the subject has ESP.

    (b) Explain how to simulate the experiment; assume for the sake of argument that H_0 is true.

    (c) Simulate 20 repetitions of the experiment; begin at line 121 of Table A.

    (d) The actual experimental result was 5 right in 10 tries. What is the event whose probability is the P-value for this experimental result? Give a (not-very-precise) estimate of the P-value based on your simulation. How convincing was the subject's performance?

4. An old farmer claims to be able to detect the presence of water with a bent stick. To test this claim, he is presented with five identical barrels, some containing water and some not. He is correct in four out of five cases. Assess the strength of this result as evidence of the farmer's special ability. (You must formulate the hypotheses and do a simulation to estimate the P-value.)

5. Read the article by Hans Zeisel and Harry Kalven, Jr., "Parking Tickets and Missing Women: Statistics and the Law," in *Statistics: A Guide to the Unknown*. These pages refer in nontechnical language to several tests of significance. In each of the following settings, state the null and alternative hypotheses. If a P-value is given in the article, state it also.

    (a) The Swedish parking-ticket case.

(b) The proportion of women in venires drawn by Dr. Spock's trial judge.

6. A study on predicting job performance reports that

> *An important predictor variable for later job performance was the score X on a screening test given to potential employees. The variable being predicted was the employee's score Y on an evaluation made after a year on the job. In a sample of 70 employees the correlation between X and Y was r = 0.4, which is statistically significant at the 1% level.*

Answer the following questions:

(a) Explain to someone who knows no statistics what information "r = 0.4" carries about the connection between screening test and later evaluation score.

(b) The null hypothesis in the test reported above is that there is *no association* between X and Y when the population of all employees is considered. What value of the correlation for the entire population does this null hypothesis correspond to?

(c) Explain to someone who knows no statistics why "statistically significant at the 1% level" means there is good reason to think that there is association between the two scores.

7. A new vaccine for a virus that now has no vaccine is to be tested. Since the disease is usually not serious, 1000 volunteers will be used and exposed to the virus.

(a) Explain how you would use these 1000 volunteers in a designed experiment to test the vaccine. Include all important details of designing the experiment (but don't actually do any random allocation).

(b) We hope to show that the vaccine is more effective than a placebo. State H_0 and H_1.

(c) The experiment gave a P-value of 0.25. Explain carefully what this means.

(d) The researchers did not consider this evidence strong enough to recommend regular use of the vaccine. Do you agree?

8. A social psychologist reports that "In our sample, ethnocentrism was significantly higher ($P < 0.05$) among church attenders than among nonattenders." Explain to someone who knows no statistics what this means.

Section 4

1. A preelection poll of 1500 registered voters finds that 781 would vote for Senator Caucus if the election were held today. Is this convincing evidence that a majority of all voters would vote for Caucus? Answer this question by using Table B to give the P-value.

2. A wholesale supplier of tree and shrub seedlings advertises that 90% of its seedlings will survive a year when given proper care. A retail nursery buys 250 dogwood seedlings to grow for later sale. After a year, 207 survive. Is this significant evidence that less than 90% of the wholesaler's seedlings will survive? State H_0 and H_1, and use Table C to assess significance.

3. The probability of rolling a 7 or 11 as the sum of the faces of two fair dice is 8/36, or 0.222. You decide to test this by watching a casino craps table. Of the first 300 rolls, 61 give 7 or 11. Is this good evidence against the hypothesis that 0.222 is the correct probability? State H_0 and H_1, and use Table C to assess the significance of the result.

4. An environmentalist group collects a liter of water from each of 45 locations along a stream and measures the amount of dissolved oxygen in each specimen. The mean is 4.62 mg and the standard deviation 0.92 mg. Is this strong evidence that the stream has a mean oxygen content of less than 5 mg per liter? Use Table B to give the P-value.

5. Scores on the SAT are approximately normally distributed with standard deviation $\sigma = 100$. When the population itself has a normal distribution, our recipe for tests about the mean μ is correct even for small samples (as long as σ is known). A random sample of 20 students from a large school system is given a training course before the SAT. Their SAT math scores are as follows:

452	438	577	421
498	450	396	743
514	520	483	328
508	398	429	450
449	547	788	593

Is there evidence that the training has raised the mean above the system mean of $\mu_0 = 483$?

6. Packages of frozen broccoli are supposed to weigh 12 ounces. Packages are automatically weighed at the end of the production line. For the last 50, $\bar{x} = 11.92$ ounces and $s = 0.11$ ounce. Is this convincing evidence that the mean weight being produced is not equal to the desired 12 ounces? (Use Table C.)

7. The method of converting a normally distributed statistic to a standard score provides tests for other hypotheses. In a comparative randomized experiment, we are often interested in testing

$$H_0\colon p_1 - p_2 = 0$$

where p_1 and p_2 are the proportions of successful outcomes in an entire population given Treatment 1 and Treatment 2. Tests of H_0 are based on the statistic $\hat{p}_1 - \hat{p}_2$, where $\hat{p}_1$ and $\hat{p}_2$ are the observed proportions of successes in the two experimental groups. When H_0 is true and the common value of p_1 and p_2 is p, $\hat{p}_1 - \hat{p}_2$ is approximately normal with mean 0 and standard deviation

$$\left[p(1 - p) \left(\frac{1}{n} + \frac{1}{m} \right) \right]^{1/2}.$$

Here n and m are the sizes of the two groups. Since p is unknown, we estimate it by the overall proportion of successes in both groups combined. You can now create a z statistic to test H_0.

In a clinical trial of the effectiveness of vitamin C in preventing colds, 408 subjects in the vitamin C group completed the experiment, of whom 106 remained free of colds. The second group received a placebo. Of the 410 subjects in this group, 74 did not get a cold. Is this good evidence that a higher proportion of people will avoid colds with vitamin C than with a placebo? Use Table C to assess significance.

8. A maker of light bulbs knows that the lifetime in service of the bulbs is normally distributed with mean 1500 hours and standard deviation 50 hours. Use Table C to fill in the blank in this advertising claim: "Ninety-five percent of our bulbs last ____ hours or more."

9. The weight of tomato juice in mechanically filled cans varies from can to can according to a normal distribution with standard deviation 8 grams. This describes the precision of the filling machinery. The mean of the distribution can be set by adjusting the machine. Use Table C to answer the following questions:

   (a) A penalty is charged if more than 10% of the cans contain less than 454 grams. What mean should be set in order to have exactly 10% of the cans weigh less than 454 grams?

   (b) Suppose instead that the penalty applies to the sample average weight $\bar{x}$ of a case of 12 cans. That is, no more than 10% of all cases may have $\bar{x}$ below 454 grams. To what mean weight should the filling machine be set to produce just 10% of cases with average can weight below 454 grams? (*Hint:* What is the standard deviation of the average weight $\bar{x}$ of the 12 cans in a case?)

Section 5

1. Which of the following questions does a test of significance help answer? Explain.

   (a) Is the sample or experiment properly designed?

   (b) Is the observed effect due to chance?

   (c) Is the observed effect important?

2. A researcher looking for ESP tests 500 subjects. (See Exercise 3 of Section 3 for the experiment employed to detect ESP.) Four of these subjects do significantly better ($P < 0.01$) than random guessing.

   (a) Is it proper for the researcher to conclude that these four people have ESP? Explain.

   (b) Is it proper to choose these four people for more tests, conducted independently of the previous tests? Explain.

3. A television news program used AT&T's "900" numbers to hold a call-in poll about a proposed ban on handgun ownership. Of the 2372 calls, 1921 oppose the ban. The station, following recommended practice, made a confidence statement: "81% of the Channel 13 Pulse Poll sample opposed the ban. We can be 95% confident that the true proportion of citizens opposing a handgun ban is within 1.6% of the sample result." Is this conclusion justified?

4. Every user of statistics should understand the distinction between statistical significance and practical significance. A sufficiently large sample will declare very small effects statistically significant. Suppose you are trying to decide whether a coin is fair when tossed. Let p be the probability of a head. If p = 0.505 rather than 0.500, this is of no practical significance to you. Test H_0: $p = 0.5$ vs. H_1: $p \neq 0.5$ in each of the following cases. Use Table C to assess significance.

   (a) 1,000 tosses give 505 heads ($\hat{p} = 0.505$).

   (b) 10,000 tosses give 5050 heads ($\hat{p} = 0.505$).

   (c) 100,000 tosses give 50,500 heads ($\hat{p} = 0.505$).

5. Exercise 4 shows that simply reporting a P-value can be misleading. A confidence interval is more informative. Give a 95% confidence interval for p in each of the cases in Exercise 4. You see that for large n the confidence interval says, "Yes, p is larger than 1/2, but it is very little larger."

6. Table 5-1 on page 182 gives the Nielsen ratings for all national prime-time television programs in the week of April 12–18, 1982. It is *not* proper to do a test of significance on these data to decide whether CBS had a significantly higher mean rating than NBC. Why not?

7. Few accounts of really complex statistical methods are readable without extensive training. One that is, and that is also an excellent essay on the abuse of statistical inference, is "The Real Error of Cyril Burt," a chapter in Stephen Jay Gould's *The Mismeasure of Man* (W.W. Norton, 1981). We met Cyril Burt under suspicious circumstances (Exercise 3 on p. 137). Gould's long chapter shows Burt and others engaged in discovering dubious patterns by complex statistics. Read it, and write a brief explanation of why "factor analysis" failed to give a firm picture of the structure of mental ability.

8. The article by Arie Y. Lewin and Linda Duchan, "Women in Academia," *Science*, Volume 173 (1971), pp. 892–895, reports an investigation in which applications of equally qualified male and female Ph.D.s were sent to aca-

demic department chairmen. The chairmen were asked which applicant they would hire. The number who chose the male was somewhat greater than the number who would hire the female. The authors concluded that "the results, although not statistically significant, showed definite trends that confirm our hypothesis that discriminatioin against women does exist at the time of the hiring decision." This conclusion was strongly attacked in letters to the editor. One irate statistician wrote, "Are the standards of *Science* the standards of science?"

Discuss the validity of the conclusion that the survey results confirm the existence of discrimination. (If possible, read the entire article first.)

Section 6

1. A criminal trial can be thought of as a decision problem, the two possible decisions being "guilty" and "not guilty." Moreover, in a criminal trial there is a null hypothesis in the sense of an assertion that we will continue to hold until we have strong evidence against it. Criminal trials are therefore similar to hypothesis testing.
   (a) What are H_0 and H_1 in a criminal trial? Explain your choice of H_0.
   (b) Describe in words the meaning of Type I error and Type II error in this setting, and display the possible outcomes in a diagram like Figures 9-8 and 9-9.
   (c) Suppose that you are a jury member. Having studied statistics, you think in terms of a significance level α, the (subjective) probability of a Type I error. What considerations would affect your personal choice of α? (For example, would the difference between a charge of murder and a charge of shoplifting affect your personal α?)

2. A computerized medical diagnostic program is being designed that will scan the results of tests conducted by technicians (pulse rate, blood pressure, urinalysis, etc.) and either clear the patient or refer the case to the attention of a doctor. This program will be used to screen many thousands of persons who do not have specific medical complaints as part of a preventive medicine system.
   (a) What are the two hypotheses and the two types of error? Display the situation in a diagram like Figures 9-8 and 9-9.
   (b) Briefly discuss the costs of each of the two types of error. These costs are not entirely monetary.
   (c) After considering these costs, which error probability would you choose to make smaller?

3. You are the consumer of bearings in an acceptance sampling situation. Your acceptance sampling plan has probability 0.01 of passing a lot of bearings that does not meet quality standards. You might think the lots that pass are almost all good. Alas, it is not so.

(a) Explain why low probabilities of error cannot ensure that lots which pass are mostly good. (*Hint:* What happens if your supplier ships all bad lots?)

(b) The paradox that most decisions can be correct (low error probabilities) and yet most lots that pass can be bad has important analogs in areas such as medical diagnosis. Explain why most conclusions that a patient has a rare disease can be false alarms even if the diagnostic system is correct 99% of the time.

4. A major advantage of the decision approach to inference is that it is not restricted to the two-decision situations characteristic of hypothesis testing. For example, suppose that three decisions are possible in an acceptance sampling setting.

Decision 1:   The lot of bearings is of high quality; accept it at full price.

Decision 2:   The lot is of medium quality; accept it at a lower price.

Decision 3:   The lot is of low quality; reject it.

The performance of a decision rule is still assessed in terms of the probabilities of error. By filling in the display below, count the different types of error now possible.

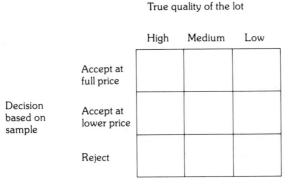

Table A. Random digits

Line								
101	19223	95034	05756	28713	96409	12531	42544	82853
102	73676	47150	99400	01927	27754	42648	82425	36290
103	45467	71709	77558	00095	32863	29485	82226	90056
104	52711	38889	93074	60227	40011	85848	48767	52573
105	95592	94007	69971	91481	60779	53791	17297	59335
106	68417	35013	15529	72765	85089	57067	50211	47487
107	82739	57890	20807	47511	81676	55300	94383	14893
108	60940	72024	17868	24943	61790	90656	87964	18883
109	36009	19365	15412	39638	85453	46816	83485	41979
110	38448	48789	18338	24697	39364	42006	76688	08708
111	81486	69487	60513	09297	00412	71238	27649	39950
112	59636	88804	04634	71197	19352	73089	84898	45785
113	62568	70206	40325	03699	71080	22553	11486	11776
114	45149	32992	75730	66280	03819	56202	02938	70915
115	61041	77684	94322	24709	73698	14526	31893	32592
116	14459	26056	31424	80371	65103	62253	50490	61181
117	38167	98532	62183	70632	23417	26185	41448	75532
118	73190	32533	04470	29669	84407	90785	65956	86382
119	95857	07118	87664	92099	58806	66979	98624	84826
120	35476	55972	39421	65850	04266	35435	43742	11937
121	71487	09984	29077	14863	61683	47052	62224	51025
122	13873	81598	95052	90908	73592	75186	87136	95761
123	54580	81507	27102	56027	55892	33063	41842	81868
124	71035	09001	43367	49497	72719	96758	27611	91596
125	96746	12149	37823	71868	18442	35119	62103	39244
126	96927	19931	36089	74192	77567	88741	48409	41903
127	43909	99477	25330	64359	40085	16925	85117	36071
128	15689	14227	06565	14374	13352	49367	81982	87209
129	36759	58984	68288	22913	18638	54303	00795	08727
130	69051	64817	87174	09517	84534	06489	87201	97245
131	05007	16632	81194	14873	04197	85576	45195	96565
132	68732	55259	84292	08796	43165	93739	31685	97150
133	45740	41807	65561	33302	07051	93623	18132	09547
134	27816	78416	18329	21337	35213	37741	04312	68508
135	66925	55658	39100	78458	11206	19876	87151	31260
136	08421	44753	77377	28744	75592	08563	79140	92454
137	53645	66812	61421	47836	12609	15373	98481	14592
138	66831	68908	40772	21558	47781	33586	79177	06928
139	55588	99404	70708	41098	43563	56934	48394	51719
140	12975	13258	13048	45144	72321	81940	00360	02428
141	96767	35964	23822	96012	94591	65194	50842	53372
142	72829	50232	97892	63408	77919	44575	24870	04178
143	88565	42628	17797	49376	61762	16953	88604	12724
144	62964	88145	83083	69453	46109	59505	69680	00900
145	19687	12633	57857	95806	09931	02150	43163	58636
146	37609	59057	66967	83401	60705	02384	90597	93600
147	54973	86278	88737	74351	47500	84552	19909	67181
148	00694	05977	19664	65441	20903	62371	22725	53340
149	71546	05233	53946	68743	72460	27601	45403	88692
150	07511	88915	41267	16853	84569	79367	32337	03316

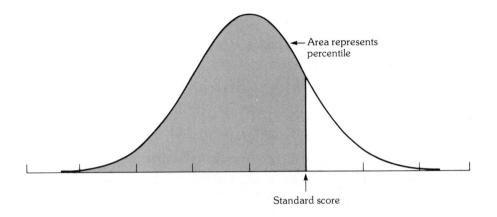

Table B. The standard normal distribution

Standard score	Percentile	Standard score	Percentile	Standard score	Percentile
−3.0	0.13	−1.0	15.87	1.0	84.13
−2.9	0.19	−0.9	18.41	1.1	86.43
−2.8	0.26	−0.8	21.19	1.2	88.49
−2.7	0.35	−0.7	24.20	1.3	90.32
−2.6	0.47	−0.6	27.42	1.4	91.92
−2.5	0.62	−0.5	30.85	1.5	93.32
−2.4	0.82	−0.4	34.46	1.6	94.52
−2.3	1.07	−0.3	38.21	1.7	95.54
−2.2	1.39	−0.2	42.07	1.8	96.41
−2.1	1.79	−0.1	46.02	1.9	97.13
−2.0	2.27	0.0	50.00	2.0	97.73
−1.9	2.87	0.1	53.98	2.1	98.21
−1.8	3.59	0.2	57.93	2.2	98.61
−1.7	4.46	0.3	61.79	2.3	98.93
−1.6	5.48	0.4	65.54	2.4	99.18
−1.5	6.68	0.5	69.15	2.5	99.38
−1.4	8.08	0.6	72.58	2.6	99.53
−1.3	9.68	0.7	75.80	2.7	99.65
−1.2	11.51	0.8	78.81	2.8	99.74
−1.1	13.57	0.9	81.59	2.9	99.81
				3.0	99.87

NOTE: The table gives the percentile corresponding to each standard score for the normal distributions. The percentile corresponding to any observation from a normal distribution can be found by converting the observation to a standard score and then looking in the table.

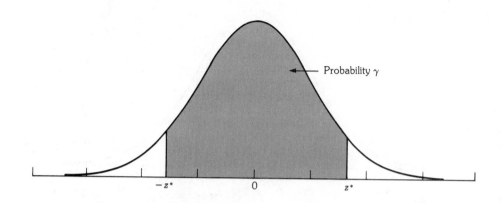

Table C-1. Two-sided normal critical values

γ	z^*	γ	z^*
0.50	0.67	0.80	1.28
0.55	0.76	0.85	1.44
0.60	0.84	0.90	1.64
0.65	0.93	0.95	1.96
0.70	1.04	0.99	2.58
0.75	1.15	0.999	3.29

NOTE: Any normal distribution has probability γ within z^* standard deviations on either side of its mean.

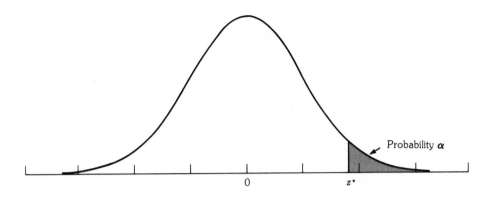

Table C-2. One-sided normal
critical values

α	z^*	α	z^*
0.20	0.84	0.02	2.05
0.15	1.04	0.01	2.33
0.10	1.28	0.005	2.58
0.05	1.64	0.001	3.09

NOTE: Any normal distribution has probability α
more than z^* standard deviations from the mean
in one direction.

Index

348